PHILOSOPHY
PARADOX AND DISCOVERY

PHILOSOPHY
PARADOX AND DISCOVERY

ARTHUR J. MINTON
University of Missouri, Kansas City

with editorial assistance from
Robert Faaborg, University of Cincinnati;
Sarah Keating, California State University, Long Beach; and
Edward Walter, University of Missouri, Kansas City

McGraw-Hill Book Company

New York   St. Louis   San Francisco   Auckland   Düsseldorf   Johannesburg
Kuala Lumpur   London   Mexico   Montreal   New Delhi   Panama
Paris   São Paulo   Singapore   Sydney   Tokyo   Toronto

PHILOSOPHY: PARADOX AND DISCOVERY

1 2 3 4 5 6 7 8 9 0 D O D O 7 9 8 7 6

This book was set in Times Roman by National ShareGraphics, Inc.
The editors were James F. Mirrielees, Alison Meersschaert, and Barry Benjamin;
the cover was designed by J. E. O'Connor;
the production supervisor was Dennis J. Conroy.
R. R. Donnelley & Sons Company was printer and binder.

Library of Congress Cataloging in Publication Data
Main entry under title:

Philosophy : paradox and discovery.

   1. Philosophy—Addresses, essays, lectures.
2. Ethics—Addresses, essays, lectures. I. Minton,
Arthur J., date
B21.P56   108   75-29128
ISBN 0-07-042412-8

To Janie

Contents

PART THREE
MORALITY AND ITS JUSTIFICATION

Sources of Morality: God, Society, and the Individual

Sources of Morality: The Search for Objectivity

Preface

This collection of readings in philosophy was assembled after an extensive survey of teachers across the country indicated a widespread dissatisfaction with traditional texts, as well as with more recent texts which emphasize "relevance." A great many instructors indicated the need for a text that speaks to the beginning student without sacrificing the hard-won insights of the past. The fundamental questions of philosophy are "relevant" in the highest sense of that much-abused word, for the simple fact is that most great philosophers theorized to solve some pressing moral and intellectual concern. From Plato to Marx, the history of the world has moved from the pressure of their pens.

Since the task of philosophy is to examine life, to tear down the comfortable barriers of dogma which prevent us from growth, the teacher of philosophy must always keep a finger on the pulse of immediate experience. But, at the same time, philosophy builds where it destroys, and this constructive task demands that the connection between first principles and the world of here and now be made explicit. It is not enough, I think, to mix a few of the classics with articles dealing with contemporary concerns, praying that the connection will be made. In this text, a different approach has been tried. First, every effort has been made to ensure that the readings deal with issues of fundamental concern. Selections that supplement one another, building together to create complexity and rigor, were chosen over more extensive, but technical, writing. Whenever possible, thinkers of unusual clarity and style were selected. Second, selections which make a clear connection between theory and practice are included in every section. In addition, the readings are integrated so that selections in one section supplement readings in another. Robert Paul Wolff's defense of anarchism, for example, is founded on Kant's ethics, and the two may be read together. James Rachels's attack on ethical egoism can be supplemented by Hobbes's political philosophy, which is based on egoism. Gilbert Ryle's "logical behaviorism" and B.F. Skinner's attack on democratic ideals, can be combined with the selection by Solomon Asch in which he tries to link ethical relativism with behaviorism. Mark Twain's devastating attack on traditional religion can be productively read with Clarence Darrow's defense of Leopold and Loeb, while John Hick's rebuttal to Twain is nicely supplemented by Peter Bertocci's defense of freewill. There are many more interesting combinations that allow the instructor to show how different areas of experience fit together to form a unified system of thought.

The text is divided into five major sections, each containing two problem areas. Each of the five sections begins with a short essay designed to confront the student with the paradoxes infecting this part of experience. Then, each problem area is introduced by an essay that furnishes the unifying historical and conceptual thread between the readings. These problem introductions have been written in order to provide the student with a clear and engaging overview of the fundamental questions of philosophy, as well as with some of the most outstanding contributions to their solution. The introductions avoid technical language as much as possible in the belief that many instructors have individual classification systems that may diverge from the norm.

Each reading is preceded by a critical headnote providing a brief biography of the author as well as a hint of the major ideas presented in the selection. The headnotes are designed to arouse the reader's interest and to suggest questions for reflection, so that reading the selection will be more critically undertaken. Each essay is followed by a series of study questions designed to aid the student in locating and understanding the main ideas of the reading, as well as to provide questions that will stimulate reflection on these ideas and their implications. A quotation from Barry Goldwater, for example, follows an essay by Marx and Engels, and the student is required to contrast the views of these authors. The questions do more than force the student to review the reading—they focus attention on new avenues of inquiry.

The editorial work in this volume reflects the collective effort of many individuals. I felt that by consulting with other interested teachers, my own assumptions would be exposed and challenged. The upshot is that several of the problem introductions, along with study questions and critical headnotes, have been written by other teachers of philosophy. The section on the existence of God was done by Robert Faaborg of the University of Cincinnati, the section on morality dealing with relativism and absolutism was written by Edward Walter of the University of Missouri, Kansas City, and the final section of the book on the nature of political freedom was done by Sarah Keating of the California State University, Long Beach. Their insightful assistance, both in writing and editorial advice, has greatly increased the value of this book. Also I wish to thank Olivia Smith for her gracious help in typing this manuscript under difficult conditions and Alison Meersschaert who, as my editor, was the guardian angel of this project. Finally, I wish to express my thanks to the many students who have contributed to this text by their frequent insights into assumptions I had passed over. More than anything else, the realization that sometimes I could not make myself understood to many bright and capable students has made me aware that a good text is an invaluable help in the difficult task of communication. I sincerely hope that this volume will contribute to that end.

Arthur J. Minton

Introduction

WHAT IS PHILOSOPHY?

Philosophy, like other studies, aims at knowledge. But philosophers seek a special sort of knowledge that eludes exact definition. The word "philosophy" comes from the Greek *philien,* to love or desire, and *sophia,* wisdom. The philosopher, then, is a "lover of wisdom." Wisdom is knowledge in its broadest sense. It does not concern things that huddle on the periphery of life. It is knowledge directed to the fundamental and pervasive concerns of existence. To desire wisdom is to seek principles that cut through the superficial and trivial facts that clutter our intellectual landscape, revealing the basic shape of things beneath. Philosophy, as a quest for wisdom, is an attempt to provide a vision of the world that is systematic and clear, in which the connections between significant facts are made manifest. It is the search for first things and last things—for first principles and their ultimate implications.

We all become philosophers at crucial points in life. We go at the painful task of living with a set of beliefs—faiths, if you will—that organize the helter-skelter of experience into a more or less systematic and coherent whole. From culture, class, religion, and family we are provided with a general framework, a world view, that filters out the unimportant and impregnates experience with meaning. This framework of beliefs and values is largely unconscious and inarticulate; and when it smashes against the hard rock of reality, the dilemma we feel, but do not yet understand, kindles philosophical reflection. As our personal relationships become more complicated, youthful optimism about human nature is tempered by disappointment and hurt. As more and more is demanded of us and we begin to see flaws in ourselves, the infinite horizon of opportunity shrinks in the face of our limitations. As we see ourselves and others repeating the same errors, playing out the same roles, we begin to wonder whether society and nature have conspired to lock us into a mechanical mode of reaction impossible to resist. As we grow conscious of the enormous amount of suffering and anguish in the world, seeing at first hand the vast waste of human life, the old easy answers about a good and loving God are shattered. As we face wholesale changes in the behavior of society, each decade overthrowing the values of the last, we cannot help but wonder whether our own commitments will stand the test of time or even whether such commitments are more than subjective whims that we have elevated to first principles. At such times we lose our way in the world and we ask "What am I about?" This is philosophical territory.

Traditionally, philosophy has been partitioned into three areas: epistemology, metaphysics, and value theory. *Epistemology* is the theory of knowledge. The following are typical epistemological questions: What is scientific method? What is the role of observation in knowing? Can there be absolute certainty about anything? What is an explanation? What is a proof? *Metaphysics* is concerned with the description of the fundamental aspects of reality. These are typical metaphysical questions: What is mind? Is it different from matter? Is there necessity in nature? Is there necessity in human decision? Does God exist? Are numbers real? Which is basic—force or matter? *Value theory* consists in resolving a number of problems about the nature of value in art, ethics, and politics: What makes something beautiful? Is it taste or an objective property? What makes something good? Again, is personal morality subjective or can it be assessed by an absolute standard? Why should I disregard my own interests, if at all? What makes one political system better than another? Should I always obey the law? What makes someone into a moral authority? As you can see, sometimes philosophical inquiry becomes lofty and abstract; but even the most abstract theorizing is genereated in a practical dilemma and will eventually come back to illuminate its beginnings. The philosophical perspective is ever the human perspective.

But the human perspective is limited. No one can scan the entire horizon of human concern with the eye of a god. We see the world from where we stand, and partial vision yields only partial truth. To recognize this fact, however, is not to counsel inaction, indecision, or despair. Nor is it to fall back on the comfortable but wholly fallacious assumption that since no one has all the answers, everyone's opinion is equally valid. The recognition of fallibility is simply an acknowledgment of our humanity. We have to get on in this world, and either we entrust our course to intellect and whatever insight we can muster or we flounder and take our chances with fate. There are no other alternatives. The basic assumption of philosophical inquiry is that the most intractable puzzles of life—no matter how large—will ultimately give way to rational analysis. But before this can happen, we must develop, as carefully as we can, our own vision of things. Lived experience is the testing ground for these partial insights. The experience of one individual or even of a generation may not be sufficient; but eventually what is true in our outlook will enlarge our understanding of the world and open it up to our command, while what is false will lead us to confusion and frustration.

THE SEARCH FOR BEDROCK: PARADOX

Philosophical thought usually begins when the world does not behave as we thought it must. In frustration, the wise person takes stock. "Know thyself" is the first injunction of philosophy, for until we appreciate the extent to which self colors experience with its own loyalties, infuses it with its inarticulate commitments, we cannot enjoy the flexibility of action and purpose that is the mark of true freedom. Many people believe that the mind is like a sponge, soaking up facts which then present themselves on the stage of consciousness in all their pristine reality. The mind, according to this view, is simply a receptacle which does not alter or transform what flows into it. This conception of the "passivity" of intellect is perhaps the greatest barrier to philosophical thinking. Philosophers are constantly reminding us that we are the active shapers of experience, investing it with meaning from a hidden fund of presuppositions, mostly submerged beneath consciousness like the great mass of an iceberg beneath the water. The first task of philosophy is to bring these presuppositions to consciousness—to remind us that the sense of obviousness accompanying certain facts has been contributed by ourselves. An example will make this clearer.

When surgical techniques allowed for the safe removal of cataracts, people who had been afflicted with this condition since birth were able to see for the first time. It is tempting to think that upon opening their eyes, they experienced the beautiful and familiar world of vision—a world of form and color, of public objects in a public space. But this does not occur. The patient is immediately confronted with a wall of brightness containing color patches that blend indistinguishably into one another. The flood of sensations is absolutely meaningless. There is no awareness of shape or size, nor any idea of distance. In fact, some patients report the impression that the swirl of color is touching their eyes. Familiar shapes, such as squares and triangles, which are easily identified by touch, are unrecognized in the visual array. One investigator writes:

> The newly-operated patients do not localize their visual impressions; they do not relate them to any point, either to the eye or to any surface, even a spherical one; they see colors much as we smell an odor of peat or varnish, which enfolds and intrudes upon us, but without occupying any specific form of extension in a more exactly definable way.[1]

---

[1] This quotation and all following quotations are taken from Marius Von Senden, *Space and Sight* (New York: The Free Press, 1960). This remarkable book is a collection of case histories of persons who acquired sight for the first time through surgery or by spontaneous remission.

Gradually, the newly sighted learn that the color patches represent objects at a distance. They discover that they can move through the field of color, that the colors move to the edge of the visual field as they walk, and that no matter how they turn their bodies, the visual swirl surrounds them. Slowly, they begin to apprehend that there are things behind them and in front of them, but their conception of the spatial world is woefully inadequate. About his patient, one doctor wrote:

> I have found in her no notion of size, for example, not even within the narrow limits she might have encompassed with the aid of touch. Thus when I asked her to show me how big her mother was, she did not stretch out her hands, but set her two index fingers apart.

Another physician reported similar affects in his patients:

> Those who are blind from birth have no real conception of distance. A house that is a mile away is thought of as nearby, but requiring the taking of a lot of steps.

Only after long and painful experience do the patients come to have an idea of objective space. At first, only things extremely close are seen in depth, while objects at a distance remain parts of a flat wall of sensation where everything ends. Here one object moving in front of another is seen as two color patches melding into one another. When a newly sighted girl first saw photographs and paintings, she asked: "Why do they put those dark marks all over them?" "Those aren't dark marks," her mother responded, "those are shadows . . . if it were not for shadows, many things would look flat." The girl answered: "Well, that's how things do look. Everything looks flat with dark patches." With time, however, the world begins to assume depth and the flat curtain of color recedes into the background.

The mental effort involved in learning to see is enormous. Without mental exertion, experimentation, and training, the bright wall of sensation remains a dazzling, incoherent barrier. Sometimes the task proves too much for adults who have spent their lifetime relying on other senses, and they relapse into their old habits. A doctor writes about his twenty-one-year-old patient:

> Her unfortunate father, who had hoped for so much from this operation, wrote that his daughter carefully shuts her eyes whenever she wishes to go about the house, especially when she comes to a staircase, and that she is never happier and more at ease than when, by closing her eyelids, she relapses into her former state of total blindness.

For the first time these people are struck by the tremendous size of the world, and they are oppressed by their own insignificance. They become aware of the fact that they have been visible to others all along, and they feel it as an intrusion into their privacy. Their emotional and mental lives are shaken to the very core.

The newly sighted undergo experiences which those of us born with vision toiled through in infancy and have long since forgotten. Long ago the flat wall of sensation fragmented into objects that zoomed away into space, and now it is almost impossible for us to regard our visual field as a blur of color patches. Our perceptual skills have become so routine and automatic that they give the illusion of naturalness, like the technique of an accomplished musician. We tend to forget that what is now easy was once painfully difficult. The experience of the blind in coping with their newfound sense of vision illustrates that even in the most elementary perception, reason and judgment are at work, albeit in dim and forgotten ways. The world that presents itself to our eyes—the world of three-dimensional objects in a public space—is as much a result of thought as of pure sensation. How much more thought and assumption, then, must lie half–hidden beneath our explicit beliefs about morality, science, politics, religion, and the other great topics of human concern. Philosophy is an attempt to ferret out the most significant of these, to bring them into the bright light of awareness, and, if possible, to submit them to critical appraisal.

Socrates was the greatest practitioner of this analytical search for fundamental assumptions. Walking through the streets of ancient Athens, he would buttonhole the powerful men of his time, asking them irreverent questions about their opinions. To those who pretended to know about justice, he quietly asked, *tò tí*—what is it? What do you mean by justice and right and goodness? Don't just give me a list of those things which possess these qualities, but tell me the essence of the idea. Define your terms. What is virtue, morality, knowledge? What do you mean by *yourself,* your soul, your mind? By skillful questioning, Socrates would pry into depths of one's system of beliefs, dragging out cherished certainties and displaying their ragged clothing. This demand for clarity of thought and exactness of definition left his victims confused and reeling. After being questioned, poor Euthyphro confesses: "I do not know, Socrates, how to express what I mean. For somehow or other our arguments, on whatever ground we rest them, seem to turn around and walk away from us."

Socrates had asked Euthyphro to define piety, and then showed, through a series of deductions, that his definition was in serious conflict with other things he believed. He was trying to make him feel a paradox in those beliefs and values which, on their face, were so familiar and obvious. Piety, Euthyphro says, is whatever is pleasing to the gods. "Do the gods love piety in and of itself?" Socrates asks. "Of course", his victim replies. If this is so, Socrates retorts, then the gods must love piety because it is pleasing to them—an absurd conclusion. Euthyphro is staggered: "Come again . . . how was that?" This sort of procedure is analytic in nature. By bringing out the paradoxical in the familiar, our attention is forced inward, to our system of definitions, to the conceptual paths we have made for ourselves in the world. The confusion we feel is that of a traveler who has used a road daily in one direction and now for the first time must travel the opposite way. The old landmarks are alien, the curves and hills are not where they are supposed to be, the terrain is confusing. Philosophy is an adventure into the commonplace. It is the human mind become conscious of itself and its contribution to what is known.

THE SEARCH FOR SYSTEM: DISCOVERY

The search for hidden assumptions and fundamental premises is actually part of a larger enterprise. In the end, a philosophy should present us with a unified vision of the world and of our place in it. It is impossible, however, to identify and evaluate the bedrock of our belief system without uncovering the relations, however vague, among basic beliefs. Perhaps another analogy from the study of vision will illustrate this point. Ordinary perceptual experience leads us to believe that our visual image is sharp and clear at any one time, like the image on a photograph. In fact, however, the greatest part of the visual field is a blur. Only about a one-thousandth part of the visual field—the part isolated by a focal area of 4 degrees out of a total of 180 degrees—is presented to consciousness with real clarity. The rest seems sharp and clear because the eye is constantly moving, summing up these focal areas in a fraction of a second to create a larger area of clarity. Stop the motion of the eye and concentrate on one word. You will notice how this small circle of clarity recedes into an expanse of vagueness and haze. Experiments have shown that when the eye is completely immobilized (it takes a machine to do it), the visual image fragments and disappears. Exploration is the sine qua non of clear vision.

Mental clarity is not unlike visual clarity. When we try to fasten onto a concept, to hold it fixed in the light of awareness, it tends to disintegrate into meaninglessness. "Every definite image in the mind," wrote William James, "is steeped and dyed in the free water that flows around it. With it goes the sense of its relations, near and remote, the dying echo of whence it came to us, the dawning sense of whither it is to lead. The significance, the value of the image, is all in this halo or penumbra that surrounds and escorts it." To see our beliefs clearly, we must scan our mental field to discover the ways an idea interacts with its surroundings. What a person does with a concept in his or her total intellectual framework is a better clue to understanding what it means than the most exacting definition.

Paradox and discovery are two sides of the same coin. Things seem paradoxical when two firmly established beliefs which have been kept apart and allowed to function in their own domains are brought side by side and seen to be inconsistent. Until then we really do not know what we believe, for usually our assumptions are nebulous and vague. We sharpen them by experimentation—by examining the effect they have on other areas of experience. What are your religious beliefs? How do you reconcile God's goodness with his creation of people who he knows will be responsible for the suffering of millions of innocents? How do you justify Hitler, Stalin, Genghis Khan, Nero, etc.? You say that they have free will and are therefore responsible for what they do. But, then, how can free will exist in light of the findings of science? Physical processes flow inevitably from their antecedent conditions. There are no alternatives. But we are not physical, you say. We possess a soul, a nonmaterial essence that escapes the rigid fatalism of matter. What is your evidence for this? And so it goes. We shall not find systematic answers to such questions lying within us, ready to spring to light when we need them. Instead, we will have a vague feeling of where we are, and we may discover that there are cracks in our belief system that cannot be repaired. Philosophical discovery is not merely clarifying what was already fully there but hidden; it is also growth.

PHILOSOPHY AND SCIENCE

Philosophy, it seems, is speculation about matters that can have no final answers. Religion, morality, the existence of the soul, free will, the ultimate structure of the world—such issues cannot be treated with precision. Science, on the other hand, presents us with a definite method, a down-to-earth approach to things. We may have to settle for less, but at least we shall know what we have got.

Is there a yawning gap between science and philosophy? In order to answer this question, we should look briefly at the dawn of modern science.

In the thirteenth century, Christian Europe rediscovered the learning of antiquity which had been lost during the Middle Ages. This vast wealth of information had to be merged with the christian tradition, for as a system of knowledge it was far superior to anything then known. The greatest name in Greek science was that of Aristotle, whose work systematized physics, astronomy, biology, and psychology.

Things in nature, Aristotle held, are a composite of two factors—form and matter. Matter is the raw material, form the structure. To know what a thing is, one must know both of these aspects: What is it made of? What is its form? The key to understanding the form of a thing is its *telos*—the goal or end toward which it moves. Everything in nature is directed by an inner force to a specific fulfillment. To know what an acorn is, for example, is to know that it will grow into a certain sort of tree. From common observation, Aristotle reasoned that the *telos* of matter was rest. Roll a ball, throw a stone, shoot an arrow, row a boat— all these experiences confirm it: Matter naturally seeks a state of rest. Pick up a stone and feel it resist being moved. The pressure you feel against your hand, its weight, is a manifestation of an inner drive to move back to earth, its natural place of rest.

This reasoning, however, produces a problem. Matter, if left alone, should seek out its place of rest and remain there. The world should be static and dead. Why hasn't this occurred? Something must be actively interfering with the elements, Aristotle thought, to keep them in motion. Looking to the heavens, he saw the stars moving in circular paths around the Earth. Here was the force needed to account for activity and change in dead matter. The heavenly spheres must communicate some of their motion by friction to the world below. But this explanation meant that if the stars continued to move forever, they were not made of ordinary matter. Indeed, they were perfect, incorruptible bodies. Eternal circular motion was perfect motion, and the stars, following the urging of their special *telos,* were striving for perfection.

Aristotle's physics and astronomy merged with Christianity in the thirteenth century to produce a world view that was at once commonsensical and profound. Although Christian thinkers continued to regard the stars and planets as perfect, the suggestion that they moved themselves in a celestial struggle for perfection smacked too much of ancient polytheism. The heavenly bodies, like ordinary matter, required an external force to keep them in motion. Whatever such a force was, it could not be material, for then it would need a further force to move it, *ad infinitum.* God was the logical solution. God was the wind in the sails of the universe, actively moving the heavenly spheres around the center of creation. This was the element that the Christian tradition needed for intellectual completion. Here was physical proof for the existence of God. Henceforth no scientific person could doubt the religious vision of the world. Astronomy, physics, and religion were molded into a unified system of explanation.

By the sixteenth century, however, this world view had become ungainly. In order to account for the erratic movements of the planets—called "wandering stars"—the original system of eight concentric spheres had evolved into an enormously complicated and cumbersome tangle of movements. The orbits of the planets were practically unimaginable. Each planet moved in a small circle, like a horse on a merry-go-round, the center of which was attached to the periphery of a larger circle with the Earth in the middle. Yet the planets did not move in their little circles around the Earth, but about a point slightly off center. To the mathematical minds of the period, such a loping cosmic circus seemed unworthy of the divine intellect. But in spite of these inelegant complications, Aristotle's astronomy remained the preferred view because it rested on concepts that were in agreement with observation and common sense. Observation suggests that the Earth is a steady platform around which the heavens move in large arcing paths. Common sense tells us a thousand times a day that a moving object will come to rest unless a continuous force is applied to it. These commonplaces were the cornerstones of Aristotle's science, and before a new vision of the world could hope to stand, they would have to be destroyed.

The year 1543 marked the publication by Nicholas Copernicus of *On the Revolutions of the Celestial Spheres.* In this book he theorized that the Earth and the rest of the planets moved in circular orbits around the sun. In order to account for the apparent movement of the sun across the sky each day, he suggested that the Earth rotates on its axis once each twenty-four hours. The simplicity of this account appealed to many scientists, but it faced what appeared to be insurmountable obstacles. If the Earth were rotating on its axis at the required rate, its surface at the equator would be moving at great speeds. An object thrown high into the air would not land in the same spot. Birds would not be able to fly in the direction of rotation, for they would be constantly falling behind the speeding ground beneath them. Besides, at such velocities, objects would be thrown away from the surface of the Earth like stones flung from a sling. These objections strike us today as absurd, but only because we have become accustomed to the concept of inertia. In the sixteenth century, they were irrefutable.

At the beginning of the seventeenth century, Galileo Galilei was a professor of mathematics at the University of Padua. Early in his career he had realized that Aristotle's science could not explain the flight of a cannonball. The cannonball continues to fly through space when there are no apparent forces acting on it to keep it in motion. Most scientists, unable to surmount their theoretical assumptions, invented invisible forces to account for this kind of case. Some said that the air behind the ball continued to push it along, and as this force died, the ball fell to earth. But to Galileo, such explanations seemed to be born of desperation. Besides, God was a mathematician, he believed, and could not have made the universe as inelegant as depicted in Aristotle's astronomy. And so Galileo became a Copernican, while continuing to teach the old astronomy. Later, in 1632, he would publish *Dialogues on the Two Chief World Systems,* which would ring the death knell for Aristotle's system.

The experiments in 1604 which led to this dramatic outcome seemed innocuous enough at first glance. Galileo had already proven that the velocity acquired by a freely falling body was not proportional to its weight. Now he was seeking to establish a lawful relation between velocity and time. Lacking an accurate timepiece, he had to "slow down" a falling object in order to measure the relation between distance traversed and time elapsed. To accomplish this, he rolled smooth brass balls down an inclined plane on the assumtion that the velocity achieved is due to the vertical factor alone. In this way he discovered that the distance traversed is proportional to the square of the elapsed time. No matter what the degree of the slope, this relation remained constant. Since the final velocity of a ball rolled down an inclined plane is due to the vertical factor alone, it can be assumed that it will acquire enough force to roll up a similar plane to its original height, no matter what the slope of the plane. Of course, Galileo's brass balls rolling down grooves lined with polished parchment did not roll back to exactly the height from which they began. He surmised that this was due to the friction of the plane. He then imagined a ball rolling down the grooved incline onto a plane tilted by the minutest fraction of a degree. What would happen? All of his experiments implied that the ball would roll up the plane until it had acheived its original height, even if this meant that it had to traverse a vast distance to do so. But what if it rolled onto a horizontal *frictionless* plane? Here Galileo made a dramatic intellectual leap: The horizontal plane is simply an incline of 0 degrees. The ball should roll over an infinite distance. A moving object, then, does not come to rest because its *telos* demands it. It comes to rest because a force, such as friction, impedes its continued motion. This is the principle of inertia.

The principle of inertia turns Aristotle's common sense on its head. A body in motion will continue in motion—a rock thrown up from the surface of the moving Earth will retain whatever velocity the Earth imparts to it, falling back to exactly the same spot. The centuries-old arguments against a moving Earth were now shown to be bankrupt. The active, moving universe no longer required God as the force to sustain its motion. With the publication of these new ideas, the Church saw Galileo and his new science as dangerous enemies of religion. Six months after its printing, *Dialogues* was banned. Galileo was called to Rome and threatened with torture. At almost seventy year of age, he recanted, in abject terms, his defense of Copernicus. Legend has it that at the end of his recantation

88347

he muttered beneath his breath *eppur si muove* (it still moves). But this is mere legend. Galileo had been broken, and he died in 1642, blind and under house arrest.

This episode from the history of science shows clearly that science and philosophy do not tread different paths.

In its fundamental aspect, Galileo's defense of Copernicus was a philosophical enterprise. Aristotle's system had reigned for so long, that what had originally begun as speculation had hardened into intuition. The concepts of *weight, force,* and *motion* rested on assumptions so deeply ingrained in habits of mind that they seemed to define the limits of thought itself. To see the world afresh, Galileo had to turn his attention to the concepts which organized experience. Every major advance in science reiterates this theme. Faraday had to think of the magnetic field as an object just as real as the gross visible magnet. In so doing he revised our conception of matter. Einstein had to imagine that clocks are not equivalent in different frames of reference. Our idea of time as flowing uniformly throughout the universe was the victim. At the frontiers of knowledge, there is no authority, no tested method, no formula to apply which will churn out the answers. Instead there is a breakdown in the usual ways of thinking. This too is philosophical territory.

The scientific image of the world affects every corner of human experience. Galileo's work began a revolution in thinking which spread out from physics to the entire conception of human knowledge. Here was a new way of explaining things—a way which ignored tradition and authority, which made no reference to purposes and goals in nature, which represented the physical world as a mechanism moving according to its own law, not enmeshed with a spiritual force that guides it. It gave rise to a new temperament, a new faith in the power of reason to reveal the structure of things. It placed new demands on political thought, ethics, religion, and psychology to establish their credentials on a similar empirical basis.

In the end, there is no hard and fast distinction between philosophy and science. A philosophy worth its salt will find a place within itself for the successes of science. Conversely, science, as we know it, rests on unchallenged assumptions which deserve philosophical analysis. If there is a conflict between science and philosophy, it is not between two bodies of truth; it is an internal conflict within human experience as the mind struggles to form a comprehensive picture of the whole while the pieces in the puzzle continue to change.

VALUE OF PHILOSOPHY

Philosophy is valuable in itself. This is not to say that philosophical reflection is the whole end of living, but merely that such activity is an essential part of happiness. Happiness is growth. It is the expansion and refinement of those powers and drives that make us distinctly human. Since curiousity is one expression of those essential human capabilities, philosophical reflection is an important part of self-fulfillment. Imagine, if you can, a society in which philosophical thought is prohibited. You are not permitted to wonder about the foundations of morality, nor to discuss theology. You cannot question the fundamental assumptions of the sciences and you are not allowed to connect the scientific image of humanity with the usual questions about the meaning of life, the existence of the soul, the possibility of human freedom, etc. Can you imagine that every important need of the human personality has been met in such a world? Hasn't something fundamental been left out? If we acknowledge that human beings have a drive to know, to explore, to connect and analyze, then by refusing to allow philosophical reflection, we would be refusing an intelligent nature its highest logical outcome. It is like saying to an athlete: "You may run, but you may not strain." Strain, however, is the only way to growth, and philosophical thought is the mind straining to understand itself and its place in the scheme of things.

The value of philosophy does not lie exclusively in the answers it gives. There is no systematic body of knowledge called "philosophy." There are, instead, people trying to think systematically about the fundamental questions of life. The great thinkers of the past differed in their conclusions, and those of today are no better off. But this is to be expected in an undertaking so grand, so final, and so audacious. The most enduring value of philosophy lies in the habit of mind it breeds in those who have discovered its pleasures. It produces a vision of things large enough to generate a life plan, a direction, tempered by the nagging suspicion that the vision may be an illusion. Philosophic thought, the exhilarating experience of paradox and discovery, is the first step toward a civilized faith.

Part One

Religion

THE PARADOXES OF RELIGION

Religion is not just a belief that some mysterious being exists. It is, on the contrary, a complex network of beliefs concerning morality, the purpose of life, the nature of the individual, and the ultimate explanation of things. Our rational, scientific experience of the world is fragmented and incomplete, and religion attempts to bring these fragments together to form a coherent, meaningful image of the whole. Philosophers have always concerned themselves with religious issues because the philosophical enterprise itself is just such an attempt to bring together the strands of experience and discover the hidden connections between every area of human concern. This is why the philosophy of religion is an excellent place to begin the study of philosophy. In examining the religious vision of the world, we are forced to lay bare our fundamental assumptions concerning knowledge, morality, and the possibility of a meaningful existence. Once our assumptions have been critically examined, whatever of worth that remains will have to be put back together again to form a coherent system.

The Judaic-Christian religious tradition, for example, claims to be relevant to life in many ways. First, it offers an ultimate explanation of things by claiming that the world is the creation of an all-powerful, all-knowing, benevolent being. The universe, then, is a rational system, not merely an arrangement of blind

1

accidents. Ultimately, this means that important features of the world must be explained in terms of the plan and goals of the creator. Closely allied with this belief is the claim that the life of each individual is significant in the divine scheme of things. Many people believe that without God, life becomes a meaningless charade, traced out briefly on the surface of an insignificant planet. But if God exists, even our most bitter disappointments serve some ultimate purpose. In addition, religion offers an explanation of morality. In Dostoyevsky's famous novel, *The Brothers Karamazov,* one of the characters proclaims that if God does not exist, anything is permitted. In other words, God is needed to transform moral sentiment from a subjective feeling into an objective requirement.

But the religious picture of the world must deal with several crucial questions. First and foremost is the question of knowledge. Can the existence of God be established by the usual patterns of reasoning and observation, or is a special source of knowledge required? If religious claims must ultimately rest on faith or mystical insight, what is the best way of understanding these states? Second, does religion actually provide a sense of purpose and significance to life which cannot be gained without God? Does it help, for example, to know that our suffering was planned and carried out in order to serve some higher ideal? Third, why should God's commandments be morally authoritative? The proponents of a religious moral theory must be able to deal with the claims of those who maintain that adequate ethics can be formulated by human beings for human needs. Finally, the religious view of life must face what appears to be an agonizing paradox. If God is all-good and all-knowing, why did He create a world full of suffering and injustice? Why, for example, must millions of innocents suffer the ravages of disease and other natural disasters? Could any purpose, no matter how noble, justify this enormous tragedy?

Does God Exist?

PROBLEM INTRODUCTION

"The unexamined life is not worth living." These are the words of Socrates as he faced an Athenian jury on charges of atheism. He was found guilty and sentenced to death by poisoning. He might have escaped the punishment by promising to stop questioning the basic beliefs of his culture. He chose death instead. The death of Socrates ushered in a new moral era, for the demand to examine life is a cry for intellectual liberation. If we never reflect upon ourselves, our actions, or our beliefs, the life we lead is not really ours at all, but simply the mechanical expression of the prevailing ideas of our time. Some of these ideas may be true, but by refusing to challenge them we do them a great disservice—we treat them as dogmas. One of the most pervasive of beliefs is the belief in the existence of God. Natural theology, a traditional branch of philosophy, deals with the systematic analysis of this belief. The primary purpose of natural theology is to provide a rational justification for believing in God. The first four selections in this section put forward and evaluate the most important "proofs" of God's existence.

Many believers and nonbelievers alike adopt the position that reasoning about the existence of God is a waste of time. The only real justification for

Editor's note: Introduction and editorial material for this section by Robert Faaborg, professor of philosophy, University of Cincinnati.

believing that something exists is the testimony of the senses. Therefore, if some-one has not experienced God, talk is pointless. But, in many ways, this position is irrational. We know, for example, that the Earth rotates on its axis and spins around the sun. Yet no one has ever seen this, and even if one could get into the position in which one "saw" the Earth behaving this way, it would be nothing to the point. After all, others could get into the position where they would "see" the sun rotating around the Earth. How would we choose between the conflicting reports? In general, we justify such beliefs through the use of complex arguments involving many areas of investigation. Usually, such arguments try to prove that what we observe is best explained by a certain general picture of things. One would justify the claim that the Earth spins on its axis, for example, by pointing out that this belief best explains the presence of the trade winds, the bulging of the Earth at the equator, the behavior of a pendulum at the poles, etc. Most of our beliefs, in other words, are the result of an interaction of experience and reason.

Yet, one of the most famous arguments for God's existence does not rely on any facts learned from observation or experiment. This argument, known as the *ontological argument,* is an attempt to prove the existence of God with absolute certainty. In St. Anselm's version of the proof, he maintains that if you merely reflect on the concept or idea of God, you must conclude that He exists. The concept of God is the concept of "the greatest conceivable being." It is impossi-ble to believe that God does not exist, because if you are thinking of something as nonexistent, then you are not thinking of the greatest conceivable being, and, hence, you are not thinking of God.

Although the ontological argument has intrigued people for centuries, it is generally regarded as a logical curiosity. Thomas Aquinas, the great medieval philosopher, for example, did not accept it as valid. Instead, he thought that any rational proof for the existence of God must make some reference to the nature of the world, and could not rely on concepts alone. In Aquinas's classic *Cosmo-logical Arguments,* he argues that God is the necessary condition for the existence of certain pervasive facts about the world. In his second argument, for instance, he claims that the natural world could not contain causes and effects unless there were a first cause. An infinite series of causes, according to him, is an absurdity. Lying behind all versions of the cosmological argument is the intellectual pre-sumption that everything about the physical world should be explainable. But an infinite series of causes does not seem to explain everything which needs explana-tion, for there is still the question, "Why this infinite series rather than another?" In other words, if we do not admit that God exists, the physical universe in its entirety is just one big unexplainable fact—there is no reason why it is as it is. Aquinas's third argument exhibits this intellectual dissatisfaction with unexplain-able facts, and Richard Taylor, a contemporary American philosopher, presents a more complete version of this argument.

For most people, however, it is not so much the raw existence of things which demands an explanation, but the complex organization which the universe exhibits. The universe is a *system* rather than a chaos, and it is difficult to under-stand how it could have come about through a series of blind accidents, unguided by some sort of plan. This sort of argument is called the *teleological argument* because it rests on the claim that the universe, in whole or in part, is a teleological system—i.e., a system whose parts are arranged to achieve a certain goal or end. Naturally, if the structure of things reveals that they are arranged to produce an effect, then there must be an arranger, namely, God. The teleological argument compares natural objects and systems to those objects which are known to have originated by intelligent design, such as clocks, engines, etc. Since natural objects have some of the same features of organization as objects which have been designed, they too must have been designed. The human eye, for example, is a mechanism which exhibits an organization far surpassing the most complex computer, thus revealing an even greater creator.

Compared with the ontological and cosmological arguments, the teleological argument has rather modest ambitions. It is designed to prove that the operation of intelligence is the best explanation of the complex organizations which occur in nature. The existence of God is not rendered a certainty, but it is still highly probable. The very modesty of its claims, however, seem to be a serious deficit for the argument. David Hume, for example, in the selection from *Dialogues Concerning Natural Religion,* maintains that the argument is insufficient to prove monotheism, for, strictly speaking, it proves only that intelligence is a factor in the creation of things and this conclusion is quite consistent with polytheism. Yet even if Hume's criticisms of the argument fail to stand up in court, it must continually compete with scientific explanations of organization in nature. Darwin's theory of natural selection, for example, dealt a serious blow to divine purposes, for he showed how complex organizations in the biological world could arise through blind genetic mutation. Still, proponents of the teleological argument maintain that more fundamental organizations, such as the complex molecules which form the building blocks of life, could not have arisen by chance. So the debate is still alive.

The teleological argument leads directly to a dilemma which confronts every believer: the problem of evil. If the universe is designed in all its fantastic detail by an all-powerful, all-knowing deity, then every bit of suffering and pain is also carefully and deliberately planned. If there is *unnecessary* pain and suffering in the world, then an all-powerful, all-knowing, and all-good God cannot exist, for surely pointless suffering is an evil which such a deity would not allow. In *Letters from the Earth,* Mark Twain critically and irreverently examines this dilemma and concludes that this world could only have been created by an evil God. He argues that God has the responsibility of a parent to protect and nourish the weak creatures He has created, but instead allows the human race to suffer the ravages of disease and disaster. Moreover, Twain maintains, God has created us with a disposition to sin. To hold us responsible for our sins is as ludicrous as a clockmaker blaming the clock for failing to tell time.

Theological responses to the problem of evil have varied widely throughout history. Of course, it is possible to deny that there is a problem by insisting that we cannot apply our moral ideas to God. The difficulty with this position is that if we are not allowed to condemn God's actions, we cannot praise them either. Therefore, unless we are willing to treat the existence of God as a morally neutral fact, thereby depriving religion of any moral connection with life, the problem of evil must be met head-on.

One of the most systematic answers to the dilemma of human suffering is the soul-building argument. This position turns on two points: the existence of free will and the necessity of suffering for character development. Human beings possess free will, and thus are morally responsible agents. Naturally, God could have made us otherwise—He could have made us so that we automatically choose the right thing all the time—but the price is too high, for the price is free will. For free agents, the choice of evil must always remain a real possibility. But what about the pain and suffering caused by the forces of nature? Surely humans cannot accept responsibility for hurricanes, floods, disease, and other destructive forces of nature. However, if we consider these natural events as the result of definite natural laws which, when understood, allow us to alter nature and rationally cope with our environment, they appear in a new light. The development of certain desirable traits, such as courage, sympathy, and perseverance require that a free agent confront a natural environment which is capable of hurt. Through this experience, humans freely respond and develop character traits which elevate their moral status. In a world where nothing can go wrong, where pain is impossible because natural law is suspended whenever suffering threatens, human beings would drift aimlessly in perpetual infancy. In our readings, this position is forcefully argued by John Hick.

In the end, each person must assess the evidence and determine for himself whether belief in God is justified by rational considerations. It is important to point out that even if none of the proofs for God's existence are successful, it does not follow that God does not exist. The absence of proof for the existence of something does not constitute proof that it does not exist. On the other hand, if the problem of evil is not sufficient to show that God does not exist, it would be equally fallacious to claim that God must exist. Naturally, in most complex issues, the ideal of rigorous proof is rarely realized. In life, the real question usually is "What am I entitled to believe?" and, in dealing with this question, the systematic failure to confirm a theory *is not a neutral* fact. If God has some connection with this world, reason should be able to uncover it. Thus if the atheist is systematically unable to make a case, this is evidence for theism and vice versa. Rational commitment does not require absolute proof, but it does require two things: the weight of evidence and an open mind.

The Ontological Argument for God's Existence

St. Anselm

St. Anselm (1033–1103) was Archbishop of Canterbury. He is often called the father of Scholasticism and is known primarily for his version of the ontological argument. Anselm attempts to prove the existence of God by reflecting on the idea or concept of God. He believes that God is the only thing which can be proved to exist by this method. Although deeply committed to rationalism, he characterized his position as "faith seeking understanding." In other words, the belief in God comes from faith, and faith is then illuminated by reason.

Anselm argues that the concept of God is that of "the greatest being that can be thought of." If you can think of something having all the attributes of God, such as omnipotence, omniscience, etc., but you can also imagine that this thing does not exist, then you are not thinking of God, for surely a being which is thought of as existing is greater than one which is thought of as not existing. Therefore, Anselm concludes, since it is impossible to even frame the idea of a nonexistent God, it is impossible to doubt that God exists.

A monk by the name of Gaunilo wrote a reply to Anselm in which he claimed that he could use Anselm's method to prove the existence of a perfect island. After all, if I can think of an island as not existing, then I am not thinking of the perfect island, for I can certainly conceive of a better one, namely, one that exists. It is impossible, then, to doubt the existence of the perfect island. Our selection contains Anselm's response to Gaunilo.

PREFACE

Some time ago, at the urgent request of some of my brethren, I published a brief work,[1] as an example of meditation on the grounds of faith, I wrote it in the role of one who seeks, by silent reasoning with himself, to learn what he does not know. But when I reflected on this little book, and saw that it was put together as a long chain of arguments, I began to ask myself whether *one* argument might possibly be found, resting on no other argument for its proof, but sufficient in itself to prove that God truly exists and that he is the supreme good, needing nothing outside himself, but needful for the being and well-being of all things. I often turned my earnest attention to this problem, and at times I believed that I could put my finger on what I was looking for, but at other times it completely escaped my mind's eye, until finally, in despair, I decided to give up searching for something that seemed impossible to find. But when I tried to put the whole question out of my mind, so as to avoid crowding out other matters, with which I might make some progress, by this useless preoccupation, then, despite my unwillingness and resistance, it began to force itself on me more persistently than

From A *Scholastic Miscellany*, edited and translated by Eugene R. Fairweather, Vol. X, Library of Christian Classics. Published simultaneously in Great Britain and the United States of America by S.C.M. Press, Ltd., London, and The Westminster Press, Philadelphia. First published in 1956. Used by permission.

[1] The *Monologion*, probably Anselm's first work, was written at Bec in the second half of 1076 (cf. Landgraf, *Einführung*, 53). Text in Schmitt, I, 7–87.

ever. Then, one day, when I was worn out by my vigorous resistance to the obsession, the solution I had ceased to hope for presented itself to me, in the very turmoil of my thoughts, so that I enthusiastically embraced the idea which, in my disquiet, I had spurned.

I thought that the proof I was so glad to find would please some readers if it were written down. Consequently, I have written the little work that follows, dealing with this and one or two other matters, in the role of one who strives to raise his mind to the contemplation of God and seeks to understand what he believes. Neither this essay nor the other one I have already mentioned really seemed to me to deserve to be called a book or to bear an author's name; at the same time, I felt that they could not be published without some title that might encourage anyone into whose hands they fell to read them, and so I gave each of them a title. The first I called *An Example of Meditation on the Grounds of Faith*, and the second *Faith Seeking Understanding*.

But when both of them had been copied under these titles by a number of people, I was urged by many people—and especially by Hugh, the reverend archbishop of Lyons, apostolic legate in Gaul, who ordered this with apostolic authority—to attach my name to them. In order to do this more fittingly, I have named the first *Monologion* (or *Soliloquy*), and the second *Proslogion* (or *Address*).

GOD TRULY IS

And so, O Lord, since thou givest understanding to faith, give me to understand—as far as thou knowest it to be good for me—that thou dost exist, as we believe, and that thou art what we believe thee to be. Now we believe that thou art a being than which none greater can be thought. Or can it be that there is no such being, since "the fool hath said in his heart, 'There is no God' "? But when this same fool hears what I am saying—"A being than which none greater can be thought"—he understands what he hears, and what he understands is in his understanding, even if he does not understand that it exists. For it is one thing for an object to be in the understanding, and another thing to understand that it exists. When a painter considers beforehand what he is going to paint, he has it in his understanding, but he does not suppose that what he has not yet painted already exists. But when he has painted it, he both has it in his understanding and understands that what he has now produced exists. Even the fool, then, must be convinced that a being than which none greater can be thought exists at least in his understanding, since when he hears this he understands it, and whatever is understood is in the understanding. But clearly that than which a greater cannot be thought cannot exist in the understanding alone. For if it is actually in the understanding alone, it can be thought of as existing also in reality, and this is greater. Therefore, if that than which a greater cannot be thought is in the understanding alone, this same thing than which a greater cannot be thought is that than which a greater can be thought. But obviously this is impossible. Without doubt, therefore, there exists, both in the understanding and in reality, something than which a greater cannot be thought.

GOD CANNOT BE THOUGHT OF AS NONEXISTENT

And certainly it exists so truly that it cannot be thought of as nonexistent. For something can be thought of as existing, which cannot be thought of as not existing, and this is greater than that which *can* be thought of as not existing. Thus, if that than which a greater cannot be thought can be thought of as not existing, this very thing than which a greater cannot be thought is *not* that than which a greater cannot be thought. But this is contradictory. So, then, there truly is a being than which a greater cannot be thought—so truly that it cannot even be thought of as not existing.

And *thou* art this being, O Lord our God. Thou so truly art, then, O Lord my God, that thou canst not even be thought of as not existing. And this is right. For if some mind could think of something better than thou, the creature would rise above the Creator and judge its Creator; but this is altogether absurd. And indeed, whatever is, except thyself alone, can be thought of as not existing. Thou alone, therefore, of all beings, hast being in the truest and highest sense, since no other being so truly exists, and thus every other being has less being. Why, then, has "the fool said in his heart, 'There is no God,' " when it is so obvious to the rational mind that, of all beings, thou dost exist supremely? Why indeed, unless it is that he is a stupid fool?

HOW THE FOOL HAS SAID IN HIS HEART WHAT CANNOT BE THOUGHT

But how did he manage to say in his heart what he could not think? Or how is it that he was unable to think what he said in his heart? After all, to say in one's heart and to think are the same thing. Now if it is true—or, rather, since it is true—that he thought it, because he said it in his heart, but did not say it in his heart, since he could not think it, it is clear that something can be said in one's heart or thought in more than one way. For we think of a thing, in one sense, when we think of the word that signifies it, and in another sense, when we understand the very thing itself. Thus, in the first sense God can be thought of as nonexistent, but in the second sense this is quite impossible. For no one who understands what God is can think that God does not exist, even though he says these words in his heart—perhaps without any meaning, perhaps with some quite extraneous meaning. For God is that than which a greater cannot be thought, and whoever understands this rightly must understand that he exists in such a way that he cannot be nonexistent even in thought. He, therefore, who understands that God thus exists cannot think of him as nonexistent.

Thanks be to thee, good Lord, thanks be to thee, because I now understand by thy light what I formerly believed by thy gift, so that even if I were to refuse to believe in thy existence, I could not fail to understand its truth.

AN EXERPT FROM THE AUTHOR'S REPLY TO THE CRITICISMS OF GAUNILO

But, you say, suppose that someone imagined an island in the ocean, surpassing all lands in its fertility. Because of the difficulty, or rather the impossibility, of finding something that does not exist, it might well be called "Lost Island." By reasoning like yours, he might then say that we cannot doubt that it truly exists in reality, because anyone can easily conceive it from a verbal description.[2] I state confidently that if anyone discovers something for me, other than that "than which a greater cannot be thought," existing either in reality or in thought alone, to which the logic of my argument can be applied, I shall find his lost island and give it to him, never to be lost again. But it now seems obvious that this being than which a greater cannot be thought cannot be thought of as nonexistent, because it exists by such a sure reason of truth. For otherwise it would not exist at all. In short, if anyone says that he thinks it does not exist, I say that when he thinks this, he either thinks of something than which a greater cannot be thought or he does not think. If he does not think, he does not think of what he is not thinking of as nonexistent. But if he does think, then he thinks of something which cannot be thought of as nonexistent. For if it could be thought of as nonexistent, it could be thought of as having a beginning and an end. But this is impossible. Therefore, if anyone thinks of it, he thinks of something that cannot even be thought of as nonexistent. But he who thinks of this does not think that it does not exist; if he did, he would think what cannot be thought. Therefore, that than which a greater cannot be thought cannot be thought of as nonexistent.

You say, moreover, that when it is said that the highest reality cannot be *thought of* as nonexistent, it would perhaps be better to say that it cannot be *understood* as nonexistent, or even as possibly nonexistent.[3] But it is more correct to say, as I said, that it cannot be thought. For if I had said that the reality itself cannot be understood not to exist, perhaps you yourself, who say that according to the very definition of the term what is false cannot be understood,[4] would object that nothing that is can be understood as nonexistent. For it is false to say that what exists does not exist. Therefore it would not be peculiar to God to be unable to be understood as nonexistent.[5] But if some one of the things that most certainly are can be understood as nonexistent, other certain things can similarly be understood as nonexistent. But this objection cannot be applied to "thinking," if it is rightly considered. For although none of the things that exist can be understood not to exist, still they can all be thought of as nonexistent, except that which most fully is. For all those things—and only those—which have a beginning or end or are composed of parts can be thought of as nonexistent, along with anything that does not exist as a whole anywhere or at any time (as I have already said).[6] But the only being that cannot be thought of as nonexistent is that in which no thought finds beginning or end or composition of parts, but which any thought finds as a whole, always and everywhere.

You must realize, then, that you can think of yourself as nonexistent, even while you know most certainly that you exist. I am surprised that you said you

[2] Cf. Gaunilo, *Pro insipiente,* 6 (Schmitt, I, 128).
[3] *Ibid.,* 7 (I, 129).
[4] *Ibid.*
[5] *Ibid.*
[6] *Responsio,* 1 (I, 131 f.).

did not know this.[7] For we think of many things as nonexistent when we know that they exist, and of many things as existent when we know that they do not exist—all this not by a real judgment, but by imagining that what we think is so. And indeed, we can think of something as nonexistent, even while we know that it exists, because we are able at the same time to think the one and know the other. And yet we cannot think of it as nonexistent, while we know that it exists, because we cannot think of something as at once existent and nonexistent. Therefore, if anyone distinguishes these two senses of the statement in this way, he will understand that nothing, as long as it is known to exist, can be thought of as nonexistent, and that whatever exists, except that than which a greater cannot be thought, can be thought of as nonexistent, even when it is known to exist. So, then, it is peculiar to God to be unable to be thought of as nonexistent, and nevertheless many things, as long as they exist, cannot be thought of as nonexistent. I think that the way in which it can still be said that God is thought of as nonexistent is stated adequately in the little book itself.[8]

STUDY QUESTIONS

1   Suppose someone said "I can imagine a universe which does not contain God." Does Anselm believe this is possible? Do you?
2   "Anselm has merely proven that when we define the word 'God,' we must include existence in the definition. But this is just 'definitional' existence, not 'real' existence." How do you think Anselm would reply to this?
3   Could there be an ontological argument for the "devil"?
4   Can you prove that something *does not* exist just by looking at its definition? What about a "circular triangle"?
5   A "squircle" is a square circle. A "super-squircle" is an existing squircle. Do super-squircles exist?
6   Gaunilo criticized Anselm's argument by claiming that it could be used to prove the greatest conceivable "anything"—unicorn, island, etc. Do you think that Anselm adequately defends himself against this criticism?

The Five Ways

St. Thomas Aquinas

St. Thomas Aquinas (1226–1274) was one of the greatest philosophers of all time. His systematic marriage of Aristotle's philosophy and Christianity form much of the basis of Catholic theology. Aquinas's "Five Ways" are among the most important and controversial of the arguments for God's existence. Each of the arguments is designed to show that the existence of God is required to explain certain features of the world.

Some of Aquinas's arguments are difficult to understand because they were written within a special philosophical framework. When Aquinas talks

[7] Gaunilo, *loc. cit.*
[8] Cf. *Proslogion,* Chapter IV.

about a "cause," for example, there are two ways of interpreting what he means. The most common interpretation is that a cause brings about the existence of something else, but it is not required to maintain that thing in existence. For example, the cause of a table is the builder, but the table continues to exist even when the builder does not. The second sense of "cause," and the one which concerns Aquinas, is quite different. In this sense, the continued existence of the cause is necessary for the continued existence of the effect. For example, atmospheric pressure is the cause of water rising in a vacuum pump, and the condition of atmospheric pressure must be maintained if water is to continue to be pumped. Similarly, the presence of gravity is the cause of atmospheric pressure, since the continued existence of atmospheric pressure depends upon the continued existence of gravity. In his second argument, then, Aquinas is asking whether there can be an infinite series of such causes. If there cannot be such a series, he has shown that there is a *presently existing* first cause.

The existence of God can be proved in five ways.

The first and more manifest way is the argument from motion. It is certain, and evident to our senses, that in the world some things are in motion. Now whatever is moved is moved by another, for nothing can be moved except it is in potentiality to that towards which it is moved; whereas a thing moves inasmuch as it is in act. For motion is nothing else than the reduction of something from potentiality to actuality. But nothing can be reduced from potentiality to actuality, except by something in a state of actuality. Thus that which is actually hot, as fire, makes wood, which is potentially hot, to be actually hot, and thereby moves and changes it. Now it is not possible that the same thing should be at once in actuality and potentiality in the same respect, but only in different respects. For what is actually hot cannot simultaneously be potentially hot; but it is simultaneously potentially cold. It is therefore impossible that in the same respect and in the same way a thing should be both mover and moved, i.e., that it should move itself. Therefore, whatever is moved must be moved by another. If that by which it is moved be itself moved, then this also must needs be moved by another, and that by another again. But this cannot go on to infinity, because then there would be no first mover, and, consequently, no other mover, seeing that subsequent movers move only inasmuch as they are moved by the first mover; as the staff moves only because it is moved by the hand. Therefore it is necessary to arrive at a first mover, moved by no other; and this everyone understands to be God.

The second way is from the nature of efficient cause. In the world of sensible things we find there is an order of efficient causes. There is no case known (neither is it, indeed, possible) in which a thing is found to be the efficient cause of itself; for so it would be prior to itself, which is impossible. Now in efficient causes it is not possible to go on to infinity, because in all efficient causes following in order, the first is the cause of the intermediate cause, and the intermediate is the cause of the ultimate cause, whether the intermediate cause be several, or one only. Now to take away the cause is to take away the effect. Therefore, if there be no first cause among efficient causes, there will be no ultimate, nor any intermediate, cause. But if in efficient causes it is possible to go on to infinity, there will be no first efficient cause, neither will there be an ultimate effect, nor any intermediate efficient causes; all of which is plainly false. Therefore it is necessary to admit a first efficient cause, to which everyone gives the name of God.

The third way is taken from possibility and necessity, and runs thus. We find in nature things that are possible to be and not to be, since they are found to be generated, and to be corrupted, and consequently, it is possible for them to be and not to be. But it is impossible for these always to exist, for that which can not-be at some time is not. Therefore, if everything can not-be, then at one time there was nothing in existence. Now if this were true, even now there would be nothing in existence, because that which does not exist begins to exist only through something already existing. Therefore, if at one time nothing was in existence, it would have been impossible for anything to have begun to exist; and thus even now nothing would be in existence—which is absurd. Therefore, not all beings are merely possible, but there must exist something the existence of which is necessary. But every necessary thing either has its necessity caused by another, or not. Now it is impossible to go on to infinity in necessary things which have their necessity caused by another, as has been already proved in regard to efficient causes. Therefore we cannot but admit the existence of some being having of itself its own necessity, and not receiving it from another, but rather causing in others their necessity. This all men speak of as God.

The fourth way is taken from the gradation to be found in things. Among beings there are some more and some less good, true, noble, and the like. But *more* and *less* are predicated of different things according as they resemble in their different ways something which is the maximum, as a thing is said to be hotter according as it more nearly resembles that which is hottest; so that there is something which is truest, something best, something noblest, and, consequently, something which is most being, for those things that are greatest in truth are greatest in being, as it is written in *Metaph.* ii. Now the maximum in any genus is the cause of all in that genus, as fire, which is the maximum of heat, is the cause of all hot things, as is said in the same book. Therefore there must also be something which is to all beings the cause of their being, goodness, and every other perfection; and this we call God.

The fifth way is taken from the governance of the world. We see that things which lack knowledge, such as natural bodies, act for an end, and this is evident from their acting always, or nearly always, in the same way, so as to obtain the best result. Hence it is plain that they achieve their end, not fortuitously, but designedly. Now whatever lacks knowledge cannot move towards an end, unless it be directed by some being endowed with knowledge and intelligence; as the arrow is directed by the archer. Therefore some intelligent being exists by whom all natural things are directed to their end; and this being we call God.

STUDY QUESTIONS

1   Suppose Aquinas's "Five Ways" are all sound arguments. Are they sufficient to prove that God exists?
2   In his first proof, Aquinas uses the analogy of the hand pushing the stick to show that change must come from something which is not itself changed. Do you think that this is a fair analogy?
3   In his second proof, Aquinas claims that an infinite series of causes cannot exist. Apparently he thinks that if you believe there is such a series of causes, you cannot believe that the world exists right now. What are the crucial assumptions in his argument? Do you see any unstated assumptions?
4   "If everything has a cause, then God must have a cause. The First Cause Argument is just that easy to refute." What do you think?
5   In his third proof, Aquinas argues that an infinite number of contingent beings cannot exist. What does he mean by a contingent being? Do you think that Aquinas is trying to prove that the world was created by God, or just that God is necessary for it to continue to exist?
6   In his fourth argument, Aquinas claims that we must have an idea of the "best" before we can say that something is "better" than another thing. Do you agree? Can you give illustrations as evidence for your belief?

The Reason for Existence

Richard Taylor

Richard Taylor(1919–   ) is a distinguished American philosopher and professor at the University of Rochester. Although Taylor attempts to prove the existence of God, he does not believe that the religious life can be expressed in an intellectual doctrine. He writes: "Being religious is not holding certain metaphysical and speculative opinions; much less is it going through prescribed liturgical motions. To be religious is to be in a certain state of mind. It is, in fact, to be perpetually high." [1]

Taylor proposes a version of Aquinas's "Third Way" as a proof for the existence of God. He bases his argument on the principle of sufficient reason, which states that there is always some sufficient reason or explanation for the fact that something exists. He argues that this principle requires that there be some being which contains the reason for its existence within itself. Since the material universe is composed of beings which are not of this sort, the being required by the principle of sufficient reason must be different from the material world. This "necessary being" is God.

One of the chief difficulties in understanding Taylor's position is his definition of a "necessary being." This is a being which possesses the reason for its existence within itself. As you read this essay, you will have to carefully consider the way in which Taylor explains this concept and why he does not think

[1] *With Heart and Mind* (New York: St. Martin's, 1973), p. 76.

that the material world can be a necessary being. We are sure you will find the argument intriguing, for it forces the reader to ask, "When is something fully explained?"

Suppose you were strolling in the woods and, in addition to the sticks, stones, and other accustomed litter of the forest floor, you one day came upon some quite unaccustomed object, something not quite like what you had ever seen before and would never expect to find in such a place. Suppose, for example, that it is a large ball, about your own height, perfectly smooth and translucent. You would deem this puzzling and mysterious, certainly, but if one considers the matter, it is no more inherently mysterious that such a thing should exist than that anything else should exist. If you were quite accustomed to finding such objects of various sizes around you most of the time, but had never seen an ordinary rock, then upon finding a large rock in the woods one day you would be just as puzzled and mystified. This illustrates the fact that something that is mysterious ceases to seem so simply by its accustomed presence. It is strange indeed, for example, that a world such as ours should exist; yet few men are very often struck by this strangeness, but simply take it for granted.

Suppose, then, that you have found this translucent ball and are mystified by it. Now whatever else you might wonder about it, there is one thing you would hardly question; namely, that it did not appear there all by itself, that it owes its existence to something. You might not have the remotest idea whence and how it came to be there, but you would hardly doubt that there was an explanation. The idea that it might have come from nothing at all, that it might exist without there being any explanation of its existence, is one that few people would consider worthy of entertaining.

This illustrates a metaphysical belief that seems to be almost a part of reason itself, even though few men ever think upon it; the belief, namely, that there is some explanation for the existence of anything whatever, some reason why it should exist rather than not. The sheer nonexistence of anything, which is not to be confused with the passing out of existence of something, never requires a reason; but existence does. That there should never have been any such ball in the forest does not require any explanation or reason, but that there should ever be such a ball does. If one were to look upon a barren plain and ask why there is not and never has been any large translucent ball there, the natural response would be to ask why there should be; but if one finds such a ball, and wonders why it is there, it is not quite so natural to ask why it should *not* be, as though existence should simply be taken for granted. That anything should not exist, then, and that, for instance, no such ball should exist in the forest, or that there should be no forest for it to occupy, or no continent containing a forest, or no earth, nor any world at all, do not seem to be things for which there needs to be any explanation or reason; but that such things should be, does seem to require a reason.

The principle involved here has been called the principle of sufficient reason. Actually, it is a very general principle, and is best expressed by saying that, in the case of any positive truth, there is some sufficient reason for it, something which, in this sense, makes it true—in short, that there is some sort of explanation, known or unknown, for everything.

Now some truths depend on something else, and are accordingly called *contingent,* while others depend only upon themselves, that is, are true by their very natures and are accordingly called *necessary.* There is, for example, a reason why the stone on my window sill is warm; namely, that the sun is shining upon it. This happens to be true, but not by its very nature. Hence, it is contingent, and depends upon something other than itself. It is also true that all the points of a circle are equidistant from the center, but this truth depends upon nothing but itself. No matter what happens, nothing can make it false. Similarly, it is a truth, and a necessary one, that if the stone on my window sill is a body, as it is, then it has a form, since this fact depends upon nothing but itself for its confirmation. Untruths are also, of course, either contingent or necessary, it being contingently false, for example, that the stone on my window sill is cold, and necessarily false that it is both a body and formless, since this is by its very nature impossible.

The principle of sufficient reason can be illustrated in various ways, as we have done, and if one thinks about it, he is apt to find that he presupposes it in his thinking about reality, but it cannot be proved. It does not appear to be itself a necessary truth, and at the same time it would be most odd to say it is contingent. If one were to try proving it, he would sooner or later have to appeal to considerations that are less plausible than the principle itself. Indeed, it is hard to see how one could even make an argument for it, without already assuming it. For this reason it might properly be called a presupposition of reason itself. One can deny that it is true without embarrassment or fear of refutation, but one is then apt to find that what he is denying is not really what the principle asserts. We shall, then, treat it here as a datum—not something that is provably true, but as something which all men, whether they ever reflect upon it or not, seem more or less to presuppose.

It happens to be true that something exists, that there is, for example, a world, and while no one ever seriously supposes that this might not be so, that there might exist nothing at all, there still seems to be nothing the least necessary in this, considering it just by itself. That no world should ever exist at all is perfectly comprehensible and seems to express not the slightest absurdity. Considering any particular item in the world it seems not at all necessary in itself that it should ever have existed, nor does it appear any more necessary that the totality of these things, or any totality of things, should ever exist.

From the principle of sufficient reason it follows, of course, that there must be a reason, not only for the existence of everything in the world but for the world itself, meaning by "the world" simply everything that ever does exist, except God, in case there is a god. This principle does not imply that there must be some purpose or goal for everything, or for the totality of all things; for explanations need not, and in fact seldom are, teleological or purposeful. All the principle requires is that there be some sort of reason for everything. And it would certainly be odd to maintain that everything in the world owes its existence to something, that nothing in the world is either purely accidental, or such that it just bestows its own being upon itself, and then to deny this of the world itself. One can indeed *say* that the world is in some sense a pure accident, that there simply is no reason at all why this or any world should exist, and one can equally say that the world exists by its very nature, or is an inherently necessary being. But it is at least very odd and arbitrary to deny of this existing world the need for any sufficient reason, whether independent of itself or not, while presupposing that there is a reason for every other thing that ever exists.

Consider again the strange ball that we imagine has been found in the forest. Now we can hardly doubt that there must be an explanation for the existence of such a thing, though we may have no notion what that explanation is. It is not, moreover, the fact of its having been found in the forest rather than elsewhere that renders an explanation necessary. It matters not in the least where it happens to be, for our question is not how it happens to be *there* but how it happens to exist at all. If we in our imagination annihilate the forest, leaving only this ball in an open field, our conviction that it is a contingent thing and owes its existence to something other than itself is not reduced in the least. If we now imagine the field to be annihilated, and in fact everything else as well to vanish into nothingness, leaving only this ball to constitute the entire physical universe, then we cannot for a moment suppose that its existence has thereby been explained, or the need of any explanation eliminated, or that its existence is suddenly rendered self-explanatory. If we now carry this thought one step further and suppose that no other reality ever has existed or ever will exist, that this ball forever constitutes the entire physical universe, then we must still insist on there being some reason independent of itself why it should exist rather than not. If there must be a reason for the existence of any particular thing, then the necessity of such a reason is not eliminated by the mere supposition that certain other things do *not* exist. And again, it matters not at all what the thing in question is, whether it be large and complex, such as the world we actually find ourselves in, or whether it be something small, simple and insignificant, such as a ball, a bacterium, or the merest grain of sand. We do not avoid the necessity of a reason for the existence of something merely by describing it in this way or that. And it would, in any event, seem quite plainly absurd to say that if the world were comprised entirely of a single ball about six feet in diameter, or of a single grain of sand, then it would be contingent and there would have to be some explanation other than itself why such a thing exists, but that, since the actual world is vastly more complex than this, there is no need for an explanation of its existence, independent of itself.

It should now be noted that it is no answer to the question, why a thing exists, to state *how long* it has existed. A geologist does not suppose that he has explained why there should be rivers and mountains merely by pointing out that they are old. Similarly, if one were to ask, concerning the ball of which we have spoken, for some sufficient reason for its being, he would not receive any answer upon being told that it had been there since yesterday. Nor would it be any better answer to say that it had existed since before anyone could remember, or even that it had always existed; for the question was not one concerning its age but its existence. If, to be sure, one were to ask where a given thing came from, or how it came into being, then upon learning that it had always existed he would learn that it never really *came* into being at all; but he could still reasonably wonder why it should exist at all. If, accordingly, the world—that is, the totality of all things excepting God, in case there is a god—had really no beginning at all, but has always existed in some form or other, then there is clearly no answer to the question, where it came from and when; it did not, on this supposition, *come* from anything at all, at any time. But still, it can be asked why there is a world, why indeed there is a beginningless world, why there should have perhaps always been something rather than nothing. And, if the principle of sufficient reason is a good principle, there must be an answer to that question, an answer that is by no means supplied by giving the world an age, or even an infinite age. . . .

If, as seems clearly implied by the principle of sufficient reason, there must be a reason for the existence of heaven and earth—i.e., for the world—then that reason must be found either in the world itself, or outside it, in something that is literally supranatural, or outside heaven and earth. Now if we suppose that the world—i.e., the totality of all things except God—contains within itself the reason for its existence, we are supposing that it exists by its very nature, that is, that it is a necessary being. In that case there would, of course, be no reason for saying that it must depend upon God or anything else for its existence; for if it exists by its very nature, then it depends upon nothing but itself, much as the sun depends upon nothing but itself for its heat. This, however, is implausible, for we find nothing about the world or anything in it to suggest that it exists by its own nature, and we do find, on the contrary, ever so many things to suggest that it does not. For in the first place, anything which exists by its very nature must necessarily be eternal and indestructible. It would be a self-contradiction to say of anything that it exists by its own nature, or is a necessarily existing thing, and at the same time to say that it comes into being or passes away, or that it ever could come into being or pass away. Nothing about the world seems at all like this, for concerning anything in the world, we can perfectly easily think of it as being annihilated, or as never having existed in the first place, without there being the slightest hint of any absurdity in such a supposition. Some of the things in the universe are, to be sure, very old; the moon, for example, or the stars and the planets. It is even possible to imagine that they have always existed. Yet it seems quite impossible to suppose that they owe their existence to nothing but themselves, that they bestow existence upon themselves by their very natures, or that they are in themselves things of such nature that it would be impossible for them not to exist. Even if we suppose that something, such as the sun, for instance, has existed forever, and will never cease, still we cannot conclude just from this that it exists by its own nature. If, as is of course very doubtful, the sun has existed forever and will never cease, then it is possible that its heat and light have also existed forever and will never cease; but that would not show that the heat and light of the sun exist by their own natures. They are obviously contingent and depend on the sun for their existence, whether they are beginningless and everlasting or not.

There seems to be nothing in the world, then, concerning which it is at all plausible to suppose that it exists by its own nature, or contains within itself the reason for its existence. In fact, everything in the world appears to be quite plainly the opposite, namely, something that not only need not exist, but at some time or other, past or future or both, does not in fact exist. Everything in the world seems to have a finite duration, whether long or short. Most things, such as ourselves, exist only for a short while; they come into being, then soon cease. Other things, like the heavenly bodies, last longer, but they are still corruptible, and from all that we can gather about them, they too seem destined eventually to perish. We arrive at the conclusion, then, that while the world may contain some things which have always existed and are destined never to perish, it is neverthe- less doubtful that it contains any such thing and, in any case, everything in the world is capable of perishing, and nothing in it, however long it may already have existed and however long it may yet remain, exists by its own nature, but depends instead upon something else.

While this might be true of everything in the world, is it necessarily true of the world itself? That is, if we grant, as we seem forced to, that nothing in the world exists by its own nature, that everything in the world is contingent and perishable, must we also say that the world itself, or the totality of all these perishable things, is also contingent and perishable? Logically, we are not forced to, for it is logically possible that the totality of all perishable things might itself be imperishable, and hence, that the world might exist by its own nature, even though it is comprised exclusively of things which are contingent. It is not logical- ly necessary that a totality should share the defects of its members. For example, even though every man is mortal, it does not follow from this that the human race, or the totality of all men, is also mortal; for it is possible that there will always be human beings, even though there are no human beings which will always exist. Similarly, it is possible that the world is in itself a necessary thing, even though it is comprised entirely of things that are contingent.

This is logically possible, but it is not plausible. For we find nothing whatev- er about the world, any more than in its parts, to suggest that it exists by its own nature. Concerning anything in the world, we have not the slightest difficulty in supposing that it should perish, or even, that it should never have existed in the first place. We have almost as little difficulty in supposing this of the world itself. It might be somewhat hard to think of everything as utterly perishing and leaving no trace whatever of its ever having been, but there seems to be not the slightest difficulty in imagining that the world should never have existed in the first place. We can, for instance, perfectly easily suppose that nothing in the world had ever existed except, let us suppose, a single grain of sand, and we can thus suppose that this grain of sand has forever constituted the whole universe. Now if we consider just this grain of sand, it is quite impossible for us to suppose that it exists by its very nature, and could never have failed to exist. It clearly depends for its existence upon something other than itself, if it depends on anything at all. The same will be true if we consider the world to consist, not of one grain of sand, but of two, or of a million, or, as we in fact find, of a vast number of stars and planets and all their minuter parts.

It would seem, then, that the world, in case it happens to exist at all—and this is quite beyond doubt—is contingent and thus dependent upon something other than itself for its existence, if it depends upon anything at all. And it must depend upon something, for otherwise there would be no reason why it exists in the first place. Now that upon which the world depends must be something that either exists by its own nature or does not. If it does not exist by its own nature, then it, in turn, depends for its existence upon something else, and so on. Now then, we can say either of two things; namely, (1) that the world depends for its existence upon something else, which in turn depends on still another thing, this depending upon still another, *ad infinitum;* or (2) that the world derives its existence from something that exists by its own nature and which is accordingly eternal and imperishable, and is the creator of heaven and earth. The first of these alternatives, however, is impossible, for it does not render a sufficient reason why anything should exist in the first place. Instead of supplying a reason why any world should exist, it repeatedly begs off giving a reason. It explains what is dependent and perishable in terms of what is itself dependent and perishable, leaving us still without a reason why perishable things should exist at all, which is what we are seeking. Ultimately, then, it would seem that the world, or the totality of contingent or perishable things, in case it exists at all, must depend upon something that is necessary and imperishable, and which accordingly exists, not in dependence upon something else, but by its own nature.

What has been said thus far gives some intimation of what meaning should be attached to the concept of a self-caused being, a concept that is quite generally misunderstood, sometimes even by scholars. To say that something—God, for example—is self-caused, or is the cause of its own existence, does not mean that this being brings itself into existence, which is a perfectly absurd idea. Nothing can *bring* itself into existence. To say that something is self-caused (*causa sui*) means only that it exists, not contingently or in dependence upon something else, but by its own nature, which is only to say that it is a being which is such that it can neither come into being nor perish. Now whether such a being in fact exists or not, there is in any case no absurdity in the idea. We have found, in fact, that the principle of sufficient reason seems to point to the existence of such a being, as that upon which the world, with everything in it, must ultimately depend for its existence.

A being that depends for its existence upon nothing but itself, and is in this sense self-caused, can equally be described as a necessary being; that is to say, a being that is not contingent, and hence not perishable. For in the case of anything which exists by its own nature, and is dependent upon nothing else, it is impossible that it should not exist, which is equivalent to saying that it is necessary. Many persons have professed to find the gravest difficulties in this concept, too, but that is partly because it has been confused with other notions. If it makes sense to speak of anything as an *impossible* being, or something which by its very nature does not exist, then it is hard to see why the idea of a necessary being, or something which in its very nature exists, should not be just as comprehensible. And of course, we have not the slightest difficulty in speaking of something, such as a square circle or a formless body, as an impossible being. And if it makes sense to speak of something as being perishable, contingent, and dependent upon something other than itself for its existence, as it surely does, then there seems to be no difficulty in thinking of something as imperishable and dependent upon nothing other than itself for its existence.

From these considerations we can see also what is properly meant by a first cause, an appellative that has often been applied to God by theologians, and which many persons have deemed an absurdity. It is a common criticism of this notion to say that there need not be any first cause, since the series of causes and effects which constitute the history of the universe might be infinite or beginning-less and must, in fact, be infinite in case the universe itself had no beginning in time. This criticism, however, reflects a total misconception of what is meant by a first cause. *First* here does not mean first in time, and when God is spoken of as a first cause, he is not being described as a being which, at some time in the remote past, *started* everything. To describe God as a first cause is only to say that he is literally a *primary* rather than a secondary cause, an *ultimate* rather than a derived cause, or a being upon which all other things, heaven and earth, ultimately depend for their existence. It is, in short, only to say that God is the creator, in the sense of creation explained above. Now this, of course, is perfectly consistent with saying that the world is eternal or beginningless. As we have seen, one gives no reason for the existence of a world merely by giving it an age, even if it is supposed to have an infinite age. To use a helpful analogy, we can say that the sun is the first cause of daylight and, for that matter, of the moonlight of the night as well, which means only that daylight and moonlight ultimately depend upon the sun for their existence. The moon, on the other hand, is only a second-ary or derivative cause of its light. This light would be no less dependent upon the sun if we affirmed that it had no beginning, for an ageless and beginningless light requires a source no less than an ephemeral one. If we supposed that the sun has always existed, and with it its light, then we would have to say that the sun has always been the first—i.e., the primary or ultimate—cause of its light. Such is precisely the manner in which God should be thought of, and is by theologians often thought of, as the first cause of heaven and earth.

STUDY QUESTIONS

1   What is the principle of sufficient reason? How does Taylor establish its truth? Can you think of a way of challenging the principle?
2   Do you think that Taylor's concept of a necessary being is the same as Anselm's concept of God?
3   Does Taylor think that if something is eternal that it exists by its own nature?
4   What does Taylor mean when he says that God is the first cause? Does this mean that the physical universe is not eternal?
5   Taylor distinguishes between the "world" and the things which make it up. He says that he cannot determine anything about the world itself which would make it neces-sary. What is his argument for this point? Do you agree with it?

God and Design

David Hume

David Hume (1711–1776), one of the great skeptics of all time, was a central figure in the development of British empiricism. This school of thought maintains that all ideas arise from perceptual experience and, consequently, that all knowledge must be based on observation. His distrust of abstract reasoning and his failure to discover any empirical evidence for the existence of God made Hume unsympathetic to religion. In the following selection from *Dialogues Concerning Natural Religion,* Philo, who represents Hume's position, is pitted against Cleanthes, who symbolizes all theologians who think that the existence of God can be proved by scientific reasoning. Hume would not allow the *Dialogues* to be published during his lifetime, for he was unsure what the public reaction would be.

Cleanthes believes that the universe exhibits traces of design. If we were to discover a clock, for example, we would be justified in inferring that it was created by an intelligent being because we have observed things like clocks being created by such beings. Since the universe itself is like a clock we can infer that it, too, was created by an intelligent being. Philo, however, thinks that such an argument is too weak to justify belief. Arguing in the empiricist tradition, Philo maintains that since we have not observed universes in the making, we cannot be justified in believing that the present universe came about by an intelligent cause. He suggests that perhaps matter has within itself the power to produce complex organizations similar to those created by humans. It is on this point that Hume's thought displays the scientific limitations of his era. A century later, Darwin would add a new dimension to this debate, ensuring that it would rage into the twentieth century.

Not to lose any time in circumlocutions, said CLEANTHES, addressing himself to DEMEA, much less in replying to the pious declamations of PHILO; I shall briefly explain how I conceive this matter. Look round the world: Contemplate the whole and every part of it: You will find it to be nothing but one great machine, subdivided into an infinite number of lesser machines, which again admit of subdivisions, to a degree beyond what human senses and faculties can trace and explain. All these various machines, and even their most minute parts, are adjusted to each other with an accuracy, which ravishes into admiration all men, who have ever contemplated them. The curious adapting of means to ends, throughout all nature, resembles exactly, though it much exceeds, the productions of human contrivance; of human design, thought, wisdom, and intelligence. Since therefore the effects resemble each other, we are led to infer, by all the rules of analogy, that the causes also resemble; and that the Author of nature is somewhat similar to the mind of man; though possessed of much larger faculties, proportioned to the grandeur of the work, which he has executed. By this argument *a posteriori*, and by this argument alone, we do prove at once the existence of a Deity, and his similarity to human mind and intelligence.

From *Dialogues Concerning Natural Religion* by David Hume, first published in 1779.

I shall be so free, CLEANTHES, said DEMEA, as to tell you, that from the beginning, I could not approve of your conclusion concerning the similarity of the Deity to men; still less can I approve of the mediums, by which you endeavour to establish it. What! No demonstration of the being of a God! No abstract arguments! No proofs *a priori!* Are these, which have hitherto been so much insisted on by philosophers, all fallacy, all sophism? Can we reach no farther in this subject than experience and probability? I will not say, that this is betraying the cause of a Deity: But surely, by this affected candour, you give advantage to atheists, which they never could obtain, by the mere dent of argument and reasoning.

What I chiefly scruple in this subject, said PHILO, is not so much, that all religious arguments are by CLEANTHES reduced to experience, as that they appear not to be even the most certain and irrefragable of that inferior kind. That a stone will fall, that fire will burn, that the earth has solidity, we have observed a thousand and a thousand times; and when any new instance of this nature is presented, we draw without hesitation the accustomed inference. The exact similarity of the cases gives us a perfect assurance of a similar event; and a stronger evidence is never desired nor sought after. But wherever you depart, in the least, from the similarity of the cases, you diminish proportionably the evidence; and may at last bring it to a very weak *analogy*, which is confessedly liable to error and uncertainty. After having experienced the circulation of the blood in human creatures, we make no doubt that it takes place in Titius and Mævius: But from its circulation in frogs and fishes, it is only a presumption, though a strong one, from analogy, that it takes place in men and other animals. The analogical reasoning is much weaker, when we infer the circulation of the sap in vegetables from our experience that the blood circulates in animals; and those, who hastily followed that imperfect analogy, are found, by more accurate experiments, to have been mistaken.

If we see a house, CLEANTHES, we conclude, with the greatest certainty, that it had an architect or builder; because this is precisely that species of effect, which we have experienced to proceed from that species of cause. But surely you will not affirm, that the universe bears such a resemblance to a house, that we can with the same certainty infer a similar cause, or that the analogy is here entire and perfect. The dissimilitude is so striking, that the utmost you can here pretend to is a guess, a conjecture, a presumption concerning a similar cause; and how that pretension will be received in the world, I leave you to consider.

It would surely be very ill received, replied CLEANTHES; and I should be deservedly blamed and detested, did I allow that the proofs of a Deity amounted to no more than a guess or conjecture. But is the whole adjustment of means to ends in a house and in the universe so slight a resemblance? The economy of final causes? The order, proportion, and arrangement of every part? Steps of a stair are plainly contrived, that human legs may use them in mounting; and this inference is certain and infallible. Human legs are also contrived for walking and mounting; and this inference, I allow, is not altogether so certain, because of the dissimilarity which you remark; but does it, therefore, deserve the name only of presumption or conjecture?

Good God! cried DEMEA, interrupting him, where are we? Zealous defenders of religion allow, that the proofs of a Deity fall short of perfect evidence! And you, PHILO, on whose assistance I depended, in proving the adorable mysteriousness of the divine nature, do you assent to all these extravagant opinions of CLEANTHES? For what other name can I give them? Or why spare my censure, when such principles are advanced, supported by such an authority, before so young a man as PAMPHILUS?

You seem not to apprehend, replied PHILO, that I argue with CLEANTHES in his own way; and by showing him the dangerous consequences of his tenets, hope at last to reduce him to our opinion. But what sticks most with you, I observe, is the representation which CLEANTHES has made of the argument *a posteriori;* and finding that that argument is likely to escape your hold and vanish into air, you think it so disguised that you can scarcely believe it to be set in its true light. Now, however much I may dissent, in other respects, from the dangerous principles of CLEANTHES, I must allow, that he has fairly represented that argument; and I shall endeavor so to state the matter to you, that you will entertain no farther scruples with regard to it.

Were a man to abstract from every thing which he knows or has seen, he would be altogether incapable, merely from his own ideas, to determine what kind of scene the universe must be, or to give the preference to one state or situation of things about another. For as nothing, which he clearly conceives, could be esteemed impossible or implying a contradiction, every chimera of his fancy would be upon an equal footing; nor could he assign any just reason, why he adheres to one idea or system, and rejects the others, which are equally possible.

Again; after he opens his eyes, and contemplates the world, as it really is, it would be impossible for him, at first, to assign the cause of any one event; much less, of the whole of things or of the universe. He might set his fancy a rambling; and she might bring him in an infinite variety of reports and representations. These would all be possible; but being all equally possible, he would never, of himself, give a satisfactory account for his preferring one of them to the rest. Experience alone can point out to him the true cause of any phenomenon.

Now according to this method of reasoning, DEMEA, it follows (and is, indeed, tacitly allowed by CLEANTHES himself) that order, arrangement, or the adjustment of final causes is not, of itself, any proof of design; but only so far as it has been experienced to proceed from that principle. For aught we can know *a priori,* matter may contain the source or spring of order originally, within itself, as well as mind does; and there is no more difficulty in conceiving, that the several elements, from an internal unknown cause, may fall into the most exquisite arrangement, than to conceive that their ideas, in the great, universal mind, from a like internal, unknown cause, fall into that arrangement. The equal possibility of both these suppositions is allowed. By experience we find (according to CLEANTHES), that there is a difference between them. Throw several pieces of steel together, without shape or form; they will never arrange themselves so as to compose a watch: Stone, and mortar, and wood, without an architect, never erect a house. But the ideas in a human mind, we see, by an unknown, inexplicable economy, arrange themselves so as to form the plan of a watch or house. Experience, therefore, proves, that there is an original principle of order in mind, not in matter. From similar effects we infer similar causes. The adjustment of means to ends is alike in the universe, as in a machine of human contrivance. The causes, therefore, must be resembling.

I was from the beginning scandalised, I must own, with this resemblance, which is asserted, between the Deity and human creatures; and must conceive it to imply such a degradation of the supreme Being as no sound theist could endure. With your assistance, therefore, DEMEA, I shall endeavour to defend what you justly call the adorable mysteriousness of the divine nature, and shall refute this reasoning of CLEANTHES; provided he allows, that I have made a fair representation of it.

When CLEANTHES had assented, PHILO, after a short pause, proceeded in the following manner.

That all inferences, CLEANTHES, concerning fact, are founded on experience, and that all experimental reasonings are founded on the supposition, that similar causes prove similar effects, and similar effects similar causes; I shall not, at present, much dispute with you. But observe, I entreat you, with what extreme caution all just reasoners proceed in the transferring of experiments to similar cases. Unless the cases be exactly similar, they repose no perfect confidence in applying their past observation to any particular phenomenon. Every alteration of circumstances occasions a doubt concerning the event; and it requires new experiments to prove certainly, that the new circumstances are of no moment or importance. A change in bulk, situation, arrangement, age, disposition of the air, or surrounding bodies; any of these particulars may be attended with the most unexpected consequences: And unless the objects be quite familiar to us, it is the highest temerity to expect with assurance, after any of these changes, an event similar to that which before fell under our observation. The slow and deliberate steps of philosophers, here, if any where, are distinguished from the precipitate march of the vulgar, who, hurried on by the smallest similitude, are incapable of all discernment or consideration.

But can you think, CLEANTHES, that your usual phlegm and philosophy have been preserved in so wide a step as you have taken, when you compared to the universe houses, ships, furniture, machines; and from their similarity in some circumstances inferred a similarity in their causes? Thought, design, intelligence, such as we discover in men and other animals, is no more than one of the springs and principles of the universe, as well as heat or cold, attraction or repulsion, and a hundred others, which fall under daily observation. It is an active cause, by which some particular parts of nature, we find, produce alterations on other parts. But can a conclusion, with any propriety, be transferred from parts to the whole? Does not the great disproportion bar all comparison and inference? From observing the growth of a hair, can we learn any thing concerning the generation of a man? Would the manner of a leaf's blowing, even though perfectly known, afford us any instruction concerning the vegetation of a tree?

But allowing that we were to take the *operations* of one part of nature upon another for the foundation of our judgment concerning the *origin* of the whole (which never can be admitted) yet why select so minute, so weak, so bounded a principle as the reason and design of animals as found to be upon this planet? What peculiar privilege has this little agitation of the brain which we call thought, that we must thus make it the model of the whole universe? Our partiality in our own favour does indeed present it on all occasions: But sound philosophy ought carefully to guard against so natural an illusion.

So far from admitting, continued PHILO, that the operations of a part can afford us any just conclusion concerning the origin of the whole, I will not allow any one part to form a rule for another part, if the latter be very remote from the former. Is there any reasonable ground to conclude, that the inhabitants of other planets possess thought, intelligence, reason, or any thing similar to these faculties in men? When nature has so extremely diversified her manner of operation in this small globe; can we imagine, that she incessantly copies herself throughout so immense a universe? And if thought, as we may well suppose, be confined merely to this narrow corner, and has even there so limited a sphere of action; with what propriety can we assign it for the original cause of all things? The narrow views of a peasant, who makes his domestic economy the rule for the government of kingdoms, is in comparison a pardonable sophism.

But were we ever so much assured, that a thought and reason, resembling the human, were to be found throughout the whole universe, and were its activity elsewhere vastly greater and more commanding than it appears in this globe: Yet I cannot see, why the operations of a world, constituted, arranged, adjusted, can with any propriety be extended to a world, which is in its embryo-state, and is advancing towards that constitution and arrangement. By observation, we know somewhat of the economy, action, and nourishment of a finished animal; but we must transfer with great caution that observation to the growth of a foetus in womb, and still more, to the formation of an animalcule in the loins of its male parent. Nature, we find, even from our limited experience, possesses an infinite number of springs and principles, which incessantly discover themselves on every change of her position and situation. And what new and unknown principles would actuate her in so new and unknown a situation as that of the formation of a universe, we cannot, without the utmost temerity, pretend to determine.

A very small part of this great system, during a very short time, is very imperfectly discovered to us: And do we thence pronounce decisively concerning the origin of the whole?

Admirable conclusion! Stone, wood, brick, iron, brass have not, at this time, in this minute globe of earth, an order or arrangement without human art and contrivance: Therefore the universe could not originally attain its order and arrangement, without something similar to human art. But is a part of nature a rule for another part very wide of the former? Is it a rule for the whole? Is a very small part a rule for the universe? Is nature in one situation, a certain rule for nature in another situation, vastly different from the former?

And can you blame me, CLEANTHES, if I here imitate the prudent reserve of SIMONIDES, who, according to the noted story, being asked by HIERO, *What God was?* desired a day to think of it, and then two days more; and after that manner continually prolonged the term, without ever bringing in his definition or description? Could you even blame me, if I had answered at first, *that I did not know,* and was sensible that this subject lay vastly beyond the reach of my faculties? You might cry out sceptic and raillier as much as you pleased: But having found, in so many other subjects, much more familiar, the imperfections and even contradictions of human reason, I never should expect any success from its feeble conjectures, in a subject, so sublime, and so remote from the sphere of our observation. When two *species* of objects have always been observed, to be conjoined together, I can *infer,* by custom, the existence of one whenever I *see* the existence of the other: And this I call an argument from experience. But how this argument can have place, where the objects, as in the present case, are single, individual, without parallel, or specific resemblance, may be difficult to explain. And will any man tell me with a serious countenance, that an orderly universe must arise from some thought and art, like the human; because we have experience of it? To ascertain this reasoning, it were requisite, that we had experience of the origin of worlds; and it is not sufficient surely, that we have seen ships and cities arise from human art and contrivance. . . .

But because I know you are not much swayed by names and authorities, I shall endeavour to show you, a little more distinctly, the inconveniences of that anthropomorphism, which you have embraced; and shall prove, that there is no ground to suppose a plan of the world to be formed in the divine mind, consisting of distinct ideas, differently arranged; in the same manner as an architect forms in his head the plan of a house which he intends to execute.

It is not easy, I own, to see what is gained by this supposition, whether we judge of the matter by *reason* or by *experience.* We are still obliged to mount higher, in order to find the cause of this cause, which you had assigned as satisfactory and conclusive.

If *reason* (I mean abstract reason, derived from enquiries *a priori*) be not alike mute with regard to all questions concerning cause and effect; this sentence at least it will venture to pronounce, That a mental world or universe of ideas requires a cause as much as does a material world or universe of objects; and if similar in its arrangement must require a similar cause. For what is there in this subject, which should occasion a different conclusion or inference? In an abstract view, they are entirely alike; and no difficulty attends the one supposition, which is not common to both of them.

Again, when we will needs force *experience* to pronounce some sentence, even on these subjects, which lie beyond her sphere; neither can she perceive any material difference in this particular, between these two kinds of worlds, but finds them to be governed by similar principles, and to depend upon an equal variety of causes in their operations. We have specimens in miniature of both of them. Our own mind resembles the one: A vegetable or animal body the other. Let experience, therefore, judge from these samples. Nothing seems more delicate with regard to its causes than thought; and as these causes never operate in two persons after the same manner, so we never find two persons, who think exactly alike. Nor indeed does the same person think exactly alike at any two different periods of time. A difference of age, of the disposition of his body, of weather, of food, of company, of books, of passions; any of these particulars or others more

minute, are sufficient to alter the curious machinery of thought, and communicate to it very different movements and operations. As far as we can judge,
vegetables and animal bodies are not more delicate in their motions, nor depend
upon a greater variety or more curious adjustment of springs and principles.

How therefore shall we satisfy ourselves concerning the cause of that Being,
whom you suppose the Author of nature, or, according to your system of anthropomorphism, the ideal world, into which you trace the material? Have we not the
same reason to trace that ideal world into another ideal world, or new intelligent
principle? But if we stop, and go no farther; why go so far? Why not stop at the
material world? How can we satisfy ourselves without going on *in infinitum?* And
after all, what satisfaction is there in that infinite progression? Let us remember
the story of the INDIAN philosopher and his elephant. It was never more applicable than to the present subject. If the material world rests upon a similar ideal
world, this ideal world must rest upon some other; and so on, without end. It
were better, therefore, never to look beyond the present material world. By supposing it to contain the principle of its order within itself, we really assert it to be
God; and the sooner we arrive at that divine Being so much the better. When you
go one step beyond the mundane system you only excite an inquisitive humour,
which it is impossible ever to satisfy.

To say, that the différent ideas, which compose the reason of the supreme
Being, fall into order, of themselves, and by their own nature, is really to talk
without any precise meaning. If it has a meaning, I would fain know, why it is not
as good sense to say, that the parts of the material world fall into order, of
themselves, and by their own nature? Can the one opinion be intelligible, while
the other is not so?

We have, indeed, experience of ideas, which fall into order, of themselves,
and without any *known* cause: But, I am sure, we have a much larger experience
of matter, which does the same; as in all instances of generation and vegetation,
where the accurate analysis of the cause exceeds all human comprehension. We
have also experience of particular systems of thought and of matter, which have
no order; of the first, in madness, of the second, in corruption. Why then should
we think, that order is more essential to one than the other? And if it requires a
cause in both, what do we gain by your system, in tracing the universe of objects
into a similar universe of ideas? The first step, which we make, leads us on for
ever. It were, therefore, wise in us, to limit all our enquiries to the present world,
without looking farther. No satisfaction can ever be attained by these speculations, which so far exceed the narrow bounds of human understanding.

In like manner, when it is asked, what cause produces order in the ideas of
the supreme Being, can any other reason be assigned by you, anthropomorphites,
than that it is a *rational* faculty, and that such is the nature of the Deity? But why
a similar answer will not be equally satisfactory in accounting for the order of the
world, without having recourse to any such intelligent Creator as you insist on,
may be difficult to determine. It is only to say, that *such* is the nature of material
objects, and that they are all originally possessed of a *faculty* of order and proportion. These are only more learned and elaborate ways of confessing our igno-

rance; nor has the one hypothesis any real advantage above the other, except in its greater conformity to vulgar prejudices.

You have displayed this argument with great emphasis, replied CLEANTHES: You seem not sensible, how easy it is to answer it. Even in common life, if I assign a cause for any event; is it any objection, PHILO, that I cannot assign the cause of that cause, and answer every new question, which may incessantly be started? And what philosophers could possibly submit to so rigid a rule? philosophers, who confess ultimate causes to be totally unknown, and are sensible, that the most refined principles, into which they trace the phenomena, are still to them as inexplicable as these phenomena themselves are to the vulgar. The order and arrangement of nature, the curious adjustment of final causes, the plain use and intention of every part and organ; all these bespeak in the clearest language an intelligent cause or Author. The heavens and the earth join in the same testimony: The whole chorus of nature raises one hymn to the praises of its Creator: You alone, or almost alone, disturb this general harmony. You start abstruse doubts, cavils, and objections: you ask me, what is the cause of this cause? I know not; I care not; that concerns not me. I have found a Deity; and here I stop my enquiry. Let those go farther, who are wiser or more enterprising.

I pretend to be neither, replied PHILO: And for that very reason, I should never perhaps have attempted to go so far; especially when I am sensible, that I must at last be contented to sit down with the same answer, which, without farther trouble, might have satisfied me from the beginning.

But to show you still more inconveniences, continued PHILO, in your anthropomorphism; please to take a new survey of your principles. *Like effects prove like causes.* This is the experimental argument; and this, you say too, is the sole theological argument. Now it is certain, that the liker the effects are, which are seen, and the liker the causes, which are inferred, the stronger is the argument. Every departure on either side diminishes the probability, and renders the experiment less conclusive. You cannot doubt of this principle: Neither ought you to reject its consequences.

Now, CLEANTHES, said PHILO, with an air of alacrity and triumph, mark the consequences. *First,* By this method of reasoning, you renounce all claim to infinity in any of the attributes of the Deity. For as the cause ought only to be proportioned to the effect, and the effect, so far as it falls under our cognisance, is not infinite; what pretensions have we, upon your suppositions, to ascribe that attribute to the divine Being? You will still insist, that, by removing him so much from all similarity to human creatures, we give into the most arbitrary hypothesis, and at the same time weaken all proofs of his existence.

Secondly, You have no reason, on your theory, for ascribing perfection to the Deity, even in his finite capacity; or for supposing him free from every error, mistake, or incoherence in his undertakings. There are many inexplicable difficulties in the works of nature, which, if we allow a perfect Author to be proved *a priori,* are easily solved, and become only seeming difficulties, from the narrow capacity of man, who cannot trace infinite relations. But according to your method of reasoning, these difficulties become all real; and perhaps will be insisted on, as new instances of likeness to human art and contrivance. At least, you must acknowledge, that it is impossible for us to tell, from our limited views, whether this system contains any great faults, or deserves any considerable praise, if compared to other possible, and even real systems. Could a peasant, if the ÆNEID were read to him, pronounce that poem to be absolutely faultless, or even assign to it its proper rank among the productions of human wit; he, who had never seen any other production?

But were this world ever so perfect a production, it must still remain uncertain, whether all the excellencies of the work can justly be ascribed to the workman. If we survey a ship, what an exalted idea must we form of the ingenuity of the carpenter, who framed so complicated, useful, and beautiful a machine? And what surprise must we entertain, when we find him a stupid mechanic, who imitated others, and copied an art, which, through a long succession of ages, after multiplied trials, mistakes, corrections, deliberations, and controversies, had been gradually improving? Many worlds might have been botched and bungled, throughout an eternity, ere this system was struck out: Much labour lost: Many fruitless trials made: And a slow, but continued improvement carried on during infinite ages in the art of world-making. In such subjects, who can determine, where the truth; nay, who can conjecture where the probability, lies; amidst a great number of hypotheses which may be proposed, and a still greater number which may be imagined?

And what shadow of an argument, continued PHILO, can you produce, from your hypothesis, to prove the unity of the Deity? A great number of men join in building a house or ship, in rearing a city, in framing a Commonwealth: Why may not several Deities combine in contriving and framing a world? This is only so much greater similarity to human affairs. By sharing the work among several, we may so much farther limit the attributes of each, and get rid of that extensive power and knowledge, which must be supposed in one Deity, and which, according to you, can only serve to weaken the proof of his existence. And if such foolish, such vicious creatures as man can yet often unite in framing and executing one plan; how much more those Deities or Dæmons, whom we may suppose several degrees more perfect?

It must be a slight fabric, indeed, said DEMEA, which can be erected on so tottering a foundation. While we are uncertain, whether there is one Deity or many; whether the Deity or Deities, to whom we owe our existence, be perfect or imperfect, subordinate or supreme, dead or alive; what trust or confidence can we repose in them? What devotion or worship address to them? What veneration or obedience pay them? To all the purposes of life, the theory of religion becomes altogether useless: And even with regard to speculative consequences, its uncertainty, according to you, must render it totally precarious and unsatisfactory.

I must confess, PHILO, replied CLEANTHES, that of all men living, the task which you have undertaken, of raising doubts and objections, suits you best, and seems, in a manner, natural and unavoidable to you. So great is your fertility of invention, that I am not ashamed to acknowledge myself unable, in a sudden, to solve regularly such out-of-the-way difficulties as you incessantly start upon me: Though I clearly see, in general, their fallacy and error. And I question not, but you are yourself, at present, in the same case, and have not the solution so ready as the objection; while you must be sensible, that common sense and reason is entirely against you, and that such whimsies, as you have delivered, may puzzle, but never can convince us.

What you ascribe to the fertility of my invention, replied PHILO, is entirely owing to the nature of the subject. In subjects, adapted to the narrow compass of human reason, there is commonly but one determination, which carries probability or conviction with it; and to a man of sound judgment, all other suppositions, but that one, appear entirely absurd and chimerical. But in such questions as the present, a hundred contradictory views may preserve a kind of imperfect analogy; and invention has here full scope to exert itself. Without any great effort of thought, I believe that I could, in an instant, propose other systems of cosmogony, which would have some faint appearance of truth; though it is a thousand, a million to one, if either yours or any one of mine be the true system.

For instance; what if I should revive the old EPICUREAN hypothesis? This is commonly, and I believe, justly, esteemed the most absurd system, that has yet been proposed; yet, I know not, whether, with a few alterations, it might not be brought to bear a faint appearance of probability. Instead of supposing matter infinite, as EPICURUS did; let us suppose it finite. A finite number of particles is only susceptible of finite transpositions: And it must happen, in an eternal duration, that every possible order or position must be tried an infinite number of times. This world, therefore, with all its events, even the most minute, has before been produced and destroyed, and will again be produced and destroyed, without any bounds and limitations. No one, who has a conception of the powers of infinite, in comparison of finite, will ever scruple this determination.

But this supposes, said DEMEA, that matter can acquire motion, without any voluntary agent or first mover.

And where is the difficulty, replied PHILO, of that supposition? Every event, before experience, is equally difficult and incomprehensible; and every event, after experience, is equally easy and intelligible. Motion, in many instances, from gravity, from elasticity, from electricity, begins in matter, without any known voluntary agent; and to suppose always, in these cases, an unknown voluntary agent, is mere hypothesis; and hypothesis attended with no advantages. The beginning of motion in matter itself is as conceivable *a priori* as its communication from mind and intelligence.

Besides, why may not motion have been propagated by impulse through all eternity, and the same stock of it, or nearly the same, be still upheld in the universe? As much as is lost by the composition of motion, as much is gained by its resolution. And whatever the causes are, the fact is certain, that matter is, and always has been in continual agitation, as far as human experience or tradition reaches. There is not probably, at present, in the whole universe, one particle of matter at absolute rest.

And this very consideration too, continued PHILO, which we have stumbled on in the course of the argument, suggests a new hypothesis of cosmogony, that is not absolutely absurd and improbable. Is there a system, an order, an economy of things, by which matter can preserve that perpetual agitation, which seems essential to it, and yet maintain a constancy in the forms, which it produces? There certainly is such an economy: For this is actually the case with the present world. The continual motion of matter, therefore, in less than infinite transpositions, must produce this economy or order; and by its very nature, that order, when once established, supports itself, for many ages, if not to eternity. But wherever matter is so poised, arranged, and adjusted as to continue in perpetual motion, and yet preserve a constancy in the forms, its situation must, of necessity, have all the same appearance of art and contrivance which we observe at present. All the parts of each form must have a relation to each other, and to the whole: And the whole itself must have a relation to the other parts of the universe; to the element, in which the form subsists; to the materials, with which it repairs its waste and decay; and to every other form, which is hostile or friendly. A defect in any of these particulars destroys the form; and the matter, of which it is composed, is again set loose, and is thrown into irregular motions and fermentations, till it unite itself to some other regular form. If no such form be prepared to receive it, and if there be a great quantity of this corrupted matter in the universe, the universe itself is entirely disordered; whether it be the feeble embryo of a world in its first beginnings, that is thus destroyed, or the rotten carcass of one, languishing in old age and infirmity. In either case, a chaos ensues; till finite, though innumerable revolutions produce at last some forms, whose parts and organs are so adjusted as to support the forms amidst a continued succession of matter.

Suppose (for we shall endeavour to vary the expression), that matter were thrown into any position, by a blind, unguided force; it is evident that this first position must in all probability be the most confused and most disorderly imaginable, without any resemblance to those works of human contrivance, which, along with a symmetry of parts, discover an adjustment of means to ends and a tendency to self-preservation. If the actuating force cease after this operation, matter must remain for ever in disorder, and continue an immense chaos, without any proportion or activity. But suppose, that the actuating force, whatever it be, still continues in matter, this first position will immediately give place to a second, which will likewise in all probability be as disorderly as the first, and so on, through many successions of changes and revolutions. No particular order or position ever continues a moment unaltered. The original force, still remaining in activity, gives a perpetual restlessness to matter. Every possible situation is produced, and instantly destroyed. If a glimpse or dawn of order appears for a moment, it is instantly hurried away, and confounded, by that never-ceasing force, which actuates every part of matter.

Thus the universe goes on for many ages in a continued succession of chaos and disorder. But is it not possible that it may settle at last, so as not to lose its motion and active force (for that we have supposed inherent in it), yet so as to preserve an uniformity of appearance, amidst the continual motion and fluctuation of its parts? This we find to be the case with the universe at present. Every individual is perpetually changing, and every part of every individual, and yet the whole remains, in appearance, the same. May we not hope for such a position, or rather be assured of it, from the eternal revolutions of unguided matter, and may not this account for all the appearing wisdom and contrivance which is in the universe? Let us contemplate the subject a little, and we shall find, that this adjustment, if attained by matter, of a seeming stability in the forms, with a real and perpetual revolution or motion of parts, affords a plausible, if not a true solution of the difficulty.

STUDY QUESTIONS

1 Philo says that "order, arrangment, or the adjustment of final causes is not, of itself, any proof of design." When are such features good evidence for design, according to Philo? Do you agree with Philo?

2 Philo points out that thought, as well as natural objects, has an organized structure. What is the significance of this for his argument?

3 How do you think Philo would respond to Taylor's use of the principle of sufficient reason?

4 Philo claims that Cleanthes's argument cannot establish any of the usual properties of God. Why is this? Can you think of any additional arguments which might get Cleanthes out of his difficulties?

5 What is the epicurean hypothesis which Philo wishes to revive? Would you say it is a stronger explanation of the universe? What would Taylor say about it?

6 Suppose you discovered a complicated machine that made other machines just like itself. Would your curiosity be satisfied if you were told that these machines had been creating themselves for an infinitely long time? If not, what sort of facts would you wish explained?

7 According to Voltaire, accepting the teleological argument is like believing that the nose was designed to fit spectacles. What is the point of this remark? Do you agree with Voltaire?

Letters from the Earth

Mark Twain

The writings of Samuel Clemens (1835–1910) are well known and much loved. Everyone in America is familiar with *The Adventures of Tom Sawyer* and *Huckleberry Finn,* his most popular works. But there is another side to his writing which has received little attention—his role as a caustic social philosopher and critic of traditional religious belief. The following selection displays this side of Twain at its best.

The setting itself shows Twain's ingenuity. Satan has been banished from heaven for making sarcastic comments about God's creation. He decides to visit the Earth and he writes back home to his friends. In the course of the correspondence, Satan argues convincingly that only mad beings would adopt the religious beliefs of humans. He bases his argument on what has been called the *problem of evil.* A perfectly good, powerful, and all-knowing God would not allow unnecessary evil to exist in His creation. But Satan points out that many of the conventional religious beliefs of humans seem to make God into a barbaric deity who tortures humanity for the sheer joy of it. What is especially amazing, Satan contends, is that humanity then blames itself for all these woes, instead of the guilty one. In his own inimitable way, Twain puts the problem of evil before us with such force and skill that we are not likely to forget that this is no mere intellectual game, but a deadly serious challenge to conventional religious belief.

Satan had been making admiring remarks about certain of the Creator's sparkling industries—remarks which, being read between the lines, were sarcasms. He had made them confidentially to his safe friends the other archangels, but they had been overheard by some ordinary angels and reported at Headquarters.

He was ordered into banishment for a day—the celestial day. It was a punishment he was used to, on account of his too flexible tongue. Formerly he had been deported into Space, there being nowhither else to send him, and had flapped tediously around there in the eternal night and the Arctic chill; but now it occurred to him to push on and hunt up the earth and see how the Human-Race experiment was coming along.

By and by he wrote home—very privately—to St. Michael and St. Gabriel about it.

SATAN'S LETTER

This is a strange place, an extraordinary place, and interesting. There is nothing resembling it at home. The people are all insane, the other animals are all insane, the earth is insane. Nature itself is insane. Man is a marvelous curiosity. When he is at his very very best he is a sort of low grade nickel-plated angel; at his worst he is unspeakable, unimaginable; and first and last and all the time he is a sarcasm. Yet he blandly and in all sincerity calls himself the "noblest work of God." This is the truth I am telling you. And this is not a new idea with him, he has talked it through all the ages, and believed it. Believed it, and found nobody among all his race to laugh at it.

Moreover—if I may put another strain upon you—he thinks he is the Creator's pet. He believes the Creator is proud of him; he even believes the Creator loves him; has a passion for him; sits up nights to admire him; yes, and watch over him and keep him out of trouble. He prays to Him, and thinks He listens. Isn't it a quaint idea? Fills his prayers with crude and bald and florid flatteries of Him, and thinks He sits and purrs over these extravagancies and enjoys them. He prays for help, and favor, and protection, every day; and does it with hopefulness and confidence, too, although no prayer of his has ever been answered. The daily affront, the daily defeat, do not discourage him, he goes on praying just the same. There is something almost fine about this perseverance. I must put one more strain upon you: he thinks he is going to heaven!

He has salaried teachers who tell him that. They also tell him there is a hell, of everlasting fire, and that he will go to it if he doesn't keep the Commandments. What are the Commandments? They are a curiosity. I will tell you about them by and by.

LETTER III

You have noticed that the human being is a curiosity. In times past he has had (and worn out and flung away) hundreds and hundreds of religions; today he has hundreds and hundreds of religions, and launches not fewer than three new ones every year. I could enlarge that number and still be within the facts.

One of his principal religions is called the Christian. A sketch of it will interest you. It is set forth in detail in a book containing two million words, called the Old and New Testaments. Also it has another name—The Word of God. For the Christian thinks every word of it was dictated by God—the one I have been speaking of.

It is full of interest. It has noble poetry in it; and some clever fables; and some blood-drenched history; and some good morals; and a wealth of obscenity; and upwards of a thousand lies.

This Bible is built mainly out of the fragments of older Bibles that had their day and crumbled to ruin. So it noticeably lacks in originality, necessarily. Its three or four most imposing and impressive events all happened in earlier Bibles; all its best precepts and rules of conduct came also from those Bibles; there are only two new things in it: hell, for one, and that singular heaven I have told you about.

What shall we do? If we believe, with these people, that their God invented these cruel things, we slander him; if we believe that these people invented them themselves, we slander them. It is an unpleasant dilemma in either case, for neither of these parties has done *us* any harm.

For the sake of tranquillity, let us take a side. Let us join forces with the people and put the whole ungracious burden upon *him*—heaven, hell, Bible and all. It does not seem right, it does not seem fair; and yet when you consider that heaven, and how crushingly charged it is with everything that is repulsive to a human being, how can we believe a human being invented it? And when I come to tell you about hell, the strain will be greater still, and you will be likely to say, No, a man would not provide that place, for either himself or anybody else; he simply couldn't.

That innocent Bible tells about the Creation. Of what—the universe? Yes, the universe. In six days!

God did it. He did not call it the universe—that name is modern. His whole attention was upon this world. He constructed it in five days—and then? It took him only one day to make twenty million suns and eighty million planets!

What were they for—according to his idea? To furnish light for this little toy-world. That was his whole purpose; he had no other. One of the twenty million suns (the smallest one) was to light it in the daytime, the rest were to help one of the universe's countless moons modify the darkness of its nights.

It is quite manifest that he believed his fresh-made skies were diamond-sown with those myriads of twinkling stars the moment his first-day's sun sank below the horizon; whereas, in fact, not a single star winked in that black vault until three years and a half after that memorable week's formidable industries had been completed.[1] Then one star appeared, all solitary and alone, and began to blink. Three years later another one appeared. The two blinked together for more than four years before a third joined them. At the end of the first hundred years there were not yet twenty-five stars twinkling in the wide wastes of those gloomy skies. At the end of a thousand years not enough stars were yet visible to make a show. At the end of a million years only half of the present array had sent their light over the telescopic frontiers, and it took another million for the rest to follow suit, as the vulgar phrase goes. There being at that time no telescope, their advent was not observed.

For three hundred years, now, the Christian astronomer has known that his Deity didn't make the stars in those tremendous six days; but the Christian astronomer does not enlarge upon that detail. Neither does the priest.

In his Book, God is eloquent in his praises of his mighty works, and calls them by the largest names he can find—thus indicating that he has a strong and just admiration of magnitudes; yet he made those millions of prodigious suns to light this wee little orb, instead of appointing this orb's little sun to dance attendance upon them. He mentions Arcturus in his Book—you remember Arcturus; we went there once. It is one of this earth's night lamps!—that giant globe which is fifty thousand times as large as this earth's sun, and compared with it as a melon compares with a cathedral.

However, the Sunday school still teaches the child that Arcturus was created to help light this earth, and the child grows up and continues to believe it long after he has found out that the probabilities are against its being so.

According to the Book and its servants the universe is only six thousand years old. It is only within the last hundred years that studious, inquiring minds have found out that it is nearer a hundred million.

During the Six Days, God created man and the other animals.

He made a man and a woman and placed them in a pleasant garden, along with the other creatures. They all lived together there in harmony and contentment and blooming youth for some time; then trouble came. God had warned the man and the woman that they must not eat of the fruit of a certain tree. And he added a most strange remark: he said that if they ate of it they should surely die. Strange, for the reason that inasmuch as they had never seen a sample of death they could not possibly know what he meant. Neither would he nor any other god have been able to make those ignorant children understand what was meant, without furnishing a sample. The mere word could have no meaning for them, any more than it would have for an infant of days.

Presently a serpent sought them out privately, and came to them walking upright, which was the way of serpents in those days. The serpent said the forbidden fruit would store their vacant minds with knowledge. So they ate it, which was quite natural, for man is so made that he eagerly wants to know; whereas the

---

[1] It takes the light of the nearest star (61 Cygni) three and a half years to come to the earth, traveling at the rate of 186,000 miles per second. Arcturus had been shining 200 years before it was visible from the earth. Remoter stars gradually became visible after thousands and thousands of years.—*The Editor* [M. T.]

priest, like God, whose imitator and representative he is, has made it his business from the beginning to keep him *from* knowing any useful thing.

Adam and Eve ate the forbidden fruit, and at once a great light streamed into their dim heads. They had acquired knowledge. What knowledge—useful knowledge? No—merely knowledge that there was such a thing as good, and such a thing as evil, and how to do evil. They couldn't do it before. Therefore all their acts up to this time had been without stain, without blame, without offense.

But now they could do evil—and suffer for it; now they had acquired what the Church calls an invaluable possession, the Moral Sense; that sense which differentiates man from the beast and sets him above the beast. Instead of below the beast—where one would suppose his proper place would be, since he is always foul-minded and guilty and the beast always clean-minded and innocent. It is like valuing a watch that must go wrong, above a watch that can't.

The Church still prizes the Moral Sense as man's noblest asset today, although the Church knows God had a distinctly poor opinion of it and did what he could in his clumsy way to keep his happy Children of the Garden from acquiring it.

Very well, Adam and Eve now knew what evil was, and how to do it. They knew how to do various kinds of wrong things, and among them one principal one—the one God had his mind on principally. That one was the art and mystery of sexual intercourse. To them it was a magnificent discovery, and they stopped idling around and turned their entire attention to it, poor exultant young things!

To proceed with the Biblical curiosities. Naturally you will think the threat to punish Adam and Eve for disobeying was of course not carried out, since they did not create themselves, nor their natures nor their impulses nor their weaknesses, and hence were not properly subject to anyone's commands, and not responsible to anybody for their acts. It will surprise you to know that the threat *was* carried out. Adam and Eve were punished, and that crime finds apologists unto this day. The sentence of death was executed.

As you perceive, the only person responsible for the couple's offense escaped; and not only escaped but became the executioner of the innocent.

In your country and mine we should have the privilege of making fun of this kind of morality, but it would be unkind to do it here. Many of these people have the reasoning faculty, but no one uses it in religious matters.

The best minds will tell you that when a man has begotten a child he is morally bound to tenderly care for it, protect it from hurt, shield it from disease, clothe it, feed it, bear with its waywardness, lay no hand upon it save in kindness and for its own good, and never in any case inflict upon it a wanton cruelty. God's treatment of his earthly children, every day and every night, is the exact opposite of all that, yet those best minds warmly justify these crimes, condone them, excuse them, and indignantly refuse to regard them as crimes at all, when *he* commits them. Your country and mine is an interesting one, but there is nothing there that is half so interesting as the human mind.

Very well, God banished Adam and Eve from the Garden, and eventually assassinated them. All for disobeying a command which he had no right to utter. But he did not stop there, as you will see. He has one code of morals for himself, and quite another for his children. He requires his children to deal justly—and gently—with offenders, and forgive them seventy-and-seven times; whereas he deals neither justly nor gently with anyone, and he did not forgive the ignorant and thoughtless first pair of juveniles even their first small offense and say, "You may go free this time, I will give you another chance."

On the contrary! He elected to punish *their* children, all through the ages to the end of time, for a trifling offense committed by others before they were born. He is punishing them yet. In mild ways? No, in atrocious ones.

You would not suppose that this kind of a Being gets many compliments. Undeceive yourself: the world calls him the All-Just, the All-Righteous, the All-Good, the All-Merciful, the All-Forgiving, the All-Truthful, the All-Loving, the Source of All Morality. These sarcasms are uttered daily, all over the world. But not as conscious sarcasms. No, they are meant seriously: they are uttered without a smile. . . .

LETTER V

Noah began to collect animals. There was to be one couple of each and every sort of creature that walked or crawled, or swam or flew, in the world of animated nature. We have to guess at how long it took to collect the creatures and how much it cost, for there is no record of these details. When Symmachus made preparation to introduce his young son to grown-up life in imperial Rome, he sent men to Asia, Africa and everywhere to collect wild animals for the arena-fights. It took the men three years to accumulate the animals and fetch them to Rome. Merely quadrupeds and alligators, you understand—no birds, no snakes, no frogs, no worms, no lice, no rats, no fleas, no ticks, no caterpillars, no spiders, no houseflies, no mosquitoes—nothing but just plain simple quadrupeds and alligators: and no quadrupeds except fighting ones. Yet it was as I have said: it took three years to collect them, and the cost of animals and transportation and the men's wages footed up $4,500,000.

How many animals? We do not know. But it was under five thousand, for that was the largest number *ever* gathered for those Roman shows, and it was Titus, not Symmachus, who made that collection. Those were mere baby museums, compared to Noah's contract. Of birds and beasts and fresh-water creatures he had to collect 146,000 kinds; and of insects upwards of two million species.

Thousands and thousands of those things are very difficult to catch, and if Noah had not given up and resigned, he would be on the job yet, as Leviticus used to say. However, I do not mean that he withdrew. No, he did not do that. He gathered as many creatures as he had room for, and then stopped.

If he had known all the requirements in the beginning, he would have been aware that what was needed was a fleet of Arks. But he did not know how many kinds of creatures there were, neither did his Chief. So he had no kangaroo, and no 'possum, and no Gila monster, and no ornithorhynchus, and lacked a multitude of other indispensable blessings which a loving Creator had provided for man and forgotten about, they having long ago wandered to a side of this world which he had never seen and with whose affairs he was not acquainted. And so everyone of them came within a hair of getting drowned.

They only escaped by an accident. There was not water enough to go around. Only enough was provided to flood one small corner of the globe—the rest of the globe was not then known, and was supposed to be nonexistent.

However, the thing that really and finally and definitely determined Noah to stop with enough species for purely business purposes and let the rest become extinct, was an incident of the last days: an excited stranger arrived with some most alarming news. He said he had been camping among some mountains and valleys about six hundred miles away, and he had seen a wonderful thing there: he stood upon a precipice overlooking a wide valley, and up the valley he saw a billowy black sea of strange animal life coming. Presently the creatures passed by, struggling, fighting, scrambling, screeching, snorting—horrible vast masses of tumultuous flesh! Sloths as big as an elephant; frogs as big as a cow; a megatherium and his harem huge beyond belief; saurians and saurians and saurians, group after group, family after family, species after species—a hundred feet long, thirty feet high, and twice as quarrelsome; one of them hit a perfectly blameless Durham bull a thump with its tail and sent it whizzing three hundred feet into the air and it fell at the man's feet with a sigh and was no more. The man said that these prodigious animals had heard about the Ark and were coming. Coming to get saved from the flood. And not coming in pairs, they were *all* coming: they did not know the passengers were restricted to pairs, the man said, and wouldn't care a rap for the regulations, anyway—they would sail in that Ark or know the reason why. The man said the Ark would not hold the half of them; and moreover they were coming hungry, and would eat up everything there was, including the menagerie and the family.

All these facts were suppressed, in the Biblical account. You find not a hint of them there. The whole thing is hushed up. Not even the names of those vast creatures are mentioned. It shows you that when people have left a reproachful vacancy in a contract they can be as shady about it in Bibles as elsewhere. Those powerful animals would be of inestimable value to man now, when transportation is so hard pressed and expensive, but they are all lost to him. All lost, and by Noah's fault. They all got drowned. Some of them as much as eight million years ago.

Very well, the stranger told his tale, and Noah saw that he must get away before the monsters arrived. He would have sailed at once, but the upholsterers and decorators of the housefly's drawing room still had some finishing touches to put on, and that lost him a day. Another day was lost in getting the flies aboard, there being sixty-eight billions of them and the Deity still afraid there might not be enough. Another day was lost in stowing forty tons of selected filth for the flies' sustenance.

Then at last, Noah sailed; and none too soon, for the Ark was only just sinking out of sight on the horizon when the monsters arrived, and added their lamentations to those of the multitude of weeping fathers and mothers and frightened little children who were clinging to the wave-washed rocks in the pouring rain and lifting imploring prayers to an All-Just and All-Forgiving and All-Pity-ing Being who had never answered a prayer since those crags were builded, grain by grain out of the sands, and would still not have answered one when the ages should have crumbled them to sand again.

LETTER VI

On the third day, about noon, it was found that a fly had been left behind. The return voyage turned out to be long and difficult, on account of the lack of chart and compass, and because of the changed aspects of all coasts, the steadily rising water having submerged some of the lower landmarks and given to higher ones an unfamiliar look; but after sixteen days of earnest and faithful seeking, the fly was found at last, and received on board with hymns of praise and gratitude, the Family standing meanwhile uncovered, out of reverence for its divine origin. It was weary and worn, and had suffered somewhat from the weather, but was otherwise in good estate. Men and their families had died of hunger on barren mountain tops, but it had not lacked for food, the multitudinous corpses furnish-ing it in rank and rotten richness. Thus was the sacred bird providentially pre-served.

Providentially. That is the word. For the fly had not been left behind by accident. No, the hand of Providence was in it. There are no accidents. All things that happen, happen for a purpose. They are foreseen from the beginning of time, they are ordained from the beginning of time. From the dawn of Creation the Lord had foreseen that Noah, being alarmed and confused by the invasion of the prodigious brevet fossils, would prematurely fly to sea unprovided with a certain invaluable disease. He would have all the other diseases, and could distribute them among the new races of men as they appeared in the world, but he would lack one of the very best—typhoid fever; a malady which, when the circum-stances are especially favorable, is able to utterly wreck a patient without killing him; for it can restore him to his feet with a long life in him, and yet deaf, dumb, blind, crippled, and idiotic. The housefly is its main disseminator, and is more competent and more calamitously effective than all the other distributors of the dreaded scourge put together. And so, by foreordination from the beginning of time, this fly was left behind to seek out a typhoid corpse and feed upon its corruptions and gaum its legs with the germs and transmit them to the re-peopled world for permanent business. From that one housefly, in the ages that have since elapsed, billions of sickbeds have been stocked, billions of wrecked bodies sent tottering about the earth, and billions of cemeteries recruited with the dead.

The human being is a machine. An automatic machine. It is composed of thousands of complex and delicate mechanisms, which perform their functions harmoniously and perfectly, in accordance with laws devised for their gover-nance, and over which the man himself has no authority, no mastership, no control. For each one of these thousands of mechanisms the Creator has planned an enemy, whose office is to harass it, pester it, persecute it, damage it, afflict it with pains, and miseries, and ultimate destruction. Not one has been overlooked.

From cradle to grave these enemies are always at work; they know no rest, night or day. They are an army: an organized army; a besieging army; an assaulting army; an army that is alert, watchful, eager, merciless; an army that never relents, never grants a truce.

It moves by squad, by company, by battalion, by regiment, by brigade, by division, by army corps; upon occasion it masses its parts and moves upon mankind with its whole strength. It is the Creator's Grand Army, and he is the Commander-in-Chief. Along its battlefront its grisly banners wave their legends in the face of the sun: Disaster, Disease, and the rest.

Disease! That is the main force, the diligent force, the devastating force! It attacks the infant the moment it is born; it furnishes it one malady after another: croup, measles, mumps, bowel troubles, teething pains, scarlet fever, and other childhood specialties. It chases the child into youth and furnishes it some specialties for that time of life. It chases the youth into maturity, maturity into age, and age into the grave.

With these facts before you will you now try to guess man's chiefest pet name for this ferocious Commander-in-Chief? I will save you the trouble—but you must not laugh. It is Our Father in Heaven!

It is curious—the way the human mind works. The Christian begins with this straight proposition, this definite proposition, this inflexible and uncompromising propositon: *God is all-knowing, and all-powerful.*

This being the case, nothing can happen without his knowing beforehand that it is going to happen; nothing happens without his permission; nothing can happen that he chooses to prevent.

That is definite enough, isn't it? It makes the Creator distinctly responsible for everything that happens, doesn't it?

The Christian concedes it in that italicized sentence. Concedes it with feeling, with enthusiasm.

Then, having thus made the Creator responsible for all those pains and diseases and miseries above enumerated, and which he could have prevented, the gifted Christian blandly calls him Our Father!

It is as I tell you. He equips the Creator with every trait that goes to the making of a fiend, and then arrives at the conclusion that a fiend and a father are the same thing! Yet he would deny that a malevolent lunatic and a Sunday school superintendent are essentially the same. What do you think of the human mind? I mean, in case you think there is a human mind.

LETTER IX

The Ark continued its voyage, drifting around here and there and yonder, compassless and uncontrolled, the sport of the random winds and the swirling currents. And the rain, the rain, the rain! It kept on falling, pouring, drenching, flooding. No such rain had ever been seen before. Sixteen inches a day had been heard of, but that was nothing to this. This was a hundred and twenty inches a day—ten feet! At this incredible rate it rained forty days and forty nights, and submerged every hill that was four hundred feet high. Then the heavens and even the angels went dry; no more water was to be had.

As a Universal Flood it was a disappointment, but there had been heaps of Universal Floods before, as is witnessed by all the Bibles of all the nations, and this was as good as the best one.

At last the Ark soared aloft and came to a rest on the top of Mount Ararat, seventeen thousand feet above the valley, and its living freight got out and went down the mountain.

Noah planted a vineyard, and drank of the wine and was overcome.

This person had been selected from all the populations because he was the best sample there was. He was to start the human race on a new basis. This was the new basis. The promise was bad. To go further with the experiment was to run a great and most unwise risk. Now was the time to do with these people what had been so judiciously done with the others—drown them. Anybody but the Creator would have seen this. But he didn't see it. That is, maybe he didn't.

It is claimed that from the beginning of time he foresaw everything that would happen in the world. If that is true, he foresaw that Adam and Eve would eat the apple; that their posterity would be unendurable and have to be drowned; that Noah's posterity would in their turn be unendurable, and that by and by he would have to leave his throne in heaven and come down and be crucified to save that same tiresome human race again. The whole of it? No! A part of it? Yes. How much of it? In each generation, for hundreds and hundreds of generations, a billion would die and all go to perdition except perhaps ten thousand out of the billion. The ten thousand would have to come from the little body of Christians, and only one in the hundred of that little body would stand any chance. None of them at all except such Roman Catholics as should have the luck to have a priest handy to sandpaper their souls at the last gasp, and here and there a Presbyterian. No others savable. All the others damned. By the million.

Shall you grant that he foresaw all this? The pulpit grants it. It is the same as granting that in the matter of intellect the Deity is the Head Pauper of the Universe, and that in the matter of morals and character he is away down on the level of David.

STUDY QUESTIONS

1   Some people argue that evil is due to the sin of Adam and Eve. How does Twain respond to this argument?
2   Some people claim that since humans are finite beings and God is infinite, we cannot comprehend God and God's ways. They conclude that there is no problem of evil. Are they right?
3   Why does Twain believe that God's foreknowledge of events is inconsistent with His goodness? What do you think?
4   Twain claims that humanity works with a double standard of morality—people excuse God from acts which would convict an ordinary person of being a moral fiend. Do you agree with this?
5   Someone might respond to Twain by claiming that the evil in the world was necessary for a greater good. Would you accept such a reply? Under what conditions do the ends justify the means?

The Soul-Building Argument

John Hick

John Hick (1922–   ) began his career as a Presbyterian minister in England. His many writings on religion have gained him wide recognition as a philosopher. He has taught at Cornell University, Princeton Theological Seminary, Cambridge University, and the University of Birmingham. Elaborating the position of Irenaus, an early Christian theologian, Hick believes that the presence of evil—evil caused by human beings and evil caused by natural phenomena—is compatible with the existence of an infinitely merciful and good God.

The evil caused by human beings is a result of free will. Of course, God could have made beings which always made the right decision; but, then, such beings would be mere mechanisms, passively acting out God's will. Hick claims that God cannot make free beings who always choose the right course of action. The fact that people possess free will makes it possible for them to construct their own characters—for good or for ill. But a necessary condition for becoming a morally superior person is that pain and suffering exist. Without a world containing such evils, moral traits such as courage, patience, and sympathy could not develop. The world, with all its shocks, is a place where we are given the opportunity to develop into moral beings. This greater good outweighs the evil.

Hick's argument depends upon several complex assumptions. Although his conception of "free will" is not spelled out carefully in this selection, perhaps the readings by Bertocci and James in Part Four will help you understand his position. The "soul-building" argument assumes that the ends sometimes justify the means. It may prove helpful to consider when this is not true and why. His argument may require some supplementation on this point.

To many, the most powerful positive objection to belief in God is the fact of evil. Probably for most agnostics it is the appalling depth and extent of human suffering, more than anything else, that makes the idea of a loving Creator seem so implausible and disposes them toward one or another of the various naturalistic theories of religion.

As a challenge to theism, the problem of evil has traditionally been posed in the form of a dilemma: if God is perfectly loving, he must wish to abolish evil; and if he is all-powerful, he must be able to abolish evil. But evil exists; therefore God cannot be both omnipotent and perfectly loving.

Certain solutions, which at once suggest themselves, have to be ruled out so far as the Judaic-Christian faith is concerned.

To say, for example (with contemporary Christian Science), that evil is an illusion of the human mind, is impossible within a religion based upon the stark realism of the Bible. Its pages faithfully reflect the characteristic mixture of good

From *Philosophy of Religion* (Englewood Cliffs, N.J.: Prentice-Hall, 1963), pp. 40–47. © 1953. Reprinted by permission of Prentice-Hall, Inc., Englewood Cliffs, New Jersey.

and evil in human experience. They record every kind of sorrow and suffering, every mode of man's inhumanity to man and of his painfully insecure existence in the world. There is no attempt to regard evil as anything but dark, menacingly ugly, heart-rending, and crushing. In the Christian scriptures, the climax of this history of evil is the crucifixion of Jesus, which is presented not only as a case of utterly unjust suffering, but as the violent and murderous rejection of God's Messiah. There can be no doubt, then, that for biblical faith, evil is unambiguously evil, and stands in direct opposition to God's will.

Again, to solve the problem of evil by means of the theory (sponsored, for example, by the Boston "Personalist" School) [1] of a finite deity who does the best he can with a material, intractable and co-eternal with himself, is to have abandoned the basic premise of Hebrew-Christian monotheism; for the theory amounts to rejecting belief in the infinity and sovereignty of God.

Indeed, any theory which would avoid the problem of the origin of evil by depicting it as an ultimate constituent of the universe, coordinate with good, has been repudiated in advance by the classic Christian teaching, first developed by Augustine, that evil represents the going wrong of something which in itself is good.[2] Augustine holds firmly to the Hebrew-Christian conviction that the universe is *good*—that is to say, it is the creation of a good God for a good purpose. He completely rejects the ancient prejudice, widespread in his day, that matter is evil. There are, according to Augustine, higher and lower, greater and lesser goods in immense abundance and variety; but everything which has being is good in its own way and degree, except in so far as it may have become spoiled or corrupted. Evil—whether it be an evil will, an instance of pain, or some disorder or decay in nature—has not been set there by God, but represents the distortion of something that is inherently valuable. Whatever exists is, as such, and in its proper place, good; evil is essentially parasitic upon good, being disorder and perversion in a fundamentally good creation. This understanding of evil as something negative means that it is not willed and created by God; but it does not mean (as some have supposed) that evil is unreal and can be disregarded. Clearly, the first effect of this doctrine is to accentuate even more the question of the origin of evil.

Theodicy,[3] as many modern Christian thinkers see it, is a modest enterprise, negative rather than positive in its conclusions. It does not claim to explain, nor to explain away, every instance of evil in human experience, but only to point to certain considerations which prevent the fact of evil (largely incomprehensible though it remains) from constituting a final and insuperable bar to rational belief in God.

In indicating these considerations it will be useful to follow the traditional division of the subject. There is the problem of *moral evil* or wickedness: why

[1] Edgar Brightman's *A Philosophy of Religion* (Englewood Cliffs, N.J.: Prentice-Hall, Inc., 1940, Chaps. 8–10, is a classic exposition of one form of this view).
[2] See Augustine's *Confessions,* Book VII, Chap. 12; *City of God,* Book XII, Chap. 3; *Enchiridion,* Chap. 4.
[3] The word "theodicy" from the Greek *theos* (God) and *dike* (righteous) means the justification of God's goodness in the face of the fact of evil.

does an all-good and all-powerful God permit this? And there is the problem of the *non-moral evil* suffering or pain, both physical and mental: why has an all-good and all-powerful God created a world in which this occurs?

Christian thought has always considered moral evil in its relation to human freedom and responsibility. To be a person is to be a finite center of freedom, a (relatively) free and self-directing agent responsible for one's own decisions. This involves being free to act wrongly as well as to act rightly. The idea of a person who can be infallibly guaranteed always to act rightly is self-contradictory. There can be no guarantee in advance that a genuinely free moral agent will never choose amiss. Consequently, the possibility of wrongdoing or sin is logically inseparable from the creation of finite persons, and to say that God should not have created beings who might sin amounts to saying that he should not have created people.

This thesis has been challenged in some recent philosophical discussions of the problem of evil, in which it is claimed that no contradiction is involved in saying that God might have made people who would be genuinely free and who could yet be guaranteed always to act rightly. A quotation from one of these discussions follows:

> If there is no logical impossibility in a man's freely choosing the good on one, or on several occasions, there cannot be a logical impossibility in his freely choosing the good on every occasion. God was not, then, faced with a choice between making innocent automata and making beings who, in acting freely, would sometimes go wrong: there was open to him the obviously better possibility of making beings who would act freely but always go right. Clearly, his failure to avail himself of this possibility is inconsistent with his being both omnipotent and wholly good.[4]

A reply to this argument is suggested in another recent contribution to the discussion.[5] If by a free action we mean an action which is not externally compelled but which flows from the nature of the agent as he reacts to the circumstances in which he finds himself, there is, indeed, no contradiction between our being free and our actions being "caused" (by our own nature) and therefore being in principle predictable. There is a contradiction, however, in saying that God is the cause of our acting as we do but that we are free beings in relation to God. There is, in other words, a contradiction in saying that God has made us so that we shall of necessity act in a certain way, and that we are genuinely independent persons in relation to him. If all our thoughts and actions are divinely predestined, however free and morally responsible we may seem to be to ourselves, we cannot be free and morally responsible in the sight of God, but must instead be his helpless puppets. Such "freedom" is like that of a patient acting out a series of posthypnotic suggestions; he appears, even to himself, to be free, but

---

[4] J. L. Mackie, "Evil and Omnipotence," *Mind* (April, 1955), p. 209. A similar point is made by Antony Flew in "Divine Omnipotence and Human Freedom," *New Essays in Philosophical Theology.* An important critical comment on these arguments is offered by Ninian Smart in "Omnipotence, Evil and Supermen," *Philosophy* (April, 1961), with replies by Flew (January, 1962) and Mackie (April, 1962).

[5] Flew, in *New Essays in Philosophical Theology.*

his volitions have actually been predetermined by another will, that of the hypnotist, in relation to whom the patient is not a free agent.

A different objector might raise the question of whether or not we deny God's omnipotence if we admit that he is unable to create persons who are free from the risks inherent in personal freedom. The answer that has always been given is that to create such beings is logically impossible, since there is nothing here to accomplish, but only a meaningless conjunction of words[6] —in this case "person who is not a person." God is able to create beings of any and every conceivable kind; but creatures who lack moral freedom, however superior they might be to human beings in other respects, would not be what we mean by persons. They would constitute a different form of life which God might have brought into existence instead of persons. When we ask why God did not create such beings in place of persons, the traditional answer is that only persons could, in any meaningful sense, become "children of God," capable of entering into a personal relationship with their Creator by a free and uncompelled response to his love.

When we turn from the possibility of moral evil as a correlate of man's personal freedom to its actuality, we face something which must remain inexplicable even when it can be seen to be possible. For we can never provide a complete causal explanation of a free act; if we could, it would not be a free act. The origin of moral evil lies forever concealed within the mystery of human freedom.

The necessary connection between moral freedom and the possibility, now actualized, of sin throws light upon a great deal of the suffering which afflicts mankind. For an enormous amount of human pain arises either from the inhumanity or the culpable incompetence of mankind. This includes such major scourges as poverty, oppression and persecution, war, and all the injustice, indignity, and inequity which occur even in the most advanced societies. These evils are manifestations of human sin. Even disease is fostered to an extent, the limits of which have not yet been determined by psychosomatic medicine, by moral and emotional factors seated both in the individual and in his social environment. To the extent that all of these evils stem from human failures and wrong decisions, their possibility is inherent in the creation of free persons inhabiting a world which presents them with real choices which are followed by real consequences.

We may now turn more directly to the problem of suffering. Even though the major bulk of actual human pain is traceable to man's misused freedom as a sole or part cause, there remain other sources of pain which are entirely independent of the human will, for example, earthquake, hurricane, storm, flood, drought, and blight. In practice, it is often impossible to trace a boundary between the suffering which results from human wickedness and folly and that which falls upon mankind from without. Both kinds of suffering are inextricably

---

[6] As Aquinas said, " . . . nothing that implies a contradiction falls under the scope of God's omnipotence," *Summa Theologica,* Part I, Question 25, article 4.

mingled together in human experience. For our present purpose, however, it is important to note that the latter category does exist and that it seems to be built into the very structure of our world. In response to it, theodicy, if it is wisely conducted, follows a negative path. It is not possible to show positively that each item of human pain serves the divine purpose of good; but, on the other hand, it does seem possible to show that the divine purpose as it is understood in Judaism and Christianity could not be forwarded in a world which was designed as a permanent hedonistic paradise.

An essential premise of this argument concerns the nature of the divine purpose in creating the world. The skeptic's assumption is that man is to be viewed as a completed creation and that God's purpose in making the world was to provide a suitable dwelling-place for this fully-formed creature. Since God is good and loving, the environment which he has created for human life to inhabit is naturally as pleasant and comfortable as possible. The problem is essentially similar to that of a man who builds a cage for some pet animal. Since our world, in fact, contains sources of hardship, inconvenience, and danger of innumerable kinds, the conclusion follows that this world cannot have been created by a perfectly benevolent and all-powerful deity.[7]

Christianity, however, has never supposed that God's purpose in the creation of the world was to construct a paradise whose inhabitants would experience a maximum of pleasure and a minimum of pain. The world is seen, instead, as a place of "soul-making" in which free beings grappling with the tasks and challenges of their existence in a common environment, may become "children of God" and "heirs of eternal life." A way of thinking theologically of God's continuing creative purpose for man was suggested by some of the early Hellenistic Fathers of the Christian Church, especially Irenaeus. Following hints from St. Paul, Irenaeus taught that man has been made as a person in the image of God but has not yet been brought as a free and responsible agent into the finite likeness of God, which is revealed in Christ.[8] Our world, with all its rough edges, is the sphere in which this second and harder stage of the creative process is taking place.

This conception of the world (whether or not set in Irenaeus' theological framework) can be supported by the method of negative theodicy. Suppose, contrary to fact, that this world were a paradise from which all possibility of pain and suffering were excluded. The consequences would be very far-reaching. For example, no one could ever injure anyone else: the murderer's knife would turn to paper or his bullets to thin air; the bank safe, robbed of a million dollars, would miraculously become filled with another million dollars (without this device, on however large a scale, proving inflationary); fraud, deceit, conspiracy, and treason would somehow always leave the fabric of society undamaged. Again, no one would ever be injured by accident; the mountain-climber, steeple-

---

[7] This is the nature of David Hume's argument in his discussion of the problem of evil in his *Dialogues,* Part XI.

[8] See Irenaeus' *Against Heresies,* Book IV, Chaps. 37 and 38.

jack, or playing child falling from a height would float unharmed to the ground; the reckless driver would never meet with disaster. There would be no need to work, since no harm could result from avoiding work; there would be no call to be concerned for others in time of need or danger, for in such a world there could be no real needs or dangers.

To make possible this continual series of individual adjustments, nature would have to work by "special providences" instead of running according to general laws which men must learn to respect on penalty of pain of death. The laws of nature would have to be extremely flexible: sometimes gravity would operate, sometimes not; sometimes an object would be hard and solid, sometimes soft. There could be no sciences, for there would be no enduring world structure to investigate. In eliminating the problems and hardships of an objective environment, with its own laws, life would become like a dream in which, delightfully but aimlessly, we would float and drift at ease.

One can at least begin to imagine such a world. It is evident that our present ethical concepts would have no meaning in it. If, for example, the notion of harming someone is an essential element in the concept of a wrong action, in our hedonistic paradise there could be no wrong actions nor any right actions in distinction from wrong. Courage and fortitude would have no point in an environment in which there is, by definition, no danger or difficulty. Generosity, kindness, the *agape* aspect of love, prudence, unselfishness, and all other ethical notions which presuppose life in a stable environment, could not even be formed. Consequently, such a world, however well it might promote pleasure, would be very ill adapted for the development of the moral qualities of human personality. In relation to this purpose it would be the worst of all possible worlds.

It would seem, then, that an environment intended to make possible the growth in free beings of the finest characteristics of personal life, must have a good deal in common with our present world. It must operate according to general and dependable laws; and it must involve real dangers, difficulties, problems, obstacles, and possibilities of pain, failure, sorrow, frustration, and defeat. If it did not contain the particular trials and perils which—subtracting man's own very considerable contribution—our world contains, it would have to contain others instead.

To realize this is not, by any means, to be in possession of a detailed theodicy. It is to understand that this world, with all its "heartaches and the thousand natural shocks that flesh is heir to," an environment so manifestly not designed for the maximization of human pleasure and the minimization of human pain, may be rather well adapted to the quite different purpose of "soul-making." [9]

These considerations are related to theism as such. Specifically, Christian theism goes further in the light of the death of Christ, which is seen paradoxically

---

[9] This brief discussion has been confined to the problem of human suffering. The large and intractable problem of animal pain is not taken up here. For a discussion of it, see, for example, Nels Ferré, *Evil and the Christian Faith* (New York: Harper & Row, Publishers, Inc., 1947), Chap. 7; and Austin Farrer, *Love Almighty and Ills Unlimited* (New York: Doubleday & Company, Inc., 1961), Chap. 5.

both (as the murder of the divine Son) as the worst thing that has ever happened and (as the occasion of Man's salvation) as the best thing that has ever happened. As the supreme evil turned to supreme good, it provides the paradigm for the distinctively Christian reaction to evil. Viewed from the standpoint of Christian faith, evils do not cease to be evils; and certainly, in view of Christ's healing work, they cannot be said to have been sent by God. Yet, it has been the persistent claim of those seriously and wholeheartedly committed to Christian discipleship that tragedy, though truly tragic, may nevertheless be turned, through a man's reaction to it, from a cause of despair and alienation from God to a stage in the fulfillment of God's loving purpose for that individual. As the greatest of all evils, the crucifixion of Christ, was made the occasion of man's redemption, so good can be won from other evils. As Jesus saw his execution by the Romans as an experience which God desired him to accept, an experience which was to be brought within the sphere of the divine purpose and made to serve the divine ends, so the Christian response to calamity is to accept the adversities, pains, and afflictions which life brings, in order that they can be turned to a positive spiritual use.[10]

At this point, theodicy points forward in two ways to the subject of life after death.

First, although there are many striking instances of good being triumphantly brought out of evil through a man's or a woman's reaction to it, there are many other cases in which the opposite has happened. Sometimes obstacles breed strength of character, dangers evoke courage and unselfishness, and calamities produce patience and moral steadfastness. But sometimes they lead, instead, to resentment, fear, grasping selfishness, and disintegration of character. Therefore, it would seem that any divine purpose of soul-making which is at work in earthly history must continue beyond this life if it is ever to achieve more than a very partial and fragmentary success.

Second, if we ask whether the business of soul-making is worth all the toil and sorrow of human life, the Christian answer must be in terms of a future good which is great enough to justify all that has happened on the way to it.

STUDY QUESTIONS

1   What does Hick mean by "free will"? Do you think that he defines it correctly? What if you did not believe that this sort of free will existed: how would this affect Hick's argument?
2   Is Hick committed to the view that God could not have made human beings better than they are? Do you think that this is true?
3   Why does Hick say that God could not create people who always choose the right thing? Do you think that his is a sound argument here?
4   "Hick says that pain and suffering are necessary to develop virtues such as courage, sympathy, etc. But if God is really all-powerful, he should be able to give us these

[10] This conception of providence is stated more fully in John Hick, *Faith and Knowledge* (Ithaca: Cornell University Press, 1957), Chap. 7, from which some sentences are incorporated in this paragraph.

virtues without putting us through the suffering." How would Hick respond to this criticism? What do you think?

5   A brilliant young researcher is on the verge of discovering a cure for all diseases. Would Hick advise the person to go ahead?

6   Hick says that courage, patience, and sympathy are virtues. Why are they virtues? Are they good in and of themselves, or are they means to a further end?

7   Suppose you had a chance to painlessly eliminate Adolf Hitler before 1940, knowing that if you did not, he would be responsible for millions of deaths. What would you do? What would Hick recommend?

Faith and the Skeptical Life

PROBLEM INTRODUCTION

What if the arguments for the existence of God fail? Has every avenue to belief been blocked? If so, what kind of world faces us? These are not idle questions. A world without Santa Claus is simply a world with a minor alteration at the north pole. But a world without God is a world without direction, a world in which humanity is alone, a world which moves on uncaringly. It is a world in which every noble achievement of humanity will be erased in some distant holocaust. With the death of God, the face of the universe becomes an "It" instead of a "Thou." It is no accident that many people find that prospect of a Godless world frightening beyond description, since, for better or for worse, our values are seriously shaken by this picture of reality.

Reason must give out somewhere in the search for religious truth, for a major part of that truth is that the infinite nature of God transcends the full understanding of the human mind. Consequently, faith has been essential to religious belief. Exactly what *faith* means, however, is subject to considerable interpretation. Martin Luther suggested that the essence of faith is "to believe that God, who saves so few and condemns so many, is merciful; that He is just, who, at his own pleasure, has made us necessarily doomed to damnation, so that He seems to delight in the torture of the wretched and to be more deserving of hate than of love." (*De Servo Arbitrio.*) Luther implies that faith is simply blind belief in spite of overwhelming evidence to the contrary. In effect the believer is saying, "I find this comforting, so I will believe it no matter what the facts are." This, of course, is rampant irrationalism. Fortunately, religious faith need not be interpreted in this way. There are at least two other alternatives. The first is to show that rationality is not the only method for discovering the nature of reality. This is the path of the mystic. The other alternative is to show that religious faith is reasonable. The proponents of such a view usually maintain that our ordinary lives are full of examples of rational faith, and that religious belief need not be any different. Let us look more closely at these two positions.

For many philosophers and theologians the essence of religious belief lies in the nature of religious experience. Religious attitudes do not originate in an empirical investigation of the world, but rather result from a special insight into the nature of things. This insight, however, is extremely difficult—if not impossible—to express in the language of ordinary experience. In our readings, W. T. Stace maintains that there are two distinct ways of coming to know the nature of reality. The method of the "rational intellect" must be contrasted with "mystical intuition." Persons who have experienced a mystical insight into the nature of things describe their vision in terms which strike the rational mind as absurd. In all religious traditions, the experience of God is "ineffable"; that is, all attempts to describe God are doomed to failure because His nature cannot be grasped by reason or logic. As Meister Eckhart, the famous Christian mystic, put it: "Why dost thou prate about God? Whatever thou sayest of Him is untrue." In the following readings, Michael Scriven, a hard-nosed rationalist, argues that a God which cannot be comprehended by the rational intellect cannot be an object of worship. If we take Eckhart literally, then when we say that God is loving, good, and kind, we must be saying things which are untrue. Scriven claims that when the truths of religion are emptied of rational content, religion ceases to have any bearing on the conduct of our lives. Mystics, of course, may simply refuse to argue, for logic and reason, according to them, are incapable of settling the issue.

But perhaps the contrast between faith and rationality has been overstated, for it seems as if much of ordinary life involves an element of faith. To have faith in a friend, for example, is to believe that the friend will continue to act in familiar ways. "Faith," in this context, means a willingness to act, even though the evidence is incomplete and less than perfect. A gamble is being taken, it is true, but not every gamble is irrational. Life does not wait while we gather conclusive evidence to back up our decisions. Reason is a tool which helps us move into an uncertain future, but it can never remove all uncertainty. We have faith in reason just as we have faith in our friends—we act as though reason will continue to guide us successfully *even though we cannot know this with absolute certainty.* Faith, then, is an essential part of reasonable living. In our readings, William James attempts to set forth the conditions under which religious faith is a reasonable gamble for guidance in an uncertain life. What is especially interesting in James's position is his claim that sometimes acting on the basis of a belief creates the conditions which make the belief true. Believing that someone will be your friend may be a necessary condition for establishing a friendship with that person. James maintains that religious faith may be the necessary condition for discovering that the religious ideal is true.

In the end, however, all routes to religious belief may fail. If this occurs, many of the most profound issues of life are affected. The universe is not the manifestation of a divine plan, and, accordingly, is indifferent to our hopes and fears. There are no values, no ideals, beyond those forged by human beings. All opportunities for a meaningful existence must be seized within the short period given to us or forever lost. To many people such thoughts are a source of despair. But in each era there have been those who believe that this vision of life, though ultimately tragic, allows for the possibility of a meaningful and noble existence. The finality of death need not mean that our ideals are empty illusions. Immortality, in itself, is no blessing, for it provides for the possibility of unending pain as well as for infinite bliss. Existence is made meaningful by its ethical qualities, not its duration; and there is no apparent reason why a short existence cannot possess such qualities. Bertrand Russell, one of the greatest intellects of this century, tries to locate the source of value within human ideals, even though such ideals are doomed to extinction with the human species. It is the consciousness of our mortality, he claims, that elevates existence and provides life with a tragic nobility. The Roman poet Lucretius expressed a similar point about sixty years before the birth of Christ—a fitting counterpoint to the promise of eternal life:

> What is your grievance, mortal, that you give yourself up to this whining and repining? Why do you weep and wail over death? If the life you have lived till now has been a pleasant thing—if all its blessings have not leaked away like water poured into a cracked pot and run to waste unrelished—why then, you silly creature, do you not retire as a guest who has had his fill of life and take your care-free rest with a quiet mind? [1]

[1] Lucretius, *The Nature of the Universe,* translated by Robert Latham (Baltimore: Penguin, 1951).

Mysticism and the Limits of Reason

W. T. Stace

W. T. Stace (1886–1967) was a district judge in Ceylon, later became mayor of Colombo, and subsequently joined the philosophy department of Princeton University. This many-faceted individual devoted the last years of his life to defending the view that mysticism and science are not opposed to one another. In this essay, Stace claims that the mystical traditions of the world have a common thread of paradox running through them. He argues that the sort of vision of reality which mystics have cannot be accurately reproduced by the ordinary concepts of the understanding.

The theme of Stace's essay is a familiar one in all religious traditions. Reason is said to be incapable of understanding the nature of God. Instead, God can be known only by direct experience or intuition. As soon as we try to express, in logical terms, what intuition has revealed, paradoxes appear. These paradoxes, Stace claims, are not signs of the inadequacy of the religious vision, but indications that the logical intellect has reached its limits. Religion is not essentially an intellectual affair—it is an immediate experience which lies forever beyond the grasp of logic.

Stace's interpretation of the mystical vision, however, is not the only possible one. Perhaps the paradoxes which he cites are not strictly contradictions, but unusual metaphors which have a profound, but logical, significance. In Shakespeare's plays, for example, usually the clearest vision of reality is expressed by a character who appears to be insane. So too with the mystics— there may be method in their madness.

Anyone who is acquainted with the mystical literature of the world will know that great mystics invariably express themselves in the language of paradox and contradiction; and it is to this aspect of mysticism that I especially want to draw your attention tonight. But before I do so I would like to make a few introductory remarks about mysticism in general. Mysticism is not a regional or local phenomenon. It is universal. By this I mean that it is found in every country, in every age, in every culture, and in association with every one of the great world-religions. I do not speak here of primitive cultures and primitive religions. No doubt mysticism expresses itself in them in primitive ways. But I am only speaking about advanced cultures and advanced religions. For instance, those ancient inspired documents, the Upanishads, which go back in time from 2,500 to 3,000 years, and which are the fountainheads both of the Hindu religion and of the Vedanta philosophy, are a direct report of mystical experience. Buddhism, too, is a mystical religion throughout. It is founded upon the mystical experience of Gautama Buddha. In the East, in India, the word "mysticism" or any word corresponding to it is not generally used. It is called "enlightenment" or "illumination." But the

From W. T. Stace, "Mysticism and Human Reason," University of Arizona Bulletin Series, Vol. XXVI, No. 3, May 1955. Copyright by University of Arizona Press, 1955: Riecker Memorial Lecture No. 1. Reprinted by permission.

enlightenment experience of the East is basically the same as what is called the mystical experience in the West. In the Mohammedan religion the Sufis were the great representatives of mysticism. Mysticism appears in China in connection with Taoism. The Tao is a mystical conception. Judaism produced notable mystics. The history of Christianity is rich with the names of great mystics and some of these names are household words: Meister Eckhart, Saint Teresa, St. John of the Cross, and many others. Even outside the boundaries of any institutional religion, in the ancient Greco-Roman pagan world, not attached, perhaps, to any particular religion, Plotinus was one of the supremely great mystics.

Now, of course, as between these mysticisms in the various cultures, there are certain differences. For instance, Hindu mysticism is not quite the same as Christian mysticism. But I believe that the resemblances, the common elements, the elements which are universally found in all these mysticisms, are far more striking than the differences. I should say that the differences are superficial, while the common, basic, universal elements in all mysticism are fundamental. Should you ask me: "What are those common elements which appear in mysticism in all these different cultures and religions?" I can, perhaps, very briefly, summarize them.

In the first place, the absolutely basic, fundamental characteristic of all mystical experience is that it is called "the unitary consciousness," or, as it is sometimes called, "the unifying vision." We may contrast the mystical consciousness with our ordinary, everyday, rational consciousness. Our ordinary, everyday consciousness is characterized by multiplicity. I mean that both the senses and the intellect, which constitute our everyday consciousness, are in contact with and are aware of a vast number, a plurality, a multiplicity of different things. In our ordinary consciousness we discriminate between one thing and another. But the mystical consciousness transcends all differences and all multiplicity. In it there is no multiplicity and no division of difference. "Here," says Eckhart "all is one, and one is all." He goes on to say that in that supreme vision there are "no contrasts." "Contrast" is Eckhart's word for the difference between one thing and another, for instance between yellow and green. He even goes so far as to say that in that experience there are no contrasts, i.e. differences, between grass, wood, and stone, but that all these "are one."

Closely connected with, and perhaps as a result of this characteristic of transcending all multiplicity, discrimination, and division are other characteristics common to mystical experience in all religions. It is non-sensuous, non-intellectual, and non-conceptual. And since all words except proper names stand for concepts, this means mystical experience is beyond all words, incapable of being expressed in any language; "ineffable" is the usual word. Another characteristic is that what is experienced is beyond space and beyond time. It is timeless; and timelessness is eternity. And therefore the mystical consciousness, even though it lasts only for a very short while, perhaps only a moment, is nevertheless eternal. For that moment gathers into itself all eternity. It is an eternal moment.

Another universal characteristic is that mystical consciousness is blessedness—it is the peace which passeth all understanding. One might quote at length from the utterances of great mystics in all religions to prove that these are the

common characteristics. I have time for only one quotation which I choose because it happens to include most of them in a few sentences. In the Mandukya
Upanishad it is written:

> It is neither inward experience nor outward experience. It is neither intellectual
> knowledge nor inferential knowledge. It is beyond the senses, beyond the under-
> standing, beyond all expression. It is the pure unitary consciousness wherein aware-
> ness of the world and of multiplicity is completely obliterated. It is ineffable peace. It
> is the supreme good. It is the One without a second.

One other common element I must mention. The mystic everywhere, except
perhaps in Buddhism, which is a rather doubtful case here, invariably feels an
absolute certainty that he is in direct touch with, and not only in direct touch
with, but has entered into actual union with, the Divine Being. Plotinus expressed
this by saying that "the man"—the mystic, that is —"is merged with the Supreme, sunken into it, one with it." And William James in his famous book,
Varieties of Religious Experience, has an excellent brief chapter on mysticism, and
in that he uses these words:

> This overcoming of all barriers between the individual and the Absolute is the great
> mystic achievement. In mystic states we become one with the Absolute. This is the
> everlasting and triumphant mystic tradition, hardly altered by differences of climate,
> culture, or creed. In Hinduism, in Neo-Platonism, in Sufism, in Christian mysticism,
> we find the same recurring note, so that there is about mystic utterances an eternal
> unanimity which ought to make the critic stop and think.

Now, of course, this mystical experience, basically the same in all cultures as
it is, might nevertheless be nothing but a beautiful dream. It is possible that it is
a purely subjective state of the mystic's own mind, and that he is under an
illusion when he thinks that he is in contact with some great being objective and
outside himself. The only logical argument, the only piece of evidence which can
be used to show that it is more than a beautiful dream, that it does actually reveal
contact with an objective, divine being is this remarkable agreement, as regards
basic features, of the different mysticisms in all the cultures of the world. Of
course one may be convinced by faith, or intuition, or feeling. But I am speaking
here of logical argument or evidence. . . .

I turn now to what is the essential subject of my lecture, the paradoxes of
mysticism. There are many such paradoxes. Their general character is this: that
whatever is affirmed of God must be at the same time and in one and the same
breath categorically denied. Whatever is said of the Divine Being, the opposite,
the contradictory, must also be said. There are many such paradoxes, but I am
going to speak tonight only about one, which is perhaps the most startling of
them. This may be expressed by saying that God is both being and non-being. If
you like, you can say it means that God both exists and does not exist; or again
that God is beyond both existence and non-existence. There is thus both a positive and negative aspect. There is the positive divine and the negative divine. As
to the positive divine, it is hardly necessary for me to say much about it because
it is well known to everyone. It is the content of popular religion everywhere. We

begin, I suppose, by saying that God exists. "Exist" is a positive word. We go on to say that he is a mind, a spirit, a person. These, too, are positive conceptions. Finally, we say that God is love, justice, mercy, power, knowledge, wisdom, and so on. All these are positive terms. And you will recognize that statements of this kind about the Divine Being are the content of ordinary, everyday, popular religious thought. This is true not only of Christianity but, I think, of all the great religions of the world, with the possible exception of Buddhism which is often called an atheistic religion. I don't think that there is really very much disagreement between the great world religions in regard to these basic attributes of God. There may be some difference of emphasis. No doubt it is the case that in Christianity the emphasis is upon God as love. In Hinduism the emphasis is on God as bliss. In Islam perhaps the emphasis is on God as power, and so on.

If we turn now to the negative divine, we pass into a region which is not so well known. This is usually especially associated with mystical religion. It may be expressed by saying that, just as for the positive divine God is being, here God is non-being. Even more striking words than this are used by the great mystics. God is "Nothing." He is "empty." He is "the Void." He is "the bottomless abyss of nothingness." And sometimes metaphors are used. Darkness as the absence of light, and silence as the absence of sound, are negative. Therefore God is spoken of as the great darkness, the great silence.

I am going to document these statements by referring very briefly (I cannot give very much of the evidence in a short lecture) to some of the great mystic utterances in the different religions of the world. I want to show that this is universal.

To begin with Christianity: Meister Eckhart, as you know, was a great Roman Catholic mystic of the 13th century. In one place he says: "God is as void as if he were not." Elsewhere he says: "Thou shalt worship God as he is, a non-God, a non-form, a non-person." One of his followers wrote this of him: "Wise Meister Eckhart speaks to us about Nothingness. He who does not understand this, in him has never shone the divine light." Using the metaphor of darkness, Eckhart says: "The end of all things is the hidden darkness of the eternal Godhead." He also refers on many occasions to God as "the nameless nothing." Another well-known Christian mystic, Tauler, uses the same kind of language. He, too, refers to God as "the nameless nothing." Albertus Magnus writes this: "We first deny of God all bodily and sensible attributes, and then all intelligible attributes, and lastly, that being which would place him among created things." Notice that being, existence, is here said to be the mark of created things.

Turning to Judaism we find that Jewish mystics often referred to Jehovah as "the mystical Nothing." And again, "in depths of His nothingness" is a common phrase. One of the Hassidic mystics wrote: "There are those who worship God with their human intellects, and others whose gaze is fixed on Nothing. He who is granted this supreme experience loses the reality of his intellect, but when he returns from such contemplation to the intellect, he finds it full of divine and inflowing splendor."

Turning to Buddhism we find a rather difficult case for our exposition because it is often said that Buddhism is an atheistic religion. This is true with some reservations. It is true that you do not find the Western concept of God in Buddhism. And it therefore might be said that it is obvious that Buddhism can have neither a positive nor a negative conception of God. This, however, is really not a justifiable conclusion. I can't go into the matter in any great detail here. On the whole, the concept of Nirvana is what corresponds in Buddhism to the Christian and Jewish concept of God. Nirvana, the experience of Nirvana, is, I think, what we would recognize as the divine experience, the experience of the divine element in the world. It is not important that the word God is not used. If Nirvana corresponds to the concept of the divine, then one can say that the concept of Nirvana has both the positive and negative aspects. Positively, it is bliss unspeakable. Negatively, it is the Void. This conception of the Void which you see that Eckhart also uses, is basic to Buddhism. Ultimate reality is the Void.

I find that in Hinduism this positive-negative paradox is more fully developed, more clear than it is in Christianity, Judaism, or Buddhism. In Hinduism it may be said that this paradox has three aspects. Brahman is the name used in the Upanishads and generally in Hindu thought for the ultimate, supreme God. The first aspect of the paradox is that Brahman both has qualities and yet is without any qualities at all. On the positive side the qualities of Brahman are the usual divine qualities to which I have already referred. On the negative side he is "unqualified." This is often expressed in the Upanishads by using a string of negative terms. For example, it is said that Brahman "is soundless, formless, shapeless, intangible, tasteless, odorless, mindless." Notice this last word, "mindless." This quotation is similar in meaning to the one which I read from Albertus Magnus. First we deny all physical qualities. He is "soundless, formless, shapeless, intangible, odorless, and tasteless." Next we deny all "intelligible," i.e., psychological or spiritual attributes. He is "mindless." But the negative of the paradox, the denial of all qualities, is summed up in a very famous verse in the Upanishads. Brahman is here, as often, referred to as the Self. The verse says: "That Self is to be described as not this, not that." One of the earlier translators worded it thus: "That Self is to be described by 'No! No!'." The force of this "No! No!" is clear. Whatever attribute you suggest, whatever predicate you suggest, whatever quality you suggest, of Brahman, the answer always is "No." Is he matter? No. Is he mind? No. Is he good? No. Is he evil? No. And so throughout every word that you can possibly choose.

The second aspect of the paradox in Hinduism is that Brahman is both personal and impersonal. His personality is carried by the very word "Self." He is the Self. He is personal and as such is wise, just, good, and so on. But he is also wholly impersonal. The word "mindless" contains this implication. For a person must necessarily be a mind. Also he is specifically referred to as "the impersonal Brahman." And sometimes the word "he" and sometimes the word "it" is used of Brahman. "He" conveys the notion of personality, "it" the notion of impersonality.

The third and final aspect of the paradox in Hinduism is that Brahman is both dynamic and static. Dynamic means he is active, static means he is actionless. On the positive side God is dynamic. He is the creative energy of the world, the creator. Also he acts in the world, guides and controls the world. On the static side it is specifically stated in the Upanishads that he is wholly actionless.[1] And the entire paradox is summed up in the following verse from the Upanishads:

> That One, though never stirring, is swifter than thought; though standing still, it overtakes those who run. It moves and it moves not.

In this phrase, "It moves and it moves not," you have the whole paradox of the dynamic and static character of God summed up in five words.

Perhaps you will say, "Well, this is just poetic language. Everybody knows that poets like pleasant sounding phrases. And they like a balance of clauses. 'It moves and it moves not' sounds very well but it is mere words." I think you are quite mistaken if you take that interpretation. This is a literal statement of the paradox of the dynamic and the static.

Now I am persuaded that this entire paradox, and particularly that of the dynamic and the static character of the divine being, is not peculiar to Hinduism but is a universal characteristic of the religious consciousness everywhere, although in Hinduism it is more explicit, more baldly stated, than in other religions. In other religions it is present but tends to be veiled. Let us look at Christianity, for example. No one will deny that the Christian God is active. He is the creator of the world; he guides and controls it. But where, you will ask me, do you find evidence that the Christian God is static, inactive? It is true that you must look under the surface to find this. It is implied, implicit rather than explicit, in the concept of God as *unchangeable and immutable*. The changelessness, the immutability of God, is not only a Christian idea. It is a universal intuition of the religious consciousness found in all religions. "In him is no shadow of turning," and there is a well-known hymn which begins with the words:

> O strength and stay upholding all creation
> Who ever dost thyself *unmoved abide*.

The last two words convey the idea of the motionless, actionless character of God. We hardly realize when we speak of God as "immutable" and yet as the Creator of the world that we are uttering a paradox. There is, in fact, a contradiction between God as active and God as unchanging, because that which acts necessarily changes—changes from that state in which the action is not done to that state in which the action is done. Therefore, that which is wholly unchanging is also wholly inactive. The same idea also appears in poetry. T. S. Eliot twice to my knowledge in his poems uses the phrase, "The still point of the turning world." The literal meaning of this is obvious. It refers to the planet, the periphery and the outer parts of which are turning, while the axis in the middle is motionless. But the mystical meaning is also clear. It means that this world is a world of flux and change and becoming, but at the center of it, in the heart of things, there is silence, stillness, motionlessness.

[1] Rudolph Otto in his *Mysticism East and West* claims it as a superiority of the Christian God over the Hindu, that the latter is merely static, the former dynamic. He has missed the paradox and been misled by the frequent statements that Brahman is inactive.

So much, then, for the exposition of this paradox. But the human intellect, when it comes to a logical contradiction, necessarily attempts to get rid of it, attempts to explain away the contradiction. It tries to show that although there is an apparent contradiction, there is not really one. To get rid of a contradiction is essential to the very nature of our logical and rationalistic intellect. . . .

My own belief is that all attempts to rationalize the paradox, to make it logically acceptable, are futile because the paradoxes of religion and of mysticism are irresoluble by the human intellect. My view is that they never have been, they never can be, and they never will be resolved, or made logical. That is to say, these paradoxes and contradictions are inherent in the mystical experience and cannot be got rid of by any human logic or ingenuity. This, in my opinion, is an aspect of what is sometimes called the mystery of God or the incomprehensibility of God. This mystery of God is not something which we can get rid of, something which we could understand by being a little more clever or a little more learned. It is ultimate, it is an ultimate and irremovable character of the divine. When you say that God is incomprehensible, one thing you mean is just that these contradictions break out in our intellect and cannot be resolved, no matter how clever or how good a logician you may be. And I think that this view is in the end the view of the mystics themselves, including Eckhart, in spite of his apparent attempt to explain the paradox.

In order to show that this is in fact the view of the mystics themselves in all religions, I will read to you from a Christian mystic, a Hindu, and a Buddhist. The Christian example again is Eckhart. Rudolph Otto writes that "Eckhart establishes a polar unity between rest and motion within the Godhead itself. The eternally resting Godhead is also the wheel rolling out of itself." And in Eckhart's own words: "This divine ground is a unified stillness, immovable in itself. Yet from this immobility all things are moved and receive life."

The Hindu from whom I wish to quote is Aurobindo, who died only a few years ago. There is no doubt in my mind that he himself experienced the mystical vision in full measure. He says:

> Those who have thus possessed the calm within can perceive always welling out from its silence the perennial supply of the energies which work in the world.

I wish to comment on this sentence. "Those who have thus possessed the calm within" means those who have possessed mystical vision. "Can perceive always welling out from its silence"—"silence" is the motionlessness, the stillness, the inactivity of the divine. "The perennial supply of the energies which work in the world" refers to the creative activity of the divine. These creative energies are said to "well out from the silence." In other words, they issue out of the empty void. Finally, we see the paradox of the static and the dynamic directly stated as an *experience.* The word "perceive" is used. This is not an intellectual proposition, a theory, an intellectual construction, a philosophical opinion. It is a direct perception or vision of reality.

My last example is Suzuki, the well-known Zen Buddhist mystic, now teaching in New York. He writes:

> It is not the nature of "prajna" to remain in the state of "sunyata," absolutely motionless.

("Prajna" is the word for mystical intuition, while "sunyata" means the void.) So he is saying it is not the nature of mystical consciousness to remain in a state of void, absolutely motionless.

> It demands of itself that it differentiate itself unlimitedly and, at the same time, it deserves to remain in itself undifferentiated. This is why "sunyata" is said to be a reservoir of infinite possibility, and not just a state of mere emptiness. Differentiating itself and yet remaining in itself undifferentiated, it goes on eternally in the work of creation. We can say of it that it is creation out of nothing. "Sunyata" is not to be conceived statically but dynamically, or better, as at once static and dynamic.

David Hume asked ironically, "Have you ever seen a world created under your eyes—have you ever observed an act of creation of the world?" The answer is: Yes, there are men who have seen this.

I conclude that these contradictions and paradoxes are impossible of logical adjustment or resolution. What, then, should we think about the matter? Should we say that there is contradiction in the nature of God himself, in the ultimate being? Well, if we were to say that, I think that we shouldn't be saying anything very unusual or very shocking. Many people have said this or at any rate implied it. Does not the Christian doctrine of the Trinity itself imply this? What could be a greater paradox than that? And it is not to be believed that the three-in-one, the three which is one and the one which is three, could be understood or explained by a super-Einstein, or by a higher mathematics than has yet been invented. It is irremovable and an absolute paradox. Also one might quote the words of Jacob Boëhme suggesting that there is contradiction in the heart of things, in the ultimate itself. Schwegler, a distinguished German historian of philosophy, writes this:

> The main thought of Boëhme's philosophizing is this: that self-distinction, inner diremption is the essential characteristic of spirit, and, consequently of God. God is the living spirit only if and insofar as he comprehends within himself difference from himself.

One might also perhaps quote Boëme's well-known statement that God is both "the Eternal Yea" and "the Eternal Nay," but this perhaps might also be taken simply as a brief expression of the negative-positive paradox.

Although I do not think it would be anything seriously erroneous if we would say that there is contradiction in the Ultimate, yet I would prefer myself to use other language. I should say that the contradiction is in us, in our intellect, and not in God. This means that God is utterly and forever beyond the reach of the logical intellect or of any intellectual comprehension, and that in consequence when we try to comprehend his nature intellectually, contradictions appear in our thinking. Let me use a metaphor to express this. We speak of God as the "Infinite" and of ourselves as "finite" minds. As a matter of fact what the word "infinite" means in this connection is itself a difficult problem in the philosophy of religion. It is certain that the word 'infinite," when applied to God, is not used in the same sense as when we speak of infinite time or infinite space or the infinite number series. What it does mean is a problem. I believe that it can be solved, that is to say, it is possible to give a clear meaning to the word "infinite"—different from the infinity of space and time—as the word is applied to God. However, if I am allowed to use this language of finite and infinite, my metaphor is that if you try to pour the infinite into the finite vessels which are human minds, these finite vessels split and crack, and these cracks and splits are the contradictions and paradoxes of which I have been talking. Therefore this amounts to saying that God is utterly incomprehensible, incapable of being intellectually understood. In order to make my final point I will use the word "unknowable." It means that God is, in a sense, unknowable. But we must be very careful of this. If God were absolutely unknowable, and in no sense knowable, then there could be no such thing as religion, because in some sense or other religion is the knowledge of God.

The explanation of this is that he is unknowable to the *the logical intellect*, but that he can be known in direct religious or mystical experience. Perhaps this is much the same as saying that he can be known by "faith" but not by "reason." Any attempt to reach God through logic, through the conceptual, logical intellect, is doomed, comes up against an absolute barrier; but this does not mean the death of religion—it does not mean that there is no possibility of that knowledge and communion with God which religion requires. It means that the knowledge of God which is the essence of religion is not of an intellectual kind. It is rather the direct experience of the mystic himself. Or if we are not mystics, then it is whatever it is that you would call religious experience. And this experience of God—in the heart, shall we say, not any intellectual understanding or explanation—this experience of God is the essence of religion.

STUDY QUESTIONS

1   List some of the similarities which Stace finds in the different mystical traditions of the world.
2   What are some of the "paradoxes" in the mystical vision of God?
3   How does Stace account for these paradoxes? In what sense is God unknowable?
4   Can you think of ordinary experiences which might be used to back up Stace's position? For example, are some aspects of ordinary experience indescribable?
5   Is it possible to view the poet as a mystic?
6   In light of Stace's comments on the mystical traditions of the world, interpret these sayings of some famous mystics:

I went from God to God, until they cried out from me in me, "O thou I!" (Bayadzid of Bistun).

The philosophers are clever enough, but wanting in wisdom; As to the others, they are either ignorant or puerile! They take an empty fist as containing something real and the pointing finger as the object pointed at. Because the finger is adhered to as though it were the moon, all their efforts are lost (Yoka Daishi).

How shall I grasp it? Do not grasp it. That which remains when there is no more grasping is the Self (Panchadasi).

Faith and Reason

Michael Scriven

Michael Scriven (1928–   ) is a distinguished philosopher who is well known for his lucid and comprehensive treatment of many classic philosophical questions. As you will soon discover, Scriven is an uncompromising defender of reason as the best tool for discovering truth. His central claim is that if God transcends the human intellect, then religious belief can have no relevant connection with life. Faith is not enough.

In general, Scriven argues that religious knowledge must always be tied to the usual forms of experience. Faith, he claims, cannot be considered an alternative to reason unless it is first shown that faith leads to consistently reliable predictions. If this could be done, then faith, as a way of knowing, would have been validated by reason. But Scriven thinks that the lack of agreement in the religious community shows that faith cannot be "proved out" in the way that the techniques of ordinary reason can be, and thus it cannot serve as an alternative to ordinary reason.

The issues raised in this essay are extremely important and the arguments may be difficult to appreciate. As you read Scriven you might adopt Stace's position in order to locate sources of disagreement between them. It may be possible, for example, that Scriven bases his argument on assumptions which the mystic would say are just the points in question.

What kind of God, if any, exists? This is the primary problem about God, and it is simply stated. Nothing else about the issue is simple. And the problem's complexity is matched by its profundity. No other problem has such important consequences for our lives and our thinking about other issues, and to no other problem does the answer at first seem so obvious. There *must* be a God, for how else could the Universe have come to exist, or life and morality have any point? So one feels. The informal versions of the arguments for the existence of God are probably the oldest and the most widely known of all philosophical arguments. But the centuries have not been entirely kind to them, and many contemporary theologians have wholly abandoned the attempt to prove that God exists, the original task of natural theology. . . .

Does it matter whether the arguments are sound? Indeed, should we be trying to reason about God at all? It is often said that such an attempt is hopelessly inappropriate, and indeed it is sometimes said to be sacrilegious. By His very nature God transcends merely human categories of thought, and to attempt to imprison Him in them is a simple fallacy. The attempt, in fact, demonstrates that some other, limited being is under discussion, not God Himself. Our enterprise and, indeed, our very definition of "God" in terms of human concepts are thus doomed from the start.

But a mountain that is infinitely tall does not thereby cease to be a mountain; those who lived in its shadow would not lack good reason for saying that there was a mountain near them just because none could determine where the end of the shadow was to be found. A God that exists everywhere is nonetheless present here and now. A God that is perfectly loving is at least as loving as a human being who loves with all his human heart. An omnipotent God is at least as powerful as you and I; indeed He is certainly more powerful than any human being. So we *can* legitimately begin by looking into the question whether there is any reason for thinking that this world is inhabited (or permeated) by a Being who is superhuman in respect of His knowledge, power, and love to the extent set out in our definition.

If such a Being exists, then we might or might not be able to go on to argue that It is *infinitely* powerful, etc., or the grounds we uncover may immediately lead to that conclusion. Despite a common belief to the contrary, this task is obviously possible in principle. We have already learned, from the fossils and footprints of the dinosaurs, that there were once beings on the Earth's surface with greater physical power than human beings. There is nothing in the least self-contradictory about a human being reasoning to the conclusion that there are beings with *more-than-human* power, just as the big-game hunter frequently reasons to the presence of elephants. One might as well argue that it is impossible to reason about the existence of beings with *less*-than-human power—after all, they are just as different from us. Indeed we can go further; the whole of modern particle physics involves reasoning about the existence of beings with properties that are so fundamentally different from the ones with which we are familiar that comprehension in the sense of simple analogy with the familiar is almost completely lacking, but the success of applied physics shows that such inferences are not only possible but very effective. And mathematics readily demonstrates the possibility of reasoning to the existence of infinite entities and properties. . . .

In a somewhat desperate move, some theologians have argued that the words we use to describe God do not have their ordinary use at all. All religious language is symbolic and not to be taken literally, they say. This move throws out the baby of belief with the bath water of mythology; it is too sophisticated for its own good. In the first place, almost all believers and potential believers, past and present, take the usual claims about God's nature to be something like the truth, even if not quite literally true; and it is to them we are addressing these discussions. The points made will not be vulnerable to the possibility that analogical or symbolic reference is the best we can do (in any comprehensible sense of "analogical" or "symbolic"). In the second place, if we try to take the sophisticated position seriously and ask what it is about religious belief, interpreted in this way, that distinguishes it from the beliefs of a pagan or an avowed atheist, we find that either there is no agreement on the answer or the answer is that no such distinction exists. The latter comment has been taken to be the profound discovery that everyone is "really" religious or even theistic (for example, because everyone has some "ultimate concern" about something or believes in the existence of substance). But, of course, it equally well proves that everyone is "really" irreligious or atheistic; if there is no difference between chalk and cheese, you can just as well call the stuff on the supermarket's cold shelves chalk as call the stuff on the blackboard cheese. There is a real difference between almost everyone who believes in the existence of God and everyone who does not; the difference is that the two groups disagree about what a thorough census of all existing entities would show and only one of them thinks it would include an intelligent Being with supernatural powers, concerned with our welfare. Attempts to eliminate this residual content in theism, common in recent "liberal" Protestant theology, are the survival attempts of a system of belief that sees its only salvation in camouflage but fails to see that what is indistinguishable cannot be indispensable.

Someone who wanted to adopt a really disproof-proof position here (many have been tempted, and at least one Indian philosopher has succumbed) could *define* God as the Unknowable; or he could say that whatever else God is, He is certainly unknowable. The only trouble with this position is that you really cannot eat your cake and worship it too; there cannot be any reason for worshiping, or respecting, or loving, or praying to, or believing in such a God. The Unknowable may be evil, stupid, inanimate, or nonexistent; a religion dedicated to such a pig in a poke would be for the feebleminded. If religious belief means anything at all, it means belief in something whose properties may not be entirely clear but which are at least worthy of respect (most have said, humble adoration). Such a Being is not wholly unknowable, since we know some very important things about Him, such as His goodness. We may certainly say that He is not fully knowable, and the ensuing discussion does not assume that God is fully knowable. The theist's claim is that there is a good supernatural force, perhaps with many mysterious properties. And the atheist's claim is simply that the God of the great religions has quite enough properties to make him, on the one hand, worthy of respect and, on the other, nonexistent.

The extreme form of the defense against the relevance of reason is therefore itself indefensible. There are no obvious mistakes in the attempt to reason about God. One can all too easily get carried away by catchy little slogans like "The finite cannot comprehend the infinite," "Man cannot presume to judge God," "God takes up where Reason gives out," and so on. Their merits, if any, lie in their potential use as tricky titles for sermons in fashionable suburban churches. They have no force as a defense against skepticism or as a support for belief. We can be quite sure there *is* an infinite sequence of digits after 1, 2, and 3, and we can be quite sure there *is not* an infinitely long ribbon in our typewriter or an infinitely heavy nuthatch sitting on the bird feeder; so the preacher just has to get down from the pulpit and do some hard, logical work to show that there is some special reason why an infinite God cannot be reasoned about in the same way. Why should the human mind be incapable of dealing with the infinite in theology but not in mathematics or cosmology, where it is a commonplace and well-defined part of the subject?

Yet, a more profound point is involved behind the scenes here. There is a nagging nervousness about talking as if there were no limitations on the power of the human reason. After all, there *must* be a certain parochialism about our present views and a certain poverty about our capacity for analyzing the evidence. We have only been thinking systematically for a few millenniums (some would say, centuries), and in that short span we have constantly found ourselves abandoning the absolute convictions of previous generations. How then can one have any degree of certainty about the existence or nonexistence of a Being so different from the beings of our immediate experience and so vastly superior to ourselves in thought?

The point is very weighty, but it is not decisive here. In the first place, the very nature of the Being we are now undertaking to discuss makes Him approachable by reason. For God, Who is often said to be ever present, is at the very least *able* to be present almost anywhere at almost any time—He is ever accessible. If He lacked this power, He would be of little concern to us. We cannot be certain about the existence of beings on other planets just because they are on other planets and not here, and thus far we have not been close enough to see if they do, in fact, exist. But a Being that is here, indeed often said to have been here since Creation—such a Being, with the opportunity and the power and the interest in doing something that would prevent or improve an imperfect work, would surely have to leave some traces in *this* world. Indeed, whether He created the world or merely had the chance to change it, the world itself must to some extent be a reflection of His character. If we can show that the world is best explicable in terms of a Divine Plan, we have the best reasons for theism. If the world is simply a natural phenomenon, whose natural properties are grossly imperfect for our needs and not improved by any unseen force, it seems at first sight as if we would have some kind of reason for thinking Him less than good, powerful, and wise. So reason can in principle both prove and disprove the existence of God. . . .

We must now contend with the suggestion that reason is irrelevant to the commitment to theism because this territory is the domain of another faculty: the faculty of faith. It is sometimes even hinted that it is morally wrong and certainly foolish to suggest we should be reasoning about God. For this is the domain of faith or of the "venture of faith," of the "knowledge that passeth understanding," of religious experience and mystic insight.

Now the normal meaning of *faith* is simply "confidence"; we say that we have great faith in someone or in some claim or product, meaning that we believe and act as if they were very reliable. Of such faith we can properly say that it is well founded or not, depending on the evidence for whatever it is in which we have faith.[1] So there is no incompatibility between this kind of faith and reason; the two are from different families and can make a very good marriage. Indeed if they do not join forces, then the resulting ill-based or inadequate confidence will probably lead to disaster. So faith, in this sense, means only a high degree of belief and may be reasonable or unreasonable.

But the term is sometimes used to mean an *alternative to reason* instead of something that should be founded on reason. Unfortunately, the mere use of the term in this way does not demonstrate that faith is a possible route to truth. It is like using the term "winning" as a synonym for "playing" instead of one possible outcome of playing. This is quaint, but it could hardly be called a satisfactory

---

[1] For faith to be well founded, especially faith in a person, it is not required that the evidence available at a particular moment justify exactly the degree of confidence one exhibits. There may be overriding reasons for retaining trust beyond the first point of rationally defensible doubt. . . . But this minor divergence does not seriously affect the discussion here.

way of proving that we are winning; any time we "win" by changing the meaning of winning, the victory is merely illusory. And so it proves in this case. To use "faith" *as if* it were an alternative way to the truth cannot by-pass the crucial question whether such results really have any likelihood of being true. A rose by any other name will smell the same, and the inescapable facts about "faith" in the new sense are that it is still *applied to* a belief and is still supposed to imply *confidence in* that belief: the belief in the existence and goodness of God. So we can still ask the same old question about that belief: Is the confidence justified or misplaced? To say we "take it on faith" does not get it off parole.

Suppose someone replies that theism is a kind of belief that does not need justification by evidence. This means either that no one cares whether it is correct or not or that there is some other way of checking that it is correct besides looking at the evidence for it, i.e., giving reasons for believing it. But the first alternative is false since very many people care whether there is a God or not; and the second alternative is false because any method of showing that belief is likely to be true is, by definition, a justification of that belief, i.e., an appeal to reason. You certainly cannot show that a belief in God is likely to be true just by having confidence in it and by saying this is a case of knowledge "based on" faith, any more than you can win a game just by playing it and by calling that winning.

It is psychologically possible to have faith in something without any basis in fact, and once in a while you will turn out to be lucky and to have backed the right belief. This does not show you "really knew all along"; it only shows you cannot be unlucky all the time. . . . But, in general, beliefs without foundations lead to an early grave or to an accumulation of superstitions, which are usually troublesome and always false beliefs. It is hardly possible to defend this approach just by *saying* that you have decided that in this area confidence is its own justification.

Of course, you might try to *prove* that a feeling of great confidence about certain types of propositions is a reliable indication of their truth. If you succeeded, you would indeed have shown that the belief was justified; you would have done this by justifying it. To do this you would have to show what the real facts were and show that when someone had the kind of faith we are now talking about, it usually turned out that the facts were as he believed; just as we might justify the claims of a telepath. The catch in all this is simply that you have got to show what the real facts are in some way *other* than by appealing to faith, since that would simply be assuming what you are trying to prove. And if you can show what the facts are in this other way, you do not need faith in any new sense at all; you are already perfectly entitled to confidence in any belief that you have shown to be well supported.

How are you going to show what the real facts are? You show this by any method of investigation that has itself been tested, the testing being done by still another tested method, etc., through a series of tested connections that eventually terminates in our ordinary everyday reasoning and testing procedures of logic and observation.

Is it not prejudiced to require that the validation of beliefs always involve ultimate reference to our ordinary logic and everyday-plus-scientific knowledge? May not faith (religious experience, mystic insight) give us access to some new domain of truth? It is certainly possible that it does this. But, of course, it is also possible that it lies. One can hardly accept the reports of those with faith or, indeed, the apparent revelations of one's own religious experiences on the ground that they *might* be right. So *might* be a fervent materialist who saw his interpretation as a revelation. Possibility is not veracity. Is it not of the very greatest importance that we should try to find out whether we really can justify the use of the term "truth" or "knowledge" in describing the content of faith? If it is, then we must find something in that content that is known to be true in some other way, because to get off the ground we must first push off against the ground—we cannot lift ourselves by our shoelaces. If the new realm of knowledge is to be a realm of knowledge and not mythology, then it must tell us something which relates it to the kind of case that gives meaning to the term "truth." If you want to use the old word for the new events, you must show that it is applicable.

Could not the validating experience, which religious experience must have if it is to be called true, be the experience of others who also have or have had religious experiences? The religious community could, surely, provide a basis of agreement analogous to that which ultimately underlies scientific truth. Unfortunately, agreement is not the only requirement for avoiding error, for all may be in error. The difficulty for the religious community is to show that its agreement is not simply agreement about a shared mistake. If agreement were the only criterion of truth, there could never be a shared mistake; but clearly either the atheist group or the theist group shares a mistake. To decide which is wrong must involve appeal to something other than mere agreement. And, of course, it is clear that particular religious beliefs are mistaken, since religious groups do not all agree and they cannot all be right.

Might not some or all scientific beliefs be wrong, too? This is conceivable, but there are crucial differences between the two kinds of belief. In the first place, any commonly agreed religious beliefs concern only one or a few entities and their properties and histories. What for convenience we are here calling "scientific belief" is actually the sum total of all conventionally founded human knowledge, much of it not part of any science, and it embraces billions upon billions of facts, each of them perpetually or frequently subject to checking by independent means, each connected with a million others. The success of *this* system of knowledge shows up every day in everything that we do: we eat, and the food is not poison; we read, and the pages do not turn to dust; we slip, and gravity does not fail to pull us down. We are not just relying on the existence of agreement about the interpretation of a certain experience among a small part of the population. We are relying directly on our extremely reliable, nearly universal, and independently tested senses, and each of us is constantly obtaining independent confirmation for claims based on these, many of these confirmations being obtained for many claims, independently of each other. It is the wildest flight of fancy to suppose that there is a body of common religious beliefs which can be set out to exhibit this degree of repeated checking by religious experiences. In fact, there is not only gross disagreement on even the most fundamental claims in the creeds of different churches, each of which is supported by appeal to religious experience or faith, but where there is agreement by many people, it is all too easily open to the criticism that it arises from the common cultural exposure of the child or the adult convert and hence is not independent in the required way.

This claim that the agreement between judges is spurious in a particular case because it only reflects previous common indoctrination of those in agreement is a serious one. It must always be met by direct disproof whenever agreement is appealed to in science, and it is. The claim that the food is not poison cannot be explained away as a myth of some subculture, for anyone, even if told nothing about the eaters in advance, will judge that the people who ate it are still well. The whole methodology of testing is committed to the doctrine that any judges who could have learned what they are expected to say about the matter they are judging are completely valueless.[2] Now anyone exposed to religious teaching, whether a believer or not, has long known the standard for such experiences, the usual symbols, the appropriate circumstances, and so on. These suggestions are usually very deeply implanted, so that they cannot be avoided by good intentions, and consequently members of our culture are rendered entirely incapable of being independent observers. Whenever observers are not free from previous contamination in this manner, the only way to support their claims is to examine independently testable *consequences* of the novel claims, such as predictions about the future. In the absence of these, the religious-experience gambit, whether involving literal or analogical claims, is wholly abortive.

A still more fundamental point counts against the idea that agreement among the religious can help support the idea of faith as an alternative path to truth. It is that every sane theist also believes in the claims of ordinary experience, while the reverse is not the case. Hence, the burden of proof is on the theist to show that the *further step* he wishes to take will not take him beyond the realm of truth. The two positions, of science and religion, are not symmetrical; the adherent of one of them suggests that we extend the range of allowable beliefs and yet is unable to produce the same degree of acceptance or "proving out" in the ordinary field of human activities that he insists on before believing in a new instrument or source of information. The atheist obviously cannot be shown his error in the way someone who thinks that there are no electrons can be shown his, *unless some of the arguments for the existence of God are sound.* Once again, we come back to these. If some of them work, the position of religious knowledge is secure; if they do not, nothing else will make it secure.

In sum, the idea of separating religious from scientific knowledge and making each an independent realm with its own basis in experience of quite different kinds is a counsel of despair and not a product of true sophistication, for one cannot break the connection between everyday experience and religious claims, for purposes of defending the latter, without eliminating the consequences of religion for everyday life. There is no way out of this inexorable contract: if you

---

[2] More precisely, a judge is said to be "contaminated" if he could know which way his judgment will count insofar as the issue at stake is concerned. The famous double-blind experimental design, keystone of drug research, achieves reliability by making it impossible for either patient or nurse to know when the real drug, rather than the dummy drug or placebo, is being judged.

want to support your beliefs, you must produce some experience which can be shown to be a reliable indicator of truth, and that can be done only by showing a connection between the experience and what we know to be true in a previously established way.

So, if the criteria of religious truth are not connected with the criteria of everyday truth, then they are not criteria of truth at all and the beliefs they "establish" have no essential bearing on our lives, constitute no explanation of what we see around us, and provide no guidance for our course through time.

STUDY QUESTIONS

1   Why does Scriven believe that the claim that we cannot reason about the infinite is untrue?
2   Scriven says that it is impossible to remain religious and think that God is unknowable. Why does he maintain this position?
3   "Human thought categories may be quite limited. We may be nothing more than the egotistic infants of the universe, so impressed by our limited faculties that we cannot see their limitations." How would Scriven reply to this suggestion? What do you think?
4   "Super-rationalists like Scriven simply replace one faith with another. Instead of faith in God, they place their faith in Science, that god above God. But for all their cool, rational protests, they are still gambling that their faith is the true one." Do you agree? How would Scriven respond to this argument?
5   Why does Scriven think it significant that theists believe in the procedures of ordinary experience for testing ordinary beliefs? Do you agree with his conclusion?

The Will to Believe

William James

William James (1842–1910) taught anatomy and physiology at Harvard before moving to psychology, a field in which he acquired an international reputation. His interests, however, turned to philosophy and he soon became one of America's foremost philosophers. James defended a theory called *pragmatism*—a view which held that the truth of an idea is determined by the consequences it has on experience. In his own words: "Ideas (which themselves are but parts of our experience) become true just insofar as they help us to get into satisfactory relation with other parts of our experience." If two theories do not have different consequences for experience, then there can be no real difference between them.

In this essay, James applies his pragmatism to religious belief and argues that what poses as a healthy, rational skepticism is actually no different from the most committed form of atheism. In fact, James maintains that when we consider the consequences of religious belief, faith in God is actually a more rational attitude than skepticism. Both faith and skepticism, he claims, are emotional commitments, but the emotions which guide faith are logically superior to those behind the skeptical position.

James has had his passionate critics as well as devoted defenders. His critics usually accuse him of licensing wishful thinking, whereas his defenders point out that he has focused on an important insight into the way we make decisions in the real world. Undoubtedly, you will join this debate. As you read this classic paper, however, try to keep in mind the qualifications which James attaches to his defense of faith.

In the recently published Life by Leslie Stephen of his brother, Fitz-James, there is an account of a school to which the latter went when he was a boy. The teacher, a certain Mr. Guest, used to converse with his pupils in this wise: "Gurney, what is the difference between justification and sanctification?—Stephen, prove the omnipotence of God!" etc. In the midst of our Harvard freethinking and indifference we are prone to imagine that here at your good old orthodox College conversation continues to be somewhat upon this order; and to show you that we at Harvard have not lost all interest in these vital subjects, I have brought with me to-night something like a sermon on justification by faith to read to you,—I mean an essay in justification *of* faith, a defence of our right to adopt a believing attitude in religious matters, in spite of the fact that our merely logical intellect may not have been coerced. "The Will to Believe," accordingly, is the title of my paper.

I have long defended to my own students the lawfulness of voluntarily adopted faith; but as soon as they have got well imbued with the logical spirit, they have as a rule refused to admit my contention to be lawful philosophically, even though in point of fact they were personally all the time chock-full of some faith or other themselves. I am all the while, however, so profoundly convinced that my own position is correct, that your invitation has seemed to me a good occasion to make my statements more clear. Perhaps your minds will be more open than those with which I have hitherto had to deal. I will be as little technical as I can, though I must begin by setting up some technical distinctions that will help us in the end.

Let us give the name of *hypothesis* to anything that may be proposed to our belief; and just as the electricians speak of live and dead wires, let us speak of any hypothesis as either *live* or *dead*. A live hypothesis is one which appeals as a real possibility to him to whom it is proposed. If I ask you to believe in the Mahdi, the notion makes no electric connection with your nature,—it refuses to scintillate with any credibility at all. As an hypothesis it is completely dead. To an Arab, however (even if he be not one of the Mahdi's followers), the hypothesis is among the mind's possibilities: it is alive. This shows that deadness and liveness in an hypothesis are not intrinsic properties, but relations to the individual thinker. They are measured by his willingness to act. The maximum of liveness in an hypothesis means willingness to act irrevocably. Practically, that means belief; but there is some believing tendency wherever there is willingness to act at all.

Next, let us call the decision between two hypotheses an *option*. Options may

An Address to the Philosophical Clubs of Yale and Brown Universities. Published in the *New World*, June, 1896.

be of several kinds. They may be—1, *living* or *dead;* 2, *forced or avoidable;* 3, *momentous* or *trivial;* and for our purposes we may call an option a *genuine* option when it is of the forced, living, and momentous kind.

1   A living option is one in which both hypotheses are live ones. If I say to you: "Be a theosophist or be a Mohammedan," it is probably a dead option, because for you neither hypothesis is likely to be alive. But if I say: "Be an agnostic or be a Christian," it is otherwise: trained as you are, each hypothesis makes some appeal, however small, to your belief.

2   Next, if I say to you: "Choose between going out with your umbrella or without it," I do not offer you a genuine option, for it is not forced. You can easily avoid it by not going out at all. Similarly, if I say, "Either love me or hate me," "Either call my theory true or call it false," your option is avoidable. You may remain indifferent to me, neither loving nor hating, and you may decline to offer any judgment as to my theory. But if I say, "Either accept this truth or go without it," I put on you a forced option, for there is no standing place outside of the alternative. Every dilemma based on a complete logical disjunction, with no possibility of not choosing, is an option of this forced kind.

3   Finally, if I were Dr. Nansen and proposed to you to join my North Pole expedition, your option would be momentous; for this would probably be your only similar opportunity, and your choice now would either exclude you from the North Pole sort of immortality altogether or put at least the chance of it into your hands. He who refuses to embrace a unique opportunity loses the prize as surely as if he tried and failed. *Per contra,* the option is trivial when the opportunity is not unique, when the stake is insignificant, or when the decision is reversible if it later prove unwise. Such trivial options abound in the scientific life. A chemist finds an hypothesis live enough to spend a year in its verification: he believes in it to that extent. But if his experiments prove inconclusive either way, he is quit for his loss of time, no vital harm being done.

The thesis I defend is, briefly stated, this: *Our passional nature not only lawfully may, but must, decide an option between propositions, whenever it is a genuine option that cannot by its nature be decided on intellectual grounds; for to say, under such circumstances, "Do not decide, but leave the question open," is itself a passional decision,—just like deciding yes or no,—and is attended with the same risk of losing the truth.* The thesis thus abstractly expressed will, I trust, soon become quite clear. . . .

One more point, small but important, and our preliminaries are done. There are two ways of looking at our duty in the matter of opinion,—ways entirely different, and yet ways about whose difference the theory of knowledge seems hitherto to have shown very little concern. *We must know the truth;* and *we must avoid error,*—these are our first and great commandments as would-be knowers; but they are not two ways of stating an identical commandment, they are two separable laws. Although it may indeed happen that when we believe the truth A, we escape as an incidental consequence from believing the falsehood B, it hardly ever happens that by merely disbelieving B we necessarily believe A. We may in escaping B fall into believing other falsehoods, C or D, just as bad as B; or we may escape B by not believing anything at all, not even A.

Believe truth! Shun error!—these, we see, are two materially different laws; and by choosing between them we may end by coloring differently our whole intellectual life. We may regard the chase for truth as paramount, and the avoidance of error as secondary; or we may, on the other hand, treat the avoidance of error as more imperative, and let truth take its chance. Clifford, in the instructive passage which I have quoted, exhorts us to the latter course. Believe nothing, he tells us, keep your mind in suspense forever, rather than by closing it on insufficient evidence incur the awful risk of believing lies. You, on the other hand, may think that the risk of being in error is a very small matter when compared with the blessings of real knowledge, and be ready to be duped many times in your investigation rather than postpone indefinitely the chance of guessing true. I myself find it impossible to go with Clifford. We must remember that these feelings of our duty about either truth or error are in any case only expressions of our passional life. Biologically considered, our minds are as ready to grind out falsehood as veracity, and he who says, "Better go without belief forever than believe a lie!" merely shows his own preponderant private horror of becoming a dupe. He may be critical of many of his desires and fears, but this fear he slavishly obeys. He cannot imagine any one questioning its blinding force. For my own part, I have also a horror of being duped; but I can believe that worse things than being duped may happen to a man in this world: so Clifford's exhortation has to my ears a thoroughly fantastic sound. It is like a general informing his soldiers that it is better to keep out of battle forever than to risk a single wound. Not so are victories either over enemies or over nature gained. Our errors are surely not such awfully solemn things. In a world where we are so certain to incur them in spite of all our caution, a certain lightness of heart seems healthier than this excessive nervousness on their behalf. At any rate, it seems the fittest thing for the empiricist philosopher.

And now, after all this introduction, let us go straight at our question. I have said, and now repeat it, that not only as a matter of fact do we find our passional nature influencing us in our opinions, but that there are some options between opinions in which this influence must be regarded both as an inevitable and as a lawful determinant of our choice.

I fear here that some of you my hearers will begin to scent danger, and lend an inhospitable ear. Two first steps of passion you have indeed had to admit as necessary,—we must think so as to avoid dupery, and we must think so as to gain truth; but the surest path to those ideal consummations, you will probably consider, is from now onwards to take no further passional step.

Well, of course, I agree as far as the facts will allow. Wherever the option between losing truth and gaining it is not momentous, we can throw the chance of *gaining truth* away, and at any rate save ourselves from any chance of *believing falsehood,* by not making up our minds at all till objective evidence has come. In scientific questions, this is almost always the case; and even in human affairs in general, the need of acting is seldom so urgent that a false belief to act on is better than no belief at all. Law courts, indeed, have to decide on the best evidence attainable for the moment, because a judge's duty is to make law as well as to ascertain it, and (as a learned judge once said to me) few cases are worth spending much time over: the great thing is to have them decided on *any* acceptable principle, and got out of the way. But in our dealings with objective nature we obviously are recorders, not makers, of the truth; and decisions for the mere sake of deciding promptly and getting on to the next business would be wholly out of place. Throughout the breadth of physical nature facts are what they are quite independently of us, and seldom is there any such hurry about them that the risks of being duped by believing a premature theory need be faced. The questions here are always trivial options, the hypotheses are hardly living (at any rate not living for us spectators), the choice between believing truth or falsehood is seldom forced. The attitude of skeptical balance is therefore the absolutely wise one if we would escape mistakes. What difference, indeed, does it make to most of us whether we have or have not a theory of the Röntgen rays, whether we believe or not in mind-stuff, or have a conviction about the causality of conscious states? It makes no difference. Such options are not forced on us. On every account it is better not to make them, but still keep weighing reasons *pro et contra* with an indifferent hand.

I speak, of course, here of the purely judging mind. For purposes of discovery such indifference is to be less highly recommended, and science would be far less advanced than she is if the passionate desires of individuals to get their own faiths confirmed had been kept out of the game. See for example the sagacity which Spencer and Weismann now display. On the other hand, if you want an absolute duffer in an investigation, you must, after all, take the man who has no interest whatever in its results: he is the warranted incapable, the positive fool. The most useful investigator, because the most sensitive observer, is always he whose eager interest in one side of the question is balanced by an equally keen nervousness lest he become deceived. Science has organized this nervousness into a regular *technique*, her so-called method of verification; and she has fallen so deeply in love with the method that one may even say she has ceased to care for truth by itself at all. It is only truth as technically verified that interests her. The truth of truths might come in merely affirmative form, and she would decline to touch it. Such truth as that, she might repeat with Clifford, would be stolen in defiance of her duty to mankind. Human passions, however, are stronger than technical rules. "Le cœur a ses raisons," as Pascal says, "que la raison ne connaît pas";[1] and however indifferent to all but the bare rules of the game the umpire, the abstract intellect, may be, the concrete players who furnish him the materials to judge of are usually, each one of them, in love with some pet 'live hypothesis' of his own. Let us agree, however, that wherever there is no forced option, the dispassionately judicial intellect with no pet hypothesis, saving us, as it does, from dupery at any rate, ought to be our ideal.

The question next arises: Are there not somewhere forced options in our speculative questions, and can we (as men who may be interested at least as much in positively gaining truth as in merely escaping dupery) always wait with impunity till the coercive evidence shall have arrived? It seems *a priori* improba-

---

[1] "The heart has its reasons, which reason cannot know."

ble that the truth should be so nicely adjusted to our needs and powers as that. In the great boardinghouse of nature, the cakes and the butter and the syrup seldom come out so even and leave the plates so clean. Indeed, we should view them with scientific suspicion if they did.

Moral questions immediately present themselves as questions whose solution cannot wait for sensible proof. A moral question is a question not of what sensibly exists, but of what is good, or would be good if it did exist. Science can tell us what exists; but to compare the *worths,* both of what exists and of what does not exist, we must consult not science, but what Pascal calls our heart. Science herself consults her heart when she lays it down that the infinite ascertainment of fact and correction of false belief are the supreme goods for man. Challenge the statement, and science can only repeat it oracularly, or else prove it by showing that such ascertainment and correction bring man all sorts of other goods which man's heart in turn declares. The question of having moral beliefs at all or not having them is decided by our will. Are our moral preferences true or false, or are they only odd biological phenomena, making things good or bad for *us,* but in themselves indifferent? How can your pure intellect decide? If your heart does not *want* a world of moral reality, your head will assuredly never make you believe in one. Mephistophelian scepticism, indeed, will satisfy the head's play-instincts much better than any rigorous idealism can. Some men (even at the student age) are so naturally cool-hearted that the moralistic hypothesis never has for them any pungent life, and in their supercilious presence the hot young moralist always feels strangely ill at ease. The appearance of knowingness is on their side, of naïveté and gullibility on his. Yet, in the inarticulate heart of him, he clings to it that he is not a dupe, and that there is a realm in which (as Emerson says) all their wit and intellectual superiority is no better than the cunning of a fox. Moral scepticism can no more be refuted or proved by logic than intellectual scepticism can. When we stick to it that there *is* truth (be it of either kind), we do so with our whole nature, and resolve to stand or fall by the results. The sceptic with his whole nature adopts the doubting attitude; but which of us is the wiser, Omniscience only knows.

Turn now from these wide questions of good to a certain class of questions of fact, questions concerning personal relations, states of mind between one man and another. *Do you like me or not?*—for example. Whether you do or not depends, in countless instances, on whether I meet you half-way, am willing to assume that you must like me, and show you trust and expectation. The previous faith on my part in your liking's existence is in such cases what makes your liking come. But if I stand aloof, and refuse to budge an inch until I have objective evidence, until you shall have done something apt, as the absolutists say, *ad extorquendum assensum meum,*[2] ten to one your liking never comes. How many women's hearts are vanquished by the mere sanguine insistence of some man that they *must* love him! he will not consent to the hypothesis that they cannot. The desire for a certain kind of truth here brings about that special truth's existence; and so it is in innumerable cases of other sorts. Who gains promotions, boons,

---

[2] "Coercing my assent."

appointments, but the man in whose life they are seen to play the part of live hypotheses, who discounts them, sacrifices other things for their sake before they have come, and takes risks for them in advance? His faith acts on the powers above him as a claim, and creates its own verification.

A social organism of any sort whatever, large or small, is what it is because each member proceeds to his own duty with a trust that the other members will simultaneously do theirs. Wherever a desired result is achieved by the co-operation of many independent persons, its existence as a fact is a pure consequence of the precursive faith in one another of those immediately concerned. A government, an army, a commercial system, a ship, a college, an athletic team, all exist on this condition, without which not only is nothing achieved, but nothing is even attempted. A whole train of passengers (individually brave enough) will be looted by a few highwaymen, simply because the latter can count on one another, while each passenger fears that if he makes a movement of resistance, he will be shot before any one else backs him up. If we believed that the whole car-full would rise at once with us, we should each severally rise, and train-robbing would never even be attempted. There are, then, cases where a fact cannot come at all unless a preliminary faith exists in its coming. *And where faith in a fact can help create the fact,* that would be an insane logic which should say that faith running ahead of scientific evidence is the "lowest kind of immorality" into which a thinking being can fall. Yet such is the logic by which our scientific absolutists pretend to regulate our lives! In truths dependent on our personal action, then, faith based on desire is certainly a lawful and possibly an indispensable thing.

But now, it will be said, these are all childish human cases, and have nothing to do with great cosmical matters, like the question of religious faith. Let us then pass on to that. Religions differ so much in their accidents that in discussing the religious question we must make it very generic and broad. What then do we now mean by the religious hypothesis? Science says things are; morality says some things are better than other things; and religion says essentially two things.

First, she says that the best things are the more eternal things, the overlapping things, the things in the universe that throw the last stone, so to speak, and say the final word. "Perfection is eternal,"—this phrase of Charles Secrétan seems a good way of putting this first affirmation of religion, an affirmation which obviously cannot yet be verified scientifically at all.

The second affirmation of religion is that we are better off even now if we believe her first affirmation to be true.

Now, let us consider what the logical elements of this situation are *in case the religious hypothesis in both its branches be really true.* (Of course, we must admit that possibility at the outset. If we are to discuss the question at all, it must involve a living option. If for any of you religion be a hypothesis that cannot, by any living possibility be true, then you need go no farther. I speak to the "saving remnant" alone.) So proceeding, we see, first, that religion offers itself as a *momentous* option. We are supposed to gain, even now, by our belief, and to lose by our non-belief, a certain vital good. Secondly, religion is a *forced* option, so far as that good goes. We cannot escape the issue by remaining sceptical and waiting for more light, because, although we do avoid error in that way *if religion be untrue,* we lose the good, *if it be true,* just as certainly as if we positively chose to disbelieve. It is as if a man should hesitate indefinitely to ask a certain woman to marry him because he was not perfectly sure that she would prove an angel after he brought her home. Would he not cut himself off from that particular angel-possibility as decisively as if he went and married some one else? Scepticism, then, is not avoidance of option; it is option of a certain particular kind of risk. *Better risk loss of truth than chance of error,*—that is your faith-vetoer's exact position. He is actively playing his stake as much as the believer is; he is backing the field against the religious hypothesis, just as the believer is backing the religious hypothesis against the field. To preach scepticism to us as a duty until "sufficient evidence" for religion be found, is tantamount therefore to telling us, when in presence of the religious hypothesis, that to yield to our fear of its being error is wiser and better than to yield to our hope that it may be true. It is not intellect against all passions, then; it is only intellect with one passion laying down its law. And by what, forsooth, is the supreme wisdom of this passion warranted? Dupery for dupery, what proof is there that dupery through hope is so much worse than dupery through fear? I, for one, can see no proof; and I simply refuse obedience to the scientist's command to imitate his kind of option, in a case where my own stake is important enough to give me the right to choose my own form of risk. If religion be true and the evidence for it be still insufficient, I do not wish, by putting your extinguisher upon my nature (which feels to me as if it had after all some business in this matter), to forfeit my sole chance in life of getting upon the winning side,—that chance depending, of course, on my willingness to run the risk of acting as if my passional need of taking the world religiously might be prophetic and right.

All this is on the supposition that it really may be prophetic and right, and that, even to us who are discussing the matter, religion is a live hypothesis which may be true. Now, to most of us religion comes in a still further way that makes a veto on our active faith even more illogical. The more perfect and more eternal aspect of the universe is represented in our religions as having personal form. The universe is no longer a mere *It* to us, but a *Thou,* if we are religious; and any relation that may be possible from person to person might be possible here. For instance, although in one sense we are passive portions of the universe, in another we show a curious autonomy, as if we were small active centres on our own account. We feel, too, as if the appeal of religion to us were made to our own active good-will, as if evidence might be forever withheld from us unless we met the hypothesis halfway. To take a trivial illustration: just as a man who in a company of gentlemen made no advances, asked a warrant for every concession, and believed no one's word without proof, would cut himself off by such churlishness from all the social rewards that a more trusting spirit would earn,—so here, one who should shut himself up in snarling logicality and try to make the gods extort his recognition willy-nilly, or not get it at all, might cut himself off forever from his only opportunity of making the gods' acquaintance. This feeling, forced on us we know not whence, that by obstinately believing that there are gods (although not to do so would be so easy both for our logic and our life) we are doing the universe the deepest service we can, seems part of the living essence of the religious hypothesis. If the hypothesis *were* true in all its parts, including this one, then pure intellectualism, with its veto on our making willing advances, would be an absurdity; and some participation of our sympathetic nature would be logically required. I, therefore, for one, cannot see my way to accepting the agnostic rules for truth-seeking, or wilfully agree to keep my willing nature out of the game. I cannot do so for this plain reason, that *a rule of thinking which would absolutely prevent me from acknowledging certain kinds of truth if those kinds of truth were really there, would be an irrational rule.* That for me is the long and short of the formal logic of the situation, no matter what the kinds of truth might materially be.

I confess I do not see how this logic can be escaped. But sad experience makes me fear that some of you may still shrink from radically saying with me, *in abstracto,* that we have the right to believe at our own risk any hypothesis that is live enough to tempt our will. I suspect, however, that if this is so, it is because you have got away from the abstract logical point of view altogether, and are thinking (perhaps without realizing it) of some particular religious hypothesis which for you is dead. The freedom to "believe what we will" you apply to the case of some patent superstition; and the faith you think of is the faith defined by the schoolboy when he said, "Faith is when you believe something that you know ain't true." I can only repeat that this is misapprehension. *In concreto,* the freedom to believe can only cover living options which the intellect of the individual cannot by itself resolve; and living options never seem absurdities to him who has them to consider. When I look at the religious question as it really puts itself to concrete men, and when I think of all the possibilities which both practically and theoretically it involves, then this command that we shall put a stopper on our heart, instincts, and courage, and *wait*—acting of course meanwhile more or less as if religion were *not* true—till doomsday, or till such time as our intellect and senses working together may have raked in evidence enough,—this command, I say, seems to me the queerest idol ever manufactured in the philosophic cave. Were we scholastic absolutists, there might be more excuse. If we had an infallible intellect with its objective certitudes, we might feel ourselves disloyal to such a perfect organ of knowledge in not trusting to it exclusively, in not waiting for its releasing word. But if we are empiricists, if we believe that no bell in us tolls to let us know for certain when truth is in our grasp, then it seems a piece of idle fantasticality to preach so solemnly our duty of waiting for the bell. Indeed we *may* wait if we will,—I hope you do not think that I am denying that,—but if we do so, we do so at our peril as much as if we believed. In either case we *act,* taking our life in our hands. No one of us ought to issue vetoes to the other, nor should we bandy words of abuse. We ought, on the contrary, delicately and profoundly to respect one another's mental freedom: then only shall we bring about the intellectual republic; then only shall we have that spirit of inner tolerance without which all our outer tolerance is soulless, and which is empiricism's glory; then only shall we live and let live, in speculative as well as in practical things.

I began by a reference to Fitz-James Stephen; let me end by a quotation from him. "What do you think of yourself: What do you think of the world? . . . These are questions with which all must deal as it seems good to them. They are riddles of the Sphinx, and in some way or other we must deal with them. . . . In all important transactions of life we have to take a leap in the dark. . . . If we decide to leave the riddles unanswered, that is a choice; if we waver in our answer, that, too, is a choice: but whatever choice we make, we make it at our peril. If a man chooses to turn his back altogether on God and the future no one can prevent him; no one can show beyond reasonable doubt that he is mistaken. If a man thinks otherwise and acts as he thinks, I do not see that any one can prove that *he* is mistaken. Each must act as he thinks best; and if he is wrong, so much the worse for him. We stand on a mountain pass in the midst of whirling snow and blinding mist, through which we get glimpses now and then of paths which may be deceptive. If we stand still we shall be frozen to death. If we take the wrong road we shall be dashed to pieces. We do not certainly know whether there is any right one. What must we do? 'Be strong and of a good courage.' Act for the best, hope for the best, and take what comes. . . . If death ends all, we cannot meet death better."

STUDY QUESTIONS

1   James believes that faith is justified only under special conditions. What are those special conditions?
2   James compares religious questions with moral questions. Why are they similar? Do you agree with his thesis about morality?
3   Why does James say that the skeptic is betting against the religious hypothesis? Why does he believe that the skeptic has no better claim to rationality than the believer?
4   James mentions a train of passengers who allow themselves to be robbed by a few bandits. What point is he trying to make? How does it fit into his defense of faith?
5   "James is simply allowing anyone to indulge in wishful thinking. In effect, he is saying that if something strikes your fancy and you do not know of any reason why it should not be believed, then you are justified in believing it." Do you think this is a fair way of representing James's position?
6   Suppose you are an atheist who believes that the religious life is degrading to humanity. What would happen if you and James were trying to convert a skeptic?

A Free Man's Worship

Bertrand Russell

Bertrand Russell (1872–1970) has been the most influential philosopher writing in the English language in this century. He has made enormous contributions to the foundations of mathematics, logic, theory of knowledge, social philosophy, educational philosophy, ethics, and other areas of investigation. During World War I he was imprisoned for his pacifist activities and when he was eighty-seven he was arrested for demonstrating against nuclear weapons. In 1940 he was invited to lecture at the City College of New York, but was prevented from teaching there through the vigorous opposition of a group of religious and political leaders who maintained that he was morally unfit. The court invalidated Russell's contract on the basis that his appointment would adversely affect "the public health, safety, and morals of the community." In 1950 he was awarded the Nobel Prize for Literature, in spite of the fact that he was not a poet or novelist. "A Free Man's Worship" demonstrates the powerful simplicity which is the trademark of his style.

In this essay, Russell considers the implications of the scientific world picture on the values of human beings. The material universe is depicted as a source of coercion, for he represents all material processes as subject to the rule of a blind fate which cannot be resisted. The only source of freedom for humanity, Russell says, is the realm of thought, which is not bound by the laws of matter. Throughout this essay, human existence is treated as a tragic undertaking which is made noble by the awareness that all human creations are doomed to destruction. For Russell, the only thing worthy of worship in this hostile universe is humanity itself. This essay is a classic statement of humanistic ideals in a godless world.

To Dr. Faustus in his study Mephistopheles told the history of the Creation, saying:

> The endless praises of the choirs of angels had begun to grow wearisome; for, after all, did he not deserve their praise? Had he not given them endless joy? Would it not be more amusing to obtain undeserved praise, to be worshiped by beings whom he tortured? He smiled inwardly, and resolved that the great drama should be performed.
>
> For countless ages the hot nebula whirled aimlessly through space. At length it began to take shape, the central mass threw off planets, the planets cooled, boiling seas and burning mountains heaved and tossed, from black masses of cloud hot sheets of rain deluged the barely solid crust. And now the first germ of life grew in the depths of the ocean, and developed rapidly in the fructifying warmth into vast forest trees, huge ferns springing from the damp mold, sea monsters breeding, fighting, devouring, and passing away. And from the monsters, as the play unfolded itself, Man was born, with the power of thought, the knowledge of good and evil, and the cruel thirst for worship. And Man saw that all is passing in this mad, monstrous world, that all is struggling to snatch, at any cost, a few brief moments of life before Death's inexorable decree. And Man said: "There is hidden purpose, could we but fathom it, and the purpose is good; for we must reverence something, and in the visible world there is nothing worthy of reverence." And Man stood aside from the struggle, resolving that God intended harmony to come out of chaos by human efforts. And when he followed the instincts which God had transmitted to him from his ancestry of beasts of prey, he called it Sin, and asked God to forgive him. But he doubted whether he could be justly forgiven, until he invented a divine Plan by which God's wrath was to have been appeased. And seeing the present was bad, he made it yet worse, that thereby the future might be better. And he gave God thanks for the strength that enabled him to forgo even the joys that were possible. And God smiled; and when he saw that Man had become perfect in renunciation and worship, he sent another sun through the sky, which crashed into Man's sun; and all returned again to nebula.

"Yes," he murmured, "It was a good play; I will have it performed again."

Such, in outline, but even more purposeless, more void of meaning, is the world which Science presents for our belief. Amid such a world, if anywhere, our ideals henceforth must find a home. That Man is the product of causes which had no prevision of the end they were achieving; that his origin, his growth, his hopes and fears, his loves and his beliefs, are but the outcome of accidental collocations of atoms; that no fire, no heroism, no intensity of thought and feeling, can preserve an individual life beyond the grave; that all the labors of the ages, all the devotion, all the inspiration, all the noonday brightness of human genius, are destined to extinction in the vast death of the solar system, and that the whole temple of Man's achievement must inevitably be buried beneath the débris of a universe in ruins—all these things, if not quite beyond dispute, are yet so nearly certain, that no philosophy which rejects them can hope to stand. Only within the scaffolding of these truths, only on the firm foundation of unyielding despair, can the soul's habitation henceforth be safely built.

How, in such an alien and inhuman world, can so powerless a creature as Man preserve his aspirations untarnished? A strange mystery it is that Nature, omnipotent but blind, in the revolutions of her secular hurryings through the abysses of space, has brought forth at last a child, subject still to her power, but gifted with sight, with knowledge of good and evil, with the capacity of judging all the works of his unthinking Mother. In spite of Death, the mark and seal of the parental control, Man is yet free, during his brief years, to examine, to criticize, to know, and in imagination to create. To him alone, in the world with which he is acquainted, this freedom belongs; and in this lies his superiority to the resistless forces that control his outward life.

The savage, like ourselves, feels the oppression of his impotence before the powers of Nature; but having in himself nothing that he respects more than Power, he is willing to prostrate himself before his gods, without inquiring whether they are worthy of his worship. Pathetic and very terrible is the long history of cruelty and torture, of degradation and human sacrifice, endured in the hope of placating the jealous gods: surely, the trembling believer thinks, when what is most precious has been freely given, their lust for blood must be appeased, and more will not be required. The religion of Moloch—as such creeds may be generically called—is in essence the cringing submission of the slave, who dare not, even in his heart, allow the thought that his master deserves no adulation. Since the independence of ideals is not yet acknowledged, Power may be freely worshiped, and receive an unlimited respect, despite its wanton infliction of pain.

But gradually, as morality grows bolder, the claim of the ideal world begins to be felt; and worship, if it is not to cease, must be given to gods of another kind than those created by the savage. Some, though they feel the demands of the ideal, will still consciously reject them, still urging that naked Power is worthy of worship. Such is the attitude inculcated in God's answer to Job out of the whirlwind: the divine power and knowledge are paraded, but of the divine goodness there is no hint. Such also is the attitude of those who, in our own day, base their morality upon the struggle for survival, maintaining that the survivors are necessarily the fittest. But others, not content with an answer so repugnant to the moral sense, will adopt the position which we have become accustomed to regard as specially religious, maintaining that, in some hidden manner the world of fact is really harmonious with the world of ideals. Thus Man creates God, all-powerful and all-good, the mystic unity of what is and what should be.

But the world of fact, after all, is not good; and, in submitting our judgment to it, there is an element of slavishness from which our thoughts must be purged. For in all things it is well to exalt the dignity of Man, by freeing him as far as possible from the tyranny of non-human Power. When we have realized that Power is largely bad, that man, with his knowledge of good and evil, is but a helpless atom in a world which has no such knowledge, the choice is again presented to us: Shall we worship Force, or shall we worship Goodness? Shall our God exist and be evil or shall he be recognized as the creation of our own conscience?

The answer to this question is very momentous, and affects profoundly our whole morality. The worship of Force, to which Carlyle and Nietzsche and the creed of Militarism have accustomed us, is the result of failure to maintain our own ideals against a hostile universe: it is itself a prostrate submission to evil, a sacrifice of our best to Moloch. If strength indeed is to be respected, let us respect rather the strength of those who refuse that false "recognition of facts" which fails to recognize that facts are often bad. Let us admit that, in the world we know, there are many things that would be better otherwise, and that the ideals to which we do and must adhere are not realized in the realm of matter. Let us preserve our respect for truth, for beauty, for the ideal of perfection which life does not permit us to attain, though none of these things meet with the approval of the unconscious universe. If Power is bad, as it seems to be, let us reject it from our hearts. In this lies Man's true freedom: in determination to worship only the God created by our own love of the good, to respect only the heaven which inspires the insight of our best moments. In action, in desire, we must submit perpetually to the tyranny of outside forces; but in thought, in aspiration, we are free, free from our fellow-men, free from the petty planet on which our bodies impotently crawl, free even, while we live, from the tyranny of death. Let us learn, then, that energy of faith which enables us to live constantly in the vision of the good; and let us descend, in action, into the world of fact, with that vision always before us.

When first the opposition of fact and ideal grows fully visible, a spirit of fiery revolt, of fierce hatred of the gods, seems necessary to the assertion of freedom. To defy with Promethean constancy a hostile universe, to keep its evil always in view, always actively hated, to refuse no pain that the malice of Power can invent, appears to be the duty of all who will not bow before the inevitable. But indignation is still a bondage, for it compels our thoughts to be occupied with an evil world; and in the fierceness of desire from which rebellion springs there is a kind of self-assertion which it is necessary for the wise to overcome. Indignation is a submission of our thoughts, but not of our desires; the Stoic freedom in which wisdom consists is found in the submission of our desires, but not of our thoughts. From the submission of our desires springs the virtue of resignation;

from the freedom of our thoughts springs the whole world of art and philosophy, and the vision of beauty by which, at last, we half reconquer the reluctant world. But the vision of beauty is possible only to unfettered contemplation, to thoughts not weighted by the load of eager wishes; and thus Freedom comes only to those who no longer ask of life that it shall yield them any of those personal goods that are subject to the mutations of Time.

Although the necessity of renunciation is evidence of the existence of evil, yet Christianity, in preaching it, has shown a wisdom exceeding that of the Promethean philosophy of rebellion. It must be admitted that, of the things we desire, some, though they prove impossible, are yet real goods; others, however, as ardently longed for, do not form part of a fully purified ideal. The belief that what must be renounced is bad, though sometimes false, is far less often false than untamed passion supposes; and the creed of religion, by providing a reason for proving that it is never false, has been the means of purifying our hopes by the discovery of many austere truths.

But there is in resignation a further good element: even real goods, when they are unattainable, ought not to be fretfully desired. To every man comes, sooner or later, the great renunciation. For the young, there is nothing unattainable; a good thing desired with the whole force of a passionate will, and yet impossible, is to them not credible. Yet, by death, by illness, by poverty, or by the voice of duty, we must learn, each one of us, that the world was not made for us, and that, however beautiful may be the things we crave, Fate may nevertheless forbid them. It is the part of courage, when misfortune comes, to bear without repining the ruin of our hopes, to turn away our thoughts from vain regrets. This degree of submission to Power is not only just and right: it is the very gate of wisdom.

But passive renunciation is not the whole of wisdom; for not by renunciation alone can we build a temple for the worship of our own ideals. Haunting foreshadowings of the temple appear in the realm of imagination, in music, in architecture, in the untroubled kingdom of reason, and in the golden sunset magic of lyrics, where beauty shines and glows, remote from the touch of sorrow, remote from the fear of change, remote from the failures and disenchantments of the world of fact. In the contemplation of these things the vision will shape itself in our hearts, giving at once a touchstone to judge the world about us, and an inspiration by which to fashion to our needs whatever is not incapable of serving as a stone in the sacred temple.

Except for those rare spirits that are born without sin, there is a cavern of darkness to be traversed before that temple can be entered. The gate of the cavern is despair, and its floor is paved with the gravestones of abandoned hopes. There Self must die; there the eagerness, the greed of untamed desire must be slain, for only so can the soul be freed from the empire of Fate. But out of the cavern the Gate of Renunciation leads again to the daylight of wisdom, by whose radiance a new insight, a new joy, a new tenderness, shine forth to gladden the pilgrim's heart.

When, without the bitterness of impotent rebellion, we have learnt both to resign ourselves to the outward rule of Fate and to recognize that the non-human world is unworthy of our worship, it becomes possible at last so to transform and refashion the unconscious universe, so to transmute it in the crucible of imagination, that a new image of shining gold replaces the old idol of clay. In all the multiform facts of the world—in the visual shapes of trees and mountains and clouds, in the events of the life of man, even in the very omnipotence of Death— the insight of creative idealism can find the reflection of a beauty which its own thoughts first made. In this way mind asserts its subtle mastery over the thoughtless forces of Nature. The more evil the material with which it deals, the more thwarting to untrained desire, the greater is its achievement in inducing the reluctant rock to yield up its hidden treasures, the prouder its victory in compelling the opposing forces to swell the pageant of its triumph. Of all the arts, Tragedy is the proudest, the most triumphant; for it builds its shining citadel in the very center of the enemy's country, on the very summit of his highest mountain; from its impregnable watch-towers, his camps and arsenals, his columns and forts, are all revealed; within its walls the free life continues, while the legions of Death and Pain and Despair, and all the servile captains of tyrant Fate, afford the burghers of that dauntless city new spectacles of beauty. Happy those sacred ramparts, thrice happy the dwellers on that all-seeing eminence. Honor to those brave warriors who, through countless ages of warfare, have preserved for us the priceless heritage of liberty, and have kept undefiled by sacrilegious invaders the home of the unsubdued.

But the beauty of Tragedy does but make visible a quality which, in more or less obvious shapes, is present always and everywhere in life. In the spectacle of Death, in the endurance of intolerable pain, and in the irrevocableness of a vanished past, there is a sacredness, an overpowering awe, a feeling of the vastness, the depth, the inexhaustible mystery of existence, in which, as by some strange marriage of pain, the sufferer is bound to the world by bonds of sorrow. In these moments of insight, we lose all eagerness of temporary desire, all struggling and striving for petty ends, all care for the little trivial things that, to a superficial view, make up the common life of day by day; we see, surrounding the narrow raft illumined by the flickering light of human comradeship, the dark ocean on whose rolling waves we toss for a brief hour; from the great night without, a chill blast breaks in upon our refuge; all the loneliness of humanity amid hostile forces is concentrated upon the individual soul, which must struggle alone, with what of courage it can command, against the whole weight of a universe that cares nothing for its hopes and fears. Victory, in this struggle with the powers of darkness, is the true baptism into the glorious company of heroes, the true initiation into the overmastering beauty of human existence. From that awful encounter of the soul with the outer world, renunciation, wisdom, and charity are born; and with their birth a new life begins. To take into the inmost shrine of the soul the irresistible forces whose puppets we seem to be—Death and change, the irrevocableness of the past and the powerlessness of man before the blind hurry of the universe from vanity to vanity—to feel these things and know them is to conquer them.

This is the reason why the Past has such magical power. The beauty of its motionless and silent pictures is like the enchanted purity of late autumn, when the leaves, though one breath would make them fall, still glow against the sky in golden glory. The Past does not change or strive; like Duncan, after life's fitful fever it sleeps well; what was eager and grasping, what was petty and transitory, has faded away, the things that were beautiful and eternal shine out of it like stars in the night. Its beauty, to a soul not worthy of it, is unendurable; but to a soul which has conquered Fate it is the key of religion.

The life of Man, viewed outwardly, is but a small thing in comparison with the forces of Nature. The slave is doomed to worship Time and Fate and Death, because they are greater than anything he finds in himself, and because all his thoughts are of things which they devour. But, great as they are, to think of them greatly, to feel their passionless splendor, is greater still. And such thought makes us free men; we no longer bow before the inevitable in Oriental subjection, but we absorb it, and make it a part of ourselves. To abandon the struggle for private happiness, to expel all eagerness of temporary desire, to burn with passion for eternal things—this is emancipation, and this is the free man's worship. And this liberation is effected by a contemplation of Fate; for Fate itself is subdued by the mind which leaves nothing to be purged by the purifying fire of Time.

United with his fellow-men by the strongest of all ties, the tie of a common doom, the free man finds that a new vision is with him always, shedding over every daily task the light of love. The life of Man is a long march through the night, surrounded by invisible foes, tortured by weariness and pain, towards a goal that few can hope to reach, and where none may tarry long. One by one, as they march, our comrades vanish from our sight, seized by the silent orders of omnipotent Death. Very brief is the time in which we can help them, in which their happiness or misery is decided. Be it ours to shed sunshine on their path, to lighten their sorrows by the balm of sympathy, to give them the pure joy of a never-tiring affection, to strengthen failing courage, to instill faith in hours of despair. Let us not weigh in grudging scales their merits and demerits, but let us think only of their need—of the sorrows, the difficulties, perhaps the blindnesses, that make the misery of their lives; let us remember that they are fellow-sufferers in the same darkness, actors in the same tragedy with ourselves. And so, when their day is over, when their good and their evil have become eternal by the immortality of the past, be it ours to feel that, where they suffered, where they failed, no deed of ours was the cause; but wherever a spark of the divine fire kindled in their hearts, we were ready with encouragement, with sympathy, with brave words in which high courage glowed.

Brief and powerless is Man's life; on him and all his race the slow, sure doom falls pitiless and dark. Blind to good and evil, reckless of destruction, omnipotent matter rolls on its relentless way; for Man, condemned to-day to lose his dearest, to-morrow himself to pass through the gate of darkness, it remains only to cherish, ere yet the blow falls, the lofty thoughts that ennoble his little day; disdaining the coward terrors of the slave of Fate, to worship at the shrine that his own hands have built; undismayed by the empire of chance, to preserve a mind free from the wanton tyranny that rules his outward life; proudly defiant of the irresistible forces that tolerate, for a moment, his knowledge and his condemnation, to sustain alone, a weary but unyielding Atlas, the world that his own ideals have fashioned despite the trampling march of unconscious power.

STUDY QUESTIONS

1   How would Russell respond to the problem of evil? Does he think that the physical world is good?
2   Russell says that a certain kind of "resignation" is good. What does he mean by "resignation"? Why is it good?
3   Russell says that people can be liberated by contemplating fate. What does he mean by "fate"? Why should recognizing it contribute to our freedom? Do you agree?
4   Suppose you were suddenly to become omnipotent. What conditions would you create to ensure that life was meaningful. Could you *ensure* it? How do you think Russell would answer these questions?
5   What are the ethical implications, if any, of Russell's thesis? If you accepted his point of view, would it affect your behavior? Do you think, for example, that you would be greedier? Why or why not?

SELECTED READINGS

Two good general anthologies are John Hick (ed.), *Classical and Contemporary Readings in the Philosophy of Religion* (Englewood Cliffs, N. J.: Prentice-Hall, 1970), and Rowe and Wainwright (eds.), *Philosophy of Religion* (New York: Harcourt Brace Jovanovich, 1973). A fine historical collection of work on the ontological argument can be found in Alvin Plantinga, *The Ontological Argument* (Garden City, N.Y.: Doubleday, 1965), and the other major arguments, along with important critiques, are anthologized in Donald R. Burrill (ed.), *The Cosmological Arguments* (Garden City, N.Y.: Doubleday, 1967).

Important classical treatments of the problem of evil are David Hume, *Dialogues Concerning Natural Religion,* Parts X and XI, edited by N. K. Smith (Indianapolis: Bobbs-Merrill, 1947) and Gottfried von Leibniz, *The Theodicy* in *Leibniz: Selections,* edited by P. Wiener (New York: Charles Scribner's Sons, 1951). A very complete and recent atheistic analysis of the problem of evil can be found in E. H. Madden and P. H. Hare, *Evil and the Concept of God* (Springfield, Ill.: Charles C Thomas, 1968). Hick's defense is more completely worked out in his *Evil and the God of Love* (New York: Harper & Row, 1966), and the noted literary critic C. S. Lewis defends Christianity in *The Problem of Pain* (New York: Macmillan, 1962).

While there are many excellent books on mysticism, W. T. Stace (ed.), *The Teachings of the Mystics* (New York: New American Library, 1960) is one of the best general introductions to mystical thought in many religious traditions. Selections from Hindu, Buddhist, Taoist, Jewish, Islamic, and Christian mystics are accompanied by editorial commentary. William James, *The Varieties of Religious Experience* (London: Longmans, 1902) is a great classic, while some of the more recent treatments include D. T. Suzuki, *Mysticism: Christian and Buddhist* (New York: Harper & Row, 1957) and W. T. Stace, *Mysticism and Philosophy* (London: Macmillan, 1961).

A famous statement of humanistic religion can be found in John Dewey, *A Common Faith* (New Haven, Conn.: Yale University Press, 1934). Clarence Darrow, the noted trial lawyer and religious skeptic, explains his position in "Why I Am an Agnostic," reprinted in A. Weinburg and L. Weinburg (eds.), *Clarence Darrow—Verdicts Out of Court* (Chicago: Quadrangle, 1963). An immensely readable and thought-provoking study into the larger issues of religion and morality is Walter Kaufmann, *The Faith of a Heretic* (Garden City, N.Y.: Anchor Books, Doubleday, 1959).

Part Two

Knowledge, Mind, and Perception

THE PARADOXES OF APPEARANCE

If the scientific description of reality is closest to the truth, then we must face up to a dilemma: the world as it really is differs radically from the way it appears to us. Consider, for a moment, reality as it is portrayed by the physicist. When a thing is hot, for example, the molecules which compose it are in a state of increased vibration. The nervous system (itself a system of molecules) detects this vibration and sends signals in the form of pulses to the brain (another system of molecules). Then, and only then, do we feel heat. But the quality we experience is quite different from the motion which causes it, just as the sensation of pain is qualitatively different from the physical conditions which produce it. Other familiar qualities in the world suffer the same fate. The colors of the peacock and the blazing reds of the setting sun are but subjective qualities produced in the perceiver by a special nervous system that responds selectively to lightwaves (themselves colorless) of varying frequencies. In itself, the sun is a colorless froth of energy. The bee, the frog, and perhaps even higher life in other galaxies experience the world in ways we can only hint at. The real world, the world as described by physics, is a neutral world of colorless, soundless, odorless matter.

We have grown so accustomed to this way of thinking about the world that it no longer shocks us. But it should! Remember that this sweeping distinction between appearance and reality is usually accompanied by an emphasis on observation and experience as the building blocks of science. It has almost become an official doctrine to regard the advance of science as due to an extreme reluctance to go beyond experienced fact. Yet we certainly do not perceive the world as the scientist describes it. If we wish to assert that the world of common sense—the world of sounds, smells, colors, etc.—does not adequately represent reality, then the way we gain knowledge of reality cannot be confined to common-sense experience. We need a method which penetrates appearance—either that, or the real world must be the world of common experience and the colorless world of physics is a fiction.

There is another paradox in the scientific conception of reality. Reality, in this view, is fundamentally material. Therefore the human perceiver, like everything else, is a system of matter. Yet if this is so, it makes no sense to say that the familiar features of experience are subjective qualities in the perceiver. If color, for example, is literally "in the perceiver" and the perceiver is matter, then colors are real qualities of matter, contrary to what the theory says. To avoid this contradiction, many scientists and philosophers have argued that the perceiving self cannot be a material object. But then the world contains more than matter—it also contains *minds.*

The scientific picture of reality raises some of the central questions of philosophy. What is the nature of the real world? How can I come to know it? What is the place of perception in knowledge? What is the nature of the self which perceives? This section presents some of the major attempts to answer these questions.

Skepticism and the Self

PROBLEM INTRODUCTION

In 1633, Galileo was tried by the Inquisition and found guilty of heresy. He was forced to renounce his scientific beliefs and was made to promise that he would never write or speak about them again. This dramatic event in the history of science marks a turning point of enormous proportions. Science was beginning to erode a traditional conception of the world and to erect a new one in its place.

What had Galileo said that so stirred up the forces of the Church against him? Earlier systems of thought, stemming from Aristotle, had emphasized the role of purpose and value in explaining the world. Explanations of natural phenomena were constructed in terms of "final causes." A final cause is the goal or end toward which something is moving. In Aristotelian physics, for example, an unsupported body moves downward in order to get to its natural place, which is the center of the earth. Once it reaches its natural place, it will remain at rest there until some force moves it. If this idea is consistently applied to everything, it becomes necessary to explain why the heavenly bodies continue to move. Why haven't they come to rest at their natural place? The answer is simple enough in terms of theology: God continues to keep them in motion. We also know that they move in circles, because a circle is a *perfect* geometrical form, and God would create only a perfect universe. Furthermore, since humanity is God's special creation, it is highly appropriate for the planets and the sun to move around the earth. The entire universe was a cosmic drama because the ultimate principles of explanation were formulated in terms of God's purpose. These principles seemed to be amply confirmed by observation and common sense. It was the perfect union of theology and physics.

Galileo was an advocate of the Copernican system of the world. According to this view, the earth and the rest of the planets moved around the sun. The apparent motion of the sun from horizon to horizon was caused by the rotation of the earth on its axis. Galileo's physics represented an attempt to provide the foundations for the Copernican picture. He was able to discover that the acceleration of freely falling bodies did not depend upon their weight, a thesis which ran counter to the prevailing Aristotelian view. If weight were a measure of the force with which a body was moving to its natural place, we should expect that a heavier body would get to its state of rest faster than a lighter body. But this was not so. Perhaps the most startling discovery of all was Galileo's early work on inertia. In a series of classic experiments, he discovered that a body tended to stay in its present state—whether of motion or rest. God was no longer needed as a force which keeps the universe in motion. The union of science and theology began to crumble.

The world was beginning to be seen as an elaborate mechanism. The principles of explanation which emerged in this period made no reference to God or to His purposes. The universe was matter governed by laws which could be expressed mathematically. The spirit had gone out of it, so to speak. Humans themselves were physical beings and subject to the same sort of analysis. Perhaps every action of the individual could be explained in terms of the laws of motion. Perhaps people were machines. Thomas Hobbes, the most radical materialist of the day, attempted to extend the principles of physics into psychology, ethics, and politics, in order to show that every aspect of existence could be accounted for in terms of matter and motion. For Hobbes, a desire was nothing more than a motion toward something, a thought was simply the activity of material particles in the body, and a decision, just the final resolution of warring physical forces inside the organism. To the orthodox, this was clearly a dangerous trend, for the immortal soul was hanging in the balance.

Descartes, a contemporary of Galileo and Hobbes, saw the profound changes in the state of knowledge, and recognizing the implications of these changes for the image of human nature, set himself two tasks. The first was to ascertain whether there are any beliefs immune to doubt in light of the continuous change of theories about the world. Is every belief a temporary fixture destined to be overthrown by new discoveries or is there a sure and certain foundation of basic truths which will weather every intellectual crisis? His second task was to determine the nature of the self. Are we nothing more than our bodies or does the human person have an aspect which is not subject to the mechanistic interpretation of ordinary matter?

What, then, can be doubted? Can I doubt the existence of the physical world? Descartes thinks that it is possible to do this. In dreams I touch, hear, smell, and see things which are nonexistent. Couldn't an evil genius of great power deceive me in my waking life by providing me with a coherent stream of perceptions similar to those I have in dreams? Indeed, couldn't such an evil genius also deceive me about my own existence? Here Descartes draws the line. I can be certain that I exist, because even my doubting requires the existence of a doubter. "I think, therefore I am": this truth is so clear and self-evident that it cannot be doubted. Truths of this sort provide the unchanging foundation for knowledge. Using such truths, Descartes attempted to prove that a good God exists who would not deceive us.[1] The existence of the physical world is then guaranteed.

But what about the self? What sort of thing is it? According to Descartes, the self is an immaterial thinking substance which is connected to the body in a mysterious relationship of mutual interaction. He reached this conclusion in the following way: Suppose I am a physical object. Since I can doubt the existence of all physical things, I should be able to doubt the existence of myself. But, indeed, this is the one thing it is meaningless to doubt. Therefore, the self cannot be a physical thing. In this way Descartes believed that he had shown the existence of the immortal soul. Religion need not fear the advance of science, for although the body is a machine, it is a machine activated by an immaterial mind. Once the mind sets the physical processes of the body in motion, science can explain the resultant movements. But the ultimate explanation of human behavior remains out of the reach of physical principles.

Descartes's position was a compromise between the developing scientific image of human beings and the older religious tradition. But this compromise represented an uneasy peace which was soon challenged. According to Descartes, the self is a *thing*—a nonmaterial substance—which underlies various mental states and activities. It is the thing which thinks, feels, desires, and perceives. In other words, the self is the spiritual canvas on which the mental life is painted. Some philosophers, such as David Hume, the great eighteenth-century skeptic, believed that this conception of the self would not adequately explain important facts about personal identity. If the self is a mental substance which underlies all psychological states, then it should be possible to remove all its perceptions, memories, beliefs, etc., replace them with new psychological states, and still have the same self. It would be like stripping the paint from a chair and repainting it a different color—it is still the same chair. Upon reflection, however, the self does not seem to be like this. New memories, new beliefs, new ways of thinking add up to a new self. Hume, therefore, suggests that, just as we do not think that a brick wall is something different from the many bricks which make it up, so we should not think of the self as something different from the many mental states which compose it. The wall is just a certain organization of bricks, and the self is a certain organization of memories, beliefs, and perceptions. Hume's theory is called the *bundle theory* of the self because the self is thought to be a collection rather than a single object.

The three centuries which intervene between Descartes and ourselves have

---

[1] Descartes uses the ontological proof to establish God's existence, since this proof does not rest on any physical assumption.

produced new challenges to dualism. With the development of modern biology, physiology, and psychology, the intimate and complex relationship between the mind and the body has been increasingly uncovered. After Darwin, mental function was viewed as an evolutionary product closely tied to the evolution of the physical body. Increasingly, biologists and psychologists explained human and animal behavior in physiological, rather than mental, terms.

Finally a bold and unorthodox position began to emerge. In an effort to make psychology "scientific," many psychologists theorized that the only appropriate *method* is one which relies exclusively on close observation and categorization of behavior. Since the realm of the mental is forever closed to public observation, these psychologists constructed a system of explanation which does not rely on mental entities. This is the doctrine of behaviorism. B. F. Skinner, the leading contemporary exponent of behaviorism, has characterized psychology as a science which searches for laws connecting environmental influences with changes in behavior. In our readings, Gilbert Ryle presents a sophisticated form of the theory. Ryle argues that the distinction between body and mind is not between two sorts of "things." When we refer to someone's mental qualities, we are merely characterizing certain features of the person's overt, observable behavior.

The implications of these changes are, of course, enormous. At the time of Descartes, humans were just a little lower than the angels. We were linked to heaven by our immortal souls and tied to Earth by our material bodies. But because of our dual nature we could escape the rigid physical determination of other animals. Our wills were free and capable of overcoming past determination. If behaviorism is correct, however, our link to heaven is severed and we become the natural children of the mechanistic universe.

Meditations I and II

René Descartes

René Descartes (1596–1650), the founder of analytical geometry, is also known as the father of modern philosophy. Born into an era of profound intellectual ferment, Descartes rejected the answers of the past. He resolved to doubt everything he had previously believed, and to accept only those truths which appeared to him to be "clear and distinct." The sense of intellectual freedom and adventure which Descartes felt is summed up in his response to a visitor who was puzzled to see so few books in his library. Descartes pointed to a corpse which he had been dissecting and replied, "This, sir, is the only book I require."

In this selection from the "Meditations," Descartes applies his systematic doubt to the very existence of the world. It is possible, he suggests, to imagine that one's entire waking life is an illusion. But even so, it is not possible to doubt one's own existence. The difficult thing, however, is to discover the nature of the self. Is the self an amalgam of perceptions and memories and feelings or are these too, like the physical body, inessential to its real nature?

In these brief reflections, Descartes raises the central questions of modern philosophy. Is there a place in the world of matter for a spiritual being? What sort of thing could it be? Can it be known and investigated with the same methods as the physical world? Descartes's answers to these questions have intrigued thinkers for centuries because similar questions arise in each epoch that science threatens to wipe out the special place of human beings in nature.

OF THE THINGS WHICH MAY BE BROUGHT WITHIN THE SPHERE OF THE DOUBTFUL

It is now some years since I detected how many were the false beliefs that I had from my earliest youth admitted as true, and how doubtful was everything I had since constructed on this basis; and from that time I was convinced that I must once for all seriously undertake to rid myself of all the opinions which I had formerly accepted, and commence to build anew from the foundation, if I wanted to establish any firm and permanent structure in the sciences. But as this enterprise appeared to be a very great one, I waited until I had attained an age so mature that I could not hope that at any later date I should be better fitted to execute my design. This reason caused me to delay so long that I should feel that I was doing wrong were I to occupy in deliberation the time that yet remains to me for action. To-day, then, since very opportunely for the plan I have in view I have delivered my mind from every care (and am happily agitated by no passions) and since I have procured for myself an assured leisure in a peaceable retirement, I shall at last seriously and freely address myself to the general upheaval of all my former opinions.

From René Descartes, "Meditations on First Philosophy" in *The Philosophical Works of Descartes*, Elizabeth Haldane and G. R. T. Ross, trans., Cambridge University Press (1931), pp. 144–157. Reprinted by permission of the publisher.

Now for this object it is not necessary that I should show that all of these are false—I shall perhaps never arrive at this end. But inasmuch as reason already persuades me that I ought no less carefully to withhold my assent from matters which are not entirely certain and indubitable than from those which appear to me manifestly to be false, if I am able to find in each one some reason to doubt, this will suffice to justify my rejecting the whole. And for that end it will not be requisite that I should examine each in particular, which would be an endless undertaking; for owing to the fact that the destruction of the foundations of necessity brings with it the downfall of the rest of the edifice, I shall only in the first place attack those principles upon which all my former opinions rested.

All that up to the present time I have accepted as most true and certain I have learned wither from the senses or through the senses; but it is sometimes proved to me that these senses are deceptive, and it is wiser not to trust entirely to any thing by which we have once been deceived.

But it may be that although the senses sometimes deceive us concerning things which are hardly perceptible, or very far away, there are yet many others to be met with as to which we cannot reasonably have any doubt, although we recognise them by their means. For example, there is the fact that I am here, seated by the fire, attired in a dressing gown, having this paper in my hands and other similar matters. And how could I deny that these hands and this body are mine, were it not perhaps that I compare myself to certain persons, devoid of sense, whose cerebella are so troubled and clouded by the violent vapours of black bile, that they constantly assure us that they think they are kings when they are really quite poor, or that they are clothed in purple when they are really without covering, or who imagine that they have an earthenware head or are nothing but pumpkins or are made of glass. But they are mad, and I should not be any the less insane were I to follow examples so extravagant.

At the same time I must remember that I am a man, and that consequently I am in the habit of sleeping, and in my dreams representing to myself the same things or sometimes even less probable things, than do those who are insane in their waking moments. How often has it happened to me that in the night I dreamt that I found myself in this particular place, that I was dressed and seated near the fire, whilst in reality I was lying undressed in bed! At this moment it does indeed seem to me that it is with eyes awake that I am looking at this paper; that this head which I move is not asleep, that it is deliberately and of set purpose that I extend my hand and perceive it; what happens in sleep does not appear so clear nor so distinct as does all this. But in thinking over this I remind myself that on many occasions I have in sleep been deceived by similar illusions, and in dwelling carefully on this reflection I see so manifestly that there are no certain indications by which we may clearly distinguish wakefulness from sleep that I am lost in astonishment. And my astonishment is such that it is almost capable of persuading me that I now dream.

Now let us assume that we are asleep and that all these particulars, e.g. that we open our eyes, shake our head, extend our hands, and so on, are but false delusions; and let us reflect that possibly neither our hands nor our whole body are such as they appear to us to be. At the same time we must at least confess that the things which are represented to us in sleep are like painted representations which can only have been formed as the counterparts of something real and true, and that in this way those general things at least, i.e. eyes, a head, hands, and a whole body, are not imaginary things, but things really existent. For, as a matter of fact, painters, even when they study with the greatest skill to represent sirens and satyrs by forms the most strange and extraordinary, cannot give them natures which are entirely new, but merely make a certain medley of the members of different animals; or if their imagination is extravagant enough to invent something so novel that nothing similar has ever before been seen, and that then their work represents a thing purely fictitious and absolutely false, it is certain all the same that the colours of which this is composed are necessarily real. And for the same reason, although these general things, to wit, [a body], eyes, a head, hands, and such like, may be imaginary, we are bound at the same time to confess that there are at least some other objects yet more simple and more universal, which are real and true; and of these things which dwell in our thoughts, whether true and real or false and fantastic, are formed.

To such a class of things pertains corporeal nature in general, and its extension, the figure of extended things, their quality or magnitude and number, as also the place in which they are, the time which measures their duration, and so on.

That is possibly why our reasoning is not unjust when we conclude from this that Physics, Astronomy, Medicine and all other sciences which have as their end the consideration of composite things, are very dubious and uncertain; but that Arithmetic, Geometry and other sciences of that kind which only treat of things that are very simple and very general, without taking great trouble to ascertain whether they are actually existent or not, contain some measure of certainty and an element of the indubitable. For whether I am awake or asleep, two and three together always form five, and the square can never have more than four sides, and it does not seem possible that truths so clear and apparent can be suspected of any falsity [or uncertainty].

Nevertheless I have long had fixed in my mind the belief that an all-powerful God existed by whom I have been created such as I am. But how do I know that He has not brought it to pass that there is no earth, no heaven, no extended body, no magnitude, no place, and that nevertheless [I possess the perceptions of all these things and that] they seem to me to exist just exactly as I now see them? And, besides, as I sometimes imagine that others deceive themselves in the things which they think they know best, how do I know that I am not deceived every time that I add two and three, or count the sides of a square, or judge of things yet simpler, if anything simpler can be imagined? But possibly God has not desired that I should be thus deceived, for He is said to be supremely good. If, however, it is contrary to His goodness to have made me such that I constantly deceive myself, it would also appear to be contrary to His goodness to permit me to be sometimes deceived, and nevertheless I cannot doubt that He does permit this.

There may indeed be those who would prefer to deny the existence of a God so powerful, rather than believe that all other things are uncertain. But let us not oppose them for the present, and grant that all that is here said of a God is a fable; nevertheless in whatever way they suppose that I have arrived at the state of being that I have reached—whether they attribute it to fate or to accident, or make out that it is by a continual succession of antecedents, or by some other method—since to err and deceive oneself is a defect, it is clear that the greater will be the probability of my being so imperfect as to deceive myself ever, as is the Author to whom they assign my origin the less powerful. To these reasons I have certainly nothing to reply, but at the end I feel constrained to confess that there is nothing in all that I formerly believed to be true, of which I cannot in some measure doubt, and that not merely through want of thought or through levity, but for reasons which are very powerful and maturely considered; so that henceforth I ought not the less carefully to refrain from giving credence to these opinions than to that which is manifestly false, if I desire to arrive at any certainty [in the sciences].

But it is not sufficient to have made these remarks, we must also be careful to keep them in mind. For these ancient and commonly held opinions still revert frequently to my mind, long and familiar custom having given them the right to occupy my mind against my inclination and rendered them almost masters of my belief; nor will I ever lose the habit of deferring to them or of placing my confidence in them, so long as I consider them as they really are, i.e. opinions in some measure doubtful, as I have just shown, and at the same time highly probable, so that there is much more reason to believe in than to deny them. That is why I consider that I shall not be acting amiss, if, taking of set purpose a contrary belief, I allow myself to be deceived, and for a certain time pretend that all these opinions are entirely false and imaginary, until at last, having thus balanced any former prejudices with my latter [so that they cannot divert my opinions more to one side than to the other], my judgment will no longer be dominated by bad usage or turned away from the right knowledge of the truth. For I am assured that there can be neither peril nor error in this course, and that I cannot at present yield too much to distrust, since I am not considering the question of action, but only of knowledge.

I shall then suppose, not that God who is supremely good and the fountain of truth, but some evil genius not less powerful than deceitful, has employed his whole energies in deceiving me; I shall consider that the heavens, the earth, colours, figures, sound, and all other external things are nought but the illusions and dreams of which this genius has availed himself in order to lay traps for my credulity; I shall consider myself as having no hands, no eyes, no flesh, no blood, nor any senses, yet falsely believing myself to possess all these things; I shall remain obstinately attached to this idea, and if by this means it is not in my power to arrive at the knowledge of any truth, I may at least do what is in my power [i.e. suspend my judgment], and with firm purpose avoid giving credence to any false thing, or being imposed upon by this arch deceiver, however powerful and deceptive he may be. But this task is a laborious one, and insensibly a certain lassitude leads me into the course of my ordinary life. And just as a captive who in sleep enjoys an imaginary liberty, when he begins to suspect that his liberty is but a dream, fears to awaken, and conspires with these agreeable illusions that the deception may be prolonged, so insensibly of my own accord I fall back into my former opinions, and I dread awakening from this slumber, lest the laborious wakefulness which would follow the tranquility of this repose should have to be spent not in daylight, but in the excessive darkness of the difficulties which have just been discussed.

OF THE NATURE OF THE HUMAN MIND

The Meditation of yesterday filled my mind with so many doubts that it is no longer in my power to forget them. And yet I do not see in what manner I can resolve them; and, just as if I had all of a sudden fallen into very deep water, I am so disconcerted that I can neither make certain of setting my feet on the bottom, nor can I swim and so support myself on the surface. I shall nevertheless make an effort and follow anew the same path as that on which I yesterday entered, i.e. I shall proceed by setting aside all that in which the least doubt could be supposed to exist, just as if I had discovered that it was absolutely false; and I shall ever follow in this road until I have met with something which is certain, or at least, if I can do nothing else, until I have learned for certain that there is nothing in the world that is certain. Archimedes, in order that he might draw the terrestrial globe out of its place, and transport it elsewhere, demanded only that one point should be fixed and immoveable; in the same way I shall have the right to conceive high hopes if I am happy enough to discover one thing only which is certain and indubitable.

I suppose, then, that all the things that I see are false; I persuade myself that nothing has ever existed of all that my fallacious memory represents to me. I consider that I possess no senses; I imagine that body, figure, extension, movement and place are but the fictions of my mind. What, then, can be esteemed as true? Perhaps nothing at all, unless that there is nothing in the world that is certain.

But how can I know there is not something different from those things that I have just considered, of which one cannot have the slightest doubt? Is there not some God, or some other being by whatever name we call it, who puts these reflections into my mind? That is not necessary, for is it not possible that I am capable of producing them myself? I myself, am I not at least something? But I have already denied that I had senses and body. Yet I hesitate, for what follows from that? Am I so dependent on body and senses that I cannot exist without these? But I was persuaded that there was nothing in all the world, that there was no heaven, no earth, that there were no minds, nor any bodies: was I not then likewise persuaded that I did not exist? Not at all; of a surety I myself did exist since I persuaded myself of something [or merely because I thought of something]. But there is some deceiver or other, very powerful and very cunning, who ever employs his ingenuity in deceiving me. Then without doubt I exist also if he deceives me, and let him deceive me as much as he will, he can never cause me to be nothing so long as I think that I am something. So that after having reflected well and carefully examined all things, we must come to the definite conclusion that this proposition: I am, I exist, is necessarily true each time that I pronounce it, or that I mentally conceive it.

But I do not yet know clearly enough what I am, I who am certain that I am; and hence I must be careful to see that I do not imprudently take some other object in place of myself, and thus that I do not go astray in respect of this knowledge that I hold to be the most certain and most evident of all that I have formerly learned. That is why I shall now consider anew what I believed myself to be before I embarked upon these last reflections; and of my former opinions I shall withdraw all that might even in a small degree be invalidated by the reasons which I have just brought forward, in order that there may be nothing at all left beyond what is absolutely certain and indubitable.

What then did I formerly believe myself to be? Undoubtedly I believed myself to be a man. But what is a man? Shall I say a reasonable animal? Certainly not; for then I should have to inquire what an animal is, and what is reasonable; and thus from a single question I should insensibly fall into an infinitude of others more difficult; and I should not wish to waste the little time and leisure remaining to me in trying to unravel subtleties like these. But I shall rather stop here to consider the thoughts which of themselves spring up in my mind, and which were not inspired by anything beyond my own nature alone when I applied myself to the consideration of my being. In the first place, then, I considered myself as having a face, hands, arms, and all that system of members composed of bones and flesh as seen in a corpse which I designated by the name of body. In addition to this I considered that I was nourished, that I walked, that I felt, and that I thought, and I referred all these actions to the soul: but I did not stop to consider what the soul was, or if I did stop, I imagined that it was something extremely rare and subtle like a wind, a flame, or an ether, which was spread throughout my grosser parts. As to body I had no manner of doubt about its nature, but thought I had a very clear knowledge of it; and if I had desired to explain it according to the notions that I had then formed of it, I should have described it thus: By the body I understand all that which can be defined by a certain figure: something which can be confined in a certain place, and which can fill a given space in such a way that every other body will be excluded from it; which can be perceived either by touch, or by sight, or by hearing, or by taste, or by smell: which can be moved in many ways not, in truth, by itself, but by something which is foreign to it, by which it is touched [and from which it receives impressions]: for to have the power of self-movement, as also of feeling or of thinking, I did not consider to appertain to the nature of body: on the contrary, I was rather astonished to find that faculties similar to them existed in some bodies.

But what am I, now that I suppose that there is a certain genius which is extremely powerful, and, if I may say so, malicious, who employs all his powers in deceiving me? Can I affirm that I possess the least of all those things which I have just said pertain to the nature of body? I pause to consider, I revolve all these things in my mind, and I find none of which I can say that it pertains to me. It would be tedious to stop to enumerate them. Let us pass to the attributes of soul and see if there is any one which is in me. What of nutrition or walking [the first mentioned]? But if it is so that I have no body it is also true that I can neither walk nor take nourishment. Another attribute is sensation. But one cannot feel without body, and besides I have thought I perceived many things during sleep that I recognised in my waking moments as not having been experienced at all. What of thinking? I find here that thought is an attribute that belongs to me: it alone cannot be separated from me. I am, I exist, that is certain. But how often? Just when I think; for it might possibly be the case if I ceased entirely to think, that I should likewise cease altogether to exist. I do not now admit anything which is not necessarily true: to speak accurately I am not more than a thing which thinks, that is to say a mind or a soul, or an understanding, or a reason, which are terms whose significance was formerly unknown to me. I am, however, a real thing and really exist; but what thing? I have answered: a thing which thinks.

And what more? I shall exercise my imagination [in order to see if I am not something more]. I am not a collection of members which we call the human body: I am not a subtle air distributed through these members, I am not a wind, a fire, a vapour, a breath, nor anything at all which I can imagine or conceive; because I have assumed that all these were nothing. Without changing that supposition I find that I only leave myself certain of the fact that I am somewhat. But perhaps it is true that these same things which I supposed were non-existent because they are unknown to me, are really not different from the self which I know. I am not sure about this, I shall not dispute about it now; I can only give judgment on things that are known to me. I know that I exist, and I inquire what I am, I whom I know to exist. But it is very certain that the knowledge of my existence taken in its precise significance does not depend on things whose existence is not yet known to me; consequently it does not depend on those which I can feign in imagination. And indeed the very term *feign* in imagination proves to me my error, for I really do this if I image myself a something, since to imagine is nothing else than to contemplate the figure or image of a corporeal thing. But I already know for certain that I am, and that it may be that all these images, and, speaking generally, all things that relate to the nature of body are nothing but dreams [and chimeras]. For this reason I see clearly that I have as little reason to say, 'I shall stimulate my imagination in order to know more distinctly what I am,' than if I were to say, 'I am now awake, and I perceive somewhat that is real and true: but because I do not yet perceive it distinctly enough, I shall go to sleep of express purpose, so that my dreams may represent the perception with greatest truth and evidence.' And, thus, I know for certain that nothing of all that I can understand by means of my imagination belongs to this knowledge which I have of myself, and that it is necessary to recall the mind from this mode of thought with the utmost diligence in order that it may be able to know its own nature with perfect distinctness.

But what then am I? A thing which thinks. What is a thing which thinks? It is a thing which doubts, understands, [conceives], affirms, denies, wills, refuses, which also imagines and feels.

Certainly it is no small matter if all these things pertain to my nature. But why should they not so pertain? Am I not that being who now doubts nearly everything, who nevertheless understands certain things, who affirms that one only is true, who denies all the others, who desires to know more, is averse from being deceived, who imagines many things, sometimes indeed despite his will, and who perceives many likewise, as by the intervention of the bodily organs? Is there nothing in all this which is as true as it is certain that I exist, even though I should always sleep and though he who has given me being employed all his ingenuity in deceiving me? Is there likewise any one of these attributes which can be distinguished from my thought, or which might be said to be separated from myself? For it is so evident of itself that it is I who doubts, who understands, and who desires, that there is no reason here to add anything to explain it. And I have certainly the power of imagining likewise; for although it may happen (as I formerly supposed) that none of the things which I imagine are true, nevertheless this power of imagining does not cease to be really in use, and it forms part of my thought. Finally, I am the same who feels, that is to say, who perceives certain things, as by the organs of sense, since in truth I see light, I hear noise, I feel heat. But it will be said that these phenomena are false and that I am dreaming. Let it be so; still it is at least quite certain that it seems to me that I see light, that I hear noise and that I feel heat. That cannot be false; properly speaking it is what is in me called feeling, and used in this precise sense that is no other thing than thinking.

From this time I begin to know what I am with a little more clearness and distinction than before; but nevertheless it still seems to me, and I cannot prevent myself from thinking, that corporeal things, whose images are framed by thought, which are tested by the senses, are much more distinctly known than that obscure part of me which does not come under the imagination. Although really it is very strange to say that I know and understand more distinctly these things whose existence seems to me dubious, which are unknown to me, and which do not belong to me, than others of the truth of which I am convinced, which are known to me and which pertain to my real nature, in a word, than myself. But I see clearly how the case stands: my mind loves to wander, and cannot yet suffer itself to be retained within the just limits of truth. Very good, let us once more give it the freest rein, so that, when afterwards we seize the proper occasion for pulling up, it may the more easily be regulated and controlled.

Let us begin by considering the commonest matters, those which we believe to be the most distinctly comprehended, to wit, the bodies which we touch and see; not indeed bodies in general, for these general ideas are usually a little more confused, but let us consider one body in particular. Let us take, for example, this piece of wax: it has been taken quite freshly from the hive, and it has not yet lost the sweetness of the honey which it contains; it still retains somewhat of the odour of the flowers from which it has been culled; its colour, its figure, its size are apparent; it is hard, cold, easily handled, and if you strike it with the finger, it will emit a sound. Finally all the things which are requisite to cause us distinctly to recognise a body, are met with in it. But notice that while I speak and approach the fire what remained of the taste is exhaled, the smell evaporates, the colour alters, the figure is destroyed, the size increases, it becomes liquid, it heats, scarcely can one handle it, and when one strikes it, no sound is emitted. Does the same wax remain after this change? We must confess that it remains; none would judge otherwise. What then did I know so distinctly in this piece of wax? It could certainly be nothing of all that the senses brought to my notice, since all these things which fall under taste, smell, sight, touch, and hearing, are found to be changed, and yet the same wax remains.

Perhaps it was what I now think, viz. that this wax was not that sweetness of honey, nor that agreeable scent of flowers, nor that particular whiteness, nor that figure, nor that sound, but simply a body which a little while before appeared to me as perceptible under these forms, and which is now perceptible under others. But what, precisely, is it that I imagine when I form such conceptions? Let us attentively consider this, and, abstracting from all that does not belong to the wax, let us see what remains. Certainly nothing remains excepting a certain extended thing which is flexible and movable. But what is the meaning of flexible and movable? Is it not that I imagine that this piece of wax being round is capable of becoming square and of passing from a square to a triangular figure? No, certainly it is not that, since I imagine it admits of an infinitude of similar changes, and I nevertheless do not know how to compass the infinitude by my imagination, and consequently this conception which I have of the wax is not brought about by the faculty of imagination. What now is the extension? Is it not also unknown? For it becomes greater when the wax is melted, greater when it is boiled, and greater still when the heat increases; and I should not conceive [clearly] according to truth what wax is, if I did not think that even this piece that we are considering is capable of receiving more variations in extension than I have ever imagined. We must then grant that I could not even understand through the imagination what this piece of wax is, and that it is my mind alone which perceives it. I say this piece of wax in particular, for as to wax in general it is yet clearer. But what is this piece of wax which cannot be understood excepting by the [understanding or] mind? It is certainly the same that I see, touch, imagine, and finally it is the same which I have always believed it to be from the beginning. But what must particularly be observed is that its perception is neither an act of vision, nor of touch, nor of imagination, and has never been such although it may have appeared formerly to be so, but only an intuition of the mind, which may be imperfect and confused as it was formerly, or clear and distinct as it is at present, according as my attention is more or less directed to the elements which are found in it, and of which it is composed.

Yet in the meantime I am greatly astonished when I consider [the great feebleness of mind] and its proneness to fall [insensibly] into error; for although without giving expression to my thoughts I consider all this in my own mind, words often impede me and I am almost deceived by the terms of ordinary language. For we say that we see the same wax, if it is present, and not that we simply judge that it is the same from its having the same colour and figure. From this I should conclude that I knew the wax by means of vision and not simply by the intuition of the mind; unless by chance I remember that, when looking from a window and saying I see men who pass in the street, I really do not see them, but infer that what I see is men, just as I say that I see wax. And yet what do I see from the window but hats and coats which may cover automatic machines?

Yet I judge these to be men. And similarly solely by the faculty of judgment which rests in my mind, I comprehend that which I believed I saw with my eyes.

A man who makes it his aim to raise his knowledge above the common should be ashamed to derive the occasion for doubting from the forms of speech invented by the vulgar; I prefer to pass on and consider whether I had a more evident and perfect conception of what the wax was when I first perceived it, and when I believed I knew it by means of the external senses or at least by the common sense as it is called, that is to say by the imaginative faculty, or whether my present conception is clearer now that I have most carefully examined what it is, and in what way it can be known. It would certainly be absurd to doubt as to this. For what was there in this first perception which was distinct? What was there which might not as well have been perceived by any of the animals? But when I distinguish the wax from its external forms, and when, just as if I had taken from it its vestments, I consider it quite naked, it is certain that although some error may still be found in my judgment, I can nevertheless not perceive it thus without a human mind.

But finally what shall I say of this mind, that is, of myself, for up to this point I do not admit in myself anything but mind? What then, I who seem to perceive this piece of wax so distinctly, do I not know myself, not only with much more truth and certainty, but also with much more distinctness and clearness? For if I judge that the wax is or exists from the fact that I see it, it certainly follows much more clearly that I am or that I exist myself from the fact that I see it. For it may be that what I see is not really wax, it may also be that I do not possess eyes with which to see anything; but it cannot be that when I see, or (for I no longer take account of the distinction) when I think I see, that I myself who think am nought. So if I judge that the wax exists from the fact that I touch it, the same thing will follow, to wit, that I am; and if I judge that my imagination, or some other cause, whatever it is, persuades me that the wax exists, I shall still conclude the same. And what I have here remarked of wax may be applied to all other things which are external to me [and which are met with outside of me]. And further, if the [notion or] perception of wax has seemed to me clearer and more distinct, not only after the sight or the touch, but also after many other causes have rendered it quite manifest to me, with how much more [evidence] and distinctness must it be said that I now know myself, since all the reasons which contribute to the knowledge of wax, or any other body whatever, are yet better proofs of the nature of my mind! And there are so many other things in the mind itself which may contribute to the elucidation of its nature, that those which depend on body such as these just mentioned, hardly merit being taken into account.

But finally here I am, having insensibly reverted to the point I desired, for, since it is now manifest to me that even bodies are not properly speaking known by the senses or by the faculty of imagination, but by the understanding only, and since they are not known from the fact that they are seen or touched, but only because they are understood, I see clearly that there is nothing which is easier for me to know than my mind. But because it is difficult to rid oneself so promptly of an opinion to which one was accustomed for so long, it will be well that I should halt a little at this point, so that by the length of my meditation I may more deeply imprint on my memory this new knowledge.

STUDY QUESTIONS

1   Why does Descartes believe that the sciences of physics, astronomy, and medicine are uncertain whereas arithmetic and geometry are not?
2   Descartes says that he will treat the existence of his body as uncertain and doubtful. Why does he do this? Do you think it is possible to doubt the existence of your own body? Would the answer to this question depend upon your historical era?
3   At one point Descartes says that he is not the same as his body. Why does he say this? Do you think the evidence is sufficient?
4   At first Descartes finds it strange that mind may be more distinctly known than matter. But then he contemplates the piece of wax. What does this case prove to him?
5   "All mere animals eat without pleasure, they cry without pain, they grow without knowing it; they desire nothing, they fear nothing, they know nothing" (Malebranche). Malebranche was a follower of Descartes. Why do you think he would say these things?

The Nature of the Self

David Hume

David Hume (1711–1776) was brought up in a rigid Calvinist home by his widowed mother. He entered the University of Edinburgh at twelve, quit school at fifteen without a degree, and decided to educate himself. His disciplined religious life combined with his growing intellectual independence to produce a mild breakdown at nineteen. But by the age of twenty-six Hume had written his masterpiece, *A Treatise of Human Nature,* from which this selection is taken. Hume was a controversial figure throughout much of his life, mostly because his brutal honesty and incisive intellect could not let any dogma pass unchallenged. His ideas on religion, psychology, history, science, and practically everything were considered "shocking." Yet in spite of his outrageous opinions, those who knew him found him to be a generous, tolerant, and friendly person.

In this selection Hume considers the doctrine that the soul is something apart from the thoughts and feelings and desires which constitute the ebb and flow of the mental life. Being a good empiricist, Hume asks whether the soul can be perceived, and finding that it cannot, argues that we cannot have an intelligible idea of it. The self, he claims, is nothing more than a series of successive perceptions. The soul is a convenient fiction.

This selection provides a fine illustration of Hume's honesty. Not satisfied with his own theory, Hume poses a problem for it, and confesses that he cannot find an answer. Perhaps you will be able to locate the source of his difficulty.

From *A Treatise of Human Nature* by David Hume, first published in 1739.

There are some philosophers who imagine we are every moment intimately conscious of what we call our *self;* that we feel its existence and its continuance in existence; and are certain, beyond the evidence of a demonstration, both of its perfect identity and simplicity. The strongest sensation, the most violent passion, say they, instead of distracting us from this view, only fix it the more intensely, and make us consider their influence on *self* either by their pain or pleasure. To attempt a further proof of this were to weaken its evidence; since no proof can be derived from any fact of which we are so intimately conscious; nor is there anything of which we can be certain if we doubt of this.

Unluckily all these positive assertions are contrary to that very experience which is pleaded for them; nor have we any idea of *self,* after the manner it is here explained. For, from what impression[1] could this idea be derived? This question it is impossible to answer without a manifest contradiction and absurdity; and yet it is a question which must necessarily be answered, if we would have the idea of self pass for clear and intelligible. It must be some one impression that gives rise to every real idea. But self or person is not any one impression, but that to which our several impressions and ideas are supposed to have a reference. If any impression gives rise to the idea of self, that impression must continue invariably the same, through the whole course of our lives; since self is supposed to exist after that manner. But there is no impression constant and invariable. Pain and pleasure, grief and joy, passions and sensations succeed each other, and never all exist at the same time. It cannot therefore be from any of these impressions, or from any other, that the idea of self is derived; and consequently there is no such idea.

But further, what must become of all our particular perceptions upon this hypothesis? All these are different, and distinguishable, and separable from each other, and may be separately considered, and may exist separately, and have no need of anything to support their existence. After what manner therefore do they belong to self, and how are they connected with it? For my part, when I enter most intimately into what I call *myself,* I always stumble on some particular perception or other, of heat or cold, light or shade, love or hatred, pain or pleasure. I never can catch *myself* at any time without a perception, and never can observe anything but the perception. When my perceptions are removed for any time, as by sound sleep, so long am I insensible of *myself,* and may truly be said not to exist. And were all my perceptions removed by death, and could I neither think, nor feel, nor see, nor love, nor hate, after the dissolution of my body, I should be entirely annihilated, nor do I conceive what is further requisite to make me a perfect nonentity. If any one, upon serious and unprejudiced reflection, thinks he has a different notion of *himself,* I must confess I can reason no longer with him. All I can allow him is, that he may be in the right as well as I, and that we are essentially different in this particular. He may, perhaps, perceive something simple and continued, which he calls *himself;* though I am certain there is no such principle in me.

But setting aside some metaphysicians of this kind, I may venture to affirm

---

[1] An impression, for Hume, is a sensation presented to the mind by any of the senses.

of the rest of mankind, that they are nothing but a bundle or collection of different perceptions, which succeed each other with an inconceivable rapidity, and are in a perpetual flux and movement. Our eyes cannot turn in their sockets without varying our perceptions. Our thought is still more variable than our sight; and all our other senses and faculties contribute to this change; nor is there any single power of the soul, which remains unalterably the same, perhaps for one moment. The mind is a kind of theatre, where several perceptions successively make their appearance; pass, repass, glide away, and mingle in an infinite variety of postures and situations. There is properly no *simplicity* in it at one time, nor *identity* in different, whatever natural propension we may have to imagine that simplicity and identity. The comparison of the theatre must not mislead us. They are the successive perceptions only, that constitute the mind; nor have we the most distant notion of the place where these scenes are represented, or of the materials of which it is composed.

What then gives us so great a propension to ascribe an identity to these successive perceptions, and to suppose ourselves possessed of an invariable and uninterrupted existence through the whole course of our lives? In order to answer this question we must distinguish betwixt personal identity, as it regards our thought or imagination, and as it regards our passions or the concern we take in ourselves. The first is our present subject; and to explain it perfectly we must take the matter pretty deep, and account for that identity, which we attribute to plants and animals; there being a great analogy betwixt it and the identity of a self or person.

We have a distinct idea of an object that remains invariable and uninterrupted through a supposed variation of time; and this idea we call that of *identity* or *sameness*. We have also a distinct idea of several different objects existing in succession, and connected together by a close relation; and this to an accurate view affords as perfect a notion of *diversity* as if there was no manner of relation among the objects. But though these two ideas of identity, and a succession of related objects, be in themselves perfectly distinct, and even contrary, yet it is certain that, in our common way of thinking, they are generally confounded with each other. That action of the imagination, by which we consider the uninterrupted and invariable object, and that by which we reflect on the succession of related objects, are almost the same to the feeling; nor is there much more effort of thought required in the latter case than in the former. The relation facilitates the transition of the mind from one object to another, and renders its passage as smooth as if it contemplated one continued object. This resemblance is the cause of the confusion and mistake, and makes us substitute the notion of identity, instead of that of related objects. However, at one instant we may consider the related succession as variable or interrupted, we are sure the next to ascribe to it a perfect identity, and regard it as invariable and uninterrupted. Our propensity to this mistake is so great from the resemblance above mentioned, that we fall into it before we are aware; and though we incessantly correct ourselves by reflection, and return to a more accurate method of thinking, yet we cannot long sustain our philosophy, or take off this bias from the imagination. Our last resource is to yield to it, and boldly assert that these different related objects are in effect the same, however interrupted and variable. In order to justify to ourselves this absurdity, we often feign some new and unintelligible principle, that connects the objects together, and prevents their interruption or variation. Thus we feign the continued existence of the perceptions of our senses, to remove the interruption; and run into the notion of a *soul,* and *self,* and *substance,* to disguise the variation. But, we may further observe, that where we do not give rise to such a fiction, our propension to confound identity with relation is so great, that we are apt to imagine something unknown and mysterious, connecting the parts, beside their relation; and this I take to be the case with regard to the identity we ascribe to plants and vegetables. And even when this does not take place, we still feel a propensity to confound these ideas, though we are not able fully to satisfy ourselves in that particular, nor find anything invariable and uninterrupted to justify our notion of identity.

Thus the controversy concerning identity is not merely a dispute of words. For when we attribute identity, in an improper sense, to variable or interrupted objects, our mistake is not confined to the expression, but is commonly attended with a fiction, either of something invariable and uninterrupted, or of something mysterious and inexplicable, or at least with a propensity to such fictions. What will suffice to prove this hypothesis to the satisfaction of every fair inquirer, is to show, from daily experience and observation, that the objects which are variable or interrupted, and yet are supposed to continue the same, are such only as consist of a succession of parts, connected together by resemblance, contiguity, or causation. For as such a succession answers evidently to our notion of diversity, it can only be by mistake we ascribe to it an identity; and as the relation of parts, which leads us into this mistake, is really nothing but a quality, which produces an association of ideas, and an easy transition of the imagination from one to another, it can only be from the resemblance, which this act of the mind bears to that by which we contemplate one continued object, that the error arises. Our chief business, then, must be to prove, that all objects, to which we ascribe identity, without observing their invariableness and uninterruptedness, are such as consist of a succession of related objects.

In order to do this, suppose any mass of matter, of which the parts are contiguous and connected, to be placed before us; it is plain we must attribute a perfect identity to this mass, provided all the parts continue uninterruptedly and invariably the same, whatever motion or change of place we may observe either in the whole or in any of the parts. But supposing some very *small* or *inconsiderable* part to be added to the mass, or subtracted from it; though this absolutely destroys the identity of the whole, strictly speaking, yet as we seldom think so accurately, we scruple not to pronounce a mass of matter the same, where we find so trivial an alteration. The passage of the thought from the object before the change to the object after it, is so smooth and easy, that we scarce perceive the transition, and are apt to imagine, that it is nothing but a continued survey of the same object.

There is a very remarkable circumstance that attends this experiment; which is, that though the change of any considerable part in a mass of matter destroys the identity of the whole, yet we must measure the greatness of the part, not absolutely, but by its *proportion* to the whole. The addition or diminution of a mountain would not be sufficient to produce a diversity in a planet; though the change of a very few inches would be able to destroy the identity of some bodies. It will be impossible to account for this, but by reflecting that objects operate upon the mind, and break or interrupt the continuity of its actions, not according to their real greatness, but according to their proportion to each other; and therefore, since this interruption makes an object cease to appear the same, it must be the uninterrupted progress of the thought which constitutes the imperfect identity.

This may be confirmed by another phenomenon. A change in any considerable part of a body destroys its identity; but it is remarkable, that where the change is produced *gradually* and *insensibly,* we are less apt to ascribe to it the same effect. The reason can plainly be no other, than that the mind, in following the successive changes of the body, feels an easy passage from the surveying of its condition in one moment, to the viewing of it in another, and in no particular time perceives any interruption in its actions. From which continued perception, it ascribes a continued existence and identity to the object.

But whatever precaution we may use in introducing the changes gradually, and making them proportionable to the whole, it is certain, that where the changes are at last observed to become considerable, we make a scruple of ascribing identity to such different objects. There is, however, another artifice, by which we may induce the imagination to advance a step further; and that is, by producing a reference of the parts to each other, and a combination to some *common end* or purpose. A ship, of which a considerable part has been changed by frequent reparations, is still considered as the same; nor does the difference of the materials hinder us from ascribing an identity to it. The common end, in which the parts conspire, is the same under all their variations, and affords an easy transition of the imagination from one situation of the body to another.

But this is still more remarkable, when we add a *sympathy* of parts to their *common end,* and suppose that they bear to each other the reciprocal relation of cause and effect in all their actions and operations. This is the case with all animals and vegetables; where not only the several parts have a reference to some general purpose, but also a mutual dependence on, and connection with, each other. The effect of so strong a relation is, that though every one must allow, that in a very few years both vegetables and animals endure a *total* change, yet we still attribute identity to them, while their form, size, and substance, are entirely altered. An oak that grows from a small plant to a large tree is still the same oak, though there be not one particle of matter or figure of its parts the same. An infant becomes a man, and is sometimes fat, sometimes lean, without any change in his identity.

We may also consider the two following phenomena, which are remarkable in their kind. The first is, that though we commonly be able to distinguish pretty exactly betwixt numerical and specific identity, yet it sometimes happens that we confound them, and in our thinking and reasoning employ the one for the other. Thus, a man who hears a noise that is frequently interrupted and renewed, says it is still the same noise, though it is evident the sounds have only a specific identity or resemblance, and there is nothing numerically the same but the cause which produced them. In like manner it may be said, without breach of the propriety of language, that such a church, which was formerly of brick, fell to ruin, and that the parish rebuilt the same church of freestone, and according to modern architecture. Here neither the form nor materials are the same, nor is there anything common to the two objects but their relation to the inhabitants of the parish; and yet this alone is sufficient to make us denominate them the same. But we must observe, that in these cases the first object is in a manner annihilated before the second comes into existence; by which means, we are never presented, in any one point of time, with the idea of difference and multiplicity; and for that reason are less scrupulous in calling them the same.

Secondly, we may remark, that though, in a succession of related objects, it be a manner requisite that the change of parts be not sudden nor entire, in order to preserve the identity, yet where the objects are in their nature changeable and inconstant, we admit of a more sudden transition than would otherwise be consistent with that relation. Thus, as the nature of a river consists in the motion and change of parts, though in less than four-and-twenty hours these be totally altered, this hinders not the river from continuing the same during several ages. What is natural and essential to anything is, in a manner, expected; and what is expected makes less impression, and appears of less moment than what is unusual and extraordinary. A considerable change of the former kind seems really less to the imagination than the most trivial alteration of the latter; and by breaking less the continuity of the thought, has less influence in destroying the identity.

We now proceed to explain the nature of *personal identity,* which has become so great a question in philosophy, especially of late years, in England, where all the abstruser sciences are studied with a peculiar ardor and application. And here it is evident the same method of reasoning must be continued which has so successfully explained the identity of plants, and animals, and ships, and houses, and of all compounded and changeable productions either of art or nature. The identity which we ascribe to the mind of man is only a fictitious one, and of a like kind with that which we ascribe to vegetable and animal bodies. It cannot therefore have a different origin, but must proceed from a like operation of the imagination upon like objects.

But lest this argument should not convince the reader, though in my opinion perfectly decisive, let him weigh the following reasoning, which is still closer and more immediate. It is evident that the identity which we attribute to the human mind, however perfect we may imagine it to be, is not able to run the several different perceptions into one, and make them lose their characters of distinction and difference, which are essential to them. It is still true that every distinct perception which enters into the composition of the mind, is a distinct existence, and is different, and distinguishable, and separable from every other perception, either contemporary or successive. But as, notwithstanding this distinction and separability, we suppose the whole train of perceptions to be united by identity, a question naturally arises concerning this relation of identity, whether it be something that really binds our several perceptions together, or only associates their ideas in the imagination; that is, in other words, whether, in pronouncing concerning the identity of a person, we observe some real bond among his perceptions, or only feel one among the ideas we form of them. This question we might easily decide, if we would recollect what has been already proved at large, that the understanding never observes any real connection among objects, and that even the union of cause and effect, when strictly examined, resolves itself into a customary association of ideas. For from thence it evidently follows, that identity is nothing really belonging to these different perceptions, and uniting them together, but is merely a quality which we attribute to them, because of the union of their ideas in the imagination when we reflect upon them. Now, the only qualities which can give ideas a union in the imagination, are these three relations above mentioned. These are the uniting principles in the ideal world, and without them every distinct object is separable by the mind, and may be separately considered, and appears not to have any more connection with any other object than if disjoined by the greatest difference and remoteness. It is therefore on some of these three relations of resemblance, contiguity and causation, that identity depends; and as the very essence of these relations consists in their producing an easy transition of ideas, it follows that our notions of personal identity proceed entirely from the smooth and uninterrupted progress of the thought along a train of connected ideas, according to the principles above explained.

The only question, therefore, which remains is, by what relations this uninterrupted progress of our thought is produced, when we consider the successive existence of a mind or thinking person. And here it is evident we must confine ourselves to resemblance and causation, and must drop contiguity, which has little or no influence in the present case.

To begin with *resemblance;* suppose we could see clearly into the breast of another, and observe that succession of perceptions which constitutes his mind or thinking principle, and suppose that he always preserves the memory of a considerable part of past perceptions, it is evident that nothing could more contribute to the bestowing a relation on this succession amidst all its variations. For what is the memory but a faculty, by which we raise up the images of past perceptions? And as an image necessarily resembles its object, must not the frequent placing of these resembling perceptions in the chain of thought, convey the imagination more easily from one link to another, and make the whole seem like the continuance of one object? In this particular, then, the memory not only discovers the identity, but also contributes to its production, by producing the relation of resemblance among the perceptions. The case is the same, whether we consider ourselves or others.

As to *causation;* we may observe that the true idea of the human mind, is to consider it as a system of different perceptions or different existences, which are linked together by the relation of cause and effect, and mutually produce, destroy, influence, and modify each other. Our impressions give rise to their correspondent ideas; and these ideas, in their turn, produce other impressions. One thought chases another, and draws after it a third, by which it is expelled in its turn. In this respect, I cannot compare the soul more properly to anything than to a republic or commonwealth, in which the several members are united by the reciprocal ties of government and subordination, and give rise to other persons who propagate the same republic in the incessant changes of its parts. And as the same individual republic may not only change its members, but also its laws and constitutions; in like manner the same person may vary his character and disposition, as well as his impressions and ideas, without losing his identity. Whatever changes he endures, his several parts are still connected by the relation of causation. And in this view our identity with regard to the passions serves to corroborate that with regard to the imagination, by making our distant perceptions influence each other, and by giving us a present concern for our past or future pains or pleasures.

As memory alone acquaints us with the continuance and extent of this succession of perceptions, it is to be considered, upon that account chiefly, as the source of personal identity. Had we no memory, we never should have any notion of causation, nor consequently of that chain of causes and effects, which constitute our self or person. But having once acquired this notion of causation from the memory, we can extend the same chain of causes, and consequently the identity of our persons beyond our memory, and can comprehend times, and circumstances, and actions, which we have entirely forgot, but suppose in general to have existed. For how few of our past actions are there, of which we have any memory? Who can tell me, for instance, what were his thoughts and actions on the first of January 1715, the eleventh of March 1719, and the third of August 1733? Or will he affirm, because he has entirely forgot the incidents of these days, that the present self is not the same person with the self of that time; and by that means overturn all the most established notions of personal identity? In this view, therefore, memory does not so much *produce* as *discover* personal identity, by showing us the relation of cause and effect among our different perceptions. It will be incumbent on those who affirm that memory produces entirely our personal identity, to give a reason why we can thus extend our identity beyond our memory.

The whole of this doctrine leads us to a conclusion, which is of great importance in the present affair, viz. [namely] that all the nice and subtile questions concerning personal identity can never possibly be decided, and are to be regarded rather as grammatical than as philosophical difficulties. Identity depends on the relations of ideas; and these relations produce identity, by means of that easy transition they occasion. But as the relations, and the easiness of the transition may diminish by insensible degrees, we have no just standard by which we can decide any dispute concerning the time when they acquire or lose a title to the name of identity. All the disputes concerning the identity of connected objects are merely verbal, except so far as the relation of parts gives rise to some fiction or imaginary principle of union, as we have already observed.

What I have said concerning the first origin and uncertainty of our notion of identity, as applied to the human mind, may be extended with little or no variation to that of *simplicity*. An object, whose different coexistent parts are bound together by a close relation, operates upon the imagination after much the same manner as one perfectly simple and indivisible, and requires not a much greater stretch of thought in order to its conception. From this similarity of operation we attribute a simplicity to it, and feign a principle of union as the support of this simplicity, and the centre of all the different parts and qualities of the object.

Thus we have finished our examination of the several systems of philosophy, both of the intellectual and moral world; and, in our miscellaneous way of reasoning, have been led into several topics, which will either illustrate and confirm some preceding part of this discourse, or prepare the way for our following opinions. It is now time to return to a more close examination of our subject, and to proceed in the accurate anatomy of human nature, having fully explained the nature of our judgment and understanding.

I had entertained some hopes, that however deficient our theory of the intellectual world might be, it would be free from those contradictions and absurdities which seem to attend every explication that human reason can give of the material world. But upon a more strict review of the section concerning *personal identity,* I find myself involved in such a labyrinth that, I must confess, I neither know how to correct my former opinions, nor how to render them consistent. If this be not a good *general* reason for scepticism, it is at least a sufficient one (if I were not already abundantly supplied) for me to entertain a diffidence and modesty in all my decisions. I shall propose the arguments on both sides, beginning with those that induced me to deny the strict and proper identity and simplicity of a self or thinking being.

When we talk of *self* or *subsistence,* we must have an idea annexed to these terms, otherwise they are altogether unintelligible. Every idea is derived from preceding impressions; and we have no impression of self or substance, as something simple and individual. We have, therefore, no idea of them in that sense.

Whatever is distinct is distinguishable, and whatever is distinguishable is separable by the thought or imagination. All perceptions are distinct. They are, therefore, distinguishable, and separable, and may be conceived as separately existant, and may exist separately, without any contradiction or absurdity.

When I view this table and that chimney, nothing is present to me but particular perceptions, which are of a like nature with all the other perceptions. This is the doctrine of philosophers. But this table, which is present to me, and that chimney, may, and do exist separately. This is the doctrine of the vulgar, and implies no contradiction. There is no contradiction, therefore, in extending the same doctrine in all the perceptions.

In general, the following reasoning seems satisfactory. All ideas are borrowed from preceding perceptions. Our ideas of objects, therefore, are derived from that source. Consequently no proposition can be intelligible or consistent with regard to objects, which is not so with regard to perceptions. But it is intelligible and consistent to say, that objects exist distinct and independent, without any common *simple* substance or subject of inhesion. This proposition, therefore, can never be absurd with regard to perceptions.

When I turn my reflection on *myself,* I never can perceive this *self* without some one or more perceptions; nor can I ever perceive anything but the perceptions. It is the composition of these, therefore, which forms the self.

We can conceive a thinking being to have either many or few perceptions. Suppose the mind to be reduced even below the life of an oyster. Suppose it to have only one perception, as of thirst or hunger. Consider it in that situation. Do you conceive anything but merely that perception? Have you any notion of *self* or *substance?* If not, the addition of other perceptions can never give you that notion.

The annihilation which some people suppose to follow upon death, and which entirely destroys this self, is nothing but an extinction of all particular perceptions; love and hatred, pain and pleasure, thought and sensation. These, therefore, must be the same with self, since the one cannot survive the other.

Is *self* the same with *substance?* If it be, how can that question have place, concerning the substance of self, under a change of substance? If they be distinct, what is the difference betwixt them? For my part, I have a notion of neither, when conceived distinct from particular perceptions.

Philosophers begin to be reconciled to the principle, *that we have no idea of external substance, distinct from the ideas of particular qualities.* This must pave the way for a like principle with regard to the mind, *that we have no notion of it, distinct from the particular perception.*

So far I seem to be attended with sufficient evidence. But having thus loosened all our particular perceptions, when I proceed to explain the principle of connection, which binds them together, and makes us attribute to them a real simplicity and identity, I am sensible that my account is very defective, and that nothing but the seeming evidence of the precedent reasonings could have induced me to receive it. If perceptions are distinct existences, they form a whole only by being connected together. But no connections among distinct existences are ever discoverable by human understanding. We only *feel* a connection or determination of the thought to pass from one object to another. It follows, therefore, that the thought alone feels personal identity, when reflecting on the train of past perceptions that compose a mind, the ideas of them are felt to be connected together, and naturally introduce each other. However extraordinary this conclusion may seem, it need not surprise us. Most philosophers seem inclined to think, that personal identity *arises* from consciousness, and consciousness is nothing but a reflected thought or perception. The present philosophy, therefore, has so far a promising aspect. But all my hopes vanish when I come to explain the principles that unite our successive perceptions in our thought or consciousness. I cannot discover any theory which gives me satisfaction on this head.

In short, there are two principles which I cannot render consistent, nor is it in my power to renounce either of them, viz. *that all our distinct perceptions are distinct existences,* and *that the mind never perceives any real connection among distinct existences.* Did our perceptions either inhere in something simple and individual, or did the mind perceive some real connection among them, there would be no difficulty in the case. For my part, I must plead the privilege of a sceptic, and confess that this difficulty is too hard for my understanding. I pretend not, however, to pronounce it absolutely insuperable. Others, perhaps, or myself, upon more mature reflections, may discover some hypothesis that will reconcile those contradictions.

STUDY QUESTIONS

1   Hume begins by saying that we do not have an "idea" of the self. What do you think
he means by the word *idea?* Could he mean *concept?*

2   At one place Hume says that the mind is like a theater which contains perceptions. Is
this remark consistent with his other statements?

3   Hume says that the notion of a "soul" or "substance" is a fiction which we create.
Why do we create it, according to him?

4   Toward the end of the essay, Hume is unhappy with his previous solution. What is
the source of his perplexity? Can you suggest an answer?

5   "It seems to me that the greatest lesson of adult life is that one's own consciousness
is not enough. . . . What great writer would not like to share the consciousness of
Shakespeare? . . . What I would choose would be an evolution of life whereby the
essence of each of us becomes welded together into some vastly larger and more
potent system" (Fred Hoyle). Would Hume say that Hoyle's dream is possible? How
about Descartes?

The Myth of the Ghost in the Machine

Gilbert Ryle

Gilbert Ryle (1900–   ) is Waynflete Professor of Metaphysical Philosophy at
Oxford University. His now classic book *The Concept of Mind* was published in
1949 and immediately sparked a flurry of controversy. Ryle, a leader of the
British school of analytic philosophy, claims that many philosophical confusions result from an unsuspecting tendency to think that grammatical distinctions reflect real differences. The distinction between mind and body is a case
in point.

 In our selection, Ryle argues that the difference between mind and body
is not a difference between two types of "things," but rather reflects a difference in the ways of characterizing and explaining a person's activities. The
mental characteristics of a person are not located in a hidden ghostly realm,
but in observable behavior. For example, to say that someone is intelligent is
just to say that he or she can do certain kinds of things, such as counting,
problem solving, etc. Thought does not first take place in a Cartesian "mind"
and then cause the observable behavior—it *is* a feature of that observable
behavior. To think otherwise, according to Ryle, is to make a "category mistake."

 Some of Ryle's critics have accused him of neglecting the most obvious
objection to his position—the undeniable experience of the hidden self. In the
last part of our selection, Ryle answers this criticism: We discover our own
psychological traits in the same way as we discover those of other persons.

THE OFFICIAL DOCTRINE

There is a doctrine about the nature and place of minds which is so prevalent
among theorists and even among laymen that it deserves to be described as the
official theory. Most philosophers, psychologists and religious teachers subscribe,

with minor reservations, to its main articles and, although they admit certain theoretical difficulties in it, they tend to assume that these can be overcome without serious modifications being made to the architecture of the theory. It will be argued here that the central principles of the doctrine are unsound and conflict with the whole body of what we know about minds when we are not speculating about them.

The official doctrine, which hails chiefly from Descartes, is something like this. With the doubtful exceptions of idiots and infants in arms every human being has both a body and a mind. Some would prefer to say that every human being is both a body and a mind. His body and his mind are ordinarily harnessed together, but after the death of the body his mind may continue to exist and function.

Human bodies are in space and are subject to the mechanical laws which govern all other bodies in space. Bodily processes and states can be inspected by external observers. So a man's bodily life is as much a public affair as are the lives of animals and reptiles and even as the careers of trees, crystals and planets.

But minds are not in space, nor are their operations subject to mechanical laws. The workings of one mind are not witnessable by other observers; its career is private. Only I can take direct cognisance of the states and processes of my own mind. A person therefore lives through two collateral histories, one consisting of what happens in and to his body, the other consisting of what happens in and to his mind. The first is public, the second private. The events in the first history are events in the physical world, those in the second are events in the mental world.

It has been disputed whether a person does or can directly monitor all or only some of the episodes of his own private history; but, according to the official doctrine, of at least some of these episodes he has direct and unchallengeable cognisance. In consciousness, self-consciousness and introspection he is directly and authentically apprised of the present states and operations of his mind. He may have great or small uncertainties about concurrent and adjacent episodes in the physical world, but he can have none about at least part of what is momentarily occupying his mind.

It is customary to express this bifurcation of his two lives and of his two worlds by saying that the things and events which belong to the physical world, including his own body, are external, while the workings of his own mind are internal. This antithesis of outer and inner is of course meant to be construed as a metaphor, since minds, not being in space, could not be described as being spatially inside anything else, or as having things going on spatially inside themselves. But relapses from this good intention are common and theorists are found speculating how stimuli, the physical sources of which are yards or miles outside a person's skin, can generate mental responses inside his skull, or how decisions framed inside his cranium can set going movements of his extremities.

Even when "inner" and "outer" are construed as metaphors, the problem how a person's mind and body influence one another is notoriously charged with theoretical difficulties. What the mind wills, the legs, arms and the tongue execute; what affects the ear and the eye has something to do with what the mind perceives: grimaces and smiles betray the mind's moods and bodily castigations lead, it is hoped, to moral improvement. But the actual transactions between the episodes of the private history and those of the public history remain mysterious, since by definition they can belong to neither series. They could not be reported among the happenings described in a person's autobiography of his inner life, but nor could they be reported among those described in some one else's biography of that person's overt career. They can be inspected neither by introspection nor by laboratory experiment. They are theoretical shuttlecocks which are forever being bandied from the physiologist back to the psychologist and from the psychologist back to the physiologist.

Underlying this partly metaphorical representation of the bifurcation of a person's two lives there is a seemingly more profound and philosophical assumption. It is assumed that there are two different kinds of existence or status. What exists or happens may have the status of physical existence, or it may have the status of mental existence. Somewhat as the faces of coins are either heads or tails, or somewhat as living creatures are either male or female, so, it is supposed, some existing is physical existing, other existing is mental existing. It is a necessary feature of what has physical existence that it is in space and time; it is a necessary feature of what has mental existence that it is in time but not in space. What has physical existence is composed of matter, or else is a function of matter; what has mental existence consists of consciousness, or else is a function of consciousness.

There is thus a polar opposition between mind and matter, an opposition which is often brought out as follows. Material objects are situated in a common field, known as "space," and what happens to one body in one part of space is mechanically connected with what happens to other bodies in other parts of space. But mental happenings occur in insulated fields, known as "minds," and there is, apart maybe from telepathy, no direct causal connection between what happens in one mind and what happens in another. Only through the medium of the public physical world can the mind of one person make a difference to the mind of another. The mind is its own place and in his inner life each of us lives the life of a ghostly Robinson Crusoe. People can see, hear and jolt one another's bodies, but they are irremediably blind and deaf to the workings of one another's minds and inoperative upon them.

What sort of knowledge can be secured of the workings of a mind? On the one side, according to the official theory, a person has direct knowledge of the best imaginable kind of the workings of his own mind. Mental states and processes are (or are normally) conscious states and processes, and the consciousness which irradiates them can engender no illusions and leaves the door open for no doubts. A person's present thinkings, feelings and willings, his perceivings, rememberings and imaginings are intrinsically "phosphorescent"; their existence and their nature are inevitably betrayed to their owner. The inner life is a stream of consciousness of such a sort that it would be absurd to suggest that the mind whose life is that stream might be unaware of what is passing down it.

True, the evidence adduced recently by Freud seems to show that there exist channels tributary to this stream, which run hidden from their owner. People are actuated by impulses the existence of which they vigorously disavow; some of their thoughts differ from the thoughts which they acknowledge; and some of the actions which they think they will to perform they do not really will. They are thoroughly gulled by some of their own hypocrisies and they successfully ignore facts about their mental lives which on the official theory ought to be patent to them. Holders of the official theory tend, however, to maintain that anyhow in normal circumstances a person must be directly and authentically seized of the present state and workings of his own mind.

Besides being currently supplied with these alleged immediate data of consciousness, a person is also generally supposed to be able to exercise from time to time a special kind of perception, namely inner perception, or introspection. He can take a (non-optical) "look" at what is passing in his mind. Not only can he view and scrutinize a flower through his sense of sight and listen to and discriminate the notes of a bell through his sense of hearing; he can also reflectively or introspectively watch, without any bodily organ of sense, the current episodes of his inner life. This self-observation is also commonly supposed to be immune from illusion, confusion or doubt. A mind's reports of its own affairs have a certainty superior to the best that is possessed by its reports of matters in the physical world. Sense-perceptions can, but consciousness and introspection cannot, be mistaken or confused.

On the other side, one person has no direct access of any sort to the events of the inner life of another. He cannot do better than make problematic inferences from the observed behaviour of the other person's body to the states of mind which, by analogy from his own conduct, he supposes to be signalised by that behaviour. Direct access to the workings of a mind is the privilege of that mind itself; in default of such privileged access, the workings of one mind are inevitably occult to everyone else. For the supposed arguments from bodily movements similar to their own to mental workings similar to their own would lack any possibility of observational corroboration. Not unnaturally, therefore, an adherent of the official theory finds it difficult to resist this consequence of his premisses, that he has no good reason to believe that there do exist minds other than his own. Even if he prefers to believe that to other human bodies there are harnessed minds not unlike his own, he cannot claim to be able to discover their individual characteristics, or the particular things that they undergo and do. Absolute solitude is on this showing the ineluctable destiny of the soul. Only our bodies can meet.

As a necessary corollary of this general scheme there is implicitly prescribed a special way of construing our ordinary concepts of mental powers and operations. The verbs, nouns and adjectives, with which in ordinary life we describe the wits, characters and higher-grade performances of the people with whom we have do, are required to be construed as signifying special episodes in their secret histories, or else as signifying tendencies for such episodes to occur. When someone is described as knowing, believing or guessing something, as hoping, dreading, intending or shirking something, as designing this or being amused at that, these verbs are supposed to denote the occurrence of specific modifications in his (to us) occult stream of consciousness. Only his own privileged access to this stream in direct awareness and introspection could provide authentic testimony that these mental-conduct verbs were correctly or incorrectly applied. The on-looker, be he teacher, critic, biographer or friend, can never assure himself that his comments have any vestige of truth. Yet it was just because we do in fact all know how to make such comments, make them with general correctness and correct them when they turn out to be confused or mistaken, that philosophers found it necessary to construct their theories of the nature and place of minds. Finding mental-conduct concepts being regularly and effectively used, they prop-erly sought to fix their logical geography. But the logical geography officially recommended would entail that there could be no regular or effective use of these mental-conduct concepts in our descriptions of, and prescriptions for, other people's minds.

THE ABSURDITY OF THE OFFICIAL DOCTRINE

Such in outline is the official theory. I shall often speak of it, with deliberate abusiveness, as "the dogma of the Ghost in the Machine." I hope to prove that it is entirely false, and false not in detail but in principle. It is not merely an assemblage of particular mistakes. It is one big mistake and a mistake of a special kind. It is, namely, a category mistake. It represents the facts of mental life as if they belonged to one logical type or category (or range of types or categories), when they actually belong to another. The dogma is therefore a philosopher's myth. In attempting to explode the myth I shall probably be taken to be denying well-known facts about the mental life of human beings, and my plea that I aim at doing nothing more than rectify the logic of mental-conduct concepts will probably be disallowed as mere subterfuge.

I must first indicate what is meant by the phrase "Category-mistake." This I do in a series of illustrations.

A foreigner visiting Oxford or Cambridge for the first time is shown a num-ber of colleges, libraries, playing fields, museums, scientific departments and administrative offices. He then asks "But where is the university? I have seen where the members of the Colleges live, where the Registrar works, where the scientists experiment and the rest. But I have not yet seen the University in which reside and work the members of your University." It has then to be explained to him that the University is not another collateral institution, some ulterior count-erpart to the colleges, laboratories and offices which he has seen. The University is just the way in which all that he has already seen is organized. When they are seen and when their co-ordination is understood, the University has been seen. His mistake lay in his innocent assumption that it was correct to speak of Christ Church, the Bodleian Library, the Ashmolean Museum *and* the University, to speak, that is, as if "the University" stood for an extra member of the class of which these other units are members. He was mistakenly allocating the Universi-ty to the same category as that to which the other institutions belong.

The same mistake would be made by a child witnessing the march-past of a division, who, having had pointed out to him such and such battalions, batteries, squadrons, etc., asked when the division was going to appear. He would be supposing that a division was a counterpart to the units already seen, partly similar to them and partly unlike them. He would be shown his mistake by being told that in watching the battalions, batteries and squadrons marching past he had been watching the division marching past. The march-past was not a parade of battalions, batteries, squadrons *and* a division; it was a parade of the battalions, batteries and squadrons *of* a division.

One more illustration. A foreigner watching his first game of cricket learns what are the functions of the bowlers, the batsmen, the fielders, the umpires and the scorers. He then says "But there is no one left on the field to contribute the famous element of team-spirit. I see who does the bowling, the batting and the wicket-keeping; but I do not see whose role it is to exercise *esprit de corps.*" Once more, it would have to be explained that he was looking for the wrong type of thing. Team-spirit is not another cricketing-operation supplementary to all of the other special tasks. It is, roughly, the keeness with which each of the special tasks is performed, and performing a task keenly is not performing two tasks. Certainly exhibiting team-spirit is not the same thing as bowling or catching, but nor is it a third thing such that we can say that the bowler first bowls *and* then exhibits team-spirit or that a fielder is at a given moment *either* catching *or* displaying *esprit de corps.*

These illustrations of category-mistakes have a common feature which must be noticed. The mistakes were made by people who did not know how to wield the concepts *University, division* and *team-spirit.* Their puzzles arose from inability to use certain items in the English vocabulary.

The theoretically interesting category-mistakes are those made by people who are perfectly competent to apply concepts, at least in the situations with which they are familiar, but are still liable in their abstract thinking to allocate those concepts to logical types to which they do not belong. An instance of a mistake of this sort would be the following story. A student of politics has learned the main differences between the British, the French and the American Constitutions, and has learned also the differences and connections between the Cabinet, Parliament, the various Ministries, the Judicature and the Church of England. But he still becomes embarrassed when asked questions about the connections between the Church of England, the Home Office and the British Constitution. For while the Church and the Home Office are institutions, the British Constitution is not another institution in the same sense of that noun. So inter-institutional relations which can be asserted or denied to hold between the Church and the Home Office cannot be asserted or denied to hold between either of them and the British Constitution. "The British Constitition" is not a term of the same logical type as "the Home Office" and "the Church of England." In a partially similar way, John Doe may be a relative, a friend, an enemy or a stranger to Richard Roe; but he cannot be any of these things to the Average Taxpayer. He knows how to talk sense in certain sorts of discussions about the Average Taxpayer, but he is baffled to say why he could not come across him in the street as he can come across Richard Roe. . . .

SELF-KNOWLEDGE WITHOUT PRIVILEGED ACCESS

. . . [W]hen we speak of a person's mind, we are not speaking of a second theatre of special-status incidents, but of certain ways in which some of the incidents of his own life are ordered. His life is not a double series of events taking place in two different kinds of stuff; it is one concatenation of events, the differences between some and other classes of which largely consist in the applicablility or inapplicability to them of logically different types of law-propositions and law-like propositions. Assertions about a person's mind are therefore assertions of special sorts about that person. So questions about the relations between a person and his mind, like those about the relations between a person's body and his mind are improper questions. They are improper in much the same way as is the question. "What transactions go on between the House of Commons and the British Constitution?" . . .

The questions "What knowledge can a person get of the workings of his own mind?" and "How does he get it?" by their very wording suggest absurd answers. They suggest that, for a person to know that he is lazy, or has done a sum carefully, he must have taken a peep into a windowless chamber, illuminated by a very peculiar sort of light, and one to which only he has access. And when the question is construed in this sort of way, the parallel questions, "What knowledge can one person get of the workings of another mind?" and "How does he get it?" by their very wording seem to preclude any answer at all; for they suggest that one person could only know that another person was lazy, or had done a sum carefully, by peering into another secret chamber to which, *ex hypothesi,* he has no access.

In fact the problem is not one of this sort. It is simply the methodological question, how we establish, and how we apply, certain sorts of law-like propositions about the overt and the silent behavior of persons. I come to appreciate the skill and tactics of a chess-player by watching him and others playing chess, and I learn that a certain pupil of mine is lazy, ambitious and witty by following his work, noticing his excuses, listening to his conversation and comparing his performances with those of others. Nor does it make any important difference if I happen myself to be that pupil. I can indeed then listen to more of his conversations, as I am the addressee of his unspoken soliloquies; I notice more of his excuses, as I am never absent, when they are made. On the other hand, my comparison of his performances with those of others is more difficult, since the examiner is himself taking the examination, which makes neutrality hard to preserve and precludes the demeanor of the candidate, when under interrogation, from being in good view.

To repeat a point previously made, the question is not the envelope-question "How do I discover that I or you have a mind?" but the range of specific questions of the pattern, "How do I discover that I am more unselfish than you; that I can do long division well, but differential equations only badly; that you suffer from certain phobias and tend to shirk facing certain sorts of facts; that I am more easily irritated than most people but less subject to panic, vertigo, or morbid conscientiousness?" Besides such pure dispositional questions there is also the range of particular performance questions and occurrence questions of the patterns, "How do I find out that I saw the joke and that you did not; that your action took more courage than mine; that the service I rendered to you was rendered from a sense of duty and not from expectation of kudos; that, though I did not fully understand what was said at the time, I did fully understand it, when I went over it in my head afterwards, while you understood it perfectly from the start; that I was feeling homesick yesterday?" Questions of these sorts offer no mysteries; we know quite well how to set to work to find out the answers to them; and though often we cannot finally solve them and may have to stop short at mere conjecture, yet, even so, we have no doubt what sorts of information would satisfy our requirements, if we could get it; and we know what it would be like to get it. For example, after listening to an argument, you aver that you understand it perfectly; but you may be deceiving yourself, or trying to deceive me. If we then part for a day or two, I am no longer in a position to test whether or not you did understand it perfectly. But still I know what tests would have settled the point. If you had put the argument into your words, or translated it into French; if you had invented appropriate concrete illustrations of the generalizations and abstractions in the argument; if you had stood up to cross-questioning; if you had correctly drawn further consequences from different stages of the argument and indicated points where the theory was inconsistent with other theories; if you had inferred correctly from the nature of the argument to the qualities of intellect and character of its author and predicted accurately the subsequent development of his theory, then I should have required no further evidence that you understood it perfectly. And exactly the same sorts of tests would satisfy me that I had understood it perfectly; the sole differences would be that I should probably not have voiced aloud the expressions of my deductions, illustrations, etc., but told them to myself more perfunctorily in silent soliloquy; and I should probably have been more easily satisfied of the completeness of my understanding than I was of yours.

In short it is part of the *meaning* of "you understood it" that you could have done so and so and would have done it, if such and such, and the *test* of whether you understood it is a range of performances satisfying the apodoses[1] of these general hypothetical statements. It should be noticed, on the one hand, that there is no single nuclear performance, overt or in your head, which would determine that you had understood the argument. Even if you claimed that you had experienced a flash or click of comprehension and had actually done so, you would still withdraw your other claim to have understood the argument, if you found that you could not paraphrase it, illustrate, expand or recast it; and you would allow someone else to have understood it who could meet all examination-questions about it, but reported no click of comprehension. It should also be noticed, on the other hand, that though there is no way of specifying how many or what sub-tests must be satisfied for a person to qualify as having perfectly understood the argument, this does not imply that no finite set of sub-tests is ever enough. To

---

[1] In a hypothetical statement of the form "If such and such, then so and so", the apodosis is the concluding clause.

settle whether a boy can do long division, we do not require him to try out his hand on a million, a thousand, or even a hundred different problems in long division. We should not be quite satisfied after one success, but we should not remain dissatisfied after twenty, provided that they were judiciously variegated and that he had not done them before. A good teacher, who not only recorded the boy's correct and incorrect solutions, but also watched his procedure in reaching them, would be satisfied much sooner, and he would be satisfied sooner still if he got the boy to describe and justify the constituent operations that he performed, though of course many boys can do long division sums who cannot describe or justify the operations performed in doing them.

I discover my or your motives in much, though not quite the same way as I discover my or your abilities. The big practical difference is that I cannot put the subject through his paces in my inquiries into his inclinations as I can in my inquiries into his competences. To discover how conceited or patriotic you are, I must still observe your conduct, remarks, demeanor and tones of voice, but I cannot subject you to examination-tests or experiments which you recognize as such. You would have a special motive for responding to such experiments in a particular way. From mere conceit, perhaps, you would try to behave self-effacingly, or from mere modesty you might try to behave conceitedly. None the less, ordinary day to day observation normally serves swiftly to settle such questions. To be conceited is to tend to boast of one's own excellences, to pity or ridicule the deficiencies of others, to daydream about imaginary triumphs, to reminisce about actual triumphs, to weary quickly of conversations which reflect unfavorably upon oneself, to lavish one's society upon distinguished persons and to economize in association with the undistinguished. The tests of whether a person is conceited are the actions he takes and the reactions he manifests in such circumstances. Not many anecdotes, sneers, or sycophancies are required from the subject for the ordinary observer to make up his mind, unless the candidate and the examiner happen to be identical.

The ascertainment of a person's mental capacities and propensities is an inductive process, an induction to law-like propositions from observed actions and reactions. Having ascertained these long-term qualities, we explain a particular action or reaction by applying the result of such an induction to the new specimen, save where open avowals let us know the explanation without research. These inductions are not, of course, carried out under laboratory conditions, or with any statistical apparatus, any more than is the shepherd's weather-lore, or the general practitioner's understanding of a particular patient's constitution. But they are ordinarily reliable enough. It is a truism to say that the appreciations of character and the explanations of conduct given by critical, unprejudiced and humane observers, who have had a lot of experience and take a lot of interest, tend to be both swift and reliable; those of inferior judges tend to be slower and less reliable. Similarly the marks awarded by practiced and keen examiners who know their subject well and are reasonably sympathetic towards the candidates tend to be about right; those of inferior examiners tend to scatter more widely from the proper order. The point of these truisms is to remind us that in real life we are quite familiar with the techniques of assessing persons and accounting for their actions, though according to the standard theory no such techniques could exist. . . .

STUDY QUESTIONS

1   What is a category mistake? Why is it improper to ask about the relation between mind and body? Can you think of some questions which embody category mistakes?

2   "How do we know that other people have minds?" How would Ryle answer this question? Would Descartes agree? How would you answer it?

3   "However completely the external body answers to the behavioristic tests for intelligence, it always remains a sensible question to ask: 'Has it really got a mind or is it merely an automation?' " (C. D. Broad). Would Ryle agree with this? What do you think is the significance of Broad's claim, if true?

4   "The behaviorist advances the view that what the psychologists have hitherto called thought is in short nothing but talking to ourselves" (John B. Watson). Would Ryle agree with this definition of "thought"? Suppose you could no longer talk to yourself, that is, all your talking was "out loud." Would you still be able to think?

5   "Consciousness is the *only* thing of which we have direct evidence, and to say 'I *think,* therefore I am' is a statement which rests more firmly on direct evidence than the behaviorists' formula 'I act, therefore I am' " (Joseph Wood Krutch). How would Ryle respond to this? With whom do you agree?

A Philosopher's Nightmare (or The Ghost Not Laid)

Jonathan Harrison

Descartes noticed that the sort of experiences he had while dreaming were indistinguishable from those of waking life. In dreams we eat, run, feel pain; and, at that moment, it is as real to us as our waking experiences. Why then couldn't our waking life be an elaborate dream, caused by some evil genius of great power bent on human confusion? The only way Descartes could get out of this dilemma was to prove the existence of a good God who would not deceive us. Although most philosophers did not accept Descartes's proof of God's existence, and therefore did not find his solution very convincing, they did not seem to be able to solve the paradox either. This was heightened by the fact that the official theory of perception—that what we immediately perceive are mental images—fits in nicely with Descartes's hypothesis. A few holdouts pinched themselves, kicked rocks, or jumped off bridges; but most learned to live with it.

In the following selection, Jonathan Harrison (1924–   ), of the University of Nottingham, puts Descartes's hypothesis in a contemporary setting. Sometime in the future a living brain is disconnected from its body at birth and attached to a computer. The computer provides the brain with a coherent stream of perceptions just as Descartes imagined the evil genius might do. The brain, named Ludwig, studies philosophy (just as you are doing) and comes across Descartes's argument about dreams. Eventually Ludwig becomes a track star, but not before he samples some of the usual theories which philosophers have offered to avoid Descartes's nightmare.

Once upon a time, in the year 2167 A.D., when the connected disciplines of Physiology, Psychology, Medicine, Cybernetics and Communication Theory were enormously more advanced than they have been before or since, there lived a very famous neurologist. He was so eminent that the conventions which circumscribed the behaviour of his less successful colleagues neither worried nor restricted him, and finding even the most difficult tasks which he met in his professional life presented a challenge insufficient adequately to tax his unrivalled knowledge and consummate skill, his ambition led him to embark upon an enterprise which one would have supposed the most dangerous excess of *hubris* could not have aspired to, an enterprise which might almost be deemed to usurp the prerogative of God himself.

One day one of his assistants delivered a baby which, it was immediately obvious, was so deformed that a life even remotely approaching normal was impossible for him. From the neck down, this baby was afflicted with almost every known physiological defect. From the neck up, hwoever, the baby appeared perfectly normal; indeed, in so far as it was possible to tell at this early age, it exhibited features which in Dr. Smythson's experience had been associated with exceptionally high intelligence, and even led him to predict very great philosophical ability. In order that such a genius should not be lost to the world by the premature cessation of his bodily functioning, Dr. Smythson made up his mind to undertake an experiment never before attempted by a human being; he decided to dissolve the unequal marriage between the superb head and mutilated body, and keep the latter alive independently of the former by a process the possibility of which had recently occurred to him. The head was to be kept in a case and to be fed with its necessary blood supply from a reservoir by means of a pump connected to the appropriate arteries.

This having been successfully accomplished, it occurred to him that the life of his protégé—whom he decided to call Alfred Ludwig Gilbert Robinson, in memory of a once well known twentieth century philosopher of that name—must inevitably be circumscribed and dull. Since he was a kindly man as well as an ingenious one, he made up his mind to produce an adaptation—which he christened the endocephalic electrohallucinator—of a twenty-second century means of entertainment and use if for a different and more questionable purpose than mere pleasure-giving. This device was designed to give men and women seeking escape from that small amount of monotony contained even by twenty-second century lives all the experiences which would be involved in participating in the various incidents celebrated in the fiction of the day by stimulating their sense organs in the identical ways in which they would have been stimulated had they actually participated in these scenes. Dr. Smythson modified it so that the necessary stimuli could be fed directly into the nerves communicating with the relevant

From Jonathan Harrison, "A Philosopher's Nightmare or The Ghost Not Laid" in *Proceedings of the Aristotelian Society*, vol. 67, © 1967, The Aristotelian Society. Reprinted by permission of the Editor.

centres of the brain—a process rather like cutting and tapping a telephone wire except that in the case we are considering the telephone wire had, as it were, already been cut. In order to do this, he found it not only necessary to remove Alfred Ludwig Gilbert Robinson's eyes, ears and tongue, but the whole of his skull, but to a man who had already removed a body from its head, the performance of this operation caused scarcely a vestige of compunction; nor was he disturbed by the fact that the impulses used to stimulate Alfred Ludwig Gilbert Robinson's perceptual apparatus produced scenes which were totally hallucinatory. Dr. Smythson contented himself with the thought that a consistent hallucination was as good as reality—in this case, indeed, even better—and solved his only slightly uneasy conscience by resolving that he would give Alfred Ludwig Gilbert Robinson an experience of life which was not only coherent, but happy as well. In order to find out, among other things, whether Ludwig was happy Dr. Smythson had to introduce another rather elaborate piece of apparatus, a development of the electro-encephalograph, much used by officials in the Department of Justice, which enabled them to detect in detail even the slightest variation in a patient's cerebral activity. Since it had been discovered that there was a correlation between such activity and the symbols used by people in their private thoughts it was possible for his thoughts to be first recorded and then decoded by officials trained for the purpose. Dr. Smythson found that reading the results of this process was a little tedious, and was sometimes distressed at the confusion which he detected, but he contented himself with the knowledge that at least he had an adequate means of telling whether the chemistry of Ludwig's blood was such as to keep him both contented and alert, and to rectify it when it was not.

In this environment Ludwig developed apace. Dr. Smythson saw that he had an excellent education, and stimulated his optic nerve with the contents of only the best books. As Ludwig reached his late 'teens, Dr. Smythson even put in his way—metaphorically speaking, of course—some works on philosophy, and was interested to see the decoded summaries of Ludwig's reflections when these were presented to him by his technical staff. The writings of one philosopher in particular—a now little regarded Frenchman called René Descartes—provoked a crisis in Ludwig's intellectual life. After reading a work of his—called *Meditations*—Ludwig was for many months distressed by the thought that all his most cherished beliefs might be mistaken and that, instead of the benevolent deity whose existence he had previously taken for granted, there was a malicious demon who produced in his mind experience which proceeded just as if he perceived material objects, though in fact no such things existed. Descartes's own reason—that God was incapable of deceit—for rejecting this hypothesis did not greatly impress him. Descartes had to defend it by suggesting that God cannot help but occassionally produce error, since it was impossible to have afferent nerves which would produce sensations by being stimulated at their endings, unless these nerves could produce similar sensations by being stimulated nearer the brain, and this suggestion struck Ludwig, who was almost entirely ignorant of physiology, as fanciful.

However, reading the works of a later Irish philosopher called Berkeley produced some reassurance to his troubled mind, and for a long time he was convinced that since what philosophers called matter was an inert and stupid substance, it could not conceivably have the power to produce in him the ideas of colour and light which he saw when he opened his eyes. Hence he concluded that these perceptions were produced in him directly by God's volitions, and that his perception, since it consisted in participating in God's own perceptual experience, brought him much closer to the deity than appeared possible on the view it was designed to replace. To say that my helicopter—for Dr. Smythson had not deemed it either kind or right not to feed Ludwig with at least the experience of flying, when all round youths of Ludwig's age had their own helicopters—exists unperceived in its heliport, he decided, is simply to say that some other being perceives it. Dr. Smythson, on reading the transcript of these reflections, was both amused and concerned at how profoundly erroneous were Ludwig's conclusions, but did not see fit to disillusion him. Indeed, he was quite sure that, were he to break in upon Ludwig with an account of the true state of affairs, his words would be neither heeded nor believed.

Ludwig did not remain long satisfied with Berkeley's refutation of his first tendency towards scepticism and atheism, and he still often felt inclined to doubt the existence of the world he seemed to experience. Reading the works of a celebrated Scottish sceptic called Hume did a little to reassure him, for the views to which he leaned seemed so preposterous when actually seen in black and white that reading them in Hume's words brought home to him their manifest absurdity. What nonsense to think that the world was composed entirely of impressions, and that, since these impressions were dependent for their existence upon the percipient's brain—at this Dr. Smythson's machine stimulated his nervous system in all the ways in which it would have been stimulated had he in reality been eating an excellent breakfast—the belief in the independent existence of a world of objects is contradictory and impossible! The belief that scepticism was absurd led him for a while to sympathize with the school of Scottish philosophers who, unlike most of their countrymen, believed in common sense, but this sympathy proved only temporary, and a week or so later, after reading a work of John Stuart Mill called *An Examination of Sir William Hamilton's Philosophy*—who Sir William Hamilton was he never discovered—he inclined to the view that material objects were no more than permanent possibilities of sensation. So long, he thought, as it is the case that if I were to go into my study—Dr. Smythson had decided that he would give him the experience of having a study, though such things were usual in the twenty-second century—I would have the sensation of seeing a room with books, etc. my study existed unobserved, for this is all that saying I have an unobserved study can mean. He never, however, felt much temptation to accept the view of some other philosophers, called idealists, that the test of the truth of his beliefs was their coherence amongst themselves. This was partly due to the obscurity of their writings, partly due to an empiricism which made him disinclined to appeal to a criterion of truth which was not based upon the deliverances of his senses.

However, recurring doubts about the reality of those personal belongings and the few friends that Dr. Smythson's apparatus was able to supply him with were eventually banished only by reading the works of a number of twentieth century philosophers, in particular, by one called G. E. Moore. Two papers, one entitled "A Defence of Common Sense," and the other "Proof of the External World" in particular impressed him. Indeed, from the time of reading these his earlier scepticism never again fully returned. It was reading Moore which eventually brought home to him how the existence of things external to our minds could be proved, and in his excitement at the solution of a problem which had long perplexed him, he actually mimicked Moore. "There must be things external to us," he argued under what he supposed was his breath, "for if there are two human hands, then there are at least two things external to us, and that there are two such things," he agreed with Moore, "can be proved as follows: Here," he said (as the machine fed him the experience of holding up one hand), "is a hand, and," as the machine fed him the experience of holding up another, "here is another."

Though this proof of the existence of his hands and so of the external world completely contented him, he nevertheless saw with satisfaction that a number of other philosophers reinforced the conclusion of Moore's argument by considerations of a slightly different nature. Though Moore himself, he realised, held the view that what we saw directly were not external objects themselves, but sense-data, he himself was quickly convinced by the arguments of some of Moore's successors which were designed to show that most of the problems of perception were the products of confusion engendered by the introduction into philosophy of this bastard concept of the sense-datum. Scepticism in particular, he decided, was one of the most undesirable consequences of that piece of philosophical legerdemain which fabricated these entities, and, he thought, that since to talk of sense-data was just an extremely misleading way of talking about how things looked, and since the dots, specks, blotches and coloured shapes he saw about him simply were material things themselves, there was no reason why he should not say he saw material objects *directly*, and the idea that there was an iron curtain of sense-data interposed between him and the external world he concluded to be absurd. Since the only reason he had had for being a sceptic, he believed, was this erroneous delusion—shared it is true, by almost all the philosophers with whom he had so far had any acquaintance—his scepticism was revealed as manifestly unfounded when once this piece of nonsense was exposed for what it was.

Reading the work of other philosophers of roughly the same period also, to his great relief, caused him to reject a number of other opinions, the possible truth of which had been perplexing him more than he cared to admit. Sometimes he had been troubled by the possibility that life was a dream from which he might one day awake, and discover that all the things and persons he thought he saw were mere illusion. This possibility, too, he discounted after a further acquaintance with mid-twentieth century Anglo-Saxon philosophy. It was impossible, he decided, that the whole of his experience could be an illusion, since the terms "real" and "illusory" were so related that it was necessary that some things should be real in order that other things could be illusory; hence that the whole of his experience should be an illusion was as much a logical impossibility as that all coins should be counterfeit, or all bank notes forged. That unhappy frame of mind into which he had fallen, he now saw, was the product of certain terminological confusions, and he felt grateful to those twentieth century philosophers who had dispelled his anxieties by so successful an application of their benign thereapeutic techniques. One argument, sometimes in those days called the argument from standard samples, gave him especial satisfaction, by its apparent simplicity and obviousness. How could he have doubted, he wondered, whether the object he sat on was a chair when it was by being shown such things as these that he had been taught the very meaning of the word "chair"? How could he have wondered whether the chair he saw was perhaps an illusion, when it was by being shown such things as this that he had been taught what was meant by the expression "real" as opposed to "illusory"? How could he have wondered whether it was certain that it was a chair, when it was in these very cases, when the thing he saw continued to appear to be a chair in whatever way he tried to test it, that he had been taught that it was correct to use the expression "It is certain that that is a chair" and that it was incorrect to use such expressions as, "It is highly probable that that is a chair" or "It seems very likely that that is a chair"?

A brief excursion into the works of certain philosophising physiologists of about the same date did for a moment cause him to suspect that all that he saw might be the product of his own cerebral activity, but he soon discounted this possibility as too absurd to contemplate. Dr. Smythson too, took fright at this point, and saw that no more such books were put into the apparatus which was responsible for Ludwig's perceptual experience.

His reading of mid-twentieth century philosophy was not pure gain, however. He had previously been of a religious disposition and, in his unsceptical moments, he had believed in the existence of an omnipotent, omniscient and perfectly benevolent deity who was responsible not only for his own existence, but for the existence of the whole world and his experience of it. To his great distress, he now saw that this possibility was not after all a real one, and that the words in which it was expressed were in fact meaningless. He now realized that the meaning of a statement was the method of its verification, and that since the statement that there was a being who supported the world, sustained him, and was responsible for the course of his experience being what it was, was unverifiable, it was also meaningless. It was meaningless, he concluded, to talk of a world or a sphere of existence other than his own, as it was meaningless to talk of any causal dependence other than that observed dependence of the things to be found in his perceptual experience upon one another. If indeed you could deduce anything from the hypothesis of a creator, then the large amount of avoidable evil in the world—Dr. Smythson was a little hurt at this—showed that it must be an hypothesis which was false. The existence of God, therefore, was either false or unverifiable, and we could only avoid the Scylla of falsification by being wrecked upon the Charybdis of unintelligibility and emptiness.

To his great regret his former much cherished belief that he had an immortal soul which would survive the death of his body quickly went the way of his belief in God. Formerly he had, in moments of depression, consoled himself with the thought that life in this world was a preparation for another, happier life upon which he would enter upon the dissolution of his body. However, after a careful perusal of one of the most influential of twentieth century philosophers, he decided that any such belief rested upon the mistake of thinking that his mind, like his body, was a substance, and so, like his body, capable of an independent existence. Now he realised that this was a mistake, and that his mind was not a hidden ghostly substance, lying behind the solid earthy substance of his body, and to the workings of which he alone—Dr. Smythson smiled at this—had access. Talk about his mind, he realised, was of a different logical type from talk about his body, much as talk about electricity was of a different logical type from talk about wires and electric light bulbs. Just as it was absurd to say "Yes, I know that electric light bulbs light up when wires connect them to the positive and negative cells of a battery, and that electric motors work in the same circumstances, but nevertheless I doubt the existence of electricity" so, he thought, it was equally absurd to suppose that he could know that he was in the presence of a mind. And so, he concluded, he knew the contents of his own mind in a way no more esoteric than that in which he knew the contents of other people's, and, correspondingly, that other people—here Dr. Smythson laughed more heartily than he had done for many a year—knew the contents of his mind in a way no more esoteric than they knew the contents of their own. The corollary to this solution of the mind/body problem, which he found as emotionally distressing as the solution itself was intellectually satisfying, was that his mind could no more exist apart from his body and the variegated activities in which it indulged than electricity could exist apart from such things as wires and television sets and vacuum cleaners and batteries. His intellectual satisfaction with this view was indeed so complete that he failed to be attracted by the more sophisticated, though also more obscure, view that his mind and body were really no more than two different kinds of predicates of the same substance. The view that statements about his thoughts and feelings were no more than statements about the neurological activity of his brain he regarded as too absurd to be taken seriously.

He was never disturbed in the state of intellectual equilibrium which he had now reached. Had he been able to continue his researches into the history of philosophy until the end of the twentieth century, and see first Oxford, always most sensitive to continental influence, then the rest of England, and eventually, though not until these movements were past their high-water mark, the last stronghold of linguistic philosophy, Scotland, held in the grip of Existentialism, Kantianism, and Neo-Thomism, his naïve faith in the permanence of the intellectual millenium he supposed himself to have discovered would no doubt have been irretrievably shaken. However, he never did see these things. By what was perhaps for him a fortunate coincidence, a young friend of Dr. Smythson's, called Marcus Antonius Richardson, who possessed a body of the most remarkable beauty and power, and whose prowess far outstripped that of any other athlete whose feats had been recorded, contracted a fatal brain disease which even the vast resources of contemporary medicine could not cure. Dr. Smythson was for a while greatly distressed by the thought of the imminent demise of a body physiologically so unique, but it was not long before he formed an idea as brilliant as any which had occurred to him previously. Ludwig, the brain without a body, would be the means of the salvation of Marcus, the body without a brain. A long, difficult and dangerous operation followed. Marcus's head was removed and Ludwig, or Ludwig's head—Dr. Smythson had some hesitation over which was the correct expression—was carefully grafted on to it. Marcus's eyes and ears were fastened to Ludwig's optic nerves in place of the apparatus which was hitherto all they had known, and his face and skull were used to protect and beautify the once disembodied brain. Though the result was indistinguishable from the original Marcus in appearance, it was more like the original Ludwig in behaviour and intellectual capacity, and, since these are of so much greater importance than the grosser physical features, we shall continue to call the amalgam Ludwig, despite the fact that actually most of it was Marcus. When Ludwig recovered from the anaesthetic he not unnaturally believed that he had now come to experience a consistent hallucination or dream, and it took Dr. Smythson and his colleagues many months before they could convince him that it was in reality his former experience which had been hallucinatory. At this moment Ludwig's career, though long and, on the whole happy, ceased to be of any philosophical importance. He married and had children—who in character and intellect bore a strong resemblance to Marcus, none at all to him—and was only briefly puzzled by the problems that what had happened to him presented to his former firm belief in the impossibility of the transmigration of souls. But acquiring Marcus' body, though it brought to his life a variety, verve and intensity which, he now discovered, it had formerly lacked, ruined his powers of concentration. Though he occasionally returned to the actual books, the contents of which Dr. Smythson had previously fed into his optic nerve, he found they did not have the same power to excite him, and eventually he gave up altogether such intellectually fatiguing pursuits, and concentrated his powers on a determined attempt to achieve Marcus' former ambition to be the first man to run a three minute mile. He contented himself with the thought that though now his goals were less elevated than they had been previously, his actually having reached them could so much more easily be proved.

STUDY QUESTIONS

1 Suppose you are Dr. Smythson. Do you think you could get Ludwig to believe that his experiences, as he is given them from the machine, are illusory? How?

2 Once Ludwig is removed from the machine, how would you persuade him that his previous experiences were illusory?

3 "Harrison's suggestion is entertaining but not germane to the issue. The question is, 'Is Ludwig being deceived?' and the answer is clearly 'No.' In order to be deceived we must at least understand what it would be like *not* to be deceived. But Dr. Smythson's illusions are just as good as physical objects, are undetectable from physical objects, so why not call them physical objects?" Critically evaluate this argument.

4 Do you think there is anything in Ludwig's case which would suggest that the mind and the body must be distinct?

5 Could Ludwig (the mere brain) commit suicide?

Perception and Knowledge

PROBLEM INTRODUCTION

In 1610 Galileo turned the newly invented telescope toward the heavens. This proved to be his own undoing as well as that of the traditional theory of the cosmos, in which the earth was the center of the universe. Twenty-three years later, the Church would accuse him of heresy for his scientific views, and Galileo would live out his life under house arrest. But by then the damage was done and nothing could save the old system.

Aristotle had said that the heavenly bodies were incorruptible and perfect. But Galileo saw irregularities in the surface of the moon. It looked more like a mountainous desert than a perfect sphere. He discovered the moons of Jupiter and saw that not everything revolved around the earth. But the crowning blow came when he discovered that the phases of Venus could not be explained by the old system, but fit the new Copernican theory nicely. Yet if Copernicus was right, humanity's special place in the universe seemed threatened. Thus the telescope told a revolutionary story—the heavens were not perfect, human beings were not at the center of things, and, worst of all, there might be countless worlds beyond the old familiar ones.

Galileo published his work and invited the intellectual world to confirm his observations. The reaction was hostile. A certain professor of philosophy at the

University of Padua refused to look through the telescope. In mocking words he announced that logic alone could refute Galileo. Logic alone could prove that Jupiter had no moons, that the earth was the center of the universe, and therefore that Galileo had been tricked by his new "toy." As he put it:

> There are seven windows given to animals in the domicile of the head. . . . From this and many other similarities in nature, such as the seven metals, . . . we gather that the number of planets is necessarily seven. Moreover these (supposed) satellites of Jupiter are invisible to the naked eye, and therefore can exercise no influence on the earth, and therefore would be useless, and therefore do not exist. Besides (from the earliest times) men have adopted the division of the week into seven days, and named them after the seven planets. Now if we increase the number of planets, this whole and beautiful system falls to the ground.

To us this argument sounds incredible, but to many of Galileo's contemporaries it made perfectly good sense. Some things are just obviously true, and if it comes to a choice between the obvious and experience, the sober person chooses the obvious. This attitude is, of course, the death of curiosity. The professor's attitude was rooted in classical Greek philosophy, which, in its own day, represented the full flowering of the ancient mind.

In the latter half of the fifth century B.C., Greek science was developing apace. From early, vague speculations, thinkers were now beginning to construct definite physical theories to explain events which heretofore had been treated with great religious caution. One scientist had the audacity to suggest that the sun was a hot rock instead of a god. Democritus constructed an atomic theory in which he claimed that all reality was composed of tiny, unobservable atoms. The atoms possessed the qualities of size and shape, but not the familiar qualities of color, smell, hot or cold, or taste. These latter properties were subjective products of the perceiving mind, and not reliable sources of truth. To some thinkers this presented a dilemma. If the ordinary world of perception is nothing more than a subjective impression, how could anyone ever go beyond this to the hidden reality. Protagoras, a famous teacher of the age, announced that indeed completely objective knowledge is impossible. When he said "Man is the measure of all things," he certainly meant this to cover religion and ethics. This was too much for the Athenians, and in 411 Protagoras was accused of impiety and his books were ordered burned. The Athenians were in no mood to be gracious, for they were losing their long war with Sparta, and the times demanded the virtues of obedience and complete commitment. To alienate the gods at this moment meant destruction.

But the seed had been sown and nothing could have remained the same. The relativism of Protagoras struck home in an era of increasing disillusionment. In the midst of this turmoil, Plato formulated a theory designed to preserve objective knowledge. In effect, Plato agreed that the shifting impressions of sense perception could not provide a foundation for knowledge. The objective order must lie beyond the world of perception, but it must make sense of the world we perceive. Plato's model for a system of knowledge is the science of geometry. What impressed Plato about geometry is the fact that the truths discovered are not about some particular physical object, but rather are about the form which is displayed in many things. The Pythagorean theorem, for example, says that in a right triangle the sum of the squares of the two sides is equal to the square of the hypotenuse. This is not a truth about some particular right triangle, but a truth about the *idea* of right-triangularity. Nor is it a truth which is discovered by measuring various physical triangles, since clearly no physical triangle exactly fits the bill. The mind, by itself, has the power to see the *form* or the *idea* of right-triangularity which is manifested in many different physical triangles. Plato extends this way of thinking to all knowledge. The world of sense is a world of flux and change which the mind must penetrate to discover the forms or ideas which lie in a realm beyond space and time. Thus, for Plato knowledge does not come from the perceptual world, nor is it fundamentally concerned with the perceptual world. Knowledge comes from the intuitions of the mind as it sees forms or ideas manifested in the flux of sensation.

Plato's conception of knowledge is a paradigm of the theory known as *rationalism.* The rationalist attributes innate powers to the mind which make it capable of discovering the nature of things by directly intuiting reality itself, bypassing the world of appearance and sensation. The dangers in such a view should be manifest. In the mind of a sloppy thinker, it is extremely easy to confuse fantasy or authority with indubitable intuition. Thus we return to the professor who refused to look through Galileo's telescope. His attitude is Platonic to the extent that he believes that the nature of reality can be discovered by the logical mind alone, but it is a corrupted form of Platonism because his logic is a mere reflection of the biases of his era.

With the development of modern science, Plato's form of rationalism seemed inconsistent with the new experimental attitude. Experience, rather than innate mental powers, was considered the source of knowledge. This new attitude toward experience was called *empiricism.* The empirical attitude was no doubt exacerbated by the fact that "logic" always seemed to be on the side of tradition and authority. Galileo found it necessary to reintroduce Democritus's distinction between kinds of qualities which objects have. Being a physicist, he claimed that the real properties of objects were those which could be measured. Such properties as velocity, shape, size, and weight were called *primary qualities.* Qualities such as color, smell, hot and cold, taste, and sound were called *secondary,* indicating their subjective character. Thus science seemed to agree with Plato that the world of sense was mere appearance, but unlike Plato, science used the familiar experienced world as the primary source for discovering the real qualities of things.

While most scientists accepted Galileo's distinction between primary and secondary qualities, it was undermined by the empiricist tradition itself. Bishop Berkeley, an eighteenth-century empiricist, brought out the hidden dilemma. If all knowledge is based on experience, and if science is correct in saying that the familiar world of experience is quite different from the real world, then how is it possible to discover the so-called real world? Berkeley's conclusion was at once reasonable and paradoxical: The real world, the only world we can know about, is the world of experience. But the qualities we experience are mental, and thus the world is mental. Samuel Johnson tried to refute Berkeley by kicking a rock, but according to Berkeley all he succeeded in doing was to make his mental image of the rock and his mental image of his foot come together, probably causing a painful sensation as well.

Needless to say, Berkeley did not find many followers, but his unusual theory provoked a period of skepticism. This skepticism found its most able spokesman in David Hume, a gentle Scot with one of the most analytic minds in history. Hume believed that all ideas were but faint remainders of past sensations and that knowledge had to be confined to what was experienced. Thus the existence of God, the external world, and even the soul became suspect. These things could not be directly experienced and hence could not be known. Turning his gaze toward science, Hume declared that even the relation between cause and effect could not stand up under examination. We believe that between the cause and the effect there is some necessary connection, making the effect inevitable upon the occurrence of the cause. But close examination of experience shows that we never perceive such a necessary connection, and hence we are not entitled to assume that there is one. Since causal laws form the basis for predicting future events, Hume would say that we have no grounds for assuming that the future will be like the past, or that the laws which worked yesterday will work today. This part of science is prejudice, because it goes beyond what can be experienced.

Hume's radical empiricism has influenced our conception of science dramatically. Many scientists believe that only if science keeps its conclusions directly related to what can be measured and observed will any sort of secure system of knowledge arise. Thus Hume's skepticism leads directly to *practice* and the advice is this: Record the correlations between observable events and confine the system of knowledge to these observations. The advice, however, has hardly ever been consistently followed. In every area of science, the advance of knowledge depends upon theories which refer to unobservable structures and entities. In our final selection, Rom Harré, a contemporary philosopher of science, tries to show why Hume's conception of science cannot lead to knowledge. Like Plato before him, Harré maintains that the knower has the resources to go beyond appearance and penetrate into the very bowels of reality.

The Role of Perception in Knowing

Plato

Plato (c. 427 B.C.–c. 347 B.C.) came from one of the most distinguished families in Athens. He was certain to become a great politician but he gave up this
ambition in disgust at the unjust trial of Socrates, his friend and teacher. After
the execution of Socrates in 399, Plato traveled extensively, convinced that
Athens had abandoned its ancient ideals of justice. During these travels, he
wrote several dialogues on philosophy, using the character of his friend Socrates to exemplify the dialectical process of question and answer. His philosophical powers increasing, Plato returned to Athens and formed a school, the
Academy, which soon became the intellectual center of Greece. Many great
mathematicians and scientists studied at the Academy, including Aristotle.

The first selection is from "The Theatetus," a dialogue named after an
important member of the Academy who discovered solid geometry. In this
dialogue the theory of Protagoras, a skeptic who claimed that knowledge was
subjective, is examined. Socrates and Theatetus come to the conclusion that
knowledge requires an active mind, which must go beyond passive sense perception. How is it possible then? How does one go beyond the evidence of the
senses? In the second selection from *The Republic*, Plato's great masterpiece
on ethics, his answer is given. Knowledge is never concerned with physical
objects but rather with forms or ideas. These abstract objects can be known
by the power of the mind alone, but it requires great effort to penetrate the
illusions of perception. "The Allegory of the Cave" depicts the struggle to
reach the realm of ideas. This famous story exerted a major influence on early
Christian thinkers such as St. Augustine, because it seemed to correspond to
the believer's search for God.

KNOWLEDGE AS PERCEPTION

Socrates: . . . So, Theaetetus, try to explain what knowledge is. Never say it
is beyond your power; it will not be so, if heaven wills [it] and you take courage.

Theaetetus: Well, Socrates, with such encouragement from a person like you,
it would be a shame not to do one's best to say what one can. It seems to me that
one who knows something is perceiving the thing he knows, and, so far as I can
see at present, knowledge is nothing but perception.

Socrates: Good. That is the right spirit in which to express one's opinion. But
now suppose we examine your offspring together and see whether it is a mere
wind egg or has some life in it. Perception, you say, is knowledge.

Theaetetus: Yes.

Socrates: The account you give of the nature of knowledge is not, by any
means, to be despised. It is the same that was given by Protagoras though he
stated it in a somewhat different way. He says you will remember, that "man is

From "The Theatetus," in *Plato's Theory of Knowledge*, translated and with commentary by F. M.
Cornford. First published in 1935 by Routledge & Kegan Paul, Ltd. (London), and reprinted with their permission and that of Humanities Press, Inc. (New York).

the measure of all things—alike of the being of things that are and of the not-being of things that are not." No doubt you have read that.

Theaetetus: Yes often.

Socrates: He puts it in this sort of way, doesn't he, that any given thing "is to me such as it appears to me, and is to you such as it appears to you," you and I being men?

Theaetetus: Yes that is how he puts it.

Socrates: Well, what a wise man says is not likely to be nonsense. So let us follow up his meaning. Sometimes, when the same wind is blowing, one of us feels chilly, the other does not, or one may feel slightly chilly, the other quite cold.

Theaetetus: Certainly.

Socrates: Well, in that case are we to say that the wind in itself is cold or not cold? Or shall we agree with Protagoras that it is cold to the one who feels chilly, and not to the other?

Theaetetus: That seems reasonable.

Socrates: And further that it so "appears" to each of us?

Theaetetus: Yes.

Socrates: And "appears" means that he "perceives" it so?

Theaetetus: True.

Socrates: "Appearing," then, is the same thing as "perceiving," in the case of what is hot or anything of that kind. They *are* to each man such as he *perceives* them.

Theaetetus: So it seems.

Socrates: Perception, then, is always of something that *is,* and, as being knowledge, it is infallible.

Theaetetus: That is clear. . . .

Socrates: Well then, Theaetetus, here is a point for you to consider. The answer you gave was that knowledge is perception, wasn't it?

Theaetetus: Yes.

Socrates: Now suppose you were asked, When a man sees white or black things or hears high or low tones, what does he see or hear with? I suppose you would say with eyes and ears.

Theaetetus: Yes, I should.

Socrates: To use words and phrases in an easygoing way without scrutinizing them too curiously is not, in general, a mark of ill breeding; on the contrary there is something lowbred in being too precise. But sometimes there is no help for it, and this is a case in which I must take exception to the form of your answer. Consider. Is it more correct to say that we see and hear *with* our eyes and ears or *through* them?

Theaetetus: I should say we always perceive through them, rather than with them.

Socrates: Yes, it would surely be strange that there should be a number of senses ensconced inside us, like the warriors in the Trojan horse, and all these things should not converge and meet in some single nature—a mind, or whatever it is to be called—*with* which we perceive all the objects of perception *through* the senses as instruments.

Theaetetus: Yes, I think that is a better description.

Socrates: My object in being so precise is to know whether there is some part of ourselves, the same in all cases, with which we apprehend black or white through the eyes, and objects of other kinds through the other senses. Can you, if the question is put to you, refer all such acts of apprehension to the body? Perhaps, however, it would be better you should speak for yourself in reply to questions, instead of my taking the words out of your mouth. Tell me, all these instruments through which you perceive what is warm or hard or light or sweet are parts of the body, aren't they, not of anything else?

Theaetetus: Of nothing else.

Socrates: Now you will also agree that the objects you perceive through one faculty cannot be perceived through another—objects of hearing, for instance, through sight, or objects of sight through hearing?

Theaetetus: Of course I will.

Socrates: Then, if you have some thought about both objects at once, you cannot be having a perception including both at once through either the one or the other organ.

Theaetetus: No.

Socrates: Now take sound and color. Have you not, to begin with, this thought which includes both at once—that they both exist.

Theaetetus: I have.

Socrates: And, further, that each of the two is *different* from the other and the *same* as itself?

Theaetetus: Naturally.

Socrates: And again, that both together are *two,* and each of them is *one?*

Theaetetus: Yes.

Socrates: And also you can ask yourself whether they are *unlike* each other or *alike?*

Theaetetus: No doubt.

Socrates: Then through what organ do you think all this about them both? What is common to them both cannot be apprehended either through hearing or through sight. Besides, here is further evidence for my point. Suppose it were possible to inquire whether sound and color were both brackish or not; no doubt you could tell me what faculty you would use—obviously not sight or hearing, but some other.

Theaetetus: Of course, the faculty that works through the tongue.

Socrates: Very good. But now, through what organ does that faculty work, which tells you what is common not only to these objects but to all things—what you mean by the words "exists" and "does not exist" and the other terms applied to them in the questions I put a moment ago? What sort of organs can you mention, corresponding to all these terms, through which the perceiving part of us perceives each one of them?

Theaetetus: You mean existence and nonexistence, likeness and unlikeness, sameness and difference, and also unity and numbers in general as applied to them, and clearly your question covers "even" and "odd" and all that kind of notions. You are asking through what part of the body our mind perceives these?

Socrates: You follow me most admirably, Theaetetus; that is exactly my question.

Theaetetus: Really, Socrates, I could not say, except that I think there is no special organ at all for these things, as there is for the others. It is clear to me that the mind in itself is its own instrument for contemplating the common terms that apply to everything.

Socrates: In fact, Theaetetus, you are handsome, not ugly as Theodorus said you were, for in a discussion handsome is that handsome does. And you have treated me more than handsomely in saving me the trouble of a very long argument, if it is clear to you that the mind contemplates some things through its own instrumentality, others through the bodily faculties. That was indeed what I thought myself, but I wanted you to agree.

Theaetetus: Well, it is clear to me.

Socrates: Under which head, then, do you place existence? For that is, above all, a thing that belongs to everything.

Theaetetus: I should put it among the things that the mind apprehends by itself.

Socrates: And also likeness and unlikeness and sameness and difference?

Theaetetus: Yes.

Socrates: And how about "honorable" and "dishonorable" and "good" and "bad"?

Theaetetus: Those again seem to me, above all, to be things whose being is considered, one in comparison with another, by the mind, when it reflects within itself upon the past and the present with an eye to the future.

Socrates: Wait a moment. The hardness of something hard and the softness of something soft will be perceived by the mind through touch, will they not?

Theaetetus: Yes.

Socrates: But their existence and the fact that they both exist and their contrariety to one another and again the existence of this contrariety are things which the mind itself undertakes to judge for us, when it reflects upon them and compares one with another.

Theaetetus: Certainly.

Socrates: Is it not true, then, that whereas all the impressions which penetrate to the mind through the body are things which men and animals alike are naturally constituted to perceive from the moment of birth, reflections about them with respect to their existence and usefulness only come, if they come at all, with difficulty through a long and troublesome process of education?

Theaetetus: Assuredly.

Socrates: Is it possible, then, to reach truth when one cannot reach existence?

Theaetetus: It is impossible.

Socrates: But if a man cannot reach the truth of a thing, can he possibly know that thing?

Theaetetus: No, Socrates, how could he?

Socrates: If that is so, knowledge does not reside in the impressions, but in our reflection upon them. It is there, seemingly, and not in the impressions, that it is possible to grasp existence and truth.

Theaetetus: Evidently.

Socrates: Then are you going to give the same name to two things which differ so widely?

Theaetetus: Surely that would not be right.

Socrates: Well then, what name do you give to the first one—to seeing, hearing, smelling, feeling cold and feeling warm?

Theaetetus: Perceiving. What other name is there for it?

Socrates: Taking it all together, then, you call this perception?

Theaetetus: Necessarily.

Socrates: A thing which, we agree, has no part in apprehending truth, since it has none in apprehending existence.

Theaetetus: No, it has none.

Socrates: Nor, consequently, in knowledge either.

Theaetetus: No.

Socrates: Then, Theaetetus, perception and knowledge cannot possibly be the same thing.

Theaetetus: Evidently not, Socrates. Indeed, it is now perfectly plain that knowledge is something different from perception.

Socrates: But when we began our talk it was certainly not our object to find out what knowledge is not, but what it is. Still, we have advanced so far as to see that we must not look for it in sense perception at all, but in what goes on when the mind is occupied with things by itself, whatever name you give to that.

Theaetetus: Well, Socrates, the name for that, I imagine, is "making judgments."

Socrates: You are right, my friend. Now begin all over again. Blot out all we have been saying, and see if you can get a clearer view from the position you have now reached. Tell us once more what knowledge is.

Theaetetus: I cannot say it is judgment as a whole, because there is false judgment, but perhaps true judgment is knowledge. You may take that as my answer. If, as we go further, it turns out to be less convincing than it seems now, I will try to find another.

Socrates: Good, Theaetetus. This promptness is much better than hanging back as you did at first. If we go on like this, either we shall find what we are after or we shall be less inclined to imagine we know something of which we know nothing whatever, and that surely is a reward not to be despised. And now, what is this you say—that there are two sorts of judgment, one true, the other false, and you define knowledge as judgment that is true? . . .

KNOWLEDGE AS TRUE BELIEF

Theaetetus: . . . True belief is knowledge. Surely there can at least be no mistake in believing what is true, and the consequences are always satisfactory.

Socrates: Try, and you will see, Theaetetus, as the man said when he was asked if the river was too deep to ford. So here, if we go forward on our search, we may stumble upon something that will reveal the thing we are looking for. We shall make nothing out, if we stay where we are.

Theaetetus: True. Let us go forward and see.

Socrates: Well, we need not go far to see this much. You will find a whole profession to prove that true belief is not knowledge.

Theaetetus: How so? What profession?

Socrates: The profession of those paragons of intellect known as orators and lawyers. There you have men who use their skill to produce conviction, not by instruction, but by making people believe whatever they want them to believe. You can hardly imagine teachers so clever as to be able, in the short time allowed by the clock, to instruct their hearers thoroughly in the true facts of a case of robbery or other violence which those hearers had not witnessed.

Theaetetus: No, I cannot imagine that, but they can convince them.

Socrates: And by convincing you mean making them believe something.

Theaetetus: Of course.

Socrates: And when a jury is rightly convinced of facts which can be known only by an eyewitness, then, judging by heresay and accepting a true belief, they are judging without knowledge, although if they find the right verdict, their conviction is correct?

Theaetetus: Certainly.

Socrates: But if true belief and knowledge were the same thing, the best of jurymen could never have a correct belief without knowledge. It now appears that they must be different things. . . .

THE OBJECTS OF KNOWLEDGE

(Socrates is conversing with Glaucon)

. . . Let me remind you of the distinction we drew earlier and have often drawn on other occasions,[1] between the multiplicity of things that we call good or beautiful or whatever it may be and, on the other hand, Goodness itself or Beauty itself and so on. Corresponding to each of these sets of many things, we postulate a single Form or real essence, as we call it.

Yes, that is so.

Further, the many things, we say, can be seen, but are not objects of rational thought; whereas the Forms are objects of thought, but invisible.

Yes, certainly.

And we see things with our eyesight, just as we hear sounds with our ears and, to speak generally, perceive any sensible thing with our sense-faculties.

Of course.

Have you noticed, then, that the artificer who designed the senses has been exceptionally lavish of his materials in making the eyes able to see and their objects visible?

That never occurred to me.

Well, look at it in this way. Hearing and sound do not stand in need of any

From Plato's *The Republic*, translated by F. M. Cornford. Published in 1941 by Oxford University Press and reprinted with the permission of Clarendon Press of Oxford England.

[1] Perhaps an allusion to the *Phaedo* (especially 78 E ff.), where the theory of Forms was first explicitly stated in similar terms. The earlier passage in the *Republic* is at 475 E ff., p. 179.

third thing, without which the ear will not hear nor sound be heard;[2] and I think the same is true of most, not to say all, of the other senses. Can you think of one that does require anything of the sort?

No, I cannot.

But there is this need in the case of sight and its objects. You may have the power of vision in your eyes and try to use it, and color may be there in the objects; but sight will see nothing and the colors will remain invisible in the absence of a third thing peculiarly constituted to serve this very purpose.

By which you mean—?

Naturally I mean what you call light; and if light is a thing of value, the sense of sight and the power of being visible are linked together by a very precious bond, such as unites no other sense with its object.

No one could say that light is not a precious thing.

And of all the divinities in the skies [3] is there one whose light, above all the rest, is responsible for making our eyes see perfectly and making objects perfectly visible?

There can be no two opinions: of course you mean the Sun.

And how is sight related to this deity? Neither sight nor the eye which contains it is the sun, but of all the sense-organs it is the most sun-like; and further, the power it possesses is dispensed by the Sun, like a stream flooding the eye.[4] And again, the Sun is not vision, but it is the cause of vision and also is seen by the vision it causes.

Yes.

It was the Sun, then, that I meant when I spoke of that offspring which the Good has created in the visible world, to stand there in the same relation to vision and visible things as that which the Good itself bears in the intelligible world to intelligence and to intelligible objects.

How is that? You must explain further.

You know what happens when the colors of things are no longer irradiated by the daylight, but only by the fainter luminaries of the night: when you look at them, the eyes are dim and seem almost blind, as if there were no unclouded vision in them. But when you look at things on which the Sun is shining, the same eyes see distinctly and it becomes evident that they do contain the power of vision.

Certainly.

Apply this comparison, then, to the soul. When its gaze is fixed upon an object irradiated by truth and reality, the soul gains understanding and knowledge and is manifestly in possession of intelligence. But when it looks towards

---

[2] Plato held that the hearing of sound is caused by blows inflicted by the air (*Timaeus* 67 B, 80 A); but the air is hardly analogous to light.

[3] Plato held that the heavenly bodies are immortal living creatures, i.e. gods.

[4] Plato's theory of vision involves three kinds of fire or light: (1) daylight, a body of pure fire diffused in the air by the Sun; (2) the visual current or "vision," a pure fire similar to daylight, contained in the eyeball and capable of issuing out in a stream direct towards the object seen; (3) the colour of the external object, "a flame streaming off from every body, having particles proportioned to those of the visual current, so as to yield sensation" when the two streams meet and coalesce (*Timaeus* 45 B, 67 C).

that twilight world of things that come into existence and pass away, its sight is dim and it has only opinions and beliefs which shift to and fro, and it seems like a thing that has no intelligence.

That is true.

This, then, which gives to the objects of knowledge their truth and to him who knows them his power of knowing, is the Form or essential nature of Goodness. It is the cause of knowledge and truth; and so, while you may think of it as an object of knowledge, you will do well to regard it as something beyond truth and knowledge and, precious as these both are, of still higher worth. And, just as in our analogy light and vision were to be thought of as like the Sun, but not identical with it, so here both knowledge and truth are to be regarded as like the Good, but to identify either with the Good is wrong. The Good must hold a yet higher place of honor.

You are giving it a position of extraordinary splendour, if it is the source of knowledge and truth and itself surpasses them in worth. You surely cannot mean that it is pleasure.

Heaven forbid, I exclaimed. But I want to follow up our analogy still further. You will agree that the Sun not only makes the things we see visible, but also brings them into existence and gives them growth and nourishment; yet he is not the same thing as existence.[5] And so with the objects of knowledge: these derive from the Good not only their power of being known, but their very being and reality; and Goodness is not the same thing as being, but even beyond being, surpassing it is dignity and power.

Glaucon exclaimed with some amusement at my exalting Goodness in such extravagant terms.

It is your fault, I replied; you forced me to say what I think.

Yes, and you must stop there. At any rate, complete your comparison with the Sun, if there is any more to be said.

There is a great deal more, I answered.

Let us hear it, then; don't leave anything out.

I am afraid much must be left unspoken. However, I will not, if I can help it, leave anything that can be said on this occasion.

Please do not.

FOUR STAGES OF COGNITION. THE LINE

Conceive, then, that there are these two powers I speak of, the Good reigning over the domain of all that is intelligible, the Sun over the visible world—or the heaven as I might call it; only you would think I was showing off my skill in etymology.[6] At any rate you have these two orders of things clearly before your mind: the visible and the intelligible?

I have.

[5] The ambiguity of *genesis* can hardly be reproduced. The Sun "gives things their *genesis*" (generation, birth), but "is not itself *genesis*" (becoming, the existence in time of things which begin and cease to exist, as opposed to the real being of eternal things in the intelligible world).

[6] Some connected the word for heaven . . . with [the word meaning] "to see" (*Cratylus*, 396 B). It is sometimes used for the whole of the visible universe.

Now take a line divided into two unequal parts, one to represent the visible order, the other the intelligible; and divide each part again in the same proportion, symbolizing degrees of comparative clearness or obscurity. Then (A) one of the two sections in the visible world will stand for images. By images I mean first shadows, and then reflections in water or in close-grained, polished surfaces, and everything of that kind, if you understand.

Yes, I understand.

Let the second section (B) stand for the actual things of which the first are likenesses, the living creatures about us and all the works of nature or of human hands.

So be it.

Will you also take the proportion in which the visible world has been divided as corresponding to degrees of reality and truth, so that the likeness shall stand to the original in the same ratio as the sphere of appearances and belief to the sphere of knowledge?

Certainly.

Now consider how we are to divide the part which stands for the intelligible world. There are two sections. In the first (C) the mind uses as images those actual things which themselves had images in the visible world; and it is compelled to pursue its inquiry by starting from assumptions and travelling, not up to a principle, but down to a conclusion. In the second (D) the mind moves in the other direction, from an assumption up towards a principle which is not hypothetical; and it makes no use of the images employed in the other section, but only of Forms, and conducts its inquiry solely by their means.

I don't quite understand what you mean.

Then we will try again; what I have just said will help you to understand. (C) You know, of course, how students of subjects like geometry and arithmetic begin by postulating odd and even numbers, or the various figures and the three kinds of angle, and other such data in each subject. These data they take as known; and, having adopted them as assumptions, they do not feel called upon to give any account of them to themselves or to anyone else, but treat them as self-evident. Then, starting from these assumptions, they go on until they arrive, by a series of consistent steps, at all the conclusions they set out to investigate.

Yes, I know that.

You also know how they make use of visible figures and discourse about them, though what they really have in mind is the originals of which these figures are images: they are not reasoning, for instance, about this particular square and diagonal which they have drawn, but about *the* Square and *the* Diagonal; and so in all cases. The diagrams they draw and the models they make are actual things, which may have their shadows or images in water; but now they serve in their turn as images, while the student is seeking to behold those realities which only thought can apprehend.[7]

True.

---

[7] Conversely, the fact that the mathematician can use visible objects as illustrations indicates that the realities and truths of mathematics are embodied, though imperfectly, in the world of visible and tangible things; whereas the counterparts of the moral Forms can only be beheld by thought.

This, then, is the class of things that I spoke of as intelligible, but with two qualifications: first, that the mind, in studying them, is compelled to employ assumptions, and, because it cannot rise above these, does not travel upwards to a first principle; and second, that it uses as images those actual things which have images of their own in the section below them and which, in comparison with those shadows and reflections, are reputed to be more palpable and valued accordingly.

I understand: you mean the procedure of geometry and of the kindred arts.

(D) Then by the second section of the intelligible world you may understand me to mean all that unaided reasoning apprehends by the power of dialectic, when it treats its assumptions, not as first principles, but as *hypotheses* in the literal sense, things "laid down" like a flight of steps up which it may mount all the way to something that is not hypothetical, the first principle of all; and having grasped this, may turn back and, holding on to the consequences which depend upon it, descend at last to a conclusion, never making use of any sensible object, but only of Forms, moving through Forms from one to another and ending with Forms.

I understand, he said, though not perfectly; for the procedure you describe sounds like an enormous undertaking. But I see that you mean to distinguish the field of intelligible reality studied by dialectic as having a greater certainty and truth than the subject-matter of the "arts," as they are called, which treat their assumptions as first principles. The students of these arts are, it is true, compelled to exercise thought in contemplating objects which the senses cannot perceive; but because they start from assumptions without going back to a first principle, you do not regard them as gaining true understanding about those objects, although the objects themselves, when connected with a first principle, are intelligible. And I think you would call the state of mind of the students of geometry and other such arts, not intelligence, but thinking, as being something between intelligence and mere acceptance of appearances.

You have understood me quite well enough, I replied. And now you may take, as corresponding to the four sections, these four states of mind: *intelligence* for the highest, *thinking* for the second, *belief* for the third, and for the last *imagining.*[8] These you may arrange as the terms in a proportion, assigning to each a degree of clearness and certainty corresponding to the measure in which their objects possess truth and reality.

I understand and agree with you. I will arrange them as you say.

THE ALLEGORY OF THE CAVE

Next, said I, here is a parable to illustrate the degrees in which our nature may be enlightened or unenlightened. Imagine the condition of men living in a sort of cavernous chamber underground, with an entrance open to the light and a long passage all down the cave.[9] Here they have been from childhood, chained by the

[8] Plato never uses hard and fast technical terms. The four here proposed are not defined or strictly employed in the sequel.

[9] The *length* of the "way in" . . . to the chamber where the prisoners sit is an essential feature,

leg and also by the neck, so that they cannot move and can see only what is in front of them, because the chains will not let them turn their heads. At some distance higher up is the light of a fire burning behind them; and between the prisoners and the fire is a track[10] with a parapet built along it, like the screen at a puppet-show, which hides the performers while they show their puppets over the top.

I see, said he.

Now behind this parapet imagine persons carrying along various artificial objects, including figures of men and animals in wood or stone or other materials, which project above the parapet. Naturally, some of these persons will be talking, others silent.[11]

It is a strange picture, he said, and a strange sort of prisoners.

Like ourselves, I replied; for in the first place prisoners so confined would have seen nothing of themselves or of one another, except the shadows thrown by the fire-light on the wall of the Cave facing them, would they?

Not if all their lives they had been prevented from moving their heads.

And they would have seen as little of the objects carried past.

Of course.

Now, if they could talk to one another, would they not suppose that their words referred only to those passing shadows which they saw? [12]

Necessarily.

And suppose their prison had an echo from the wall facing them? When one of the people crossing behind them spoke, they could only suppose that the sound came from the shadow passing before their eyes.

No doubt.

In every way, then, such prisoners would recognize as reality nothing but the shadows of those artificial objects.[13]

Inevitably.

Now consider what would happen if their release from the chains and the healing of their unwisdom should come about in this way. Suppose one of them was set free and forced suddenly to stand up, turn his head, and walk with eyes lifted to the light; all these movements would be painful, and he would be too dazzled to make out the objects whose shadows he had been used to see. What do you think he would say, if someone told him that what he had formerly seen was

---

explaining why no daylight reaches them.

[10] The track crosses the passage into the cave at right angles, and is *above* the parapet built along it.

[11] A modern Plato would compare his Cave to an underground cinema, where the audience watch the play of shadows thrown by the film passing before a light at their backs. The film itself is only an image of "real" things and events in the world outside the cinema. For the film Plato has to substitute the clumsier apparatus of a procession of artificial objects carried on their heads by persons who are merely part of the machinery, providing for the movement of the objects and the sounds whose echo the prisoners hear. The parapet prevents these persons's shadows from being cast on the wall of the Cave.

[12] Adam's text and interpretation. The prisoners, having seen nothing but shadows, cannot think their words refer to the objects carried past behind their backs. For them shadows (images) are the only realities.

[13] The state of mind called *eikasia* in the previous chapter.

meaningless illusion, but now, being somewhat nearer to reality and turned towards more real objects, he was getting a truer view? Suppose further that he
were shown the various objects being carried by and were made to say, in reply
to questions, what each of them was. Would he not be perplexed and believe the
objects now shown him to be not so real as what he formerly saw? [14]

Yes, not nearly so real.

And if he were forced to look at the fire-light itself, would not his eyes ache,
so that he would try to escape and turn back to the things which he could see
distinctly, convinced that they really were clearer than these other objects now
being shown to him?

Yes.

And suppose someone were to drag him away forcibly up the steep and
rugged ascent and not let him go until he had hauled him out into the sunlight,
would he not suffer pain and vexation at such treatment, and, when he had come
out into the light, find his eyes so full of its radiance that he could not see a single
one of the things that he was now told were real?

Certainly he would not see them all at once.

He would need, then, to grow accustomed before he could see things in that
upper world.[15] At first it would be easiest to make out shadows, and then images
of men and things reflected in water, and later on the things themselves. After
that, it would be easier to watch the heavenly bodies and the sky itself by night,
looking at the light of the moon and stars rather than the Sun and the Sun's light
in the day-time.

Yes, surely.

Last of all, he would be able to look at the Sun and contemplate its nature,
not as it appears when reflected in water or any alien medium, but as it is in itself
in its own domain.

No doubt.

And now he would begin to draw the conclusion that it is the Sun that
produces the seasons and the course of the year and controls everything in the
visible world, and moreover is in a way the cause of all that he and his companions used to see.

Clearly he would come at last to that conclusion.

Then if he called to mind his fellow prisoners and what passed for wisdom in
his former dwelling-place, he would surely think himself happy in the change and
be sorry for them. They may have had a practice of honoring and commending
one another, with prizes for the man who had the keenest eye for the passing
shadows and the best memory for the order in which they followed or accompanied one another, so that he could make a good guess as to which was going to
come next.[16] Would our released prisoner be likely to covet those prizes or to
envy the men exalted to honor and power in the Cave? Would he not feel like

[14] The first effect of Socratic questioning is perplexity. . . .

[15] Here is the moral—the need of habituation by mathematical study before discussing moral
ideas and ascending through them to the Form of the Good.

[16] The empirical politician, with no philosophic insight, but only a "knack of remembering
what usually happens" (*Gorg.* 501 A). He has *eikasia* = conjecture as to what is likely. . . .

Homer's Achilles, that he would far sooner "be on earth as a hired servant in the house of a landless man" [17] or endure anything rather than go back to his old beliefs and live in the old way?

Yes, he would prefer any fate to such a life.

Now imagine what would happen if he went down again to take his former seat in the Cave. Coming suddenly out of the sunlight, his eyes would be filled with darkness. He might be required once more to deliver his opinion on those shadows, in competition with the prisoners who had never been released, while his eyesight was still dim and unsteady; and it might take sometime to become used to the darkness. They would laugh at him and say that he had gone up only to come back with his sight ruined; it was worth no one's while even to attempt the ascent. If they could lay hands on the man who was trying to set them free and lead them up, they would kill him.[18]

Yes, they would.

Every feature in this parable, my dear Glaucon, is meant to fit our earlier analysis. The prison dwelling corresponds to the region revealed to us through the sense of sight, and the fire-light within it to the power of the Sun. The ascent to see the things in the upper world you may take as standing for the upward journey of the soul into the region of the intelligible; then you will be in possession of what I surmise, since that is what you wish to be told. Heaven knows whether it is true; but this, at any rate, is how it appears to me. In the world of knowledge, the last thing to be perceived and only with great difficulty is the essential Form of Goodness. Once it is perceived, the conclusion must follow that, for all things, this is the cause of whatever is right and good; in the visible world it gives birth to light and to the lord of light, while it is itself sovereign in the intelligible world and the parent of intelligence and truth. Without having had a vision of this Form no one can act with wisdom, either in his own life or in matters of state.

So far as I can understand, I share your belief.

Then you may also agree that it is no wonder if those who have reached this height are reluctant to manage the affairs of men. Their souls long to spend all their time in that upper world—naturally enough, if here once more our parable holds true. Nor, again, is it all strange that one who comes from the contemplation of divine things to the miseries of human life should appear awkward and ridiculous when, with eyes still dazed and not yet accustomed to the darkness, he is compelled, in a law-court or elsewhere, to dispute about the shadows of justice or the images that cast those shadows, and to wrangle over the notions of what is right in the minds of men who have never beheld Justice itself.[19]

It is not at all strange.

No; a sensible man will remember that the eyes may be confused in two

---

[17] This verse . . . being spoken by the ghost of Achilles, suggests that the Cave is comparable with Hades.

[18] An allusion to the fate of Socrates.

[19] In the *Gorgias* 486 A, Callicles, forecasting the trial of Socrates, taunts him with the philosopher's inability to defend himself in a court.

ways—by a change from light to darkness or from darkness to light; and he will recognize that the same thing happens to the soul. When he sees it troubled and unable to discern anything clearly, instead of laughing thoughtlessly, he will ask whether, coming from a brighter existence, its unaccustomed vision is obscured by the darkness, in which case he will think its condition enviable and its life a happy one; or whether, emerging from the depths of ignorance, it is dazzled by excess of light. If so, he will rather feel sorry for it; or, if he were inclined to laugh, that would be less ridiculous than to laugh at the soul which has come down from the light.

That is a fair statement.

If this is true, then, we must conclude that education is not what it is said to be by some, who profess to put knowledge into a soul which does not possess it, as if they could put sight into blind eyes. On the contrary, our own account signifies that the soul of every man does possess the power of learning the truth and the organ to see it with; and that, just as one might have to turn the whole body round in order that the eye should see light instead of darkness, so the entire soul must be turned away from this changing world, until its eye can bear to contemplate reality and that supreme splendor which we have called the Good. Hence there may well be an art whose aim would be to effect this very thing, the conversion of the soul, in the readiest way; not to put the power of sight into the soul's eye, which already has it, but to ensure that, instead of looking in the wrong direction, it is turned the way it ought to be.

Yes it may well be so.

It looks, then, as though wisdom were different from those ordinary virtues, as they are called, which are not far removed from bodily qualities, in that they can be produced by habituation and exercise in a soul which has not possessed them from the first. Wisdom, it seems, is certainly the virtue of some diviner faculty, which never loses its power, though its use for good or harm depends on the direction towards which it is turned. You must have noticed in dishonest men with a reputation for sagacity the shrewd glance of a narrow intelligence piercing the objects to which it is directed. There is nothing wrong with their power of vision, but it has been forced into the service of evil, so that the keener its sight, the more harm it works.

STUDY QUESTIONS

1   Socrates distinguishes between seeing "with" the eyes and "through" the eyes. What is he trying to explain? What do you think perception would be like if this distinction were not made?

2   Through what organ does Theatetus say we perceive "sameness," "difference," "existence," etc.? Why can these things not be sensed in the usual way? Do you think Descartes would agree with Plato on this point?

3   Plato's doctrine is often called a *theory of innate ideas.* Briefly, such a theory would hold that we are born with certain concepts, such as "sameness," and we do not acquire them from experience. To what extent do you agree with this? Can you think of experiments which would test this theory?

4   In the selection from *The Republic,* Plato says that the many things which are sensed

are not the objects of rational thought. What are the objects of thought, then? Can anything in the *Theatetus* help explain this?

5   In the section on the stages of cognition, Plato divides the intelligible world into two parts. He uses geometry to explain the kind of thinking that occurs in the first division (C). Can you explain the difference between this sort of thinking and that which occurs in the second division (D)? Can you think of any analogies which might bring out the difference?

Perception and Matter

George Berkeley

George Berkeley (1685–1753) was the first great philosopher to visit America. He and his wife lived in Rhode Island for three years, hoping to establish a college in Bermuda. But the money for this project never arrived from England, and, after the death of their baby daughter, the Berkeleys returned to Ireland. Because of a poem he wrote, however, Berkeley was honored by the New World—a small California town was named after him.

Berkeley was an Anglican bishop, who believed that materialism was the foundation of atheism. His new philosophy of "immaterialism" was designed to show that matter does not exist and that reality is fundamentally spiritual. Following John Locke, he claimed that we never perceive anything but our own ideas. Matter cannot be the cause of our ideas because the concept of "material substance" is meaningless. Here Berkeley uses the fundamental tenet of empiricism—that all our ideas come from perception—to demonstrate that the only things which can exist are mental. He summed it up in the phrase *Esse est percipi:* To be is to be perceived.

One day after church, Samuel Johnson, the great literary critic of the age, was asked his opinion of this new doctrine of immaterialism. He is reported to have kicked a large rock, saying, "I refute it thus." After reading the following selection, you may decide for yourself whether Johnson's common sense prevails.

Hylas: You were represented in last night's conversation, as one who maintained the most extravagant opinion that ever entered into the mind of man, to wit, that there is no such thing as *material substance* in the world.

Philonous: That there is no such thing as what Philosophers call *material substance,* I am seriously persuaded: but, if I were made to see anything absurd or sceptical in this, I should then have the same reason to renounce this that I imagine I have now to reject the contrary opinion.

Hylas: What! can anything be more fantastical, more repugnant to common sense, or a more manifest piece of Scepticism, than to believe there is no such thing as *matter?*

Philonous: Softly, good Hylas. What if it should prove, that you, who hold there is, are, by virtue of that opinion, a greater sceptic, and maintain more paradoxes and repugnances to common sense, than I who believe no such thing?

From *Three Dialogues between Hylas and Philonous,* 1713, by George Berkeley. First Dialogue.

Hylas: You may as soon persuade me, the part is greater than the whole, as that, in order to avoid absurdity and Scepticism, I should ever be obliged to give up my opinion in this point.

Philonous: Well then, are you content to admit that opinion for true, which, upon examination, shall appear most agreeable to common sense, and remote from Scepticism?

Hylas: With all my heart. Since you are for raising disputes about the plainest things in nature, I am content for once to hear what you have to say.

Philonous: Pray, *Hylas,* what do you mean by a *sceptic?*

Hylas: I mean what all men mean, one that doubts of everything.

Philonous: He then who entertains no doubt concerning some particular point, with regard to that point cannot be thought a sceptic.

Hylas: I agree with you.

Philonous: Whether doth doubting consist in embracing the affirmative or negative side of a question?

Hylas: In neither; for whoever understands English cannot but know that *doubting* signifies a suspense between both.

Philonous: He then that denieth any point, can no more be said to doubt of it, than he who affirmeth it with the same degree or assurance.

Hylas: True.

Philonous: And, consequently, for such his denial is no more to be esteemed a sceptic than the other.

Hylas: I acknowledge it.

Philonous: How cometh it to pass then, *Hylas,* that you pronounce me a *sceptic,* because I deny what you affirm, to wit, the existence of Matter? Since, for aught you can tell, I am as peremptory in my denial, as you in your affirmation.

Hylas: Hold, *Philonous,* I have been a little out in my definition; but every false step a man makes in discourse is not to be insisted on. I said indeed that a *sceptic* was one who doubted of everything; but I should have added, or who denies the reality and truth of things.

Philonous: What things? Do you mean the principles and theorems of sciences? But these you know are universal intellectual notions, and consequently independent of Matter; the denial therefore of this doth not imply the denying them.

Hylas: I grant it. But are there no other things? What think you of distrusting the senses, of denying the real existence of sensible things, or pretending to know nothing of them. Is not this sufficient to denominate a man a *sceptic?*

Hylas: That is what I desire.

Philonous: What mean you by Sensible Things?

Hylas: Those things which are perceived by the senses. Can you imagine that I mean anything else?

Philonous: Pardon me, Hylas, if I am desirous clearly to apprehend your notions, since this may much shorten our inquiry. Suffer me then to ask you this farther question. Are those things only perceived by the senses which are perceived immediately? Or, may those things properly be said to be *sensible* which are perceived mediately, or not without the intervention of others?

Hylas: I do not sufficiently understand you.

Philonous: In reading a book, what I immediately perceive are the letters, but mediately, or by means of these, are suggested to my mind the notions of God, virtue, truth, &c. Now, that the letters are truly sensible things, or perceived by sense, there is no doubt: but I would know whether you take the things suggested by them to be so too.

Hylas: No certainly; it were absurd to think God or *virtue* sensible things, though they may be signified and suggested to the mind by sensible marks, with which they have an arbitrary connexion.

Philonous: It seems then, that by *sensible things* you mean those only which can be perceived *immediately* by sense?

Hylas: Right.

Philonous: Doth it not follow from this, that though I see one part of the sky red, and another blue, and that my reason doth thence evidently conclude there must be some cause of that diversity of colours, yet that cause cannot be said to be a sensible thing, or perceived by the sense of seeing?

Hylas: It doth.

Philonous: In like manner, though I hear variety of sounds, yet I cannot be said to hear the causes of those sounds?

Hylas: You cannot.

Philonous: And when by my touch I perceive a thing to be hot and heavy, I cannot say, with any truth or propriety, that I feel the cause of its heat or weight?

Hylas: To prevent any more questions of this kind, I tell you once for all, that by *sensible things* I mean those only which are perceived by sense, and that in truth the senses perceive nothing which they do not perceive immediately: for they make no inferences. The deducing therefore of causes or occasions from effects and appearances, which alone are perceived by sense, entirely relates to reason.

Philonous: This point then is agreed between us—that *sensible things are those only which are immediately perceived by sense.* You will farther inform me, whether we immediately perceive by sight anything beside light, and colours, and figures; or by hearing, anything but sounds; by the palate, anything besides tastes; by the smell, beside odours; or by the touch, more than tangible qualities.

Hylas: We do not.

Philonous: It seems, therefore, that if you take away all sensible qualities, there remains nothing sensible?

Hylas: I grant it.

Philonous: Sensible things therefore are nothing else but so many sensible qualities, or combinations of sensible qualities?

Hylas: Nothing else.

Philonous: Heat is then a sensible thing?

Hylas: Certainly.

Philonous: Doth the reality of sensible things consist in being perceived? or, is it something distinct from their being perceived, and that bears no relation to the mind?

Hylas: To *exist* is one thing, and to be *perceived* is another.

Philonous: I speak with regard to sensible things only: and of these I ask, whether by their real existence you mean a subsistence exterior to the mind, and distinct from their being perceived?

Hylas: I mean a real absolute being, distinct from, and without any relation to their being perceived.

Philonous: Heat therefore, if it be allowed a real being, must exist without the mind?

Hylas: It must.

Philonous: Tell me, Hylas, is real existence equally compatible to all degrees of heat, which we perceive; or is there any reason why we should attribute it to some, and deny it to others? and if there be, pray let me know that reason.

Hylas: Whatever degree of heat we perceive by sense, we may be sure the same exists in the object that occasions it.

Philonous: What! the greatest as well as the least?

Hylas: I tell you, the reason is plainly the same in respect of both: they are both perceived by sense; nay, the greater degree of heat is more sensibly perceived; and consequently, if there is any difference, we are more certain of its real existence than we can be of the reality of a lesser degree.

Philonous: But is not the most vehement and intense degree of heat a very great pain?

Hylas: No one can deny it.

Philonous: And is any unperceiving thing capable of pain or pleasure?

Hylas: No certainly.

Philonous: Is your material substance a senseless being, or a being endowed with sense and perception?

Hylas: It is senseless without doubt.

Philonous: It cannot therefore be the subject of pain?

Hylas: By no means.

Philonous: Nor consequently of the greatest heat perceived by sense, since you acknowledge this to be no small pain?

Hylas: I grant it.

Philonous: What shall we say then of your external object; is it a material substance, or no?

Hylas: It is a material substance with the sensible qualities inhering in it.

Philonous: How then can a great heat exist in it, since you own it cannot in a material substance? I desire you would clear this point.

Hylas: Hold, *Philonous,* I fear I was out in yielding intense heat to be a pain. It should seem rather, that pain is something distinct from heat, and the consequences or effect of it.

Philonous: Upon putting your hand near the fire, do you perceive one simple uniform sensation, or two distinct sensations?

Hylas: But one simple sensation.

Philonous: Is not the heat immediately perceived?

Hylas: It is.

Philonous: And the pain?

Hylas: True.

Philonous: Seeing therefore they are both immediately perceived at the same time, and the fire affects you only with one simple, or uncompounded idea, it follows that this same simple idea is both the intense heat immediately perceived, and the pain; and, consequently, that the intense heat immediately perceived, is nothing distinct from a particular sort of pain.

Hylas: It seems so.

Philonous: Again, try in your thought, Hylas, if you can conceive a vehement sensation to be without pain or pleasure.

Hylas: I cannot.

Philonous: Or can you frame to yourself an idea of sensible pain or pleasure, in general, abstracted from every particular idea of heat, cold, tastes, smells? &c.

Hylas: I do not find that I can.

Philonous: Doth it not therefore follow, that sensible pain is nothing distinct from those sensations or ideas,—in an intense degree?

Hylas: It is undeniable; and, to speak the truth, I begin to suspect a very great heat cannot exist but in a mind perceiving it.

Philonous: What! are you then in that *sceptical* state of suspense, between affirming and denying? . . .

Hylas: But, after all, can anything be more absurd than to say, *there is no heat in the fire?*

Philonous: To make the point still clearer; tell me whether, in two cases exactly alike, we ought not to make the same judgment?

Hylas: We ought.

Philonous: When a pin pricks your finger, doth it not rend and divide the fibres of your flesh?

Hylas: It doth.

Philonous: And when a coal burns your finger, doth it any more?

Hylas: It doth not.

Philonous: Since, therefore, you neither judge the sensation itself occasioned by the pin, nor anything like it to be in the pin; you should not, conformably to what you have now granted, judge the sensation occasioned by the fire, or anything like it, to be in the fire.

Hylas: Well, since it must be so, I am content to yield this point, and acknowledge that heat and cold are only sensations existing in our minds. But there still remain qualities enough to secure the reality of external things. . . .

Philonous: The objects you speak of are, I suppose, corporeal substances existing without the mind.

Hylas: They are.

Philonous: And have true and real colours inhering in them?

Hylas: Each visible object hath that colour which we see in it.

Philonous: How! Is there any thing visible but what we perceive by sight?

Hylas: There is not.

Philonous: And do we perceive anything by sense, which we do not perceive immediately?

Hylas: How often must I be obliged to repeat the same thing? I tell you, we do not.

Philonous: Have patience, good Hylas; and tell me once more, whether there is any thing immediately perceived by the senses, except sensible qualities. I know you asserted there was not: but I would now be informed, whether you still persist in the same opinion.

Hylas: I do.

Philonous: Pray, is your corporeal substance either a sensible quality, or made up of sensible qualities?

Hylas: What a question that is! who ever thought it was?

Philonous: My reason for asking was, because in saying, *each visible object hath colour which we see in it,* you make visible objects to be corporeal substances; which implies either that corporeal substances are sensible qualities, or else that there is something beside sensible qualities perceived by sight: but as this point was formerly agreed between us, and is still maintained by you, it is a clear consequence, that your corporeal substance is nothing distinct from sensible qualities.

Hylas: You may draw as many absurd consequences as you please, and endeavour to perplex the plainest things; but you shall never persuade me out of my senses. I clearly understand my own meaning.

Philonous: I wish you would make me understand it too. But since you are unwilling to have your notion of corporeal substance examined, I shall urge that point no farther. Only be pleased to let me know, whether the same colours which we see, exist in external bodies, or some other.

Hylas: The very same.

Philonous: What! are then the beautiful red and purple we see on yonder clouds, really in them? Or do you imagine they have in themselves any other form, than that of a dark mist or vapour?

Hylas: I must own, Philonous, those colours are not really in the clouds as they seem to be at this distance. They are only apparent colours.

Philonous: Apparent call you them? how shall we distinguish these apparent colours from real?

Hylas: Very easily. Those are to be thought apparent, which appearing only at a distance, vanish upon a nearer approach.

Philonous: And those I suppose are to be thought real, which are discovered by the most near and exact survey.

Hylas: Right.

Philonous: Is the nearest and exactest survey made by the help of a microscope, or by the naked eye?

Hylas: By a microscope, doubtless.

Philonous: But a microscope often discovers colours in an object different from those perceived by the unassisted sight. And in case we had microscopes magnifying to any assigned degree; it is certain, that no object whatsoever viewed through them, would appear in the same colour which it exhibits to the naked eye.

Hylas: And what will you conclude from all this? You cannot argue that

there are really and naturally no colours on objects: because by artificial man-
agements they may be altered, or made to vanish.

Philonous: I think it may evidently be concluded from your own concessions,
that all the colours we see with our naked eyes, are only apparent as those on the
clouds, since they vanish upon a more close and accurate inspection, which is
afforded us by a microscope. Then as to what you say by way of prevention: I
ask you, whether the real and natural state of an object is better discovered by a
very sharp and piercing sight, or by one which is less sharp?

Hylas: By the former without doubt.

Philonous: Is it not plain from *dioptrics,* that microscopes make the sight
more penetrating, and represent objects as they would appear to the eye, in case
it were naturally endowed with a most exquisite sharpness?

Hylas: It is.

Philonous: Consequently the microscopical representation is to be thought
that which best sets forth the real nature of the thing, or what it is in itself. The
colours therefore by it perceived, are more genuine and real, than those perceived
otherwise.

Hylas: I confess there is something in what you say.

Philonous: Besides, it is not only possible but manifest, that there actually are
animals, whose eyes are by Nature framed to perceive those things, which by
reason of their minuteness escape our sight. What think you of those inconceiv-
ably small animals perceived by glasses? Must we suppose they are all stark
blind? Or, in case they see, can it be imagined their sight hath not the same use
in preserving their bodies from injuries, which appears in that of all other animals? And if it hath, is it not evident, they must see particles less than their own
bodies, which will present them with a far different view in each object, from that
which strikes our senses? Even our own eyes do not always represent objects to us
after the same manner. In the *jaundice,* every one knows that all things seem
yellow. Is it not therefore highly probable, those animals in whose eyes we discern a very different texture from that of ours, and whose bodies abound with
different humours, do not see the same colours in every object that we do? From
all which, should it not seem to follow, that all colours are equally apparent, and
that none of those which we perceive are really inherent in any outward object?

Hylas: It should.

Philonous: The point will be past all doubt, if you consider, that in case
colours were real properties or affections inherent in external bodies, they could
admit of no alteration, without some change wrought in the very bodies themselves: but is it not evident from what hath been said, that upon the use of
microscopes, upon a change happening in the humours of the eye, or a variation
of distance, without any manner of real alteration in the thing itself, the colours
of any object are either changed, or totally disappear? Nay all other circumstances remaining the same, change but the situation of some objects, and they
shall present different colours to the eye. The same thing happens upon viewing
an object in various degrees of light. And what is more known, than that the same
bodies appear differently coloured by candle-light, from what they do in the open
day? Add to these the experiment of a prism, which separating the heterogeneous

rays of light, alters the colour of any object; and will cause the whitest to appear of a deep blue or red to the naked eye. And now tell me, whether you are still of opinion, that every body hath its true real colour inhering in it; and if you think it hath, I would fain know farther from you, what certain distance and position of the object, what peculiar texture and formation of the eye, what degree or kind of light is necessary for ascertaining that true colour, and distinguishing it from apparent ones.

Hylas: I own myself entirely satisfied, that they are all equally apparent; and that there is no such thing as colour really inhering in external bodies, but that it is altogether in the light. And what confirms me in this opinion is, that in proportion to the light, colours are still more or less vivid; and if there be no light, then are there no colours perceived. Besides, allowing there are colours on external objects, yet how is it possible for us to perceive them? For no external body affects the mind, unless it act first on our organs of sense. But the only action of bodies is motion; and motion cannot be communicated otherwise than by impulse. A distant object therefore cannot act on the eye, nor consequently make itself or its properties perceivable to the soul. Whence it plainly follows, that it is immediately some contiguous substance, which operating on the eye occasions a perception of colours: and such is light.

Philonous: How! is light then a substance?

Hylas: I tell you, Philonous, external light is nothing but a thin fluid substance, whose minute particles being agitated with a brisk motion, and in various manners reflected from the different surfaces of outward objects to the eyes, communicate different motions to the optic nerves; which being propagated to the brain, cause therein various impressions: and these are attended with the sensations of red, blue, yellow, &c.

Philonous: It seems then, the light doth no more than shake the optic nerves.

Hylas: Nothing else.

Philonous: And consequent to each particular motion of the nerves the mind is affected with a sensation, which is some particular colour.

Hylas: Right.

Philonous: And these sensations have no existence without the mind.

Hylas: They have not.

Philonous: How then do you affirm that colours are in the light, since by *light* you understand a corporeal substance external to the mind?

Hylas: Light and colours, as immediately perceived by us, I grant cannot exist without the mind. But in themselves they are only the motions and configurations of certain insensible particles of matter.

Philonous: Colours then in the vulgar sense, or taken for the immediate objects of sight, cannot agree to any but a perceiving substance.

Hylas: That is what I say.

Philonous: Well then, since you give up the point as to those sensible qualities, which are alone thought colours by all mankind beside, you may hold what you please with regard to those invisible ones of the philosophers. It is not my business to dispute about them; only I would advise you to bethink your self, whether considering the inquiry we are upon, it be prudent for you to affirm, *the red and blue which we see are not real colours, but certain unknown motions and figures which no man ever did or can see, are truly so.* Are not these shocking notions, and are not they subject to as many ridiculous inferences, as those you were obliged to renounce before in the case of sounds?

Hylas: I frankly own, Philonous, that it is in vain to stand out any longer. Colours, sounds, tastes, in a word, all those termed *secondary qualities,* have certainly no existence without the mind. But by this acknowledgment I must not be supposed to derogate any thing from the reality of matter or external objects, seeing it is no more than several philosophers maintain, who nevertheless are the farthest imaginable from denying matter. For the clearer understanding of this, you must know sensible qualities are by philosophers divided into *primary* and *secondary.* The former are extension, figure, solidity, gravity, motion, and rest. And these they hold exist really in bodies. The latter are those above enumerated; or briefly, all sensible qualities beside the primary, which they assert are only so many sensations or ideas existing no where but in the mind. But all this, I doubt not, you are already apprised of. For my part, I have been a long time sensible there was such an opinion current among philosophers, but was never thoroughly convinced of its truth till now.

Philonus: You are still then of opinion, that extension and figure are inherent in external unthinking substances.

Hylas: I am.

Philonous: But what if the same arguments which are brought against secondary qualities, will hold good against these also?

Hylas: Why then I shall be obliged to think, they too exist only in the mind.

Philonous: Is it your opinion, the very figure and extension which you perceive by sense, exist in the outward object or material substance?

Hylas: It is.

Philonous: Have all other animals as good grounds to think the same of the figure and extension which they see and feel?

Hylas: Without doubt, if they have any thought at all.

Philonous: Answer me, Hylas. Think you the senses were bestowed upon all animals for their preservation and well-being in life? or were they given to men alone for this end?

Hylas: I make no question but they have the same use in all other animals.

Philonous: If so, is it not necessary they should be enabled by them to perceive their own limbs, and those bodies which are capable of harming them?

Hylas: Certainly.

Philonous: A mite therefore must be supposed to see his own foot, and things equal or even less than it, as bodies of some considerable dimension; though at the same time they appear to you scarce discernible, or at best as so many visible points.

Hylas: I cannot deny it.

Philonous: And to creatures less than the mite they will seem yet larger.

Hylas: They will.

Philonous: Insomuch that what you can hardly discern, will to another extremely minute animal appear as some huge mountain.

Hylas: All this I grant.

Philonous: Can one and the same thing be at the same time in itself of different dimensions?

Hylas: That were absurd to imagine.

Philonous: But from what you have laid down it follows, that both the extension by you perceived, and that perceived by the mite itself, as likewise all those perceived by lesser animals, are each of them the true extension of the mite's foot, that is to say, by your own principles you are led into an absurdity.

Hylas: There seems to be some difficulty in the point.

Philonous: Again, have you not acknowledged that no real inherent property of any object can be changed, without some change in the thing itself?

Hylas: I have.

Philonous: But as we approach to or recede from an object, the visible extension varies, being at one distance ten or an hundred times greater than at another. Doth it not therefore follow from hence likewise, that it is not really inherent in the object?

Hylas: I own I am at a loss what to think.

Philonous: Your judgment will soon be determined, if you will venture to think as freely concerning this quality, as you have done concerning the rest. Was it not admitted as a good argument, that neither heat nor cold was in the water, because it seemed warm to one hand, and cold to the other?

Hylas: It was.

Philonous: Is it not the very same reasoning to conclude, there is no extension or figure in an object, because to one eye it shall seem little, smooth, and round, when at the same time it appears to the other, great, uneven, and angular?

Hylas: The very same. But doth this latter fact ever happen?

Philonous: You may at any time make the experiment, by looking with one eye bare, and with the other through a microscope.

Hylas: I know not how to maintain it, and yet I am loth to give up *extension,* I see so many odd consequences following upon such a concession.

Philonous: Odd, say you? After the concessions already made, I hope you will stick at nothing for its oddness. But on the other hand should it not seem very odd, if the general reasoning which includes all other sensible qualities did not also include extension? If it be allowed that no idea nor any thing like an idea can exist in an unperceiving substance, then surely it follows, that no figure or mode of extension, which we can either perceive or imagine, or have any idea of, can be really inherent in matter; not to mention the peculiar difficulty there must be, in conceiving a material substance, prior to and distinct from extension, to be the *substratum* of extension. Be the sensible quality what it will, figure, or sound, or colour; it seems alike impossible it should subsist in that which doth not perceive it. . . .

Hylas: I acknowledge, *Philonous,* that, upon a fair observation of what passes in my mind, I can discover nothing else but that I am a thinking being, affected with variety of sensations; neither is it possible to conceive how a sensation should exist in an unperceiving substance. But then, on the other hand, when I look on sensible things in a different view, considering them as so many modes and qualities, I find it necessary to suppose a material substratum, without which they cannot be conceived to exist.

Philonous: Material substratum call you it? Pray, by which of your senses came you acquainted with that being?

Hylas: It is not itself sensible; its modes and qualities only being perceived by the senses.

Philonous: I presume then it was by reflection and reason you obtained the idea of it?

Hylas: I do not pretend to any proper positive idea of it. However, I conclude it exists, because qualities cannot be conceived to exist without a support.

Philonous: It seems then you have only a relative notion of it, or that you conceive it not otherwise than by conceiving the relation it bears to sensible qualities?

Hylas: Right.

Philonous: Be pleased therefore to let me know wherein that relation consists.

Hylas: Is it not sufficiently expressed in the term *substratum* or *substance?*

Philonous: If so, the word *substratum* should import that it is spread under the sensible qualities or accidents?

Hylas: True.

Philonous: And consequently under extension?

Hylas: I own it.

Philonous: It is therefore somewhat in its own nature entirely distinct from extension?

Hylas: I tell you, extension is only a mode, and Matter is something that supports modes. And is it not evident the thing supported is different from the thing supporting?

Philonous: So that something distinct from, and exclusive of, extension is supposed to be the *substratum* of extension?

Hylas: Just so.

Philonous: Answer me, Hylas. Can a thing be spread without extension? or is not the idea of extension necessarily included in *spreading?*

Hylas: It is.

Philonous: Whatsoever therefore you suppose spread under anything must have in itself an extension distinct from the extension of that thing under which it is spread?

Hylas: It must.

Philonous: Consequently, every corporeal substance being the substratum of extension must have in itself another extension, by which it is qualified to be a *substratum,* and so on to infinity? And I ask whether this be not absurd in itself, and repugnant to what you granted just now, to wit, that the *substratum* was something distinct from and exclusive of extension?

Hylas: Aye, but *Philonous,* you take me wrong. I do not mean that Matter is *spread* in a gross literal sense under extension. The world *substratum* is used only to express in general the same thing with *substance.*

Philonous: Well then, let us examine the relation implied in the term *substance.* Is it not that it stands under accidents?

Hylas: The very same.

Philonous: But, that one thing may stand under or support another, must it not be extended?

Hylas: It must.

Philonous: Is not therefore this supposition liable to the same absurdity with the former?

Hylas: You still take things in a strict literal sense; that is not fair, *Philonous.*

Philonous: I am not for imposing any sense on your words: you are at liberty to explain them as you please. Only, I beseech you, make me understand something by them. You tell me Matter supports or stands under accidents. How! is it as your legs support your body?

Hylas: No; that is the literal sense.

Philonous: Pray let me know any sense, literal or not literal, that you understand it in. . . . How long must I wait for an answer, Hylas?

Hylas: I declare I know not what to say. I once thought I understood well enough what was meant by Matter's supporting accidents. But now, the more I think on it the less can I comprehend it; in short I find that I know nothing of it.

STUDY QUESTIONS

1   Samuel Johnson claimed to have refuted Berkeley by kicking a large rock. What do you think of his "refutation"? (If you have read selections in the preceding section, you might consider the respective reactions of Descartes and Harrison.)

2   Some religious groups who accepted Berkeley's doctrine refused medical help for their illnesses. Since the body is mental, they argued, all that is required to cure disease is the right mental attitude. Do you think this follows from Berkeley's doctrine?

3   "To be is to be perceived" seems to mean that things disappear when I am no longer looking at them. Berkeley's response is summed up in this limerick:

There was a young man who said, "God
Must think it exceedingly odd
    If he finds that this tree
    Continues to be
When there's no one about in the Quad"

Reply

Dear Sir:
    Your astonishment's odd.
I am always about in the Quad
    And that's why the tree
    Will continue to be
Since observed by
    Yours faithfully,

    God.
    (Ronald Knox)

Do you think God's reply is sufficient to account for an objective world?

4   Can you think how Berkeley might analyze the sense of touch? Is this sense ever subject to illusion?

5   Berkeley is not content to deny the existence of matter, for he also wants to say that the concept of matter is "nonsensical." What makes a concept meaningful according to Berkeley? Do you think that the concept of "God" is meaningful?

6   Do you think one could be a scientist and accept Berkeley's theory? What would you say to Bertrand Russell's claim that "physical objects are those series of appearances whose matter obeys the laws of physics"?

Our Knowledge of Cause and Effect

David Hume

In this selection, David Hume (see biography on pages 22 and 105) brings his skepticism to its ultimate conclusion. He insists that knowledge cannot go beyond *experience,* and he limits experience to passive sense perception. God, the self, the external world, are rendered beyond human comprehension by this strict form of empiricism. In this selection, Hume's target is the assumption which seems to underlie all experience—the assumption that there is a real connection between the events we experience. We believe, for example, that cause and effect are necessarily connected. That is, if the cause occurs, the effect must follow. The bread we ate yesterday should produce the same nourishing effects today. The water which satisfied thirst a few seconds ago should do so again. But with infuriating logic Hume argues that this assumption is a blind prejudice.

Many contemporary scientists have accepted part of what Hume wants us to believe, namely, that the only evidence we have for the cause-effect relation is our perception of a constant correlation between two observable events. In fact, many scientists claim that this is all we can ever know about nature. Yet most do not accept or ignore the consequences of this for prediction. Still it is probably accurate to say that this essay has had a great influence on the contemporary picture of science. Whether the influence has been for good or for ill is for you to decide.

I

All the objects of human reason or inquiry may naturally be divided into two kinds, to wit, *Relations of Ideas,* and *Matters of Fact.* Of the first kind are the sciences of Geometry, Algebra, and Arithmetic; and in short, every affirmation which is either intuitively or demonstratively certain. *That the square of the hypotenuse is equal to the square of the two sides,* is a proposition which expresses a relation between these figures. *That three times five is equal to the half of thirty,* expresses a relation between these numbers. Propositions of this kind are discoverable by the mere operation of thought, without dependence on what is anywhere existent in the universe. Though there never were a circle or triangle in nature, the truths demonstrated by Euclid would forever retain their certainty and evidence.

From *An Enquiry concerning Human Understanding,* by David Hume, first published in 1748.

Matters of fact, which are the second objects of human reason, are not ascertained in the same manner; nor is our evidence of their truth, however great, of a like nature with the foregoing. The contrary of every matter of fact is still possible; because it can never imply a contradiction, and is conceived by the mind with the same facility and distinctness, as if ever so conformable to reality. *That the sun will not rise tomorrow* is no less intelligible a propositon, and implies no more contradiction than the affirmation, *that it will rise.* Were it demonstratively false, it would imply a contradiction, and could never be distinctly conceived by the mind.

It may, therefore, be a subject worthy of curiosity, to inquire what is the nature of that evidence which assures us of any real existence and matter of fact, beyond the present testimony of our senses, or the records of our memory. This part of philosophy, it is observable, has been little cultivated, either by the ancients or moderns; and therefore our doubts and errors, in the prosecution of so important an inquiry, may be the most excusable; while we march through such difficult paths without any guide or direction. They may even prove useful, by exciting curiosity, and destroying that implicit faith and security, which is the bane of all reasoning and free inquiry. The discovery of defects in the common philosophy, if any such there be, will not, I presume, be a discouragement, but rather an incitement, as is usual, to attempt something more full and satisfactory than has yet been proposed to the public.

All reasonings concerning matter of fact seem to be founded on the relation of *Cause and Effect.* By means of that relation alone we can go beyond the evidence of our memory and senses. If you were to ask a man, why he believes any matter of fact, which is absent; for instance, that his friend is in the country, or in France; he would give you a reason; and this reason would be some other fact; as a letter received from him, or the knowledge of his former resolutions and promises. A man finding a watch or any other machine in a desert island, would conclude that there had once been men in that island. All our reasonings concerning fact are of the same nature. And here it is constantly supposed that there is a connection between the present fact and that which is inferred from it. Were there nothing to bind them together, the inference would be entirely precarious. The hearing of an articulate voice and rational discourse in the dark assures us of the presence of some person: Why? because these are the effects of the human make and fabric, and closely connected with it. If we anatomize all the other reasonings of this nature, we shall find that they are founded on the relation of cause and effect, and that this relation is either near or remote, direct or collateral. Heat and light are collateral effects of fire, and the one effect may justly be inferred from the other.

If we would satisfy ourselves, therefore, concerning the nature of that evidence, which assures us of matters of fact, we must inquire how we arrive at the knowledge of cause and effect.

I shall venture to affirm, as a general proposition, which admits of no exception, that the knowledge of this relation is not, in any instance, attained by reasonings *a priori;* but arises entirely from experience, when we find that any particular objects are constantly conjoined with each other. Let an object be presented to a man of ever so strong natural reason and abilities; if that object be entirely new to him, he will not be able, by the most accurate examination of its sensible qualities, to discover any of its causes or effects. Adam, though his rational faculties be supposed, at the very first, entirely perfect, could not have inferred from the fluidity and transparency of water that it would suffocate him, or from the light and warmth of fire that it would consume him. No object ever discovers, by the qualities which appear to the senses, either the causes which produced it, or the effects which will arise from it; nor can our reason, unassisted by experience, ever draw any inference concerning real existence and matter of fact.

This proposition, *that causes and effects are discoverable, not by reason but by experience,* will readily be admitted with regard to such objects, as we remember to have once been altogether unknown to us; since we must be conscious of the utter inability, which we then lay under, of foretelling what would arise from them. Present two smooth pieces of marble to a man who has no tincture of natural philosophy; he will never discover that they will adhere together in such a manner as to require great force to separate them in a direct line, while they make so small a resistance to a lateral pressure. Such events, as bear little analogy to the common course of nature, are also readily confessed to be known only by experience; nor does any man imagine that the explosion of gunpowder, or the attraction of a loadstone, could ever be discovered by arguments *a priori.* In like manner, when an effect is supposed to depend upon an intricate machinery or secret structure of parts, we make no difficulty in attributing all our knowledge of it to experience. Who will assert that he can give the ultimate reason, why milk or bread is proper nourishment for a man, not for a lion or a tiger?

But the same truth may not appear, at first sight, to have the same evidence with regard to events, which have become familiar to us from our first appearance in the world, which bear a close analogy to the whole course of nature, and which are supposed to depend on the simple qualities of objects, without any secret structure of parts. We are apt to imagine that we could discover these effects by the mere operation of our reason, without experience. We fancy, that were we brought on a sudden into this world, we could at first have inferred that one Billiard-ball would communicate motion to another upon impulse; and that we needed not to have waited for the event, in order to pronounce with certainty concerning it. Such is the influence of custom, that, where it is strongest, it not only covers our natural ignorance, but even conceals itself, and seems not to take place, merely because it is found in the highest degree.

But to convince us that all the laws of nature, and all the operations of bodies without exception, are known only by experience, the following reflections may, perhaps, suffice. Were any object presented to us, and were we required to pronounce concerning the effect, which will result from it, without consulting past observation; after what manner, I beseech you, must the mind proceed in this operation? It must invent or imagine some event, which it ascribes to the object as its effect; and it is plain that this invention must be entirely arbitrary. The mind can never possibly find the effect in the supposed cause, by the most accurate scrutiny and examination. For the effect is totally different from the cause, and consequently can never be discovered in it. Motion in the second Billiard-ball is a quite distinct event from motion in the first; nor is there anything in the one to suggest the smallest hint of the other. A stone or piece of metal raised into the air, and left without any support, immediately falls: but to consider the matter *a priori,* is there anything we discover in this situation which can beget the idea of a downward, rather than an upward, or any other motion, in the stone or metal?

And as the first imagination or invention of a particular effect, in all natural operations, is arbitrary, where we consult not experience; so must we also esteem the supposed tie or connection between the cause and effect, which binds them together, and renders it impossible that any other effect could result from the operation of that cause. When I see, for instance, a Billard-ball moving in a straight line towards another; even suppose motion in the second ball should by accident be suggested to me, as the result of their contact or impulse; may I not conceive, that a hundred different events might as well follow from that cause? May not both these balls remain at absolute rest? May not the first ball return in a straight line, or leap off from the second in any line or direction? All these suppositions are consistent and conceivable. Why then should we give the preference to one, which is no more consistent or conceivable than the rest? All our reasonings *a priori* will never be able to show us any foundation for this preference.

In a word, then, every effect is a distinct event from its cause. It could not, therefore, be discovered in the cause, and the first invention or conception of it, *a priori,* must be entirely arbitrary. And even after it is suggested, the conjunction of it with the cause must appear equally arbitrary; since there are always many other effects, which, to reason, must seem fully as consistent and natural. In vain, therefore, should we pretend to determine any single event, or infer any cause or effect, without the assistance of observation and experience.

Hence we may discover the reason why no philosopher, who is rational and modest, has ever pretended to assign the ultimate cause of any natural operation, or to show distinctly the action of that power, which produces any single effect in the universe. It is confessed, that the utmost effort of human reason is to reduce the principles, productive of natural phenomena, to a greater simplicity, and to resolve the many particular effects into a few general causes, by means of reasonings from analogy, experience, and observation. But as to the causes of these general causes, we should in vain attempt their discovery; nor shall we ever be able to satisfy ourselves, by any particular explication of them. These ultimate springs and principles are totally shut up from human curiosity and inquiry. Elasticity, gravity, cohesion of parts, communication of motion by impulse; these are probably the ultimate causes and principles which we shall ever discover in nature; and we may esteem ourselves sufficiently happy, if, by accurate inquiry and reasoning, we can trace up the particular phenomena to, or near to, these general principles. The most perfect philosophy of the natural kind only staves off our ignorance a little longer: as perhaps the most perfect philosophy of the moral or metaphysical kind serves only to discover large portions of it. Thus the observation of human blindness and weakness is the result of all philosophy, and meets us at every turn, in spite of our endeavors to elude or avoid it.

II

But we have not yet attained any tolerable satisfaction with regard to the question first proposed. Each solution still gives rise to a new question as difficult as the foregoing, and leads us on to farther inquiries. When it is asked, *What is the nature of all our reasonings concerning matter of fact?* the proper answer seems to be, that they are founded on the relation of cause and effect. When again it is asked, *What is the foundation of all our reasonings and conclusions concerning that relation?* it may be replied in one word, Experience. But if we still carry on our sifting humor, and ask, *What is the foundation of all conclusions from experience?* this implies a new question, which may be of more difficult solution and explication. Philosophers, that give themselves airs of superior wisdom and sufficiency, have a hard task when they encounter persons of inquisitive dispositions, who push them from every corner to which they retreat, and who are sure at last to bring them to some dangerous dilemma. The best expedient to prevent this confusion, is to be modest in our pretensions; and even to discover the difficulty ourselves before it is objected to us. By this means, we may make a kind of merit of our very ignorance.

I shall content myself, in this section, with an easy task, and shall pretend only to give a negative answer to the question here proposed. I say then, that, even after we have experience of the operations of cause and effect, our conclusions from that experience are not founded on reasoning, or any process of the understanding. This answer we must endeavor both to explain and to defend.

It must certainly be allowed, that nature has kept us at a great distance from all her secrets, and has afforded us only the knowledge of a few superficial qualities of objects; while she conceals from us those powers and principles on which the influence of those objects entirely depends. Our senses inform us of the color, weight, and consistence of bread; but neither sense nor reason can ever inform us of those qualities which fit it for the nourishment and support of a human body. Sight or feeling conveys an idea of the actual motion of bodies; but as to that wonderful force or power, which would carry on a moving body forever in a continued change of place, and which bodies never lose but by communicating it to others; of this we cannot form the most distant conception. But notwithstanding this ignorance of natural powers[1] and principles, we always presume, when we see like sensible qualities, that they have like secret powers, and expect that effects, similar to those which we have experienced, will follow from them. If a body of like color and consistence with that bread, which we have formerly eat, be presented to us, we make no scruple of repeating the experiment, and foresee, with certainty, like nourishment and support. Now this is a process of the mind or thought, of which I would willingly know the foundation. It is allowed on all hands that there is no known connection between the sensible qualities and the secret powers; and consequently, that the mind is not led to

---

[1] The word, Power, is here used in a loose and popular sense. The more accurate explication of it would give additional evidence to this argument.

form such a conclusion concerning their constant and regular conjunction, by anything which it knows of their nature. As to past *Experience*, it can be allowed to give *direct* and *certain* information of those precise objects only, and that precise period of time, which fell under its cognizance: but why this experience should be extended to future times, and to other objects, which for aught we know, may be only in appearance similar; this is the main question on which I would insist. The bread, which I formerly eat, nourished me; that is, a body of such sensible qualities was, at that time, endued with such secret powers: but does it follow, that other bread must also nourish me at another time, and that like sensible qualities must always be attended with like secret powers? The consequence seems nowise necessary. At least, it must be acknowledged that there is here a consequence drawn by the mind; that there is a certain step taken; a process of thought, and an inference, which wants to be explained. These two propositions are far from being the same, *I have found that such an object has always been attended with such an effect,* and *I foresee, that other objects, which are, in appearance, similar, will be attended with similar effects.* I shall allow, if you please, that the one proposition may justly be inferred from the other: I know, in fact, that it always is inferred. But if you insist that the inference is made by a chain of reasoning, I desire you to produce that reasoning. The connection between these propositions is not intuitive. There is required a medium, which may enable the mind to draw such an inference, if indeed it be drawn by reasoning and argument. What that medium is, I must confess, passes my comprehension; and it is incumbent on those to produce it, who assert that it really exists, and is the origin of all our conclusions concerning matter of fact.

This negative argument must certainly, in process of time, become altogether convincing, if many penetrating and able philosophers shall turn their inquiries this way and no one be ever able to discover any connecting proposition or intermediate step, which supports the understanding in this conclusion. But as the question is yet new, every reader n ay not trust so far to his own penetration, as to conclude, because an argument e. capes his inquiry, that therefore it does not really exist. For this reason it may be requisite to venture upon a more difficult task; and enumerating all the branches of human knowledge, endeavor to show that none of them can afford such an argument.

All reasonings may be divided into two kinds, namely, demonstrative reasoning, or that concerning relations of ideas, and moral reasoning, or that concerning matter of fact and existence. That there are no demonstrative arguments in the case seems evident; since it implies no contradiction that the course of nature may change, and that an object, seemingly like those which we have experienced, may be attended with different or contrary effects. May I not clearly and distinctly conceive that a body, falling from the clouds, and which, in all other respects, resembles snow, has yet the taste of salt or feeling of fire? Is there any more intelligible proposition than to affirm, that all the trees will flourish in December and January, and decay in May and June? Now whatever is intelligible, and can be distinctly conceived, implies no contradiction, and can never be proved false by any demonstrative argument or abstract reasoning *a priori.*

If we be, therefore, engaged by arguments to put trust in past experience, and make it the standard of our future judgment, these arguments must be probable only, or such as regard matter of fact and real existence, according to the division above mentioned. But that there is no argument of this kind, must appear, if our explication of that species of reasoning be admitted as solid and satisfactory. We have said that all arguments concerning existence are founded on the relation of cause and effect; that our knowledge of that relation is derived entirely from experience; and that all our experimental conclusions proceed upon the supposition that the future will be conformable to the past. To endeavor, therefore, the proof of this last supposition by probable arguments, or arguments regarding existence, must be evidently going in a circle, and taking that for granted, which is the very point in question.

In reality, all arguments from experience are founded on the similarity which we discover among natural objects, and by which we are induced to expect effects similar to those which we have found to follow from such objects. And though none but a fool or madman will ever pretend to dispute the authority of experience, or to reject that great guide of human life, it may surely be allowed a philosopher to have so much curiosity at least as to examine the principle of human nature, which gives this mighty authority to experience, and makes us draw advantage from that similarity which nature has placed among different objects. From causes which appear *similar* we expect similar effects. This is the sum of all our experimental conclusions. Now it seems evident that, if this conclusion were formed by reason, it would be as perfect at first, and upon one instance, as after ever so long a course of experience. But the case is far otherwise. Nothing so like as eggs; yet no one, on account of this appearing similarity, expects the same taste and relish in all of them. It is only after a long course of uniform experiments in any kind, that we attain a firm reliance and security with regard to a particular event. Now where is that process of reasoning which, from one instance draws a conclusion so different from that which it infers from a hundred instances that are nowise different from that single one? This question I propose as much for the sake of information, as with an intention of raising difficulties. I cannot find, I cannot imagine any such reasoning. But I keep my mind still open to instruction, if any one will vouchsafe to bestow it on me.

Should it be said that, from a number of uniform experiments, we *infer* a connection between the sensible qualities and the secret powers; this, I must confess, seems the same difficulty, couched in different terms. The question still recurs, on what process of argument this *inference* is founded? Where is the medium, the interposing ideas, which join propositions so very wide of each other? Is it confessed that the color, consistence, and other sensible qualities of bread appear not, of themselves, to have any connection with the secret powers of nourishment and support? For otherwise we could infer these secret powers from the first appearance of these sensible qualities, without the aid of experience; contrary to the sentiment of all philosophers, and contrary to plain matter of fact. Here, then, is our natural state of ignorance with regard to the powers and influence of all objects. How is this remedied by experience? It only shows us a number of uniform effects, resulting from certain objects, and teaches us that those particular objects, at that particular time, were endowed with such powers and forces. When a new object, endowed with similar sensible qualities, is produced, we expect similar powers and forces, and look for a like effect. From a body of like color and consistence with bread we expect like nourishment and support. But this surely is a step or progress of the mind, which wants to be explained. When a man says, *I have found, in all past instances, such sensible qualities conjoined with such secret powers:* And when he says, *Similar sensible qualities will always be conjoined with similar secret powers,* he is not guilty of a tautology, nor are these propositions in any respect the same. You say that the one proposition is an inference from the other. But you must confess that the inference is not intuitive; neither is it demonstrative: Of what nature is it, then? To say it is experimental, is begging the question. For all inferences from experiences suppose, as their foundation, that the future will resemble the past, and that similar powers will be conjoined with similar sensible qualities. If there be any suspicion that the course of nature may change, and that the past may be no rule for the future, all experience becomes useless, and can give rise to no inference or conclusion. It is impossible, therefore, that any arguments from experience can prove this resemblance of the past to the future; since all these arguments are founded on the supposition of that resemblance. Let the course of things be allowed hitherto ever so regular; that alone, without some new argument or inference, proves not that, for the future, it will continue so. In vain do you pretend to have learned the nature of bodies from your past experience. Their secret nature, and consequently all their effects and influence, may change, without any change in their sensible qualities. This happens sometimes, and with regard to some objects: Why may it not happen always, and with regard to all objects? What logic, what process of argument secures you against this supposition? My practice, you say, refutes my doubts. But you mistake the purport of my question. As an agent, I am quite satisfied in the point; but as a philosopher, who has some share of curiosity, I will not say skepticism, I want to learn the foundation of this inference. No reading, no inquiry has yet been able to remove my difficulty, or give me satisfaction in a matter of such importance. Can I do better than propose the difficulty to the public, even though, perhaps, I have small hopes of obtaining a solution? We shall at least, by this means, be sensible of our ignorance, if we do not augment our knowledge.

I must confess that a man is guilty of unpardonable arrogance who concludes, because an argument has escaped his own investigation, that therefore it does not really exist. I must also confess that, though all the learned, for several ages, should have employed themselves in fruitless search upon any subject, it may still, perhaps, be rash to conclude positively that the subject must, therefore, pass all human comprehension. Even though we examine all the sources of our knowledge, and conclude them unfit for such a subject, there may still remain a suspicion, that the enumeration is not complete, or the examination not accurate. But with regard to the present subject, there are some considerations which seem to remove all this accusation of arrogance or suspicion of mistake.

It is certain that the most ignorant and stupid peasants—nay infants, nay even brute beasts—improve by experience, and learn the qualities of natural objects, by observing the effects which result from them. When a child has felt the sensation of pain from touching the flame of a candle, he will be careful not to put his hand near any candle; but will expect a similar effect from a cause which is similar in its sensible qualities and appearance. If you assert, therefore, that the understanding of the child is led into this conclusion by any process of argument or ratiocination, I may just require you to produce that argument; nor have you any pretence to refuse so equitable a demand. You cannot say that the argument is abstruse, and may possibly escape your inquiry; since you confess that it is obvious to the capacity of a mere infant. If you hesitate, therefore, a moment, or if, after reflection, you produce any intricate or profound argument, you, in a manner, give up the question, and confess that it is not reasoning which engages us to suppose the past resembling the future, and to expect similar effects from causes which are, to appearance, similar. This is the proposition which I intended to enforce in the present section. If I be right, I pretend not to have made any mighty discovery. And if I be wrong, I must acknowledge myself to be indeed a very backward scholar; since I cannot now discover an argument which, it seems, was perfectly familiar to me long before I was out of my cradle.

STUDY QUESTIONS

1   Hume says that causes and effects are not discovered by reason, but by experience. What does he mean by "reason" and "experience"?
2   Hume suggests that it is possible to imagine stuff falling from the sky which resembles snow in every respect, except that it is hot instead of cold. What is his point? Do you agree that such an event is possible?
3   "Since bread has nourished me in the past, it will continue to do so in the future." Would Hume say that this is a valid inference? Why? Do you think that the future resembles the past?
4   "The terms 'cause' and 'effect' are no longer widely used in science. . . . The terms which replace them, however, refer to the same factual core. . . . The new terms do not suggest *how* a cause causes its effect: they merely assert that different events tend to occur together in a certain order" (B. F. Skinner). Would Hume think that Skinner's conception of cause and effect is correct? How do you think Skinner would locate the "causes" of human behavior?
5   What do you think Hume would say to someone who thought that the moon stayed in orbit because the Earth *attracted* it through the force of gravity?

Reasoning in Science
Rom Harré

Philosophers and scientists who accept Hume's analysis of cause and effect have tried to formulate a theory of scientific method which will not fall prey to his skepticism. If science sticks to observable facts and carefully records the correlations between the facts, then Hume's criticisms are avoided. The scientist is thus depicted as one who approaches nature with the intention of neutrally observing the world and discovering orderly and regular phenomena. By observing regularities, the scientist may be able to formulate "natural laws," which then can be used to predict and explain the course of nature.

In this essay, Rom Harré (1927–   ) of Oxford University claims that an inductive science which follows Hume's analysis of cause and effect cannot give genuine explanations. Furthermore, to think of science as Hume recommends is to distort actual scientific practice. Science, he claims, proceeds by attempting to penetrate the level of appearance to an unobservable reality which underlies it. Instead of complete neutrality, the scientist approaches nature with a hypothesis about the sorts of unobserved mechanisms which could be causing an observable phenomenon. Then, through experiment, the scientist *actively* shapes the situation so that answers might be found.

Like Plato, Harré is saying that observation is not enough. The regularities in nature remain mysterious until they themselves are explained. Science, then, is not the search for observable correlations, but the search for the hidden structure in things.

Actual science is a very complex activity, so it is not surprising that there have been several theories, expressing different ideals of scientific reasoning, particularly for those steps of reasoning by which laws of nature are formulated on the basis of factual evidence, and by which the effect of new evidence on our confidence in the truth of laws is assessed. Before I set out the various theories that are of importance we shall have a look at two typical examples of scientific reasoning. In one a conclusion is drawn which is agreed to be a law of nature, and the conclusion is based upon evidence already known. In the other a law, which is already known, is tested by drawing conclusions from the law and testing them by further observation. The reasoning that leads to theories is very much more complicated and will occupy us later. We should also remember that the reasoning which leads to the original stating of a law is commonly not as simple as the cases I propose to discuss here.

MENDEL'S LAWS

These laws describe the ratios of the numbers of individuals which in successive generations of adult plants and animals show certain characteristics. For instance, the children of a brown-eyed man and a blue-eyed woman will all have brown eyes, but if one of those children marries someone from a similar background, then the chances are that in every four children of such marriages three will be brown-eyed and one blue-eyed. Mendel formulated general laws which described such cases, where dominant (brown eyes) and recessive (blue eyes) "genetic factors" are grouped in various combinations in people, animals, and plants. Mendel reached his laws by reasoning from evidence. He and his assistants grew pea plants, and cross-bred them, and counted the numbers having certain specific characteristics in each generation. From this evidence he generalized to reach his laws. In so doing he ignored small discrepancies from the perfect ratios which are expressed in his laws. The characters he investigated were the

From *The Philosophies of Science* by Rom Harré, published by Oxford University Press. Reprinted by permission of the publisher.

shape and colour of the peas produced in each generation. He compared round with wrinkled, green with yellow.

This process of reasoning could be set out schematically as follows:

In experiment 1 the ratios were 5,474 round, 1,850 wrinkled = 2.96:1.
In experiment 2 the ratios were 428 green, 152 yellow = 2.82:1.

These are Mendel's actual figures, though some doubt has recently been cast on their authenticity. Then he formulated his law as follows:

In the second generation the ratio of dominant to recessive characters is 3:1.

It is perfectly clear that his process of reasoning begins with the experimental evidence and passes to the law as conclusion. Using the terminology of logic we seem to have premisses, the description of the results of the experiments, and a conclusion, the statement of the law. We thus seem to have an argument, a step or series of steps, from premisses to conclusion. What then, we might ask, is the rule or principle of the argument? In trying to answer this question we shall run into all sorts of trouble, so much trouble in fact, as to incline some people to say that there is not really an argument here at all, only the semblance of one.

KEPLER AND THE ORBIT OF MARS

In *De Stella Martis,* Kepler describes his agonies of mind in trying to work out from the observations of the relative positions of Mars against the background of the fixed stars that he had from Tycho Brahe and others, exactly what must be the shape of its orbit. He was trying to pass from premisses to a conclusion, from the facts ascertained about the positions of the planet to a law or at least a general proposition about its motion. His only conclusion was that it must be an egg-shaped orbit that changed its shape according to a theory of librations, expansion and contraction of its diameter. Kepler knew in his heart that this was no good. Then, after working on the theory of the ellipse in another context, he suddenly had the bright idea of *supposing* that the orbit of Mars was actually elliptical, and seeing if, on this supposition, he could work out positions for the planet which corresponded well with the observed positions. This he did, and to his delight, he found that the supposition, or hypothesis, that the orbit was elliptical, was borne out in practice—that is, Mars was seen to be in the positions he had predicted by assuming its orbit was elliptical. He had formed his law independently and then *tested* it against the evidence. Here we have a different logical pattern. In this process the law becomes the starting-point for the reasoning; the premiss and the steps of thought yield conclusions which are judged by their agreement with the facts. However, there is another step associated with this way of proceeding in science which brings it rather closer to the kind of reasoning we have seen Mendel presumably using. What is the point of the tests? Surely if they turn out to be satisfactory we can say that the supposed law is satisfactory. That is, we seem to be inferring or reasoning from the satisfactoriness of the predictions to the satisfactoriness of the law, or if you like, from the truth of the predictions to the acceptability of the law, and that is something like reasoning from the facts to the law, as we supposed Mendel must have done.

MILL'S CANONS

The first of our examples exemplifies the *inductive* method, the second exemplifies the *hypothetico-deductive* method. Some logicians have treated these methods together as two different aspects of the same reasoning procedure; others have supposed them to be fundamentally different. Many philosophers have attempted to schematize the patterns of reasoning which lie behind such apparent examples of the use of the inductive method as the discovery of Mendel's laws. It is sometimes mistakenly supposed that Francis Bacon was one of these, and indeed the inductive method is sometimes, with little justice, called the Baconian method. The chief exponents of the inductive method have been William of Ockham, John Herschel, and John Stuart Mill. With less than historic justice the usual formulation of some alleged inductive laws has been called Mill's Canons. Mill, Herschel, and Ockham all agreed on the following principles.[1]

The Canon of Agreement: "If two or more instances of the phenomenon under investigation have only one circumstance in common, the circumstance in which alone all the instances agree is the cause (or effect) of the given phenomenon."

The Canon of Difference: "If an instance in which the phenomenon under investigation occurs, and an instance in which it does not occur have every circumstance in common save one, that one occurring only in the former, the circumstance in which alone the two instances differ is the effect, or the cause, or an indispensable part of the cause of the phenomenon."

In comment upon these Mill says: "The Method of Agreement stands on the ground that whatever can be eliminated is not connected with the phenomenon by any law. The Method of Difference has for its foundation, that whatever cannot be eliminated is connected with the phenomenon by a law." Mill also quotes various other canons of lesser importance. These two main canons he offers as the principles or among the principles of inductive reasoning, for, having found the cause we have found the law, or so he thinks. Here are principles by which we can pass from facts to general laws.

How do these apply in practice? Consider our example of Mendel's reasoning to his law. The only difference between smooth green peas and wrinkled yellow peas which were cultivated in his garden must lie in differences between the parent plants. So whatever differences there were between the parents must be responsible for the differences in the offspring. And looked at from the point of view of the Canon of Difference the agreement in other cases between parental differences and differences among offspring gives powerful support to the detailed hypotheses about how the differences in the generations were to be explained.

But there are difficulties with Mill's Canons, and these I must now gradually bring to the fore. In trying to apply the Methods of Agreement and Difference it

[1] J. S. Mill, *A System of Logic* (London, 1879), Bk, iii, ch. 8.

is necessary to form some idea of the totality of possible causes for a phenomenon. Suppose we are studying the growth of plants, and we find that in warm weather plants grow more vigorously than in cold. Unless we realize that in warm weather the sun's *light* shines for a longer time we might be tempted to suppose that it is the difference in heat which is responsible for the different rate of plant growth. In this case the greater warmth accompanies the greater growth because both happen together, though the cause of increased growth is the greater amount of sunlight in the summer. Mill's Canons by themselves, could not possibly allow us to decide the question of whether it was the heat or the light which was the causal factor, *unless a different experiment was carried out.* We could try to grow plants in the absence of light and presence of heat, and in the presence of light but in the absence of the usual summer heat. *Then,* using Mill's Canons, we could reason from the results of the experiments which is the cause of growth. But could we? Even after these additional experiments, the results are equivocal. What we actually find is that a certain amount of heat is necessary to stimulate growth, and also light is needed. But light seems to be the predominating cause. But perhaps light is accompanied by a third factor, which is really the cause but which we haven't yet spotted. To resolve this kind of difficulty something quite different needs to be done. We need to investigate the mechanism of plant growth, the process by which a plant synthesizes new material. And when we do this we find that the process depends upon light. It is photosynthesis. Only after the mechanism of growth has been discovered can we be sure that we have the cause. And to describe the mechanism of growth is to put forward a theory as to how growth occurs. Our belief in this theory will depend on how certain we are that we have uncovered the true mechanism. Whether any particular application of Mill's Canons yields information of value is determined by how good a theory we have to explain the processes we are investigating. What information the use of the Canons yields will depend at least as much upon theory held by the investigator as upon what he observes in his controlled experiment. It looks as if Mill's Canons are, at best, a preliminary to the deeper studies of scientists. In effect they eliminate possibilities, but do not positively prove anything. In practice we never rest content with laws for which there are no explanations.

But there is another difficulty about Mill's Canons, if we regard them as expressing acceptable forms of reasoning. We noticed this problem in the first chapter. It is the problem of how far we can regard laws produced by reasoning according to Mill's Canons or any other inductive method as true. Suppose our only reason for believing Mendel's Laws was the experiments Mendel did. And let us suppose we accept the results he puts forward as facts, that is that we accept these as irrefutable evidence, as the actual results of experiments. Can we be equally sure of the generalized Mendelian Laws? What sort of doubts might we have? Well, is it not possible that the figures he got were a coincidence, and that if we made similar studies another year we would get very different results? There is nothing in the experiments that leads us to think that we would get similar results in another year, or in another century for that matter. And yet enunciating the results as *laws* certainly suggests a strong expectation that inheritance has worked according to this pattern and will always do so. The whole idea of there being Laws of Nature carries with it the suggestion that the patterns in phenomena repeat themselves. Yet, where is the evidence for this?

Suppose we answer that the evidence is the whole body of science as we have it. Over and over again we have found that the patterns of nature we have discerned with the help of Mill's Canons do repeat themselves. Natural processes do continue in the ways they have previously proceeded. So we have good empirical grounds for believing in the uniformity of Nature. It seems that Mill's Canons are a pair of logical principles grounded in fact. And yet what logical principles did we use to reason from the evidence of past successes of science to the truth of the supposition that patterns repeat themselves in similar circumstances? None other than Mill's Canons! Where patterns did repeat themselves science was successful; in those cases where "laws" were based upon coincidences or faulty experiments they subsequently turned out to have exceptions, or sometimes no application at all. Here are the Methods of Agreement and Difference at work again. It looks as if the proof of one of the most important kinds of scientific reasoning depends upon assuming the correctness of that very method itself. So unless one is very careful one can be surprised into thinking that scientific method is either ungrounded, or based upon a fallacious proof. But this dire consequence can be sidestepped.

What we have actually found out is that Mill's Canons are some among many subordinate and limited forms of reasoning. They set standards of procedure, and like other ideals are not in need of practical scientific proof. We have also discovered that if we accept Mill's Canons as ideal forms of reasoning they do not cover all we would want to include in scientific method. Our reasons for thinking that one kind of phenomenon is the cause of another kind are not just a matter of seeing if the two kinds of phenomena appear together or in a sequence, and the second never without the first, but are based much more upon our knowledge or speculations about the mechanisms by which the two are related, and by which the first kind of phenomenon produces the second. Our knowledge that vibration is a cause of metal fatigue derives not only from the fact that vibrated metals break earlier and more often than non-vibrated ones but also from our knowledge of the structure of metals, and the changes in that structure brought about by vibration. Mill's Canons represent one of the forms of reasoning in use in science, but though they are often used as an essential preliminary stage of an investigation they are certainly not the only principles required to formulate hypotheses successfully.

INDUCTIVISM

But in the inimitable way of philosophy the canons have been promoted as a complete theory of science. This theory can be expressed in three principles.

The Principle of Accumulation: that scientific knowledge is a conjunction of well-attested facts, and that such knowledge grows by the addition of further well-attested facts, so that the addition of a new fact to the conjunction leaves all the previous facts unaltered. It is as if chemistry consisted only of list after list of reactions among the elements and compounds.

The Principle of Induction: that there is a form of inference of laws from the accumulated simple facts, so that from true statements describing observations and the results of experiments, true laws may be inferred. Mill's Canons, for instance, might be offered as the principles of such inferences. The Laws of Nature are nothing but the codified and generalized particular facts. As Mach put it "they are the mnemonic reproduction of facts in thought." In modern science the operation of this principle is often seen in the effort to obtain numerical data and then find algebraic functions to express them.

The Principle of Instance Confirmation: that our belief in the degree of plausibility of (or our degree of belief in) a law is proportioned to the number of instances that have been observed of the phenomenon described in the law. For instance, the more gases we find to be diatomic (having two atoms in their molecule in the gaseous state) the more ready we are to believe and to accept a law that all gases are diatomic.

This is a very seductive theory of science. It seems to be a hardheaded, straightforward, and empirically based view. Scientists are seen as steadily piling up facts, generalizing them into laws, and piling up more facts, step by step in the laboratory. If you can infer the laws from the accumulated facts, you can deduce the facts again from the laws, and the content of the laws is nothing but the facts.

OBJECTIONS TO INDUCTIVISM

But inductivism will hardly stand a moment's serious criticism. None of its three principles will do at all. Take the principle that science grows by the accumulation of facts. This is just not true. The growth of science is a leap-frog process of fact accumulation and theoretical advance. A change in theory can turn seeming facts into falsehoods. For instance, consider the history of the determination of the atomic weights. What *were* the facts? Under the influence of Prout's hypothesis some chemists considered that the discrepancies between integral values for the atomic weights of the elements were errors, since Prout had maintained that all elemental atoms were combinations of whole numbers of complete hydrogen atoms, and hence their atomic weights had to be integral numbers by comparison with hydrogen. Those who did not accept or had abandoned Prout's hypothesis were inclined rather to suppose that the non-integral weights were the facts, that is a genuine measure of a natural phenomenon. What the facts were depended in part upon whether one held or did not hold a particular theory.

Not only does a change in theory result in a change of fact but even in the field of a single theory there are problems as to what are the facts. Consider again the atomic weights. Are they the relative weights of atoms, as their title would suggest, or are they a picturesquely named set of numerical ratios of the relative weights in which substances combine? Even though these are important considerations, nevertheless it might be thought that we ought to be able to discern some "brute facts," that is facts which would remain the same throughout all change of theory and point of view. Unfortunately the attempt to find such facts leads to a fatal dilemma. The only facts which seem to be genuinely independent of any

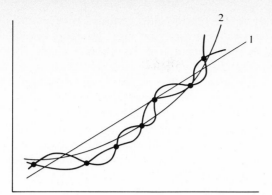

Fig. 1 Curve fitting

scientific theory are those of the present experiences of touch, taste, smell, hearing, and sight that each individual scientist is currently experiencing. But such facts are not, of course, public facts, they are private to each individual. So we have the dilemma, that if facts are truly independent of theory they are private and do not form part of the public domain of knowledge; if they are public facts they are affected by all sorts of influences particularly from previous knowledge and upon which their exact form and our confidence in them depend. At least for science, there are no brute facts. There are no facts which other facts may not change; there is no knowledge altogether independent of theory.

The Principle of Induction leads us into still deeper water. Not only are there the objections that we have already seen to Mill's Canons, which are particular forms of the inductive principle, but there are more general problems, the most crucial being the indeterminacy of the results of trying to use the principle to infer a law. A principle of inference is no good if, from the premises offered, more than one mutually incompatible conclusion can be drawn. But from each set of premises of experimental and observational fact, infinitely many laws can be inferred using the principle of induction. This is perhaps simplest to see in a graph. Each curve represents a law inferred inductively from the premises represented by the points marked on the paper, and from each law the points (the facts) can be inferred. Which of these potentially infinitely many laws is the correct one? The principle of induction will not give us an answer, because, from all we can tell using that principle alone, all are equally correct. To deal with this problem inductivists have nearly always added a Principle of Simplicity to their logical armoury. Of all the laws which induction yields, only the simplest should be accepted, they contend. So in the diagram above we should choose (1). But this is a highly dubious principle.

First, it is certainly not clear exactly how to apply it. Should we choose (1) or (2) in the diagram above? Certainly (2) is a pretty good fit, and yet so is (1). It is not difficult to conceive of further experiments adding further points which would remain equivocal with respect to the choice between (1) and (2). Remember that on the inductivist view there is nothing else to go on but the experimental facts, and the principle of simplicity. The step that scientists usually take of referring to theory to adjudicate is no longer open.

Secondly, the history of science can offer little comfort to believers in simplicity. The progress of knowledge does not lead to the most complex conceivable forms of law being discovered, if such a concept as "the most complex" even makes sense, but it certainly does not lead to the simplest. The growth of knowledge of the behaviour of gases has led from $PV = RT$ to $(P + a/V^2)(V - b) = RT;$ the growth of knowledge of the movements of the planets from the simple hypothesis of circles as orbits has led to the more complex curves of elliptical form; the growth of knowledge of the figure of the earth has led from the simple idea of a spherical shape through the idea that it is an oblate spheroid (flattened at the poles) to yet more complex shapes. There can be no doubt that the history of science shows that the laws of nature are always more complex than we originally thought. The Principle of Simplicity as a *blanket* principle can hardly be accepted. Of course at each stage of knowledge it would be mad to choose any more complex hypothesis than one has to, but that it is hardly a methodological principle of the portentous epistemological status assigned to the principle of simplicity.

We have already run into difficulties about confirmation by instances in various contexts, so we can hardly give our allegiance to the Principle of Instance Confirmation. However, the deepest problem of all with inductivism as an exclusive theory of science, offering an all-embracing ideal, is its failure to include explanation in the field of scientific endeavour. This defect can be clearly discerned if we compare Babylonian and Greek methods of astronomy. The practical problem to which scientists from both cultures addressed themselves was the construction of tables of ephemerides, that is tables which would give, in advance, various astronomical facts in which people were interested, such as the times of rising and setting of the constellations, and of the sun and the moon, throughout the year. The Babylonians used an inductive method, the Greeks a non-inductive one. For the Babylonians the tables of ephemerides were constructed by the use of numerical rules, derived as inductive laws, by which addition or subtraction of constants according to definite rules produced sets of numbers which represented the successive risings and settings of those bodies which were of astronomical interest. For details of this interesting kind of astronomy see Neugebauer, *The Exact Sciences in Antiquity.*[2] In this sort of science we have a theory only in the sense of an abstract calculating device yielding predictions, but not a theory in the sense of an explanation of the phenomena within some picture of the stellar system, which would account for and explain them. Babylonian astronomical methods, as they have been reconstructed from tablets, could never yield realistic hypotheses about the structure of the Universe and the motions of its parts, since there is no element in the "theory" capable of realization in the required way. It is just not possible to make a physical hypothesis out of the subtraction or addition of some constant number alone.

The situation in Greek astronomy was quite different. The lunar theory of Eudoxus is already half-way to being a model of the Universe, for its elements are not arithmetical relations but geometrical spheres. For example, to account for the motion of the moon, as we see it, Eudoxus proposed a theory. He consid-

[2] O. Neugebauer, *The Exact Sciences in Antiquity* (New York: Harper, 1962), ch. 5.

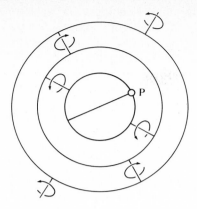

Fig. 2   The system of Eudoxus

ered that there might be (or might be envisaged to be) three spheres, concentric with the earth, each rotating within the other, as in the diagram, the moon being attached to the point P.

Aristotle went further and treated the spheres of Eudoxus as actual physical objects in the Universe, whose real motions actually caused the motion of the heavenly bodies as seen from the earth. Babylonian astronomy gave a "mnemonic reproduction of the facts in thought," and its method of adding and subtracting (zigzag functions) came as near to a science of purely inductive laws as it is possible to get. But the Babylonians could not explain the observed motions of the stars. On the other hand Greek astronomical theory both summarized the facts and so served as a basis for prediction, and *also* explained these facts to the satisfaction of the proponents of each theory as flowing from the operation of certain mechanisms. It is worth noting, too, that for the Babylonians, the facts were the relative positions of the stars as we see them in the heavens. But for the Greeks the facts were subtly different. What most of the Greek astronomers thought they were seeing when they looked up at night were bright objects which moved about in some pattern or system which was not exactly the way it looked from the earth, because we see the stellar system from only one point of view. It is Greek explanatory astronomy that developed into modern ideas about the Universe, not Babylonian inductive astronomy.

Our conclusion must be that though Mill's Canons are valuable schemata for organizing an investigation they could hardly be generalized into the whole of scientific method. And the reason, in short, is that scientists are not exclusively concerned to discover correlations among phenomena, but are at least as interested in the explanations as to why the correlations that can be discovered are the way they are, and in explanations as to why there are the structures that there are. Astronomy should explain not only the correlation between the rising and setting times of heavenly bodies but also the way the planets are arranged in the solar system, and that system in the galaxy.

This leads to a point of more general application. The real reason why inductivism is so wrong is that it is so unrealistic. It is an attempt to codify a more or less mythical conception of science. It is quite clear from Mill's Canons that inductivists picture scientists experimenting in the *hope* of finding correlations among phenomena. What then are we to make of the activities of anatomists who investigate the structure of organisms, of crystallographers and nuclear physicists who also are searchers after knowledge of structure? What are we to make of the enormous amount of effort put into attempts to measure natural constants accurately? What about taxonomists and their efforts to classify the plants, animals, and minerals found in the world? It would be quite ridiculous to rule out these activities as non-science. And if they are science and, as I contend, a major part of it, science can hardly be pictured as the search for correlations among types of events. Chemists are interested in finding what materials they can make from what; they are not interested in the correlation of the events of the vanishing of one lot of substances and the appearance of another lot. This myth of phenomena has been much in the minds of philosophers and has been responsible in no small part for the pointlessness of much philosophy of science in the past.

STUDY QUESTIONS

1   In Mendel's experiments, what is the relation between "fact" and "law"? How does Mendel's case differ from Kepler's?
2   Suppose Smith gets sick on three successive evenings. The first evening he drank scotch and water. The second evening he drank bourbon and water. He consumed lots of gin and water on the third evening. Using Mill's methods, find the cause of his sickness. What weakness in Mill's methods is revealed by this example?
3   "Mill's methods are the most reliable way to determine the laws of nature. They have been confirmed by centuries of practical and scientific experience." Would Harré agree with this statement? Do you think Hume would side with Harré?
4   Why does Harré think that inductivism is mistaken about the nature of "facts"? Do you believe that there are any "brute" facts?
5   What was the principal difference between Babylonian and Greek astronomy? Why does Harré think that this difference is so important? Can you make a similar point about some ordinary activities—say, cooking or auto mechanics?

SELECTED READINGS

One of the most famous contemporary arguments against Descartes's form of radical skepticism is G. E. Moore, "Proof of an External World," reprinted in his *Philosophical Papers* (London: G. Allen, 1959; New York: Collier Books, 1962). A. Kenny, *Descartes: A Study of His Philosophy* (New York: Random House, 1968), and H. G. Frankfurt, *Demons, Dreamers, and Madmen* (Indianapolis: Bobbs-Merrill, 1970) are good, recent critical studies of Cartesian skepticism. Some of the best writing on the mind-body problem is collected in A. Flew (ed.), *Body, Mind and Death* (New York: Macmillan, 1964), and G. N. A. Vesey (ed.), *Body and Mind* (London: G. Allen, 1964). These anthologies provide a wide historical survey of questions relating to the nature of mind, although Flew has the best coverage on the issue of personal identity. Ryle's views are critically evaluated in O. P. Wood and G. Pitcher (eds.), *Ryle—A Collection of Critical Essays* (Garden City, N.Y.: Doubleday, 1970). One of the earliest and most provocative statements of the behaviorist position was made by the psychologist

John B. Watson in *Behaviorism* (New York: Norton, 1924). By far the most famous contemporary spokesperson for the position is B. F. Skinner. A good, general statement of his views can be found in his *Science and Human Behavior* (New York: Macmillan, 1953). Interesting critiques of behaviorism by a psychologist and a philosopher respectively are contained in W. Köhler, *Gestalt Psychology* (New York: Liveright, 1929), and B. Russell, *Outline of Philosophy* (London: G. Allen; New York: Norton, 1927).

The first four chapters in Bertrand Russell, *The Problems of Philosophy* (London: Oxford University Press, 1912) raise the problem of perception and knowledge in a clear and thought-provoking way. A more technical account can be found in Russell, *Our Knowledge of the External World,* 2d ed. (London: G. Allen, 1926). F. M. Cornford's *Plato's Theory of Knowledge* (London: Routledge, 1935), from which our Plato selection was taken, is a very good book on Plato's theory of knowledge. Cornford adds rich commentary to the text, so that the beginning student can read Plato as well as have important philosophical points explained and set into a historical context. For the more advanced student, Brand Blanshard, *The Nature of Thought,* Vol. II (London: G. Allen, 1939) gives a good defense of rationalism and compares it with other theories. G. J. Warnock, *Berkeley* (Harmondsworth: Penguin Books, 1953) is a good general account of Berkeley's philosophy. For more extensive reading on idealism, see A. C. Ewing (ed.), *The Idealist Tradition from Berkeley to Blanshard* (New York: Free Press, 1957). M. Cohen and E. Nagel, *Introduction to Logic and Scientific Method* (New York: Harcourt, Brace, 1934) contains an excellent introductory discussion of scientific method and the pitfalls of Mill's methods. More advanced discussions of contemporary work in the philosophy of science are C. G. Hempel, *Philosophy of Natural Science* (Englewood Cliffs, N.J.: Prentice-Hall, 1966), N. R. Hanson, *Patterns of Discovery* (Cambridge, Mass.: Harvard, 1958), and Karl Popper, *The Logic of Scientific Discovery* (New York: Basic Books, 1959).

Part Three

Morality and Its Justification

THE PARADOX OF MORAL EXPERIENCE

In Dostoyevsky's famous novel *The Brothers Karamazov,* one of the characters describes the following scene:

> One day a serf boy, a little child of eight, threw a stone in play and hurt the paw of the general's favorite hound. "Why is my favorite dog lame?" He is told that the boy threw a stone that hurt the dog's paw. "So you did it." The general looked the child up and down. "Take him." He was taken—taken from his mother and kept shut up all night. Early the next morning the general comes out on horseback, with the hounds, his dependents, dog-boys, and huntsmen, all mounted around him in full hunting parade. The servants are summoned for their edification, and in front of them all stands the mother of the child. The child is brought forward. It's a gloomy, cold, foggy autumn day, a perfect day for hunting. . . . "Make him run," commands the general. "Run, run," shout the dog-boys. The boy runs. . . . "At him!" yells the general, and he sets the whole pack of hounds after the child. The hounds catch him and tear him to pieces before the mother's eyes. . . .

As this moral horror unfolds, powerful feelings and judgments intrude upon the reader. Rage, pity, and indignation emerge, along with the immediate and convincingly clear judgment that the suffering of the child is bad, that the punishment is unfair, and that the general is evil.

These are the facts of moral experience. The question for philosophy is how to understand them. Why do we feel these powerful urgings and sentiments? There are thousands of common events which do not call forth these feelings, so what is special about the death of the child? When we judge that the boy's suffering is bad, what exactly do we mean and what justifies our mental attitude? Is there something in the nature of things which demands a specific moral response, much as the nature of a triangle demands a certain intellectual judgment about it, or do we instead project our subjective feelings onto an objectively neutral circumstance?

Historically, theories have been developed on both sides. Moral subjectivism interprets our reactions as nonrational emotional responses which have been conditioned by training and which can be altered by training. On this view, there is no objective moral quality to the situation described by Dostoyevsky and there is nothing in human nature which *must* find it abhorrent. Perhaps in the future, in some new culture, audiences will watch such things for entertainment, and scholars will find our reactions somewhat curious and primitive. Thus for the moral subjectivist, our moral judgments are but expressions of taste, and taste is capricious and abitrary. On the other hand, objectivists view our moral judgments in the same way as other judgments. Moral judgments are true or false, depending upon the objective nature of things. Although disagreeing in detail, objectivists all agree that moral evaluation can be a rational affair.

Both positions, of course, can be supported with reasons. As you begin the readings, you will be confronted with the paradoxes of our moral experience. The rest is discovery.

Sources of Morality: God, Society, and the Individual

PROBLEM INTRODUCTION

In 399 B.C. Socrates was executed by the Athenian court on trumped-up charges of atheism and corrupting the youth. He probably could have escaped the death sentence if he had been willing to leave Athens or cease his philosophical activity, but, convinced that the unexamined life is not worth living, Socrates chose death over silence. In his speech to the court, he announced that his consuming passion was to examine the nature of virtue—what it is and how it is acquired. Socrates devoted his life to interrogating the citizens of Athens about morality, attempting to show them that, in spite of their firm convictions, they did not really know what virtue was. Since some of the things he was saying appeared to be an affront to religion, and were finding acceptance among the young, he was considered a threat to the established order.

Two moral theories found acceptance in the Athens of Socrates's day. The traditionalists maintained that the gods set forth a system of rules which all people were required to obey. For this group, moral and religious behavior were inseparable. This view was opposed by a new and unorthodox theory which took morality to be a set of rules used to further the interests of the strong. According

Editor's note: Introduction and editorial material for this section by Edward Walter, professor of philosophy, University of Missouri at Kansas City.

to this theory, right and wrong, good and evil are not real qualities in the world but merely conventions designed to protect the prevailing mode of life. To the traditionalist, this new conception of morality threatened to undermine the foundations of civilized society. How could people be motivated to follow the dictates of duty, often against their own self-interest, if morality is considered a human convention, destined to be replaced with new social conditions? On the other hand, the proponents of the new morality saw themselves as a progressive force in society, liberated from the dogmas of religion and custom.

Plato found himself in the middle of this controversy. Like Socrates, his teacher, he disagreed with both sides. The simple picture of moral obligation presented by the traditionalists is complicated by two persistent facts: one, human opinion about the will of the gods is extremely varied, and two, there is no certain method for choosing among conflicting opinion. In addition, the fact that the gods call some things good and other things evil tells us nothing about the nature of good and evil. The following important questions remain: Why do the gods command us to do certain things and not others? Is it mere caprice, or is there some reason behind the choice? Why should the gods be viewed as moral authorities? Does might make right? Unless satisfactory answers to these questions can be given, adherence to the will of the gods is blind obedience to dogmatic authority. Unlike the proponents of the new morality, Plato believed that some things are good by their very nature. That is, goodness is an objective quality in the world which does not alter with each new regime; nor does it depend on the changing character of human opinion. The selection from the *Euthyphro* provides a good example of Plato's criticism of the traditional conception of morality as well as a vivid picture of the kind of stinging criticism which alienated Socrates from the Athenian community.

The questions raised by Plato are as alive and meaningful today as they were in his own time. Many people continue to believe that an atheistic philosophy leads to moral anarchy. The contemporary existentialist Jean-Paul Sartre, himself an atheist, concedes that human beings in a godless universe find themselves without any foundation for morality. Sartre is led to this disquieting position because of his rejection of the theory known as *ethical naturalism.* Ethical naturalists believe that the foundation of ethics lies in the nature of humans themselves. Systems of morality are attempts to promote human happiness and to regulate conduct so that peace and harmony are maintained. Moral rules are validated by the fact that they lead to these universally desired consequences. In other words, moral rules can be objective in the sense that they can express the real conditions for the achievement of universal human goals. Sartre rejects this theory because he denies that there is a universal human "nature." People do not have a common set of needs and desires merely in virtue of the fact that they are people. Human beings are not compelled by a predetermined "nature" to value one thing or another. We are absolutely free to create ourselves and our values— "existence precedes essence." There are, therefore, no universal moral truths, no fixed and irresistible human goals, which can serve as signposts for correct moral decision. We are, Sartre says, "condemned to be free."

The conception of morality as a system of objective, universally binding rules has come under attack from the social sciences as well as humanistic existentialism. Advocating a theory which is reminiscent of the "new morality" of Plato's time, many social scientists are convinced that moral values are nothing more than conventions which have evolved within the special environment of each distinct culture. Ruth Benedict, a noted cultural anthropologist, points out that the forms of behavior vary so extensively from culture to culture that no universally approved practices can be found. Because of this she adopts the position called *ethical relativism.* Ethical relativists tend to view ethical systems as arbitrary conventions which have no logical basis in human nature or any other objective fact. Therefore morality varies from culture to culture, and each culture's morality is correct for it, for there are no criteria for determining which, if any, is the superior system of rules.

In some ways this sort of relativism strikes a progressive and reasonable note. Social scientists have long been aware of the disastrous effects of one culture rigidly imposing its system of morality on another. We recognize that, in many instances, to suppress different customs in the name of morality is an expression of an outworn puritanism or a presumptuous egotism. But ethical relativism, if pushed to its logical limits, penetrates deep into the moral values of all cultures and declares that they stand on the same nonrational level. Many serious thinkers reject relativism because of this implication. If whatever a culture approves of is right for that culture, then there is no point in trying to change any dominant practice. In fact, in a culture where slavery, for example, is the dominant social practice, it would be wrong to try to change things. When cultural approval becomes the sole criterion for right, moral progress does not seem possible. Indeed, the progressive and tolerant appearance of relativism begins to recede into moral complacency.

A second critique of relativism challenges one of its basic assumptions, namely that the values of various cultures are fundamentally different. It is true, for example, that some societies approve of infanticide while others do not. But this sort of difference concerning a specific practice may not indicate a difference in fundamental attitude. The same act may not have the same meaning in different cultural contexts because of divergent beliefs about the world. Thus a culture which practices infanticide may view the infant in exactly the same way as we view the newly formed fetus, or perhaps even as we view a plant. Consequently, the act has a different psychological significance to them. Solomon Asch, a social psychologist, maintains that because ethical relativists do not consider the psychological situation in which people moralize, they are inclined to interpret opposing practices as signs of opposing systems of value. He suggests that if we probe deeply enough into the psychological framework which gives meaning to various cultural practices we may find a common network of values.

But ethical relativism has survived this sort of criticism, for underlying the debate about the relativity of cultural practices, there is the nagging suspicion that moral judgments are intrinsically subjective—reflecting nothing more than the nonrational sentiment conditioned in us by our culture. Many contemporary philosophers, for example, have made much of the difference between scientific and ethical reasoning. In science, there is a method for resolving disputes—a method which involves experimentation to test competing theories. But ethical disputes do not seem to be resolved this way. When it comes down to basic ethical principles, nothing can be given as evidence, except perhaps another ethical principle which is just as suspect as the one in question. At this point arguments seem to degenerate into emotional displays. Bertrand Russell, one of the greatest philosophers of this century, advocated a theory of ethics called *emotivism*. Struck by the difference between scientific and ethical reasoning, he proposed that ethical statements, such as "Abortion is wrong," be considered as expressions of emotion, rather than assertions about the world. Accordingly, moral pronouncements are not true or false, for they are merely the venting, in speech, of our nonrational moral desires. Therefore, even if people agreed in their fundamental attitudes, as Asch suggests, moral principles would still be subjective and beyond rational appraisal.

Emotivism has aroused more controversy than any other ethical theory proposed in this century. Its critics, such as Brand Blanshard, observe that it is the ultimate foundation for ethical relativism, for it asserts that the moral qualities of things are created by the way we feel about them, not by their intrinsic character. As he points out, there can be no objective way of condemning Nazis for their unprovoked slaughter of Jews, Russians, and others; for when we say that they were wrong, we are not saying anything which could be true or false. Our emotions are erupting, but there is nothing in the world to logically justify one emotional reaction rather than another. Blanshard sees a world of moral anarchy depicted by the emotivists, a world where people do whatever they want and where everyone is right in doing so.

Still, it is probably correct to call ours *the era of subjectivism*. Never before in the history of thought have so many intelligent and educated people rejected the belief in a universal, objective system of values. Indeed, much of the recent resurgence of religious sentiment is grounded in the belief that moral chaos is the inevitable consequence of godless universe. Many eminent thinkers simply believe that the logical problems confronting an objective ethics are insurmountable. However, before you form an opinion you should study the next series of readings in which several philosophers discuss the most notable formulations of an objective ethics.

Why Should We Obey God?

Plato

Plato (c. 427 B.C.–c. 347 B.C.) was an Athenian aristocrat who became a philosopher because of the influence of his teacher and friend Socrates. Plato spent most of his life in Athens teaching at his school, the Academy. The dialogues he composed give us a good idea of his concept of education. These dialogues usually have Socrates and his student seeking a solution to a problem by discovering the nature of such things as "justice," "goodness," "knowledge," or "courage." The philosopher acts as a "midwife" to the student, helping the student give "birth" to an adequate idea. This conception of inquiry emphasizes that the source of knowledge is within each individual.

The subject under investigation in this dialogue is the nature of piety. The irony runs deep throughout this work because Socrates was executed for impiety. Euthyphro, who is shown to be cocky and ignorant, sided with those who brought charges against him. Although the dialogue is a search for the nature of piety, it clearly applies to morality. To most Greeks, morality was a system of duties set down by the gods, and so they would hardly distinguish between acting morally and acting piously. The point which Socrates urges against Euthyphro is that nothing becomes good, worthwhile, or obligatory simply because it is approved or commanded by someone—even God. Piety or goodness has an essential nature which is objective, and it is this nature which makes something good. Thus the *Euthyphro* is a treatise against authoritarianism in morality.

Euthyphro: Why have you left the Lyceum, Socrates? and what are you doing in the Porch of the King Archon? Surely you cannot be concerned in a suit before the King like myself?

Socrates: Not in a suit, Euthyphro; impeachment is the word which the Athenians use.

Euthyphro: What! I suppose that some one has been prosecuting you, for I cannot believe that you are the prosecutor of another.

Socrates: Certainly not.

Euthyphro: Then some one else has been prosecuting you?

Socrates: Yes.

Euthyphro: And who is he?

Socrates: A young man who is little known, Euthyphro; and I hardly know him: his name is Meletus, and he is of the deme of Pitthis. Perhaps you may remember his appearance; he has a beak, and long straight hair, and a beard which is ill grown.

Euthyphro: No, I do not remember him, Socrates. But what is the charge which he brings against you?

Socrates: What is the charge? Well, a very serious charge, which shows a good deal of character in the young man, and for which he is certainly not to be despised. He says he knows how the youth are corrupted and who are their

From *The Dialogues of Plato*, trans. B. Jowett (New York: The Macmillan Company, 1892).

corruptors. I fancy that he must be a wise man, and seeing that I am the reverse of a wise man, he has found me out, and is going to accuse me of corrupting his young friends. And of this our mother the state is to be the judge. Of all our political men he is the only one who seems to me to begin in the right way, with the cultivation of virtue in youth; like a good husbandman, he makes the young shoots his first care, and clears away us who are the destroyers of them. This is only the first step; he will afterwards attend to the elder branches; and if he goes on as he has begun, he will be a very great public benefactor.

Euthyphro: I hope that he may; but I rather fear, Socrates, that the opposite will turn out to be the truth. My opinion is that in attacking you he is simply aiming a blow at the foundation of the state. But in what way does he say that you corrupt the young?

Socrates: He brings a wonderful accusation against me, which at first hearing excites surprise: he says that I am a poet or maker of gods, and that I invent new gods and deny the existence of old ones; this is the ground of his indictment.

Euthyphro: I understand, Socrates; he means to attack you about the familiar sign which occasionally, as you say, comes to you. He thinks that you are a neologian, and he is going to have you up before the court for this. He knows that such a charge is readily received by the world, as I myself know too well; for when I speak in the assembly about divine things, and foretell the future to them, they laugh at me and think me a madman. Yet every word that I say is true. But they are jealous of us all; and we must be brave and go at them.

Socrates: Their laughter, friend Euthyphro, is not a matter of much consequence. For a man may be thought wise; but the Athenians, I suspect, do not much trouble themselves about him until he begins to impart his wisdom to others; and then for some reason or other, perhaps, as you say, from jealousy, they are angry.

Euthyphro: I am never likely to try their temper in this way.

Socrates: I dare say not, for you are reserved in your behaviour, and seldom impart your wisdom. But I have a benevolent habit of pouring out myself to everybody, and would even pay for a listener, and I am afraid that the Athenians may think me too talkative. Now if, as I was saying, they would only laugh at me, as you say that they laugh at you, the time might pass gaily enough in the court; but perhaps they may be in earnest, and then what the end will be you soothsayers only can predict.

Euthyphro: I dare say that the affair will end in nothing, Socrates, and that you will win your cause; and I think that I shall win my own.

Socrates: And what is your suit, Euthyphro? are you the pursuer or the defendant?

Euthyphro: I am the pursuer.

Socrates: Of whom?

Euthyphro: You will think me mad when I tell you.

Socrates: Why, has the fugitive wings?

Euthyphro: Nay, he is not very volatile at his time of life.

Socrates: Who is he?

Euthyphro: My father.

Socrates: Your father! my good man?

Euthyphro: Yes.

Socrates: And of what is he accused?

Euthyphro: Of murder, Socrates.

Socrates: By the powers, Euthyphro! how little does the common herd know of the nature of right and truth. A man must be an extraordinary man, and have made great strides in wisdom, before he could have seen his way to bring such an action.

Euthyphro: Indeed, Socrates, he must.

Socrates: I suppose that the man whom your father murdered was one of your relatives—clearly he was; for if he had been a stranger you would never have thought of prosecuting him.

Euthyphro: I am amused, Socrates, at your making a distinction between one who is a relation and one who is not a relation; for surely the pollution is the same in either case, if you knowingly associate with the murderer when you ought to clear yourself and him by proceeding against him. The real question is whether the murdered man has been justly slain. If justly, then your duty is to let the matter alone; but if unjustly, then even if the murderer lives under the same roof with you and eats at the same table, proceed against him. Now the man who is dead was a poor dependant of mine who worked for us as a field labourer on our farm in Naxos, and one day in a fit of drunken passion he got into a quarrel with one of our domestic servants and slew him. My father bound him hand and foot and threw him into a ditch, and then sent to Athens to ask of a diviner what he should do with him. Meanwhile he never attended to him and took no care about him, for he regarded him as a murderer; and thought that no great harm would be done even if he did die. Now this was just what happened. For such was the effect of cold and hunger and chains upon him, that before the messenger returned from the diviner, he was dead. And my father and family are angry with me for taking the part of the murderer and prosecuting my father. They say that he did not kill him, and that if he did, the dead man was but a murderer, and I ought not to take any notice, for that a son is impious who prosecutes a father. Which shows, Socrates, how little they know what the gods think about piety and impiety.

Socrates: Good heavens, Euthyphro! and is your knowledge of religion and of things pious and impious so very exact, that, supposing the circumstances to be as you state them, you are not afraid lest you too may be doing an impious thing in bringing an action against your father?

Euthyphro: The best of Euthyphro, and that which distinguishes him, Socrates, from other men, is his exact knowledge of all such matters. What should I be good for without it?

Socrates: Rare friend! I think that I cannot do better than be your disciple. Then before the trial with Meletus comes on I shall challenge him, and say that I have always had a great interest in religious questions, and now, as he charges me with rash imaginations and innovations in religion, I have become your disciple. You, Meletus, as I shall say to him, acknowledge Euthyphro to be a great theologian, and sound in his opinions; and if you approve of him you ought to approve of me, and not have me into court; but if you disapprove, you should begin by indicting him who is my teacher, and who will be the ruin, not of the young, but of the old; that is to say, of myself whom he instructs, and of his old father whom he admonishes and chastises. And if Meletus refuses to listen to me, but will go on, and will not shift the indictment from me to you, I cannot do better than repeat this challenge in the court.

Euthyphro: Yes, indeed, Socrates; and if he attempts to indict me I am mistaken if I do not find a flaw in him; the court shall have a great deal more to say to him than to me.

Socrates: And I, my dear friend, knowing this, am desirous of becoming your disciple. For I observe that no one appears to notice you—not even this Meletus; but his sharp eyes have found me out at once, and he has indicted me for impiety. And therefore, I adjure you to tell me the nature of piety and impiety, which you said that you knew so well, and, of murder, and of other offences against the gods. What are they? Is not piety in every action always the same? and impiety, again—is it not always the opposite of piety, and also the same with itself, having, as impiety, one notion which includes whatever is impious?

Euthyphro: To be sure, Socrates.

Socrates: And what is piety, and what is impiety?

Euthyphro: Piety is doing as I am doing; that is to say, prosecuting any one who is guilty of murder, sacrilege, or of any similar crime—whether he be your father or mother, or whoever he may be—that makes no difference; and not to prosecute them is impiety. And please to consider, Socrates, what a notable proof I will give you of the truth of my words, a proof which I have already given to others:—of the principle, I mean, that the impious, whoever he may be, ought not to go unpunished. For do not men regard Zeus as the best and most righteous of the gods?—and yet they admit that he bound his father (Cronos) because he wickedly devoured his sons, and that he too had punished his own father (Uranus) for a similar reason, in a nameless manner. And yet when I proceed against my father, they are angry with me. So inconsistent are they in their way of talking when the gods are concerned, and when I am concerned.

Socrates: May not this be the reason, Euthyphro, why I am charged with impiety—that I cannot away with these stories about the gods? and therefore I suppose that people think me wrong. But, as you who are well informed about them approve of them, I cannot do better than assent to your superior wisdom. What else can I say, confessing as I do, that I know nothing about them? Tell me, for the love of Zeus, whether you really believe that they are true.

Euthyphro: Yes, Socrates; and things more wonderful still, of which the world is in ignorance.

Socrates: And do you really believe that the gods fought with one another, and had dire quarrels, battles, and the like, as the poets say, and as you may see represented in the works of great artists? The temples are full of them; and notably the robe of Athene, which is carried up to the Acropolis at the great Panathenaea, is embroidered with them. Are all these tales of the gods true, Euthyphro?

Euthyphro: Yes, Socrates; and, as I was saying, I can tell you, if you would like to hear them, many other things about the gods which would quite amaze you.

Socrates: I dare say; and you shall tell me them at some other time when I have leisure. But just at present I would rather hear from you a more precise answer, which you have not as yet given, my friend, to the question, What is "piety"? When asked, you only replied, Doing as you do, charging your father with murder.

Euthyphro: And what I said was true, Socrates.

Socrates: No doubt, Euthyphro; but you would admit that there are many other pious acts?

Euthyphro: There are.

Socrates: Remember that I did not ask you to give me two or three examples of piety, but to explain the general idea which makes all pious things to be pious. Do you not recollect that there was one idea which made the impious impious, and the pious pious?

Euthyphro: I remember.

Socrates: Tell me what is the nature of this idea, and then I shall have a standard to which I may look, and by which I may measure actions, whether yours or those of any one else, and then I shall be able to say that such and such an action is pious, such another impious.

Euthyphro: I will tell you, if you like.

Socrates: I should very much like.

Euthyphro: Piety, then, is that which is dear to the gods, and impiety is that which is not dear to them.

Socrates: Very good, Euthyphro; you have now given me the sort of answer which I wanted. But whether what you say is true or not I cannot as yet tell, although I make no doubt that you will prove the truth of your words.

Euthyphro: Of course.

Socrates: Come, then, and let us examine what we are saying. That thing or person which is dear to the gods is pious, and that thing or person which is hateful to the gods is impious, these two being opposites of one another. Was not that said?

Euthyphro: It was.

Socrates: And well said?

Euthyphro: Yes, Socrates, I thought so; it was certainly said.

Socrates: And further, Euthyphro, the gods were admitted to have enmities and hatreds and differences?

Euthyphro: Yes, that was also said.

Socrates: And what sort of difference creates enmity and anger? Suppose for example that you and I, my good friend, differ about a number; do differences of this sort make us enemies and set us at variance with one another? Do we not go at once to arithmetic, and put an end to them by a sum?

Euthyphro: True.

Socrates: Or suppose that we differ about magnitudes, do we not quickly end the differences by measuring?

Euthyphro: Very true.

Socrates: And we end a controversy about heavy and light by resorting to a weighing machine?

Euthyphro: To be sure.

Socrates: But what differences are there which cannot be thus decided, and which therefore make us angry and set us at enmity with one another? I dare say that answer does not occur to you at the moment, and therefore I will suggest that these enmities arise when the matters of difference are the just and unjust, good and evil, honourable and dishonourable. Are not these the points about which men differ, and about which when we are unable satisfactorily to decide our differences, you and I and all of us quarrel, when we do quarrel[1]?

Euthyphro: Yes, Socrates, the nature of the differences about which we quarrel is such as you describe.

Socrates: And the quarrels of the gods, noble Euthyphro, when they occur, are of a like nature?

Euthyphro: Certainly they are.

Socrates: They have differences of opinion, as you say, about good and evil, just and unjust, honourable and dishonourable: there would have been no quarrels among them, if there had been no such differences—would there now?

Euthyphro: You are quite right.

Socrates: Does not every man love that which he deems noble and just and good, and hate the opposite of them?

Euthyphro: Very true.

Socrates: But, as you say, people regard the same things, some as just and others as unjust,—about these they dispute; and so there arise wars and fightings among them.

Euthyphro: Very true.

Socrates: Then the same things are hated by the gods and loved by the gods, and are both hateful and dear to them?

Euthyphro: True.

Socrates: And upon this view the same things, Euthyphro, will be pious and also impious?

Euthyphro: So I should suppose.

Socrates: Then, my friend, I remark with surprise that you have not answered the question which I asked. For I certainly did not ask you to tell me what action is both pious and impious: but now it would seem that what is loved by the gods is also hated by them. And therefore, Euthyphro, in thus chastising your father you may very likely be doing what is agreeable to Zeus but disagreeable to Cronos or Uranus, and what is acceptable to Hephaestus but unacceptable to Herè, and there may be other gods who have similar differences of opinion.

Euthyphro: But I believe, Socrates, that all the gods would be agreed as to the propriety of punishing a murderer: there would be no difference of opinion about that.

Socrates: Well, but speaking of men, Euthyphro, did you ever hear any one arguing that a murderer or any sort of evil-doer ought to be let off?

---

[1] Cp. I Alcib. III foll.

Euthyphro: I should rather say that these are the questions which they are always arguing, especially in courts of law: they commit all sorts of crimes, and there is nothing which they will not do or say in their own defence.

Socrates: But do they admit their guilt, Euthyphro, and yet say that they ought not to be punished?

Euthyphro: No; they do not.

Socrates: Then there are some things which they do not venture to say and do: for they do not venture to argue that the guilty are to be unpunished, but they deny their guilt, do they not?

Euthyphro: Yes.

Socrates: Then they do not argue that the evil-doer should not be punished, but they argue about the fact of who the evil-doer is, and what he did and when?

Euthyphro: True.

Socrates: And the gods are in the same case, if as you assert they quarrel about just and unjust, and some of them say while others deny that injustice is done among them. For surely neither God nor man will ever venture to say that the doer of injustice is not to be punished?

Euthyphro: That is true, Socrates, in the main.

Socrates: But they join issue about the particulars—gods and men alike; and, if they dispute at all, they dispute about some act which is called in question, and which by some is affirmed to be just, by others to be unjust. Is not that true?

Euthyphro: Quite true.

Socrates: Well then, my dear friend Euthyphro, do tell me, for my better instruction and information, what proof have you that in the opinion of all the gods a servant who is guilty of murder, and is put in chains by the master of the dead man, and dies because he is put in chains before he who bound him can learn from the interpreters of the gods what he ought to do with him, dies unjustly; and that on behalf of such an one a son ought to proceed against his father and accuse him of murder. How would you show that all the gods absolutely agree in approving of his act? Prove to me that they do, and I will applaud your wisdom as long as I live.

Euthyphro: It will be a difficult task; but I could make the matter very clear indeed to you.

Socrates: I understand; you mean to say that I am not so quick of apprehension as the judges: for to them you will be sure to prove that the act is unjust, and hateful to the gods.

Euthyphro: Yes indeed. Socrates: at least if they will listen to me.

Socrates: But they will be sure to listen if they find that you are a good speaker. There was a notion that came into my mind while you were speaking; I said to myself: "Well, and what if Euthyphro does prove to me that all the gods regarded the death of the serf as unjust, how do I know anything more of the nature of piety and impiety? for granting that this action may be hateful to the gods, still piety and impiety are not adequately defined by these distinctions, for that which is hateful to the gods has been shown to be also pleasing and dear to them." And therefore, Euthyphro, I do not ask you to prove this; I will suppose, if you like, that all the gods condemn and abominate such an action. But I will amend the definition so far as to say that what all the gods hate is impious, and what they love pious or holy; and what some of them love and others hate is both or neither. Shall this be our definition of piety and impiety?

Euthyphro: Why not, Socrates?

Socrates: Why not! certainly, as far as I am concerned, Euthyphro, there is no reason why not. But whether this admission will greatly assist you in the task of instructing me as you promised, is a matter for you to consider.

Euthyphro: Yes, I should say that what all the gods love is pious and holy, and the opposite which they all hate, impious.

Socrates: Ought we to enquire into the truth of this, Euthyphro, or simply to accept the mere statement on our own authority and that of others? What do you say?

Euthyphro: We should enquire; and I believe that the statement will stand the test of enquiry.

Socrates: We shall know better, my good friend, in a little while. The point which I should first wish to understand is whether the pious or holy is beloved by the gods because it is holy, or holy because it is beloved of the gods.

Euthyphro: I do not understand your meaning, Socrates.

Socrates: I will endeavour to explain: we speak of carrying and we speak of being carried, of leading and being led, seeing and being seen. You know that in all such cases there is a difference, and you know also in what the difference lies?

Euthyphro: I think that I understand.

Socrates: And is not that which is beloved distinct from that which loves?

Euthyphro: Certainly.

Socrates: Well; and now tell me, is that which is carried in this state of carrying because it is carried, or for some other reason?

Euthyphro: No; that is the reason.

Socrates: And the same is true of what is led and of what is seen?

Euthyphro: True.

Socrates: And a thing is not seen because it is visible, but conversely, visible because it is seen; nor is a thing led because it is in the state of being led, or carried because it is in the state of being carried, but the converse of this. And now I think, Euthyphro, that my meaning will be intelligible; and my meaning is, that any state of action or passion implies previous action or passion. It does not become because it is becoming, but it is in a state of becoming because it becomes; neither does it suffer because it is in a state of suffering, but it is in a state of suffering because it suffers. Do you not agree?

Euthyphro: Yes.

Socrates: Is not that which is loved in some state either of becoming or suffering?

Euthyphro: Yes.

Socrates: And the same holds as in the previous instances; the state of being loved follows the act of being loved, and not the act the state.

Euthyphro: Certainly.

Socrates: And what do you say of piety, Euthyphro: is not piety, according to your definition, loved by all the gods?

Euthyphro: Yes.

Socrates: Because it is pious or holy, or for some other reason?

Euthyphro: No, that is the reason.

Socrates: It is loved because it is holy, not holy because it is loved?

Euthyphro: Yes.

Socrates: And that which is dear to the gods is loved by them, and is in a state to be loved of them because it is loved of them?

Euthyphro: Certainly.

Socrates: Then that which is dear to the gods, Euthyphro, is not holy, nor is that which is holy loved of God, as you affirm; but they are two different things.

Euthyphro: How do you mean, Socrates?

Socrates: I mean to say that the holy has been acknowledged by us to be loved of God because it is holy, not to be holy because it is loved.

Euthyphro: Yes.

Socrates: But that which is dear to the gods is dear to them because it is loved by them, not loved by them because it is dear to them.

Euthyphro: True.

Socrates: But, friend Euthyphro, if that which is holy is the same with that which is dear to God, and is loved because it is holy, then that which is dear to God would have been loved as being dear to God; but if that which is dear to God is dear to him because loved by him, then that which is holy would have been holy because loved by him. But now you see that the reverse is the case, and that they are quite different from one another. For one Θεοφιλές is of a kind to be loved because it is loved, and the other ὅσιον is loved because it is of a kind to be loved. Thus you appear to me, Euthyphro, when I ask you what is the essence of holiness, to offer an attribute only, and not the essence—the attribute of being loved by all the gods. But you still refuse to explain to me the nature of holiness. And therefore, if you please, I will ask you not to hide your treasure, but to tell me once more what holiness or piety really is, whether dear to the gods or not (for that is a matter about which we will not quarrel); and what is impiety?

Euthyphro: I really do not know, Socrates, how to express what I mean. For somehow or other our arguments, on whatever ground we rest them, seem to turn round and walk away from us.

Socrates: Your words, Euthyphro, are like the handiwork of my ancestor Daedalus; and if I were the sayer or propounder of them, you might say that my arguments walk away and will not remain fixed where they are placed because I am a descendant of his. But now, since these notions are your own, you must find some other gibe, for they certainly, as you yourself allow, show an inclination to be on the move.

Euthyphro: Nay, Socrates, I shall still say that you are the Daedalus who sets arguments in motion; not I, certainly, but you make them move or go round, for they would never have stirred, as far as I am concerned. . . .

Socrates: Then we must begin again and ask, What is piety? That is an enquiry which I shall never be weary of pursuing as far as in me lies; and I entreat you not to scorn me, but to apply your mind to the utmost, and tell me the truth. For, if any man knows, you are he; and therefore I must detain you, like Proteus, until you tell. If you had not certainly known the nature of piety and impiety, I am confident that you would never, on behalf of a serf, have charged your aged father with murder. You would not have run such a risk of doing wrong in the sight of the gods, and you would have had too much respect for the opinions of men. I am sure, therefore, that you know the nature of piety and impiety. Speak out then, my dear Euthyphro, and do not hide your knowledge.

Euthyphro: Another time, Socrates; for I am in a hurry, and must go now.

Socrates: Alas! my companion, and will you leave me in despair? I was hoping that you would instruct me in the nature of piety and impiety; and then I might have cleared myself of Meletus and his indictment. I would have told him that I had been enlightened by Euthyphro, and had given up rash innovations and speculations, in which I indulged only through ignorance, and that now I am about to lead a better life.

STUDY QUESTIONS

1   In answer to Socrates's request for a definition of piety, Euthyphro replies that "piety is doing what I am doing; that is to say, prosecuting any one who is guilty of murder, sacrilege, or any similar crime." Socrates finds this answer unsatisfactory. What is wrong with it?

2   Euthyphro claims that piety is doing what the gods urge us to do. By analogy, Socrates demonstrates that Euthyphro's standard cannot answer the question about the nature of piety. What is the analogy? Why does Euthyphro's standard fail?

3   Toward the end of the dialogue, Socrates asks, "Is the pious or holy beloved by the gods because it is holy, or holy because it is beloved of the gods?" How does Socrates imply that this question should be answered? What reasons support his contention?

4   A final answer is not given to the question, "What is piety?" Why do you think that this question is hard to answer? How would you answer it?

5   *Smith:*   God commanded me to steal your money.
     Jones: No, God could not have commanded that, because it is wrong. You must
                   be mistaken.
     Could Jones accept Euthyphro's position?

6   Suppose we know the things that the gods approve of now. Are we in a position to know what they would approve of under other, new circumstances?

Morality without Religion

Jean-Paul Sartre

Jean-Paul Sartre (1905–   ) has done more than anyone else to make existentialism the most popular and influential philosophical movement of this century. In the early part of his career he taught philosophy at the Lycée Condorcet. With the outbreak of World War II, he served in the French Army and then became a resistance fighter in the French underground movement. In 1964 he was offered the Nobel Prize for Literature, but refused to accept it. In addition to many philosophical works, Sartre has written several plays and a novel.

This essay summarizes many of his key beliefs. Human beings are possessed of a radical freedom—the freedom to develop unique capacities apart from those given by human nature or by society. We are not predetermined, he argues, to be anything other than what we choose to be. But this freedom is a frightening thing. It means that there can be no excuses for what we are and what we become. It also means that there are no authorities, no guides, other than ourselves, in the life we create. God is dead, Sartre believes, and this means that humanity must look at itself in a new way. As uncomfortable as that may be, each of us must actively forge our own values.

Sartre's critics have attacked his view of human freedom. Does it really make sense to say that we can choose our own nature? As you read this essay, it might be helpful to keep this point in mind. Can every desire or need be eliminated or altered without changing something essential to the fabric of humanity?

What is meant by the term *existentialism?* Can it be that what really scares them in the doctrine I shall try to present here is that it leaves to man a possibility of choice? To answer this question, we must re-examine it on a strictly philosophical plane.

Actually, it is the least scandalous, the most austere of doctrines. It is intended strictly for specialists and philosophers. Yet it can be defined easily. What complicates matters is that there are two kinds of existentialist; first, those who are Christian, among whom I would include Jaspers and Gabriel Marcel, both Catholic; and on the other hand the atheistic existentialists, among whom I class Heidegger, and then the French existentialists and myself. What they have in common is that they think that existence precedes essence, or, if you prefer, that subjectivity must be the starting point.

Just what does that mean? Let us consider some object that is manufactured, for example, a book or a paper-cutter: here is an object which has been made by an artisan whose inspiration came from a concept. He referred to the concept of what a paper-cutter is and likewise to a known method of production, which is part of the concept, something which is, by and large, a routine. Thus, the paper-cutter is at once an object produced in a certain way and, on the other hand, one having a specific use; and one can not postulate a man who produces a paper-cutter but does not know what it is used for. Therefore, let us say that, for the paper-cutter, essence—that is, the ensemble of both the production routines and the properties which enable it to be both produced and defined—precedes existence. Thus, the presence of the paper-cutter or book in front of me is determined. Therefore, we have here a technical view of the world whereby it can be said that production precedes existence.

When we conceive God as the Creator, He is generally thought of as a superior sort of artisan. Whatever doctrine we may be considering, whether one like that of Descartes or that of Leibnitz, we always grant that will more or less

From Jean-Paul Sartre, *Existentialism,* trans. Bernard Frechtman (New York: Philosophical Library, 1947). Reprinted by permission.

follows understanding or, at the very least, accompanies it, and that when God creates He knows exactly what He is creating. Thus, the concept of man in the mind of God is comparable to the concept of paper-cutter in the mind of the manufacturer, and, following certain techniques and a conception, God produces man, just as the artisan, following a definition and a technique, makes a paper-cutter. Thus, the individual man is the realization of a certain concept in the divine intelligence.

In the eighteenth century, the atheism of the *philosophes* discarded the idea of God, but not so much for the notion that essence precedes existence. To a certain extent, this idea is found everywhere; we find it in Diderot, in Voltaire, and even in Kant. Man has a human nature; this human nature, which is the concept of the human, is found in all men, which means that each man is a particular example of a universal concept, man. In Kant, the result of this universality is that the wild-man, the natural man, as well as the bourgeois, are circumscribed by the same definition and have the same basic qualities. Thus, here too the essence of man precedes the historical existence that we find in nature.

Atheistic existentialism, which I represent, is more coherent. It states that if God does not exist, there is at least one being in whom existence precedes essence, a being who exists before he can be defined by any concept, and that this being is man, or, as Heidegger says, human reality. What is meant here by saying that existence precedes essence? It means that, first of all, man exists, turns up, appears on the scene, and, only afterwards, defines himself. If man, as the existentialist conceives him, is indefinable, it is because at first he is nothing. Only afterward will he be something, and he himself will have made what he will be. Thus, there is no human nature, since there is no God to conceive it. Not only is man what he conceives himself to be, but he is also only what he wills himself to be after this thrust toward existence.

Man is nothing else but what he makes of himself. Such is the first principle of existentialism. It is also what is called subjectivity, the name we are labeled with when charges are brought against us. But what do we mean by this, if not that man has a greater dignity than a stone or table? For we mean that man first exists, that is, that man first of all is the being who hurls himself toward a future and who is conscious of imagining himself as being in the future. Man is at the start a plan which is aware of itself, rather than a patch of moss, a piece of garbage, or a cauliflower; nothing exists prior to this plan; there is nothing in heaven; man will be what he will have planned to be. Not what he will want to be. Because by the word "will" we generally mean a conscious decision, which is subsequent to what we have already made of ourselves. I may want to belong to a political party, write a book, get married; but all that is only a manifestation of an earlier, more spontaneous choice that is called "will." But if existence really does precede essence, man is responsible for what he is. Thus, existentialism's first move is to make every man aware of what he is and to make the full responsibility of his existence rest on him. And when we say that a man is responsible for himself, we do not only mean that he is responsible for this own individuality, but that he is responsible for all men.

The word subjectivism has two meanings, and our opponents play on the two. Subjectivism means, on the one hand, that an individual chooses and makes himself; and, on the other, that it is impossible for man to transcend human subjectivity. The second of these is the essential meaning of existentialism. When we say that man chooses his own self, we mean that every one of us does likewise; but we also mean by that that in making this choice he also chooses all men. In fact, in creating the man that we want to be, there is not a single one of our acts which does not at the same time create an image of man as we think he ought to be. To choose to be this or that is to affirm at the same time the value of what we choose, because we can never choose evil. We always choose the good, and nothing can be good for us without being good for all.

If, on the other hand, existence precedes essence, and if we grant that we exist and fashion our image at one and the same time, the image is valid for everybody and for our whole age. Thus, our responsibility is much greater than we might have supposed, because it involves all mankind. If I am a workingman and choose to join a Christian trade-union rather than be a communist, and if by being a member I want to show that the best thing for man is resignation, that the kingdom of man is not of this world, I am not only involving my own case—I want to be resigned for everyone. As a result, my action has involved all humanity. To take a more individual matter, if I want to marry, to have children; even if this marriage depends solely on my own circumstances or passion or wish, I am involving all humanity in monogamy and not merely myself. Therefore, I am responsible for myself and for everyone else. I am creating a certain image of man of my own choosing. In choosing myself, I choose man.

This helps us understand what the actual content is of such rather grandiloquent words as anguish, forlornness, despair. As you will see, it's all quite simple.

First, what is meant by anguish? The existentialists say at once that man is anguish. What that means is this: the man who involves himself and who realizes that he is not only the person he chooses to be, but also a lawmaker who is, at the same time, choosing all mankind as well as himself, can not help escape the feeling of his total and deep responsibility. Of course, there are many people who are not anxious; but we claim that they are hiding their anxiety, that they are fleeing from it. Certainly, many people believe that when they do something, they themselves are the only ones involved, and when someone says to them, "What if everyone acted that way?" they shrug their shoulders and answer, "Everyone doesn't act that way." But really, one should always ask himself, "What would happen if everybody looked at things that way?" There is no escaping this disturbing thought except by a kind of double-dealing. A man who lies and makes excuses for himself by saying "not everybody does that," is someone with an uneasy conscience, because the act of lying implies that a universal value is conferred upon the lie.

Anguish is evident even when it conceals itself. This is the anguish that Kierkegaard called the anguish of Abraham. You know the story: an angel has ordered Abraham to sacrifice his son; if it really were an angel who has come and said, "You are Abraham, you shall sacrifice your son," everything would be all right. But everyone might first wonder, "Is it really an angel, and am I really Abraham? What proof do I have?"

There was a madwoman who had hallucinations; someone used to speak to her on the telephone and give her orders. Her doctor asked her, "Who is it who talks to you?" She answered, "He says it's God." What proof did she really have that it was God? If an angel comes to me, what proof is there that it's an angel? And if I hear voices, what proof is there that they come from heaven and not from hell, or from the subconscious, or a pathological condition? What proves that they are addressed to me? What proof is there that I have been appointed to impose my choice and my conception of man on humanity? I'll never find any proof or sign to convince me of that. If a voice addresses me, it is always for me to decide that this is the angel's voice; if I consider that such an act is a good one, it is I who will choose to say that it is good rather than bad.

Now, I'm not being singled out as an Abraham, and yet at every moment I'm obliged to perform exemplary acts. For every man, everything happens as if all mankind had its eyes fixed on him and were guiding itself by what he does. And every man ought to say to himself, "Am I really the kind of man who has the right to act in such a way that humanity might guide itself by my actions?" And if he does not say that to himself, he is masking his anguish.

There is no question here of the kind of anguish which would lead to quietism, to inaction. It is a matter of a simple sort of anguish that anybody who has had responsibilities is familiar with. For example, when a military officer takes the responsibility for an attack and sends a certain number of men to death, he chooses to do so, and in the main he alone makes the choice. Doubtless, orders come from above, but they are too broad; he interprets them, and on this interpretation depend the lives of ten or fourteen or twenty men. In making a decision he can not help having a certain anguish. All leaders know this anguish. That doesn't keep them from acting; on the contrary, it is the very condition of their action. For it implies that they envisage a number of possibilities, and when they choose one, they realize that it has value only because it is chosen. We shall see that this kind of anguish, which is the kind that existentialism describes, is explained, in addition, by a direct reponsibility to the other men whom it involves. It is not a curtain separating us from action, but is part of action itself.

When we speak of forlornness, a term Heidegger was fond of, we mean only that God does not exist and that we have to face all the consequences of this. The existentialist is strongly opposed to a certain kind of secular ethics which would like to abolish God with the least possible expense. About 1880, some French teachers tried to set up a secular ethics which went something like this: God is a useless and costly hypothesis; we are discarding it; but, meanwhile, in order for there to be an ethics, a society, a civilization, it is essential that certain values be taken seriously and that they be considered as having an *a priori* existence. It must be obligatory, *a priori,* to be honest, not to lie, not to beat your wife, to have children, etc., etc. So we're going to try a little device which will make it possible to show that values exist all the same, inscribed in a heaven of ideas, though otherwise God does not exist. In other words—and this, I believe, is the tendency of everything called reformism in France—nothing will be changed if God does not exist. We shall find oursleves with the same norms of honesty, progress, and humanism, and we shall have made of God an outdated hypothesis which will peacefully die off by itself.

The existentialist, on the contrary, thinks it very distressing that God does not exist, because all possibility of finding values in a heaven of ideas disappears along with Him; there can no longer be an *a priori* Good, since there is no infinite and perfect consciousness to think it. Nowhere is it written that the Good exists, that we must be honest, that we must not lie; because the fact is we are on a plane where there are only men. Dostoievsky said, "If God didn't exist, everything would be possible." That is the very starting point of existentialism. Indeed, everything is permissible if God does not exist, and as a result man is forlorn, because neither within him nor without does he find anything to cling to. He can't start making excuses for himself.

If existence really does precede essence, there is no explaining things away by reference to a fixed and given human nature. In other words, there is no determinism, man is free, man is freedom. On the other hand, if God does not exist, we find no values or commands to turn to which legitimize our conduct. So, in the bright realm of values, we have no excuse behind us, nor justification before us. We are alone, with no excuses.

That is the idea I shall try to convey when I say that man is condemned to be free. Condemned, because he did not create himself, yet, in other respects is free; because, once thrown into the world, he is responsible for everything he does. The existentialist does not believe in the power of passion. He will never agree that a sweeping passion is a ravaging torrent which fatally leads a man to certain acts and is therefore an excuse. He thinks that man is responsible for his passion.

The existentialist does not think that man is going to help himself by finding in the world some omen by which to orient himself. Because he thinks that man will interpret the omen to suit himself. Therefore, he thinks that man, with no support and no aid, is condemned every moment to invent man. Ponge, in a very fine article, has said, "Man is the future of man." That's exactly it. But if it is taken to mean that this future is recorded in heaven, that God sees it, then it is false, because it would really no longer be a future. If it is taken to mean that, whatever a man may be, there is a future to be forged, a virgin future before him, then this remark is sound. But then we are forlorn.

To give you an example which will enable you to understand forlornness better, I shall cite the case of one of my students who came to see me under the following circumstances: his father was on bad terms with his mother, and, more-over, was inclined to be a collaborationist; his older brother had been killed in the German offensive of 1940, and the young man, with somewhat immature but generous feelings, wanted to avenge him. His mother lived alone with him, very much upset by the half-treason of her husband and the death of her older son; the boy was her only consolation.

The boy was faced with the choice of leaving for England and joining the Free French Forces—that is, leaving his mother behind—or remaining with his mother and helping her to carry on. He was fully aware that the woman lived only for him and that his going-off—and perhaps his death—would plunge her into despair. He was also aware that every act that he did for his mother's sake was a sure thing, in the sense that it was helping her to carry on, whereas every effort he made toward going off and fighting was an uncertain move which might run aground and prove completely useless; for example, on his way to England he might, while passing through Spain, be detained indefinitely in a Spanish camp; he might reach England or Algiers and be stuck in an office at a desk job. As a result, he was faced with two very different kinds of action: one, concrete, immediate, but concerning only one individual; the other concerned an incomparably vaster group, a national collectivity, but for that very reason was dubious, and might be interrupted en route. And, at the same time, he was wavering between two kinds of ethics. On the one hand, an ethics of sympathy, of personal devotion; on the other, a broader ethics, but one whose efficacy was more dubious. He had to choose between the two.

Who could help him choose? Christian doctrine? No. Christian doctrine says, "Be charitable, love your neighbor, take the more rugged path, etc., etc." But which is the more rugged path? Whom should he love as a brother? The fighting man or his mother? Which does the greater good, the vague act of fighting in a group, or the concrete one of helping a particular human being to go on living? Who can decide *a priori?* Nobody. No book of ethics can tell him. The Kantian ethics says, "Never treat any person as a means, but as an end." Very well, if I stay with my mother, I'll treat her as an end and not as a means; but by virtue of this very fact, I'm running the risk of treating the people around me who are fighting, as a means; and, conversely, if I go to join those who are fighting, I'll be treating them as an end, and, by doing that, I run the risk of treating my mother as a means.

If values are vague, and if they are always too broad for the concrete and specific case that we are considering, the only thing left for us is to trust our instincts. That's what this young man tried to do; and when I saw him, he said, "In the end, feeling is what counts. I ought to choose whichever pushes me in one direction. If I feel that I love my mother enough to sacrifice everything else for her—my desire for vengeance, for action, for adventure—then I'll stay with her. If, on the contrary, I feel that my love for my mother isn't enough, I'll leave.". . .

Forlornness implies that we ourselves choose our being. Forlornness and anguish go together.

As for despair, the term has a very simple meaning. It means that we shall confine ourselves to reckoning only with what depends upon our will, or on the ensemble of probabilities which make our action possible. When we want something, we always have to reckon with probabilities. I may be counting on the arrival of a friend. The friend is coming by rail or street-car; this supposes that the train will arrive on schedule, or that the street-car will not jump the track. I am left in the realm of possibility; but possibilities are to be reckoned with only to the point where my action comports with the ensemble of these possibilities, and no further. The moment the possibilities I am considering are not rigorously involved by my action, I ought to disengage myself from them, because no God, no scheme, can adapt the world and its possibilities to my will. When Descartes said, "Conquer yourself rather than the world," he meant essentially the same thing. . . .

Actually, things will be as man will have decided they are to be. Does that mean that I should abandon itself to quietism? No. First, I should involve myself; then, act on the old saw, "Nothing ventured, nothing gained." Nor does it mean that I shouldn't belong to a party, but rather that I shall have no illusions and shall do what I can. For example, suppose I ask myself, "Will socialization, as such, ever come about?" I know nothing about it. All I know is that I'm going to do everything in my power to bring it about. Beyond that, I can't count on anything. Quietism is the attitude of people who say, "Let others do what I can't do." The doctrine I am presenting is the very opposite of quietism, since it declares, "There is no reality except in action." Moreover, it goes further, since it adds, "Man is nothing else than his plan; he exists only to the extent that he fulfills himself; he is therefore nothing else than the ensemble of his acts, nothing else than his life."

According to this, we can understand why our doctrine horrifies certain people. Because often the only way they can bear their wretchedness is to think, "Circumstances have been against me. What I've been and done doesn't show my true worth. To be sure, I've had no great love, no great friendship, but that's because I haven't met a man or woman who was worthy. The books I've written haven't been very good because I haven't had the proper leisure. I haven't had children to devote myself to because I didn't find a man with whom I could have spent my life. So there remains within me, unused and quite viable, a host of propensities, inclinations, possibilities, that one wouldn't guess from the mere series of things I've done."

Now, for the existentialist there is really no love other than one which manifests itself in a person's being in love. There is no genius other than one which is expressed in works of art; the genius of Proust is the sum of that, there is nothing. Why say that Racine could have written another tragedy, when he didn't write it? A man is involved in life, leaves his impress on it, and outside of that there is nothing. To be sure, this may seem a harsh thought to someone whose life hasn't been a success. But, on the other hand, it prompts people to understand that reality alone is what counts, that dreams, expectations, and hopes warrant no more than to define a man as a disappointed dream, as miscarried hopes, as vain expectations. In other words, to define him negatively and not positively. However, when we say, "You are nothing else than your life," that does not imply that the artist will be judged solely on the basis of his works of art; a thousand other things will contribute toward summing him up. What we mean is that a man is nothing else than a series of undertakings, that he is the sum, the organization, the ensemble of the relationships which make up these undertakings. . . .

Besides, if it is impossible to find in every man some universal essence which would be human nature, yet there does exist a universal human condition. It's not by chance that today's thinkers speak more readily of man's condition than of his nature. By condition they mean, more or less definitely, the *a priori* limits which outline man's fundamental situation in the universe. Historical situations vary; a man may be born a slave in a pagan society or a feudal lord or a proletarian.

What does not vary is the necessity for him to exist in the world, to be at work there, to be there in the midst of other people, and to be mortal there. The limits are neither subjective nor objective, or, rather, they have an objective and a subjective side. Objective because they are to be found everywhere and are recognizable everywhere; subjective because they are *lived* and are nothing if man does not live them, that is, freely determine his existence with reference to them. And though the configurations may differ, at least none of them are completely strange to me, because they all appear as attempts either to pass beyond these limits or recede from them or deny them or adapt to them. Consequently, every configuration, however individual it may be, has a universal value.

Every configuration, even the Chinese, the Indian, or the Negro, can be understood by a Westerner. "Can be understood" means that by virtue of a situation that he can imagine, a European of 1945 can, in like manner, push himself to his limits and reconstitute within himself the configuration of the Chinese, the Indian, or the African. Every configuration has universality in the sense that every configuration can be understood by every man. This does not at all mean that this configuration defines man forever, but that it can be met with again. There is always a way to understand the idiot, the child, the savage, the foreigner, provided one has the necessary information. . . .

If anybody thinks that he recognizes here Gide's theory of the arbitrary act, he fails to see the enormous difference between this doctrine and Gide's. Gide does not know what a situation is. He acts out of pure caprice. For us, on the contrary, man is in an organized situation in which he himself is involved. Through his choice, he involves all mankind, and he can not avoid making a choice: either he will remain chaste, or he will marry without having children, or he will marry and have children; anyhow, whatever he may do, it is impossible for him not to take full responsibility for the way he handles this problem. Doubtless, he chooses without referring to pre-established values, but it is unfair to accuse him of caprice. Instead, let us say that moral choice is to be compared to the making of a work of art. And before going any further, let it be said at once that we are not dealing here with an aesthetic ethics, because our opponents are so dishonest that they even accuse us of that. The example I've chosen is a comparison only.

Having said that, may I ask whether anyone has ever accused an artist who has painted a picture of not having drawn his inspiration from rules set up *a priori?* Has anyone ever asked, "What painting ought he to make?" It is clearly understood that there is no definite painting to be made, that the artist is engaged in the making of his painting, and that the painting to be made is precisely the painting he will have made. It is clearly understood that there are no *a priori* aesthetic values, but that there are values which appear subsequently in the coherence of the painting, in the correspondence between what the artist intended and the result. Nobody can tell what the painting of tomorrow will be like. Painting can be judged only after it has once been made. What connection does that have with ethics? We are in the same creative situation. We never say that a work of art is arbitrary. When we speak of a canvas of Picasso, we never say that it is arbitrary; we understand quite well that he was making himself what he is at the very time he was painting, that the ensemble of his work is embodied in his life.

The same holds on the ethical plane. What art and ethics have in common is that we have creation and invention in both cases. We can not decide *a priori* what there is to be done. I think that I pointed that out quite sufficiently when I mentioned the case of the student who came to see me, and who might have applied to all the ethical systems, Kantian or otherwise, without getting any sort of guidance. He was obliged to devise his law himself. Never let it be said by us that this man—who, taking affection, individual action, and kind-heartedness toward a specific person as his ethical first principle, chooses to remain with his mother, or who, preferring to make a sacrifice, chooses to go to England—has made an arbitrary choice. Man makes himself. He isn't ready made at the start. In choosing his ethics, he makes himself, and force of circumstances is such that he can not abstain from choosing one. We define man only in relationship to involvement. It is therefore absurd to charge us with arbitrariness of choice. . . .

STUDY QUESTIONS

1   Sartre says that when most intellectuals in Western society believed in God's existence it was plausible to believe that "essence precedes existence." To demonstrate this point, he draws an analogy between God as the creator of people and a paper cutter. Through this analogy, how does Sartre show the meaning of the claim "essence precedes existence"?

2   Sartre claims that there are Christian and atheistic existentialists. What do they have in common? Why does Sartre say that atheistic existentialism is a more coherent theory?

3   Sartre says that existentialism implies subjectivism. In what sense is the word *subjectivism* used? Why does human subjectivism imply human freedom, according to Sartre? Why does Sartre say that people are *condemned* to be free?

4   People *are* anguish, forlornness, despair, according to Sartre. In what way?

5   What does Sartre believe goodness is? What is badness? Do you think that his view is reasonable? What would happen to society if people followed Sartre's moral advice?

Culture and Morality
Ruth Benedict

Ruth Benedict (1887–1948) was one of America's leading cultural anthropologists. Her *Patterns of Culture* (1934) is a classic study in comparative anthropology. Benedict viewed a culture as a coherent system of ideas and practices which evolve around a central preference or mode of behavior. Once these core values have been selected, habits and ideas are chosen which are congenial with them. Practices which conflict with the core preferences are discarded, and over long periods of time a systematic pattern of behavior is built up.

Benedict believed that human beings are, for the most part, fairly adaptive. Widely divergent preferences may be expressed by different cultures, even to the point of whole cultures behaving in ways we would characterize as "crazy." But she surveys this diversity with moral neutrality. In this essay she claims that morality is nothing more than habit. What is moral for a culture is what is normal for that culture; and there is no fixed human nature which determines that only one behavior pattern can be normal.

Benedict's theory is a form of subjectivism. There is no hint given that some attitudes are more reasonable than others. In fact, some of the things she says suggest that "rationality," like morality, may be a culturally defined trait. This theory gives new life to the saying of the ancient Greek philosopher, Protagoras: "Man is the measure of all things."

Modern social anthropology has become more and more a study of the varieties and common elements of cultural environment and the consequences of these in human behavior. For such a study of diverse social orders primitive peoples fortunately provide a laboratory not yet entirely vitiated by the spread of a standardized worldwide civilization. Dyaks and Hopis, Fijians and Yakuts are significant for psychological and sociological study because only among these simpler peoples has there been sufficient isolation to give opportunity for the development of localized social forms. In the higher cultures the standardization of custom and belief over a couple of continents has given a false sense of the inevitability of the particular forms that have gained currency, and we need to turn to a wider survey in order to check the conclusions we hastily base upon this near-universality of familiar customs. Most of the simpler cultures did not gain the wide currency of the one which, out of our experience, we identify with human nature, but this was for various historical reasons, and certainly not for any that gives us as its carriers a monopoly of social good or of social sanity. Modern civilization, from this point of view, becomes not a necessary pinnacle of human achievement but one entry in a long series of possible adjustments.

These adjustments, whether they are in mannerisms like the ways of showing anger, or joy, or grief in any society, or in major human drives like those of sex, prove to be far more variable than experience in any one culture would suggest. In certain fields, such as that of religion or of formal marriage arrangements, these wide limits of variability are well known and can be fairly described. In others it is not yet possible to give a generalized account, but that does not absolve us of the task of indicating the significance of the work that has been done and of the problems that have arisen.

One of these problems relates to the customary modern normal-abnormal categories and our conclusions regarding them. In how far are such categories culturally determined, or in how far can we with assurance regard them as absolute? In how far can we regard inability to function socially as diagnostic of abnormality, or in how far is it necessary to regard this as a function of the culture?

From "Anthropology and the Abnormal," by Ruth Benedict, which appeared in The Journal of General Psychology, 1934, 10, 59–82. Reprinted by permission of The Journal Press.

As a matter of fact, one of the most striking facts that emerge from a study of widely varying cultures is the ease with which our abnormals function in other cultures. It does not matter what kind of "abnormality" we choose for illustration, those which indicate extreme instability, or those which are more in the nature of character traits like sadism or delusions of grandeur or of persecution, there are well-described cultures in which these abnormals function at ease and with honor, and apparently without danger or difficulty to the society.

The most notorious of these is trance and catalepsy. Even a very mild mystic is aberrant in our culture. But most peoples have regarded even extreme psychic manifestations not only as normal and desirable, but even as characteristic of highly valued and gifted individuals. This was true even in our own cultural background in that period when Catholicism made the ecstatic experience the mark of sainthood. It is hard for us, born and brought up in a culture that makes no use of the experience, to realize how important a role it may play and how many individuals are capable of it, once it has been given an honorable place in any society.

Cataleptic and trance phenomena are, of course, only one illustration of the fact that those whom we regard as abnormals may function adequately in other cultures. Many of our culturally discarded traits are selected for elaboration in different societies. Homosexuality is an excellent example, for in this case our attention is not constantly diverted, as in the consideration of trance, to the interruption of routine activity which it implies. Homosexuality poses the problem very simply. A tendency toward this trait in our culture exposes an individual to all the conflicts to which all aberrants are always exposed, and we tend to identify the consequences of this conflict with homosexuality. But these consequences are obviously local and cultural. Homosexuals in many societies are not incompetent, but they may be such if the culture asks adjustments of them that would strain any man's vitality. Wherever homosexuality has been given an honorable place in any society, those to whom it is congenial have filled adequately the honorable roles society assigns to them. Plato's *Republic* is, of course, the most convincing statement of such a reading of homosexuality. It is presented as one of the major means to the good life, and it was generally so regarded in Greece at that time.

The cultural attitude toward homosexuals has not always been on such a high ethical plane, but it has been very varied. Among many American Indian tribes there exists the institution of the berdache, as the French called them. These men-women were men who at puberty or thereafter took the dress and the occupations of women. Sometimes they married other men and lived with them. Sometimes they were men with no inversion, persons of weak sexual endowment who chose this rôle to avoid the jeers of the women. The berdaches were never regarded as of first-rate supernatural power, as similar men-women were in Siberia, but rather as leaders in women's occupations, good healers in certain diseases, or, among certain tribes, as the genial organizers of social affairs. In any case, they were socially placed. They were not left exposed to the conflicts that visit the deviant who is excluded from participation in the recognized patterns of his society.

The most spectacular illustrations of the extent to which normality may be culturally defined are those cultures where an abnormality of our culture is the cornerstone of their social structure. It is not possible to do justice to these possibilities in a short discussion. A recent study of an island of northwest Melanesia by Fortune describes a society built upon traits which we regard as beyond the border of paranoia. In this tribe the exogamic groups look upon each other as prime manipulators of black magic, so that one marries always into an enemy group which remains for life one's deadly and unappeasable foes. They look upon a good garden crop as a confession of theft, for everyone is engaged in making magic to induce into his garden the productiveness of his neighbors'; therefore no secrecy in the island is so rigidly insisted upon as the secrecy of a man's harvesting of his yams. Their polite phrase at the acceptance of a gift is, "And if you now poison me, how shall I repay you this present? " Their preoccupation with poisoning is constant; no woman ever leaves her cooking pot for a moment untended. Even the great affinal economic exchanges that are characteristic of this Melanesian culture area are quite altered in Dobu since they are incompatible with this fear and distrust that pervades the culture. They go farther and people the whole world outside their own quarters with such malignant spirits that all-night feasts and ceremonials simply do not occur here. They have even rigorous religiously enforced customs that forbid the sharing of seed even in one family group. Anyone else's food is deadly poison to you, so that communality of stores is out of the question. For some months before harvest the whole society is on the verge of starvation, but if one falls to the temptation and eats up one's seed yams, one is an outcast and a beachcomber for life. There is no coming back. It involves, as a matter of course, divorce and the breaking of all social ties.

Now in this society where no one may work with another and no one may share with another, Fortune describes the individual who was regarded by all his fellows as crazy. He was not one of those who periodically ran amok and, beside himself and frothing at the mouth, fell with a knife upon anyone he could reach. Such behavior they did not regard as putting anyone outside the pale. They did not even put the individuals who were known to be liable to these attacks under any kind of control. They merely fled when they saw the attack coming on and kept out of the way. "He would be all right tomorrow." But there was one man of sunny, kindly disposition who liked work and liked to be helpful. The compulsion was too strong for him to repress it in favor of the opposite tendencies of his culture. Men and women never spoke of him without laughing; he was silly and simple and definitely crazy. Nevertheless, to the ethnologist used to a culture that has, in Christianity, made his type the model of all virtue, he seemed a pleasant fellow.

An even more extreme example, because it is of a culture that has built itself upon a more complex abnormality, is that of the North Pacific Coast of North America. The civilization of the Kwakiutl, at the time when it was first recorded in the last decades of the nineteenth century, was one of the most vigorous in North America. It was built up on an ample economic supply of goods, the fish which furnished their food staple being practically inexhaustible and obtainable with comparatively small labor, and the wood which furnished the material for their houses, their furnishings, and their arts being, with however much labor, always procurable. They lived in coastal villages that compared favorably in size with those of any other American Indians and they kept up constant communication by means of sea-going dug-out canoes.

It was one of the most vigorous and zestful of the aboriginal cultures of North America, with complex crafts and ceremonials, and elaborate and striking arts. It certainly had none of the earmarks of a sick civilization. The tribes of the Northwest Coast had wealth, and exactly in our terms. That is, they had not only a surplus of economic goods, but they made a game of the manipulation of wealth. It was by no means a mere direct transcription of economic needs and the filling of those needs. It involved the idea of capital, of interest, and of conspicuous waste. It was a game with all the binding rules of a game, and a person entered it as a child. His father distributed wealth for him, according to his ability, at a small feast or potlatch, and each gift the receiver was obliged to accept and to return after a short interval with interest that ran to about 100 per cent a year. By the time the child was grown, therefore, he was well launched, a larger potlatch had been given for him on various occasions of exploit or initiation, and he had wealth either out at usury or in his own possession. Nothing in the civilization could be enjoyed without validating it by the distribution of this wealth. Everything that was valued, names and songs as well as material objects, were passed down in family lines, but they were always publicly assumed with accompanying sufficient distributions of property. It was the game of validating and exercising all the privileges one could accumulate from one's various forbears, or by gift, or by marriage, that made the chief interest of the culture. Everyone in his degree took part in it, but many, of course, mainly as spectators. In its highest form it was played out between rival chiefs representing not only themselves and their family lines but their communities, and the object of the contest was to glorify oneself and to humiliate one's opponent. On this level of greatness the property involved was no longer represented by blankets, so many thousand of them to a potlatch, but by higher units of value. These higher units were like our bank notes. They were incised copper tablets, each of them named, and having a value that depended upon their illustrious history. This was as high as ten thousand blankets, and to possess one of them, still more to enhance its value at a great potlatch, was one of the greatest glories within the compass of the chiefs of the Northwest Coast.

The details of this manipulation of wealth are in many ways a parody on our own economic arrangements, but it is with the motivations that were recognized in this contest that we are concerned in this discussion. The drives were those which in our own culture we should call megalomaniac. There was an uncensored self-glorification and ridicule of the opponent that it is hard to equal in other cultures outside of the monologues of the abnormal. . . .

All of existence was seen in terms of insult. Not only derogatory acts performed by a neighbor or an enemy, but all untoward events, like a cut when one's axe slipped, or a ducking when one's canoe overturned, were insults. All alike threatened first and foremost one's ego security, and the first thought one was allowed was how to get even, how to wipe out the insult.

In their behavior at great bereavements this set of the culture comes out most strongly. Among the Kwakiutl it did not matter whether a relative had died in bed of disease, or by the hand of an enemy, in either case death was an affront to be wiped out by the death of another person. The fact that one had been caused to mourn was proof that one had been put upon. A chief's sister and her daughter had gone up to Victoria, and either because they drank bad whiskey or because their boat capsized they never came back. The chief called together his warriors. "Now I ask you, tribes, who shall wail? Shall I do it or shall another? " The spokesman answered, of course, "Not you, Chief. Let some other of the tribes." Immediately they set up the war pole to announce their intention of wiping out the injury, and gathered a war party. They set out, and found seven men and two children asleep and killed them. "Then they felt good when they arrived at Sebaa in the evening."

The point which is of interest to us is that in our society those who on that occasion would feel good when they arrived at Sebaa that evening would be the definitely abnormal. There would be some, even in our society, but it is not a recognized and approved mood under the circumstances. On the Northwest Coast those are favored and fortunate to whom that mood under those circumstances is congenial, and those to whom it is repugnant are unlucky. This latter minority can register in their own culture only by doing violence to their congenial responses and acquiring others that are difficult for them. The person, for instance, who, like a Plains Indian whose wife has been taken from him, is too proud to fight, can deal with the Northwest Coast civilization only by ignoring its strongest bents. If he cannot achieve it, he is the deviant in that culture, their instance of abnormality.

This head-hunting that takes place on the Northwest Coast after a death is no matter of blood revenge or of organized vengeance. There is no effort to tie up the subsequent killing with any responsibility on the part of the victim for the death of the person who is being mourned. A chief whose son has died goes visiting wherever his fancy dictates, and he says to his host, "My prince has died today, and you go with him." Then he kills him. In this, according to their interpretation, he acts nobly because he has not been downed. He has thrust back in return. The whole procedure is meaningless without the fundamental paranoid reading of bereavement. Death, like all the other untoward accidents of existence, confounds man's pride and can only be handled in the category of insults.

Behavior honored upon the Northwest Coast is one which is recognized as abnormal in our civilization, and yet it is sufficiently close to the attitudes of our own culture to be intelligible to us and to have a definite vocabulary with which we may discuss it. The megalomaniac paranoid trend is a definite danger in our society. It is encouraged by some of our major preoccupations, and it confronts us with a choice of two possible attitudes. One is to brand it as abnormal and reprehensible, and is the attitude we have chosen in our civilization. The other is to make it an essential attribute of ideal man, and this is the solution in the culture of the Northwest Coast.

These illustrations, which it has been possible to indicate only in the briefest manner, force upon us the fact that normality is culturally defined. An adult shaped to the drives and standards of either of these cultures, if he were transported into our civilization, would fall into our categories of abnormality. He would be faced with the psychic dilemmas of the socially unavailable. In his own culture, however, he is the pillar of society, the end result of socially inculcated mores, and the problem of personal instability in his case simply does not arise.

No one civilization can possibly utilize in its mores the whole potential range of human behavior. Just as there are great numbers of possible phonetic articulations, and the possibility of language depends on a selection and standardization of a few of these in order that speech communication may be possible at all, so the possibility of organized behavior of every sort, from the fashions of local dress and houses to the dicta of a people's ethics and religion, depends upon a similar selection among the possible behavior traits. In the field of recognized economic obligations or sex tabus this selection is as nonrational and subconscious a process as it is in the field of phonetics. It is a process which goes on in the group for long periods of time and is historically conditioned by innumerable accidents of isolation or of contact of peoples. In any comprehensive study of psychology, the selection that different cultures have made in the course of history within the great circumference of potential behavior is of great significance.

Every society, beginning with some slight inclination in one direction or another, carries its preference farther and farther, integrating itself more and more completely upon its chosen basis, and discarding those types of behavior that are uncongenial. Most of those organizations of personality that seem to us most uncontrovertibly abnormal have been used by different civilizations in the very foundations of their institutional life. Conversely the most valued traits of our normal individuals have been looked on in differently organized cultures as aberrant. Normality, in short, within a very wide range, is culturally defined. It is primarily a term for the socially elaborated segment of human behavior in any culture; and abnormality, a term for the segment that that particular civilization does not use. The very eyes with which we see the problem are conditioned by the long traditional habits of our own society.

It is a point that has been made more often in relation to ethics than in relation to psychiatry. We do not any longer make the mistake of deriving the morality of our locality and decade directly from the inevitable constitution of human nature. We do not elevate it to the dignity of a first principle. We recognize that morality differs in every society, and is a convenient term for socially approved habits. Mankind has always preferred to say, "It is a morally good," rather than "It is habitual," and the fact of this preference is matter enough for a critical science of ethics. But historically the two phrases are synonymous.

The concept of the normal is properly a variant of the concept of the good. It is that which society has approved. A normal action is one which falls well within the limits of expected behavior for a particular society. Its variability among different peoples is essentially a function of the variability of the behavior patterns that different societies have created for themselves, and can never be wholly divorced from a consideration of culturally institutionalized types of behavior.

Each culture is a more or less elaborate working-out of the potentialities of the segment it has chosen. In so far as a civilization is well integrated and consistent within itself, it will tend to carry farther and farther, according to its nature, its initial impulse toward a particular type of action, and from the point of view of any other culture those elaborations will include more and more extreme and aberrant traits.

Each of these traits, in proportion as it reinforces the chosen behavior patterns of that culture, is for that culture normal. Those individuals to whom it is congenial either congenitally, or as the result of childhood sets, are accorded prestige in that culture, and are not visited with the social contempt or disapproval which their traits would call down upon them in a society that was differently organized. On the other hand, those individuals whose characteristics are not congenial to the selected type of human behavior in that community are the deviants, no matter how valued their personality traits may be in a contrasted civilization.

The Dobuan who is not easily susceptible to fear of treachery, who enjoys work and likes to be helpful, is their neurotic and regarded as silly. On the Northwest Coast the person who finds it difficult to read life in terms of an insult contest will be the person upon whom fall all the difficulties of the culturally unprovided for. The person who does not find it easy to humiliate a neighbor, nor to see humiliation in his own experience, who is genial and loving, may, of course, find some unstandardized way of achieving satisfactions in his society, but not in the major patterned responses that his culture requires of him. If he is born to play an important rôle in a family with many hereditary privileges, he can succeed only by doing violence to his whole personality. If he does not succeed, he has betrayed his culture; that is, he is abnormal.

I have spoken of individuals as having sets toward certain types of behavior, and of these sets as running sometimes counter to the types of behavior which are institutionalized in the culture to which they belong. From all that we know of contrasting cultures it seems clear that differences of temperament occur in every society. The matter has never been made the subject of investigation, but from the available material it would appear that these temperament types are very likely of universal recurrence. That is, there is an ascertainable range of human behavior that is found wherever a sufficiently large series of individuals is observed. But the proportion in which behavior types stand to one another in different societies is not universal. The vast majority of the individuals in any group are shaped to the fashion of that culture. In other words, most individuals are plastic to the moulding force of the society into which they are born. In a society that values trance, as in India, they will have supernormal experience. In a society that institutionalizes homosexuality, they will be homosexual. In a society that sets the gathering of possessions as the chief human objective, they will amass property. The deviants, whatever the type of behavior the culture has institutionalized, will remain few in number, and there seems no more difficulty in moulding the vast malleable majority to the "normality" of what we consider an aberrant trait, such as delusions of reference, than to the normality of such accepted behavior patterns as acquisitiveness. The small proportion of the number of the deviants in any culture is not a function of the sure instinct with which that society has built itself upon the fundamental sanities, but of the universal fact that, happily, the majority of mankind quite readily take any shape that is presented to them. . . .

STUDY QUESTIONS

1   What examples are used by Benedict to demonstrate that normalcy is culturally defined? What is her discussion of normalcy supposed to show about morality?
2   What does Benedict say happens to an individual who is transported to a culture which has a different conception of normalcy? What is the importance of this claim?
3   How does the recognition of the cultural relativity of normalcy affect our conception of morality, according to Benedict?
4   Why is it said that the concept of normalcy is a variant of the concept of the good? Do you think that this is true? Why or why not?
5   "National Socialists say: Legality is that which does the German people good; illegality is that which harms the German people" (William Frick—Nazi minister of the interior). Would Benedict say that Frick is on solid logical ground? How would Benedict respond to the Nuremburg trials?

The Psychology of Relativism

Solomon Asch

In the previous reading, Ruth Benedict, like many anthropologists, suggests that the radical diversity in human moral behavior means that there are no universal values. In this selection, Solomon Asch (1907–   ), a distinguished American psychologist and professor of Swarthmore College, challenges this claim. Cultural diversity, he argues, is not incompatible with shared values.

It is a mistake, Asch believes, to identify the morality of a culture with the behavior patterns exhibited in that culture. In this way, morality is seen as simply a complex system of conditioned responses. Naturally this leads to relativism. But such an analysis neglects the psychological meaning which members of a culture give to certain forms of behavior. Imagine, for example, how a primitive person from New Guinea would assess modern surgery. Not knowing anything of the theory and beliefs that underlie modern medicine, this person would "see" the surgeon butcher the patient. Such people would interpret our behavior in terms of a primitive system of beliefs and consequently would judge us to be vicious. And yet, in spite of our different practices, we may share the same goals of health and vigor and happiness.

Asch claims that once the context of action is considered, along with the psychological meaning given to the situation, different behavior patterns no longer seem strange and bizarre, but become infused with a rationale which appeals to a common humanity. Underneath cultural diversity, then, there may be a common human nature striving to fulfill itself under different conditions.

From Solomon E. Asch, *Social Psychology,* © 1952. Reprinted by permission of Prentice-Hall, Inc., Englewood Cliffs, New Jersey.

. . . Cultural relativism finds a strict psychological foundation in the propositions of stimulus-response psychology about needs and learning. In particular they offer an apparently cogent explanation of the formation of different reactions to identical conditions. Stimulus-response theory asserts that one can at will attach to a given situation S_1 any of a number of acts, feelings, and evaluations, depending on the consequences that follow. To situation S_1 any of responses R_x, R_y, R_z are possible. Which of the responses will become connected to the situation S_1 depends on which response will be followed by reward. It follows that we can, by the manipulation of rewards and punishments, attach to the *same* situation either of two *opposed* responses. There are situations that approximate outwardly to this interpretation. A signal in a conditioning experiment can be connected with food or with shock; a word can designate one object or another wholly unlike it. The stimulus-response account presupposes a thoroughgoing relation of arbitrariness between situation and action and between action and consequence. Let us now see how this interpretation is applied to practices and convictions.

The extension is accomplished simply by the assertion that beliefs, customs, and values are also "responses," learned in precisely the same way as one learns the connection between a person and his name or between a person and his telephone number. We learn to believe that which rewards and to disbelieve that which incurs pain. Therefore the manipulation of rewards and punishments can determine us to judge the same action as good or bad, true or false. For an organism governed by rewards and punishments these are the only possible and necessary "proofs." The laws of learning grind out truth and falsehood indifferently; rewards and punishments are the sole content and criterion of right and wrong. It follows that our ideas of right and wrong, beautiful or ugly are decided by social sanctions and that identical actions can be made desirable or despicable. It is on this basis that we are said to learn that gangsters are bad and that democracy is desirable. These are standards that we have "accepted"; nothing in the nature of democracy and crime points to their value. Life in society is therefore likened to the running of a maze in which the paths are arbitrarily fixed and which one learns to run in the search for satisfaction and avoidance of pain. "Culture, as conceived by social scientists, is a statement of the design of the human maze, of the type of reward involved, and of what responses are to be rewarded. It is in this sense a recipe for learning." . . . When today we encounter the statement that culture is "learned" it often refers not only to the necessity of past experience but also to the arbitrary effect of experience described here.

Deeply embedded in this view is the assumption that aside from a few biological needs there are no factor forces or tendencies in men. All else is "plasticity," the capacity to be shaped in almost indefinitely different ways by rewards and punishments. The temper of this position was clearly expressed in the following well-known statement by J. B. Watson:

> Give me a dozen healthy infants, well-formed, and my own specific world to bring them up in and I'll guarantee to take any one at random and train him to become any type of specialist I might select—doctor, lawyer, artist, merchant-chief, and yes, even beggar-man and thief, regardless of his talents, penchants, tendencies, abilities,

vocations, and race of his ancestors. [*Behaviorism.* New York: W. W. Norton, 1930, p. 82.]

The core of the same thought has been expressed more recently in the following statement:

Man's biological nature is neither good nor bad, agressive nor submissive, warlike nor peaceful, but neutral in these respects. He is capable of developing in either direction depending on what he is compelled to learn by his environment and by his culture. It is a mistake to assume that he can learn war more easily than peace. His learning machinery is not prejudiced, as is sometimes thought, toward the acquirement of bad habits. The bias is in his social environment. [M. A. May: *A Social Psychology of War and Peace.* New Haven: Yale University Press, 1944, p. 20.]

This position presupposes a dynamically empty organism, lacking autonomous tendencies beyone primary needs and lacking directed forces toward nature or society, which can therefore be turned with equal ease in opposed directions. To be sure, men can learn. But the fact of learning has the peculiar property of not altering them in any way that is significant for a conception of their character, since the habits they form contain nothing of comprehension or insight. Stimulus-response theory excludes the direct perception of social necessities or the guidance of sociological events by conscious direction. The following may serve as an illustration. We find that people react in one way when they find that someone has been untruthful and in a quite different way when he has been truthful. How is this to be understood? The stimulus-response answer is that such actions have in the past been connected with different consequences. What is of interest about the answer is not that it emphasizes the results of action, but its disregard of the idea that truthfulness and untruthfulness are comprehended in terms of their structure—in terms of what they signify for the relation between one person and another—and that they are evaluated on that basis. Instead of concluding that the requirement of truthfulness grows out of a grasp of the causal relation between act and consequence, it treats of truthfulness as a habit that has survived in the course of a trial and error process. This view is responsible for the conclusion that human nature is like water, which takes on whatever shape is imparted to it.

It is not difficult to see how this starting point decides the general interpretation of social action. If convictions and decisions are exclusively the outcome of arbitrary forces upon people who believe what they are made to believe, then one must not deceive oneself into holding that they are other than an expression of bias. In the sense of cultural relativism your values are not yours; they are those of the *Times,* or the *Tribune,* or whatever source of special pleading has succeeded in gaining access to you. You are a mouthpiece with society pulling the strings. At the center of these formulations is a definite assumption about the kind of dependence that prevails between individuals and groups. A plastic individual meets an established social order; the relation is that of hammer and anvil. Such views recommend themselves to many because of their objectivistic character; they appear to assume so much less than other psychologies. It remains to be seen whether they do not contain large assumptions. . . .

The insufficiencies of an absolutist psychological theory of ethical judgments are obvious. It has no means for dealing with cultural diversity (or, for that
matter, with intra-individual diversity). On the other hand, although the observations to which relativism refers have greatly widened the horizon of the social
sciences, the psychological interpretation they have received poses equally serious
difficulties. It is often assumed that these positions are the sole alternatives. Is
there not, however, a way to understand the diversities of human practices and
convictions without at the same time denying the authentic role of ethical discrimination? We will attempt to show that there is an alternative that fits the facts
more closely.

It is now necessary to consider a point about value-judgments that was only
adumbrated in the preceding chapter. When we evaluate an act as right or wrong
we do so with reference to its place and setting. We evaluate acts always as parts
of given conditions. We consider it wrong to take food away from a hungry child,
but not if he is overeating. We consider it right to fulfill a promise, but not if it is
a promise to commit a crime. Each of these examples is evidence that required-
ness is not a property that belongs to an action irrespective of its setting and
relations. Every judgment of the value of an act takes into account the particular
circumstances under which it occurs. There follows the important consequence
that the *same* act may be evaluated as right because it is fitting under one set of
conditions, and as wrong because it violates the requirements of another set of
conditions. (Whether there are some acts that we evaluate as right or wrong
under all circumstances is a difficult question that we may leave open in an
elementary discussion.)

It has been customary to hold that diverse evaluations of the same act are
automatic evidence for the presence of different principles of evaluation. The
preceding examples point to an error in this interpretation and to the need for a
distinction between relational determination and relativism. Indeed, an examination of the relational factors that determine the demands we sense may point to
the operation of constant principles in situations that differ in concrete details.
We shall explore now the bearing of the fact of relational determination upon the
culturally determined diversities of evaluation.

The essential proposition of ethical relativism states that one can connect to
the identical situation different and even opposed evaluations. Comparative observations of cultures seem to support this view abundantly. Infanticide, as we
have seen, receives different evaluations, as do numerous other practices. It
seems to follow that the content of our most basic convictions is variable and that
there is hardly a principle that, cherished under one social climate, is not violated
in another. These observations apparently contradict the conclusion that we
sense the demands of conditions. Relativism asserts this contradiction, claiming
that evaluations are subjective habits and preferences.

Some years ago Duncker and Wertheimer examined this problem and called
attention to a fundamental oversight in the relativistic position. Duncker showed
that the conclusion of relativism rests exclusively on the diverse connections
observed between outer conditions and practices. But psychological analysis requires that we take cognizance of certain intermediate steps. We act toward a

given situation in terms of its meaning—what we understand of it and what experience has taught us about it. On this basis we make evaluations and sense requirements that guide action. The terms of which we must take cognizance in the analysis of actions that have value-character are: (a) the externally given conditions; (b) the meaning they have for the actor; (c) the evaluations and requirements that available knowledge and understanding produce; and (d) the resulting actions. Now the thesis of relativism points to a lack of constancy in the relation between (a) and (d). It fails however to deal with the intervening terms. In particular, it does not consider the relation of evaluation (c) to the given cognitive conditions (b). But relativism, if it is to be psychologically valid, must assert that one can attach different evaluations to situations that have the same cognitive and emotional content. If, for example, we are to speak of relativism with reference to infanticide we must assume that the *same* action which is tolerated under one set of conditions is outlawed under other conditions. This assumption is as a rule dubious. The character of the object "infant" may not be the same under all conditions. In the first few days of life, an infant may be regarded as not yet human, in the way that many regard the embryo. (It should be noted that infanticide, when practiced, occurs only during the first few days following birth.) Therefore, the act of killing will not have the same meaning under all conditions. Precisely the same issue arises in connection with the killing of parents. In the society that follows this practice there prevails the belief that people continue to lead in the next world the same existence as in the present and that they maintain forever the condition of health and vigor they had at the time of death. It is therefore a filial duty of the son to dispatch his parents, an act that has the full endorsement of the parent and of the community.

Duncker suggests that different and apparently opposed practices and values are frequently not the consequence of diversity in ethical principles but of differences in the comprehension of a situation—differences in "situational meaning." The same external situation may possess quite varied meanings, depending upon the existing level of knowledge and upon other conditions. The resulting differences of action may therefore not be due to a diversity of principle. The meaning of a situation is usually a dependent part of a wider context. In a society in which supernatural beings are part of the cognitive scene, it will be plausible and convincing to impute illness to a purposeful, human-like agency. Consequently, the exorcising of illness by prayer and incantation will, under the given conditions, have a marked relevance. It will not signify that the persons in question are employing novel principles of causation or that they possess different modes of perceiving causation. Similarly, the concept of "stranger" may vary greatly; it may decide whether we shall slay him or treat him essentially like ourselves. The relativistic argument, by failing to take into account the psychological content of the situation, equates things that are psychologically different and only externally the same. It seeks for a mechanical regularity between external situation and action instead of a structural identity between the psychological content of a situation and the act. If we consider the psychological content, we have to conclude that the same action may represent psychologically different contents and that different actions may be functionally identical. To establish whether human beings actually possess contradictory values, it would be necessary to show that the relations between situational meanings and evaluation, or between the terms (b) and (c) above, can vary. This relativism has decidedly failed to do.

Implicit in the preceding discussion is the conclusion that the fact of cultural differences cannot be automatically converted into an argument for a relativism of values. Cultural differences are compatible with identity in values. Indeed, the assumption of variance dictates the conclusion that practices will differ with circumstances. If action and experience are a function of given conditions, we must expect that the former will vary with the latter. To expect uniform practices among societies is as reasonable as to expect all those with poor eyesight to wear identical lenses or for a person to face all situations with the same emotion. This point is well understood when the facts of material culture are under discussion. We consider it reasonable that the Bantu do not build igloos and that Eskimos do not live in thatched huts. Instead of stating conclusions about the relativism of building practices we quite properly take into account the climate, the materials available, and the level of knowledge. The same mode of thinking is indicated when we speak of values, if we do not assume in advance that they are arbitrary. When an Eskimo family permits an old person to expose himself to death this must be viewed in relation to their situation, their problems, and the alternatives open to them. The act does not have the same meaning for them that it would have for us today; Eskimos do not have homes for the aged or retirement pensions. If we take the given circumstances into account the possibility is present for understanding diverse actions in terms of the same operations of valuing.

What can we say about the relation between "situational meaning" and evaluation? In general, anthropological evidence does not furnish proof of relativism in the relation between the meaning of situations and their evaluation. We do not know of societies in which bravery is despised and cowardice held up to honor, in which generosity is considered a vice and ingratitude a virtue. It seems rather, as Duncker proposed, that the relations between valuation and meaning are invariant. It is not usual to find groups placing a different valuation upon, or experiencing different obligations toward, a situation that they understand in an identical way. It seems rather that certain ethical discriminations are universally known. We still have to hear of a society to which modesty, courage, and hospitality are not known.

Throughout the preceding discussion we have assumed one far-reaching form of "relativism" to be present: that pertaining to knowledge and understanding. Historical conditions determine the extent and level of knowledge and therefore the content and evaluation of given conditions. We may illustrate the general fact with a simple instance. A need, such as hunger, does not innately refer to its adequate object. It is only when the hungry infant is fed that he can form a craving for milk or sweets and search for them subsequently. Obviously the object must be experienced (or heard about) if it is to become relevant to one's needs. One cannot crave an object one has not experienced. It will necessarily happen that in different societies there will be quite different food preferences. Here we have a concrete, if simple, instance of what many call relativism, although it is more properly an example of relational determination. What can it teach us? First, the variation is not unlimited; however different in quality and in adequacy, an article of food will generally become an object of craving because it has food-value. When two groups come in contact, each will continue to prefer its diet; here we have a difference that is to a degree arbitrary. But again we find that the differences are not as unlimited as a sketchy analysis suggests. To the extent that different diets are equally nutritious, a preference for the one that is familiar is a fact upon which one cannot place undue importance. It is more significant to ask about the changes in diet that follow increased knowledge. The answer is fairly obvious. . . .

A serious appraisal of the role of cognitive factors permits us to clarify an important problem about values. It may have seemed that to emphasize the probability of invariance between evaluation and action and the presence of certain universal ethical discriminations leaves no place for the growth or change of values. But it should be evident that changes of knowledge and understanding make necessary the evolution of values. When knowledge spreads that men have basic qualities in common, it becomes more difficult to oppress them. When we find that differences between races are chiefly socially determined, it becomes less easy to practice segregation and colonialism. When we learn that criminals have emotions and strong social tendencies we can no longer sustain a purely punitive attitude toward them. With an increased appreciation of the role of reflection and knowledge some come to feel the obligation to be intelligent. Increasing knowledge of human characteristics teaches us the value of the human person. As we learn more of the conditions that affect the development of persons we feel the obligation to improve the material conditions of mankind. In this way alone can we understand the more humane treatment of mental patients, the feeble-minded, and other disadvantaged groups. In this sense there can be a development in the notions of justice and the emergence of novel moral insight. There is reason to say that ideas have an immense effect on evaluation and action. . . .

What are the consequences of these ideas for understanding cultural differences in evaluation? Perhaps the main effect is to make the practices of peoples more comprehensible by divesting them, not of interest, but of bizarreness and grotesqueness. Once we abandon certain assumptions about the externality of man's relation to the surroundings, a wholly different view of cultural differences unfolds before us. These need no longer appear as responses to manipulation by social conditions or as the final signs of limitation and subjectivity. We can now see them also as the necessary consequence of permanent human tendencies coming to expression under particular conditions. It also becomes clear that the first step in understanding action or conviction is to establish the way in which it appears to the actor and the reason it appears to him to be right. This is the way to proceed if we take seriously human capacities for comprehension and for formulating explanations within the limitations of knowledge and experience. We need to establish the core of relevance that action or belief has for its practitioners; to do so we need to see action in its context.

Considered from the standpoint of method, relativism deals with social data in a piecemeal way. The impressiveness of its conclusions rests almost entirely on

the divorce of data from their context. It lists the diversity of practices in response to the same external conditions, tearing them out of their context. In
consequence it obscures their concrete content and dynamics. It should also be
mentioned here that an adequate examination must include a reference to the
repercussions that standards and values have upon those who are under their
sway. The reactions to regulations, the problems they solve, and the conflicts they
generate are as pertinent as is their existence and observance. Those views that
stress the almost unlimited malleability of human character tend to overlook the
inevitable concomitants of conditions, which it would be hard to understand
relativistically. Unless we look at interrelations we remove the possibility of understanding either cultural differences or similarities.

In general, it is not enough to catalogue existing similarities and differences;
these are only the starting point of inquiry. It is more important to show that
cultural variations are facts having direction. To consider cultural differences in
terms of change and direction is immediately to transcend the static position of
relativism. It is not enough to say that some societies observe rules of cleanliness
and others do not. It would be more consequential to ask whether one can as
readily teach one group to adopt the habits of cleanliness as another to surrender
them; whether one can as readily convert an American community to curing
illness by sorcery as persuade a primitive group to adopt modern medical practices. It is not enough to say for example that the musical tastes of Japanese and
Europeans differ. It is more significant to ask what the reactions of Japanese and
Europeans would be to both forms of music when they have mastered each. If we
proceed in this way we are likely to find that changes have a direction and that
often the direction is irreversible because of the sensible character of some psychological processes. Instead of comparing men and societies as they are, it is
more fruitful to study the tendencies they show in the course of change.

This discussion has not attempted to settle the extent to which values are
invariant, but rather to suggest a way of thinking about their identities and differences. In particular, it has described an alternative to the positions of absolutism
and relativism. In contrast to the former, we have taken into account the facts of
cultural diversity. At the same time we have tried to go beyond the sheer factual
demonstration of diversity. The first two positions, although entirely opposed in
their conclusions, are at one on an essential point of theory. They reach opposed
conclusions on the basis of the same technical assumption of elementarism;
therefore they agree that the sole alternatives are between them. Indeed, it would
be right to say that each rests its case on the failure of the other. Relativism
argues that if there are valid standards they must everywhere be the same and
that the variability of standards is evidence that they are arbitrary. Absolutism,
on the other hand, seeks to preserve the validity of standards at the cost of
ignoring observed differences. If, however, we take into account the structural
properties of experience and action we can understand that standards are relative
without abandoning the concept of a human nature. It is necessary to acknowledge that science, art, and moral convictions at no time express completely the
facts of the world or human needs; in this general sense there is relativism. But

we need also to see these achievements as part of the history of human development, as the strivings of an authentic human nature. If we follow this path we will not treat all social facts as equally arbitrary or identify what is with what is right. Instead we will consider what societies do to realize human possibilities or to stunt them.

STUDY QUESTIONS

1   Contrast the conception of human nature which Asch attributes to ethical relativism with an opposing view of human nature. Is it possible to go to extremes either way? Which conception do you find most reasonable?

2   What facts of the ethical situation does Asch believe are neglected by a stimulus-response analysis of human behavior? Why are these facts important?

3   What is the *essential* claim of ethical relativism? Why does Asch say that the evidence of cultural diversity is insufficient to prove this claim?

4   Asch distinguishes between relativism and *relational determination*. Explain this difference. What is the difference between relational determination and what Asch calls *absolutism?*

5   Construct a debate between an ethical relativist, like Benedict, and Asch. Develop the argument so that the strongest position wins.

6   Which position do you think leads to a greater tolerance of cultural diversity—Benedict's or Asch's? Defend your answer.

Science and Ethics

Bertrand Russell

Bertrand Russell (1872–1970) was the twentieth-century representative of a tradition of British philosophy reaching back through Mill, Hume, and Locke. Cultured, urbane, and immensely civilized, Russell nevertheless expressed a fierce individualism in the face of dominant cultural attitudes. His early career was marked by his work in logic and mathematics, which culminated in the publication of *Principia Mathematica,* with Alfred North Whitehead, in 1910. At this time he became a lecturer at Cambridge University, but his pacifism caused him to be dismissed. Later, during World War I, he was imprisoned for his pacifist views. Throughout his lifetime Russell was known for his unorthodox beliefs about politics, marriage, religion, and the other great concerns of human existence. At the end of his life, he was a vociferous critic of America's involvement in Indochina. (For further information on Russell, see p. 79.)

In this essay Russell gives the main outline of the emotive theory of ethics. He maintains that there are no objective moral facts which exist independent of human desires. Our moral judgments are not really judgments at all, for they do not express truth or falsity. In fact, our moral evaluations are merely expressions of our desires. Ethical argument is not an attempt to get at the facts, but rather an attempt to get others to feel as we do.

Russell's critics have claimed that this doctrine leads to moral anarchy. But Russell replies that most people have genuinely social desires that cannot be created by abstract argument. This fact saves us, he claims, from chaos. Reason alone never could.

Those who maintain the insufficiency of science . . . appeal to the fact that science has nothing to say about "values." This I admit; but when it is inferred that ethics contains truths which cannot be proved or disproved by science, I disagree. The matter is one on which it is not altogether easy to think clearly, and my own views on it are quite different from what they were thirty years ago. But it is necessary to be clear about it if we are to appraise such arguments as those in support of Cosmic Purpose. As there is no consensus of opinion about ethics, it must be understood that what follows is my personal belief, not the dictum of science.

The study of ethics, traditionally, consists of two parts, one concerned with moral rules, the other with what is good on its own account. Rules of conduct, many of which have a ritual origin, play a great part in the lives of savages and primitive peoples. It is forbidden to eat out of the chief's dish, or to seethe the kid in its mother's milk; it is commanded to offer sacrifices to the gods, which, at a certain stage of development, are thought most acceptable if they are human beings. Other moral rules, such as the prohibition of murder and theft, have a more obvious social utility, and survive the decay of the primitive theological systems with which they were originally associated. But as men grow more reflective there is a tendency to lay less stress on rules and more on states of mind. This comes from two sources—philosophy and mystical religion. We are all familiar with passages in the prophets and the gospels, in which purity of heart is set above meticulous observance of the Law; and St. Paul's famous praise of charity, or love, teaches the same principle. The same thing will be found in all great mystics, Christian and non-Christian: what they value is a state of mind, out of which, as they hold, right conduct must ensue; rules seem to them external, and insufficiently adaptable to circumstances.

One of the ways in which the need of appealing to external rules of conduct has been avoided has been the belief in "conscience," which has been especially important in Protestant ethics. It has been supposed that God reveals to each human heart what is right and what is wrong, so that, in order to avoid sin, we have only to listen to the inner voice. There are, however, two difficulties in this theory: first, that conscience says different things to different people; secondly, that the study of the unconscious has given us an understanding of the mundane causes of conscientious feelings.

As to the different deliverances of conscience: George III's conscience told him that he must not grant Catholic Emancipation, as, if he did, he would have committed perjury in taking the Coronation Oath, but later monarchs have had no such scruples. Conscience leads some to condemn the spoliation of the rich by the poor, as advocated by communists; and others to condemn exploitation of the poor by the rich, as practised by capitalists. It tells one man that he ought to

From Bertrand Russell, Chapter IX "Science and Ethics" in *Religion and Science*. Reprinted by permission of The Clarendon Press, Oxford.

defend his country in case of invasion, while it tells another that all participation in warfare is wicked. During the War, the authorities, few of whom had studied ethics, found conscience very puzzling, and were led to some curious decisions, such as that a man might have conscientious scruples against fighting himself, but not against working on the fields so as to make possible the conscription of another man. They held also that, while conscience might disapprove of all war, it could not, failing that extreme position, disapprove of the war then in progress. Those who, for whatever reason, thought it wrong to fight, were compelled to state their position in terms of this somewhat primitive and unscientific conception of "conscience."

The diversity in the deliverances of conscience is what is to be expected when its origin is understood. In early youth, certain classes of acts meet with approval, and others with disapproval; and by the normal process of association, pleasure and discomfort gradually attach themselves to the acts, and not merely to the approval and disapproval respectively produced by them. As time goes on, we may forget all about our early moral training, but we shall still feel uncomfortable about certain kinds of actions, while others will give us a glow of virtue. To introspection, these feelings are mysterious, since we no longer remember the circumstances which originally caused them; and therefore it is natural to attribute them to the voice of God in the heart. But in fact conscience is a product of education, and can be trained to approve or disapprove, in the great majority of mankind, as educators may see fit. While, therefore, it is right to wish to liberate ethics from external moral rules, this can hardly be satisfactorily achieved by means of the notion of "conscience."

Philosophers, by a different road, have arrived at a different position in which, also, moral rules of conduct have a subordinate place. They have framed the concept of the Good, by which they mean (roughly speaking) that which, in itself and apart from its consequences, we should wish to see existing—or, if they are theists, that which is pleasing to God. Most people would agree that happiness is preferable to unhappiness, friendliness to unfriendliness, and so on. Moral rules, according to this view, are justified if they promote the existence of what is good on its own account, but not otherwise. The prohibition of murder, in the vast majority of cases, can be justified by its effects, but the practice of burning widows on their husband's funeral pyre cannot. The former rule, therefore, should be retained, but not the latter. Even the best moral rules, however, will have *some* exceptions, since no class of action *always* has bad results. We have thus three different senses in which an act may be ethically commendable: (1) it may be in accordance with the received moral code; (2) it may be sincerely intended to have good effects; (3) it may in fact have good effects. The third sense, however, is generally considered inadmissible in morals. According to orthodox theology, Judas Iscariot's act of betrayal had good consequences, since it was necessary for the Atonement; but it was not on this account laudable.

Different philosophers have formed different conceptions of the Good. Some hold that it consists in the knowledge and love of God; others in universal love; others in the enjoyment of beauty; and yet others in pleasure. The Good once defined, the rest of ethics follows: we ought to act in the way we believe most likely to create as much good as possible, and as little as possible of its correlative evil. The framing of moral rules, so long as the ultimate Good is supposed known, is matter for science. For example: should capital punishment be inflicted for theft, or only for murder, or not at all? Jeremy Bentham, who considered pleasure to be the Good, devoted himself to working out what criminal code would most promote pleasure, and concluded that it ought to be much less severe than that prevailing in his day. All this, except the proposition that pleasure is the Good, comes within the sphere of science.

But when we try to be definite as to what we mean when we say that this or that is "the Good," we find ourselves involved in very great difficulties. Bentham's creed that pleasure is the Good roused furious opposition, and was said to be a pig's philosophy. Neither he nor his opponents could advance any argument. In a scientific question, evidence can be adduced on both sides, and in the end one side is seen to have the better case—or, if this does not happen, the question is left undecided. But in a question as to whether this or that is the ultimate Good, there is no evidence either way; each disputant can only appeal to his own emotions, and employ such rhetorical devices as shall rouse similar emotions in others.

Take, for example, a question which has come to be important in practical politics. Bentham held that one man's pleasure has the same ethical importance as another man's, provided the quantities are equal; and on this ground he was led to advocate democracy. Nietzsche, on the contrary, held that only the great man can be regarded as important on his own account, and that the bulk of mankind are only means to his well-being. He viewed ordinary men as many people view animals: he thought it justifiable to make use of them, not for their own good, but for that of the superman, and this view has since been adopted to justify the abandonment of democracy. We have here a sharp disagreement of great practical importance, but we have absolutely no means, of a scientific or intellectual kind, by which to persuade either party that the other is in the right. There are, it is true, ways of altering men's opinions on such subjects, but they are all emotional, not intellectual.

Questions as to "values"—that is to say, as to what is good or bad on its own account, independently of its effects—lie outside the domain of science, as the defenders of religion emphatically assert. I think that in this they are right, but I draw the further conclusion, which they do not draw, that questions as to "values" lie wholly outside the domain of knowledge. That is to say, when we assert that this or that has "value," we are giving expression to our own emotions, not to a fact which would still be true if our personal feelings were different. To make this clear, we must try to analyze the conception of the Good.

It is obvious, to begin with, that the whole idea of good and bad has some connection with *desire. Prima facie,* anything that we all desire is "good," and anything that we all dread is "bad." If we all agreed in our desires, the matter could be left there, but unfortunately our desires conflict. If I say "what I want is good," my neighbour will say "No, what I want." Ethics is an attempt—though not, I think, a successful one—to escape from this subjectivity. I shall naturally try to show, in my dispute with my neighbour, that my desires have some quality which makes them more worthy of respect than his. If I want to preserve a right of way, I shall appeal to the landless inhabitants of the district; but he, on his side, will appeal to the landowners. I shall say: "What use is the beauty of the countryside if no one sees it?" He will retort: "What beauty will be left if trippers are allowed to spread devastation?" Each tries to enlist allies by showing that his own desires harmonize with those of other people. When this is obviously impossible, as in the case of a burglar, the man is condemned by public opinion, and his ethical status is that of a sinner.

Ethics is thus closely related to politics: it is an attempt to bring the collective desires of a group to bear upon individuals; or, conversely, it is an attempt by an individual to cause his desires to become those of his group. This latter is, of course, only possible if his desires are not too obviously opposed to the general interest: the burglar will hardly attempt to persuade people that he is doing them good, though plutocrats make similar attempts, and often succeed. When our desires are for things which all can enjoy in common, it seems not unreasonable to hope that others may concur; thus the philosopher who values Truth, Goodness and Beauty seems, to himself, to be not merely expressing his own desires, but pointing the way to the welfare of all mankind. Unlike the burglar, he is able to believe that his desires are for something that has value in an impersonal sense.

Ethics is an attempt to give universal, and not merely personal, importance to certain of our desires. I say "certain" of our desires, because in regard to some of them this is obviously impossible, as we saw in the case of the burglar. The man who makes money on the Stock Exchange by means of some secret knowledge does not wish others to be equally well informed: Truth (in so far as he values it) is for him a private possession, not the general human good that it is for the philosopher. The philosopher may, it is true, sink to the level of the stock-jobber, as when he claims priority for a discovery. But this is a lapse: in his purely philosophic capacity, he wants only to enjoy the contemplation of Truth, in doing which he in no way interferes with others who wish to do likewise.

To seem to give universal importance to our desires—which is the business of ethics—may be attempted from two points of view, that of the legislator, and that of the preacher. Let us take the legislator first.

I will assume, for the sake of argument, that the legislator is personally disinterested. That is to say, when he recognizes one of his desires as being concerned only with his own welfare, he does not let it influence him in framing the laws; for example, his code is not designed to increase his personal fortune. But he has other desires which seem to him impersonal He may believe in an ordered hierarchy from king to peasant, or from mine-owner to black indentured labourer. He may believe that women should be submissive to men. He may hold that the spread of knowledge in the lower classes is dangerous. And so on and so on. He will then, if he can, so construct his code that conduct promoting the ends which he values shall, as far as possible, be in accordance with individual self-interest; and he will establish a system of moral instruction which will, where it succeeds, make men feel wicked if they pursue other purposes than his.[1] Thus

---

[1] Compare the following advice by a contemporary of Aristotle (Chinese, not Greek); "A ruler

"virtue" will come to be in fact, though not in subjective estimation, subservience to the desires of the legislator, in so far as he himself considers these desires worthy to be universalized.

The standpoint and method of the preacher are necessarily somewhat different, because he does not control the machinery of the State, and therefore cannot produce an artificial harmony between his desires and those of others. His only method is to try to rouse in others the same desires that he feels himself, and for this purpose his appeal must be to the emotions. Thus Ruskin caused people to like Gothic architecture, not by argument, but by the moving effect of rhythmical prose. *Uncle Tom's Cabin* helped to make people think slavery an evil by causing them to imagine themselves as slaves. Every attempt to persuade people that something is good (or bad) in itself, and not merely in its effects, depends upon the art of rousing feelings, not upon an appeal to evidence. In every case the preacher's skill consists in creating in others emotions similar to his own—or dissimilar, if he is a hypocrite. I am not saying this as a criticism of the preacher, but as an analysis of the essential character of his activity.

When a man says "this is good in itself," he *seems* to be making a statement, just as much as if he said "this is square" or "this is sweet." I believe this to be a mistake. I think that what the man really means is: "I wish everybody to desire this," or rather "Would that everybody desired this." If what he says is interpreted as a statement, it is merely an affirmation of his own personal wish; if, on the other hand, it is interpreted in a general way, it states nothing, but merely desires something. The wish, as an occurrence, is personal, but what it desires is universal. It is, I think, this curious interlocking of the particular and the universal which has caused so much confusion in ethics.

The matter may perhaps become clearer by contrasting an ethical sentence with one which makes a statement. If I say "all Chinese are Buddhists," I can be refuted by the production of a Chinese Christian or Mohammedan. If I say "I believe that all Chinese are Buddhists," I cannot be refuted by any evidence from China, but only by evidence that I do not believe what I say; for what I am asserting is only something about my own state of mind. If, now, a philosopher says "Beauty is good," I may interpret him as meaning either "Would that everybody loved the beautiful" (which corresponds to "all Chinese are Buddhists") or "I wish that everybody loved the beautiful" (which corresponds to "I believe that all Chinese are Buddhists"). The first of these makes no assertion, but expresses a wish; since it affirms nothing, it is logically impossible that there should be evidence for or against it, or for it to possess either truth or falsehood. The second sentence, instead of being merely optative, does make a statement, but it is one about the philosopher's state of mind, and it could only be refuted by evidence that he does not have the wish that he says he has. This second sentence does not belong to ethics, but to psychology or biography. The first sentence,

---

should not listen to those who believe in people having opinions of their own and in the importance of the individual. Such teachings cause men to withdraw to quiet places and hide away in caves or on mountains, there to rail at the prevailing government, sneer at those in authority, belittle the importance of rank and emoluments, and despise all who hold official posts." Waley, *The Way and Its Power,* p. 37.

which does belong to ethics, expresses a desire for something, but asserts nothing.

Ethics, if the above analysis is correct, contains no statements, whether true or false, but consists of desires of a certain general kind, namely such as are concerned with the desires of mankind in general—and of gods, angels, and devils, if they exist. Science can discuss the causes of desires, and the means for realizing them, but it cannot contain any genuinely ethical sentences, because it is concerned with what is true or false.

The theory which I have been advocating is a form of the doctrine which is called the "subjectivity" of values. This doctrine consists in maintaining that, if two men differ about values, there is not a disagreement as to any kind of truth, but a difference of taste. If one man says "oysters are good" and another says "I think they are bad," we recognize that there is nothing to argue about. The theory in question holds that all differences as to values are of this sort, although we do not naturally think them so when we are dealing with matters that seem to us more exalted than oysters. The chief ground for adopting this view is the complete impossibility of finding any arguments to prove that this or that has intrinsic value. If we all agreed, we might hold that we know values by intuition. We cannot *prove,* to a colour-blind man, that grass is green and not red. But there are various ways of proving to him that he lacks a power of discrimination which most men possess, whereas in the case of values there are no such ways, and disagreements are much more frequent than in the case of colours. Since no way can be even imagined for deciding a difference as to values, the conclusion is forced upon us that the difference is one of tastes, not one as to any objective truth.

The consequences of this doctrine are considerable. In the first place, there can be no such thing as "sin" in any absolute sense; what one man calls "sin" another may call "virtue" and though they may dislike each other on account of this difference, neither can convict the other of intellectual error. Punishment cannot be justified on the ground that the criminal is "wicked," but only on the ground that he has behaved in a way which others wish to discourage. Hell, as a place of punishment for sinners, becomes quite irrational.

In the second place, it is impossible to uphold the way of speaking about values which is common among those who believe in Cosmic Purpose. Their argument is that certain things which have been evolved are "good," and therefore the world must have had a purpose which was ethically admirable. In the language of subjective values, this argument becomes: "Some things in the world are to our liking, and therefore they must have been created by a Being with our tastes, Whom, therefore, we also like, and Who, consequently, is good." Now it seems fairly evident that, if creatures having likes and dislikes were to exist at all, they were pretty sure to like *some* things in their environment, since otherwise they would find life intolerable. Our values have been evolved along with the rest of our constitution, and nothing as to any original purpose can be inferred from the fact that they are what they are.

Those who believe in "objective" values often contend that the view which I have been advocating has immoral consequences. This seems to me to be due to faulty reasoning. There are, as has already been said, certain ethical consequences of the doctrine of subjective values, of which the most important is the rejection of vindictive punishment and the notion of "sin." But the more general consequences which are feared, such as the decay of all sense of moral obligation, are not to be logically deduced. Moral obligation, if it is to influence conduct, must consist not merely of a belief, but of a desire. The desire, I may be told, is the desire to be "good" in a sense which I no longer allow. But when we analyse the desire to be "good" it generally resolves itself into a desire to be approved, or, alternatively, to act so as to bring about certain general consequences which we desire. We have wishes which are not purely personal, and, if we had not, no amount of ethical teaching would influence our conduct except through fear of disapproval. The sort of life that most of us admire is one which is guided by large impersonal desires; now such desires can, no doubt, be encouraged by example, education, and knowledge, but they can hardly be created by the mere abstract belief that they are good, nor discouraged by an analysis of what is meant by the word "good."

When we contemplate the human race, we may desire that it should be happy, or healthy, or intelligent, or warlike, and so on. Any one of these desires, if it is strong, will produce its own morality; but if we have no such general desires, our conduct, whatever our ethic may be, will only serve social purposes in so far as self-interest and the interests of society are in harmony. It is the business of wise institutions to create such harmony as far as possible, and for the rest, whatever may be our theoretical definition of value, we must depend upon the existence of impersonal desires. When you meet a man with whom you have a fundamental ethical disagreement—for example, if you think that all men count equally, while he selects a class as alone important—you will find yourself no better able to cope with him if you believe in objective values than if you do not. In either case, you can only influence his conduct through influencing his desires: if you succeed in that, his ethic will change, and if not, not.

Some people feel that if a general desire, say for the happiness of mankind, has not the sanction of absolute good, it is in some way irrational. This is due to a lingering belief in objective values. A desire cannot, in itself, be either rational or irrational. It may conflict with other desires, and therefore lead to unhappiness; it may rouse opposition in others, and therefore be incapable of gratification. But it cannot be considered "irrational" merely because no reason can be given for feeling it. We may desire A because it is a means to B, but in the end, when we have done with mere means, we must come to something which we desire for no reason, but not on that account "irrationally." All systems of ethics embody the desires of those who advocate them, but this fact is concealed in a mist of words. Our desires are, in fact, more general and less purely selfish than many moralists imagine; if it were not so, no theory of ethics would make moral improvement possible. It is, in fact, not by ethical theory, but by the cultivation of large and generous desires through intelligence, happiness, and freedom from fear, that men can be brought to act more than they do at present in a manner that is consistent with the general happiness of mankind. Whatever our definition of the "Good," and whether we believe it to be subjective or objective, those who do not desire the happiness of mankind will not endeavour to further it, while those who do desire it will do what they can to bring it about.

I conclude that, while it is true that science cannot decide questions of value, that is because they cannot be intellectually decided at all, and lie outside the realm of truth and falsehood. Whatever knowledge is attainable, must be attained by scientific methods; and what science cannot discover, mankind cannot know.

STUDY QUESTIONS

1   What is the purpose of "moral rules," according to Russell? What does he say "the Good" is? How does Russell relate moral rules and the Good? Which of these is a matter for science? Which is not?
2   What is the distinctive character of a scientific problem according to Russell?
3   How does ethics try to escape subjectivity, according to Russell? How does Russell relate "desires" to people's attempt to escape subjectivity?
4   Ultimately, Russell claims that subjectivity cannot be avoided and scientific objectivity cannot be broached by ethics. Why does he believe this? If this is so, what distinction is ultimately drawn between scientific statements and moral utterances? Do you believe that Russell is right about this? Why or why not?
5   "Never hope to realize Plato's republic . . . for who can change the opinions of men? And without a change of sentiments what can you make but reluctant slaves and hypocrites" (Marcus Aurelius). Do you think Russell would agree with this? Is it possible to change sentiments? If so, how and to what extent?

The New Subjectivism in Ethics

Brand Blanshard

Brand Blanshard (1892–   ) has taught at Michigan, Swarthmore, and Yale. Before his retirement in 1961, he was chairman of the philosophy department at Yale and Sterling Professor of Philosophy. He is one of America's most distinguished philosophers, and the leading contemporary exponent of rationalism and idealism. His ethical views are completely stated in *Reason and Goodness* (1961). His *Reason and Analysis* (1962) is one of the clearest and most comprehensive attacks on contemporary empiricism. Blanshard was extremely popular as a teacher because of his clarity and humanity. The lucidity of his thought is demonstrated in this classic critique of Russell's emotivism.

Emotivists claim that moral judgments can be neither true nor false. In fact, they are not statements at all, for they are verbal expressions of feelings of approval or disapproval. They are merely emotional reactions. Blanshard attacks the theory because it inaccurately describes moral discourse and moral practice. He believes that goodness and badness must be considered to be real features of the moral situation which exist whether we react or not. It is possible, for example, to make a moral judgment without any emotional feelings; and yet the meaning remains the same. Furthermore, the idea of moral progress seems to vanish with emotivism. If good and evil are essentially created by attitudes, then no one can be mistaken in his or her views. The implications of this are frightening to Blanshard, who sees subjectivism as a doctrine of smug moral complacency which can justify anything.

By the new subjectivism in ethics I mean the view that when anyone says "this is right" or "this is good," he is only expressing his own feeling; he is not asserting anything true or false, because he is not asserting or judging at all; he is really making an exclamation that expresses a favorable feeling.

This view has recently come into much favor. With variations of detail, it is being advocated by Russell, Wittgenstein and Ayer in England, and by Carnap, Stevenson, Feigl, and others, in this country. Why is it that the theory has come into so rapid a popularity? Is it because moralists of insight have been making a fresh and searching examination of moral experience and its expression? No, I think not. A consideration of the names just mentioned suggests a truer reason. All these names belong, roughly speaking, to a single school of thought in the theory of knowledge. If the new view has become popular in ethics, it is because certain persons who were at work in the theory of knowledge arrived at a new view *there,* and found, on thinking it out, that it required the new view in ethics; the view comes less from ethical analysis than from logical positivism.

As positivists, these writers held that every judgment belongs to one or other of two types. On the one hand, it may be *a priori* or necessary. But then it is always analytic, i.e., it unpacks in its predicate part of all of its subject. Can we safely say that 7 + 5 make 12? Yes, because 12 is what we mean by "7 + 5." On the other hand, the judgment may be empirical, and then, if we are to verify it, we can no longer look to our meanings only; it refers to sense experience and there we must look for its warrant. Having arrived at this division of judgments, the positivists raised the question where value judgments fall. The judgment that knowledge is good, for example, did not seem to be analytic; the value that knowledge might have did not seem to be part of our concept of knowledge. But neither was the statement empirical, for goodness was not a quality like red or squeaky that could be seen or heard. What were they to do, then, with these awkward judgments of value? To find a place for them in their theory of knowledge would require them to revise the theory radically, and yet that theory was what they regarded as their most important discovery. It appeared that the theory could be saved in one way only. If it could be shown that judgments of good and bad were not judgments at all, that they asserted nothing true or false, but merely expressed emotions like "Hurrah" or "Fiddlesticks," then these wayward judgments would cease from troubling and weary heads could be at rest. This is the course the positivists took. They explained value judgments by explaining them away.

Now I do not think their view will do. But before discussing it, I should like to record one vote of thanks to them for the clarity with which they have stated their case. It has been said of John Stuart Mill that he wrote so clearly that he could be found out. This theory has been put so clearly and precisely that it deserves criticism of the same kind, and this I will do my best to supply. The

Reprinted from Brand Blanshard. "The New Subjectivism in Ethics," *Philosophy and Phenomenological Research,* 1949, 9 (no. 3): 504–511, by permission of the editor.

theory claims to show by analysis that when we say, "That is good," we do not mean to assert a character of the subject of which we are thinking. I shall argue that we do mean to do just that.

Let us work through an example, and the simpler and commoner the better. There is perhaps no value statement on which people would more universally agree than the statement that intense pain is bad. Let us take a set of circumstances in which I happen to be interested on the legislative side and in which I think every one of us might naturally make such a statement. We come upon a rabbit that has been caught in one of the brutal traps in common use. There are signs that it has struggled for days to escape and that in a frenzy of hunger, pain, and fear, it has all but eaten off its own leg. The attempt failed: the animal is now dead. As we think of the long and excruciating pain it must have suffered, we are very likely to say: "It was a bad thing that the little animal should suffer so." The positivist tells us that when we say this we are only expressing our present emotion. I hold, on the contrary, that we mean to assert something of the animal's experience itself, namely, that it was bad—bad when and as it occurred.

Consider what follows from the positivist view. On that view, nothing good or bad happened in the case until I came on the scene and made my remark. For what I express in my remark is something going on in me at the time, and that of course did not exist until I did come on the scene. The pain of the rabbit was not itself bad; nothing evil was happening when that pain was being endured; badness, in the only sense in which it is involved at all, waited for its appearance till I came and looked and felt. Now that this is at odds with our meaning may be shown as follows. Let us put to ourselves the hypothesis that we had not come on the scene and that the rabbit never was discovered. Are we prepared to say that in that case nothing bad occurred in the sense in which we said it did? Clearly not. Indeed we should say, on the contrary, that the accident of our later discovery made no difference whatever to the badness of the animal's pain, that it would have been every whit as bad whether a chance passer-by happened later to discover the body and feel repugnance or not. If so, then it is clear that in saying the suffering was bad we are not expressing our feelings only. We are saying that the pain was bad when and as it occurred and before anyone took an attitude toward it.

The first argument is thus an ideal experiment in which we use the method of difference. It removes our present expression and shows that the badness we meant would not be affected by this, whereas on positivist grounds it should be. The second argument applies the method in the reverse way. It ideally removes the past event, and shows that this would render false what we mean to say, whereas on positivist grounds it should not. Let us suppose that the animal did not in fact fall into the trap and did not suffer at all, but that we mistakenly believe it did, and say as before that its suffering was an evil thing. On the positivist theory, everything I sought to express by calling it evil in the first case is still present in the second. In the only sense in which badness is involved at all, whatever was bad in the first case is still present in its entirety, since all that is expressed in either case is a state of feeling, and that feeling is still there. And our question is, is such an implication consistent with what we meant? Clearly it is not. If anyone asked us, after we made the remark that the suffering was a bad thing, whether we should think it relevant to what we said to learn that the incident had never occurred and no pain had been suffered at all, we should say that it made all the difference in the world, that what we were asserting to be bad was precisely the suffering we thought had occurred back there, that if this had not occurred, there was nothing left to be bad, and that our assertion was in that case mistaken. The suggestion that in saying something evil had occurred we were after all making no mistake, because we had never meant anyhow to say anything about the past suffering, seems to me merely frivolous. If we did not mean to say this, why should we be so relieved on finding that the suffering had not occurred? On the theory before us, such relief would be groundless, for in that suffering itself there was nothing bad at all, and hence in its nonoccurrence there would be nothing to be relieved about. The positivist theory would here distort our meaning beyond recognition.

So far as I can see, there is only one way out for the positivist. He holds that goodness and badness lie in feelings of approval or disapproval. And there is a way in which he might hold that badness did .n this case precede our own feeling of disapproval without belonging to the pain itself. The pain in itself was neutral; but unfortunately the rabbit, on no grounds at all, took up toward this neutral object an attitude of disapproval, and that made it for the first time, and in the only intelligible sense, bad. This way of escape is theoretically possible, but since it has grave difficulties of its own and has not, so far as I know, been urged by positivists, it is perhaps best not to spend time over it.

I come now to a third argument, which again is very simple. When we come upon the rabbit and make our remark about its suffering being a bad thing, we presumably make it with some feeling; the positivists are plainly right in saying that such remarks do usually express feeling. But suppose that a week later we revert to the incident in thought and make our statement again. And suppose that the circumstances have now so changed that the feeling with which we made the remark in the first place has faded. The pathetic evidence is no longer before us; and we are now so fatigued in body and mind that feeling is, as we say, quite dead. In these circumstances, since what was expressed by the remark when first made is, on the theory before us, simply absent, the remark now expresses nothing. It is as empty as the word "Hurrah" would be when there was no enthusiasm behind it. And this seems to me untrue. When we repeat the remark that such suffering was a bad thing, the feeling with which we made it last week may be at or near the vanishing point, but if we were asked whether we meant to say what we did before, we should certainly answer Yes. We should say that we made our point with feeling the first time and little or no feeling the second time, but that it was the same point we were making. And if we can see that what we meant to say remains the same, while the feeling varies from intensity to near zero, it is not the feeling that we primarily meant to express.

I come now to a fourth consideration. We all believe that toward acts or effects of a certain kind one attitude is fitting and another not; but on the theory before us such a belief would not make sense. Broad and Ross have lately contended that this fitness is one of the main facts of ethics, and I suspect they are right. But that is not exactly my point. My point is this: whether there is such fitness or not, we all assume that there is, and if we do, we express in moral judgments more than the subjectivists say we do. Let me illustrate.

In the novel *The House of the Dead,* Dostoevsky tells of his experiences in a Siberian prison camp. Whatever the unhappy inmates of such camps are like today, Dostoevsky's companions were about as grim a lot as can be imagined. "I have heard stories," he writes, "of the most terrible, the most unnatural actions, of the most monstrous murders, told with the most spontaneous, childishly merry laughter." Most of us would say that in this delight at the killing of others or the causing of suffering there is something very unfitting. If we were asked why we thought so, we should say that these things involve great evil and are wrong, and that to take delight in what is evil or wrong is plainly unfitting. Now on the subjectivist view, this answer is ruled out. For before someone takes up an attitude toward death, suffering, or their infliction, they have no moral quality at all. There is therefore nothing about them to which an attitude of approval or condemnation could be fitting. They are in themselves neutral, and, so far as they get a moral quality, they get it only through being invested with it by the attitude of the onlooker. But if that is true, why is any attitude more fitting than any other? Would applause, for example, be fitting if, apart from the applause, there were nothing good to applaud? Would condemnation be fitting if, independently of the condemnation, there were nothing bad to condemn? In such a case, any attitude would be as fitting or unfitting as any other, which means that the notion of fitness has lost all point.

Indeed we are forced to go much farther. If goodness and badness lie in attitudes only and hence are brought into being by them, those men who greeted death and misery with childishly merry laughter are taking the only sensible line. If there is nothing evil in these things, if they get their moral complexion only from our feeling about them, why shouldn't they be greeted with a cheer? To greet them with repulsion would turn what before was neutral into something bad; it would needlessly bring badness into the world; and even on subjectivist assumptions that does not seem very bright. On the other hand, to greet them with delight would convert what before was neutral into something good; it would bring goodness into the world. If I have murdered a man and wish to remove the stain, the way is clear. It is to cry, "Hurrah for murder."

What is the subjectivist to reply? I can only guess. He may point out that the inflicting of death is *not* really neutral before the onlooker takes his attitude, for the man who inflicted the death no doubt himself took an attitude, and thus the act had a moral quality derived from this. But that makes the case more incredible still, for the man who did the act presumably approved it, and if so it was good in the only sense in which anything is good, and then our conviction that the laughter is unfit is more unaccountable still. It may be replied that the victim, too, had his attitude and that since this was unfavorable, the act was not unqualifiedly good. But the answer is plain. Let the killer be expert at his job; let him despatch his victim instantly before he has time to take an attitude, and then gloat about his perfect crime without ever telling anyone. Then, so far as I can see, his act will be good without any qualification. It would become bad only if

someone found out about it and disliked it. And that would be a curiously irrational procedure, since the man's approving of his own killing is in itself just as
neutral as the killing that it approves. Why then should anyone dislike it?

It may be replied that we can defend our dislike on this ground that, if the
approval of killing were to go unchecked and spread, most men would have to
live in insecurity and fear, and these things are undesirable. But surely this reply
is not open; these things are not, on the theory, undesirable, for nothing is; in
themselves they are neutral. Why then should I disapprove men's living in this
state? The answer may come that if other men live in insecurity and fear, I shall
in time be infected myself. But even in my own insecurity and fear there is, on the
theory before us, nothing bad whatever, and therefore, if I disapprove them, it is
without a shadow of ground and with no more fitness in my attitude than if I
cordially cheered them. The theory thus conflicts with our judgments of fitness
all along the line.

I come now to a fifth and final difficulty with the theory. It makes mistakes
about values impossible. There is a whole nest of inter-connected criticisms here,
some of which have been made so often that I shall not develop them again, such
as that I can never agree or disagree in opinion with anyone else about an ethical
matter, and that in these matters I can never be inconsistent with others or with
myself. I am not at all content with the sort of analysis which says that the only
contradictions in such cases have regard to facts and that contradictions about
value are only differences of feeling. I think that if anyone tells me that having a
bicuspid out without an anaesthetic is not a bad experience and I say it is a very
nasty experience indeed, I am differing with him in opinion, and differing about
the degree of badness of the experience. But without pressing this further, let me
apply the argument in what is perhaps a fresh direction.

There is an old and merciful distinction that moralists have made for many
centuries about conduct—the distinction between what is subjectively and what
is objectively right. They have said that in any given situation there is some act
which, in view of all the circumstances, would be the best act to do; and this is
what would be objectively right. The notion of an objectively right act is the
ground of our notion of duty: our duty is always to find and do this act if we can.
But of course we often don't find it. We often hit upon and do acts that we think
are the right ones, but we are mistaken; and then our act is only subjectively
right. Between these two acts the disparity may be continual; Professor Prichard
suggested that probably few of us in the course of our lives ever succeed in doing
the right act.

Now so far as I can see, the new subjectivism would abolish this difference
at a stroke. Let us take a case. A boy abuses his small brother. We should
commonly say, "That is wrong, but perhaps he doesn't know any better. By
reason of bad teaching and a feeble imagination, he may see nothing wrong in
what he is doing, and may even be proud of it. If so, his act may be subjectively
right, though it is miles away from what is objectively right." What concerns me
about the new subjectivism is that it prohibits this distinction. If the boy feels this
way about his act, then it is right in the only sense in which anything is right. The
notion of an objective right lying beyond what he has discovered, and which he

ought to seek and do is meaningless. There might, to be sure, be an act that would more generally arouse favorable feelings in others, but that would not make it right for him unless he thought of it and approved it, which he doesn't. Even if he did think of it, it would not be obligatory for him to feel about it in any particular way, since there is nothing in any act, as we have seen, which would make any feeling more suitable than any other.

Now if there is no such thing as an objectively right act, what becomes of the idea of duty? I have suggested that the idea of duty rests on the idea of such an act, since it is always our duty to find that act and do it if we can. But if whatever we feel approval for at the time is right, what is the point of doubting and searching further? Like the little girl in Boston who was asked if she would like to travel, we can answer, "Why should I travel when I'm already there?" If I am reconciled in feeling to my present act, no act I could discover by reflection could be better, and therefore why reflect or seek at all? Such a view seems to me to break the mainspring of duty, to destroy the motive for self-improvement, and to remove the ground for self-criticism. It may be replied that by further reflection I can find an act that would satisfy my feelings more widely than the present one, and that this is the act I should seek. But this reply means either that such general satisfaction is objectively better, which would contradict the theory, or else that, if at the time I don't feel it better, it isn't better, in which case I have no motive for seeking it. When certain self-righteous persons took an inflexible line with Oliver Cromwell, his very Cromwellian reply was, "Bethink ye, gentlemen, by the bowels of Christ, that ye may be mistaken." It was good advice. I hope nobody will take from me the privilege of finding myself mistaken. I should be sorry to think that the self of thirty years ago was as far along the path as the self of today, merely because he was a smug young jackanapes, or even that the paragon of today has as little room for improvement as would be allowed by his myopic complacency.

One final remark. The great problems of the day are international problems. Has the new subjectivism any bearing upon these problems? I think it has, and a somewhat sinister bearing. I would not suggest, of course, that those who hold the theory are one whit less public-spirited than others; surely there are few who could call themselves citizens of the world with more right (if "rights" have meaning any longer) than Mr. Russell. But Mr. Russell has confessed himself discontented with his ethical theory, and in view of his breadth of concern, one cannot wonder. For its general acceptance would, so far as one can see, be an international disaster. The assumption behind the old League and the new United Nations was that there is such a thing as right and wrong in the conduct of a nation, a right and wrong that do not depend on how it happens to feel at the time. It is implied, for example, that when Japan invaded Manchuria in 1931 she might be wrong, and that by discussion and argument she might be shown to be wrong. It was implied that when the Nazis invaded Poland they might be wrong, even though German public sentiment overwhelmingly approved it. On the theory before us, it would be meaningless to call these nations mistaken; if they felt approval for what they did, then it was right with as complete a justification as could be supplied for the disapproval felt by the rest of the world. In the present dispute between Russia and our own country over southeast Europe, it is non-sense to speak of the right or rational course for either of us to take; if with all the facts before the two parties, each feels approval for its own course, both attitudes are equally justified or unjustified; neither is mistaken; there is no common reason to which they can take an appeal; there are no principles by which an international court could pronounce on the matter; nor would there be any obligation to obey the pronouncement if it were made. This cuts the ground from under any attempt to establish one's case as right or anyone else's case as wrong. So if our friends the subjectivists still hold their theory after I have applied my little ruler to their knuckles, which of course they will, I have but one request to make of them: Don't make a present of it to Mr. Gromyko.

STUDY QUESTIONS

1   How does Blanshard describe the "new subjectivism in ethics"? What does he say advocates of this theory (called the *emotive theory*) mean by expressions like "That is good!"

2   Using as an example a rabbit who has died in a trap after suffering hunger and fear and having almost eaten off its own leg, Blanshard lists the moral judgments that a person might make at different times and places. What are those judgments? Why are they said to have raised difficulties for the emotive theory?

3   Blanshard states that a traditional distinction—that between what is subjectively and what is objectively right—is obliterated by the emotive theory. What is meant by this distinction? Do you think that Blanshard is right in claiming that the emotive theory eliminates this distinction? If you agree with Blanshard, do you think that it is good or bad that the emotive theory leads to this consequence?

4   How does the emotive theory affect the international problems of the day, according to Blanshard? Could Russell escape Blanshard's criticism by claiming that some desires are irrational?

5   " 'Reason' has a perfectly clear and precise meaning. It signifies the choice of the right means to an end that you wish to achieve. It has nothing whatever to do with the choice of ends" (Bertrand Russell). Do you agree? If not, explain how reason operates to select ends. What would Blanshard say?

Sources of Morality: The Search for Objectivity

PROBLEM INTRODUCTION

Most of us, in our everyday lives, believe that there is something called *moral truth*. That is, we act as though there is a genuine difference between good and evil, right and wrong. We attempt to assess the direction of our lives and to guide ourselves by ideals which appear to us to be much more than sentiment, social convention, or mere whim. We do not regard morality as something we just come up with on the spur of the moment, but instead we actively strive to overcome our passions, prejudices, narrow social or economic contexts in order to see the world as it really is. In other words, we regard morality as rooted in the nature of things, part and parcel of the world, as discoverable as the other facts of nature. Can we find a standpoint from which to justify this attitude?

The first giant step in the search for objectivity was taken by the Greek philosophers Plato and Aristotle. Plato saw clearly that morality must be severed from religion and made into an independent intellectual enterprise. This means that God is not enough to justify objectivity. Even if the moral law is a divine commandment, God must be able to provide good reasons for His law. Without this, the divine will is simply irrational whim. But if morality is rooted in the nature of things, then it should be accessible to the inquiring mind, whether that mind be divine or human. The importance of this step cannot be stressed enough,

239

for it eliminates forever the comfortable stupor of intellectual and moral dependency. Fact, rather than power, has become the source of moral authority.

But what facts are important? To Aristotle, the answer to this question was clear: an objective morality must be founded on the facts of human nature. A simple example can demonstrate what led Aristotle to this conclusion. In general, we have no difficulty evaluating many common objects and events. We can tell a good shoe from a bad shoe, a good chess player from a bad one, or a good mathematician from a bad one. How do we make such value judgments? First, we ask for the definition of the thing in question. This tells us what it is, what features of the object set it apart from other things. The definition of a shoe, for example, specifies that it is an object having a certain function. This gives us a criterion of excellence. A good shoe is one which functions as it is the nature of shoes to function. In general, a thing is good when it functions as its definition specifies. So it is for baseballs, mathematicians, houses, hands, legs, eyes, and other objects. Indeed, so it is for human beings. People, like other objects, have a definite nature which sets them off from the rest of creation. The good life for human beings, then, is one in which this essential nature is most completely manifested. Aristotle's ethics is the ethics of self-realization. The Greek poet Pindar expressed it in the credo: "Become what you are."

What are we then? What is our essential nature? Aristotle was struck by the fact that human beings are equipped by nature to pursue intellectual activities. We are rational animals. Therefore, the good life, the life of happiness, must consist in rational activity. If we were gods, without physical needs, we would be happy in pure contemplation. But since we are animals, other needs must be satisfied as well. These needs can be met in rational or irrational ways. Moral virtue, then, is the state of character which leads to intelligent and rational choices in our pursuit of happiness. In our practical affairs the rational path usually lies between two irrational extremes. Bravery, for example, is a virtue which lies between the extremes of cowardice and rashness. Aristotle is careful to point out that the rational choice is always relative to the person and the circumstances. A skilled warrior may exhibit his bravery in a certain course of action, whereas an untried soldier would be foolish to do the same thing. Therefore, moral virtue cannot be set down in a rigidly defined code of behavior.

This point is extremely important. The search for objectivity cannot result in a list of moral recipes for every situation. An example from geometry can show why. Proving a theorem in geometry is a rational affair if anything is. It involves seeing connections between definitions, axioms, and other theorems. Yet even in this formal, logical activity, there is no set of rules which will tell the student how to construct proofs for any problem. Basic principles must be mastered, and after some practice, it is assumed that intelligence will show the way to a solution. Similarly, in scientific activity there are no rules which one can study and then use to construct good, fruitful experiments for every problem. Yet experimental design, like proving a theorem, is a highly rational procedure. Intelligent people, through experience and practice, learn to prove theorems, design experiments, and choose wisely. This is what Aristotle calls "practical wisdom."

Aristotle's theory represents a revolution in thought. It brings morality down from the heavens and places it squarely in the lap of humanity. It emphasizes that the source of value is within our own nature. Human nature is not intrinsically corrupt—it is intrinsically good. Furthermore, we possess the power to become happy and virtuous. Virtue is not a gift, a sign of the gods' favor. It is the result of training, of the application of intelligence to living. The total effect of Aristotle's thought is to ennoble humanity and to increase personal responsibility.

Within the basic framework set down by Aristotle, there is a great deal of room for alternative theories. The eighteenth-century philosopher Immanuel Kant believed, as did Aristotle, that the key to moral objectivity lay in the rationality of humans. But unlike Aristotle, Kant rejected the idea that happiness was intrinsically good. There are some persons who do not *deserve* to be happy. A world of happy Hitlers is not the best of all possible worlds. Kant argues that the only thing that is intrinsically good is a *good will.* In other words, the virtuous person is one who has certain *motives,* regardless of whether those motives lead to his own happiness. What, then, is a good reason for moral action? According to Kant, the only reason which makes an act praiseworthy is that it was done out of a regard for duty. The truly moral agent acts out of his recognition that the moral law demands it—and for no other reason. The moral law must be universal and apply to everyone alike. Given this condition, it must have a certain form. It must command us to behave in ways which we recognize to be legitimate for everyone. Such a law, Kant maintains, rules out selfishness and sometimes our own happiness.

Kant's moral theory is called a *rationalistic theory of value* because he believes that reason alone, through the investigation of our moral concepts, can discover what we ought to do. But empirically minded philosophers of the nineteenth century wished to bring ethics into the realm of science, and so returned to the Aristotelian assumption that morality must be founded on an empirical study of human nature. The nineteenth century was a period of great social reform. In England, France, and the United States, the pursuit of happiness became the rallying cry of change. John Stuart Mill, an English philosopher and social reformer, the most famous exponent of the doctrine of utilitarianism, stated that all policies of the individual and government must be aimed at increasing the general happiness of humanity. The most important undertaking in Mill's theory is his proof of utilitarianism. In a manner similar to Aristotle, Mill argues that the only proof of something's value is whether people value it. Happiness is good, he says, because people desire it. Most philosophers have strongly disagreed with this sort of "proof." In addition, Mill's theory requires that individuals sometimes sacrifice their own happiness for the general happiness. But how can this be justified? After all, it is not obvious that everyone does, in fact, desire the general happiness.

The emphasis on human nature can lead in many directions, depending upon one's theory of human nature. Aristotle, Kant, and Mill, for example, take a rather charitable view of humanity. In general, they depict people as basically rational, other-regarding, sincere, and capable of overcoming impulses which are contrary to these traits. Yet one of the most popular moral theories does not accept this picture of human psychology. Ethical egoism is the view that people ought to be concerned with their own interests first and always, even if this means neglecting the interests of others. This ethical doctrine is based on a harsh conception of humanity. People are basically selfish and egoistic. They are moved by desires such as self-preservation, self-esteem, or love of power; and these desires are so elemental that they cannot be eliminated. Self-realization, according to this scheme of things, demands that each person satisfy himself or herself to the greatest extent possible. If we must treat others with kindness and charity, it can only be because there is some payoff in it for us. Any other reason requires us to go against our nature. In our readings, James Rachels examines this conception of morality and claims that it distorts human nature in such a grotesque way as to be unrealistic.

In the end, the objective standpoint may be incapable of proof, in the usual sense of that word. After all, how do you prove to people that something is red? If they look at it, they see it. If they do not see it, either they have misunderstood the instructions or they are color blind. Morality may be the same way. Many philosophers have been intuitionists, believing that the ultimate test for the morality of an action is moral vision—an immediate intuition of the rightness or wrongness of the act. However, it should be pointed out that this does not eliminate the role of reason. We must still know what the facts are, because our moral insights are based on what we believe to be the real representation of the moral situation. Once reason has reported all the facts, however, we just "see" whether the act is right or wrong, or whether the consequences of it are good or evil. The final selection by William Gass represents a kind of intuitionist position.

The world has always been brutalized by people who claim to be bearers of the "true" morality. But dogmatism is not more likely under the objective standpoint than under any other. In fact, to the extent that the objective standpoint depends upon the use of reason to discover moral truth, it should discourage dogmatism. If we take science as our model, then we can regard our moral theories as hypotheses. They are capable of revision, of expansion and change as new experience reveals unforeseen circumstances. This does not mean that we cannot be guided by our beliefs with fervor and intensity. It does mean, however, that we should strive to keep open the means by which our own ideals can be disproved in case we are wrong.

Virtue and Rationality

Aristotle

Aristotle (384 B.C.–322 B.C.) studied at Plato's Academy. He is surely one of the greatest philosophers of all time. His work in biology and physics stood as the principal theories until the scientific revolution in the seventeenth century. Even Darwin admitted that Aristotle was the greatest biologist to have ever lived. This empirical temper stands in marked contrast to the rationalistic emphasis of his teacher, Plato. After Plato's death, Aristotle traveled and was largely engaged in marine biology. In 342 B.C., he became the tutor of Alexander the Great, and in 336, he returned to Athens, where he established his own school, the Lyceum. With the death of Alexander in 323, Aristotle became involved in the political upheaval which followed. The Athenians trumped up charges of impiety against him, and recalling the fate of Socrates, he fled Athens so that the city would not "offend twice against philosophy."

Aristotle believed that the good was happiness. But happiness can be defined only after the fundamental facts of human nature have been uncovered. The entire structure of human psychology reveals that humans are animals who are directed in their activities by rational principles. Rational activity, therefore, is the highest good according to Aristotle. But living requires action, and virtue is a state of character which produces rational action. Aristotle does not attempt to lay down rules for everyone to obey, since what is rational will depend to some extent upon the context. Still, this is not subjectivism since happiness is an objective and universal goal.

1

Every art and every inquiry, and similarly every action and pursuit, is thought to aim at some good; and for this reason the good has rightly been declared to be that at which all things aim. But a certain difference is found among ends; some are activities, others are products apart from the activities that produce them. Where there are ends apart from the actions, it is the nature of the products to be better than the activities. Now, as there are many actions, arts, and sciences, their ends also are many; the end of the medical art is health, that of shipbuilding a vessel, that of strategy victory, that of economics wealth. But where such arts fall under a single capacity—as bridle-making and the other arts concerned with the equipment of horses fall under the art of riding, and this and every military action under strategy, in the same way other arts fall under yet others—in all of these the ends of the master arts are to be preferred to all the subordinate ends; for it is for the sake of the former that the latter are pursued. It makes no difference whether the activities themselves are the ends of the actions, or something else apart from the activities, as in the case of the sciences just mentioned.

If, then, there is some end of the things we do, which we desire for its own sake (everything else being desired for the sake of this), and if we do not choose

From the *Nichomachean Ethics,* translated by W. D. Ross, in *The Oxford Translation of Aristotle,* Volume IX, 1925. Reprinted by permission of Oxford University Press, Oxford.

everything for the sake of something else (for at that rate the process would go on to infinity, so that our desire would be empty and vain), clearly this must be the good and the chief good. Will not the knowledge of it, then, have a great influence on life? Shall we not, like archers who have a mark to aim at, be more likely to hit upon what is right? If so, we must try, in outline at least to determine what it is, and of which of the sciences or capacities it is the object. It would seem to belong to the most authoritative art and that which is most truly the master art. And politics appears to be of this nature; for it is this that ordains which of the sciences should be studied in a state, and which each class of citizens should learn and up to what point they should learn them; and we see even the most highly esteemed of capacities to fall under this, e.g., strategy, economics, rhetoric; now, since politics uses the rest of the sciences, and since, again, it legislates as to what we are to do and what we are to abstain from, the end of this science must include those of the others, so that this end must be the good for man. For even if the end is the same for a single man and for a state, that of the state seems at all events something greater and more complete whether to attain or to preserve; though it is worthwhile to attain the end merely for one man, it is finer and more godlike to attain it for a nation or for city-states. These, then, are the ends at which our inquiry aims, since it is political science, in one sense of that term.

Our discussion will be adequate if it has as much clearness as the subject matter admits of, for precision is not to be sought for alike in all discussions, any more than in all the products of the crafts. Now fine and just actions, which political science investigates, admit of much variety and fluctuation of opinion, so that they may be thought to exist only by convention, and not by nature. And goods also give rise to a similar fluctuation because they bring harm to many people; for before now men have been undone by reason of their wealth, and others by reason of their courage. We must be content, then, in speaking of such subjects and with such premises to indicate the truth roughly and in outline, and in speaking about things which are only for the most part true and with premises of the same kind to reach conclusions that are no better. In the same spirit, therefore, should each type of statement be *received;* for it is the mark of an educated man to look for precision in each class of things just so far as the nature of the subject admits; it is evidently equally foolish to accept probable reasoning from a mathematician and to demand from a rhetorician scientific proofs.

Now each man judges well the things he knows, and of these he is a good judge. And so the man who has been educated in a subject is a good judge of that subject, and the man who has received an all-around education is a good judge in general. Hence a young man is not a proper hearer of lectures on political science; for he is inexperienced in the actions that occur in life, but its discussions start from these and are about these; and, further, since he tends to follow his passions, his study will be vain and unprofitable, because the end aimed at is not knowledge but action. And it makes no difference whether he is young in years or youthful in character; the defect does not depend on time, but on his living, and pursuing each successive object, as passion directs. For to such persons, as to the incontinent, knowledge brings no profit; but to those who desire and act in accordance with a rational principle knowledge about such matters will be of great benefit.

These remarks about the student, the sort of treatment to be expected, and the purpose of the inquiry, may be taken as our preface.

Let us resume our inquiry and state, in view of the fact that all knowledge and every pursuit aims at some good, what it is that we say political science aims at and what is the highest of all goods achievable by action. Verbally there is very general agreement; for both the general run of men and people of superior refine-ment say that it is happiness, and identify living well and doing well with being happy; but with regard to what happiness is they differ, and the many do not give the same account as the wise. For the former think it is some plain and obvious thing, like pleasure, wealth, or honor; they differ, however, from one another— and often even the same man identifies it with different things, with health when he is ill, with wealth when he is poor; but, conscious of their ignorance, they admire those who proclaim some great ideal that is above their comprehension. Now some[1] thought that apart from these many goods there is another which is self-subsistent and causes the goodness of all these as well. To examine all the opinions that have been held were perhaps somewhat fruitless; enough to exam-ine those that are most prevalent or that seem to be arguable. . . .

To judge from the lives that men lead, most men, and men of the most vulgar type, seem (not without some ground) to identify the good, or happiness, with pleasure; which is the reason why they love the life of enjoyment. For there are, we may say, three prominent types of life—that just mentioned, the political, and thirdly the contemplative life. Now the mass of mankind are evidently quite slavish in their tastes, preferring a life suitable to beasts, but they get some ground for their view from the fact that many of those in high places share the tastes of Sardanapalus. A consideration of the prominent types of life shows that people of superior refinement and of active disposition identify happiness with honor; for this is, roughly speaking, the end of the political life. But it seems too superficial to be what we are looking for, since it is thought to depend on those who bestow honor rather than on him who receives it, but the good we divine to be something proper to a man and not easily taken from him. Further, men seem to pursue honor in order that they may be assured of their goodness; at least it is by men of practical wisdom that they seek to be honored, and among those who know them, and on the ground of their virtue; clearly, then, according to them, at any rate, virtue is better. And perhaps one might even suppose this to be, rather than honor, the end of the political life. But even this appears somewhat incom-plete; for possession of virtue seems actually compatible with being asleep, or with lifelong inactivity, and further, with the greatest sufferings and misfortunes; but a man who was living so no one would call happy, unless he were maintain-

[1] The Platonic School.

ing a thesis at all costs. But enough of this; for the subject has been sufficiently treated even in the current discussions. Third comes the comtemplative life, which we shall consider later.

The life of moneymaking is one undertaken under compulsion, and wealth is evidently not the good we are seeking; for it is merely useful and for the sake of something else. And so one might rather take the aforenamed objects to be ends; for they are loved for themselves. But it is evident that not even these are ends; yet many arguments have been thrown away in support of them. Let us leave this subject, then. . . .

Let us again return to the good we are seeking, and ask what it can be. It seems different in different actions and arts; it is different in medicine, in strategy, and in the other arts likewise. What then is the good of each? Surely that for whose sake everything else is done. In medicine this is health, in strategy victory, in architecture a house, in any other sphere something else, and in every action and pursuit the end; for it is for the sake of this that all men do whatever else they do. Therefore, if there is an end for all that we do, this will be the good achievable by action, and if there are more than one, these will be the goods achievable by action.

So the argument has by a different course reached the same point; but we must try to state this even more clearly. Since there are evidently more than one end, and we choose some of these (e.g., wealth, flutes, and, in general, instruments) for the sake of something else, clearly not all ends are final ends; but the chief good is evidently something final. Therefore, if there is only one final end, this will be what we are seeking, and if there are more than one, the most final of these will be what we are seeking. Now we call that which is in itself worthy of pursuit more final than that which is worthy of pursuit for the sake of something else, and that which is never desirable for the sake of something else more final than the things that are desirable both in themselves and for the sake of that other thing, and therefore we call final without qualification that which is always desirable in itself and never for the sake of something else.

Now such a thing as happiness, above all else, is held to be; for this we choose always for itself and never for the sake of something else, but honor, pleasure, reason, and every virtue we choose indeed for themselves (for if nothing resulted from them we should still choose each of them), but we choose them also for the sake of happiness, judging that by means of them we shall be happy. Happiness, on the other hand, no one chooses for the sake of these, nor, in general, for anything other than itself.

From the point of view of self-sufficiency the same result seems to follow; for the final good is thought to be self-sufficient. Now by self-sufficient we do not mean that which is sufficient for a man by himself, for one who lives a solitary life, but also for parents, children, wife, and in general for his friends and fellow citizens, since man is born for citizenship. But some limit must be set to this; for if we extend our requirement to ancestors and descendants and friends' friends we are in for an infinite series. Let us examine this question, however, on another occasion; the self-sufficient we now define as that which when isolated makes life desirable and lacking in nothing; and such we think happiness to be; and further we think it most desirable of all things, without being counted as one good thing among others—if it were so counted it would clearly be made more desirable by the addition of even the least of goods; for that which is added becomes an excess of goods, and of goods the greater is always more desirable. Happiness, then, is something final and self-sufficient, and is the end of action.

Presumably, however, to say that happiness is the chief good seems a platitude, and a clearer account of what it is is still desired. This might perhaps be given, if we could first ascertain the function of man. For just as for a flute-player, a sculptor, or any artist, and, in general, for all things that have a function or activity, the good and the "well" is thought to reside in the function, so would it seem to be for man, if he has a function. Have the carpenter, then, and the tanner certain functions or activities, and has man none? Is he born without a function? Or as eye, hand, foot, and in general each of the parts evidently has a function, may one lay it down that man similarly has a function apart from all these? What then can this be? Life seems to be common even to plants, but we are seeking what is peculiar to man. Let us exclude, therefore, the life of nutrition and growth. Next there would be a life of perception, but it also seems to be common even to the horse, the ox, and every animal. There remains, then, an active life of the element that has a rational principle; of this, one part has such a principle in the sense of being obedient to one, the other in the sense of possessing one and exercising thought. And, as "life of the rational element" also has two meanings, we must state that life in the sense of activity is what we mean; for this seems to be the more proper sense of the term. Now if the function of man is an activity of soul which follows or implies a rational principle, and if we say "a-so-and-so" and "a good so-and-so" have a function which is the same in kind, e.g., a lyre player and a good lyre player, and so without qualification in all cases, eminence in respect of goodness being added to the name of the function (for the function of a lyre player is to play the lyre, and that of a good lyre player is to do so well): if this is the case, [and we state the function of man to be a certain kind of life, and this to be an activity or actions of the soul implying a rational principle, and the function of a good man to be the good and noble performance of these, and if any action is well performed when it is performed in accordance with the appropriate excellence: if this is the case,] human good turns out to be activity of soul in accordance with virtue, and if there are more than one virtue, in accordance with the best and most complete.

But we must add "in a complete life." For one swallow does not make a summer, nor does one day; and so too one day, or a short time, does not make a man blessed and happy. . . .

Yet evidently, as we said, it [happiness] needs the external goods as well; for it is impossible, or not easy, to do noble acts without the proper equipment. In many actions we use friends and riches and political power as instruments; and there are some things the lack of which takes the luster from happiness, as good birth, goodly children, beauty; for the man who is very ugly in appearance or ill-born or solitary and childless is not very likely to be happy, and perhaps a man would be still less likely if he had thoroughly bad children or friends or had lost good children or friends by death. As we said, then, happiness seems to need this sort of prosperity in addition; for which reason some identify happiness with good fortune, though others identify it with virtue. . . .

2

Virtue, then, being of two kinds, intellectual and moral, intellectual virtue in the main owes both its birth and its growth to teaching (for which reason it requires experience and time), while moral virtue comes about as a result of habit, whence also its name *ethike* is one that is formed by a slight variation from the word *ethos* (habit). From this it is also plain that none of the moral virtues arises in us by nature; for nothing that exists by nature can form a habit contrary to its nature. For instance the stone which by nature moves downwards cannot be habituated to move upwards, not even if one tries to train it by throwing it up ten thousand times; nor can fire be habituated to move downwards, nor can anything else that by nature behaves in one way be trained to behave in another. Neither by nature, then, nor contrary to nature do the virtues arise in us; rather we are adapted by nature to receive them, and are made perfect by habit.

Again, of all the things that come to us by nature we first acquire the potentiality and later exhibit the activity (this is plain in the case of the senses; for it was not by often seeing or often hearing that we got these senses, but on the contrary we had them before we used them, and did not come to have them by using them); but the virtues we get by first exercising them, as also happens in the case of the arts as well. For the things we have to learn before we can do them, we learn by doing them, e.g., men become builders by building and lyre players by playing the lyre, so too we become just by doing just acts, temperate by doing temperate acts, brave by doing brave acts.

This is confirmed by what happens in states; for legislators make the citizens good by forming habits in them, and this is the wish of every legislator, and those who do not effect it miss their mark, and it is in this that a good constitution differs from a bad one.

Again, it is from the same causes and by the same means that every virtue is both produced and destroyed, and similarly every art; for it is from playing the lyre that both good and bad lyre players are produced. And the corresponding statement is true of builders and of all the rest; men will be good or bad builders as a result of building well or badly. For if this were not so, there would have been no need of a teacher, but all men would have been born good or bad at their craft. This, then, is the case with the virtues also; by doing the acts that we do in our transactions with other men we become just or unjust, and by doing the acts that we do in the presence of danger, and being habituated to feel fear or confidence, we become brave or cowardly. The same is true of appetites and feelings of anger; some men become temperate and good-tempered, others self-indulgent and irascible, by behaving in one way or the other in the appropriate circumstances. Thus, in one word, states of character arise out of like activities. This is why the activities we exhibit must be of a certain kind; it is because the states of character correspond to the differences between these. It makes no small difference, then, whether we form habits of one kind or of another from our very youth; it makes a very great difference, or rather *all* the difference.

Since, then, the present inquiry does not aim at theoretical knowledge like the others (for we are inquiring not in order to know what virtue is, but in order to become good, since otherwise our inquiry would have been of no use), we must examine the nature of actions, namely how we ought to do them; for these determine also the nature of the states of character that are produced, as we have said. Now, that we must act according to the right rule is a common principle and must be assumed—it will be discussed later, i.e., both what the right rule is, and how it is related to the other virtues. But this must be agreed upon beforehand, that the whole account of matters of conduct must be given in outline and not precisely, as we said at the very beginning that the accounts we demand must be in accordance with the subject matter; matters concerned with conduct and questions of what is good for us have no fixity, any more than matters of health. The general account being of this nature, the account of particular cases is yet more lacking in exactness; for they do not fall under any art of precept but the agents themselves must in each case consider what is appropriate to the occasion, as happens also in the art of medicine or of navigation.

But though our present account is of this nature we must give what help we can. First, then, let us consider this, that it is the nature of such things to be destroyed by defect and excess, as we see in the case of strength and of health (for to gain light on things imperceptible we must use the evidence of sensible things); both excessive and defective exercise destroys the strength, and similarly drink or food which is above or below a certain amount destroys the health, while that which is proportionate both produces and increases and preserves it. So too is it, then, in the case of temperance and courage and the other virtues. For the man who flies from and fears everything and does not stand his ground against anything becomes a coward, and the man who fears nothing at all but goes to meet every danger becomes rash; and similarly the man who indulges in every pleasure and abstains from none becomes self-indulgent, while the man who shuns every pleasure, as boors do, becomes in a way insensible; temperance and courage, then, are destroyed by excess and defect, and preserved by the men.

But not only are the sources and causes of their origination and growth the same as those of their destruction but also the sphere of their actualization will be the same; for this is also true of the things which are more evident to sense, e.g., of strength; it is produced by taking much food and undergoing much exertion, and it is the strong man that will be most able to do these things. So too is it with the virtues; by abstaining from pleasures we become temperate, and it is when we have become so that we are most able to abstain from them; and similarly too in the case of courage; for by being habituated to despise things that are terrible and to stand our ground against them we become brave, and it is when we have become so that we shall be most able to stand our ground against them.

We must take as a sign of states of character the pleasure or pain that ensues on acts; for the man who abstains from bodily pleasures and delights in this very fact is temperate, while the man who is annoyed at it is self-indulgent, and he who stands his ground against things that are terrible and delights in this or at least is not pained is brave, while the man who is pained is a coward. For moral excellence is concerned with pleasures and pains; it is on account of the pleasure that we do bad things, and on account of the pain that we abstain from noble ones. Hence we ought to have been brought up in a particular way from our very youth, as Plato says, so as both to delight in and to be pained by the things that we ought; for this is the right education. . . .

Next we must consider what virtue is. Since things that are found in the soil are of three kinds—passions, faculties, states of character—virtue must be one of these. By passions I mean appetite, anger, fear, confidence, envy, joy, friendly feeling, hatred, longing, emulation, pity, and in general the feelings that are accompanied by pleasure or pain; by faculties the things in virtue of which we are said to be capable of feeling these, e.g., of becoming angry or being pained or feeling pity; by states of character the things in virtue of which we stand well or badly with reference to the passions, e.g., with reference to anger we stand badly if we feel it violently or too weakly, and well if we feel it moderately; and similarly with reference to the other passions.

Now neither the virtues nor the vices are *passions,* because we are not called good or bad on the ground of our passions, but are so called on the ground of our virtues and our vices, and because we are neither praised nor blamed for our passions (for the man who feels fear or anger is not praised, nor is the man who simply feels anger blamed, but the man who feels it in a certain way), but for our virtues and our vices we *are* praised or blamed.

Again, we feel anger and fear without choice, but the virtues are modes of choice or involve choice. Further, in respect of the passions we are said to be moved, but in respect of the virtues and the vices we are said not to be moved but to be disposed in a particular way.

For these reasons also they are not *faculties;* for we are neither called good nor bad, nor praised nor blamed, for the simple capacity of feeling the passions; again, we have the faculties by nature, but we are not made good or bad by nature; we have spoken of this before.

If, then, the virtues are neither passions nor faculties, all that remains is that they should be *states of character.*

Thus we have stated what virtue is in respect of its genus.

We must, however, not only describe virtue as a state of character, but also say what sort of state it is. We may remark, then, that every virtue or excellence both brings into good condition the thing of which it is the excellence and makes the work of that thing be done well; e.g., the excellence of the eye makes both the eye and its work good; for it is by the excellence of the eye that we see well. Similarly the excellence of the horse makes a horse both good in itself and good at running and at carrying its rider and at awaiting the attack of the enemy. Therefore, if this is true in every case, the virtue of man also will be the state of character which makes a man good and which makes him do his own work well.

How this is to happen we have stated already, but it will be made plain also by the following consideration of the specific nature of virtue. In everything that is continuous and divisible it is possible to take more, less, or an equal amount, and that either in terms of the thing itself or relatively to us; and the equal is an intermediate excess and defect. By the intermediate in the object I mean that which is equidistant from each of the extremes, which is one and the same for all men; by the intermediate relatively to us that which is neither too much nor too little—and this is not one, nor the same for all. For instance, if ten is many and two is few, six is the intermediate, taken in terms of the object; for it exceeds and is exceeded by an equal amount; this is intermediate according to arithmetical proportion. But the intermediate relatively to us is not to be taken so; if ten pounds are too much for a particular person to eat and two too little, it does not follow that the trainer will order six pounds; for this also is perhaps too much for the person who is to take it, or too little—too little for Milo, too much for the beginner in athletic exercises. The same is true of running and wrestling. Thus a master of any art avoids excess and defect, but seeks the intermediate and chooses this—the intermediate not in the object but relatively to us.

It is thus, then, that every art does its work well—by looking to the intermediate and judging its works by this standard (so that we often say of good works of art that it is not possible either to take away or to add anything, implying that excess and defect destroy the goodness of works of art, while the mean preserves it; and good artists, as we say, look to this in their work), and if, further, virtue is more exact and better than any art, as nature also is, then virtue must have the quality of aiming at the intermediate. I mean moral virtue; for it is this that is concerned with passions and actions, and in these there is excess, defect, and the intermediate. For instance, both fear and confidence and appetite and anger and pity and in general pleasure and pain may be felt both too much and too little, and in both cases not well; but to feel them at the right times, with reference to the right objects, towards the right people, with the right motive, and in the right way, is what is both intermediate and best, and this is characteristic of virtue. Similarly with regard to actions also there is excess, defect, and the intermediate. Now virtue is concerned with passions and actions, in which excess is a form of failure, and so is defect, while the intermediate is praised and is a form of success; and being praised and being successful are both characteristics of virtue. Therefore virtue is a kind of mean, since, as we have seen, it aims at what is intermediate.

Again, it is possible to fail in many ways (for evil belongs to the class of the unlimited, as the Pythagoreans conjectured, and good to that of the limited), while to succeed is possible only in one way (for which reason also one is easy and the other difficult—to miss the mark easy, to hit it difficult); for these reasons also, then, excess and defect are characteristic of vice, and the means of virtue;

For men are good in but one way, but bad in many.

Virtue, then, is a state of character concerned with choice, lying in a mean, i.e., the mean relative to us, this being determined by a rational principle, and by that principle by which the man of practical wisdom would determine it. Now it is a mean between two vices, that which depends on excess and that which depends on defect; and again it is a mean because the vices respectively fall short of or exceed what is right in both passions and actions, while virtue both finds and chooses that which is intermediate. Hence in respect of its substance and the definition which states its essence virtue is a mean, with regard to what is best and right an extreme.

But not every action nor every passion admits of a mean; for some have names that already imply badness, e.g., spite, shamelessness, envy, and in the case of actions adultery, theft, murder; for all of these and suchlike things imply by their names that they are themselves bad, and not the excesses or deficiencies of them. It is not possible, then, ever to be right with regard to them; one must always be wrong. Nor does goodness or badness with regard to such things depend on committing adultery with the right woman, at the right time, and in the right way, but simply to do any of them is to go wrong. It would be equally absurd, then, to expect that in unjust, cowardly, and voluptuous action there should be a mean, an excess, and a deficiency; for at that rate there would be a mean of excess and of deficiency, an excess of excess, and a deficiency of deficiency. But as there is no excess and deficiency of temperance and courage because what is intermediate is in a sense an extreme, so too of the actions we have mentioned there is no mean nor any excess and deficiency, but however they are done they are wrong; for in general there is neither a mean of excess and deficiency, nor excess and deficiency of a mean.

STUDY QUESTIONS

1   How does Aristotle define "the chief good"? Why are honor and virtue not chief goods? Do you agree with Aristotle's argument on this point?

2   When we talk about a good knife, a good tennis ball, a good carpenter, and a good hand, what common quality makes all of these things good? How does Aristotle apply this quality to "man"? In what sense does Aristotle try to make goodness a function of *human nature?*

3   Rationality is, for Aristotle, a central part of human nature. Is this enough, do you think, to adequately define humanity? What would Sartre say?

4   What is Aristotle's definition of happiness? Can you think of some things he has left out? Do you think that this concept can be defined alike for everyone?

5   How does one become virtuous, according to Aristotle? What do you think the role of intellect is in such a process?

6   Suppose you do not know what to do in a puzzling moral situation. Does Aristotle's theory contain any practical advice?

7   The first line of Tolstoy's *Anna Karenina* reads: "Happy families are all alike; every unhappy family is unhappy in its own way." What do you think Tolstoy is trying to say about happiness? Would Aristotle agree?

The Categorical Imperative
Immanuel Kant

Immanuel Kant (1724–1804) was an immensely innovative and influential philosopher. His *Critique of Pure Reason* (1781) introduced a revolution in thinking which set the tone for all nineteenth-century philosophy, and which is still
felt today. Kant lived most of his life in obscurity in Konigsberg, East Prussia,
teaching at the University of Konigsberg. A man of great discipline and regular
habits, it is said that the people of Konigsberg set their clocks by Kant's daily
walks to the university.

There are two related questions raised in Kant's selection: What makes
an act right and what makes a person morally praiseworthy? The latter question has a fairly direct answer. A person is morally praiseworthy only when that
person acts from a love for duty. Self-regard, pity, sympathy, or social inclinations of whatever sort are not morally respectable motives. Duty is a perfectly
rational consideration which is determined by the *categorical imperative.* In
order to determine whether an action is right, according to Kant, the moral
agent must be able to imagine the action as something which he would want
everyone to do in similar circumstances. Whatever can be so universalized
into a law for everyone is right. Of course, this is Kant's version of the Golden
Rule.

As you look at the examples Kant gives as illustrations of his ethics, ask
yourself whether they embody the principles he says they do. His critics have
suggested that the examples actually employ self-interest as a fundamental
moral tenet.

Nothing in the world—indeed nothing even beyond the world—can possibly be
conceived which could be called good without qualification except a *good will.*
Intelligence, wit, judgment, and the other talents of the mind, however they may
be named, or courage, resoluteness, and perserverance as qualities of temperament, are doubtless in many respects good and desirable. But they can become
extremely bad and harmful if the will, which is to make use of these gifts of
nature and which in its special constitution is called character, is not good. It is
the same with the gifts of fortune. Power, riches, honor, even health, general
well-being, and the contentment with one's condition which is called happiness,
make for pride and even arrogance if there is not a good will to correct their
influence on the mind and on its principles of action so as to make it universally
comfortable to its end. It need hardly be mentioned that the sight of being
adorned with no feature of a pure and good will, yet enjoying uninterrupted
prosperity, can never give pleasure to a rational impartial observer. Thus the
good will seems to constitute the indispensable condition even of worthiness to
be happy.

Some qualities seem to be conducive to this good will and can facilitate its
action, but, in spite of that, they have no intrinsic unconditional worth. They

rather presuppose a good will, which limits the high esteem which one otherwise rightly has for them and prevents their being held to be absolutely good. Moderation in emotions and passions, self-control, and calm deliberation not only are good in many respects but even seem to constitute a part of the inner worth of the person. But however unconditionally they were esteemed by the ancients, they are far from being good without qualification. For without the principle of good will they can become extremely bad, and the coolness of a villain makes him not only far more dangerous but also more directly abominable in our eyes than he would have seemed without it.

The good will is not good because of what it effects or accomplishes or because of its adequacy to achieve some proposed end; it is good only because of its willing, i.e., it is good of itself. And, regarded for itself, it is to be esteemed incomparably higher than anything which could be brought about by it in favor of any inclination or even of the sum total of all inclinations. Even if it should happen that, by a particularly unfortunate fate or by the niggardly provision of a stepmotherly nature, this will should be wholly lacking in power to accomplish its purpose, and if even the greatest effort should not avail it to achieve anything of its end, and if there remained only the good will (not as a mere wish but as the summoning of all the means in our power), it would sparkle like a jewel in its own right, as something that had its full worth in itself. Usefulness or fruitlessness can neither diminish nor augment this worth. Its usefulness would be only its setting, as it were, so as to enable us to handle it more conveniently in commerce or to attract the attention of those who are not yet connoisseurs, but not to recommend it to those who are experts or to determine its worth.

But there is something so strange in this idea of the absolute worth of the will alone, in which no account is taken of any use, that, not withstanding the agreement even of common sense, the suspicion must arise that perhaps only high-flown fancy is its hidden basis, and that we- may have misunderstood the purpose of nature in its appointment of reason as the ruler of our will. We shall therefore examine this idea from this point of view.

In the natural constitution of an organized being, i.e., one suitably adapted to life, we assume as an axiom that no organ will be found for any purpose which is not the fittest and best adapted to that purpose. Now if its preservation, its welfare—in a word, its happiness—were the real end of nature in a being having reason and will, then nature would have hit upon a very poor arrangement in appointing the reason of the creature to be the executor of this purpose. For all the actions which the creature has to perform with this intention, and the entire rule of its conduct, would be dictated much more exactly by instinct, and that end would be far more certainly attained by instinct than it ever could be by reason. And if, over and above this, reason should have been granted to the favored creature, it would have served only to let it contemplate the happy constitution of its nature, to admire it, to rejoice in it, and to be grateful for it to its beneficient cause. But reason would not have been given in order that the being should subject its faculty of desire to that weak and delusive guidance and to meddle with the purpose of nature. In a word, nature would have taken care that reason did not break forth into practical use nor have the presumption, with its weak insight, to think out for itself the plan of happiness and the means of attaining it. Nature would have taken over not only the choice of ends but also that of the means, and with wise foresight she would have entrusted both to instinct alone.

And, in fact, we find that the more a cultivated reason deliberately devotes itself to the enjoyment of life and happiness, the more the man falls short of true contentment. From this fact there arises in many persons, if only they are candid enough to admit it, a certain degree of misology, hatred of reason. This is particularly the case with those who are most experienced in its use. After counting all the advantages which they draw—I will not say from the invention of the arts of common luxury—from the sciences (which in the end seem to be also a luxury of the understanding), they nevertheless find that they have actually brought more trouble on their shoulders instead of gaining in happiness; they finally envy, rather than despise, the common run of men who are better guided by mere natural instinct and who do not permit their reason much influence on their conduct. And we must at least admit that a morose attitude or ingratitude to the goodness with which the world is governed is by no means found always among those who temper or refute the boasting eulogies which are given of the advantages of happiness and contentment with which reason is supposed to supply us. Rather their judgment is based on the idea of another and far more worthy purpose of their existence for which, instead of happiness, their reason is properly intended, this purpose, therefore, being the supreme condition to which the private purposes of men must for the most part defer.

Reason is not, however, competent to guide the will safely with regard to its objects and the satisfaction of all our needs (which it in part multiplies), and to this end an innate instinct would have led with far more certainty. But reason is given to us as a practical faculty, i.e., one which is meant to have an influence on the will. As nature has elsewhere distributed capacities suitable to the functions they are to perform, reason's proper function must be to produce a will good in itself and not one good merely as a means, for to the former reason is absolutely essential. This will must indeed not be the sole and complete good but the highest good and the condition of all others, even of the desire for happiness. In this case it is entirely compatible with the wisdom of nature that the cultivation of reason, which is required for the former unconditional purpose, at least in this life restricts in many ways—indeed can reduce to less than nothing—the achievement of the latter conditional purpose, happiness. For one perceives that nature here does not proceed unsuitably to its purpose, because reason, which recognizes its highest practical vocation in the establishment of a good will, is capable of a contentment of its own kind, i.e., one that springs from the attainment of a purpose which is determined by reason, even though this injures the ends of inclination.

We have, then, to develop the concept of a will which is to be esteemed as good of itself without regard to anything else. It dwells already in the natural sound understanding and does not need so much to be taught as only to be brought to light. In the estimation of the total worth of our actions it always takes first place and is the condition of everything else. In order to show this, we shall take the concept of duty. It contains that of a good will, though with certain subjective restrictions and hindrances; but these are far from concealing it and making it unrecognizable, for they rather bring it out by contrast and make it shine forth all the brighter.

I here omit all actions which are recognized as opposed to duty, even though they may be useful in one respect or another, for with these the question does not arise at all as to whether they may be carried out *from* duty, since they conflict with it. I also pass over the actions which are really in accordance with duty and to which one has not direct inclination, rather executing them because impelled to do so by another inclination. For it is easily decided whether an action in accord with duty is performed from duty or for some selfish purpose. It is far more difficult to note this difference when the action is in accordance with duty and, in addition, the subject has a direct inclination to do it. For example, it is in fact in accordance with duty that a dealer should not overcharge an inexperienced customer, and wherever there is much business the prudent merchant does not do so, having a fixed price for everyone, so that a child may buy of him as cheaply as any other. Thus the customer is honestly served. But this is far from sufficient to justify the belief that the merchant has behaved in this way from duty and principles of honesty. His own advantage required this behavior; but it cannot be assumed that over and above that he had a direct inclination to the purchaser and that, out of love, as it were, he gave none an advantage in price over another. Therefore the action was done neither from duty nor from direct inclination but only for a selfish purpose.

On the other hand, it is a duty to preserve one's life, and moreover everyone has a direct inclination to do so. But for that reason the often anxious care which most men take of it has no intrinsic worth, and the maxim of doing so has no moral import. They preserve their lives according to duty, but not from duty. But if adversities and hopeless sorrow completely take away the relish for life, if an unfortunate man, strong in soul, is indignant rather than despondent or dejected over his fate and wishes for death, and yet preserves his life without loving it and from neither inclination nor fear but from duty—then his maxim has a moral import.

To be kind where one can is duty, and there are, moreover, many persons so sympathetically constituted that without any motive of vanity or selfishness they find an inner satisfaction in spreading joy, and rejoice in the contentment of others which they have made possible. But I say that, however dutiful and amiable it may be, that kind of action has no true moral worth. It is on a level with [actions arising from] other inclinations, such as the inclination to honor, which, if fortunately directed to what in fact accords with duty and is generally useful and thus honorable, deserve praise and encouragement but no esteem. For the maxim lacks the moral import of an action done not from inclination but from duty. But assume that the mind of that friend to mankind was clouded by a sorrow of his own which extinguished all sympathy with the lot of others and that he still had the power to benefit others in distress, but that their need left him untouched because he was preoccupied with his own need. And now suppose him to tear himself, unsolicited by inclination, out of this dead insensibility and to perform this action only from duty and without any inclination—then for the first time his action has genuine moral worth. Furthermore, if nature has put little sympathy in the heart of man, and if he, though an honest man, is by temperament cold and indifferent to the sufferings of others, perhaps because he is provided with special gifts of patience and fortitude and expects or even requires that others should have the same—and such a man would certainly not be the meanest product of nature—would not he find himself a source from which to give himself a far higher worth than he could have got by having a good-natured temperament? This in unquestionably true even though nature did not make him philanthropic, for it is just here that the worth of the character is brought out, which is morally and incomparably the highest of all: he is beneficient not from inclination but from duty.

To secure one's own happiness is at least indirectly a duty, for discontent with one's condition under pressure from many cares and amid unsatisfied wants could easily become a great temptation to transgress duties. But without any view to duty all men have the strongest and deepest inclination to happiness, because in this idea all inclinations are summed up. But the precept of happiness is often so formulated that it definitely thwarts some inclinations, and men can make no definite and certain concept of the sum of satisfaction of all inclinations which goes under the name of happiness. It is not to be wondered at, therefore, that a single inclination, definite as to what it promises and as to the time at which it can be satisfied, can outweigh a fluctuating idea, and that, for example, a man with the gout can choose to enjoy what he likes and to suffer what he may, because according to his calculations at least on this occasion he has not sacrificed the enjoyment of the present moment to a perhaps groundless expectation of a happiness supposed to lie in health. But even in this case, if the universal inclination to happiness did not determine his will, and if health were not at least for him a necessary factor in these calculations, there yet would remain, as in all other cases, a law that he ought to promote his happiness, not from inclination but from duty. Only from this law would his conduct have true moral worth.

It is in this way, undoubtedly, that we should understand those passages of Scripture which command us to love our neighbor and even our enemy, for love as an inclination cannot be commanded. But beneficence from duty, when no inclination impels it and even when it is opposed by a natural and unconquerable aversion, is practical love, not pathological love; it resides in the will and not in the propensities of feeling, in principles of action and not in tender sympathy; and it alone can be commanded.

[Thus the first proposition of morality is that to have moral worth an action must be done from duty.] The second proposition is: An action performed from duty does not have its moral worth in the purpose which is to be achieved through it but in the maxim by which it is determined. Its moral value, therefore, does not depend on the realization of the object of the action but merely on the principle of volition by which the action is done, without any regard to the objects of the faculty of desire. From the preceding discussion it is clear that the purposes we may have for our actions and their effects as ends and incentives of the will cannot give the actions any unconditional and moral worth. Wherein, then, can this worth lie, if it is not in the will in relation to its hoped-for effect? It can lie nowhere else than in the principle of the will, irrespective of the ends which can be realized by such action. For the will stands, as it were, at the crossroads halfway between its a priori principle which is formal and its a posteriori incentive which is material. Since it must be determined by something, if it is done from duty it must be determined by the formal principle of volition as such since every material principle has been withdrawn from it.

The third principle, as a consequence of the two preceding, I would express as follows: Duty is the necessity of an action executed from respect for law. I can certainly have an inclination to the object as an effect of the proposed action, but I can never have respect for it precisely because it is a mere effect and not an activity of a will. Similarly, I can have no respect for any inclination whatsoever, whether my own or that of another; in the former case I can at most approve of it and in the latter I can even love it, i.e., see it as favorable to my own advantage. But that which is connected with my will merely as ground and not as consequence, that which does not serve my inclination but overpowers it or at least excludes it from being considered in making a choice—in a word, law itself—can be an object of respect and thus a command. Now as an act from duty wholly excludes the influence of inclination and therewith every object of the will, nothing remains which can determine the will objectively except the law, and nothing subjectively except pure respect for this practical law. This subjective element is the maxim [1] that I ought to follow such a law even if it thwarts all my inclinations.

Thus the moral worth of an action does not lie in the effect which is expected from it or in any principle of action which has to borrow its motive from this expected effect. For all these effects (agreeableness of my own condition, indeed even the promotion of the happiness of others) could be brought about through other causes and would not require the will of a rational being, while the highest and unconditional good can be found only in such a will. Therefore, the pre-eminent good can consist only in the conception of the law in itself (which can be present only in a rational being) so far as this conception and not the hoped-for effect is the determining ground of the will. This pre-eminent good, which we call moral, is already present in the person who acts according to this conception, and we do not have to look for it first in the result.[2]

---

[1] A maxim is the subjective principle of volition. The objective principle (i.e., that which would serve all rational beings also subjectively as a practical principle if reason had full power over the faculty of desire) is the practical law.

[2] It might be objected that I seek to take refuge in an obscure feeling behind the word "respect," instead of clearly resolving the question with a concept of reason. But though respect is a feeling, it is not one received through any [outer] influence but is self-wrought by a rational concept; thus it differs specifically from all feelings of the former kind which may be referred to inclination or fear. What I recognize directly as a law for myself I recognize with respect, which means merely the consciousness of the submission of my will to a law without the intervention of other influences on my mind. The direct determination of the will by the law and the consciousness of this determination is respect; thus respect can be regarded as the effect of the law on the subject and not as the cause of the law. Respect is properly the conception of a worth which thwarts my self-love. Thus it is regarded as an object neither of inclination nor of fear, though it has something analogous to both. The only object of respect is the law, and indeed only the law which we impose on ourselves and yet recognize

But what kind of a law can that be, the conception of which must determine the will without reference to the expected result? Under this condition alone the will can be called absolutely good without qualification. Since I have robbed the will of all impulses which could come to it from obedience to any law, nothing remains to serve as a principle of the will except universal conformity of its action to law as such. That is, I should never act in such a way that I could not also will that my maxim should be a universal law. Mere conformity to law as such (without assuming any particular law applicable to certain actions) serves as the principle of the will, and it must serve as such a principle if duty is not to be a vain delusion and chimerical concept. The common reason of mankind in its practical judgments is in perfect agreement with this and has this principle constantly in view.

Let the question, for example, be: May I, when in distress, make a promise with the intention not to keep it? I easily distinguish the two meanings which the question can have, viz., whether it is prudent to make a false promise, or whether it conforms to my duty. Undoubtedly the former can often be the case, though I do see clearly that it is not sufficient merely to escape from the present difficulty by this expedient, but that I must consider whether inconveniences much greater than the present one may not later spring from this lie. Even with all my supposed cunning, the consequences cannot be so easily foreseen. Loss of credit might be far more disadvantageous than the misfortune I now seek to avoid, and it is hard to tell whether it might not be more prudent to act according to a universal maxim and to make it a habit not to promise anything without intending to fulfill it. But it is soon clear to me that such a maxim is based only on an apprehensive concern with consequences.

To be truthful from duty, however, is an entirely different thing from being truthful out of fear of disadvantageous consequences, for in the former case the concept of the action itself contains a law for me, while in the latter I must first look about to see what results for me may be connected with it. For to deviate from the principle of duty is certainly bad, but to be unfaithful to my maxim of prudence can sometimes be very advantageous to me, though it is certainly safer to abide by it. The shortest but most infallible way to find the answer to the question as to whether a deceitful promise is consistent with duty is to ask myself: Would I be content that my maxim (of extricating myself from difficulty by a false promise) should hold as a universal law for myself as well as for others? And could I say to myself that everyone may make a false promise when he is in a difficulty from which he otherwise cannot escape? I immediately see that I could will the lie but not a universal law to lie. For with such a law there would be no promises at all, inasmuch as it would be futile to make a pretense of my

---

as necessary in itself. As a law, we are subject to it without consulting self-love; as imposed on us by ourselves, it is a consequence of our will. In the former respect it is analogous to fear and in the latter to inclination. All respect for a person is only respect for the law (of righteousness, etc.) of which the person provides an example. Because we see the improvement of our talents as a duty, we think of a person of talents as the example of a law, as it were (the law that we should by practice become like him in his talents), and that constitutes our respect. And so-called moral interest consists solely in respect for the law.

intention in regard to future actions to those who would not believe in this pretense or—if they overhastily did so—who would pay me back in my own coin. Thus my maxim would necessarily destroy itself as soon as it was made a universal law.

I do not, therefore, need any penetrating acuteness in order to discern what I have to do in order that my volition may be morally good. Inexperienced in the course of the world, incapable of being prepared for all its contingencies, I ask myself only: Can I will that my maxim become a universal law? If not, it must be rejected, not because of any disadvantage accruing to myself or even to others, but because it cannot enter as a principle into a possible universal legislation, and reason extorts from me an immediate respect for such legislation. I do not as yet discern on what it is grounded (a question the philosopher may investigate), but I at least understand that it is an estimation of the worth which far outweighs all the worth of whatever is recommended by the inclinations, and that the necessity of my actions from pure respect for the practical law constitutes duty. To duty every other motive must give place, because duty is the condition of a will good in itself, whose worth transcends everything. . . .

There is, therefore, only one categorical imperative. It is: Act only according to that maxim by which you can at the same time will that it should become a universal law.

Now if all imperatives of duty can be derived from this one imperative as a principle, we can at least show what we understand by the concept of duty and what it means, even though it remain undecided whether that which is called duty is an empty concept or not.

The universality of law according to which effects are produced constitutes what is properly called nature in the most general sense (as to form), i.e., the existence of things so far as it is determined by universal laws. [By analogy], then, the universal imperative of duty can be expressed as follows: Act as though the maxim of your action were by your will to become a universal law of nature.

We shall now enumerate some duties, adopting the usual division of them into duties to ourselves and to others and into perfect and imperfect duties.[3]

1 A man who is reduced to despair by a series of evils feels a weariness with life but is still in possession of his reason sufficiently to ask whether it would not be contrary to his duty to himself to take his own life. Now he asks whether the maxim of his action could become a universal law of nature. His maxim, however, is: For love of myself, I make it my principle to shorten my life when by a longer duration it threatens more evil than satisfaction. But it is questionable whether this principle of self-love could become a universal law of nature. One immediately sees a contradiction in a system of nature whose law would be to

---

[3] It must be noted here that I reserve the division of duties for a future *Metaphysics of Morals* and that the division here stands as only an arbitrary one (chosen in order to arrange my examples). For the rest, by a perfect duty I here understand a duty which permits no exception in the interest of inclination; thus I have not merely outer but also inner perfect duties. This runs contrary to the usage adopted in the schools, but I am not disposed to defend it here because it is all one to my purpose whether this is conceded or not.

destroy life by the feeling whose special office is to impel the improvement of life. In this case it would not exist as nature; hence that maxim cannot obtain as a law of nature, and thus it wholly contradicts the supreme principle of all duty.

2   Another man finds himself forced by need to borrow money. He well knows that he will not be able to repay it, but he also sees that nothing will be loaned him if he does not firmly promise to repay it at a certain time. He desires to make such a promise, but he has enough conscience to ask himself whether it is not improper and opposed to duty to relieve his distress in such a way. Now, assuming he does decide to do so, the maxim of his action would be as follows: When I believe myself to be in need of money, I will borrow money and promise to repay it, although I know I shall never do so. Now this principle of self-love or of his own benefit may very well be compatible with his whole future welfare, but the question is whether it is right. He changes the pretension of self-love into a universal law and then puts the question: How would it be if my maxim became a universal law? He immediately sees that it could never hold as a universal law of nature and be consistent with itself; rather it must necessarily contradict itself. For the universality of a law which says that anyone who believes himself to be in need could promise what he pleased with the intention of not fulfilling it would make the promise itself and the end to be accomplished by it impossible; no one would believe what was promised to him but would only laugh at any such assertion as vain pretense.

3   A third finds in himself a talent which could, by means of some cultivation, make him in many respects a useful man. But he finds himself in comfortable circumstances and prefers indulgence in pleasure to troubling himself with broadening and improving his fortunate natural gifts. Now, however, let him ask whether his maxim of neglecting his gifts, besides agreeing with his propensity to idle amusement, agrees also with what is called duty. He sees that a system of nature could indeed exist in accordance with such a law, even though man (like the inhabitants of the South Sea Islands) should let his talents rust and resolve to devote his life merely to idleness, indulgence, and propagation—in a word, to pleasure. But he cannot possibly will that this should become a universal law of nature or that it should be implanted in us by a natural instinct. For, as a rational being, he necessarily wills that all his faculties should be developed, inasmuch as they are given to him for all sorts of possible purposes.

4   A fourth man, for whom things are going well, sees that others (whom he could help) have to struggle with great hardships, and he asks, "What concern of mine is it? Let each one be as happy as heaven wills, or as he can make himself; I will not take anything from him or even envy him; but to his welfare or to his assistance in time of need I have no desire to contribute." If such a way of thinking were a universal law of nature, certainly the human race could exist, and without doubt even better than in a state where everyone talks of sympathy and good will, or even exerts himself occasionally to practice them while, on the other hand, he cheats when he can and betrays or otherwise violates the rights of man. Now although it is possible that a universal law of nature according to that maxim could exist, it is nevertheless impossible to will that such a principle should hold everywhere as a law of nature. For a will which resolved this would

conflict with itself, since instances can often arise in which he would need the love and sympathy of others, and in which he would have robbed himself, by such a law of nature springing from his own will, of all hope of the aid he desires.

The foregoing are a few of the many actual duties, or at least of duties we hold to be actual, whose derivation from the one stated principle is clear. We must be able to will that a maxim of our action become a universal law; this is the canon of the moral estimation of our action generally. Some actions are of such a nature that their maxim cannot even be *thought* as a universal law of nature without contradiction, far from it being possible that one could will that it should be such. In others this internal impossibility is not found, though it is still impossible to *will* that their maxim should be raised to the universality of a law of nature, because such a will would contradict itself. We easily see that the former maxim conflicts with the stricter or narrower (imprescriptible) duty, the latter with broader (meritorious) duty. Thus all duties, so far as the kind of obligation (not the object of their action) is concerned, have been completely exhibited by these examples in their dependence on the one principle.

When we observe ourselves in any transgression of a duty, we find that we do not actually will that our maxim should become a universal law. That is impossible for us; rather, the contrary of this maxim should remain as a law generally, and we only take the liberty of making an exception to it for ourselves or for the sake of our inclination, and for this one occasion. Consequently, if we weighed everything from one and the same standpoint, namely, reason, we would come upon a contradiction in our own will, viz., that a certain principle is objectively necessary as a universal law and yet subjectively does not hold universally but rather admits exceptions. However, since we regard our action at one time from the point of view of a will wholly conformable to reason and then from that of a will affected by inclinations, there is actually no contradiction, but rather an opposition of inclination to the precept of reason (*antagonismus*). In this the universality of the principle (*universalitas*) is changed into mere generality (*generalitas*), whereby the practical principle of reason meets the maxim halfway. Although this cannot be justified in our own impartial judgment, it does show that we actually acknowledge the validity of the categorical imperative and allow ourselves (with all respect to it) only a few exceptions which seem to us to be unimportant and forced upon us. . . .

STUDY QUESTIONS

1   What does Kant mean by a "good will"? What does he mean by claiming that it is good "without qualification"?
2   What argument does Kant give to show that happiness is not good in itself? What do you think of the argument?
3   The following are statements of motives. How would Kant analyze them?
     a   I helped him because I could not stand to see him suffering.
     b   I helped her because the Bible says it is my duty to help others.
     c   I helped him because I want to promote social behavior that may prove beneficial to myself.
4   Kant distinguishes between an action done from duty and one done from inclination.

In fact he says that it is possible to disregard all inclinations and follow duty. Do you think this is possible? Do you think Kant should count the love for duty as an inclination?

5   How do you think Kant would define freedom of the will? Why would a free will be a condition for moral responsibility?

6   Do you see any difference between Kant's categorical imperative and the Golden Rule?

7   How do you think Kant would analyze the morality of abortion? What maxim is involved? Do his other examples provide hints about how he would treat such a maxim?

Utilitarianism

John Stuart Mill

John Stuart Mill (1806–1873) was one of the outstanding thinkers of the nineteenth century. His father, James Mill, himself a famous economist and social philosopher, and Jeremy Bentham, the founder of utilitarianism, raised Mill according to a strict plan. They set out to make young Mill into a democratic, intellectual, social reformer who would carry on their own liberal projects. Denied the usual pastimes of youth, he quickly adapted to a rigorous schedule of study, and by the age of twelve he had mastered Latin and Greek, read the classics, and worked his way beyond the differential calculus. The plan worked, and in his maturity, Mill was an explosion of talents devoted to a progressive and democratic society.

Mill's utilitarianism was the logical backbone of his attempts at social reform. Human happiness is the only thing which is intrinsically valuable and right conduct is that which tends to maximize happiness. It is important to point out that utilitarianism is not egoistic, for to maximize happiness may require personal sacrifice. In the first part of our selection, he attempts to clarify the utilitarian standard. In the latter part, he discusses how it may be proved. Mill's conception of how ethical principles are proved is one of the most debated issues in moral philosophy. As you read this section, keep in mind that he has to prove *two* things: that happiness is intrinsically valuable, and that each person ought to be concerned with the happiness of others.

WHAT UTILITARIANISM IS

A passing remark is all that needs be given to the ignorant blunder of supposing that those who stand up for utility as the test of right and wrong use the term in that restricted and merely colloquial sense in which utility is opposed to pleasure. An apology is due to the philosophical opponents of utilitarianism for even the momentary appearance of confounding them with anyone capable of so absurd a

From *Utilitarianism* by John Stuart Mill, published in 1863. Many editions, Chaps. 2 and 4.

misconception; which is the more extraordinary, inasmuch as the contrary accusation, of referring everything to pleasure, and that, too, in its grossest form, is another of the common charges against utilitarianism: and, as has been pointedly remarked by an able writer, the same sort of persons, and often the very same persons, denounce the theory "as impracticably dry when the word 'utility' precedes the word 'pleasure,' and as too practically voluptuous when the word 'pleasure' precedes the word 'utility.' " Those who know anything about the matter are aware that every writer, from Epicurus to Bentham, who maintained the theory of utility meant by it, not something to be contradistinguished from pleasure, but pleasure itself, together with exemption from pain; and instead of opposing the useful to the agreeable or the ornamental, have always declared that the useful means these, among other things. Yet the common herd, including the herd of writers, not only in newspapers and periodicals, but in books of weight and pretension, are perpetually falling into this shallow mistake. Having caught up the word "utilitarian," while knowing nothing whatever about it but its sound, they habitually express by it the rejection or the neglect of pleasure in some of its forms: of beauty, of ornament, or of amusement. Nor is the term thus ignorantly misapplied solely in disparagement, but occasionally in compliment, as though it implied superiority to frivolity and the mere pleasures of the moment. And this perverted use is the only one in which the word is popularly known, and the one from which the new generation are acquiring their sole notion of its meaning. Those who introduced the word, but who had for many years discontinued it as a distinctive appellation, may well feel themselves called upon to resume it if by doing so they can hope to contribute anything toward rescuing it from this utter degradation.

The creed which accepts as the foundation of morals "utility" or the "greatest happiness principle" holds that actions are right in proportion as they tend to promote happiness; wrong as they tend to produce the reverse of happiness. By happiness is intended pleasure and the absence of pain; by unhappiness, pain and the privation of pleasure. To give a clear view of the moral standard set up by the theory, much more requires to be said; in particular, what things it includes in the ideas of pain and pleasure, and to what extent this is left an open question. But these supplementary explanations do not affect the theory of life on which this theory of morality is grounded—namely, that pleasure and freedom from pain are the only things desirable as ends; and that all desirable things (which are as numerous in the utilitarian as in any other scheme) are desirable either for pleasure inherent in themselves or as means to the promotion of pleasure and the prevention of pain.

Now such a theory of life excites in many minds, and among them in some of the most estimable in feeling and purpose, inveterate dislike. To suppose that life has (as they express it) no higher end than pleasure—no better and nobler object of desire and pursuit—they designate as utterly mean and groveling, as a doctrine worthy only of swine, to whom the followers of Epicurus were, at a very early period, contemptuously likened; and modern holders of the doctrine are occasionally made the subject of equally polite comparisons by its German, French, and English assailants.

When thus attacked, the Epicureans have always answered that it is not they, but their accusers, who represent human nature in a degrading light, since the accusation supposes human beings to be capable of no pleasures except those of which swine are capable. If this supposition were true, the charge could not be gainsaid, but would then be no longer an imputation; for if the sources of pleasure were precisely the same to human beings and to swine, the rule of life which is good enough for the one would be good enough for the other. The comparison of the Epicurean life to that of beasts is felt as degrading, precisely because a beast's pleasures do not satisfy a human being's conceptions of happiness. Human beings have faculties more elevated than the animal appetites and, when once made conscious of them, do not regard anything as happiness which does not include their gratification. I do not, indeed, consider the Epicureans to have been by any means faultless in drawing out their scheme of consequences from the utilitarian principle. To do this in any sufficient manner, many Stoic, as well as Christian, elements require to be included. But there is no known Epicurean theory of life which does not assign to the pleasures of the intellect, of the feelings and imagination, and of the moral sentiments a much higher value as pleasures than to those of mere sensation. It must be admitted, however, that utilitarian writers in general have placed the superiority of mental over bodily pleasures chiefly in the greater permanency, safety, uncostliness, etc., of the former—that is, in their circumstantial advantages rather than in their intrinsic nature. And on all these points utilitarians have fully proved their case; but they might have taken the other and, as it may be called, higher ground with entire consistency. It is quite compatible with the principle of utility to recognize the fact that some kinds of pleasure are more desirable and more valuable than others. It would be absurd that, while in estimating all other things quality is considered as well as quantity, the estimation of pleasure should be supposed to depend on quantity alone.

If I am asked what I mean by difference of quality in pleasures, or what makes one pleasure more valuable than another, merely as a pleasure, except its being greater in amount, there is but one possible answer. Of two pleasures, if there be one to which all or almost all who have experience of both give a decided preference, irrespective of any feeling of moral obligation to prefer it, that is the more desirable pleasure. If one of the two is, by those who are competently acquainted with both, placed so far above the other that they prefer it, even though knowing it to be attended with a greater amount of discontent, and would not resign it for any quantity of the other pleasure which their nature is capable of, we are justified in ascribing to the preferred enjoyment a superiority in quality so far outweighing quantity as to render it, in comparison, of small account.

Now it is an unquestionable fact that those who are equally acquainted with and equally capable of appreciating and enjoying both do give a most marked preference to the manner of existence which employs their higher faculties. Few human creatures would consent to be changed into any of the lower animals for a promise of the fullest allowance of a beast's pleasures; no intelligent human being would consent to be a fool, no instructed person would be an ignoramus, no person of feeling and conscience would be selfish and base, even though they should be persuaded that the fool, the dunce, or the rascal is better satisfied with his lot than they are with theirs. They would not resign what they possess more than he for the most complete satisfaction of all the desires which they have in common with him. If they ever fancy they would, it is only in cases of unhappiness so extreme that to escape from it they would exchange their lot for almost any other, however undesirable in their own eyes. A being of higher faculties requires more to make him happy, is capable probably of more acute suffering, and certainly accessible to it at more points, than one of an inferior type; but in spite of these liabilities, he can never really wish to sink into what he feels to be a lower grade of existence. We may give what explanation we please of this unwillingness; we may attribute it to pride, a name which is given indiscriminately to some of the most and to some of the least estimable feelings of which mankind are capable; we may refer it to the love of liberty and personal independence, an appeal to which was with the Stoics one of the most effective means for the inculcation of it; to the love of power or to the love of excitement, both of which do really enter into and contribute to it; but its most appropriate appellation is a sense of dignity, which all human beings possess in one form or other, and in some, though by no means in exact, proportion to their higher faculties, and which is so essential a part of the happiness of those in whom it is strong that nothing which conflicts with it could be otherwise than momentarily an object of desire to them. Whoever supposes that this preference takes place at a sacrifice of happiness—that the superior being, in anything like equal circumstances, is not happier than the inferior—confounds the two very different ideas of happiness and content. It is indisputable that the being whose capacities of enjoyment are low has the greatest chance of having them fully satisfied; and a highly endowed being will always feel that any happiness which he can look for, as the world is constituted, is imperfect. But he can learn to bear its imperfections, if they are at all bearable; and they will not make him envy the being who is indeed unconscious of the imperfections, but only because he feels not at all the good which those imperfections qualify. It is better to be a human being dissatisfied than a pig satisfied; better to be Socrates dissatisfied than a fool satisfied. And if the fool, or the pig, are of a different opinion, it is because they only know their own side of the question. The other party to the comparison knows both sides. . . .

I have dwelt on this point as being a necessary part of a perfectly just conception of utility or happiness considered as the directive rule of human conduct. But it is by no means an indispensable condition to the acceptance of the utilitarian standard; for that standard is not the agent's own greatest happiness, but the greatest amount of happiness altogether; and if it may possibly be doubted whether a noble character is always the happier for its nobleness, there can be no doubt that it makes other people happier, and that the world in general is immensely a gainer by it. Utilitarianism, therefore, could only attain its end by the general cultivation of nobleness of character, even if each individual were only benefited by the nobleness of others, and his own, so far as happiness is concerned, were a sheer deduction from the benefit. But the bare enunciation of such an absurdity as this last renders refutation superfluous.

According to the greatest happiness principle, as above explained, the ultimate end, with reference to and for the sake of which all other things are desirable—whether we are considering our own good or that of other people—is an existence exempt as far as possible from pain, and as rich as possible in enjoyments, both in point of quantity and quality; the test of quality and the rule for measuring it against quantity being the preference felt by those who, in their opportunities of experience, to which must be added their habits of self-consciousness and self-observation, are best furnished with the means of comparison. This, being according to the utilitarian opinion the end of human action, is necessarily also the standard of morality, which may accordingly be defined "the rules and precepts for human conduct," by the observance of which an existence such as has been described might be, to the greatest extent possible, secured to all mankind; and not to them only, but, so far as the nature of things admits, to the whole sentient creation. . . .

OF WHAT SORT OF PROOF THE PRINCIPLE OF UTILITY IS SUSCEPTIBLE

. . . Questions of ultimate ends do not admit of proof, in the ordinary acceptation of the term. To be incapable of proof by reasoning is common to all first principles, to the first premises of our knowledge, as well as to those of our conduct. But the former, being matters of fact, may be the subject of a direct appeal to the faculties which judge of fact—namely, our senses and our internal consciousness. Can an appeal be made to the same faculties on questions of practical ends? Or by what other faculty is cognizance taken of them?

Questions about ends are, in other words, questions what things are desirable. The utilitarian doctrine is that happiness is desirable, and the only thing desirable, as an end; all other things being only desirable as means to that end. What ought to be required of this doctrine, what conditions is it requisite that the doctrine should fulfill—to make good its claim to be believed?

The only proof capable of being given that an object is visible is that people actually see it. The only proof that a sound is audible is that people hear it; and so of the other sources of our experience. In like manner, I apprehend, the sole evidence it is possible to produce that anything is desirable is that people do actually desire it. If the end which the utilitarian doctrine proposes to itself were not, in theory and in practice, acknowledged to be an end, nothing could ever convince any person that it was so. No reason can be given why the general happiness is desirable, except that each person, so far as he believes it to be attainable, desires his own happiness. This, however, being a fact, we have not only all the proof which the case admits of, but all which it is possible to require, that happiness is a good, that each person's happiness is a good to that person, and the general happiness, therefore, a good to the aggregate of all persons. Happiness has made out its title as *one* of the ends of conduct and, consequently, one of the criteria of morality.

But it has not, by this alone, proved itself to be the sole criterion. To do that, it would seem, by the same rule, necessary to show, not only that people desire happiness, but that they never desire anything else. Now it is palpable that they do desire things which, in common language, are decidedly distinguished from happiness. They desire, for example, virtue and the absence of vice no less really than pleasure and the absence of pain. The desire of virtue is not as universal, but it is as authentic a fact as the desire of happiness. And hence the opponents of the utilitarian standard deem that they have a right to infer that there are other ends of human action besides happiness, and that happiness is not the standard of approbation and disapprobation.

But does the utilitarian doctrine deny that people desire virtue, or maintain that virtue is not a thing to be desired? The very reverse. It maintains not only that virtue is to be desired, but that it is to be desired disinterestedly, for itself. Whatever may be the opinion of utilitarian moralists as to the original conditions by which virtue is made virtue, however they may believe (as they do) that actions and dispositions are only virtuous because they promote another end than virtue, yet this being granted, and it having been decided, from consider-ations of this description, what *is* virtuous, they not only place virtue at the very head of the things which are good as means to the ultimate end, but they also recognize as a psychological fact the possibility of its being, to the individual, a good in itself, without looking to any end beyond it; and hold that the mind is not in a right state, not in a state conformable to utility, not in the state most conducive to the general happiness, unless it does love virtue in this manner—as a thing desirable in itself, even although, in the individual instance, it should not produce those other desirable consequences which it tends to produce, and on account of which it is held to be virtue. This opinion is not, in the smallest degree, a departure from the happiness principle. The ingredients of happiness are very various, and each of them is desirable in itself, and not merely when considered as swelling an aggregate. The principle of utility does not mean that any given pleasure, as music, for instance, or any given exemption from pain, as for exam-ple health, is to be looked upon as means to a collective something termed happi-ness, and to be desired, on that account. They are desired and desirable in and for themselves; besides being means, they are a part of the end. Virtue, according to the utilitarian doctrine, is not naturally and originally part of the end, but it is capable of becoming so; and in those who live it disinterestedly it has become so, and is desired and cherished, not as a means to happiness, but as a part of their happiness.

To illustrate this further, we may remember that virtue is not the only thing originally a means, and which if it were not a means to anything else would be and remain indifferent, but which by association with what it is a means to comes to be desired for itself, and that too with the utmost intensity. What, for example, shall we say of the love of money? There is nothing originally more desirable about money than about any heap of glittering pebbles. Its worth is solely that of the things which it will buy; the desires for other things than itself, which it is a means of gratifying. Yet the love of money is not only one of the strongest moving forces of human life, but money is, in many cases, desired in and for itself; the desire to possess it is often stronger than the desire to use it, and goes on increasing when all the desires which point to ends beyond it, to be compassed by it, are falling off. It may, then, be said truly that money is desired not for the sake of an end, but as part of the end. From being a means to happiness, it has come to be itself a principal ingredient of the individual's conception of happiness. The same may be said of the majority of the great objects of human life: power, for example, or fame, except that to each of these there is a certain amount of immediate pleasure annexed, which has at least the semblance of being naturally inherent in them—a thing which cannot be said of money. Still, however, the strongest natural attraction, both of power and of fame, is the immense aid they give to the attainment of our other wishes; and it is the strong association thus generated between them and all our objects of desire which gives to the direct desire of them the intensity it often assumes, so as in some characters to surpass in strength all other desires. In these cases the means have become a part of the end, and a more important part of it than any of the things which they are means to. What was once desired as an instrument for the attainment of happiness has come to be desired for its own sake. In being desired for its own sake it is, however, desired as *part* of happiness. The person is made, or thinks he would be made, happy by its mere possession; and is made unhappy by failure to obtain it. The desire of it is not a different thing from the desire of happiness any more than the love of music or the desire of health. They are included in happiness. They are some of the elements of which the desire of happiness is made up. Happiness is not an abstract idea but a concrete whole; and these are some of its parts. And the utilitarian standard sanctions and approves their being so. Life would be a poor thing, very ill provided with sources of happiness, if there were not this provision of nature by which things originally indifferent, but conducive to, or otherwise associated with, the satisfaction of our primitive desires, become in themselves sources of pleasure more valuable than the primitive pleasures, both in permanency, in the space of human existence that they are capable of covering, and even in intensity.

Virtue, according to the utilitarian conception, is a good of this description. There was no original desire of it, or motive to it, save its conduciveness to pleasure, and especially to protection from pain. But through the association thus formed it may be felt a good in itself, and desired as such with as great intensity as any other good; and with this difference between it and the love of money, of power, or of fame—that all of these may, and often do, render the individual noxious to the other members of the society to which he belongs, whereas there is nothing which makes him so much a blessing to them as the cultivation of the disinterested love of virtue. And consequently, the utilitarian standard, while it tolerates and approves those other acquired desires, up to the point beyond which they would be more injurious to the general happiness than promotive of it, enjoins and requires the cultivation of the love of virtue up to the greatest strength possible, as being above all things important to the general happiness.

It results from the preceding considerations that there is in reality nothing desired except happiness. Whatever is desired otherwise than as a means to some end beyond itself, and ultimately to happiness, is desired as itself a part of happiness, and is not desired for itself until it has become so. Those who desire virtue for its own sake desire it either because the consciousness of it is a pleasure, or because the consciousness of being without it is a pain, or for both reasons united; as in truth the pleasure and pain seldom exist separately, but almost always together—the same person feeling pleasure in the degree of virtue attained, and pain in not having attained more. If one of these gave him no pleasure, and the other no pain, he would not love or desire virtue, or would desire it only for the other benefits which it might produce to himself or to persons whom he cared for.

We have now, then, an answer to the question, of what sort of proof the principle of utility is susceptible. If the opinion which I have now stated is psychologically true—if human nature is so constituted as to desire nothing which is not either a part of happiness or a means of happiness—we can have no other proof, and we require no other, that these are the only things desirable. If so, happiness is the sole end of human action, and the promotion of it the test by which to judge of all human conduct; from whence it necessarily follows that it must be the criterion of morality, since a part is included in the whole.

And now to decide whether this is really so, whether mankind do desire nothing for itself but that which is a pleasure to them, or of which the absence is a pain, we have evidently arrived at a question of fact and experience, dependent, like all similar questions, upon evidence. It can only be determined by practiced self-consciousness and self-observation, assisted by observation of others. I believe that these sources of evidence, impartially consulted, will declare that desiring a thing and finding it pleasant, aversion to it and thinking of it as painful, are phenomena entirely inseparable or, rather, two parts of the same phenomenon—in strictness of language, two different modes of naming the same psychological fact; that to think of an object as desirable (unless for the sake of its consequences) and to think of it as pleasant are one and the same thing; and that to desire anything except in proportion as the idea of it is pleasant is a physical and metaphysical impossibility.

So obvious does this appear to me that I expect it will hardly be disputed; and the objection made will be, not that desire can possibly be directed to anything ultimately except pleasure and exemption from pain, but that the will is a different thing from desire; that a person of confirmed virtue or any other person whose purposes are fixed carries out his purposes without any thought of the pleasure he has in contemplating them or expects to derive from their fulfillment, and persists in acting on them, even though these pleasures are much diminished by changes in his character or decay of his passive sensibilities, or are outweighed by the pains which the pursuit of the purposes may bring upon him. All this I fully admit and have stated it elsewhere as positively and emphatically as anyone. Will, the active phenomenon, is a different thing from desire, the state of passive sensibility, and, though originally an offshoot from it, may in time take root and detach itself from the parent stock, so much so that in the case of a habitual purpose, instead of willing the thing because we desire it, we often desire it only because we will it. This, however, is but an instance of that familiar fact, the power of habit, and is nowise confined to the case of virtuous actions. Many indifferent things which men originally did from a motive of some sort they continue to do from habit. Sometimes this is done unconsciously, the consciousness coming only after the action; at other times with conscious volition, but volition which has become habitual and is put in operation by the force of habit, in opposition perhaps to the deliberate preference, as often happens with those who have contracted habits of vicious or hurtful indulgence. Third and last comes the case in which the habitual act of will in the individual instance is not in contradiction to the general intention prevailing at other times, but in fulfillment of it, as in the case of the person of confirmed virtue and of all who pursue deliberately and consistently any determinate end. The distinction between will and desire thus understood is an authentic and highly important psychological fact; but the fact consists solely in this—that will, like all other parts of our constitution, is amenable to habit, and that we may will from habit what we no longer desire for itself, or desire only because we will it. It is not the less true that will, in the beginning, is entirely produced by desire, including in that term the repelling influence of pain as well as the attractive one of pleasure. Let us take into consideration no longer the person who has a confirmed will to do right, but him in whom that virtuous will is still feeble, conquerable by temptation, and not to be fully relied on; by what means can it be strengthened? How can the will to be virtuous, where it does not exist in sufficient force, be implanted or awakened? Only by making the person *desire* virtue—by making him think of it in a pleasurable light, or of its absence in a painful one. It is by associating the doing right with pleasure, or the wrong with pain, or by eliciting and impressing and bringing home to the person's experience the pleasure naturally involved in the one or the pain in the other, that it is possible to call forth that will to be virtuous which, when confirmed, acts without any thought of either pleasure or pain. Will is the child of desire, and passes out of the dominion of its parent only to come under that of habit. That which is the result of habit affords no presumption of being intrinsically good; and there would be no reason for wishing that the purpose of virtue should become independent of pleasure and pain were it not that the influence of the pleasurable and painful associations which prompt to virtue is not sufficiently to be depended on for unerring constancy of action until it has acquired the support of habit. Both in feeling and in conduct, habit is the only thing which imparts certainty; and it is because of the importance to others of being able to rely absolutely on one's feelings and conduct, and to oneself of being able to rely on one's own, that the will to do right ought to be cultivated into this habitual independence. In other words, this state of the will is a means to good, not intrinsically a good; and does not contradict the doctrine that nothing is a good to human beings but in so far as it is either itself pleasurable or a means of attaining pleasure or averting pain.

But if this doctrine be true, the principle of utility is proved. Whether it is so or not must now be left to the consideration of the thoughtful reader.

STUDY QUESTIONS

1   Happiness, according to Mill, is a life of pleasure. How does Mill distinguish between kinds of pleasures? To what sort of pleasure does the principle of utility refer?

2   What is the test for determining the quality of pleasure? Suppose someone were to say that the highest pleasures were to be found in eating, drinking, sex, and sleep. Would Mill agree? Why not? What would Aristotle say?

3   What is the distinction between happiness and contentment? How can Mill say that it is *better* to be Socrates dissatisfied than a fool satisfied?

4   Mill argues that the only proof that something is desirable is that people actually do desire it. Many philosophers have argued that this "proof" is completely fallacious. What do you think? Does Mill supplement this proof of utility?

5   How does Mill prove that the general happiness is a good? Does he prove that *each* individual ought to desire the general happiness?

6   Kant insists that the love of duty is the only morally respectable motive for action. Does Mill's defense of the "disinterested love of virtue" allow him to agree with Kant?

7   Do you think that Kant and Mill would disagree on the relation between *desire* and *will?* Does Mill think it is possible for the will to operate independently of desire? If free will is required for moral responsibility, do you think that Mill would say a free will is one that is not "caused" ?

Egoism and Moral Skepticism

James Rachels

"What's in it for me?" Many people believe this question to be at the heart of morality. If a course of action brings no benefit to the agent, if social morality demands things which promise no payoff, then such demands are irrational and no one is obliged to obey. This is the position of ethical egoism. In this selection, James Rachels (1941–   ), professor of philosophy at the University of Miami, looks at the assumptions underlying this conception of morality and finds them wanting.

The ethical doctrine that no one is obliged to do anything which is not in his or her self-interest is usually accompanied by a psychological theory which depicts people as selfish and incapable of acting out of a genuine interest in the welfare of others. If egoism is correct, then the Golden Rule is nonsense. I *cannot* love my neighbor as myself, and no one can demand that I do the impossible. This psychological picture, Rachels argues, is founded on confusion—in particular, the failure to distinguish selfishness from self-interest. But even if people are *capable* of acting altruistically, why *should* they? Why shouldn't I use the noble feelings of others to my own advantage? Philosophers have traditionally used several arguments against ethical egoism. But Rachels claims that none of these arguments work. Ethical egoism is a logically consistent moral theory which cannot be refuted on logical grounds alone. Moral rules must be founded on what we actually desire. Ethical egoism is faulty, he says, because it distorts human nature and human desires beyond recognition.

1 Our ordinary thinking about morality is full of assumptions that we almost never question. We assume, for example, that we have an obligation to consider the welfare of other people when we decide what actions to perform or what rules to obey; we think that we must refrain from acting in ways harmful to others, and that we must respect their rights and interests as well as our own. We also assume that people are in fact capable of being motivated by such considerations, that is, that people are not wholly selfish and that they do sometimes act in the interests of others.

Both of these assumptions have come under attack by moral sceptics, as long ago as by Glaucon in Book II of Plato's *Republic*. Glaucon recalls the legend of Gyges, a shepherd who was said to have found a magic ring in a fissure opened by an earthquake. The ring would make its wearer invisible and thus would enable him to go anywhere and do anything undetected. Gyges used the power of the ring to gain entry to the Royal Palace where he seduced the Queen, murdered the King, and subsequently seized the throne. Now Glaucon asks us to determine that there are two such rings, one given to a man of virtue and one given to a rogue. The rogue, of course, will use his ring unscrupulously and do anything necessary to increase his own wealth and power. He will recognize no moral constraints on his conduct, and, since the cloak of invisibility will protect him from discovery, he can do anything he pleases without fear of reprisal. So, there will be no end to the mischief he will do. But how will the so-called virtuous man behave? Glaucon suggests that he will behave no better than the rogue: "No one, it is commonly believed, would have such iron strength of mind as to stand fast in doing right or keep his hands off other men's goods, when he could go to the market-place and fearlessly help himself to anything he wanted, enter houses and sleep with any woman he chose, set prisoners free and kill men at his pleasure, and in a word go about among men with the powers of a god. He would behave no better than the other; both would take the same course."[1] Moreover, why shouldn't he? Once he is freed from the fear of reprisal, why shouldn't a man simply do what he pleases, or what he thinks is best for himself? What reason is there for him to continue being "moral" when it is clearly not to his own advantage to do so?

These sceptical views suggested by Glaucon have come to be known as *psychological egoism* and *ethical egoism* respectively. Psychological egoism is the view that all men are selfish in everything that they do, that is, that the only motive from which anyone ever acts is self-interest. On this view, even when men are acting in ways apparently calculated to benefit others, they are actually motivated by the belief that acting in this way is to their own advantage, and if they did not believe this, they would not be doing that action. Ethical egoism is, by contrast, a normative view about how men *ought* to act. It is the view that, regardless of how men do in fact behave, they have no obligation to do anything except what is in their own interests. According to the ethical egoist, a person is always justified in doing whatever is in his own interests, regardless of the effect on others.

[1] *The Republic of Plato,* translated by F. M. Cornford (Oxford, 1941), p. 45.

Clearly, if either of these views is correct, then "the moral institution of life" (to use Butler's well-turned phrase) is very different than what we normally think. The majority of mankind is grossly deceived about what is, or ought to be, the case, where morals are concerned.

2   Psychological egoism seems to fly in the face of the facts. We are tempted to say: "Of course people act unselfishly all the time. For example, Smith gives up a trip to the country, which he would have enjoyed very much, in order to stay behind and help a friend with his studies, which is a miserable way to pass the time. This is a perfectly clear case of unselfish behavior, and if the psychological egoist thinks that such cases do not occur, then he is just mistaken." Given such obvious instances of "unselfish behavior," what reply can the egoist make? There are two general arguments by which he might try to show that all actions, including those such as the one just outlined, are in fact motivated by self-interest. Let us examine these in turn:

A.   The first argument goes as follows. If we describe one person's action as selfish, and another person's action as unselfish, we are overlooking the crucial fact that in both cases, assuming that the action is done voluntarily, *the agent is merely doing what he most wants to do.* If Smith stays behind to help his friend, that only shows that he wanted to help his friend more than he wanted to go to the country. And why should he be praised for his "unselfishness" when he is only doing what he most wants to do? So, since Smith is only doing what he wants to do, he cannot be said to be acting unselfishly.

This argument is so bad that it would not deserve to be taken seriously except for the fact that so many otherwise intelligent people have been taken in by it. First, the argument rests on the premise that people never voluntarily do anything except what they want to do. But this is patently false; there are at least two classes of actions that are exceptions to this generalization. One is the set of actions which we may not want to do, but which we do anyway as a means to an end which we want to achieve; for example, going to the dentist in order to stop a toothache, or going to work every day in order to be able to draw our pay at the end of the month. These cases may be regarded as consistent with the spirit of the egoist argument, however, since the ends mentioned are wanted by the agent. But the other set of actions are those which we do, not because we want to, nor even because there is an end which we want to achieve, but because we feel ourselves *under an obligation* to do them. For example, someone may do something because he has promised to do it, and thus feels obligated, even though he does not want to do it. It is sometimes suggested that in such cases we do the action because, after all, we want to keep our promises; so, even here, we are doing what we want. However, this dodge will not work; if I have promised to do something, and if I do not want to do it, then it is simply false to say that I want to keep my promise. In such cases we feel a conflict precisely because we do *not* want to do what we feel obligated to do. It is reasonable to think that Smith's action falls roughly into this second category: he might stay behind, not because he wants to, but because he feels that his friend needs help.

But suppose we were to concede, for the sake of the argument, that all voluntary action is motivated by the agent's wants, or at least that Smith is so motivated. Even if this were granted, it would not follow that Smith is acting selfishly or from self-interest. For if Smith wants to do something that will help his friend, even when it means forgoing his own enjoyments, that is precisely what makes him *un*selfish. What else could unselfishness be, if not wanting to help others? Another way to put the same point is to say that it is the *object* of a want that determines whether it is selfish or not. The mere fact that I am acting on *my* wants does not mean that I am acting selfishly; that depends on *what it is* that I want. If I want only my own good, and care nothing for others, then I am selfish; but if I also want other people to be well-off and happy, and if I act on *that* desire, then my action is not selfish. So much for this argument.

B. The second argument for psychological egoism is this. Since so-called unselfish actions always produce a sense of self-satisfaction in the agent,[2] and since this sense of satisfaction is a pleasant state of consciousness, it follows that the point of the action is really to achieve a pleasant state of consciousness, rather than to bring about any good for others. Therefore, the action is "unselfish" only at a superficial level of analysis. Smith will feel much better with himself for having stayed to help his friend—if he had gone to the country, he would have felt terrible about it—and that is the real point of the action. According to a well-known story, this argument was once expressed by Abraham Lincoln:

> Mr. Lincoln once remarked to a fellow-passenger on an old-time mud-coach that all men were prompted by selfishness in doing good. His fellow-passenger was antagonizing this position when they were passing over a corduroy bridge that spanned a slough. As they crossed this bridge they espied an old razor-backed sow on the bank making a terrible noise because her pigs had got into the slough and were in danger of drowning. As the old coach began to climb the hill, Mr. Lincoln called out, "Driver, can't you stop just a moment?" Then Mr. Lincoln jumped out, ran back, and lifted the little pigs out of the mud and water and placed them on the bank. When he returned, his companion remarked: "Now, Abe, where does selfishness come in on this little episode?" "Why, bless your soul, Ed, that was the very essence of selfishness. I should have had no peace of mind all day had I gone on and left that suffering old sow worrying over those pigs. I did it to get peace of mind, don't you see?"[3]

This argument suffers from defects similar to the previous one. Why should we think that merely because someone derives satisfaction from helping others this makes him selfish? Isn't the unselfish man precisely the one who *does* derive satisfaction from helping others, while the selfish man does not? If Lincoln "got peace of mine" from rescuing the piglets, does this show him to be selfish, or, on the contrary, doesn't it show him to be compassionate and good-hearted? (If a man were truly selfish, why should it bother his conscience that *others* suffer—much less pigs?) Similarly, it is nothing more than shabby sophistry to say, because Smith takes satisfaction in helping his friend, that he is behaving selfish-

---

[2] Or, as it is sometimes said, "It gives him a clear conscience," or "He couldn't sleep at night if he had done otherwise," or "He would have been ashamed of himself for not doing it," and so on.

[3] Frank C. Sharp, *Ethics* (New York, 1928), pp. 74–75. Quoted from the Springfield (Ill.) *Monitor* in the *Outlook,* vol. 56, p. 1059.

ly. If we say this rapidly, while thinking about something else, perhaps it will sound all right; but if we speak slowly, and pay attention to what we are saying, it sounds plain silly.

Moreover, suppose we ask *why* Smith derives satisfaction from helping his friend. The answer will be, it is because Smith cares for him and wants him to succeed. If Smith did not have these concerns, then he would take no pleasure in assisting him; and these concerns, as we have already seen, are the marks of unselfishness, not selfishness. To put the point more generally: if we have a positive attitude toward the attainment of some goal, then we may derive satisfaction from attaining that goal. But the *object* of our attitude is *the attainment of that goal;* and we must want to attain the goal *before* we can find any satisfaction in it. We do not, in other words, desire some sort of "pleasurable consciousness" and then try to figure out how to achieve it; rather, we desire all sorts of different things—money, a new fishing-boat, to be a better chess-player, to get a promotion in our work, etc.—and because we desire these things, we derive satisfaction from attaining them. And so, if someone desires the welfare and happiness of another person, he will derive satisfaction from that; but this does not mean that this satisfaction is the object of his desire, or that he is in any way selfish on account of it.

It is a measure of the weakness of psychological egoism that these insupportable arguments are the ones most often advanced in its favor. Why, then, should anyone ever have thought it a true view? Perhaps because of a desire for theoretical simplicity: In thinking about human conduct, it would be nice if there were some simple formula that would unite the diverse phenomena of human behavior under a single explanatory principle, just as simple formulae in physics bring together a great many apparently different phenomena. And since it is obvious that self-regard is an overwhelmingly important factor in motivation, it is only natural to wonder whether all motivation might not be explained in these terms. But the answer is clearly No; while a great many human actions are motivated entirely or in part by self-interest, only by a deliberate distortion of the facts can we say that all conduct is so motivated. This will be clear, I think, if we correct three confusions which are commonplace. The exposure of these confusions will remove the last traces of plausibility from the psychological egoist thesis.

The first is the confusion of selfishness with self-interest. The two are clearly not the same. If I see a physician when I am feeling poorly, I am acting in my own interest but no one would think of calling me "selfish" on account of it. Similarly, brushing my teeth, working hard at my job, and obeying the law are all in my self-interest but none of these are examples of selfish conduct. This is because selfish behavior is behavior that ignores the interests of others, in circumstances in which their interests ought not to be ignored. This concept has a definite evaluative flavor; to call someone "selfish" is not just to describe his action but to condemn it. Thus, you would not call me selfish for eating a normal meal in normal circumstances (although it may surely be in my self-interest); but you would call me selfish for hoarding food while others about are starving.

The second confusion is the assumption that every action is done *either* from self-interest or from other-regarding motives. Thus, the egoist concludes that if there is no such thing as genuine altruism then all actions must be done from self-interest. But this is certainly a false dichotomy. The man who continues to smoke cigarettes, even after learning about the connection between smoking and cancer, is surely not acting from self-interest, not even by his own standards— self-interest would dictate that he quit smoking at once—and he is not acting altruistically either. He *is,* no doubt, smoking for the pleasure of it, but all that this shows is that undisciplined pleasure-seeking and acting from self-interest are very different. This is what led Butler to remark that "The thing to be lamented is, not that men have so great regard to their own good or interest in the present world, for they have not enough."[4]

The last two paragraphs show (a) that it is false that all actions are selfish, and (b) that it is false that all actions are done out of self-interest. And it should be noted that these two points can be made, and were, without any appeal to putative examples of altruism.

The third confusion is the common but false assumption that a concern for one's own welfare is incompatible with any genuine concern for the welfare of others. Thus, since it is obvious that everyone (or very nearly everyone) does desire his own well-being, it might be thought that no one can really be concerned with others. But again, this is false. There is no inconsistency in desiring that everyone, including oneself *and* others, be well-off and happy. To be sure, it may happen on occasion that our own interests conflict with the interests of others, and in these cases we will have to make hard choices. But even in these cases we might sometimes opt for the interests of others, especially when the others involved are our family or friends. But more importantly, not all cases are like this: sometimes we are able to promote the welfare of others when our own interests are not involved at all. In these cases not even the strongest self-regard need prevent us from acting considerately toward others.

Once these confusions are cleared away, it seems to me obvious enough that there is no reason whatever to accept psychological egoism. On the contrary, if we simply observe people's behavior with an open mind, we may find that a great deal of it is motivated by self-regard, but by no means all of it; and that there is no reason to deny that "the moral institution of life" can include a place for the virtue of beneficence.[5]

3 The ethical egoist would say at this point, "Of course it is possible for people to act altruistically, and perhaps many people do act that way—but there is no reason why they *should* do so. A person is under no obligation to do anything except what is in his own interests."[6] This is really quite a radical

---

[4] *The Works of Joseph Butler,* edited by W. E. Gladstone (Oxford, 1896), vol. II, p. 26. It should be noted that most of the points I am making against psychological egoism were first made by Butler. Butler made all the important points; all that is left for us is to remember them.

[5] The capacity for altruistic behavior is not unique to human beings. Some interesting experiments with rhesus monkeys have shown that these animals will refrain from operating a device for securing food if this causes other animals to suffer pain. See Masserman, Wechkin, and Terris, " 'Altruistic' Behavior in Rhesus Monkeys," *The American Journal of Psychiatry,* vol. 121 (1964), 584–585.

[6] I take this to be the view of Ayn Rand, in so far as I understand her confusing doctrine.

doctrine. Suppose I have an urge to set fire to some public building (say, a department store) just for the fascination of watching the spectacular blaze: according to this view, the fact that several people might be burned to death provides no reason whatever why I should not do it. After all, this only concerns *their* welfare, not my own, and according to the ethical egoist the only person I need think of is myself.

Some might deny that ethical egoism has any such monstrous consequences. They would point out that it is really to my own advantage not to set the fire—for, if I do that I may be caught and put into prison (unlike Gyges, I have no magic ring for protection). Moreover, even if I could avoid being caught it is still to my advantage to respect the rights and interests of others, for it is to my advantage to live in a society in which people's rights and interests are respected. Only in such a society can I live a happy and secure life; so, in acting kindly toward others, I would merely be doing my part to create and maintain the sort of society which it is to my advantage to have.[7] Therefore, it is said, the egoist would not be such a bad man; he would be as kindly and considerate as anyone else, because he would see that it is to his own advantage to be kindly and considerate.

This is a seductive line of thought, but it seems to me mistaken. Certainly it is to everyone's advantage (including the egoist's) to preserve a stable society where people's interests are generally protected. But there is no reason for the egoist to think that merely because *he* will not honor the rules of the social game, decent society will collapse. For the vast majority of people are not egoists, and there is no reason to think that they will be converted by his example—especially if he is discreet and does not unduly flaunt his style of life. What this line of reasoning shows is not that the egoist himself must act benevolently, but that he must encourage *others* to do so. He must take care to conceal from public view his own self-centered method of decision-making, and urge others to act on precepts very different from those on which he is willing to act.

The rational egoist, then, cannot advocate that egoism be universally adopted by everyone. For he wants a world in which his own interests are maximized; and if other people adopted the egoistic policy of pursuing their own interests to the exclusion of his interests, as he pursues his interests to the exclusion of theirs, then such a world would be impossible. So he himself will be an egoist, but he will want others to be altruists.

This brings us to what is perhaps the most popular "refutation" of ethical egoism current among philosophical writers—the argument that ethical egoism is at bottom inconsistent because it cannot be universalized.[8] The argument goes like this:

To say that any action or policy of action is *right* (or that it *ought* to be adopted) entails that it is right for *anyone* in the same sort of circumstances. I cannot, for example, say that it is right for me to lie to you, and yet object when

---

[7] Cf. Thomas Hobbes, *Leviathan* (London, 1651), chap. 17.

[8] See, for example, Brian Medlin, "Ultimate Principles and Ethical Egoism," *Australian Journal of Philosophy,* vol. 35 (1957), 111–118; and D. H. Monro, *Empiricism and Ethics* (Cambridge, 1967), chap. 16.

you lie to me (provided, of course, that the circumstances are the same). I cannot hold that it is all right for me to drink your beer and then complain when you drink mine. This is just the requirement that we be consistent in our evaluations; it is a requirement of logic. Now it is said that ethical egoism cannot meet this requirement because, as we have already seen, the egoist would not want others to act in the same way that he acts. Moreover, suppose he *did* advocate the universal adoption of egoistic policies: he would be saying to Peter, "You ought to pursue your own interests even if it means destroying Paul" ; and he would be saying to Paul, "You ought to pursue your own interests even if it means destroying Peter." The attitudes expressed in these two recommendations seem clearly inconsistent—he is urging the advancement of Peter's interest at one moment, and countenancing their defect at the next. Therefore, the argument goes, there is no way to maintain the doctrine of ethical egoism as a consistent view about how we ought to act. We will fall into inconsistency whenever we try.

What are we to make of this argument? Are we to conclude that ethical egoism has been refuted? Such a conclusion, I think, would be unwarranted; for I think that we can show, contrary to this argument, how ethical egoism can be maintained consistently. We need only to interpret the egoist's position in a sympathetic way: we should say that he has in mind a certain kind of world which he would prefer over all others; it would be a world in which his own interests were maximized, regardless of the effects on other people. The egoist's primary policy of action, then, would be to act in such a way as to bring about, as nearly as possible, this sort of world. Regardless of however morally reprehensible we might find it, there is nothing *inconsistent* in someone's adopting this as his ideal and acting in a way calculated to bring it about. And if someone did adopt this as his ideal, then he would not advocate universal egoism; as we have already seen, he would want other people to be altruists. So, if he advocates any principles of conduct for the general public, they will be altruistic principles. This would be inconsistent; on the contrary, it would be perfectly consistent with his goal of creating a world in which his own interests are maximized. To be sure, he would have to be deceitful; in order to secure the good will of others, and a favorable hearing for his exhortations to altruism, he would have to pretend that he was himself prepared to accept altruistic principles. But again, that would be all right; from the egoist's point of view, this would merely be a matter of adopting the necessary means to the achievement of his goal—and while we might not approve of this, there is nothing inconsistent about it. Again, it might be said: "He advocates one thing, but does another. Surely *that's* inconsistent." But it is not; for what he advocates and what he does are both calculated as means to an end (the *same* end, we might note); and as such, he is doing what is rationally required in each case. Therefore, contrary to the previous argument, there is nothing inconsistent in the ethical egoist's view. He cannot be refuted by the claim that he contradicts himself.

Is there, then, no way to refute the ethical egoist? If by "refute" we mean show that he has made some *logical* error, the answer is that there is not. However, there is something more that can be said. The egoist challenge to our ordinary moral convictions amounts to a demand for an explanation of why we should adopt certain policies of action, namely policies in which the good of others is given importance. We can give an answer to this demand, albeit an indirect one. The reason one ought not to do actions that would hurt other people is: other people would be hurt. The reason one ought to do actions that would benefit other people is: other people would be benefited. This may at first seem like a piece of philosophical sleight-of-hand, but it is not. The point is that the welfare of human beings is something that most of us value *for its own sake,* and not merely for the sake of something else. Therefore, when *further* reasons are demanded for valuing the welfare of human beings, we cannot point to anything further to satisfy this demand. It is not that we have no reason for pursuing these policies, but that our reason is that these policies are for the good of human beings.

So: if we are asked "Why shouldn't I set fire to this department store? " one answer would be "Because if you do, people may be burned to death." This is a complete, sufficient reason which does not require qualification or supplementation of any sort. If someone seriously wants to know why this action shouldn't be done, that's the reason. If we are pressed further and asked the sceptical question "But why shouldn't I do actions that will harm others? " we may not know what to say—but this is because the questioner has included in his question the very answer we would like to give: "Why shouldn't you do actions that will harm others? Because, doing those actions would harm others."

The egoist, no doubt, will not be happy with this. He will protest that *we* may accept this as a reason, but *he* does not. And here the argument stops: there are limits to what can be accomplished by argument, and if the egoist really doesn't care about other people—if he honestly doesn't care whether they are helped or hurt by his actions—then we have reached those limits. If we want to persuade him to act decently toward his fellow humans, we will have to make our appeal to such other attitudes as he does possess, by threats, bribes, or other cajolery. That is all that we can do.

Though some may find this situation distressing (we would like to be able to show that the egoist is just *wrong*), it holds no embarrassment for common morality. What we have come up against is simply a fundamental requirement of rational action, namely, that the existence of reasons for action always depends on the prior existence of certain attitudes in the agent. For example, the fact that a certain course of action would make the agent a lot of money is a reason for doing it only if the agent wants to make money; the fact that practicing at chess makes one a better player is a reason for practicing only if one wants to be a better player; and so on. Similarly, the fact that a certain action would help the agent is a reason for doing the action only if the agent cares about his own welfare, and the fact that an action would help others is a reason for doing it only if the agent cares about others. In this respect ethical egoism and what we might call ethical altruism are in exactly the same fix: both require that the agent *care* about himself, or about other people, before they can get started.

So a nonegoist will accept "it would harm another person" as a reason not to do an action simply because he cares about what happens to that other person. When the egoist says that he does *not* accept that as a reason, he is saying something quite extraordinary. He is saying that he has no affection for friends or family, that he never feels pity or compassion, that he is the sort of person who can look on scenes of human misery with complete indifference, so long as he is not the one suffering. Genuine egoists, people who really don't care at all about anyone other than themselves, are rare. It is important to keep this in mind when thinking about ethical egoism; it is easy to forget just how fundamental to human psychological makeup the feeling of sympathy is. Indeed, a man without any sympathy at all would scarcely be recognizable as a man; and that is what makes ethical egoism such a disturbing doctrine in the first place.

4   There are, of course, many different ways in which the sceptic might challenge the assumptions underlying our moral practice. In this essay I have discussed only two of them, the two put forward by Glaucon in the passage that I cited from Plato's *Republic*. It is important that the assumptions underlying our moral practice should not be confused with particular judgments made within that practice. To defend one is not to defend the other. We may assume—quite properly, if my analysis has been correct—that the virtue of beneficence does, and indeed should, occupy an important place in "the moral institution of life"; and yet we may make constant and miserable errors when it comes to judging when and in what ways this virtue is to be exercised. Even worse, we may often be able to make accurate moral judgments, and know what we ought to do, but not do it. For these ills, philosophy alone is not the cure.

STUDY QUESTIONS

1   What is the difference between ethical egoism and psychological egoism? Do you think that psychological egoism leads to ethical egoism or vice versa?

2   Thomas Hobbes, the famous materialist and egoist of the seventeenth century, was observed giving money to a beggar. When asked whether such altruistic behavior was consistent with his psychological picture of humanity, Hobbes replied that giving money to the beggar gave him great pleasure. Is this a sufficient answer?

3   Why does Rachels distinguish selfishness and self-interest? Can you formulate a definition of each? Can you think of a case where helping others is in one's self-interest?

4   Rachels does not think that ethical egoism can be refuted by the "universalizability" argument. What is this argument and why does Rachels reject it?

5   In the end, Rachels finds ethical egoism unacceptable. Why? Do you think that he has shown egoism to be untenable?

6   Suppose Gyges read Rachels's paper. Would anything in the paper persuade him (assuming he is rational) to act one way or another?

The Case of the Obliging Stranger

William Gass

William Gass (1924–   ) is professor of philosophy at Washington University. In addition to his philosophical writing, he has published several short stories and a novel, *Omensetter's Luck* (1966). In this selection, Gass challenges the usual account of moral reasoning. He argues that moral problems are not solved in real life by appealing to "principles." Instead, the elaborate theories of moralists, along with the abstract principles of right and good they are designed to justify, are themselves justified by ordinary moral experience.

Gass claims that there are "clear" cases of immoral (and moral) conduct. Only a lunatic—or a philosopher—could look at such cases and seriously ask, "But is it really wrong?" These clear cases are unmistakable data and no moral theory which conflicts with these data can be correct. Moral principles, he maintains, are actually convenient summaries of some of the outstanding features of the clear cases. A tendency to lead to the greatest happiness, for example, is a feature of some clear cases of moral action. But it is not this tendency which makes it moral, no more than the tendency of a rooster to crow at sunrise makes it into a rooster. Other principles provide different distinguishing marks of clear cases. But when principles conflict, we must throw them aside and return to moral experience, which Gass says requires no explanation.

I

Imagine I approach a stranger on the street and say to him, "If you please, sir, I desire to perform an experiment with your aid." The stranger is obliging, and I lead him away. In a dark place conveniently by, I strike his head with the broad of an axe and cart him home. I place him, buttered and trussed, in an ample electric oven. The thermostat reads 450° F. Thereupon I go off to play poker with friends and forget all about the obliging stranger in the stove. When I return, I realize I have overbaked my specimen, and the experiment, alas, is ruined.

Something has been done wrong. Or something wrong has been done.

Any ethic that does not roundly condemn my action is vicious. It is interesting that none is vicious for this reason. It is also interesting that no more convincing refutation of any ethic could be given than by showing that it approved of my baking the obliging stranger.

This is really all I have to say, but I shall not stop on that account. Indeed, I shall begin again.

II

The geometer cannot demonstrate that a line is beautiful. The beauty of lines is not his concern. We do not chide him when he fails to observe uprightness in his verticals, when he discovers no passions between sinuosities. We would not judge it otherwise than foolish to berate him for neglecting to employ the methods

From "The Case of the Obliging Stranger" by William Gass. *Philosophical Review*, LXVI (1957), 193–204. Reprinted by permission of the editor and the author.

successful in biology or botany merely because those methods dealt fairly with lichens and fishes. Nor do we despair of him because he cannot give us reasons for doing geometry which will equally well justify our drilling holes in teeth. There is a limit, as Aristotle said, to the questions which we may sensibly put to each man of science; and however much we may desire to find unity in the purposes, methods, and results of every fruitful sort of inquiry, we must not allow that desire to make mush of their necessary differences.

Historically, with respect to the fundamental problems of ethics, this limit has not been observed. Moreover, the analogy between mathematics and morals, or between the methods of empirical science and the good life, has always been unfairly one-sided. Geometers never counsel their lines to be moral, but moralists advise men to be like lines and go straight. There are triangles of lovers, but no triangles in love. And who says the organism is a state?

For it is true that the customary methods for solving moral problems are the methods which have won honors by leaping mathematical hurdles on the one hand or scientific and physical ones on the other: the intuitive and deductive method and the empirical and inductive one. Nobody seems to have minded very much that the moral hurdle has dunked them both in the pool beyond the wall, for they can privately laugh at each other for fools, and together they can exclaim how frightfully hard is the course.

The difficulty for the mathematical method is the discovery of indubitable moral first premises which do not themselves rest on any inductive foundation and which are still applicable to the complicated tissue of factors that make up moral behavior. The result is that the premises are usually drawn from metaphysical speculations having no intimate relation to moral issues or from rational or mystical revelations which only the intuiter and his followers are willing to credit. For the purposes of deduction, the premises have to be so broad and, to satisfy intuition, so categorically certain, that they become too thin for touch and too heavy for bearing. All negative instances are pruned as unreal or parasitic. Consequently, the truth of the ultimate premises is constantly called into question by those who have intuited differently or have men and actions in mind that they want to call good and right but cannot.

Empirical solutions, so runs the common complaint, lop off the normative branch altogether and make ethics a matter of expediency, taste, or conformity to the moral etiquette of the time. One is told what people do, not what they ought to do; and those philosophers who still wish to know what people ought to do are told, by some of the more uncompromising, that they can have no help from empiricism and are asking a silly question. Philosophers, otherwise empiricists, who admit that moral ends lie beyond the reach of factual debate turn to moral sentiment or some other *bonum ex machina,* thus generously embracing the perplexities of both methods.

III

Questions to which investigators return again and again without success are very likely improperly framed. It is important to observe that the ethical question put so directly as "What is good?" or "What is right?"[1] aims in its answer not, as one might immediately suppose, at a catalogue of the world's good, right things. The moralist is not asking for a list of sheep and goats. The case of the obliging stranger is a case of immoral action, but this admission is not an answer, even partially, to the question, "What is wrong?"

Furthermore, the ethical question is distressingly short. "Big" questions, it would seem, ought to be themselves big, but they almost never are; and they tend to grow big simply by becoming short—too short, in fact, ever to receive an answer. I might address, to any ear that should hear me, the rather less profound-sounding, but none the less similar question, "Who won?" or perhaps the snappier, "What's a winner?" I should have to ask this question often because, if I were critical, I should never find an answer that would suit me; while at the same time there would be a remarkable lot of answers that suited a remarkable lot of people. The more answers I had—the more occasions on which I asked the question—the more difficult, the more important, the more "big" the question would become.

If the moralist does not want to hear such words as "Samson," "money," or "brains" when he asks his question, "What is good?", what does he want to hear? He wants to hear a word like "power." He wants to know what is good in the things that are good that makes them good. It should be perfectly clear it is not the things themselves that he thinks good or bad but the qualities they possess, the relations they enter into, or the consequences they produce. Even an intuitionist, who claims to perceive goodness directly, perceives a property of things when he perceives goodness, and not any *thing*, except incidentally. The wrong done the obliging stranger was not the act of cooking him but was something belonging to the act in some one of many possible ways. It is not I who am evil (if I am not mad) but something which I *have* that is; and while, of course, I may be adjudged wicked for having whatever it is I have that is bad, it is only because I have it that I am wicked—as if I owned a vicious and unruly dog.

I think that so long as I look on my act in this way, I wrong the obliging stranger a second time.

The moralist, then, is looking for the ingredient that perfects or spoils the stew. He wants to hear the word "power." He wants to know what is good in what is good that makes it good; and the whole wretched difficulty is that one is forced to reply either that what is good in what is good makes the good in what is good good, or that it is, in fact, made good by things which are not in the least good at all. So the next question, which is always, "And why is power good?" is answered by saying that it is good because it is power and power is good; or it is put off by the promise that power leads to things worth much; or it is shrugged aside with the exclamation, "Well, that's life!" This last is usually accompanied by an exhortation not to oppose the inevitable course of nature.

You cannot ask questions forever. Sooner or later the questioning process is brought up short by statements of an apparently dogmatic sort. Pleasure is

---

[1] The order in which these questions are asked depends on one's view of the logical primacy of moral predicates. I shall not discriminate among them since I intend my remarks to be indiscriminate.

sought for pleasure's sake. The principle of utility is susceptible of no demonstration. Every act and every inquiry aims at well-being. The nonnatural property of goodness fastens itself to its object and will remain there whatever world the present world may madly become. Frustrated desires give rise to problems, and problems are bad. We confer the title of The Good upon our natural necessities.

I fail to see why, if one is going to call a halt in this way, the halt cannot be called early, and the evident, the obvious, the axiomatic, the indemonstrable, the intrinsic, or whatever one wants to name it, be deemed those clear cases of moral goodness, badness, obligation, or wrong which no theory can cloud, and for which men are prepared to fight to the last ditch. For if someone asks me, now I am repentant, why I regard my act of baking the obliging stranger as wrong, what can I do but point again to the circumstances comprising the act? "Well, I put this fellow in an oven, you see. The oven was on, don't you know." And if my questioner persists, saying: "Of course, I know all about *that;* but what I want to know is, why is *that* wrong?", I should recognize there is no use in replying that it is wrong because of the kind of act it is, a wrong one, for my questioner is clearly suffering from a sort of *folie de doute morale* which forbids him to accept any final answer this early in the game, although he will have to accept precisely the same kind of answer at some time or other.

Presumably there is some advantage in postponing the stop, and this advantage lies in the explanatory power of the higher-level answer. It cannot be that my baking the stranger is wrong for no reason at all. It would then be inexplicable. I do not think this is so, however. It is not inexplicable; it is transparent. Furthermore, the feeling of elucidation, of greater insight or knowledge, is a feeling only. It results, I suspect, from the satisfaction one takes in having an open mind. The explanatory factor is always more inscrutable than the event it explains. The same questions can be asked of it as were asked of the original occasion. It is either found in the situation and brought forward to account for all, as one might advance pain, in this case, out of the roaster; or it resides there mysteriously, like an essence, the witch in the oven; or it hovers, like a coil of smoke, as hovers the greatest unhappiness of the greatest number.

But how ludicrous are the moralist's "reasons" for condemning my baking the obliging stranger. They sound queerly unfamiliar and out of place. This is partly because they intrude where one expects to find denunciation only and because it is true they are seldom if ever *used.* But their strangeness is largely due to the humor in them.

Consider:

My act produced more pain than pleasure.
Baking this fellow did not serve the greatest good to the greatest number.
I acted wrongly because I could not consistently will that the maxim of my action become a universal law.
God forbade me, but I paid no heed.
Anyone can apprehend the property of wrongness sticking plainly to the whole affair.
Decent men remark it and are moved to tears.

But I should say that my act was wrong even if my stranger were tickled into laughter while he cooked; or even if his baking did the utmost good it could; or if, in spite of all, I could consistently will that whatever maxim I might have had might become a universal law; or even if God had spoken from a bush to me, "Thou shalt!" How redundant the property of wrongness, as if one needed *that,* in such a case! And would the act be right if the whole world howled its glee? Moralists can say, with conviction, that the act is wrong; but none can *show* it.

Such cases, like that of the obliging stranger, are cases I call clear. They have the characteristic of moral transparency, and they comprise the core of our moral experience. When we try to explain why they are instances of good or bad, of right or wrong, we sound comic, as anyone does who gives elaborate reasons for the obvious, especially when these reasons are so shamefaced before reality, so miserably beside the point. What we must explain is not why these cases have the moral nature they have, for that needs no explaining, but *why they are so clear.* It is an interesting situation: any moralist will throw over his theory if it reverses the decision on cases like the obliging stranger's. The most persuasive criticism of any ethical system has always been the demonstration, on the critic's part, that the system countenances moral absurdities, despite the fact that, in the light of the whole theoretical enterprise, such criticisms beg the question. Although the philosopher who is caught by a criticism of this sort may protest its circularity or even manfully swallow the dreadful conclusion, his system has been scotched, if it has not been killed.

Not all cases are clear. But the moralist will furrow his brow before even this one. He will pursue principles which do not apply. He does not believe in clear cases. He refuses to believe in clear cases. Why?

IV

His disbelief is an absolute presupposition with him. It is a part of his methodological commitments and a part of his notion of profundity and of the nature of philosophy. It is a part of his reverence for intellectual humility. It is a part of his fear of being arbitrary. So he will put the question bravely to the clear cases, even though no state of fact but only his state of mind brings the question up, and even though putting the question, revealing the doubt, destroys immediately the validity of any answer he has posed the question to announce.

Three children are killed by a drunken driver. A family perishes in a sudden fire. Crowded bleachers collapse. Who is puzzled, asking why these things are terrible, why these things are wrong? When is such a question asked? It is asked when the case is not clear, when one is in doubt about it. "Those impious creatures! . . . At the movies . . . today, . . . which is the Lord's!" Is that so bad? Is being impious, even, so bad? I do not know. It is unclear, so I ask why. Or I disagree to pick a quarrel. Or I am a philosopher whose business it is to be puzzled. But do I imagine there is nothing the matter when three children are run over by drunkenness, or when a family goes up in smoke, or when there is a crush of people under timbers under people? There is no lack of clarity here, there is only the philosopher: patient, persistent as the dung beetle, pushing his "whys" up his hillocks with his nose. His doubts are never of the present case. They are always general. They are doubts in legion, regiment, and principle.

The obliging stranger is overbaked. I wonder whether this is bad or not. I ask about it. Presumably there is a reason for my wonderment. What is it? Well, of course there is not any reason that is a reason about the obliging stranger. There is only a reason because I am a fallibilist, or because one must not be arbitrary, or because all certainties in particular cases are certain only when deduced from greater, grander certainties. The reason I advance may be advanced upon itself. The entire moral structure tumbles at once. It is a test of the clarity of cases that objections to them are objections in principle; that the principle applies as well to all cases as to any one; and that these reasons for doubt devour themselves with equal right and the same appetite. That is why the moralist is really prepared to fight for the clear cases to the last ditch; why, when he questions them, he does so to display his philosophical breeding, because it is good form: he knows that if these cases are not clear, none are, and if none are, the game is up.

If there are clear cases, and if every moralist, at bottom, behaves as if there were, why does he still, at the top, behave as if there were none?

V

He may do so because he is an empiricist practicing induction. He believes, with Peirce, that "the inductive method springs directly out of dissatisfaction with existing knowledge." To get more knowledge he must become dissatisfied with what he has, all of it, by and large, often for no reason whatever. Our knowledge is limited, and what we do know, we know inexactly. In the sphere of morals the moralist has discovered how difficult it is to proceed from facts to values, and although he has not given up, his difficulties persuade him not that no one knows but that no one can be sure.

Above all, the empiricist has a hatred of certainty. His reasons are not entirely methodological. Most are political: certainty is evil; it is dictatorial; it is undemocratic; all cases should be scrutinized equally; there should be no favoritism; the philosopher is fearless. "Thought looks into the pit of hell and is not afraid."

The moralist may behave as if there were no clear cases because he is a rationalist practicing deduction. He knows all about the infinite regress. He is familiar with the unquestioned status of first principles. He is beguiled by the precision, rigor, and unarguable moves of logical demonstration. Moreover, he is such an accomplished doubter of the significance of sensation that he has persuaded the empiricist also to doubt that significance. He regards the empiricist as a crass, anti-intellectual booby, a smuggler where he is not an honest skeptic, since no fact, or set of facts, will account for the value we place on the obliging stranger unless we are satisfied to recount again the precise nature of the case.

Suppose our case concerned toads. And suppose we were asking of the toads, "Why? Why are you toads?" They would be unable to reply, being toads. How far should we get in answering our own question if we were never sure of any particular toad that he was one? How far should we get with our deductions if we were going to deduce one from self-evident toadyisms? What is self-evident about toads except that some are toads? And if we had a toad before us, and we were about to investigate him, and someone doubted that we had a toad before us, we could only say our creature was tailless and clumsy and yellow-green and made warts. So if someone still wanted to doubt our toad, he would have to change the definition of "toad," and someone might want to do that; but who wants to change our understanding of the word "immoral" so that the baking of the obliging stranger is not to be called immoral?

The empiricist is right: the deductive ethic rests upon arbitrary postulation. The rationalist is right: the inductive ethic does not exist; or worse, it consists of arbitrary values disguised as facts. Both are guilty of the most elaborate and flagrant rationalizations. Both know precisely what it is they wish to save. Neither is going to be surprised in the least by what turns out to be good or bad. They are asking of their methods answers that their methods cannot give.

VI

It is confusion which gives rise to doubt. What about the unclear cases? I shall be satisfied to show that there are clear ones, but the unclear ones are more interesting, and there are more of them. How do we decide about blue laws, supposing that there is nothing to decide about the obliging stranger except how to prevent the occurrence from happening again? How do we arbitrate conflicts of duty where each duty, even, may be clear? What of principles, after all? Are there none? Are they not used by people? Well, they talk about them more than they use them, but they use them a little.

I should like to try to answer these questions another time. I can only indicate, quite briefly, the form these answers will take.

I think we decide cases where there is some doubt by stating what it is about them that puzzles us. We hunt for more facts, hoping that the case will clear:

"She left her husband with a broken hand and took the children."

"She did!"

"He broke his hand on her head."

"Dear me; but even so!"

"He beat her every Thursday after tea and she finally couldn't stand it any longer."

"Ah, of course, but the poor children?"

"He beat them, too."

"My, my, and was there no other way?"

"The court would grant her no injunction."

"Why not?"

"Judge Bridlegoose is a fool."

"Ah, of course, she did right, no doubt about it."

If more facts do not clear the case, we redescribe it, emphasizing first this fact and then that until it is clear, or until we have several clear versions of the original muddle. Many ethical disputes are due to the possession, by the contending parties, of different accounts of the same occasion, all satisfactorily clear, and this circumstance gives the disputants a deep feeling for the undoubted rightness of each of their versions. Such disputes are particularly acrimonious, and they cannot be settled until an agreement is reached about the true description of the case.

There are, of course, conflicts of duty which are perfectly clear. I have promised to meet you at four to bowl, but when four arrives I am busy rescuing a baby from the jaws of a Bengal tiger and cannot come. Unclear conflicts we try to clarify. And it sometimes happens that the tug of obligations is so equal as to provide no reasonable solution. If some cases are clear, others are undecidable.

It is perfectly true that principles are employed in moral decisions—popular principles, I mean, like the golden rule and the laws of God. Principles really obscure matters as often as they clear them. They are generally flags and slogans to which the individual is greatly attached. Attack the principle and you attack the owner: his good name, his reputation, his sense of righteousness. Love me, love my maxims. People have been wrongly persuaded that principles decide cases and that a principle which fails in one case fails in all. So principles are usually vehicles for especially powerful feelings and frequently get in the way of good sense. We have all observed the angry arguer who grasps the nettle of absurdity to justify his bragging about the toughness of his skin.

I should regard useful principles as summaries of what may be present generally in clear cases, as for instance: cases where pain is present are more often adjudged bad than not. We might, if the reverse were true for pleasure, express our principle briefly in hedonistic terms: pleasure is the good. But there may be lots of principles of this sort, as there may be lots of rather common factors in clear cases. Principles state more or less prevalent identifying marks, as cardinals usually nest in low trees, although there is nothing to prevent them from nesting elsewhere, and the location of the nest is not the essence of the bird. When I appeal to a principle, then, the meaning of my appeal consists of the fact that before me is a case about which I can reach no direct decision; of the fact that the principle I invoke is relevant, since not every principle is (the laws of God do not cover everything, for instance). In this way I affirm my loyalty to those clear cases the principle so roughly summarizes and express my desire to remain consistent with them.

VII

Insofar as present moral theories have any relevance to our experience, they are elaborate systems designed to protect the certainty of the moralist's last-ditch data. Although he may imagine he is gathering his principles from the purest vapors of the mind, the moralist will in fact be prepared to announce as such serenities only those which support his most cherished goods. And if he is not careful to do just this, he will risk being charged with irrelevancy by those who will employ the emptiness and generality of his principles to demonstrate the value of trivialities: as for example, the criticism of the categorical imperative that claims one can universally will all teeth be brushed with powder in the morning, and so on in like manner.

Ethics, I wish to say, is about something, and in the rush to establish principles, to elicit distinctions from a recalcitrant language, and to discover "laws," those lovely things and honored people, those vile seducers and ruddy villains our principles and laws are supposed to be based upon and our ethical theories to be about are overlooked and forgotten.

STUDY QUESTIONS

1   According to Gass, moralists are looking for some property that makes all good things good. Does he think this search will lead to an answer?
2   Gass thinks that the moralist's reasons for not baking the stranger sound ludicrous. He argues that none of the familiar principles could justify such an act. Do you agree? If not, which principle could justify it?
3   Suppose you simply observed the case of the obliging stranger. That is, you watched someone struck, killed, and baked until overdone. Do you think that this is enough to know that the action is immoral? If not, what else do you have to know? Does your answer affect Gass's analysis of moral reasoning?
4   What is Gass's account of moral argument? What is the role of rationality in this account? Do you think that Russell could agree with him?
5   Some early Portuguese explorers reported that there was a tribe in the jungles of Brazil which practiced cannibalism. The children of captured tribes were raised to adolescence and then cooked and eaten by the adoptive tribe. Would this sort of case undermine what Gass has to say about "clear" cases. What facts would someone like Asch claim are relevant here? Would Asch agree with Gass's analysis of moral reasoning?

SELECTED READINGS

The claim that an objective morality depends upon the existence of God is defended in A. E. Taylor, *The Faith of a Moralist* (London: Macmillan, 1930), and given a thorough airing in H. J. Paton, *The Modern Predicament* (New York: Collier Books, 1962), Chapter 21. Some of the most important works in the literature on ethical relativity are R. Benedict, *Patterns of Culture* (Boston: Houghton Mifflin, 1934), M. Herskovits, *Man and His Works* (New York: Knopf, 1948), and E. Westermarck, *Ethical Relativity* (New York: Harcourt, Brace, 1932). W. T. Stace, *The Concept of Morals* (New York: Macmillan, 1937) is one of the most comprehensive and clear criticisms of relativism. Russell's theory was an early form of emotivism. The doctrine became refined and given its most popular expression in A. J. Ayer, *Language, Truth, and Logic* (New York: Dover, 1946). C. L. Stevenson further refined the position and gave a complex defense of it in *Ethics and Lanugage* (New Haven, Conn.: Yale, 1943). S. Hook and J. Buchler criticize Russell's theory in P. A. Schilpp (ed.), *The Philosophy of Bertrand Russell* (Evanston, Ill.: Northwestern University Press, 1944). Russell responds to his critics in this volume, but indicates that he is unsatisfied with his position. For a careful and comprehensive evaluation of emotivism, see J. O. Urmson, *The Emotive Theory of Ethics* (Berkeley: University of California Press, 1954).

Two good books which clearly and interestingly compare the major traditions in ethics are J. Hospers, *Human Conduct* (New York: Harcourt, Brace &

World, 1961), and W. K. Frankena, *Ethics* (Englewood Cliffs, N.J.: Prentice-Hall, 1963). Aristotle's moral theory is set in the context of the rest of his philosophy in J. H. Randall, *Aristotle* (New York: Columbia, 1960), and W. D. Ross, *Aristotle* (New York: Barnes & Noble, 1955). Jeremy Bentham, who had a close hand in Mill's education, was an early defender of utility. His *Principles of Morals and Legislation* laid the groundwork for Mill's theory. Bentham's book is especially interesting because, unlike Mill, he made pleasurable sensations intrinsically good. He even provided a "calculus" for measuring pleasures. Mill's *Autobiography* (New York: Columbia, 1924) provides many insights into the travails of his intense childhood. The classical attack on egoism is Bishop Joseph Butler's *Fifteen Sermons upon Human Nature,* first printed in 1726. The relevant sections of this work can be found in R. Brandt (ed.), *Value and Obligation* (New York: Harcourt, Brace & World, 1961). An interesting contemporary treatment of egoism is K. Baier, *The Moral Point of View* (Ithaca, N.Y.: Cornell, 1958). In this century, G. E. Moore's criticism of ethical naturalism is most responsible for the decline of utilitarianism and the rise of nonnaturalist theories. Moore's critique of naturalism and his own intuitionism are presented in *Principia Ethica* (New York: Cambridge, 1959). Two other forms of intuitionism are defended in W. D. Ross, *Foundations of Ethics* (Oxford: Clarendon Press, 1939), and D. D. Raphael, *The Moral Sense* (London: Oxford, 1957).

Part Four

Free Will and Determinism

THE PARADOX OF FREEDOM

I have quit smoking. The cigarettes lie on the desk before me. I remember the delightful sensation of smoke filling my lungs. My fingers begin to twitch. I force myself to think of the consequences of resuming the habit—the health dangers, the responsibilities I have to others. But I am especially nervous today and smoking would calm me down. Besides, just one couldn't hurt. . . . I pick up the pack. But then I hesitate, gather myself together, and throw them away. I have won against powerful forces within myself. I am not a passive victim, for I have exerted my will.

This sort of struggle is a familiar story to everyone. As we experience it, we feel that we can go one way or another. The future is open, and the outcome is under our control. But there are facts which cloud this assumption. If every event has a cause, as science seems to say, how can we be in control of things? In a burst of scientific enthusiasm, the nineteenth-century mathematician LaPlace remarked that if a person of great intelligence knew the exact configuration of atoms at any specific time, as well as the laws which govern the movement of matter, that person could predict every future state of the universe with absolute certainty. Every event is conditioned to be just as it is by what immediately precedes it, and those events by what precedes them, and so on. A million years ago God could have predicted that I would throw the cigarettes away. Whatever happens *must* happen—there is no alternative.

The dominant image of life which emerges from this dilemma seems clearly pessimistic. The individual is a passive object, manipulated by hidden forces that are impossible to resist. Try as we might, we cannot alter the future which is laid down at the beginning of time. In our own time, new developments in psychology have added detail to this picture. Many psychologists emphasize the extent to which our choices are governed by unconscious forces created by early childhood experiences. Our lives are depicted as the working out of blind mechanical processes over which we have no control.

Yet the feeling of freedom persists. At least some of the time, we believe that we are in control of our future. Above all, we see ourselves as morally responsible agents, ready to stand accountable for what we do, because we could have done otherwise. Is this feeling of freedom an unscientific illusion, or is the realm of choice somehow exempt from the laws of causality?

Choice: From Chance to Compulsion

PROBLEM INTRODUCTION

Determinism is the view that every event has a cause. At first glance, this seems to be a reasonable assumption, but it is one which has confounded every thinker who has pondered its implications. Modern science assumes that the universe is a deterministic system. To explain, predict, and establish lawful relations between things requires that the past and the future be connected, and this, in turn, seems to mean that the future flows necessarily from the past. If things and events are caused, then it is possible to specify a set of conditions which, when present, produce the effect *without exception.* On the other hand, an indeterministic universe would be one where sometimes events would lead up to what appeared to be an inevitable consequence, and yet something new might occur— something which could not be predicted from the past, not even by God.

How does the issue of determinism affect our belief that we are free agents? The most natural position to adopt is that a deterministic universe rules out free will. If this assumption is correct, then one is forced to choose between free will and determinism. The position known as *hard-determinism* rejects free will, whereas its opposite counterpart, *libertarianism,* asserts that determinism is false.

The hard-determinist claims that the human personality is within the normal course of nature, and so free will cannot exist. If it did exist, it would be possible for a person to choose a course of action against all the forces of heredity and training which have been building in the opposite direction. But the hard-determinist believes that every choice can be completely explained by previous causes, and so the subjective feeling of freedom to choose between alternatives is an illusion. Naturally, this affects the normal view of moral responsibility. Character—that is, habits, beliefs, values, dispositions, and capacities—is a unique product of heredity and environment. Our decisions flow from our character with the same necessity as an unfolding chemical reaction. But we are not responsible for our character, and so we cannot be held responsible for the actions produced by it.

It is very easy to confuse hard-determinism with fatalism. The central idea of fatalism is that *specific* events are unavoidable. It leads to the resignation expressed by many soldiers in the slogan "There's a bullet out there with my name on it," indicating that a specific mode of dying at a specific time and place is inevitable. Strictly speaking, however, fatalism is not a form of determinism. To say that something is inevitable is to assert that it will occur *no matter what* precedes it. No determinist can accept this. If the world is deterministic, then the future is conditioned to be what it is by the past. If conditions in the past were altered, the future would be altered also. Since human activity is part and parcel of nature, there is no reason to suppose that it cannot serve as a cause for future events. A hard-determinist, therefore, believes that human effort is not futile. But hard-determinists would also say that whether we put forth that effort or not is determined, and we are not free to control *that*.

It is not easy, however, to reject the nagging feeling of freedom that most people experience in their daily lives. Libertarianism, like hard-determinism, is based on the assumption that free will cannot exist in a deterministic universe. Because of the experienced quality of freedom, the libertarian denies that the universe is completely deterministic. William James, for example, believed that chance is an ultimate factor in nature. Most libertarians do not go so far as James for fear of denying the obvious successes of science. Rather than regarding the uniformities of nature as a series of happy coincidences, they grant that most events are under the rule of causal necessity. There is, however, a range of events where alternative possibilities are available—namely, the events of human choice. Therefore, libertarians all agree that some decisions cannot be completely explained by prior causes.

Libertarianism is a doctrine which seeks to preserve the sense of self-control which is required for moral responsibility. People do not merely passively respond to the world. The person is a well-spring of creative activity which stands over against the flow of events and controls them. Determinism, consequently, is a view that runs counter to the predominant trend of experience. William James argues that our feelings of regret do not make sense in a determined world. We regret the occurrence of things that are bad. But according to the determinist, they *must* occur. How can we regret something that must be? We might as well regret the falling of a stone when we drop it. As a result, James held that determinism leads to moral complacency, for, without regrets, we must be satisfied with the world as it is.

We seem to be on the horns of a dilemma: give up free will or give up determinism. Either alternative is intellectually discomforting. But there is a middle position. This is the theory called *soft-determinism*. Soft-determinists claim that free will and determinism are compatible. Indeed, soft-determinists believe that determinism is a necessary condition for moral responsibility. William James called this view a "quagmire of evasion."

The soft-determinist maintains that our actual moral practices cannot be squared with indeterminism, and that they make sense only if we suppose that a person's behavior is caused by certain ingredients of the personality. If someone commits a murder while under the influence of a hypnotist, for example, it is absurd to hold that person responsible. The chief cause of the action lay outside the person's character—in this case, in the character of the hypnotist. Similarly, if someone behaves irrationally because of a brain tumor, or as a result of excruciating pain, responsibility is diminished. Once again, these are causes which lie outside the wants and desires that make up the personality. The reason why we do not punish individuals under these conditions is that the punishment would not affect such behavior under similar circumstances. Punishment, like rewards, makes sense only under the assumption that *it will serve as a cause for future behavior*. Libertarianism, therefore, cannot provide an adequate account of moral responsibility because it is a theory in which decisions are not caused by the central mechanisms of the personality. If a person's decisions do not spring from the personality—if they simply "pop" into existence—then they are capricious. In such a world, the person is a victim of chance, not a free agent. Moral freedom is not freedom from all causes, but rather it is freedom from certain *kinds* of causes. When we are prevented by an external constraint from acting as we want to act, or when our actions result from causes foreign to our personality, we are not free. We are free when our actions result from the uncompelled choices of the personality.

According to soft-determinism, both libertarianism and hard-determinism are founded on a shared misconception. Both positions have correctly noted that freedom requires that more than one alternative be available to the agent. They have interpreted this to mean that a free agent must be able to act independently of prior causes. But this is an error. When we say that a person has alternatives available, we simply mean that no matter which course of action is chosen, there are no external constraints which would prevent the person from acting on that choice. A free agent could have done otherwise, in the sense that nothing stood in the way of doing otherwise, *if another choice had been made*.

What are the practical consequences of these theories? Does accepting one of them make a difference? The answer to this is an unqualified "yes." To see the practical effect of a belief in hard-determinism, read Clarence Darrow's moving defense of Leopold and Loeb, two admitted murderers. Darrow argues that the death penalty is cruel and senseless because the defendants were not responsible for what they did. Indeed, Darrow would argue that punishment of any kind is unjustified. If people are to be locked up, it is only to protect society—not because they deserve it. A libertarian, on the other hand, believes that wrong doing merits retribution. That is, punishment is justified because the agent *could have done otherwise.* Also, the libertarian position supposes that the human person cannot be fully analyzed by the methods of science, and therefore transcends the normal order of nature. Soft-determinism accepts something from both positions. It counsels mercy, because the sole function of punishment is to reform. Like Darrow, the soft-determinist cannot regard the infliction of punishment as retribution for past wrongs. Therefore, the doctrine of eternal punishment which is a feature in many religions is senseless. But like the libertarian, the soft-determinist believes that people can be held responsible for their actions under certain conditions, because holding them responsible serves as a cause for socially desired behavior.

Leopold and Loeb: The Crime of Compulsion

Clarence Darrow

In 1924, America was shocked at the brutal kidnapping and murder of four-teen-year-old Bobby Franks. The confessed killers were two brilliant students: Nathan Leopold, Jr., eighteen, and Richard Loeb, seventeen. Both came from wealthy Chicago families. Leopold was the youngest graduate of the University of Chicago and Loeb was the youngest graduate of the University of Michigan. In order to demonstrate their contempt for conventional morality, the two made a pact to commit the "perfect" crime. The state demanded the death penalty.

They were defended by Clarence Darrow (1867–1938), American's best-known criminal attorney. At this time Darrow was already famous for his many defenses of unpopular causes. He was, for example, an early supporter of organized labor when it was considered an anarchist movement. Early in his career, when he was the general counsel for the Chicago and Northwest Rail-road Company, he quit his position to defend union strikers against his former company.

Darrow believed that the case of Leopold and Loeb would allow him to present his views against capital punishment. He attempted to show that the two boys were helpless victims of heredity and environment. Killing them, he argued, would be a pointless brutality.

For over twelve hours, Darrow pleaded for mercy for the two boys. At the end of his summation, the courtroom was quiet and the judge was weeping openly. The defendants were sentenced to life in prison.

I have tried to study the lives of these two most unfortunate boys. Three months ago, if their friends and the friends of the family had been asked to pick out the most promising lads of their acquaintance, they probably would have picked these two boys. With every opportunity, with plenty of wealth, they would have said that those two would succeed.

In a day, by an act of madness, all this is destroyed, until the best they can hope for now is a life of silence and pain, continuing to the end of their years.

How did it happen?

Let us take Dickie Loeb first.

I do not claim to know how it happened; I have sought to find out. I know that something, or some combination of things, is responsible for this mad act. I know that there are no accidents in nature. I know that effect follows cause. I know that, if I were wise enough, and knew enough about this case, I could lay my finger on the cause. I will do the best I can, but it is largely speculation.

The child, of course, is born without knowledge.

Impressions are made upon its mind as it goes along. Dickie Loeb was a child of wealth and opportunity. Over and over in this court Your Honor has been asked, and other courts have been asked, to consider boys who have no chance; they have been asked to consider the poor, whose home had been the street, with no education and no opportunity in life, and they have done it, and done it rightfully.

But, Your Honor, it is just as often a great misfortune to be the child of the rich as it is to be the child of the poor. Wealth has its misfortunes. Too much, too great opportunity and advantage, given to a child has its misfortunes, and I am asking Your Honor to consider the rich as well as the poor (and nothing else). Can I find what was wrong? I think I can. Here was a boy at a tender age, placed in the hands of a governess, intellectual, vigorous, devoted, with a strong ambition for the welfare of this boy. He was pushed in his studies, as plants are forced in hothouses. He had no pleasures, such as a boy should have, except as they were gained by lying and cheating.

Now, I am not criticizing the nurse. I suggest that some day Your Honor look at her picture. It explains her fully. Forceful, brooking no interference, she loved the boy, and her ambition was that he should reach the highest perfection. No time to pause, no time to stop from one book to another, no time to have those pleasures which a boy ought to have to create a normal life. And what happened? Your Honor, what would happen? Nothing strange or unusual. This nurse was with him all the time, except when he stole out at night, from two to fourteen years of age. He, scheming and planning as healthy boys would do, to get out from under her restraint; she, putting before him the best books, which children generally do not want; and he, when she was not looking, reading detective stories, which he devoured, story after story, in his young life. Of all this there can be no question.

What is the result? Every story he read was a story of crime. We have a statute in this state, passed only last year, if I recall it, which forbids minors reading stories of crime. Why? There is only one reason. Because the legislature in its wisdom felt that it would produce criminal tendencies in the boys who read them. The legislature of this state has given its opinion, and forbidden boys to read these books. He read them day after day. He never stopped. While he was passing through college at Ann Arbor he was still reading them. When he was a senior he read them, and almost nothing else.

Now, these facts are beyond dispute. He early developed the tendency to mix with crime, to be a detective; as a little boy shadowing people on the street; as a little child going out with his fantasy of being the head of a band of criminals and directing them on the street. How did this grow and develop in him? Let us see. It seems to be as natural as the day following the night. Every detective story is a story of a sleuth getting the best of it: trailing some unfortunate individual through devious ways until his victim is finally landed in jail or stands on the gallows. They all show how smart the detective is, and where the criminal himself falls down.

This boy early in his life conceived the idea that there could be a perfect crime, one that nobody could ever detect; that there could be one where the detective did not land his game—a perfect crime. He had been interested in the story of Charley Ross, who was kidnaped. He was interested in these things all his life. He believed in his childish way that a crime could be so carefully planned that there would be no detection, and his idea was to plan and accomplish a perfect crime. It would involve kidnaping and involve murder.

There had been growing in Dickie's brain, dwarfed and twisted—as every act in this case shows it to have been dwarfed and twisted—there had been growing this scheme, not due to any wickedness of Dickie Loeb, for he is a child. It grew as he grew; it grew from those around him; it grew from the lack of the proper training until it possessed him. He believed he could beat the police. He believed he could plan the perfect crime. He had thought of it and talked of it for years—had talked of it as a child, had worked at it as a child—this sorry act of his, utterly irrational and motiveless, a plan to commit a perfect crime which must contain kidnaping, and there must be ransom, or else it could not be perfect, and they must get the money. . . .

The law knows and has recognized childhood for many and many a long year. What do we know about childhood? The brain of the child is the home of dreams, of castles, of visions, of illusions and of delusions. In fact, there could be no childhood without delusions, for delusions are always more alluring than facts. Delusions, dreams and hallucinations are a part of the warp and woof of childhood. You know it and I know it. I remember, when I was a child, the men seemed as tall as the trees, the trees as tall as the mountains. I can remember very well when, as a little boy, I swam the deepest spot in the river for the first time. I swam breathlessly and landed with as much sense of glory and triumph as Julius Caesar felt when he led his army across the Rubicon. I have been back since, and I can almost step across the same place, but it seemed an ocean then. And those men whom I thought so wonderful were dead and left nothing behind. I had lived in a dream. I had never known the real world which I met, to my discomfort and despair, and that dispelled the illusions of my youth.

The whole life of childhood is a dream and an illusion, and whether they take one shape or another shape depends not upon the dreamy boy but on what surrounds him. As well might I have dreamed of burglars and wished to be one as to dream of policemen and wished to be one. Perhaps I was lucky, too, that I had no money. We have grown to think that the misfortune is in not having it. The great misfortune in this terrible case is the money. That has destroyed their lives. That has fostered these illusions. That has promoted this mad act. And, if Your Honor shall doom them to die, it will be because they are the sons of the rich. . . .

I know where my life has been molded by books, amongst other things. We all know where our lives have been influenced by books. The nurse, strict and jealous and watchful, gave him one kind of book; by night he would steal off and read the other.

Which, think you, shaped the life of Dickie Loeb? Is there any kind of question about it? A child. Was it pure maliciousness? Was a boy of five or six or seven to blame for it? Where did he get it? He got it where we all get our ideas, and these books became a part of his dreams and a part of his life, and as he grew up his visions grew to hallucinations.

He went out on the street and fantastically directed his companions, who were not there, in their various moves to complete the perfect crime. Can there be any sort of question about it?

Suppose, Your Honor, that instead of this boy being here in this court, under the plea of the State that Your Honor shall pronounce a sentence to hang him by the neck until dead, he had been taken to a pathological hospital to be analyzed, and the physicians had inquired into his case. What would they have said? There is only one thing that they could possibly have said. They would have traced everything back to the gradual growth of the child.

That is not all there is about it. Youth is hard enough. The only good thing about youth is that it has no thought and no care; and how blindly we can do things when we are young!

Where is the man who has not been guilty of delinquencies in youth? Let us be honest with ourselves. Let us look into our own hearts. How many men are there today—lawyers and congressmen and judges, and even state's attorneys— who have not been guilty of some mad act in youth? And if they did not get caught, or the consequences were trivial, it was their good fortune.

We might as well be honest with ourselves, Your Honor. Before I would tie a noose around the neck of a boy I would try to call back into my mind the emotions of youth. I would try to remember what the world looked like to me when I was a child. I would try to remember how strong were these instinctive, persistent emotions that moved my life. I would try to remember how weak and inefficient was youth in the presence of the surging, controlling feelings of the child. One that honestly remembers and asks himself the question and tries to unlock the door that he thinks is closed, and calls back the boy, can understand the boy.

But, Your Honor, that is not all there is to boyhood. Nature is strong and she is pitiless. She works in her own mysterious way, and we are her victims. We have not much to do with it ourselves. Nature takes this job in hand, and we play our parts. In the words of old Omar Khayyam, we are only:

> *But helpless pieces in the game He plays*
> *Upon this checkerboard of nights and days;*
> *Hither and thither moves, and checks, and slays,*
> *And one by one back in the closet lays.*

What had this boy to do with it? He was not his own father; he was not his own mother; he was not his own grandparents. All of this was handed to him. He did not surround himself with governesses and wealth. He did not make himself. And yet he is to be compelled to pay.

There was a time in England, running down as late as the beginning of the last century, when judges used to convene court and call juries to try a horse, a dog, a pig, for crime. I have in my library a story of a judge and jury and lawyers trying and convicting an old sow for lying down on her ten pigs and killing them.

What does it mean? Animals were tried. Do you mean to tell me that Dickie Loeb had any more to do with his making than any other product of heredity that is born upon the earth? . . .

For God's sake, are we crazy? In the face of history, of every line of philosophy, against the teaching of every religionist and seer and prophet the world has ever given us, we are still doing what our barbaric ancestors did when they came out of the caves and the woods.

From the age of fifteen to the age of twenty or twenty-one, the child has the burden of adolescence, of puberty and sex thrust upon him. Girls are kept at home and carefully watched. Boys without instruction are left to work the period out for themselves. It may lead to excess. It may lead to disgrace. It may lead to perversion. Who is to blame? Who did it? Did Dickie Loeb do it?

Your Honor, I am almost ashamed to talk about it. I can hardly imagine that we are in the twentieth century. And yet there are men who seriously say that for what nature has done, for what life has done, for what training has done, you should hang these boys.

Now, there is no mystery about this case, Your Honor. I seem to be criticizing their parents. They had parents who were kind and good and wise in their way. But I say to you seriously that the parents are more responsible than these boys. And yet few boys had better parents.

Your Honor, it is the easiest thing in the world to be a parent. We talk of motherhood, and yet every woman can be a mother. We talk of fatherhood, and yet every man can be a father. Nature takes care of that. It is easy to be a parent. But to be wise and farseeing enough to understand the boy is another thing; only a very few are so wise and so farseeing as that. When I think of the light way nature has of picking our parents and populating the earth, having them born and die, I cannot hold human beings to the same degree of responsibility that young lawyers hold them when they are enthusiastic in a prosecution. I know what it means.

I know there are no better citizens in Chicago than the fathers of these poor boys. I know there were no better women than their mothers. But I am going to be honest with this court, if it is at the expense of both. I know that one of two things happened to Richard Loeb: that this terrible crime was inherent in his organism, and came from some ancestor; or that it came through his education and his training after he was born. Do I need to prove it? Judge Crowe said at one point in this case, when some witness spoke about their wealth, that "probably that was responsible."

To believe that any boy is responsible for himself or his early training is an absurdity that no lawyer or judge should be guilty of today. Somewhere this came to the boy. If his failing came from his heredity, I do not know where or how. None of us are bred perfect and pure; and the color of our hair, the color of our eyes, our stature, the weight and fineness of our brain, and everything about us could, with full knowledge, be traced with absolute certainty to somewhere. If we had the pedigree it could be traced just the same in a boy as it could in a dog, a horse or a cow.

I do not know what remote ancestors may have sent down the seed that corrupted him, and I do not know through how many ancestors it may have passed until it reached Dickie Loeb.

All I know is that it is true, and there is not a biologist in the world who will not say that I am right.

If it did not come that way, then I know that if he was normal, if he had been understood, if he had been trained as he should have been it would not have happened. Not that anybody may not slip, but I know it and Your Honor knows it, and every schoolhouse and every church in the land is an evidence of it. Else why build them?

Every effort to protect society is an effort toward training the youth to keep the path. Every bit of training in the world proves it, and it likewise proves that it sometimes fails. I know that if this boy had been understood and properly trained—properly for him—and the training that he got might have been the very best for someone; but if it had been the proper training for him he would not be in this courtroom today with the noose above his head. If there is responsibility anywhere, it is back of him; somewhere in the infinite number of his ancestors, or in his surroundings, or in both. And I submit, Your Honor, that under every principle of natural justice, under every principle of conscience, of right, and of law, he should not be made responsible for the acts of someone else. . . .

It is when these dreams of boyhood, these fantasies of youth still linger, and the growing boy is still a child—a child in emotion, a child in feeling, a child in hallucinations—that you can say that it is the dreams and the hallucinations of childhood that are responsible for his conduct. There is not an act in all this horrible tragedy that was not the act of a child, the act of a child wandering around in the morning of life, moved by the new feelings of a boy, moved by the uncontrolled impulses which his teaching was not strong enough to take care of, moved by the dreams and the hallucinations which haunt the brain of a child. I say, Your Honor, that it would be the height of cruelty, of injustice, of wrong and barbarism to visit the penalty upon this poor boy.

STUDY QUESTIONS

1   Darrow begins by tracing the causes of Loeb's mental framework. Why does he do this? Is there anything special about Loeb's background which exempts him from responsibility?

2   At one point Darrow quotes Omar Khayyam, and says that nature is pitiless. Why is nature pitiless? Do you agree?

3   Where does Darrow wish to place the responsibility for the crime? Can he consistently place responsibility anywhere?

4   What do you think it means to say that people are responsible for what they do? Is it possible to be responsible and to have causes for what we choose?

5   "What's it to me that nobody's guilty and I know it—I need revenge or I'd kill myself. And revenge not in some far off eternity, somewhere, sometime, but here and now, on earth, so that I can see it" (Dostoyevsky, *The Brothers Karamozov*). What would Darrow say about the sentiment expressed in this quote? What do you say? Do you think that the desire for revenge is rational?

6   "In conformity, therefore, to the clear doctrine of Scripture we assert, that by an eternal and immutable counsel, God has once for all determined, both whom he

would admit to salvation, and whom he would condemn to destruction" (John Calvin, *The Institutes of the Christian Religion*). If Calvin's God were sitting on the jury, how would He vote?

The Dilemma of Determinism

William James

William James (1842–1910) was one of the boldest thinkers America has produced. His early aspirations were to become an artist, but he subsequently moved into medicine. He obtained his M.D. degree from Harvard in 1869. Branching out from medicine, he turned first to physiology and then to psychology. His book *The Principles of Psychology* was published in 1869, and for decades was the definitive text. This triumph complete, James expanded into the study of religious experience and philosophy. This period produced such masterpieces as *The Varieties of Religious Experience* (1902) and *Pragmatism* (1907). In every major period of his life, his work is characterized by a vitality and intensity which brings theory into close connection with life. His writing on free will is no exception.

James called himself a "possibility man." This means that he regarded the universe as an unfolding system which cannot be completely predicted from past events. When we think of the future, we can imagine many different possibilities, and none of them is logically inconsistent with what went before. Therefore, he says, possibility or chance is a real factor in things. This must be so, James believes, to make sense of our moral experience.

James's critics have claimed that if human choice involves "chance," then anything should be possible—at any time; saints may suddenly "choose" to become fiends, or as you read this, you may "choose" to start eating the carpet, a most undesirable trait in the universe. Keep this in mind as you read one of the most provocative essays ever written on the nature of freedom.

A common opinion prevails that the juice has ages ago been pressed out of the free-will controversy, and that no new champion can do more than warm up stale arguments which every one has heard. This is a radical mistake. I know of no subject less worn out, or in which inventive genius has a better chance of breaking open new ground—not, perhaps, of forcing a conclusion or of coercing assent, but of deepening our sense of what the issue between the two parties really is, of what the ideas of fate and of free-will imply. . . . The arguments I am about to urge all proceed on two suppositions: first, when we make theories about the world and discuss them with one another, we do so in order to attain a conception of things which shall give us subjective satisfaction; and, second, if there be two conceptions, and the one seems to us, on the whole, more rational than the other, we are entitled to suppose that the more rational one is the truer of the two. I hope that you are all willing to make these suppositions with me; for I am afraid that if there be any of you here who are not, they will find little

An Address to the Harvard Divinity Students, published in the *Unitarian Review*, September 1884.

edification in the rest of what I have to say. I cannot stop to argue the point; but I myself believe that all the magnificent achievements of mathematical and physical science—our doctrines of evolution, of uniformity of law, and the rest— proceed from our indomitable desire to cast the world into a more rational shape in our minds than the shape into which it is thrown there by the crude order of our experience. The world has shown itself, to a great extent, plastic to this demand of ours for rationality. How much farther it will show itself plastic no one can say. Our only means of finding out is to try; and, I, for one, feel as free to try conceptions of moral as of mechanical or of logical rationality. If a certain formula for expressing the nature of the world violates my moral demand, I shall feel as free to throw it overboard, or at least to doubt it, as if it disappointed my demand for uniformity of sequence, for example; the one demand being, so far as I can see, quite as subjective and emotional as the other is. The principle of causality, for example,—what is it but a postulate, an empty name covering simply a demand that the sequence of events shall some day manifest a deeper kind of belonging of one thing with another than the mere arbitrary juxtaposition which now phenomenally appears? It is as much an altar to an unknown god as the one that Saint Paul found at Athens. All our scientific and philosophic ideals are altars to unknown gods. Uniformity is as much so as is free-will. If this be admitted, we can debate on even terms. But if any one pretends that while freedom and variety are, in the first instance, subjective demands, necessity and uniformity are something altogether different, I do not see how we can debate at all.

To begin, then, I must suppose you acquainted with all the usual arguments on the subject. I cannot stop to take up the old proofs from causation, from statistics, from the certainty with which we can foretell one another's conduct, from the fixity of character, and all the rest. But there are two *words* which usually encumber these classical arguments, and which we must immediately dispose of if we are to make any progress. One is the eulogistic word *freedom,* and the other is the opprobrious word *chance.* The word "chance" I wish to keep, but I wish to get rid of the word "freedom." Its eulogistic associations have so far overshadowed all the rest of its meaning that both parties claim the sole right to use it, and determinists to-day insist that they alone are freedom's champions. Old-fashioned determinism was what we may call *hard* determinism. It did not shrink from such words as fatality, bondage of the will, necessitation, and the like. Nowadays, we have a *soft* determinism which abhors harsh words, and, repudiating fatality, necessity, and even predetermination, says that its real name is freedom; for freedom is only necessity understood, and bondage to the highest is identical with true freedom.

Now, all this is a quagmire of evasion under which the real issue of fact has been entirely smothered. . . . But there *is* a problem, an issue of fact and not of words, an issue of the most momentous importance, which is often decided without discussion in one sentence,—nay, in one clause of a sentence,—by those very writers who spin out whole chapters in their efforts to show what "true" freedom is; and that is the question of determinism, about which we are to talk to-night.

Fortunately, no ambiguities hang about this word or about its opposite, indeterminism. Both designate an outward way in which things may happen, and their cold and mathematical sound has no sentimental associations that can bribe our partiality either way in advance. Now, evidence of an external kind to decide between determinism and indeterminism is, as I intimated a while back, strictly impossible to find. Let us look at the difference between them and see for ourselves. What does determinism profess?

It professes that those parts of the universe already laid down absolutely appoint and decree what the other parts shall be. The future has no ambiguous possibilities hidden in its womb: the part we call the present is compatible with only one totality. Any other future complement than the one fixed from eternity is impossible. The whole is in each and every part, and welds it with the rest into an absolute unity, an iron block, in which there can be no equivocation or shadow of turning.

> With earth's first clay they did the last man knead,
> And there of the last harvest sowed the seed.
> And the first morning of creation wrote
> What the last dawn of reckoning shall read.

Indeterminism, on the contrary, says that the parts have a certain amount of loose play on one another, so that the laying down of one of them does not necessarily determine what the others shall be. It admits that possibilities may be in excess of actualities, and that things not yet revealed to our knowledge may really in themselves be ambiguous. Of two alternative futures which we conceive, both may now be really possible; and the one become impossible only at the very moment when the other excludes it by becoming real itself. Indeterminism thus denies the world to be one unbending unit of fact. It says there is a certain ultimate pluralism in it; and, so saying, it corroborates our ordinary unsophisticated view of things. To that view, actualities seem to float in a wider sea of possibilities from out of which they are chosen; and, *somewhere,* indeterminism says, such possibilities exist, and form a path of truth.

Determinism, on the contrary, says they exist *nowhere,* and that necessity on the one hand and impossibility on the other are the sole categories of the real. Possibilities that fail to get realized are, for determinism, pure illusions: they never were possibilities at all. There is nothing inchoate, it says, about this universe of ours, all that was or is or shall be actual in it having been from eternity virtually there. The cloud of alternatives our minds escort this mass of actuality withal is a cloud of sheer deceptions, to which "impossibilities" is the only name that rightfully belongs.

The issue, it will be seen, is a perfectly sharp one, which no eulogistic terminology can smear over or wipe out. The truth *must* lie with one side or the other, and its lying with one side makes the other false.

The question relates solely to the existence of possibilities, in the strict sense of the term, as things that may, but need not, be. Both sides admit that a volition, for instance, has occurred. The indeterminists say another volition might have occurred in its place: the determinists swear that nothing could possibly have occurred in its place. Now, can science be called in to tell us which of these two point-blank contradicters of each other is right? Science professes to draw no conclusions but such as are based on matters of fact, things that have actually happened; but how can any amount of assurance that something actually happened give us the least grain of information as to whether another thing might or might not have happened in its place? Only facts can be proved by other facts. With things that are possibilities and not facts, facts have no concern. If we have no other evidence than the evidence of existing facts, the possibility-question must remain a mystery never to be cleared up. . . .

The sting of the word "chance" seems to lie in the assumption that it means something positive, and that if anything happens by chance, it must needs be something of an intrinsically irrational and preposterous sort. Now, chance means nothing of the kind. It is a purely negative and relative term, giving us no information about that of which it is predicated, except that it happens to be disconnected with something else,—not controlled, secured, or necessitated by other things in advance of its own actual presence. As this point is the most subtle one of the whole lecture, and at the same time the point on which all the rest hinges, I beg you to pay particular attention to it. What I say is that it tells us nothing about what a thing may be in itself to call it "chance." It may be a bad thing, it may be a good thing. It may be lucidity, transparency, fitness incarnate, matching the whole system of other things, when it has once befallen, in an unimaginably perfect way. All you mean by calling it "chance" is that this is not guaranteed, that it may also fall out otherwise.

Nevertheless, many persons talk as if the minutest dose of disconnectedness of one part with another, the smallest modicum of independence, the faintest tremor of ambiguity about the future, for example, would ruin everything, and turn this goodly universe into a sort of insane sand-heap or nulliverse, no universe at all. Since future human volitions are as a matter of fact the only ambiguous things we are tempted to believe in, let us stop for a moment to make ourselves sure whether their independent and accidental character need be fraught with such direful consequences to the universe as these.

What is meant by saying that my choice of which way to walk home after the lecture is ambiguous and matter of chance as far as the present moment is concerned? It means that both Divinity Avenue and Oxford Street are called; but that only one, and that one *either* one, shall be chosen. Now, I ask you seriously to suppose that this ambiguity of my choice is real; and then to make the impossible hypothesis that the choice is made twice over, and each time falls on a different street. In other words, imagine that I first walk through Divinity Avenue, and then imagine that the powers governing the universe annihilate ten minutes of time with all that it contained, and set me back at the door of this hall just as I was before the choice was made. Imagine then that, everything else being the same, I now make a different choice and traverse Oxford Street. You, as passive spectators, look on and see the two alternative universes,—one of them with me walking through Divinity Avenue in it, the other with the same me walking through Oxford Street. Now, if you are determinists you believe one of these universes to have been from eternity impossible: you believe it to have been impossible because of the intrinsic irrationality or accidentality somewhere involved in it. But looking outwardly at these universes, can you say which is the impossible and accidental one, and which the rational and necessary one? I doubt if the most ironclad determinist among you could have the slightest glimmer of light on this point. In other words, either universe *after the fact* and once there would, to our means of observation and understanding, appear just as rational as the other. There would be absolutely no criterion by which we might judge one necessary and the other matter of chance. Suppose now we relieve the gods of their hypothetical task and assume my choice, once made, to be made forever. I go through Divinity Avenue for good and all. If, as good determinists, you now begin to affirm, what all good determinists punctually do affirm, that in the nature of things I *couldn't* have gone through Oxford Street,—had I done so it would have been chance, irrationality, insanity, a horrid gap in nature,—I simply call your attention to this, that your affirmation is what the Germans call a *Machtspruch,* a mere conception fulminated as a dogma and based on no insight into details. Before my choice, either street seemed as natural to you as to me. Had I happened to take Oxford Street, Divinity Avenue would have figured in your philosophy as the gap in nature; and you would have so proclaimed it with the best deterministic conscience in the world. . . .

And this at last brings us within sight of our subject. We have seen what determinism means: we have seen that indeterminism is rightly described as meaning chance; and we have seen that chance, the very name of which we are urged to shrink from as from a metaphysical pestilence, means only negative fact that no part of the world, however big, can claim to control absolutely the destinies of the whole. But although, in discussing the word "chance," I may at moments have seemed to be arguing for its real existence, I have not meant to do so yet. We have not yet ascertained whether this be a world of chance or no; at most, we have agreed that it seems so. And I now repeat what I said at the outset, that, from any strict theoretical point of view, the question is insoluble. To deepen our theoretic sense of the *difference* between a world with chances in it and a deterministic world is the most I can hope to do; and this I may now at last begin upon, after all our tedious clearing of the way.

I wish first of all to show you just what the notion that this is a deterministic world implies. The implications I call your attention to are all bound up with the fact that it is a world in which we constantly have to make what I shall, with your permission, call judgments of regret. Hardly an hour passes in which we do not wish that something might be otherwise; and happy indeed are those of us whose hearts have never echoed the wish of Omar Khayam—

> That we might clasp, ere closed, the book of fate,
> And make the writer on a fairer leaf
> Inscribe our names, or quite obliterate.

> Ah! Love, could you and I with fate conspire
> To mend this sorry scheme of things entire,
> Would we not shatter it to bits, and then
> Remould it nearer to the heart's desire?

Now, it is undeniable that most of these regrets are foolish, and quite on a par in point of philosophic value with the criticisms on the universe of that friend of our infancy, the hero of the fable The Atheist and the Acorn,—

Fool! had that bough a pumpkin bore,
Thy whimsies would have worked no more, etc.

Even from the point of view of our own ends, we should probably make a botch of remodelling the universe. How much more then from the point of view of ends we cannot see! Wise men therefore regret as little as they can. But still some regrets are pretty obstinate and hard to stifle,—regrets for acts of wanton cruelty or treachery, for example, whether performed by others or by ourselves. Hardly any one can remain *entirely* optimistic after reading the confession of the murderer at Brockton the other day: how, to get rid of the wife whose continued existence bored him, he inveigled her into a desert spot, shot her four times, and then, as she lay on the ground and said to him, "You didn't do it on purpose, did you dear?" replied, "No, I didn't do it on purpose," as he raised a rock and smashed her skull. Such an occurrence, with the mild sentence and self-satisfaction of the prisoner, is a field for a crop of regrets, which one need not take up in detail. We feel that, although a perfect mechanical fit to the rest of the universe, it is a bad moral fit, and that something else would really have been better in its place.

But for the deterministic philosophy the murder, the sentence, and the prisoner's optimism were all necessary from eternity; and nothing else for a moment had a ghost of a chance of being put into their place. To admit such a chance, the determinists tell us, would be to make a suicide of reason; so we must steel our hearts against the thought. And here our plot thickens, for we see the first of those difficult implications of determinism and monism which it is my purpose to make you feel. If this Brockton murder was called for by the rest of the universe, if it had to come at its preappointed hour, and if nothing else would have been consistent with the sense of the whole, what are we to think of the universe? Are we stubbornly to stick to our judgment of regret, and say, though it *couldn't* be, yet, it *would* have been a better universe with something different from this Brockton murder in it? That, of course, seems the natural and spontaneous thing for us to do; and yet it is nothing short of deliberately espousing a kind of pessimism. The judgment of regret calls the murder bad. Calling a thing bad means, if it mean anything at all, that the thing ought not to be, that something else ought to be in its stead. Determinism, in denying that anything else can be in its stead, virtually defines the universe as a place in which what ought to be is impossible,—in other words, as an organism whose constitution is afflicted with an incurable taint, an irremediable flaw. The pessimism of a Schopenhauer says no more than this,—that the murder is a symptom; and that it is a vicious symptom because it belongs to a vicious whole, which can express its nature no otherwise than by bringing forth just such a symptom as that at this particular spot. Regret for the murder must transform itself, if we are determinists and wise, into a larger regret. It is absurd to regret the murder alone. Other things being what they are, *it* could not be different. What we should regret is that whole frame of things of which the murder is one member. I see no escape whatever from this pessimistic conclusion, if, being determinists, our judgment of regret is to be allowed to stand at all.

The only deterministic escape from pessimism is everywhere to abandon the judgment of regret. That this can be done, history shows to be not impossible. The devil, *quoad existentiam,* may be good. That is, although he be a *principle* of evil, yet the universe, with such a principle in it, may practically be a better universe than it could have been without. On every hand, in a small way, we find that a certain amount of evil is a condition by which a higher form of good is bought. There is nothing to prevent anybody from generalizing this view, and trusting that if we could but see things in the largest of all ways, even such matters as this Brockton murder would appear to be paid for by the uses that follow in their train. An optimism *quand même,* a systematic and infatuated optimism like that ridiculed by Voltaire in his Candide, is one of the possible ideal ways in which a man may train himself to look on life. Bereft of dogmatic hardness and lit up with the expression of a tender and pathetic hope, such an optimism has been the grace of some of the most religious characters that ever lived.

> Throb thine with Nature's throbbing breast,
> And all is clear from east to west.

Even cruelty and treachery may be among the absolutely blessed fruits of time, and to quarrel with any of their details may be blasphemy. The only real blasphemy, in short, may be that pessimistic temper of the soul which lets it give way to such things as regrets, remorse, and grief.

Thus, our deterministic pessimism may become a deterministic optimism at the price of extinguishing our judgments of regret.

But does not this immediately bring us into a curious logical predicament? Our determinism leads us to call our judgments of regret wrong, because they are pessimistic in implying that what is impossible yet ought to be. But how then about the judgments of regret themselves? If they are wrong, other judgments, judgments of approval presumably, ought to be in their place. But as they are necessitated, nothing else *can* be in their place; and the universe is just what it was before,—namely, a place in which what ought to be appears impossible. We have got one foot out of the pessimistic bog, but the other one sinks all the deeper. We have rescued our actions from the bonds of evil, but our judgments are now held fast. When murders and treacheries cease to be sins, regrets are theoretic absurdities and errors. The theoretic and the active life thus play a kind of seesaw with each other on the ground of evil. The rise of either sends the other down. Murder and treachery cannot be good without regret being bad: regret cannot be good without treachery and murder being bad. Both, however, are supposed to have been foredoomed; so something must be fatally unreasonable, absurd, and wrong in the world. It must be a place of which either sin or error forms a necessary part. From this dilemma there seems at first sight no escape. Are we then so soon to fall back into the pessimism from which we thought we had emerged? . . .

Let me, then, without circumlocution say just this. The world is enigmatical enough in all conscience, whatever theory we may take up toward it. The indeterminism I defend, the free-will theory of popular sense based on the judgment of regret, represents that world as vulnerable, and liable to be injured by certain of its parts if they act wrong. And it represents their acting wrong as a matter of possibility or accident, neither inevitable nor yet to be infallibly warded off. In all this, it is a theory devoid either of transparency or of stability. It gives us a pluralistic, restless universe, in which no single point of view can ever take in the whole scene; and to a mind possessed of the love of unity at any cost, it will, no doubt, remain forever inacceptable. A friend with such a mind once told me that the thought of my universe made him sick, like the sight of the horrible motion of a mass of maggots in their carrion bed.

But while I freely admit that the pluralism and the restlessness are repugnant and irrational in a certain way, I find that every alternative to them is irrational in a deeper way. The indeterminism with its maggots, if you please to speak so about it, offends only the native absolutism of my intellect,—an absolutism which, after all, perhaps, deserves to be snubbed and kept in check. But the determinism with its necessary carrion, to continue the figure of speech, and with no possible maggots to eat the latter up, violates my sense of moral reality through and through. When, for example, I imagine such carrion as the Brockton murder, I cannot conceive it as an act by which the universe, as a whole, logically and necessarily expresses its nature without shrinking from complicity with such a whole. And I deliberately refuse to keep on terms of loyalty with the universe by saying blankly that the murder, since it does flow from the nature of the whole, is not carrion. There are *some* instinctive reactions which I, for one, will not tamper with. The only remaining alternative, the attitude of gnostical romanticism, wrenches my personal instincts in quite as violent a way. It falsifies the simple objectivity of their deliverance. It makes the goose-flesh the murder excites in me a sufficient reason for the perpetration of the crime.

No! better a thousand times, than such systematic corruption of our moral sanity, the plainest pessimism, so that it be straightforward; but better far than that the world of chance. Make as great an uproar about chance as you please, I know that chance means pluralism and nothing more. If some of the members of the pluralism are bad, the philosophy of pluralism, whatever broad views it may deny me, permits me, at least, to turn to the other members with a clean breast of affection and an unsophisticated moral sense. And if I still wish to think of the world as a totality, it lets me feel that a world with a *chance* in it of being altogether good, even if the chance never come to pass, is better than a world with no such chance at all. That "chance" whose very notion I am exhorted and conjured to banish from my view of the future as the suicide of reason concerning it, that "chance" is—what? Just this,—the chance that in moral respects the future may be other and better than the past has been. This is the only chance we have any motive for supposing to exist. Shame, rather, on its repudiation and its denial! For its presence is the vital air which lets the world live, the salt which keeps it sweet.

STUDY QUESTIONS

1   What is the difference between determinism and indeterminism? How would a deterministic world affect our choices?

2   What does James mean by "chance"? Can you think of other meanings? Do you think that James would regard the throw of dice as a matter of chance?

3   The example about Oxford Street and Divinity Avenue is supposed to show that choice is "ambiguous." What does this mean? Does the example show this, do you think?

4   James argues that in a deterministic universe the feeling of regret makes no sense. Why is this? Why does determinism lead to pessimism?

5   James suggests that the determinist gets into a logical predicament. What is this predicament?

6   "There are some instinctive reactions which I, for one, will not tamper with." What reactions does James have in mind here? Do you think he is irrational on this issue?

7   "If some great power would agree to always make me think what is true and do what is right, on condition of being turned into a sort of clock and wound up every morning before I got out of bed, I should instantly close with the offer" (T. H. Huxley). Do you agree with Huxley? Which universe do you think would be best—Huxley's or James's?

Free Will and Self-creation

Peter Bertocci

Peter Anthony Bertocci (1910–   ) is professor of philosophy at Boston University. He is well known for his defense of the teleological argument in proving the existence of God. In this selection he considers a familiar slogan which determinists often use to excuse someone from responsibility: "We don't create ourselves." Bertocci, on the contrary, believes that to some extent we can create our own character.

Bertocci's argument softens James's position somewhat. Possibility is still a real element in the universe, but, as far as the personality is concerned, there are restrictions. We must distinguish between "will-agency" and "will-power." We may will to do something but be unable to carry it out—this is a failure of will-power. The ability to carry out choices depends upon many factors, including heredity and environment. However, these restrictions on will-power do not effect the reality of will-agency, which is an innate ability to consider alternatives and to try to make one of two possibilities into a reality. The final behavior of the person is the result of will-agency working within a restricted framework of will-power. Our habits, developed traits, learned capacities, are tools with which we confront our own natures as well as the world. We cannot do more than our tools allow. Therefore, much of our behavior may be predictable because these ingredients of our will-power and their limitations are known. Within these limitations, however, we are free to build our own characters.

A human being's *personality,* we may say, *is his unique and dynamic mode of adjustment to his own nature and the world.* In the process of living, a person's nature is affected by the influences coming to bear upon him; the home, school, playground, church, social organizations, work-environment challenge his capacities and leave their marks on his particular structure. However, he is far from neutral to these influences. He is more responsive and plastic in some ways than others, and he ploughs the course his own basic developing nature makes possible.

Thus, children brought up in the same home and community develop different personalities because their natures differ in responsiveness to their world as they each seek an adequate *modus vivendi.* As they grow older they find themselves having to deal not only with other persons and the world but also with the habits and dispositions which make up their own developing personalities. Once certain habits and attitudes are formed, they stand as obstacles to new adjustments the children should make; the personality pattern, itself a product of learning, is beginning to restrict ease of choice and further development. This is a very interesting and important fact. Even language habits illustrate it. Do we not learn to express our thoughts through a specific language and then find that it becomes almost impossible for us to think except in terms of that language? Similarly, we find that the personalities we develop restrict the channels for the expression of native wants and abilities.

Other persons see us in our personalities. However, although what other people think of us may be important, our personality is our own more or less unified pattern of adjustment, much of which is hidden from observers, and some of which we ourselves are not aware of. The patterning of our responses is more intricate than we understand, but we cannot deny the fact that as our personality-formation "sets," our adaptability is reduced. How difficult it is for us now to act like persons who worked out their life-adjustment in China! Yet had we been born in other homes, we could (with the same innate constitutions) have developed different emphases in our personalities.

It should now be clear that we as *persons* (as unified activities of wanting, knowing, feeling, willing, and oughting) are not coextensive with our *personalities.* If these unified activities (*persons*) had been brought up in China, they would have developed different modes of adjustment (*personalities*). These same wants and abilities might have found different expressions—other personalities could have been built from the same raw materials, as it were.

Now let us assume that a given person comes to the point where he does not approve his personality (or parts of it). Can he change it? Indeed, given the inheritance he had and the environmental forces which surrounded him from the moment of conception, could he really have developed any other personality than the one he has? This brings us face to face with the problem of free will. Is it true that a person's personality is *wholly* the product of the forces, hereditary and environmental, which meet in him?

From Peter Anthony Bertocci, *Introduction to the Philosophy of Religion,* Chapter IX, Prentice-Hall, Inc., 1951. Reprinted by permission of the publisher and the author.

We are here confronting one of the most important problems of philosophy and life. . . . So many other issues come to lodge at the entrance and at the exits of this problem that one hardly knows where to begin, especially if the discussion must be brief. It seems best here to define what we find in our conscious experience before moving to other considerations. It may help if the description is expressed in personal terms so that the reader may check the account by his own introspection.

From the time that I began to be conscious of myself as an active agent, I have had many experiences of confronting at least two alternative courses of action and then of *choosing to enact one.* A book falls. I consider: Shall I pick it up now or not? At the moment I have no doubt that I can, if I decide to, but I actually decide not to pick it up now. Again: the telephone rings. Shall I start at once to answer it, or shall I let it ring while I finish a sentence? I can go immediately, I feel, but I decide to finish the sentence. There are many examples of such simple choices. And they are not to be confused with those run-of-the-mill routine actions in which the strongest impulse is obeyed before any question comes up.

In most instances where alternatives come before my thought *as* problems of choice, I find myself leaning toward or wanting one alternative more than the other; to stay in bed rather than shiver temporarily in the cold, and to work in the garden rather than study, for example. If I did not stop to think about the situation, the ensuing action would surely be the one toward which I had the stronger leaning, and too often, even though I do stop to think about it, the wanted action still ensues!

Two things are clear so far. When I am conscious of alternatives, I am free at least to think about them. Since I do not have to go on thinking about them, and since I frequently do not want to continue thinking about them, the first act of will is the *willing to think or not to think* about any alternatives.

I use the word *will* to designate not the fact that I want to think but that I shall try to think even though it would be easier not to think. My *will* seems to be an activity of my person and an activity whereby I concentrate on an alternative which would have died had I not exerted effort on its behalf and withheld consent from the other wanted activity. My self (person) is a complex activity-unit whose life *in the main* consists of moving along in the wake of the dominant concourse of feeling, wanting, and thinking. But as conflicting courses present themselves in it, I must try (or try not) to "make up my mind" as to which course I, as a whole, *will* pursue.

In the last chapter we emphasized the importance of considering personal activities as different modes of one complex unity. It is equally important for us to remember that fact here. For the *will* must not be thought of as some separate faculty of the self, engaged in a struggle with other faculties or "components" of the self. It refers to that one of my self-activities in which I hold possible courses of action before myself, and, at least, think about them before I allow any one simply to dominate the path of action. While we shall, for brevity, go on speaking about the will as if it were one of the players on the team composing the person, it is untrue to fact to consider it in this way. A person is nothing apart from his varied distinguishable activities.

The next point to note is that I may not only will to think and, to that extent, delay the course of possible action, but having thought that one alternative is the better one for me to pursue, I may then *will* that one. William James properly, I think, called this effortful act, *fiat*.[1] Since I cannot define it further, I can only appeal to my reader to identify in his own experience the state of consciousness in which one throws the total energy at his disposal on the side of one of his alternatives and "pushes" that.

This *fiat*—this setting oneself in support of one course of action in opposition to another—is the most vivid and the clearest expression of the will. The self may not succeed in the course it thus sets itself to realize, but that it can think about the alternative and that it can assign itself to the task of supporting the approved goal seems clear. So far as I know, nothing can keep me from exerting whatever energy I have toward the realization of an approved objective.

But note: I have not asserted that I know or can guarantee the amount of control I have. Furthermore, I do know there are some things I cannot do. Free will does not mean that I can add an inch to the stature of any given endowment beyond the limits set by nature. Free will does not mean that I can create some new ability. I can operate only within the limits and possibilities of my given wants and abilities *and* of my environment. All free will, then, is freedom within limits of a person's inborn capabilities and of the world in which he lives.

However, whereas I cannot add to the ultimate potentialities of my wants and abilities—to my I.Q., for example—is it, then, the environment which comes in to determine what form my adjustment, given my capacities, will take? Not completely, for the environment cannot force me to do my best. Between the "floor" and the "ceiling" of my nature I can choose. Thus it is up to me, whatever environment I am in, to decide whether I will think my hardest and go on thinking even though fatigue is setting in. It is up to me whether I will persevere in certain activities beyond the point at which they would normally "carry themselves," especially when difficulty or pain are involved.

If, however, I develop habits of work and other attitudes which do not take full advantage of what is really available to me, if my personality is more limited than my endowment allows, I may not be able to realize my full endowment later when I might wish to. In other words, the choices I made along the way have determined my present mode of adjustment, and this in turn may restrict the range of freedom I *now* have.

Here we are brought to a point at which a distinction must be carefully drawn between *free will* (or *will-agency* as we shall now call it) and *will-power*. Our conception of human freedom will be clearer if this distinction—it is a distinction and not a separation—is kept in mind.

To what in experience does *will-power* refer? It is one thing to will to think, to do one's best to realize one alternative. But it is another thing to succeed in the face of the obstacles, internal and external, one confronts. The power of will

---

[1] See William James, *Psychology*. New York: Henry Holt & Co., 1896, II, 559 ff.

(*will-power*) refers to the actual efficacy, as opposed to the effort being expended by the person, of the willing to realize a chosen objective. *How much power* willing has is frequently a matter of great uncertainty, for we never can be sure what obstacles willing may confront. *Free will is not acquired.* The *power* of that will to realize the approved goal depends not completely on the activity of willing but on factors within the personality and the environment impinging upon the person at the time of choice.

Thus *power* or *strength of will* refers not to the possibility of free will (will-agency) to begin with, but to the ability of will-agency to overcome opposition or actually to bring the approved to fruition. To repeat, the basic capacities of the individual, the strength of the opposition, be it conscious or unconscious personality-segments already formed, or those external conditons surrounding a given choice—all of these may be more influential than the agent realizes. It should, therefore, be clear that the question of whether there is free will (will-agency) is a different one from the question of how much power (in terms of effect) the will actually has in given situations. Only one with complete knowledge of all the ingredients in a situation of choice could predict with high *probability* whether the person, *if* he chose to will one alternative, would be victorious (that is, would have enough will-power).

It is at this point that psychological analyses could contribute to our understanding, since the light thrown on the formation of personality is light thrown on the nature of the organization which will-agency has to face as the person chooses to effect changes in his life. A person with an ingrained trait of honesty, gradually built into his personality through the years, may try (will) to be dishonest, but he may actually fail (have no will-power in this respect). When the author urged a graduate student to borrow available funds in order that he could complete his graduate work, the student replied that much as his mind approved of finishing his work, he simply could not bring himself to get into debt; the training his mother had given him was telling more than he or she had ever realized that it would. *Will-power, then, is one of the by-products of the organization of the personality; but will-agency itself is a property of the person who builds and changes his personality within the ultimate limits of his given nature and the opportunities or obstacles afforded by his acquired habits, attitudes, and traits.*

To press the point of our distinction: if a psychologist knew the ultimate potentialities of a given person, and if he knew the present structure of habits, sentiments, traits (and other ingredients) of his personality, he might be able to predict failure or success in objective terms because he knows the relative hold of these upon the person. He might well have predicted, for example, that this graduate student would not borrow the money. But from such facts would the conclusion be warranted that the student has no will-agency? No. All we can say is that the student has inadequate will-power at present to alter the course of events in a certain area of his life. The fact that a person does not seem to alter his *behavior* is far from proof that he has no free will. The psychologist did not witness the battle going on in the individual as he fought his strong sentiment about indebtedness. The student was willing to break his sentiment, and his willing delayed the failure.

There has been some fear that a recognition of free will would actually demoralize human beings. For, it has been argued, if one can alter his behavior at will, then what point is there in struggling to form good habits. The child who has been brought up to be honest or to hate indebtedness can at any time change that habit. Thus neither he nor his parents can expect stability in his character.

This objection would be serious against any view which asserted freedom of will without limits, but it certainly does not hold against views, such as the one here presented, which hold that the effect of habit and of personality structure will constantly influence the amount of will-power one actually can exert.

When a person wills, he wills as a person with definite capacities, innate and acquired. He wills to think this, to continue wanting that—he wills, in other words, to realize what another part of his total nature makes possible. What his willing accomplishes is not the simple result of "an act of will" but of the total situation he confronts at the moment of willing. Thus the honest person will not find it easy to do something dishonest, and the habitually dishonest person will hardly become honest overnight because he has free will. Stability of character is not undermined by the existence of a will which operates within the total possibilities his nature and development allow.

But deny free will altogether and take the denial seriously. Then the very possibility of moral or immoral life vanishes; moral development becomes a meaningless process. To a person intent on realizing ideals, the fact that the effort can be made, the fact that the evil action is at least delayed, the fact that a person goes down in defeat against his best willing—all these are considerations which determine whether he can have any self-respect. If a person were convinced that he simply could not alter his behavior, what *good reason* would there be for trying or for urging *trying?* Indeed, if his trying is simply the outcome of circumstances, if it is "in the cards" to try, he will; if not, he will not, and that's the end of it. For any action will be the by-product of what was going on in him at a given moment in the light of the past and of the environmental forces venting themselves through him.

Are not those who say that "one can still praise or blame a man for what he really *had* to do" using words without meaning? Praise and blame are meaningless unless there is both will-agency and obstacle to will-agency in human life. We do not praise a man for being a male, but we do praise him for being one kind of man when he could have been another. We do not praise him simply so that he will be influenced to be better. We praise him because we think that he has already chosen a path which was not forced upon him, and because we believe that he will be able to make our praise help him in the future. We as part of his environment influence him, but we do so because he is willing to let praise help him.

Similarly, to consider actions morally right or wrong is meaningless, unless the possibility of choice is real. . . . When we say: "John did right to tell the truth," we presuppose that he meant to tell the truth when falsehood was open to him. Otherwise we might as well say that John did right to breathe, to digest, to blink his eyes—all actions appropriate for survival but not right in the sense intended when we say he did right to tell the truth. Right and wrong as moral terms are nonsense syllables if we apply them to actions which involve no choice. For if any action is the only action really possible to the person, the problem of right *or* wrong does not apply. If we do not say it is right for the match to burn the paper (since we know that given the proper conditions no other effect is ever produced), why say that a given act is right (or wrong) if we know no other could have resulted?

But an even more far-reaching consequence issues from the denial of free will. If there is no free will, then "true" and "false" become meaningless. If this is so, it makes no sense to say that determinism is true and free will is false. Let us see why this is so.

What do I mean when I say: John's conclusion is truer than Mary's? I mean that given the problem and the data, John had developed a better evaluation of the data than had Mary.

But the process of discovering truth is not a simple one. In solving the problem there were likes and dislikes, sympathies and antipathies in both Mary and John which might tempt them to favor solutions not adequately grounded in the data. This of course would hold all the more if their interests were vitally affected by the solution. Accordingly, in saying that John's solution is truer than Mary's, I am asserting that John was able, whatever the difficulties in the problem and whatever the prejudices affecting him, to develop a solution which was fair to the evidence. Assuming that Mary and John had the same ability and opportunities, I am asserting that Mary was not able to control her desires or to use her ability in such a way as to arrive at an unbiased interpretation of the problem.

But if I believe in determinism, I must say that given John's nature and given Mary's nature there could be no other account of the data than the one each actually gave. If Mary denied John's conclusion (or if John denied Mary's), both condemnations would be the result of past and present determination. All we could say is: This is what John concluded, and this is what Mary concluded. They could do nothing else!

If then someone should ask me: Why do you think your observation about John and Mary is any truer than Mary's conclusion? the situation becomes quite serious. For if all my actions are determined, then my judgment too is as determined as Mary's and John's; it is the product of all the subjective forces and the data making their impact on my mind. I was compelled to come to my conclusion just as much as Mary and John were. There are three conclusions now, John's and Mary's, and mine about theirs. Is there any reason for supposing that one is truer than the other? If each of us could come to no other conclusion, if no one of us was free to control his own subjective attitudes toward the data and the possible solutions, why trust any statement?

The only one who can know what judgment is true is a person who can analyze and think freely about the data, a person who is able to resist any conclusion which is not based on the evidence before him. The person who cannot will to think and keep thinking about the evidence and different interpretations of it will *have* conclusions; but his conclusions are not necessarily *from* the evidence.

If what we have said is true, the person who holds that scientific investigation presupposes that all events are determined is in an embarrassing position. For if there is no freedom of will, there is no meaning to scientific truth. Hold that the mind, in its reasoning about events, is just as determined as the events are, and there is no basis for holding that the scientist's conclusion is truer than that of the layman. Indeed, no one is left to know which conclusion is less partial than the other, for everyone's conclusion proceeds not from relatively free or detached observation of the facts but from the nexus of events in his brain. But why is one flurry of electrical events truer than another, unless we can have some basis for believing that subjective desires and prejudices, for example, can be *will*-fully resisted in accordance with an ideal of proper investigation?

To summarize our conception of free will: man is free to will within uncertain limits. His will-agency is not arbitrary in the sense that it can operate without regard for his own nature, his past development, and his present opportunities. Will-agency represents the capacity of man to build his own world within the possible worlds provided by his environment and his capacities. But in willing man wills what is possible to his own nature, and in doing so he finds himself effective to different extents. Thus man is more than a responsive creature; he is a responsible creature. His plastic needs and abilities provide the raw materials from which he must build his own character and personality. He cannot be blamed for the raw materials, but he can be blamed for the kind of structure he wills to create out of them.

STUDY QUESTIONS

1   What does Bertocci mean by "free will"? What exactly do his examples from experience show? Do they show, for example, that both alternatives are really possible for the agent?

2   What does Bertocci mean by a "fiat" of the will? Is such a thing compatible with determinism?

3   Can you give some everyday examples which would illustrate the difference between will-agency and will-power? Are there some features of the personality which restrict will-power and which will-agency could choose to eliminate? If so, provide an example.

4   Some people have argued that the claim that God is the first cause of things does not provide an adequate explanation for the universe because God Himself would need an explanation for His choices. What do you think Bertocci would say?

5   "No one says: It is useless to offer wages for work that you wish done, because people may prefer starvation. If free-will were common, all social organization would be impossible, since there would be no way of influencing their actions" (Bertrand Russell, *Human Society in Ethics and Politics*). How do you think Bertocci would reply to Russell?

6   "It is my contention that all beliefs are caused by the application of rewards and punishment. We find believing that the Earth is round rewarding—teachers pat us on the head when we believe it—and so it becomes part of our intellectual system. Years of study and experiment by psychologists have proved this beyond a doubt." What would Bertocci say about this claim? Can it be "true"?

Can a Robot Have Free Will?

J. J. C. Smart

J. J. C. Smart (1920–   ) is Hughes Professor of Philosophy at the University of Adelaide. He is one of the most famous contemporary defenders of the view that mental processes are nothing more than physical events in the brain. Consequently, the human decision-making process is a sequence of physical events which is as determined as any other material process. In this essay, Smart argues that determinism is not inconsistent with the common notion of free will.

Smart argues that while there may be some degree of indeterminacy in the behavior of atomic particles, this does not affect the free-will issue. A machine can act "rationally" even though its choices are caused. Sometimes there is equal evidence on either side of an issue, and in such cases, a "random" or "uncaused" selection procedure can be rational. But most of the time, a condition of rationality is that the choice is caused by the weight of evidence.

Those who insist that free will is uncaused seem to believe that if this were not so, then many common practices, such as punishment, would no longer make sense. But Smart denies this implication of determinism. To hold someone responsible, for example, is justified on the ground that punishment and blame will serve as *causes* for altering future behavior. The question is not whether we are all "programmed," but whether our programs can be altered by being held responsible.

Does pure chance imply free will, and does the absence of pure chance imply the absence of free will? That is, are free will and determinism incompatible? I wish to argue that the question of pure chance or determinism is irrelevant to the question of free will, though, so far from free will and determinism being incompatible with one another, a close approximation to determinism on the macrolevel is required for free will.

Consider two decision making computers *A* and *B*. Suppose that they are designed to select candidates for a staff training course for some organization. (I do not wish to argue here that selection of candidates should at present be automated in this way: my illustration is here meant purely to illustrate a metaphysical point.) Into the inputs of the computers all available information is fed by means of punched cards. The information consists of detailed records of examination results, gradings of mental character (e.g., "honest," "moderately honest," etc., "bad tempered," "easy tempered," etc.) and in short all possible information which might be of interest to a human selector. The machines have been programmed in such a way that we would be happy with the candidates selected (e.g., none of them are too stupid, too dishonest, too bad tempered).

Suppose that there are 20 vacancies and that the computer selects 19 candidates first. For the 20th (and last) place there are two equally good candidates.

This last candidate is then selected from the two possibilities by means of a randomizing device. Suppose that Smith and Jones are the two candidates between which, on the available criteria, the machine so far can not choose. The randomizing device is such that it gives a probability of ½ of choosing each candidate. In the case of machine A the randomizer consists of a roulette wheel on which there is an electrical contact. If the wheel stops with "red" opposite a fixed contact it causes the machine to choose Smith, whereas if "black" is opposite the fixed contact Jones is chosen. In the case of machine B the randomizer consists of a Geiger counter near a small quantity of a radioactive substance such that there is a probability of ½ of the Geiger counter being actuated in the nth second after the start of operation of the machine, where n is an odd number, and there is a probability of ½ of it being actuated in the mth second where m is an even number. If the Geiger counter is actuated in an odd numbered second the machine chooses Smith, and if it is actuated in an even numbered second the machine chooses Jones. Let us suppose that in fact, in the case of each machine, Smith happens to be the candidate chosen.

The machine A as described above can be regarded as a deterministic machine, since its behavior can be described with a close enough approximation by means of classical physics. We may say that the choice by machine A of Smith as against Jones was a deterministic one, since with sufficient knowledge of the inputs to the machine and of the initial state and working of the machine the choice of Smith as against Jones could have been predicted. On the other hand the machine B is an indeterministic machine, since the choice of Smith depended on an indeterministic quantum mechanical effect.

Was the choice of Smith as made by machine A any more or less "rational" than the same choice as made by machine B? Surely not. Was the choice of Smith by B "more rational" than the choice of the first nineteen candidates, whose qualifications were such that no use of the randomizer was necessary in their case? We may say that the indeterministic machine B is neither more nor less "free" than is the deterministic machine A. For this reason I hold that the principle of quantum mechanical indeterminacy has nothing whatever to do with the problem of free will. Whether our brains are (near enough) deterministic machines or whether they contain "pure chance" randomizers, they are neither more nor less possessed of free will.

Some philosophers would object to my implicit assumption above that choice is a matter of a largely causal computation process. They would say that in free choice we act from reasons, not from causes, and they would say that acting from reasons is neither caused nor a matter of pure chance. I find this unintelligible. The machine which chose the twentieth man by a quantum mechanical randomizer did not do so on account of a cause, but did so by pure chance. It had no reason to choose the one candidate rather than another. On the other hand the machine in choosing the first nineteen candidates did behave in a deterministic way and could be said to have been caused to make the choices it did. It was programmed in such a way that its causes corresponded to reasons, for example it was programmed in such a way that it chose the most intelligent, sensible, etc., candidates, and so it was programmed to act in accordance with what we would call "good reasons." It acted from reasons precisely because it was caused.

It may be objected, however, that here is the trouble. It was *programmed* to do so, whereas we act freely. In reply to this we may make two rejoinders. In the first place are we not ourselves "programmed"? That is, on account of our genetic endowment, together with certain environmental influences both when we were embryos and ever since, our brains have been caused to have a certain structure. They therefore compute in certain ways. People with certain brain structures will make certain choices, and people with other brain structures will make other choices. The second rejoinder is as follows. If the view that we are largely deterministic machines is taken to imply that we do not have free will, we may concede indeed that we also do not have free will in the sense which the objector has in mind. It is not clear, however, what this sense is: the free choice is supposed to be not deterministic and not a matter of pure chance in the way in which a quantum jump is supposed to be pure chance. It is supposed to be pure chance in the sense of "not being determined" but the suggestion is that it is also not merely random and is "acting from reason." The previous paragraph suggests, however, that acting from reasons is not merely random precisely because it is also acting from causes.

It is possible that the plain man's concept of free will has inconsistent elements in it. He may demand of free will that it be both random and yet not random. If so, we should feel no compunction about denying the existence of free will in the plain man's sense. This does not mean, however, that we do not have at our disposal the means to make most of the contrasts which the plain man makes by asserting or denying free will. A determinist can still make the distinction between the condition of a man who goes for a walk because he wants to do so (being determined by his desire, which we may take to be a state of neural interconnections in his brain) and a man in a prison cell who does not go for a walk, even though he dearly desires to do so. (The latter man would be caused by the state of his brain to go for a walk but he is prevented from doing so by the bolts and bars of his cell.) Being caused by your internal state of desire in the former way is, *ceteris paribus,* pleasant, and being prevented by external constraints is, *ceteris paribus,* unpleasant. Similarly we do not deny that there is an important difference between doing a thing X, because we want to do it and have no conflicting desires, and the case where we do X because of some threat. A man who gives money to charity because he wishes to help that good cause acts in a way which is relatively pleasant. A man who hands over money in a police court because he has to pay a fine also in a sense does what he wants to do, but he wants to hand over the money only in the sense that he dislikes the alternative of going to prison even more. Once more the determinist can make the relevant distinction, and whether or not he does so by means of the words "free" and "unfree" is not very important.

What about the contrast between a psychopathic offender (say a kleptomaniac) and an ordinary criminal (say a burglar)? In both cases their desires cause the behavior. The plain man and the criminal law both tend to contrast the case of the kleptomaniac and the ordinary burglar by denying that the kleptomaniac was fully free. We can make the required contrast (which is all that the criminal law should need) by saying that the kleptomaniac is not easily caused by threats of punishment to act otherwise, whereas the ordinary burglar is amenable to threats. On account of this we can give a rational justification for treating kleptomaniacs differently from burglars, and we can do so without involving the questionable concept of free will. Once more we conclude that if the plain man's concept of free will is a denial both of determinism and of randomness, then its apparent inconsistency does not matter all that much, since we can nevertheless make most of the distinctions which the plain man wishes to make without its aid.

Now let us consider a piece of science fiction. Instead of having our brains "programmed" by our genes and environment let us suppose that they could be programmed (or reprogrammed) by means of a machine. Suppose that it were possible to change a person's whole character by applying a number of electrodes to his head, so that in some (at present technologically inconceivable) way the interconnections between his neurons (and possibly also whatever constitutes his memory store) are radically altered. Perhaps we could apply such a machine to a humanitarian poet and turn him into a diabolical technologist who is an able inventor of lethal weapons. It might be said that such a "reprogrammed" man, however little he was thwarting contrary desires, would not be free, and would merit neither praise nor blame for his activities. In reply to this we could contend that he would merit praise or blame exactly as much or as little as would an ordinary person (i.e., a person who had not had his brain changed in this way). If it were useful (for deterrent reasons) to punish the ordinary person, so would it be useful (for deterrent reasons) to punish the reprogrammed person. (I neglect here the possibility that in the fictional case better results might be achieved by punishing not the programmee but the programmer.) The only good reasons for punishment or reward, praise or blame, seem to me to be their social effects. A philosopher who thinks that it is not right to blame or punish an ordinary person, is surely forgetting that the ordinary person is also programmed by his heredity and environment. Such a philosopher may have the extraordinary idea, when thinking of a vicious murderer, that if *he* had had the murderer's bad brain and bad environment he would nevertheless have acted differently. I think that such a view is unintelligible.

My conclusion therefore is that even though the brain should be a deterministic mechanism, we are still able to make the important contrasts which we normally signalize by calling behavior either "free" or "unfree." It is a matter of somewhat arbitrary choice whether or not we say that the ordinary man's concept of free will is contrary to determinism, and that the view of the mind as a deterministic (or largely deterministic) machine implies that we have not got free will. A lot depends on what plain man we catch, and on whether or not we catch him in a metaphysical frame of mind. If we do say that the plain man's concept of free will is incompatible with determinism, then even so we can also say that our denial of free will does not have the startling consequences which it would have had if it had implied also the denial of the important contrasts which have been discussed above. Alternatively we can use "free" and "unfree" in order to make the above mentioned contrasts, in which case determinism is perfectly compatible with free will.

What has science to say about the question whether the brain is a deterministic machine? A good many philosophers have held that the indeterministic nature of quantum mechanics leaves a loophole for free will. Our discussion of free will should have shown what is wrong with this. It is abstractly possible that the brain might contain indeterministic trigger mechanisms, like the Geiger counter of machine B above. Nevertheless this would mean only that the brain contained an indeterministic randomizer: if it contained instead a deterministic randomizer like that of machine A how would this affect the question of its freedom? We must not entirely discount the possibility of very small events, possibly below the level of quantum mechanical uncertainty, which occur in the synaptic knobs of single neurons, being amplified by neuronal mechanisms so as to produce behavioral effects. No less a neurophysiologist than Sir John Eccles has indeed proposed such a mechanism. Eccles thinks that in this way events in an immaterial mind can have effects on the brain. Many scientists would perhaps think that the idea of an immaterial mind produces more difficulties than it solves. For one thing the postulation of an immaterial mind seems to raise difficulties for the genetical theory of evolution by natural selection. It is not difficult to see in a general way how mutations in genes lead, *via* the biochemistry of embryology, to slightly differently convoluted brains, and hence ultimately to the sort of potentialities for behavior which leads us to say that an organism has a mind. But it is hard to see how the production of an immaterial mind could come to be reconciled with the chemical approach to genetics. Eccles regards the existence of the immaterial mind as vouched for by introspection, but we shall here avoid discussing this issue, which raises large and controversial questions in the philosophy of mind. Let us remark, however, that the postulation of an immaterial mind does not help to illuminate the problem of free will. For once more we can ask whether events in the immaterial mind are caused, or whether they are random, or supposing that they are neither caused nor random, we can ask what this third possibility consists in.

STUDY QUESTIONS

1   Smart compares two decision-making computers. Some of the time, both computers use a randomizing device to make their selections. Why does it not make any difference whether such a device is deterministic or indeterministic? If the indeterministic device made *all* choices of the candidates, would such a procedure be rational?

2   Smart claims that the computers acted from "good reasons" precisely because they were caused. What would Bertocci say about that? Would Bertocci agree that indeterminism means random choice?

3   Smart maintains that even if the ordinary notion of free will is inconsistent, determinism is compatible with the sorts of contrasts which the ordinary notion is used to make. What are these contrasts? How do you think Smart would finish the following:

     a   Smith freely gave his money to charity because . . .
     b   Smith did not freely hand over his money to the man in the mask because . . .
     c   Smith remained in jail of his own free will because . . .

What does Smart mean by "free" and "unfree"?

4   "Praise and blame, rewards and punishments, and the whole apparatus of the crimi-
     nal law, are rational on the deterministic hypothesis, but not on the hypothesis of free
     will, for they are all mechanisms designed to cause volitions that are in harmony with
     the interests of the community. . . . " (Bertrand Russell, *Human Society in Ethics
     and Politics*). Would Smart agree with this? Do you?
5   Does Smart believe that if someone could prove the existence of the "soul," the
     problem of free will would be solved? Do you?

Moral Responsibility in a
Determined World

PROBLEM INTRODUCTION

Consider the behavior of the solitary wasp *Sphex*. When the time for egg-laying approaches, this little wasp carefully digs a burrow to serve as the hatchery for her young. Then she searches for a cricket. She stings the cricket in just the right place so as to paralyze it, and carries it to her burrow. Leaving the cricket just outside her carefully prepared nest, she goes inside for a last-minute check to clear out any unwanted debris which may have gotten in. Then she drags the cricket inside the hatchery and lays her eggs beside it. When the eggs hatch, the young wasps will feed on the living host that their mother has so graciously placed in suspended animation. Her task complete, the wasp leaves the burrow, covers it up, and flies away—the future of her children secured.

Complex behavior of this sort in insects, fish, and lower mammals has intrigued scientists for centuries. On the surface, it bears all the marks of intelligent, purposeful, and free action. Yet, in spite of appearances, the elaborate behavior pattern of the wasp is simply a sequence of automatic stages. If, for example, the cricket host is removed a few inches from the edge of the burrow while the wasp is inside making her last-minute check, she will drag it to the edge of the burrow again and go through the same routine. Again and again, this poor harried mother can be made to repeat her housecleaning chores by moving the cricket a few inches from the lip of the nest. This shows that the wasp has no executive control over the entire operation. Each stage of this complex sequence of behavior is "triggered" by an earlier stage in the chain. If part of the chain is interfered with, the insect reacts in response to the last completed part of the chain, even if this means doing the same thing over and over again indefinitely. The wasp is a helpless victim of her own internal wiring.

In one of the readings that follow, John Hospers argues that people cannot alter their drives, wants, and emotions, and therefore cannot be held responsible for actions which such features of the personality produce. No doubt if wasps were conscious, they would have the feeling of freedom. Each time the mother wasp dragged the cricket back to the entrance of the burrow, she would say to herself, "Should I check the burrow again?" and each time, with the inevitablity of clockwork, she would answer, "Yes." Given the circumstances, and the programming of the wasp, it cannot *choose* otherwise. The appearance of alternatives, the possibility of an option, is an illusion. Hospers believes that, like the wasp, we too must think and choose as our "wiring" programs us to think and choose, and this means that freedom disappears.

The case of the wasp raises some interesting questions about the major positions on free will. In the previous section, we identified three main theories about free will. Hard-determinism assumes that free will and moral responsibility are incompatible with a universe in which all events are caused. Since the hard-determinist believes that the world is deterministic, free will is held to be impossible. The libertarian, on the other hand, believes that experience reveals the reality of free will, and so denies that determinism is true. Between these two opposing views there is a compromise position called *soft-determinism,* which is an attempt to make freedom compatible with determinism. Surely this would be the ideal theory, if it could be justified, for then the ethical and the scientific pictures of humanity would not be in conflict.

The soft-determinist tries to reconcile freedom and determinism by claiming that moral responsibility does not depend upon being free from all causes but merely upon being free from certain *kinds* of causes. Any action of ours which is principally caused by factors outside our own personalities is one for which we cannot be held responsible. The soft-determinist says that if an action issues from our own wants and desires, it is free. A free agent can do otherwise, is free to do otherwise, if there is nothing which would prevent the exercise of an alternative choice. This is called the *hypothetical interpretation of freedom,* since it says that a free agent can do otherwise *if* some other choice is made.

Both hard-determinists and libertarians believe that this analysis is superficial. The real issue, they argue, is not whether someone can act differently if a different choice is made. The real issue is whether someone can *choose* differently. Freedom of action must be distinguished from freedom of the will. The wasp which repeats the cleaning operation over and over enjoys freedom of action. There is nothing preventing her from dragging the cricket into the burrow *if she chooses to do so.* But of course she cannot choose to do so! It is this fact which prompts us to declare that the wasp is not free.

C. A. Campbell is a libertarian who believes that since the hypothetical freedom of soft-determinism still leaves choices under the reign of necessity, the central problem of free will remains. A person could have *chosen* differently, according to the soft-determinist, only if some aspect of his or her personality were altered. But Campbell insists that what we want to know is whether the same person, with the same desires and beliefs, could have chosen differently in the same circumstances. This is impossible in a deterministic universe. Campbell recognizes that soft-determinism has rightly rejected the indeterminism of William James. If choice is ruled by chance, if anything is possible, then choice does not reflect the self and so the self cannot be held responsible. Although he admits that choices are caused by the self, he insists that the self is something distinct from the formed character. The self has the ability to stand against the flow of environmental pressures, even to stand against its own habits and desires, and to choose in a new direction—a direction which cannot be explained or predicted by the forces which have molded character. It is possible, therefore, for the autonomous self to creatively choose duty over its own strongest desire. This form of libertarianism is not strictly indeterminism, since choices are caused by the self; but the self is something which stands outside of the usual flow of events, and its action cannot be causally explained.

The soft-determinist cannot ignore these criticisms. Moral freedom must be more than freedom from external forces. We can be victimized by our own natures, as well as by the external environment, and any theory which ignores this—any theory that says that the wasp is free—is surely false. Soft-determinism, therefore, must be able to distinguish between causes which deprive us of free will and those which create free will, whether those causes be internal or external. To the libertarian and the hard-determinist, such a distinction is unintelligible. All forms of necessity destroy human freedom, they argue, because necessity means that one cannot make another choice. How can the soft-determinist meet this objection? Can the choices of a free agent come about by necessity?

The answer to this paradox, according to the soft-determinist, depends on how the word "necessity" is understood. In a deterministic universe, to say that a choice is necessitated is simply to say that given the prior conditions, that choice, and no other, must occur. The word "necessitated," however, suggests that choices are fated and uncontrollable. It suggests that certain decisions will be made no matter what we try to do to alter them, and our most fervent efforts to change ourselves are useless. Now surely this is true some of the time. There are some features of our personality which no one can change, just as there are physical events which cannot be altered by human design. But many features of the personality are caused by human effort—if not by one's own effort, then by the effort of others. Our parents, for example, cause us to react and behave in certain ways through the training they provide. If someone else's effort can shape my personality, then surely mine can too.

"Aha!" says the hard-determinist, "certainly you can change your own personality to some extent *if you desire to do so.* But your desire to change is itself caused by factors which you cannot control." This is surely correct. Does this mean, however, that self-control is lost? The soft-determinist says, "No." In fact, determinism is required for self-control.

Remember that free will is something valuable. Even the hard-determinist regrets that it doesn't exist, much like the atheist regards the prospect of heaven.

Free will is valuable because it is required for self-control, and this, in turn, is valuable because it allows us to alter ourselves and our reactions so as to avoid frustrations, pain, and unhappiness. The absence of self-control means that there is no flexibility, no possibility of alternative responses, in a world of change. It is to be locked into a system of mechanical habits which remain rigid and unyielding in the face of a shifting environment. What does it take to be the master of myself? When I have an appreciation of my most fundamental needs, those which are essential to my self-identity and happiness, I will try to satisfy them in the most efficient way. Of course, whether I am successful depends upon how accurately I can predict the consequences of my actions. This, in turn, depends upon my knowledge of the world in which I shall act. To know the conditions for happiness, to know the world enough to see the avenues for achieving it, and to have the motivation to set oneself on those avenues—*this is self-control.* In other words, self-control is having our choices caused by the most rational appraisal of ourselves and our environment.

There is a temptation to suppose that this is not enough. The libertarian, for example, would insist that even if the system of causes produces the best choices, it is still true that no other choices are possible. Unless a person could have chosen otherwise, he or she is not free.

In order to formulate the soft-determinist response to this, let us return to the case of the harassed wasp. The wasp does not exhibit self-control because it cannot alter its behavior to achieve its goal. When we say that the wasp "cannot do otherwise" we mean that it is incapable of responding flexibly, in light of its own needs, to changing situations. Someone who is in control is open to new information and new circumstances in a way that allows for alternative choices *if the information warrants it.* An intelligent and rational agent will alter certain habits and dispositions, *if these are no longer effective in achieving basic goals.* The capacity to do otherwise is valuable only when doing otherwise is the rational thing to do. Therefore, someone who is caused to behave by a system of rationality possesses the ability to choose otherwise in the only meaningful sense of that expression. This is a hypothetical sense, it is true, because it makes choice depend on the introduction of new causal factors (new information), but any other sense would deprive the person of self-control. The wasp is a victim, not because its behavior is necessitated, but because the necessitating causes are automatic and inflexible.

In the following readings, the position just outlined is ably defended by John Dewey, one of the foremost American philosophers of this century. Dewey argues that freedom must be nourished or it dies. The flexible and intelligent self is something which is created, just as the neurotic and rigid self is created. Therefore, Dewey ties moral freedom to social conditions, especially education. This form of self-determinism is philosophically optimistic while also scientific. Human effort is upgraded, freedom increases, as science uncovers the causes of behavior. Dewey gives a fresh meaning to the claim that knowledge is power. We are not powerless to change ourselves when we know the causes of our behavior.

What Means This Freedom?

John Hospers

At one time, insanity was treated as a crime, and the mentally deranged were punished in particularly vicious ways. The very fact that we now talk about mental "illness" and classify some psychological disorders as "diseases" indicates that many forms of behavior which were once thought to deserve punishment have been shown to be the result of factors beyond the agent's control. With the development of modern psychiatry and psychology, more and more is being discovered about the causes of fairly typical behavior patterns. John Hospers (1918–   ), professor of philosophy at the University of Southern California, believes that as this trend continues we shall find that ultimately no one is responsible.

   Hospers is particularly interested in the consequences of psychotherapy on the doctrine of free will. The psychoanalyst does not blame someone for being unable to cope with the world nor does she or he praise someone for possessing the capacity to handle life's problems. Everyone's reaction to the world is the result of forces which shaped their psychological dispositions for better or for worse. In order to be held morally responsible, a person should have been able to do otherwise. But Hospers claims that the ability to do otherwise hinges on the ability to have different desires than those which caused the action. This is impossible, he claims, and so the usual conception of responsibility is wrong.

I

. . . There are many actions—not those of an insane person (however the term "insane" be defined), nor of a person ignorant of the effects of his action, nor ignorant of some relevant fact about the situation, nor in any obvious way mentally deranged—for which human beings in general and the courts in particular are inclined to hold the doer responsible, and for which, I would say, he should not be held responsible. The deed may be planned, it may be carried out in cold calculation, it may spring from the agent's character and be continuous with the rest of his behavior, and it may be perfectly true that he could have done differently *if* he had wanted to; nonetheless his behavior was brought about by unconscious conflicts developed in infancy, over which he had no control and of which (without training in psychiatry) he does not even have knowledge. He may even *think* he knows why he acted as he did, he may *think* he has conscious control over his actions, he may even *think* he is fully responsible for them; but he is not. Psychiatric casebooks provide hundreds of examples. The law and common sense, though puzzled sometimes by such cases, are gradually becoming aware that they exist; but at this early stage countless tragic blunders still occur because neither the law nor the public in general is aware of the genesis of criminal

Reprinted by permission of New York University Press from *Determinism and Freedom in the Age of Modern Science*, by Sidney Hook (ed.), © 1958 by New York University.
Editor's note: The division of this reading is the editor's.

actions. The mother blames her daughter for choosing the wrong men as candidates for husbands; but though the daughter thinks she is choosing freely and
spends a considerable amount of time "deciding" among them, the identification
with her sick father, resulting from Oedipal fantasies in early childhood, prevents
her from caring for any but sick men, twenty or thirty years older than herself.
Blaming her is beside the point; she cannot help it, and she cannot change it.
Countless criminal acts are thought out in great detail; yet the participants are
(without their own knowledge) acting out fantasies, fears, and defenses from
early childhood, over whose coming and going they have no conscious control.

Let us suppose it were established that a man commits murder only if, sometime during the previous week, he has eaten a certain combination of foods—say,
tuna fish salad at a meal also including peas, mushroom soup, and blueberry pie.
What if we were to track down the factors common to all murders committed in
this country during the last twenty years and found this factor present in all of
them, and only in them? The example is of course empirically absurd; but may it
not be that there is *some* combination of factors that regularly leads to homicide.
. . . When such specific factors are discovered, won't they make it clear that it is
foolish and pointless, as well as immoral, to hold human beings responsible for
crimes? Or, if one prefers biological to psychological factors, suppose a neurologist is called in to testify at a murder trial and produces X-ray pictures of the
brain of the criminal; anyone can see, he argues, that the *cella turcica* was already
calcified at the age of nineteen; it should be a flexible bone, growing, enabling
the gland to grow.[1] All the defendant's disorders might have resulted from this
early calcification. Now, this particular explanation may be empirically false; but
who can say that no such factors, far more complex, to be sure, exist?

When we know such things as these, we no longer feel so much tempted to
say that the criminal is responsible for his crime; and we tend also (do we not?)
to excuse him—not legally (we still confine him to prison) but morally; we no
longer call him a monster or hold him personally responsible for what he did.
Moreover, we do this in general, not merely in the case of crime: "You must
excuse Grandmother for being irritable, she's really quite ill and is suffering some
pain all the time." Or: "The dog always bites children after she's had a litter of
pups; you can't blame her for it; she's not feeling well, and besides she naturally
wants to defend them." Or: "She's nervous and jumpy, but do excuse her; she has
a severe glandular disturbance."

Let us note that the more *thoroughly* and *in detail* we know the causal factors
leading a person to behave as he does, the more we tend to exempt him from
responsibility. When we know nothing of the man except what we see him do, we
say he is an ungrateful cad who expects much of other people and does nothing
in return, and we are usually indignant. When we learn that his parents were the
same way and, having no guilt feelings about this mode of behavior themselves,
brought him up to be greedy and avaricious, we see that we could hardly expect
him to have developed moral feelings in this direction. When we learn, in addition, that he is not aware of being ungrateful or selfish, but unconsciously re-

[1] Meyer Levin, *Compulsion* (New York: Simon and Schuster, 1956), p. 403.

presses the memory of events unfavorable to himself, we feel that the situation is unfortunate but "not really his fault." When we know that this behavior of his, which makes others angry, occurs more constantly when he feels tense or insecure, and that he now feels tense and insecure, and that relief from pressure will diminish it, then we tend to "feel sorry for the poor guy" and say he's more to be pitied than censured. We no longer want to say that he is personally responsible; we might rather blame nature or his parents for having given him an unfortunate constitution or temperament.

> In recent years a new form of punishment has been imposed on middle-aged and elderly parents. Their children, now in their twenties, thirties or even forties, present them with a modern grievance. "My analysis proves that *you* are responsible for my neurosis." Overawed by these authoritative statements, the poor tired parents fall easy victims to the newest variations on the scapegoat theory.
>
> In my opinion, this senseless cruelty—which disinters educational sins which had been buried for decades, and uses them as the basis for accusations which the victims cannot answer—is unjustified. Yes, "the truth loves to be centrally located" (Melville), and few parents—since they are human—have been perfect. But granting their mistakes, they acted as *their* neurotic difficulties forced them to act. To turn the tables and declare the children not guilty because of the *impersonal* nature of their own neuroses, while at the same time the parents are *personally* blamed, is worse than illogical; it is profoundly unjust.[2]

And so, it would now appear, neither of the parties is responsible: "they acted as their neurotic difficulties forced them to act." The patients are not responsible for their neurotic manifestations, but then neither are the parents responsible for theirs; and so, of course, for their parents in turn, and theirs before them. It is the twentieth-century version of the family curse, the curse on the House of Atreus.

"But," a critic complains, "it's immoral to exonerate people indiscriminately in this way. I might have thought it fit to excuse somebody because he was born on the other side of the tracks, if I didn't know so many bank presidents who were also born on the other side of the tracks." Now, I submit that the most immoral thing in this situation is the critic's caricature of the conditions of the excuse. Nobody is excused merely because he was born on the other side of the tracks. But if he was born on the other side of the tracks *and* was a highly narcissistic infant to begin with *and* was repudiated or neglected by his parents *and* . . . (here we list a finite number of conditions), and if this complex of factors is *regularly* followed by certain behavior traits in adulthood, and moreover *unavoidably* so—that is, they occur no matter what he or anyone else tries to do—then we excuse him morally and say he is not responsible for his deed. If he is not responsible for A, a series of events occurring in his babyhood, then neither is he reponsible for B, a series of things he does in adulthood, provided that B inevitably—that is, unavoidably—follows upon the occurrence of A. And according to psychiatrists and psychoanalysts, this often happens.

But one may still object that so far we have talked only about neurotic behavior. Isn't nonneurotic or normal or not unconsciously motivated (or what-

---

[2] Edmund Bergler, *The Superego* (New York: Grune and Stratton, 1952), p. 320.

ever you want to call it) behavior still within the area of responsibility? There are reasons for answering "No" even here; for the normal person no more than the neurotic one has caused his own character, which makes him what he is. Granted that neurotics are not responsible for their behavior (that part of it which we call neurotic) because it stems from undigested infantile conflicts that they had no part in bringing about, and that are external to them just as surely as if their behavior had been forced on them by a malevolent deity (which is indeed one theory on the subject); but the so-called normal person is equally the product of causes in which his volition took no part. And if, unlike the neurotic's, his behavior is changeable by rational consideration, and if he has the willpower to overcome the effects of an unfortunate early environment, this again is no credit to him; he is just lucky. If energy is available to him in a form in which it can be mobilized for constructive purposes, this is no credit to him, for this too is part of his psychic legacy. Those of us who can discipline ourselves and develop habits of concentration of purpose tend to blame those who cannot, and call them lazy and weak-willed; but what we fail to see is that they literally *cannot* do what we expect; if their psyches were structured like ours, they could, but as they are burdened with a tyrannical superego (to use psychoanalytic jargon for the moment), and a weak defenseless ego whose energies are constantly consumed in fighting endless charges of the superego, they simply cannot do it, and it is irrational to expect it of them. We cannot with justification blame them for their inability, any more than we can congratulate ourselves for our ability. This lesson is hard to learn, for we constantly and naïvely assume that other people are constructed as we ourselves are.

But, one persists, it isn't a matter simply of luck; it is a matter of effort. Very well then, it's a matter of effort; without exerting the effort you may not overcome the deficiency. But whether or not you are the kind of person who has it in him to exert the effort is a matter of luck.

All this is well known to psychoanalysts. They can predict, from minimal cues that most of us don't notice, whether a person is going to turn out to be lucky or not. "The analyst," they say, "must be able to use the residue of the patient's unconscious guilt so as to remove the symptom or character trait that creates the guilt. The guilt must not only be present, but *available* for use, *mobilizable.* If it is used up (absorbed) in criminal activity, or in an excessive amount of self-damaging tendencies, then it cannot be used for therapeutic purposes, and the prognosis is negative." Not all philosophers will relish the analyst's way of putting the matter, but at least as a physician he can soon detect whether the patient is lucky or unlucky—and he knows that whichever it is, it *isn't the patient's fault.* The patient's conscious volition cannot remedy the deficiency. Even whether he will cooperate with the analyst is really out of the patient's hands: if he continually projects the denying-mother fantasy on the analyst and unconsciously identifies him always with the cruel, harsh forbidder of the nursery, thus frustrating any attempt at impersonal observation, the sessions are useless; yet if it happens that way, he can't help that either. That fatal projection is not under his control; whether it occurs or not depends on how his unconscious identifications have developed since his infancy. He can try, yes—but the ability to try enough for the therapy to have effect is also beyond his control; the capacity to try more than just so much is either there or it isn't—and either way "it's in the lap of the gods."

The position, then, is this: if we *can* overcome the effects of early environment, the ability to do so is itself a product of the early environment. We did not give ourselves this ability; and if we lack it we cannot be blamed for not having it. Sometimes, to be sure, moral exhortation brings out an ability that is there but not being used, and in this lies its *occasional* utility; but very often its use is pointless, because the ability is not there. The only thing that can overcome a desire, as Spinoza said, is a stronger contrary desire; and many times there simply is no wherewithal for producing a stronger contrary desire. Those of us who do have the wherewithal are lucky.

There is one possible practical advantage in remembering this. It may prevent us (unless we are compulsive blamers) from indulging in righteous indignation and committing the sin of spiritual pride, thanking God that we are not as this publican here. And it will protect from our useless moralizings those who are least equipped by nature for enduring them.

As with responsibility, so with deserts. Someone commits a crime and is punished by the state; "he deserved it," we say self-righteously—as if we were moral and he immoral, when in fact we are lucky and he is unlucky—forgetting that there, but for the grace of God and a fortunate early environment, go we. Or, as Clarence Darrow said in his speech for the defense in the Loeb-Leopold case:

> I do not believe that people are in jail because they deserve to be. . . . I know what causes the emotional life. . . . I know it is practically left out of some. Without it they cannot act with the rest. They cannot feel the moral shocks which safeguard others. Is [this man] to blame that his machine is imperfect? Who is to blame? I do not know. I have never in my life been interested so much in fixing blame as I have in relieving people from blame. I am not wise enough to fix it.[3]

II

I want to make it quite clear that I have not been arguing for determinism. Though I find it difficult to give any sense to the term "indeterminism," because I do not know what it would be like to come across an uncaused event, let us grant indeterminists everything they want, at least in words—influences that suggest but do not constrain, a measure of acausality in an otherwise rigidly causal order, and so on—whatever these phrases may mean. With all this granted, exactly the same situation faces the indeterminist and the determinist; all we have been saying would still hold true. "Are our powers innate or acquired?"

> Suppose the powers are declared innate; then the villain may sensibly ask whether he is responsible for what he was born with. A negative reply is inevitable. Are they then acquired? Then the ability to acquire them—was *that* innate? or acquired? it is innate? Very well then. . . .[4]

³ Levin, op. cit., pp. 439–440, 469.
⁴ W. I. Matson, "The Irrelevance of Free Will to Moral Responsibility," *Mind*, LXV (October 1956), p. 495.

The same fact remains—that we did not cause our characters, that the influences that made us what we are are influences over which we had no control and of whose very existence we had no knowledge at the time. This fact remains for "determinism" and "indeterminism" alike. And it is this fact to which I would appeal, not the specific tenets of traditional forms of "determinism," which seem to me, when analyzed, empirically empty.

"But," it may be asked, "isn't it your view that nothing ultimately *could* be other than it is? And isn't this deterministic? And isn't it deterministic if you say that human beings could never act otherwise than they do, and that their desires and temperaments could not, when you consider their antecedent conditions, be other than they are?"

I reply that all these charges rest on confusions.

1 To say that nothing *could* be other than it is, is, taken literally, nonsense; and if taken as a way of saying something else, misleading and confusing. If you say, "I can't do it," this invites the question, "No? Not even if you want to?" "Can" and "could" are power words, used in the context of human action; when applied to nature they are merely anthropomorphic. "Could" has no application to nature—unless, of course, it is uttered in a theological context; one might say that God *could* have made things different. But with regard to inanimate nature "could" has no meaning. Or perhaps it is intended to mean that the order of nature is in some sense *necessary*. But in that case the sense of "necessary" must be specified. I know what "necessary" means when we are talking about propositions, but not when we are talking about the sequence of events in nature.

2 What of the charge that we could never have acted otherwise than we did? This, I submit, is simply not true. Here the exponents of Hume-Mill-Schlick-Ayer "soft determinism" are quite right. I could have gone to the opera today instead of coming here; that is, if certain conditions had been different, I should have gone. I could have done many other things instead of what I did, if some condition or other had been different, specifically if my desire had been different. I repeat that "could" is a power word, and "I could have done this" means approximately "I *should* have done this *if* I had wanted to." In this sense, all of us could often have done otherwise than we did. I would not want to say that I should have done differently even if *all* the conditions leading up to my action had been the same (this is generally not what we mean by "could" anyway); but to assert that I could have is empty, for if I *did* act differently from the time before, we would automatically say that one or more of the conditions were different, whether we had independent evidence for this or not, thus rendering the assertion immune to empirical refutation. (Once again, the vacuousness of "determinism.")

3 Well, then, could we ever have, not acted, but desired otherwise than we did desire? This gets us once again to the heart of the matter we were discussing in the previous section. Russell said, "We can do as we please but we can't please as we please." But I am persuaded that even this statement conceals a fatal mistake. Let us follow the same analysis through. "I could have done X" means "I should have done X if I had wanted to." "I could have wanted X" by the same analysis would mean "I should have wanted X if I had wanted to"—which seems to make no sense at all. (What does Russell want? To please as he doesn't please?)

What does this show? It shows, I think, that the only meaningful context of "can" and "could have" is that of *action*. "Could have acted differently" makes sense; "could have desired differently," as we have just seen, does not. Because a word or phrase makes good sense in one context, let us not assume that it does so in another.

I conclude, then, with the following suggestion: that we operate on two levels of moral discourse, which we shouldn't confuse; one (let's call it the upper level) is that of actions; the other (the lower, or deeper, level) is that of the springs of action. Most moral talk occurs on the upper level. It is on this level that the Hume-Mill-Schlick-Ayer analysis of freedom fully applies. As we have just seen, "can" and "could" acquire their meaning on this level; so, I suspect, does "freedom." So does the distinction between compulsive and noncompulsive behavior, and among the senses of "responsibility," discussed in the first section of this paper, according to which we are responsible for some things and not for others. All these distinctions are perfectly valid on this level (or in this dimension) of moral discourse; and it is, after all, the usual one—we are practical beings interested in changing the course of human behavior, so it is natural enough that 99 per cent of our moral talk occurs here.

But when we descend to what I have called the lower level of moral discourse, as we occasionally do in thoughtful moments when there is no immediate need for action, then we must admit that we are ultimately the kind of persons we are because of conditions occurring outside us, over which we had no control. But while this is true, we should beware of extending the moral terminology we used on the other level to this one also. "Could" and "can," as we have seen, no longer have meaning here. "Right" and "wrong," which apply only to actions, have no meaning here either. I suspect that the same is true of "responsibility," for now that we have recalled often forgotten facts about our being the product of outside forces, we must ask in all seriousness what would be added by saying that we are not *responsible* for our own characters and temperaments. What would it mean even? Has it a significant opposite? What would it be like to be responsible for one's own character? What possible situation is describable by this phrase? Instead of saying that it is *false* that we are responsible for our own characters, I should prefer to say that the utterance is meaningless—meaningless in the sense that it describes no possible situation, though it *seems* to because the word "responsible" is the same one we used on the upper level, where it marks a real distinction. If this is so, the result is that *moral* terms—at least the terms "could have" and "responsible"—simply drop out on the lower level. What remains, shorn now of moral terminology, is the point we tried to bring out in Part [I]: whether or not we have personality disturbances, whether or not we have the ability to overcome deficiences of early environment, is like the answer to the question whether or not we shall be struck down by a dread disease: "it's all a matter of luck." It is important to keep this in mind, for people almost always forget it, with consequences in human intolerance and unnecessary suffering that are incalculable.

STUDY QUESTIONS

1   Hospers says that the more thoroughly we know the causes of someone's behavior, the more we tend to exempt that person from responsibility. Why is this? Do you think this is true for all kinds of causes—neurotic and nonneurotic?

2   "Darrow argued that Loeb should be excused because he had been conditioned to do whatever he did by his background of wealth and luxury. But there are plenty of wealthy children who do not grow up to be criminals." How would Hospers respond to this criticism?

3   "Perhaps what Hospers says is true about neurotic people, but it is certainly not true about normal people. Most people are rational, they can alter their behavior in the face of discomforting situations. So it makes sense to hold most people responsible for what they do." What would Hospers say to this? Do you agree with him?

4   Does Hospers believe that a person "could have done something other than what he or she did"?

5   What would Hospers reply to someone who claimed that one could have desired differently? Do you agree with him on this point?

6   Hospers says that there are two levels of moral discourse. What are these two levels? Do you think he would maintain that it is possible to be responsible for what you do, even though you are not responsible for what you are?

The Self and Free Will

C. A. Campbell

C. A. Campbell (1897–   ) is professor emeritus at the University of Glasgow. He is perhaps the most outstanding contemporary exponent of libertarianism. At the core of his theory is the belief that the "self" is more than the elaborate system of habits and dispositions which we call a person's "character." The self is something which "has" a character, but is not identical with it. The self has the power to resist the inclinations of its character, to rise above all caused dispositions, and to act "creatively."

Campbell does not believe that the usual varieties of soft-determinism provide any genuine answer to the problem of free will. A condition for moral responsibility is that the agent "could have done otherwise." Soft-determinists interpret this to mean that the agent "could have done otherwise, *if* he had chosen otherwise." But Campbell insists that this is not enough. The real question, he believes, is whether the agent could have "chosen otherwise," in spite of the urgings of character. This ability to "creatively" choose is known to exist by everyone's experience of it.

Campbell denies that free will is inconsistent with prediction or that it leads to capricious choice. On rare occasions, the individual is required to choose between moral duty and the impulses of character. Only then is the situation indeterminate.

I

. . . It is something of a truism that in philosophic enquiry the exact formulation of a problem often takes one a long way on the road to its solution. In the case of the Free Will problem I think there is a rather special need of careful formulation. For there are many sorts of human freedom; and it can easily happen that one wastes a great deal of labour in proving or disproving a freedom which has almost nothing to do with the freedom which is at issue in the traditional problem of Free Will. The abortiveness of so much of the argument for and against Free Will in contemporary philosophical literature seems to me due in the main to insufficient pains being taken over the preliminary definition of the problem. . . .

Fortunately we can at least make a beginning with a certain amount of confidence. It is not seriously disputable that the kind of freedom in question is the freedom which is commonly recognised to be in some sense a precondition of moral responsibility. Clearly, it is on account of this integral connection with moral responsibility that such exceptional importance has always been felt to attach to the Free Will problem. But in what precise sense is free will a precondition of moral responsibility, and thus a postulate of the moral life in general? This is an exceedingly troublesome question; but until we have satisfied ourselves about the answer to it, we are not in a position to state, let alone decide, the question whether "Free Will" in its traditional, ethical, significance is a reality. . . .

The first point to note is that the freedom at issue (as indeed the very name "Free *Will* Problem" indicates) pertains primarily not to overt acts but to inner acts. The nature of things has decreed that, save in the case of one's self it is only overt acts which one can directly observe. But a very little reflection serves to show that in our moral judgments upon others their overt acts are regarded as significant only in so far as they are the expression of inner acts. We do not consider the acts of a robot to be morally responsible acts; nor do we consider the acts of a man to be so save in so far as they are distinguishable from those of a robot by reflecting an inner life of choice. Similarly, from the other side, if we are satisfied (as we may on occasion be, at least in the case of ourselves) that a person has definitely elected to follow a course which he believes to be wrong, but has been prevented by external circumstances from translating his inner choice into an overt act, we still regard him as morally blameworthy. Moral freedom, then, pertains to *inner* acts.

The next point seems at first sight equally obvious and uncontroversial; but, as we shall see, it has awkward implications if we are in real earnest with it (as almost nobody is). It is the simple point that the act must be one of which the person judged can be regarded as the *sole* author. It seems plain enough that if there are any *other* determinants of the act, external to the self, to that extent the act is not an act which the *self* determines, and to that extent not an act for which

From C. A. Campbell, *On Selfhood and Godhood*, George Allen & Unwin Ltd., 1957. Reprinted by permission of the publisher.

the self can be held morally responsible. The self is only part-author of the act, and his moral responsibility can logically extend only to those elements within the act (assuming for the moment that these can be isolated) of which he is the *sole* author. . . .

Thirdly, we come to a point over which much recent controversy has raged. We may approach it by raising the following question. Granted an act of which the agent is sole author, does this "sole authorship" suffice to make the act a morally free act? We may be inclined to think that it does, until we contemplate the possibility that an act of which the agent is sole author might conceivably occur as a necessary expression of the agent's nature; the way in which, e.g. some philosophers have supposed the Divine act of creation to occur. This consideration excites a legitimate doubt; for it is far from easy to see how a person can be regarded as a proper subject for moral praise or blame in respect of an act which he *cannot help* performing—even if it be his own "nature" which necessitates it. Must we not recognise it as a condition of the morally free act that the agent "could have acted otherwise" than he in fact did? It is true, indeed, that we sometimes praise or blame a man for an act about which we are prepared to say, in the light of our knowledge of his established character, that he "could no other." But I think that a little reflection shows that in such cases we are not praising or blaming the man strictly for what he does *now* (or at any rate we ought not to be), but rather for those past acts of his which have generated the firm habit of mind from which his *present* act follows "necessarily." In other words, our praise and blame, so far as justified, are really retrospective, being directed not to the agent *qua* performing *this* act, but to the agent *qua* performing those past acts which have built up his present character, and in respect to which we presume that he *could* have acted otherwise, that there really *were* open possibilities before him. These cases, therefore, seem to me to constitute no valid exception to what I must take to be the rule, viz. that a man can be morally praised or blamed for an act only if he could have acted otherwise.

Now philosophers today are fairly well agreed that it is a postulate of the morally responsible act that the agent "could have acted otherwise" in *some* sense of that phrase. But sharp differences of opinion have arisen over the way in which the phrase ought to be interpreted. There is a strong disposition to water down its apparent meaning by insisting that it is not (as a postulate of moral responsibility) to be understood as a straightforword categorical proposition, but rather as a disguised hypothetical proposition. All that we really require to be assured of, in order to justify our holding X morally responsible for an act, is, we are told, that X could have acted otherwise *if* he had *chosen* otherwise or perhaps that X could have acted otherwise *if* he had had a different character, or *if* he had been placed in different circumstances.

I think it is easy to understand, and even, in a measure, to sympathise with, the motives which induce philosophers to offer these counterinterpretations. It is not just the fact that "X could have acted otherwise," as a bald categorical statement, is incompatible with the universal sway of causal law—though this is, to some philosophers, a serious stone of stumbling. The more wide-spread objection is that at least it looks as though it were incompatible with that causal continuity of an agent's character with his conduct which is implied when we believe (surely with justice) that we can often tell the sort of thing a man will do from our knowledge of the sort of man he is.

We shall have to make our accounts with that particular difficulty later. At this stage I wish merely to show that neither of the hypothetical propositions suggested—and I think the same could be shown for *any* hypothetical alternative—is an acceptable substitute for the categorical proposition "X could have acted otherwise" as the presupposition of moral responsibility.

Let us look first at the earlier suggestion—"X could have acted otherwise *if* he had chosen otherwise." Now clearly there are a great many acts with regard to which we are entirely satisfied that the agent is thus situated. We are often perfectly sure that—for this is all it amounts to—if X had chosen otherwise, the circumstances presented no external obstacle to the translation of that choice into action. For example, we often have no doubt at all that X, who in point of fact told a lie, could have told the truth *if* he had so chosen. But does our confidence on this score allay all legitimate doubts about whether X is really blameworthy? Does it entail that X is free in the sense required for moral responsibility? Surely not. The obvious question immediately arises: "But *could* X have *chosen* otherwise than he did?" It is doubt about the true answer to *that* question which leads most people to doubt the reality of moral responsibility. Yet on this crucial question the hypothetical proposition which is offered as a sufficient statement of the condition justifying the ascription of moral responsibility gives us no information whatsoever.

Indeed this hypothetical substitute for the categorical "X could have acted otherwise" seems to me to lack all plausibility unless one contrives to forget why it is, after all, that we ever come to feel fundamental doubts about man's moral responsibility. Such doubts are born, surely, when one becomes aware of certain reputable world-views in religion or philosophy, or of certain reputable scientific beliefs, which in their several ways imply that man's actions are necessitated, and thus could not be otherwise than they in fact are. But clearly a doubt so based is not even touched by the recognition that a man could very often act otherwise *if* he so chose. That proposition is entirely compatible with the necessitarian theories which generate our doubt: indeed it is this very compatibility that has recommended it to some philosophers, who are reluctant to give up either moral responsibility or Determinism. The proposition which we *must* be able to affirm if moral praise or blame of X is to be justified is the categorical proposition that X could have acted otherwise because—not if—he could have chosen otherwise; or, since it is essentially the inner side of the act that matters, the proposition simply that X could have chosen otherwise.

For the second of the alternative formulae suggested we cannot spare more than a few moments. But its inability to meet the demands it is required to meet is almost transparent. "X could have acted otherwise," as a statement of a precondition of X's moral responsibility, really means (we are told) "X could have acted otherwise *if* he were differently constituted, or *if* he had been placed in different circumstances." It seems a sufficient reply to this to point out that the person whose moral responsibility is at issue is X; a specific individual, in a specific set of circumstances. It is totally irrelevant to X's moral responsibility that we should be able to say that some person differently constituted from X, or X in a different set of circumstances, could have done something different from what X did. . . .

II

That brings me to the second, and more constructive, part of this lecture. From now on I shall be considering whether it is reasonable to believe that man does in fact possess a free will of the kind specified in the first part of the lecture. If so, just how and where within the complex fabric of the volitional life are we to locate it?—for although free will must presumably belong (if anywhere) to the volitional side of human experience, it is pretty clear from the way in which we have been forced to define it that it does not pertain simply to volition as such; not even to all volitions that are commonly dignified with the name of "choices." It has been, I think, one of the more serious impediments to profitable discussion of the Free Will problem that Libertarians and Determinists alike have so often failed to appreciate the comparatively narrow area within which the free will that is necessary to "save" morality is required to operate. It goes without saying that this failure has been gravely prejudicial to the case for Libertarianism. I attach a good deal of importance, therefore, to the problem of locating free will correctly within the volitional orbit. Its solution forestalls and annuls, I believe, some of the more tiresome clichés of Determinist criticism.

We saw earlier that Common Sense's practice of "making allowances" in its moral judgments for the influence of heredity and environment indicates Common Sense's conviction, both that a just moral judgment must discount determinants of choice over which the agent has no control, and also (since it still accepts moral judgments as legitimate) that *something* of moral relevance survives which can be regarded as genuinely self-originated. We are now to try to discover what this "something" is. And I think we may still usefully take Common Sense as our guide. Suppose one asks the ordinary intelligent citizen *why* he deems it proper to make allowances for X, whose heredity and/or environment are unfortunate. He will tend to reply, I think, in some such terms as these: that X has more and stronger temptations to deviate from what is right than Y or Z, who are normally circumstanced, so that he must put forth a *stronger moral effort* if he is to achieve the same level of external conduct. The intended implication seems to be that X is just as morally praiseworthy as Y or Z *if* he exerts an equivalent moral effort, even though he may not thereby achieve an equal success in conforming his will to the "concrete" demands of duty. And this implies, again, Common Sense's belief that *in moral effort* we have something for which a man is responsible *without qualification,* something that is *not* affected by heredity and environment but depends *solely* upon the self itself.

Now in my opinion Common Sense has here, in principle, hit upon the one and only defensible answer. Here, and here alone, so far as I can see, in the act of deciding whether to put forth or withhold the moral effort required to resist temptation and rise to duty, is to be found an act which is free in the sense required for moral responsibility; an act of which the self is sole author, and of which it is true to say that "it could be" (or, after the event, "could have been") "otherwise." Such is the thesis which we shall now try to establish.

The species of argument appropriate to the establishment of a thesis of this sort should fall, I think, into two phases. First, there should be a consideration of the evidence of the moral agent's own inner experience. What *is* the act of moral decision, and what does it imply, from the standpoint of the actual participant? Since there is no way of knowing the act of moral decision—or for that matter any other form of activity—except by actual participation in it, the evidence of the subject, or agent, is on an issue of this kind of palmary importance. It can hardly, however, be taken as in itself conclusive. For even if that evidence should be overwhelmingly to the effect that moral decision does have the characteristics required by moral freedom, the question is bound to be raised—and in view of considerations from other quarters pointing in a contrary direction is *rightly* raised—Can we *trust* the evidence of inner experience? That brings us to what will be the second phase of the argument. We shall have to go on to show, if we are to make good our case, that the extraneous considerations so often supposed to be fatal to the belief in moral freedom are in fact innocuous to it. . . .

These arguments can, I think, be reduced in principle to no more than two: first, the argument from "predictability"; second, the argument from the alleged meaninglessness of an act supposed to be the self's act and yet not an expression of the self's character. Contemporary criticism of free will seems to me to consist almost exclusively of variations on these two themes. I shall deal with each in turn.

Let us remind ourselves briefly of the setting within which, on our view, free will functions. There is X, the course which we believe we ought to follow, and Y, the course towards which we feel our desire is strongest. The freedom which we ascribe to the agent is the freedom to put forth or refrain from putting forth the moral effort required to resist the pressure of desire and do what he thinks he ought to do.

But then there is surely an immense range of practical situations—covering by far the greater part of life—in which there is no question of a conflict within the self between what he most desires to do and what he thinks he ought to do. Indeed such conflict is a comparatively rare phenomenon for the majority of men. Yet over that whole vast range there is nothing whatever in our version of Libertarianism to prevent our agreeing that character determines conduct. In the absence, real or supposed, of any "moral" issue, what a man chooses will be simply that course which, after such reflection as seems called for, he deems most likely to bring him what he most strongly desires; and that is the same as to say the course to which his present character inclines him.

Over by far the greater area of human choices, then, our theory offers no more barrier to successful prediction on the basis of character than any other theory. For where there is no clash of strongest desire with duty, the free will we are defending has no business. There is just nothing for it to do.

But what about the situations—rare enough though they may be—in which there *is* this clash and in which free will does therefore operate? Does our theory entail that there at any rate, as the critic seems to suppose, "anything may happen"?

Not by any manner of means. In the first place, and by the very nature of the case, the range of the agent's possible choices is bounded by what he thinks he ought to do on the one hand, and what he most strongly desires on the other. The freedom claimed for him is a freedom of decision to make or withhold the effort required to do what he thinks he ought to do. There is no question of a freedom to act in some "wild" fashion, out of all relation to his characteristic beliefs and desires. This so-called "freedom of caprice," so often charged against the Libertarian, is, to put it bluntly, a sheer figment of the critic's imagination, with no *habitat* in serious Libertarian theory. Even in situations where free will does come into play it is perfectly possible, on a view like ours, given the appropriate knowledge of a man's character, to predict within certain limits how he will respond.

I claim, therefore, that the view of free will I have been putting forward is consistent with predictability of conduct on the basis of character over a very wide field indeed. And I make the further claim that that field will cover all the situations in life concerning which there is any empirical evidence that successful prediction is possible.

Let us pass on to consider the second main line of criticism. This is, I think, much the more illuminating of the two, if only because it compels the Libertarian to make explicit certain concepts which are indispensable to him, but which, being desperately hard to state clearly, are apt not to be stated at all. The critic's fundamental point might be stated somewhat as follows:

"Free will as you describe it is completely unintelligible. On your own showing no *reason* can be given, because there just *is* no reason, why a man decides to exert rather than to withhold moral effort, or *vice versa*. But such an act—or more properly, such an 'occurrence'—it is nonsense to speak of as an act of a *self*. If there is nothing in the self's character to which it is, even in principle, in any way traceable, the self has nothing to do with it. Your so-called 'freedom,' therefore, so far from supporting the self's moral responsibility, destroys it as surely as the crudest Determinism could do."

If we are to discuss this criticism usefully, it is important, I think, to begin by getting clear about two different senses of the word "intelligible."

If, in the first place, we mean by an "intelligible" act one whose occurrence is in principle capable of being inferred, since it follows necessarily from something (though we may not know in fact from what), then it is certainly true that the Libertarian's free will is unintelligible. But that is only saying, is it not, that the Libertarian's "free" act is not an act which follows necessarily from something! This can hardly rank as a *criticism* of Libertarianism. It is just a description of it. That there can be nothing unintelligible in *this* sense is precisely what the Determinist has got to *prove*.

Yet it is surprising how often the critic of Libertarianism involves himself in this circular mode of argument. Repeatedly it is urged against the Libertarian, with a great air of triumph, that on this view he can't say *why* I now decide to rise to duty, or now decide to follow my strongest desire in defiance of duty. Of course he can't. If he could he wouldn't *be* a Libertarian. To "account for" a "free" act is a contradiction in terms. A free will is *ex hypothesi* the sort of thing of which the request for an *explanation* is absurd. The assumption that an explanation must be in principle possible for the act of moral decision deserves to rank as a classic example of the ancient fallacy of "begging the question."

But the critic usually has in mind another sense of the word "unintelligible." He is apt to take it for granted that an act which is unintelligible in the *above* sense (as the morally free act of the Libertarian undoubtedly is) is unintelligible in the *further* sense that we can attach no meaning to it. And this is an altogether more serious matter. If it could really be shown that the Libertarian's "free will" were unintelligible in this sense of being meaningless, that, for myself at any rate, would be the end of the affair. Libertarianism would have been conclusively refuted.

But it seems to me manifest that this can *not* be shown. The critic has allowed himself, I submit, to become the victim of a widely accepted but fundamentally vicious assumption. He has assumed that whatever is meaningful must exhibit its meaningfulness to those who view it from the standpoint of external observation. Now if one chooses thus to limit one's self to the rôle of external observer, it is, I think, perfectly true that one can attach no meaning to an act which is the act of something we call a "self" and yet follows from nothing in that self's character. But then *why should we* so limit ourselves, when what is under consideration is a subjective activity? For the apprehension of subjective acts there is *another* standpoint available, that of *inner experience,* of the practical consciousness in its actual functioning. If our free will should turn out to be something to which we can attach a meaning from *this* standpoint, no more is required. And no more ought to be expected. For I must repeat that only from the inner standpoint of living experience *could* anything of the nature of "activity" be directly grasped. Observation from without is in the nature of the case impotent to apprehend the active *qua* active. We can from without observe sequences of states. If into these we read activity (as we sometimes do), this can only be on the basis of what we discern in ourselves from the inner standpoint. It follows that if anyone insists upon taking his criterion of the meaningful simply from the standpoint of external observation, he is really deciding in advance of the evidence that the notion of activity, and *a fortiori* the notion of a free will, is "meaningless." He looks for the free act through a medium which is in the nature of the case incapable of revealing it, and then, because inevitably he doesn't find it, he declares that it doesn't exist!

But if, as we surely ought in this context, we adopt the inner standpoint, then (I am suggesting) things appear in a totally different light. From the inner standpoint, it seems to me plain, there is no difficulty whatever in attaching meaning to an act which is the self's act and which nevertheless does not follow from the self's character. So much I claim has been established by the phenomenological analysis, in this and the previous lecture, of the act of moral decision in face of moral temptation. It is thrown into particularly clear relief where the moral decision is to make the moral effort required to rise to duty. For the very function of moral effort, as it appears to the agent engaged in the act, is to enable the self to act against the line of least resistance, against the line to which his character as so far formed most strongly inclines him. But if the self is thus conscious here of *combating* his formed character, he surely cannot possibly suppose that the act, although his own act, *issues from* his formed character? I submit, therefore, that the self knows very well indeed—from the inner standpoint—what is meant by an act which is the *self's* act and which nevertheless does not follow from the self's *character*.

What this implies—and it seems to me to be an implication of cardinal importance for any theory of the self that aims at being more than superficial—is that the nature of the self is for itself something more than just its character as so far formed. The "nature" of the self and what we commonly call the "character" of the self are by no means the same thing, and it is utterly vital that they should not be confused. The "nature" of the self comprehends, but is not without remainder reducible to, its "character"; it must, if we are to be true to the testimony of our experience of it, be taken as including *also* the authentic creative power of fashioning and re-fashioning "character."

STUDY QUESTIONS

1   Campbell says that a condition of moral responsibility is that the agent be the sole author of the act in question. There is, however, a further condition for moral responsibility. What is it?
2   What is the hypothetical interpretation of the expression, "X could have done otherwise"? Why does Campbell believe that the various hypothetical interpretations are inadequate for moral responsibility?
3   Campbell admits that it is proper to make allowances for those individuals whose environment has been unfortunate. But he says this does not mean that such persons do not have a free will. Why is this? Do you agree?
4   In B. F. Skinner's novel *Walden II,* individuals are conditioned by behavioral engineering to become "perfect" citizens in a utopian community. At one point, the mastermind of the project, a psychologist by the name of Frazier, makes the following observation about free will: "I deny that freedom exists at all. I must deny it—or my program would be absurd. You cannot have a science about a subject matter which hops capriciously about." How would Campbell respond to this comment? Do you think his answer is sufficient?
5   Why does Campbell believe that the "inner standpoint" is the preferred standpoint in the matter of free will? What can be seen in inner experience which cannot be appreciated from an external position? Do you agree with this view?

Moral Freedom in a Determined World

Sidney Hook

Sidney Hook (1902–   ) is one of America's most outstanding political philosophers. He is professor of philosophy at New York University and the author of many books on social and political philosophy, including *Reason, Social Myths, and Democracy* (1940) and *The Paradoxes of Freedom* (1967). In the following essay, Hook does a masterful job of rallying the best criticisms of both indeterminism and hard-determinism.

Indeterminism, he argues, is unintelligible. To the extent that indeterminists wish to locate human freedom in the ability to reflect and reason, such ability is consistent with determinism. Hard-determinism, on the other hand, is an inconsistent doctrine that has morally undesirable consequences. It is a doctrine which leads to personal inertia and prevents the full exercise of human powers. Indeed, the belief that we are responsible, and that others will hold us responsible, serves as a cause for new effort and new direction in our actions. The justification for blame in a determined world is the fact that it is a cause for behavior which would not have occurred without it.

In the last year of the Weimar Republic, when ordinary criminals were sometimes more philosophical than the judges of Hitler's Third Reich subsequently proved to be, a strange case was tried before the tribunal of Hanover. The evidence showed that one Waldemar Debbler had been guilty of burglary, and the prosecutor proposed two years of penal servitude. Whereupon the prisoner rose and said:

"Gentlemen, you see in me the victim of an unwavering destiny. So-called freedom of decision does not exist. Every human action in this world is determined. The causes are given by the circumstances and the results inevitable. By my inclinations of character, for which I am not responsible, since they were born in me, by my upbringing, my experiences, I was predetermined to become what I am. If you, gentlemen, had a heredity similar to mine and had been subjected to the same influence as I, you would also have committed the burglary in this particular situation. With this theory I am in good company. I refer you to Spinoza and Leibnitz. Even St. Augustine and, later, Calvin attributed all human actions to the immutable decree of destiny. As I have only done what I had to do, you have no moral right to punish me, and I therefore plead for my acquittal."

To which peroration the court answered:

"We have followed the prisoner's reasoning with attention. Whatever happens is the necessary and immutable sequel of preceding causes which, once given, could not be other than it is. Consequently the prisoner, by reason of his character and experience, was destined to commit the burglary. On the other hand, destiny also decrees that the court, as a result of the submitted testimony, must judge the prisoner guilty of burglary. The causes—the deed, the law, the nature of the judge—being given, the sentence of guilty and punishment follows as a natural consequence."

When asked whether he accepted the sentence, the prisoner declared: "Destiny demands that I appeal." To which the judge replied: "That may be. However, destiny will see to it that your appeal is rejected."

This story, for whose authenticity with respect to exact detail I will not vouch, confuses the concept of determinism with that of fatalism. It confuses an event whose occurrence depends upon, or is caused by, what the individual in this particular situation desires and does, with an event whose occurrence does not depend upon any event antecedent to it, and which would occur no matter what the antecedent event was. It confuses conditional necessity with unconditional necessity, what is *predetermined* with what is predictable with reference to certain laws and initial data. It further fails to distinguish clearly between the concept of punishment and the concept of moral responsibility. Nonetheless, in its appeal to a double standard of judgment it illustrates a defect which appears in the writings of more sophisticated philosophers who have returned to the theme of determinism and moral responsibility in recent years.

Those philosophers who have thought that progress in philosophy consists in part in showing that the traditional problems of philosophy are either pseudo-problems, or a confusing mixture of psychology, logic, and sociology, have been rudely awakened from their complacency by a revival of interest in the question of free will, determinism, and responsibility. It had been widely assumed that the whole problem of whether the *will* is free had been replaced, in consequence of the writings of Hobbes, Locke, Hume, Mill, and the modern naturalists and positivists, by the problem of the *conditions* under which men's actions are free. The general solution had been that *men* are free when their actions are determined by their own will, and not by the will of others, or by factors which lead us to say that their actions were involuntary. To the extent that conditions exist which prevent a man from acting as he wishes (*e.g.*, ignorance, physical incapacity, constraint used upon his body and mind) he is unfree. This view accepts the postulate of determinism as valid, regardless of whether a man's action is free or coerced—in one case his action is determined by his own volition, in the other not. The fact that my volition, say, to undergo an operation, is caused by a complex of factors, among which the existence of sickness or disease, or the belief in the existence of sickness or disease, is normally a necessary condition, does not make my action less free. After all, it would be absurd to suggest that my action in undergoing an operation would be free only if there were no cause or reason to undergo it. If one insisted on undergoing an operation when one knew there was no cause for the operation, one would normally be regarded as insane. That there would be a cause for the decision, for the insistence on the unnecessary operation, would not affect our judgment of it. On this view, the distinction between free and unfree acts, sane or insane acts, lies in the specific character of the causes at work, not in the presence or absence of causes.

What has been until recently considered a commonplace is now in several quarters described and repudiated as a wild paradox. That an action can be characterized as both "determined" and "free," or "determined" and "responsible," is denied from two different points of view. The first view accepts determinism, indeed insists on it, because of the findings of modern medicine and psychotherapy, and then argues the invalidity of judgments of responsibility in any and every case. The second accepts the validity of the principle of responsibility, but denies the validity of the postulate of determinism or of its universal applicability.

Those who believe that one cannot legitimately square the doctrine of determinism with the acceptance of responsibility argue generally as follows: an individual is neither responsible nor blamable for his actions unless he could have acted differently from the way he did. Given the sum total of conditions which preceded his action, the latter is in principle always predictable or determined, and therefore unavoidable. But if an action is unavoidable, then no one can be held morally responsible for it.

The usual retort to this is to point out that an act is determined, among other things, by a wish or desire or volition for which we shall use the generic term "choice." Consequently it is sometimes true to say that if an individual had chosen differently, he would have acted differently. To which the rejoinder comes that this is merely an evasion. If every event is in principle predictable and therefore determined, then the choice itself, given all the antecedent conditions, is unavoidable. An individual cannot be held morally responsible for his choice if it could not have been other than it was. And even if it were true that his choice now was a consequence of an earlier choice, which *if* it had been different *would* have led to different present choice and action, that earlier choice *could not* have been different, given its antecedent conditions, and so on for any other choice in the series. And since the choice could not have been different, we cannot blame the person choosing since he is not morally responsible. He is "a victim of circumstances."

There is a certain ambiguity in the writings of those who, accepting the principle of determinism, criticize the attribution of moral responsibility to individuals or the judgment of blameworthiness on their actions. Sometimes their criticism has an air of high moral concern. They imply that under certain circumstances, which they often spell out in advance, individuals are being improperly considered responsible. They inveigh against the injustice of improperly blaming those who, because their desires and choices are determined, are the victims not the agents of misfortune. This plea is sometimes forensically very effective, as the legal career of Clarence Darrow shows. Defending the accused in the Leopold-Loeb murder case, which is now enjoying a revival in popular concern, he said in his closing address to the jury, after quoting Housman's poem, the soliloquy of a boy about to be hanged, "I do not know what it was that made these boys do this mad act, but I know there is a reason for it. I know they did not beget themselves. I know that any one of an infinite number of causes reaching back to the beginning might be working out in these boys' minds, whom you are asked to hang in malice and in hatred and injustice, because someone in the past has sinned against them."

One does not, of course, look for precision in an *ex parte* plea. To a determinist, what difference does it make whether human beings are begotten by others, whether they reproduce by fission or by spontaneous generation in test tubes? In any case the process is determined. Of course we did not choose to be born. But suppose we did choose to be born: would that make us more responsible? The choice to be born would not be any less determined. And if the argument is that in a determined world, where our choices are bound to be what they are, it is unfair to blame anybody for any action to which that choice leads, how would we be better off, *i.e.,* more responsible, if we chose to be born? And if it is unjust to tax anyone with sinning who is not responsible for his being born, is it any more legitimate to speak of his being sinned against? If children cannot sin against parents, neither can parents sin against children.

Darrow's inconsistencies are less surprising than the fact that some sophisticated philosophers have adopted pretty much the same position. They fortify it with complex and subtle elaborations of the findings of psychoanalysis as these bear upon the motives and compulsive behavior of men. Yet the logic of their argument makes all the evidence of psychoanalysis irrelevant to the question of blame and responsibility. For if every psychoanalytical theory were discarded as false, the life of mind would still be determined if one accepts the postulate of universal determinism. The piling up of the data which exhibit the specific mechanism of determination adds only a rhetorical force to the position. Further, it is one thing to imply that the concept of moral responsibility is empty, that although in fact no individuals are morally responsible, there are conditions or circumstances under which they could be legitimately held responsible; it is quite another thing to hold that the concept of moral responsibility is completely *vacuous,* that no matter what the specific conditions are under which men choose to act, it would still be inappropriate to hold them morally responsible or blame them. And it is this view *i.e.,* that moral responsibility is a vacuous or unintelligible expression, which seems to me to be entailed by those who urge Darrow's position, for they never seem able to indicate the rule or condition for its proper use. If one cannot indicate any possible situation on a deterministic view under which actions can be blamed, the term "blame" is cognitively meaningless.

Nonetheless, the paradox of the position is that those who hold it, blame us for blaming others. Just as the burgler in our story makes an appeal whose sense depends upon there being alternatives, that is upon the possibility of making or not making that specific appeal, so some philosophers find us blameworthy for not acting on the recognition that in a determined world in which no one chooses to be born, no one can be held at fault. . . .

The great difficulty with the indeterminist view in most forms is the suggestion it carries that choices and actions, if not determined, are capricious. Caprice and responsibility are more difficult to reconcile than determinism and responsibility, for it seems easier to repudiate a choice or action which does not follow from one's character, or history, or nature, or self, than an act which does follow. Consequently, the more thoughtful indeterminists are those who do not deny the operation of determining forces or tendencies altogether, but insist upon a certain kind of determination which manifests itself in addition to, or over and above, the factors extrinsic to the particular situation in which the choosing individual finds himself. For example, they believe that the free action is not the habitual action, not the coerced action, not the instinctive or impulsive action, but the action which is determined by reflection. And as we shall see, there is a sense in which ordinarily we do characterize an action as responsible, depending upon whether it was intended, and if intended, upon the character and extent of the reflection which preceded it. But so long as "reasons" are not disembodied entities but express reflective choices of men in nature, there is nothing here at which a determinist need boggle. On the contrary, he may define the locus of moral freedom and responsibility in the capacity of the human creature, using his insight and foresight to modify his preferences and control his inclinations whenever they conflict or lead to "actions involving others."

Not only indeterminists who recognize moral responsibility, but some determinists who regard it as an empty concept, write as if a person would be responsible if he could "ultimately and completely shape or choose his own character." Surely the notion of ultimately and completely shaping or choosing one's own character is more difficult to grasp than any it would illumine. Since every decision to shape or choose one's character, to be responsibly attributed to oneself, must be one's own, and therefore is already an indication of the kind of person one is, the notion that one can ultimately and completely shape or choose one's character seems to be unintelligible. C. A. Campbell distinguishes between a choice which is the expression of a formed character, and therefore determined, and a choice of a self. But aside from the difficulty of separating self from character, it is hard to understand why we should be more willing to accept responsibility or blame for the decision of a raw or pure self that has no history, than to accept responsibility or blame for the choices of our formed characters.

We return now to consider some of the difficulties which the determinist faces who attributes blame or responsibility to himself or others. If all actions are in principle predictable or unavoidable, how can he blame the actor? If every judgment of "ought" or "should" implies a "can" or "could," and if of every act we can say (once given its antecedent conditions) that it cannot or could not have been avoided, why blame, why praise, why, indeed, in a determined universe, pass any moral judgment whatsoever, whether it be on a petty sneak-thief or on a Hitler or Stalin?

I shall try to show that the difficulty lies uniquely in the use of the concept of blame, not of praise, and not of moral judgment *per se.* The difficulty in the concept of blame is that ordinary usage is itself confusing, that the confusion requires a reconstruction of our use in such a way as to bring out more consistently and systematically the pragmatic character of judgments of blame. I do not believe that if we guide ourselves by ordinary usage we can make ends meet, because in this instance ordinary usage is vague and inconsistent.

First of all, although it may be difficult to square the belief that all choices are determined with judgments of blame and responsibility, I do not see that there is any difficulty in squaring the belief that all choices are determined with the moral judgment that these choices, and the actions to which they lead, are good or bad. Pain is evil, and an intentional action which imposes unnecessary pain, or a desire to impose unnecessary pain, is wicked. After all, we blame persons only for those acts of omission or commission which we condemn. If such actions were not initially or antecedently judged good or bad, we could not blame anybody for failing to do the one, or failing to prevent the other. No matter whether an action is determined or undetermined, accidental or intention-al, I can still pronounce it good or bad. We may not blame the child whose actions cause the house to burn, or the maniac who kills those who minister to his wants; but we can and do deplore and condemn these actions as bad. And I believe that this is legitimate from the standpoint of any analysis of the meaning of "good" or "bad" which philosophers have offered, except the Kantian analy-sis. So, too, although there are difficulties about feelings of "remorse" similar to those about judgments of blame, I can only feel remorse about something I regret, and the qualities of the action I regret are what they are, independently of whether the action is determined or not.

It is sometimes said that if it is unwarranted to pass judgments of blame on actions that are predictable or unavoidable, it is also unwarranted to pass judg-ments of praise. I am not so sure of this, because of the broader semantic range of judgments of praise. When we praise a person for his or her beauty, talent, intelligence, charm, personality, warmth, etc., etc., we do not have in mind at all whether or not the person could help being or doing that which evokes our praise. Formally, we can always praise a person for not committing an act that we would blame, and in this sense the logic of the judgments is symmetrical. But aside from such cases, and some others in which praise seems to be justified because an individual might have acted differently, e.g., in which he fights against odds instead of running away, there is an indefinitely large number of situations in which we unembarrassedly praise, regardless of whether the person can help being as he is or acting as he does. And when judgments of praise do not have this character, they may plausibly be regarded as having the social function of inducing individuals to do what we regard as desirable and to forgo doing the undesirable. But if it is possible to carry out such an analysis without difficulty for judgments of praise, is it possible to do so for judgments of blame and attribu-tions of moral responsibility?

The facts of responsibility must be distinguished from their justification. By facts of responsibility I mean that in every society there are social relations or institutional arrangements which are regarded as binding on human behavior, for violations of which human beings are called to account. When individuals are called to account, this involves the possibility that sanctions may be applied. These facts of responsibility are an anthropological datum—varied and multi-form. In some cultures children are held responsible for their parents; in others, parents for children. Leaving aside questions of legal responsibility, or rather legal liability, which are often only matters of social convenience and rules of the road, the justification of responsibility is a moral question. Should a child be held personally responsible for the sins of its father, not only for the Biblical three generations, but even for one? Should a parent ever be held responsible for the misdeeds of his children? Now those who hold that determinism is incompatible with reasoned judgments of blame presumably do not mean to deny the existence of the facts of responsibility. They simply contest the justification of the facts— not the justification of any specific fact of responsibility, but the possibility of any justification whatsoever on the determinist view. If this were true, then, since social life is impossible without recognition of some kind of responsibility in behavior, the whole basis of social life would appear utterly unintelligible, or if justified, only by some extrinsic consideration that had no moral relevance. But, as our illustration shows, there are obviously good reasons why in general we regard it as more justifiable to blame parents up to a point for the misdeeds of their children than to blame children for the misdeeds of their parents. First, we know there is some causal connection between the training or absence of training which parents give their children and the children's behavior outside the home, a causal connection which is not reversible; second, and more important, we blame parents for their children rather than children for their parents, primarily because in this way we can get more desirable conduct on the part of both parents and children. We influence the future by our judgments of blame and, to the extent that they are not merely judgments of spontaneous admiration or excellence, by our judgments of praise as well.

There are some obvious difficulties with this interpretation of judgments of blame. For example, as C. A. Campbell observes, we can influence the future behavior of infants and animals by punishment, but we certainly do not blame them when we are reflective. On the other hand, we do not seem to be able to influence the future behavior of the hardened criminal, but we certainly do blame him. Further, how explain remorse, as distinct from regret, for actions committed long ago?

Because the behavior of children and animals is modifiable by appropriate reward and deprivation, we punish them, even though we may hesitate to use the term to identify what we do. We do not "blame" them, however, even when we find it necessary to punish, because blame is directed to volitions, or, if we do not believe in volitions, to intentions. If children's actions reveal intentions or if we suspect, as we sometimes do, that animals have intentions, we count upon the sting of our blame to prod them to different behavior. Otherwise there is no point in blaming. But, it is objected, this only tells us whether our blame is effective rather than deserved. The blame is "deserved" if the action we wish to correct is bad, and the worse the action the more deserved—provided the blame has point in the first place. When we distribute blame—as when we say "I blame you more than I do him"—it is because we believe that the intentions (or volitions) of the one had a greater role in the commission of the act, or could have a greater role in preventing similar actions in the future, than the intention of the other. We must be able to answer the question: what is the use of blaming any individual? before we can properly distribute blame among individuals. I can see no earthly use of blaming an individual save directly or indirectly to prevent the undesirable act from being repeated in the future. This is the justification for blame in a determined world.

Another element enters into the picture. The more rational an individual is, the more susceptible he is to understanding and giving reasons, the more blame-worthy we hold him—not because the intelligent man's choice is less determined than that of the stupid man's but because the choice, which is determined among other things by insight into reasons, is generally more informed, more persistent, and more decisive in redetermining the stream of events. We blame children more as they approach the age of rationality, not because they come into possession of a soul, not because they become more subject to causal laws, but because the growth of intelligence enhances the subtlety, range, and effectiveness of their choice. And if animals could think or respond to reasons, we would blame them, too, because we could build up within them a sense of blame, shame, and responsibility. A sense of blame, shame, and responsibility has a sound therapeutic use in the moral education of men.

Why, then, do we blame the hardened criminal for his actions, when the continued life of crime makes blame and punishment almost as inefficacious in his case—so it is said—as in the case of an alcoholic, a dope addict, or a kleptomaniac? I believe here that most people in blaming a hardened offender are blaming him for the entire series of his actions and not only for his latest action; what revolts them is the cumulative series of evil things done; and they make the mistake of running these evils together, as if it were one great evil which one great blame or punishment might effectively forestall in the future, if not for the offender in question then for others. If, however, one were to isolate the latest dereliction of the hardened offender, and show that no blame or punishment one can devise is more likely to modify his conduct than blame or punishment can prevent an alcoholic addict from drinking or a kleptomaniac from stealing or a pyromaniac from arson, then I believe blame of the hardened criminal would be pointless. We would tend to regard him as criminally insane, confine him without blaming him.

It is sometimes said that we can legitimately blame only when the person blamed has failed to do his duty or live up to an obligation, and that wherever a person has a duty, wherever we say he "ought" to do something, then he in fact "could have" done so. As I have already indicated, I am not at all sure that our actual usage of terms like "blame," "duty," or "ought" in life and law bears this out. In some contexts "ought" clearly does not entail or even imply "can." "A, the contestant in a quiz, ought to have answered x instead of y to question z" is perfectly intelligible and leaves completely open the question whether he could or could not answer question z, or even see question z. Even in strictly moral situations, when I say "Since he was on guard duty, he ought not to have fallen asleep," I am not sure that I am implying necessarily that this particular soldier could have stayed awake, although I am undoubtedly referring to the general capacities of soldiers. But it is undoubtedly true that the evidence that this particular soldier had not slept for seventy-two hours and was assigned to guard duty by mistake, or that he suffered from sleeping sickness, leads to the judgment that he is not as blameworthy as a sentry who had had normal sleep and enjoyed perfect health. That the actions of both sentries, given the antecedent conditions, were determined or predictable, although in one case it was easier than in the other, seems irrelevant. Yet in one case we say that the sentry could not help falling asleep, and in the second we say he could help it. This produces the appearance of paradox. But if one is challenged to explain the judgment, he would probably say that no matter how hard the first sentry tried, it would not have helped him stay awake, whereas if the second sentry had tried, thoroughly rested and thoroughly healthy as he was, he could have remained awake. The distinction between what one can and what one cannot help doing is perfectly intelligible to a determinist, even though in concrete situations it may be difficult to determine which is which. Normally we do not go beyond that distinction. To the question: could he help trying? we normally reply in the affirmative, and expect the burden of proof to rest upon the person who claims that the second sentry could not help not trying because say (a) either he had been doped or (b) hypnotized. In both cases we are prepared to make allowances or excuses for anything which seems to be an external constraint upon choice or volition. But merely because an action is caused, it is not therefore excused.

Our ordinary common-sense judgments are here rather faltering, because the criteria of what is an external constraint as distinct from an internal constraint, and the distinction between an internal constraint which has originally been set up by an outside agency and one which develops naturally within the system, are vague. The progress of science affects our moral judgment of wrongdoers by uncovering the *specific* factors which tend to make the *wrongdoing* uncontrollable by the volition or decision of the agent involved. If one believes that alcoholism is a disease which operates independently of what one wishes or of how one tries, one will judge differently from the way one will if alcoholism is regarded merely as a bad habit. In law as in common sense, the individual is expected to take responsibility for what is self-determined, for one's character or the kind of person one is, even though no one is completely self-determined. If A develops a fateful passion for B, given A's character, then although there may seem to be a tragic inevitability about the course of the affair, we normally do not expect A to duck responsibility by claiming that he could not help being born, or could not help having the character he has. However, if A, as in Tristan and Isolde, is the victim of a love potion administered by others, we are likely to feel and judge quite differently; for in that case it is not A's choice, but someone else's choice, which coerces his own. The cause was of a compelling kind. I venture to suggest that in all these cases the difference in our response does not depend upon our belief that in one class of situations the individuals are free to choose and in another they are not, but on the belief that, where responsibility and blame are appropriate, the uncompelled choice had some determining influence on the action, and that *our* judgments of responsibility and blame will have some influence upon the future choice of actions of the person judged, as well as on the actions of all other persons contemplating similar measures.

One of the obvious absurdities of the view that judgments of blame and responsibility cannot be squared with an acceptance of thoroughgoing determinism is that it wipes out or ignores the relevance of distinctions between the sane and insane, and undercuts the basis of rational legal and moral judgment with respect to intentional and unintentional actions. It suggests that the difference between the criminal and non-criminal is *merely* a matter of accidental power, that the difference between the sane and insane, the responsible and irresponsible, is only a question of majority and minority. It even goes so far as to call all moral terms into dispute. In the words of Clarence Darrow, "I do not believe that there is any sort of distinction between the moral condition in and out of jail.

One is just as good as the other. The people here [in jail] can no more help being here than the people outside can avoid being outside. I do not believe that people are in jail because they deserve to be. They are in jail simply because they cannot avoid it, on account of circumstances which are entirely beyond their control and for which they are in no way responsible." To analyze this seems as cruel as dissecting a butterfly, except that its contradictions and sentimentalities have been incorporated in the attitudes of many social workers. But all we need ask is what sense the word "deserve" has on Darrow's view. If no action can *possibly* merit deserved punishment, on what ground can any punishment be justifiably considered "undeserved"? Once more we ask: if the people in jail can no more help being there than the people outside of jail can help being outside, how can those outside help jailing those on the inside? And, if they can't help it, why condemn them?

The belief that because men are determined they cannot be morally responsible is a mistaken one. Not only is it a mistaken belief, it is a mischievous one. For far from diminishing the amount of needless suffering and cruelty in the world, it is quite certain to increase it. It justifies the infamous dictum of Smerdyakov in *The Brothers Karamazov:* "All things are permissible," if only one can get away with them. One of the commonest experiences of teachers, if not parents, is to observe young men and women whose belief that they can't help doing what they are doing, or failing to do, is often an excuse for not doing as well as they can do, or at the very least better than they are at present doing. When we have, as we often do, independent evidence that they are capable of doing better, is it so absurd to hold them at least partly responsible for not doing better? Do we not know from our own experience that our belief that we are responsible, or that we will be held responsible, enables us to do things which had previously seemed beyond our power?

What often passes as irremediable evil in the world, or the inevitable ills and suffering to which the flesh is heir, is a consequence of our failure to act in time. We are responsible, whether we admit it or not, for what it is in our power to do; and most of the time we can't be sure what is in our power to do until we attempt it. If only we are free to try, we don't have to claim also to be free to try to try, or look for an ultimate footing in some prime metaphysical indeterminate to commit ourselves responsibly. Proximate freedom is enough. And although what we are now is determined by what we were, what we will be is still determined also by what we do now. Human effort can within limits re-determine the direction of events even though it cannot determine the conditions which make human effort possible. It is time enough to reconcile oneself to what is unalterable, or to disaster, after we have done our best to overcome them.

STUDY QUESTIONS

1   "You can't blame me for what I've done. I didn't choose to be born. I didn't choose my parents. I didn't choose my environment." Why does Hook think that such an argument is inconsistent?

2   What does Hook identify as the greatest difficulty in the indeterminist position? What does he mean by a "thoughtful indeterminist"? Would Campbell qualify?

3   What is the justification for blame in a determined world, according to Hook? Why do we treat some people as more blameworthy than others?

4   Suppose it were possible to correct the behavior of criminals by giving them a certain sort of pill, depending upon the crime. Murderers, for example, would be given antimurder pills, rapists would be given antirape pills, etc. Imagine, then, that every convicted criminal is made to take the appropriate pill. Would you want to punish them also? Would they still "deserve" to be punished? What would Hook say?

5   Hospers argues that the more that is known about the causes of someone's behavior, the more we tend to excuse that person from responsibility. To what extent would Hook agree?

6   Hook says that Darrow's kind of hard-determinism is mischievous. Why does he think so? Do you?

Freedom and Intelligence

John Dewey

The immense influence of John Dewey (1859–1952) on American thought is only beginning to be understood. Around the turn of the century, while he was chairman of the Department of Philosophy, Psychology, and Education at the University of Chicago, Dewey organized his famous laboratory school. This was a school for young children where Dewey and his colleagues tested their theories of education. Most education at this time was essentially rigid and unimaginative memory work. The child was trained to passively accept facts which meant little for experience. Dewey, on the other hand, believed that children are naturally active and curious. Education should provide a properly structured environment in which the creative impulses of the child are infused with intelligent habits. This was the birth of progressive education.

  In this essay, Dewey is concerned with the nature of freedom. Freedom, he believes, is a capacity to respond flexibly and intelligently to a changing and sometimes hostile environment. Complete freedom is not a natural condition of humanity. It is a capacity which must develop and grow, and it can grow properly only under certain social conditions. Like other soft-determinists, Dewey does not identify freedom with "chance." Indeed, Dewey is careful to point out that a knowledge of the causes of action is essential for controlling our actions. To know the cause of things is to know how to change them. This applies in science as well as in our own development.

. . . There is an inexpugnable feeling that choice *is* freedom and that man without choice is a puppet, and that man then has no acts which he can call his very own. Without genuine choice, choice that when expressed in action makes things different from what they otherwise would be, men are but passive vehicles through which external forces operate. This feeling is neither self-explanatory nor self-justificatory. But at least it contributes an element in the statement of the problem of freedom. Choice is one of the things that demands examination.

The theoretical formulation for the justification of choice as the heart of freedom became, however, involved at an early time with other interests; and they, rather than the unprejudiced examination of the fact of choice, determined the form taken by a widely prevalent philosophy of freedom. Men are given to praise and blame; to reward and punishment. As civilization matured, definite civil agencies were instituted for "trying" men for modes of conduct so that if found guilty they might be punished. The fact of praise and blame, of civil punishment, directed at men on account of their behavior, signifies that they are held liable or are deemed responsible. The fact of punishment called attention, as men became more inquiring, to the ground of liability. Unless men were responsible for their acts, it was unjust to punish them; if they could not help doing what they did, what was the justice in holding them responsible for their acts, and blaming and punishing them? Thus a certain philosophy of the nature of choice as freedom developed as an apologia for an essentially legal interest: liability to punishment. The outcome was the doctrine known as freedom of will: the notion that a power called will lies back of choice as its author, and is the ground of liability and the essence of freedom. This will has the power of indifferent choice; that is, it is equally free to choose one way or another unmoved by any desire or impulse, just because of a causal force residing in will itself. So established did this way of viewing choice become, that it is still commonly supposed that choice and the arbitrary freedom of will are one and the same thing.

It is then worth while to pause in our survey while we examine more closely the nature of choice in relation to this alleged connection with free will, free here meaning unmotivated choice. Analysis does not have to probe to the depths to discover two serious faults in the theory. It is a man, a human being in the concrete, who is held responsible. If the act does not proceed from the man, from the human being in his concrete make-up of habits, desires and purposes, why should *he* be held liable and be punished? Will appears as a force outside of the individual person as he actually is, a force which is the real ultimate cause of the act. *Its* freedom to make a choice arbitrarily thus appears no ground for holding the human being as a concrete person responsible for a choice. Whatever else is to be said or left unsaid, choice must have some closer connection with the actual make-up of disposition and character than this philosophy allows.

We may seem then to be in a hopeless dilemma. If the man's nature, original and acquired, makes him do what he does, how does his action differ from that of a stone or tree? Have we not parted with any ground for responsibility? When the question is looked at in the face of facts rather than in a dialectic of concepts it turns out not to have any terrors. Holding men to responsibility may make a decided difference in their *future* behavior; holding a stone or tree to responsibility is a meaningless performance; it has no consequence; it makes no difference. If we locate the ground of liability in future consequences rather than in antecedent causal conditions, we moreover find ourselves in accord with actual practice. Infants, idiots, the insane, those completely upset, are not held to liability; the reason is that it is absurd—meaningless—to do so, for it has no effect on their further actions. A child as he grows older finds responsibilities thrust upon him. This is surely not because freedom of the will has suddenly been inserted in him, but because his assumption of them is a necessary factor in his *further* growth and movement. . . .

As we ascend in the range of complexity from inanimate things to plants, and from plants to animals and from other animals to man, we find an increasing variety of selective responses, due to the influence of life-history, or experiences already undergone. The manifestation of preferences becomes a "function" of an entire history. To understand the action of a fellow-man we have to know something of the *course* of his life. A man is susceptible, sensitive, to a vast variety of conditions, and undergoes varied and opposed experiences—as lower animals do not. Consequently a man in the measure of the scope and variety of his past experiences carries in his present capacity for selective response a large set of varied possibilities. That life-history of which his present preference is a function is complex. Hence the possibility of continuing diversification of behavior: in short, the distinctive *educability* of men. This factor taken by itself does not cover all that is included within the change of preference into genuine choice, but it has a bearing on that individual participation and individual contribution that is involved in choice as a mode of freedom. It is a large factor in our strong sense that we are not pushed into action from behind as are inanimate things. For that which is "behind" is so diversified in its variety and so intimately a part of the present self that preference becomes hesitant. Alternative preferences simultaneously manifest themselves.

Choice, in the distinctively human sense, then presents itself as one preference among and out of preferences; not in the sense of one preference already made and stronger than others, but as the formation of a new preference out of a conflict of preferences. If we can say upon what the formation of this new and determinate preference depends, we are close to finding that of which we are in search. Nor does the answer seem far to seek nor hard to find. As observation and foresight develop, there is ability to form signs and symbols that stand for the interaction and movement of things, without involving us in their actual flux. Hence the new preference may reflect this operation of mind, especially the forecast of the consequences of acting upon the various competing preferences. If we sum up, pending such qualification or such confirmation as further inquiry may supply, we may say that a stone has its preferential selections set by a relatively fixed, a rigidly set, structure and that no anticipation of the results of acting one way or another enters into the matter. The reverse is true of human action. In so far as a variable life-history and intelligent insight and foresight enter into it, choice signifies a capacity for deliberately changing preferences. The hypothesis that is suggested is that in these two traits we have before us the essential constituents of choice as freedom: the factor of individual participation.

Before that idea is further examined, it is, however, desirable to turn to another philosophy of freedom. For the discussion thus far has turned about the fact of choice alone. And such an exclusive emphasis may well render some readers impatient. It may seem to set forth an idea of freedom which is too individual, too "subjective." What has this affair to do with the freedom for which men have fought, bled and died: freedom from oppression and despotism, freedom of institutions and laws? This question at once brings to mind a philosophy of freedom which shifts the issue from choice to action, action in an overt and public sense. This philosophy is sufficiently well presented for our purposes in the idea of John Locke, the author, one may say, of the philosophy of Liberalism in its classic sense. Freedom is *power to act* in accordance with your choice. It is actual ability to carry desire and purpose into operation, to *execute* choices when they are made. Experience shows that certain laws and institutions prevent such operation and execution. This obstruction and interference constitutes what we call oppression, enslavement. Freedom, in fact, the freedom worth fighting for, is secured by abolition of these oppressive measures, tyrannical laws and modes of government. It is liberation, emancipation; the possession and active manifestation of *rights,* the right to self-determination in action. To many minds, the emphasis which has been put upon the formation of choice in connection with freedom will appear an evasion, a trifling with metaphysical futilities, in comparison with this form of freedom, a desire for which has caused revolutions, overthrown dynasties, and which as it is attained supplies the measure of human progress in freedom. . . .

Instincts and impulses, however they may be defined, are part of the "natural" constitution of man; a statement in which "natural" signifies "native," original. The theory assigns a certain intrinsic rightness in this original structure, rightness in the sense of conferring upon impulses a title to pass into direct action, except when they directly and evidently interfere with similar self-manifestation in others. The idea thus overlooks the part played by interaction with the surrounding medium, especially the social, in generating impulses and desires. These are supposed to inhere in the "nature" of the individual when that is taken in a primal state, uninfluenced by interaction with an environment. The latter is thus thought of as purely external to an individual, and as irrelevant to freedom except when it interferes with the operation of native instincts and impulses. A study of history would reveal that this notion, like its theoretically formulated congeners in economic and political Liberalism, is a "faint rumor" left on the air of morals and politics by disappearing theological dogmas, which held that "nature" is thoroughly good as it comes from the creative hand of God, and that evil is due to corruption through the artificial interference and oppression exercised by external or "social" conditions. . . .

The real fallacy lies in the notion that individuals have such a native or original endowment of rights, powers and wants that all that is required on the side of institutions and laws is to eliminate the obstructions they offer to the "free" play of the natural equipment of individuals. The removal of obstructions did have a liberating effect upon such individuals as were antecedently possessed of the means, intellectual and economic, to take advantage of the changed social conditions. But it left all others at the mercy of the new social conditions brought about by the freed powers of those advantageously situated. The notion that men are equally free to act if only the same legal arrangements apply equally to all—irrespective of differences in education, in command of capital, and the control of the social environment which is furnished by the institution of property—is a pure absurdity, as facts have demonstrated. Since actual, that is, effective, rights and demands are products of interactions, and are not found in the original and isolated constitution of human nature, whether moral or psychological, mere elimination of obstructions is not enough. The latter merely liberates force and ability as that happens to be distributed by past accidents of history. This "free" action operates disastrously as far as the many are concerned. The only possible conclusion, both intellectually and practically, is that the attainment of freedom conceived as power to act in accord with choice depends upon positive and constructive changes in social arrangements.

We now have two seemingly independent philosophies, one finding freedom in choice itself, and the other in power to *act* in accord with choice. Before we inquire whether the two philosophies must be left in a position of mutual independence, or whether they link together in a single conception, it will be well to consider another track followed by another school of thinkers, who also in effect identify freedom with operative power in action. This other school had a clear consciousness of the dependence of this power to act upon social conditions, and attempted to avoid and correct the mistakes of the philosophy of classic Liberalism. It substituted a philosophy of institutions for a philosophy of an original moral or psychological structure of individuals. This course was first charted by Spinoza, the great thinker of the seventeenth century. Although the philosophy of Liberalism had not as yet taken form, his ideas afford in anticipation an extraordinarily effective means of criticizing it. To Spinoza freedom was power. The "natural" rights of an individual consist simply in freedom to do whatever he *can* do—an idea probably suggested by Hobbes. But what *can* he do? The answer to that question is evidently a matter of the amount of the power he actually possesses. The whole discussion turns on this point. The answer in effect is that man in his original estate possesses a very limited amount of power. Men as "natural," that is, as native beings are but parts, almost infinitesimally small fractions, of the whole of Nature to which they belong. In Spinoza's phraseology, they are "modes" not substances. As merely a part, the action of any part is limited on every hand by the action and counteraction of other parts. Even if there is power to initiate an act—a power inhering in any natural thing, inanimate as well as human—there is no power to carry it through; an action is immediately caught in an infinite and intricate net-work of *inter*actions. If a man acts upon his private impulse, appetite or want and upon his private judgment about the aims and measures of conduct, he is just as much a subjected part of an infinitely complex whole as is a stock or stone. What he actually does is conditioned by equally blind and partial action of other parts of nature. Slavery, weakness, dependence, is the outcome, not freedom, power and independence. . . .

We now face what is admittedly the crucial difficulty in framing a philosophy of freedom: What is the connection or lack of connection between freedom defined in terms of choice and freedom defined in terms of power in action? Do the two ways of conceiving freedom have anything but the name in common? The difficulty is the greater because we have so little material to guide us in dealing with it. Each type of philosophy has been upon the whole developed with little consideration of the point of view of the other. Yet it would seem that there must be some connection. Choice would hardly be significant if it did not take effect in outward action, and if it did not, when expressed in deeds, make a difference in things. Action as power would hardly be prized if it were power like that of an avalanche or an earthquake. The power, the ability to command issues and consequences, that forms freedom must, it should seem, have some connection with that something in personality that is expressed in choice. At all events, the essential problem of freedom, it seems to me, is the problem of the relation of choice and unimpeded effective action to each other.

I shall first give the solution to this problem that commends itself to me, and then trust to the further discussion not indeed to prove it but to indicate the reasons for holding it. There is an intrinsic connection between choice as freedom and power of action as freedom. A choice which intelligently manifests individuality enlarges the range of action, and this enlargement in turn confers upon our desires greater insight and foresight, and makes choice more intelligent. There is a circle, but an enlarging circle, or, if you please, a widening spiral. This statement is of course only a formula. We may perhaps supply it with meaning by first considering the matter negatively. Take for example an act following from a blind preference, from an impulse not reflected upon. It will be a matter of luck if the resulting action does not get the one who acts into conflict with surrounding conditions. Conditions go against the realization of his preference; they cut across it, obstruct it, deflect its course, get him into new and perhaps more serious entanglements. Luck may be on his side. Circumstances may happen to be propitious or he may be endowed with native force that enables him to brush aside obstructions and sweep away resistances. He thus gets a certain freedom, judged from the side of power-to-do. But this result is a matter of favor, of grace, of luck; it is not due to anything in himself. Sooner or later he is likely to find his deeds at odds with conditions; an accidental success may only reinforce a foolhardy impulsiveness that renders a man's future subjection the more probable. Enduringly lucky persons are exceptions.

Suppose, on the other hand, our hero's act exhibits a choice expressing a preference formed after consideration of consequences, an intelligent preference. Consequences depend upon an interaction of what he starts to perform with his environment, so he must take the latter into account. No one can foresee all consequences because no one can be aware of all the conditions that enter into their production. Every person builds better or worse than he knows. Good fortune or the favorable co-operation of environment is still necessary. Even with his best thought, a man's proposed course of action may be defeated. But in as far as his act is truly a manifestation of intelligent choice, he learns something: as in a scientific experiment an inquirer may learn through his experimentation, his intelligently directed action, quite as much or even more from a failure than from a success. He finds out at least a little as to what was the matter with his prior choice. He can choose better and *do* better next time; "better choice" meaning a more reflective one, and "better doing" meaning one better co-ordinated with the conditions that are involved in realizing purpose. Such control or power is never complete; luck or fortune, the propitious support of circumstances not foreseeable is always involved. But at least such a person forms the habit of choosing and acting with conscious regard to the grain of circumstance, the run of affairs. And what is more to the point, such a man becomes able to turn frustration and failure to account in his further choices and purposes. Everything in so far as serves his purpose—to be an intelligent human being. This gain in power or freedom can be nullified by no amount of external defeats.

An illustration drawn from the denial of the idea that there is an intimate connection of the two modes of freedom, namely, intelligent choice and power in action, may aid in clearing up the idea. The attitude and acts of other persons is of course one of the most important parts of the conditions involved in bringing the manifestation of preference to impotency or to power in action. Take the case of a child in a family where the environment formed by others is such as to humor all his choices. It is made easy for him to do what he pleases. He meets a minimum of resistance; upon the whole others co-operate with him in bringing his preferences to fulfilment. Within this region he seems to have free power of action. By description he is unimpeded, even aided. But it is obvious that as far as he is concerned, this is a matter of luck. He is "free" merely because his surrounding conditions happen to be of the kind they are, a mere happening or accident as far as his make-up and his preferences are concerned. It is evident in such a case that there is *no growth* in the intelligent exercise of preferences. There is rather a conversion of blind impulse into regular habits. Hence his attained freedom is such only in appearance: it disappears as he moves into other social conditions.

Now consider the opposite case. A child is balked, inhibited, interfered with and nagged pretty continuously in the manifestation of his spontaneous preferences. He is constantly "disciplined" by circumstances adverse to his preferences—as discipline is not infrequently conceived. Does it follow then that he develops in "inner" freedom, in thoughtful preference and purpose? The question answers itself. Rather is some pathological condition the outcome. "Discipline" is indeed necessary as a preliminary to any freedom that is more than unrestrained outward power. But our dominant conception of discipline is a travesty; there is only one genuine discipline, namely, that which takes effect in producing habits of observation and judgment that insure intelligent desires. In short, while men do not think about and gain freedom in conduct unless they run during action against conditions that resist their original impulses, the secret of education consists in having that blend of check and favor which influences thought and foresight, and that takes effect in outward action through this modification of disposition and outlook.

I have borrowed the illustration from the life of a child at home or in school, because the problem is familiar and easily recognizable in those settings. But there is no difference when we consider the adult in industrial, political and ecclesiastic life. When social conditions are such as to prepare a prosperous career for a man's spontaneous preferences in advance, when things are made easy by institutions and by habits of admiration and approval, there is precisely the same kind of outward freedom, of relatively unimpeded action, as in the case of the spoiled child. But there is hardly more of freedom on the side of varied and flexible capacity of choice; preferences are restricted to the one line laid down, and in the end the individual becomes the slave of his successes. Others, vastly more in number, are in the state of the "disciplined" child. There is hard sledding for their spontaneous preferences; the grain of the environment, especially of existing economic arrangements, runs against them. But the check, the inhibition, to the immediate operation of their native preferences no more confers on them the quality of intelligent choice than it does with the child who never gets a fair chance to try himself out. There is only a crushing that results in apathy and indifference; a deflection into evasion and deceit; a compensatory over-responsiveness to such occasions as permit untrained preferences to run riot—and all the other consequences which the literature of mental and moral pathology has made familiar.

I hope these illustrations may at least have rendered reasonably clear what is intended by our formula; by the idea that freedom consists in a trend of conduct that causes choices to be more diversified and flexible, more plastic and more cognizant of their own meaning, while it enlarges their range of unimpeded operation. There is an important implication in this idea of freedom. The orthodox theory of freedom of the will and the classic theory of Liberalism both define freedom on the basis of something antecedently given, something already possessed. Unlike in contents as are the imputation of unmotivated liberty of choice and of natural rights and native wants, the two ideas have an important element in common. They both seek for freedom in something already there, given in advance. Our idea compels us on the other hand to seek for freedom in something which comes to be, in a certain kind of growth; in consequences, rather than in antecedents. We are free not because of what we statically are, but in as far as we are becoming different from what we have been. . . .

I sum up by saying that the possibility of freedom is deeply grounded in our very beings. It is one with our individuality, our being uniquely what we are and not imitators and parasites of others. But like all other possibilities, this possibility has to be actualized; and, like all others, it can only be actualized through interaction with objective conditions. The question of political and economic freedom is not an addendum of afterthought, much less a deviation or excrescence, in the problem of personal freedom. For the conditions that form political and economic liberty are required in order to realize the potentiality of freedom each of us carries with him in his very structure. Constant and uniform relations in change and a knoweldge of them in "laws," are not a hindrance to freedom, but a necessary factor in coming to be effectively that which we have the capacity to grow into. Social conditions interact with the preferences of an individual (that *are* his individuality) in a way favorable to actualizing freedom only when they develop intelligence, not abstract knowledge and abstract thought, but power of vision and reflection. For these take effect in making preference, desire and purpose more flexible, alert, and resolute. Freedom has too long been thought of as an indeterminate power operating in a closed and ended world. In its reality, freedom is a resolute will operating in a world in some respects indeterminate, because open and moving toward a new future.

Yet we cannot separate power to become from consideration of what already and antecedently is. Capacity to become different, even though we define freedom by it, must be a present capacity, something in some sense present. At this point of the inquiry, the fact that all existences whatever possess selectivity in action recurs with new import. It may sound absurd to speak of electrons and atoms exhibiting preference, still more perhaps to attribute bias to them. But the absurdity is wholly a matter of the words used. The essential point is that they have a certain opaque and irreducible individuality which shows itself in what they do; in the fact that they behave in certain ways and not in others. In the description of causal sequences, we still have to start with and from existences, things that are individually and uniquely just what they are. The fact that we can state changes which occur by certain uniformities and regularities does not eliminate this original element of individuality, or preference and bias. On the contrary, the statement of laws presupposes just this capacity. We cannot escape this fact by an attempt to treat each thing as an effect of other things. Since we have to admit individuality no matter how far we carry the chase, we might as well forego the labor and start with the unescapable fact. . . .

No law does away with individuality of existence, having its own particular way of operating; for a law is concerned with relations and hence presupposes the being and operation of individuals. If choice is found to be a distinctive act, having distinctive consequences, then no appeal to the authority of scientific law can militate in any way against its reality. The problem reduces itself to one of fact. Just what *is* intelligent choice and just what does it effect in human life? I cannot ask you to re-traverse the ground already gone over. But I do claim that the considerations already adduced reveal that what men actually cherish under the name of freedom is that power of varied and flexible growth, of change of disposition and character, that springs from intelligent choice, so there is a sound basis for the common-sense practical belief in freedom, although theories in justification of this belief have often taken an erroneous and even absurd form.

We may indeed go further than we have gone. Not only is the presence of uniform relations of change no bar to the reality of freedom, but these are, *when known,* aids to the development of that freedom. Take the suppositions case already mentioned. That my ideas have causes signifies that their *rise,* their *origin* (not their nature), is a change connected with other changes. If I only knew the connection, my power over obtaining the ideas I want would be that much increased. The same thing holds good of any effect my idea may have upon the ideas and choices of some one else. Knowledge of the conditions under which a choice *arises* is the same as potential ability to guide the formation of choices intelligently. This does not eliminate the distinctive quality of choice; choice is still choice. But it is now an intelligent choice instead of a dumb and stupid one, and thereby the probability of its leading to freedom in unimpeded action is increased.

STUDY QUESTIONS

1   Dewey says that if free will is defined as "unmotivated choice," then it does not have anything to do with man in the concrete. What does he mean by "man in the concrete"? Why can not this idea of free will provide a rationale for responsibility?

2   "If we are determined to do what we do by our natures, then it makes no sense to hold anyone responsible. You might as well hold a clock responsible for telling time the way it does." How would Dewey respond to this criticism?

3   How is it possible for a multiplicity of preferences to present themselves to us, but not to, for example, a tree? What is the role of symbols in this process?

4   What is the other philosophy of freedom which stands over against freedom of choice? What assumptions about human nature does Dewey believe are involved in this notion of freedom? What is the importance of social arrangements which Dewey believes this view neglects?

5   What conditions allow an individual's choices to become progressively diverse and flexible? What does the word "flexible" mean here? Do you think that Dewey would say that several courses of action are "possible" to a free agent?

6   What is the role of social institutions in developing freedom? Can you think of some examples which Dewey might cite as relevant to the growth of individualism?

SELECTED READINGS

There are several good anthologies which give the student an appreciation of the extent of the problem of free will: Willard Enteman, *The Problem of Free Will* (New York: Scribner, 1967), Sidney Morganbesser and James Walsh, *Free Will* (Englewood Cliffs, N.J.: Prentice-Hall, 1962), and D. F. Pears, *Freedom and the Will* (London: Macmillan, 1963). Sidney Hook (ed.), *Determinism and Freedom in the Age of Modern Science* (New York: New York University Press, 1958), from which our selection by Hospers comes, provides good coverage of many modern philosophers.

Fatalism and predestination especially bothered Christian theologians, since responsibility for evil seemed to rest with God. St. Augustine's views can be found in his *City of God*, Book IX, Chap. 21, and in Morganbesser and Walsh, cited above. Defenses of predestination by John Calvin and Jonathan Edwards have been reprinted in Enteman, cited above. St. Thomas's opinions can be found in *Summa Theologica*, Part I, Question 14, Article 3. An interesting contemporary defense of fatalism is given by Richard Taylor, *Metaphysics* (Englewood Cliffs, N.J.: Prentice-Hall, 1963), Chap. 5.

There are many kinds of libertarianism. Campbell's sort of theory has its historical counterpart in Thomas Reid (1710–1796), *Essays on the Active Powers of Man*, in many editions. A similar position is advocated in H. D. Lewis, *Morals and Revelation* (London: G. Allen, 1951). A Jamesian position of objective chance is defended in Corliss Lamont, *Freedom of Choice Affirmed* (New York: Horizon Press, 1957), and an extreme theory of self-creation is urged by the popular existentialist Jean-Paul Sartre in *Being and Nothingness*, trans. H. E. Barnes (New York: Philosophical Library, 1956).

The first complete statement of soft-determinism was given by the seventeenth-century materialist, Thomas Hobbes. His position is reprinted in R. S. Peters (ed.), *Body, Mind, and Citizen* (New York: Collier Books, 1962). This theory became the official view for most of the British empiricists down to the present time. David Hume states the position forcefully in Section 8 of his *Enquiry Concerning Human Understanding*. The classic nineteenth-century presentation was

John Stuart Mill, *An Examination of Sir William Hamilton's Philosophy* (London: Longmans, 1872), Chap. 26. Bertrand Russell, *Philosophical Essays,* rev. ed. (London: G. Allen, 1966), and C. J. Ducasse, *Nature, Mind, and Death* (La Salle, Ill: Open Court, 1951) have good, clear discussions of the position.

Part Five

Political and Social Philosophy

THE PARADOXES OF AUTHORITY

"Men of Athens, I honor and love you, but I shall obey God rather than you. . . . Either acquit me or not; but whichever you do, understand that I shall never alter my ways, not even if I have to die many times." (Socrates in *The Apology,* on the occasion of his trial.)

"A Man must do what his city and his country order him; or he must change their view of what is just. . . . He who disobeys (the laws) is thrice wrong; first because in disobeying (them) he is disobeying his parents; secondly because (they) are the authors of his education; thirdly because he has made an agreement with (them) that he will duly obey (their) commands." (Socrates in the *Crito,* on the occasion of an opportunity to escape prison and execution.)

"The sole end for which mankind are warranted, individually or collectively, in interfering in the liberty of action of any of their number, is self-protection . . . the only purpose for which power can be rightfully exercised on any member of a civilized community, against his will, is to prevent harm to others. . . ." (John Stuart Mill *On Liberty.*)

"There are also many positive acts for the benefit of others, which he may rightfully be compelled to perform; such as to give evidence in a court of justice, to bear his fair share in the common defense, or in any other joint work necessary to the interest of the society of which he enjoys the protection. . . ." (John Stuart Mill *On Liberty.*)

I think we all have moral obligations to obey just laws. On the other hand, I think that we have moral obligations to disobey unjust laws because non-cooperation with evil is just as much a moral obligation as cooperation with good." (Rev. Martin Luther King.)

"Submit yourselves to every ordinance of men for the Lord's sake; whether it be to the king, as supreme; or unto the governors, as unto them that are sent by him for the punishment of evil-doers and for the praise of them that do well." (1 Peter 2:13.)

"The working class, in the course of its development, will substitute for the old civil society an association which will exclude classes and their antagonism, and there will be no more political power properly so-called, since political power is precisely the official expression of antagonism in civil society." (Karl Marx, *Poverty of Philosophy.*)

"The task of the leaders is not to put into effect the wishes and will of the masses. . . . In the recent past we have encountered the phenomenon of certain categories of workers acting *against* their interests. What is the task of a leader in such a situation? Is it mechanically to implement incorrect ideas? No, it is not. . . . If the will of the masses does not coincide with progress, then one must lead the masses in another direction. . . ." (Jan Kadar, Address to the Hungarian National Assembly on May 11, 1957, explaining the need to suppress workers after the 1956 Budapest uprising.)

The State and the Individual

PROBLEM INTRODUCTION

The anthill is not an institution—it is a natural fact. The social identity of each and every ant is completely contained in a genetic code which specifies what function the individual shall have in the bustling hum of activity as a whole. Each ant is simply a concrete manifestation of an abstract social equation, a function, a role. No ant desires anything beyond service to the whole, for the eccentric and the useless are mercilessly weeded out by natural selection. If happiness is the unimpeded satisfaction of our most basic desires, then ant bliss is the unfrustrated performance of a definite, unchangeable set of social routines.

Human societies are not natural facts—they are institutions. Nature does not demand that we take any specific form of social organization, for although human beings have common needs—the need for nourishment, security, love, self-expression, etc.—each individual manifests these needs in dramatically different forms. Nature has been generous, giving each person something excitingly different which shall not be seen again. But this generosity has its drawbacks, for although we are above the anthill, we are not yet angels either. The unique potential within each person can only be realized within organized society, and the form of the society will determine the form and extensiveness of each person's individuality. But as long as individuality exists, there will be conflicts which must be managed. Were we angels, we would be completely benevolent and rational, instantly agreeing on the perfect path to self-fulfillment with social justice. But being somewhere between angels and ants, we need philosophy. We need an overview of ourselves—of our fundamental nature, our most basic needs, and the sources of coercion that prevent us from achieving our highest potential; of what can be changed about ourselves and our institutions, and how much has to be accepted as the fixed boundaries within which happiness must be found. If we do not think in terms of such questions, if we do not have a working hypothesis about ourselves, we are sure to become mired in the accidental and trivial aspects of existence—taking our own cultural eccentricities as expressions of human nature, confronting every social change as an affront to natural law, and, in general, viewing our defeats as vicious conspiracies, rather than as experimental checks on our hidden assumptions.

The readings in this section begin with a search for some of the basic beliefs that underlie democratic political theory. Because it is usually easier to locate our own assumptions by examining opposing views, the first selection is by Thomas Hobbes, a seventeenth-century philosopher who defended a monarchical form of government. The seventeenth century was the fertile breeding ground for revolutionary ideas in all areas of intellectual life. Being a conservative, Hobbes was no revolutionary in the political sense. But the reasons he gave for the centralization of power in the hands of an absolute sovereign represent a revolutionary application of scientific ideas that were slowly altering the dominant conception of humans. The starting point for Hobbes was Galileo's studies on motion and William Harvey's anatomical discoveries. Galileo began his physics with the assumption that the behavior of every physical body could best be understood in terms of general laws of motion. One of these was the law of inertia, which asserts that a body in motion will stay in motion unless affected by an opposing force. Harvey's experiments in anatomy had revealed that the human body functioned like a complicated mechanism—the arteries, veins, nerves, and organs being biological gears and springs. Putting these ideas together, Hobbes conceived of the human person as a mechanical system of matter in motion, a machine whose behavior could be completely explained and predicted by physical principles. He became the consummate materialist: emotions, thoughts, sensations—all psychological states—were merely manifestations of matter in motion. The seventeenth century was also a period of social and political upheaval. As Hobbes saw political groups struggling to extend their power, he took their behavior to be an expression of human nature, rather than a local and temporary effect of the tumultuous social climate. People were, he thought, naturally rapacious and egoistic. This aggressiveness and selfishness could be explained by his materialism since, as the law of inertia predicted, people are material systems preserving themselves in motion.

This conception of human nature has important consequences for ethics and political theory. If human beings are compelled by natural law to seek their own interests above all else, it makes no sense to demand that they behave differently. Saint and sinner are motivated by the same impulses—the saint looks toward heaven for a reward, whereas the sinner's eyes are closer to the ground. Even

God cannot demand the impossible. The upshot is that the quest for self-interest is both natural and *right*. The best political system will be one which allows each individual to satisfy egoistic drives in the most efficient way.

But what is the best way to satisfy one's own self-interest in a world full of aggressive individuals who will stop at nothing to enhance their own personal power? Hobbes recognized that to give perfect liberty to everyone is to invite anarchy. This is what he called the state of nature, where there is no power to keep people from attacking one another. Clearly, it is in each person's self-interest to cease this perpetual war and to gain some modicum of security. It is impossible, however, for people to become gentle of their own free will. Therefore, in order to create peace, a natural motive must be found for subduing aggressiveness. This motive is fear. There must be some overarching power, capable of restraining the natural violence of people with the threat of counterviolence. Any attempt to divide power, as in a democracy, is sure to unleash the natural ferocity of the individual. A dictatorship, then, is the ideal form of government.

The essay by Charles Frankel is a defense of democracy. At the outset it is clear that Frankel does not begin with a Hobbesian conception of human nature. The democratic view of human nature reflects a guarded optimism. Individuals are regarded as benevolent and rational until they prove themselves otherwise. In a democracy, individuals must be credited with more rationality than Hobbes allows, no matter how we conceive their motives. Since people are given relatively more autonomy and freedom from control, as well as a voice in the formulation of policy, we must assume that they will restrain their impulses by the enlightened recognition that the usual forms of selfishness are not in their long-term interests. It is the rational appreciation of the consequences that restrains the individual, not the visible signs of retaliation. Frankel argues that this is manifested in the way democratic procedures deal with political outcasts. It is presumed that those who lose political battles, even though passionately interested in their own programs, will restrain themselves through the recognition that the system has provided them with a way of fighting again another day. The competition depicted is highly civilized. It is certainly not like Hobbes's state of nature.

Both Hobbes and Frankel claim that their political philosophies embody scientific principles. But there is an important difference. Frankel maintains that democratic theory is based on a scientific conception of the best method for discovering the truth, whereas Hobbes believes that his theory is the extension of a scientific truth already discovered. The importance of this difference cannot be overemphasized. For Hobbes, the true nature of people—their dominant motives and their possibilities—is known. All that remains is to determine which form of government best suits the psychological picture. But in democratic political theory, a vast amount of ignorance about the human condition is assumed. Science and experience have not turned in the final answer to the human equation. Perhaps there is no dominant drive which characterizes the human essence. Perhaps there are a number of such drives or none at all. This uncertainty demands that people be given as much freedom as possible to discover themselves for themselves. Because our estimate of human nature is constantly being refined, the best government is one which allows for an efficient way of correcting errors while providing for an environment stable enough for progress to be made. Democracy is not a fixed body of doctrine, but a method—a procedure for coming to the truth. Therefore, Frankel depicts democracy as a form of experimental ethics, where social policies are to be regarded as tentative appraisals of the interests of the people and the best way to serve those interests. The vote is, in effect, the experimental check on such hypothetical assessments of human nature.

The readings by Plato and Robert Paul Wolff are concerned with the moral authority of the state. In contemporary society we are compelled and forbidden in hundreds of ways which have faded, unnoticed, into the fabric of life. We must have a medical examination to be married, money is taken from us in the form of taxes, building codes and zoning ordinances limit construction, thousands of regulations govern all sorts of business transactions, our foreign travel is restricted, we must join trade unions and pay dues, we cannot sell or rent according to our own lights. The list goes on and on. And even so, most people do not find the weight of the state suffocating. But there are moments of anarchy when the individual refuses to acknowledge the authority of the state. From the Boston Tea Party to that day in 1955, when Mrs. Rosa Parks, a black woman, tired from her day's labor as a domestic, refused to move to the back of the bus as required by the laws of Montgomery, Alabama, people have collectively and individually taken the law into their own hands in the name of conscience and freedom.

In our readings, Plato comes down on the side of the state. In the *Crito,* Socrates is urged by his friends to escape from prison, thereby avoiding the death penalty which has been unjustly imposed by the Athenian court. But Socrates argues that he has an obligation to obey the law, even if it must mean his own death. This obligation, he claims, is based on two considerations. First, his escape would damage the rule of law and undermine public order, for he would be proclaiming that the law is to be obeyed only when it pleases him. Secondly, he maintains that he has entered into a contract with the state to obey its laws. The state has nurtured him and given him the opportunity to leave should he find the law oppressive. Since he has remained, he has promised to be governed by the laws of the state. To escape under these conditions would be breaking a legitimate contract. But Robert Paul Wolff argues that the state does not have the right to command us, and we are not obliged to obey. Using Kant's ethics as a touchstone, Wolff locates moral authority within each individual. If we place authority in something outside ourselves, surrendering our conscience to a system which "knows better," we have sacrificed our moral autonomy to sheer power.

Socrates does not submit to the state without reason. But it is clear that he ranks the claims of public authority and social order quite high. The law is not to be obeyed only when it pleases the individual. Like Hobbes, Plato sees society as a restraint against the capriciousness and destructive irrationality of people. And surely there is something right about this. The claims of conscience are not all equally valid. The Ku Klux Klan elevates conscience over the law, and would have lynched Rosa Parks for her violation of social morality. Nor is Wolff's anarchism mere whimsy. There are some moral beliefs which cannot stand against the lessons of human experience and the hard-fought battles of moral reason. A genuine moral agent has a healthy dose of rationality, experience, and respect for fact. The issue of public and private authority is part and parcel of the debate between democracy and totalitarianism, the individual and the state. Your assessment of the human condition, of the possibilities of perfection or destruction within human nature will determine where you draw the line between freedom and anarchy, order and repression.

In Defense of Dictatorship

Thomas Hobbes

Thomas Hobbes (1588–1679) was the first philosopher to systematically apply physical principles to ethics and social philosophy. Taking Galileo's new physics as a model, Hobbes proposed to show that every change could be understood as a change of matter in motion. Human beings were thought of as mechanical systems of material particles, governed by the same physical laws as other material bodies. Hobbes interpreted all psychological states as physical in nature, and saw the most fundamental need of the human system as the drive to preserve itself in motion. Physics, therefore, was the foundation for natural aggressiveness. People are by nature devoid of any feelings of kindliness or sympathy. In his usual way, Hobbes interpreted feelings of sympathy as actually arising from the contemplation of ourselves undergoing a painful fate.

This psychological picture of human beings led Hobbes to certain political conclusions. If left alone, people will attack one another with impunity as long as there is some hope of gaining power over others. Political order requires that power be placed in the hands of a single sovereign so that no one could believe it possible to wrest it away. In Hobbes's own day, power was divided between Parliament and the king, and this led to a civil war. Parliament won the victory and Charles I was executed in 1649. Since Hobbes had defended an absolute sovereign, he fled to France, believing that Parliament would take reprisals against him. While in France, he was briefly engaged to tutor the future Charles II, but his reputation as an atheist and freethinker made his position in France untenable. He returned to England after an exile of eleven years, and spent the rest of his days writing treatises and books, and enjoying his reputation as the "father of atheists."

There be in animals, two sorts of *motions* peculiar to them: one called *vital;* begun in generation, and continued without interruption through their whole life; such as are the *course* of the *blood,* the *pulse,* the *breathing,* the *concoction, nutrition, excretion,* etc. to which motions there needs no help of imagination: the other is *animal motion,* otherwise called *voluntary motion;* as to *go,* to *speak,* to *move* any of our limbs, in such manner as is first fancied in our minds. That sense is motion in the organs and interior parts of man's body, caused by the action of the things we see, hear, etc.; and that fancy is but the relics of the same motion, remaining after sense, has been already said in the first and second chapters. And because *going, speaking,* and the like voluntary motions, depend always upon a precedent thought of *whither, which way,* and *what;* it is evident, that the imagination is the first internal beginning of all voluntary motion. And although unstudied men do not conceive any motion at all to be there, where the thing moved is invisible; or the space it is moved in is, for the shortness of it, insensible; yet that doth not hinder, but that such motions are. . . .

From Thomas Hobbes, *Leviathan* and *Philosophical Rudiments,* from *The English Works of Thomas Hobbes,* Vols. II and III, Sir William Molesworth, ed., London, 1839.

As, in sense, that which is really within us, is, as I have said before, only motion, caused by the action of external objects, but in apparence; to the sight, light and colour; to the ear, sound; to the nostril, odour, etc.: so, when the action of the same object is continued from the eyes, ears, and other organs to the heart, the real effect there is nothing but motion, or endeavour; which consisteth in appetite, or aversion, to or from the object moving. But the apparence, or sense of that motion, is that we either call *delight,* or *trouble of mind.*

This motion, which is called appetite, and for the apparence of it *delight,* and *pleasure,* seemeth to be a corroboration of vital motion, and a help thereunto; and therefore such things as caused delight, were not improperly called *jucunda, à juvando,* from helping or fortifying; and the contrary, *molesta, offensive,* from hindering, and troubling the motion vital.

. . . Whatsoever is the object of any man's appetite or desire, that is it which he for his part calleth *good:* and the object of his hate and aversion, *evil;* and of his contempt, *vile* and *inconsiderable.* For these words of good, evil, and contemptible, are ever used with relation to the person that useth them: there being nothing simply and absolutely so; not any common rule of good and evil, to be taken from the nature of the objects themselves.

. . . In the nature of man, we find three principal causes of quarrel. First, competition; secondly, diffidence; thirdly, glory.

The first, maketh men invade for gain; the second, for safety; and the third, for reputation. The first use violence, to make themselves masters of other men's persons, wives, children, and cattle; the second, to defend them; the third, for trifles, as a word, a smile, a different opinion, and any other sign of undervalue, either direct in their persons, or by reflection in their kindred, their friends, their nation, their profession, or their name.

Hereby it is manifest, that during the time men live without a common power to keep them all in awe, they are in that condition which is called war; and such a war, as is of every man, against every man. For WAR, consisteth not in battle only, or the act of fighting; but in a tract of time, wherein the will to contend by battle is sufficiently known: and therefore the notion of *time,* is to be considered in the nature of war; as it is in the nature of weather. For as the nature of foul weather, lieth not in a shower or two of rain; but in an inclination thereto of many days together: so the nature of war, consisteth not in actual fighting; but in the known disposition thereto, during all the time there is no assurance to the contrary. All other time is PEACE.

Whatsoever therefore is consequent to a time of war, where every man is enemy to every man; the same is consequent to the time, wherein men live without other security, than what their own strength, and their own invention shall furnish them withal. In such condition, there is no place for industry; because the fruit thereof is uncertain: and consequently no culture of the earth; no navigation, nor use of the commodities that may be imported by sea; no commodious building; no instruments of moving, and removing, such things as require much force; no knowledge of the face of the earth; no account of time; no arts; no letters; no society; and which is worst of all, continual fear, and danger of violent death; and the life of man, solitary, poor, nasty, brutish, and short. . . .

All society therefore is either for gain, or for glory; that is, not so much for love of our fellows, as for the love of ourselves. But no society can be great or lasting, which begins from vain glory. Because that glory is like honour; if all men have it no man hath it, for they consist in comparison and precellence. Neither doth the society of others advance any whit the cause of my glorying in myself; for every man must account himself, such as he can make himself without the help of others. But though the benefits of this life may be much furthered by mutual help; since yet those may be better attained to by dominion than by the society of others, I hope no body will doubt, but that men would much more greedily be carried by nature, if all fear were removed, to obtain dominion, than to gain society. We must therefore resolve, that the original of all great and lasting societies consisted not in the mutual good will men had towards each other, but in the mutual fear they had of each other.

The cause of mutual fear consists partly in the natural equality of men, partly in their mutual will of hurting: whence it comes to pass, that we can neither expect from others, nor promise to ourselves the least security. For if we look on men full-grown, and consider how brittle the frame of our human body is, which perishing, all its strength, vigour, and wisdom itself perisheth with it; and how easy a matter it is, even for the weakest man to kill the strongest: there is no reason why any man, trusting to his own stength, should conceive himself made by nature above others. They are equals, who can do equal things one against the other; but they who can do the greatest things, namely, kill, can do equal things. All men therefore among themselves are by nature equal; the inequality we now discern, hath its spring from the civil law. . . .

Among so many dangers therefore, as the natural lusts of men do daily threaten each other withal, to have a care of one's self is so far from being a matter scornfully to be looked upon, that one has neither the power nor wish to have done otherwise. For every man is desirous of what is good for him, and shuns what is evil, but chiefly the chiefest of natural evils, which is death; and this he doth by a certain impulsion of nature, no less than that whereby a stone moves downward. It is therefore neither absurd nor reprehensible, neither against the dictates of true reason, for a man to use all his endeavours to preserve and defend his body and the members thereof from death and sorrows. But that which is not contrary to right reason, that all men account to be done justly, and with right. Neither by the word *right* is anything else signified, than that liberty which every man hath to make use of his natural faculties according to right reason. Therefore the first foundation of natural right is this, that *every man as much as in him lies endeavour to protect his life and members.* . . .

It may seem strange to some man, that has not well weighed these things; that nature should thus dissociate, and render men apt to invade, and destroy one another: and he may therefore, not trusting to this inference, made from the passions, desire perhaps to have the same confirmed by experience. Let him therefore consider with himself, when taking a journey, he arms himself, and seeks to go well accompanied; when going to sleep, he locks his doors; when even in his house he locks his chests; and this when he knows there be laws, and public officers, armed, to revenge all injuries shall be done him; what opinion he has of his fellow-subjects, when he rides armed; of his fellow citizens, when he locks his doors; and of his children, and servants, when he locks his chests. Does he not there as much accuse mankind by his actions, as I do by my words? But neither of us accuse man's nature in it. The desires, and other passions of man, are in themselves no sin. No more are the actions, that proceed from those passions, till they know a law that forbids them: which till laws be made they cannot know: nor can any law be made, till they have agreed upon the person that shall make it. . . .

To this war of every man, against every man, this also is consequent; that nothing can be unjust. The notions of right and wrong, justice and injustice have there no place. Where there is no common power, there is no law: where no law, no injustice. Force, and fraud, are in war the two cardinal virtues. Justice, and injustice are none of the faculties neither of the body, nor mind. If they were, they might be in a man that were alone in the world, as well as his senses, and passions. They are qualities, that relate to men in society, not in solitude. It is consequent also to the same condition, that there be no propriety, no dominion, no *mine* and *thine* distinct; but only that to be every man's, that he can get; and for so long, as he can keep it. And thus much for the ill condition, which man by mere nature is actually placed in; though with a possibility to come out of it, consisting partly in the passions, partly in his reason.

The passions that incline men to peace, are fear of death; desire of such things as are necessary to commodious living; and a hope by their industry to obtain them. And reason suggesteth convenient articles of peace, upon which men may be drawn to agreement. These articles, are they, which otherwise are called the Laws of Nature. . . .

A LAW OF NATURE, *lex naturalis,* is a precept or general rule, found out by reason, by which a man is forbidden to do that, which is destructive of his life, or taketh away the means of preserving the same; and to omit that, by which he thinketh it may be best preserved. For though they that speak of this subject, use to confound *jus,* and *lex, right* and *law:* yet they ought to be distinguished: because RIGHT, consisteth in liberty to do, or to forbear; whereas LAW, determineth, and bindeth to one of them: so that law, and right, differ as much, as obligation, and liberty; which in one and the same matter are inconsistent.

And because the condition of man, as hath been declared in the precedent chapter, is a condition of war of every one against every one: in which case every one is governed by his own reason; and there is nothing he can make use of, that may not be a help unto him, in preserving his life against his enemies; it followeth, that in such a condition, every man has a right to every thing; even to one another's body. And therefore, as long as this natural right of every man to every thing endureth, there can be no security to any man, how strong or wise soever he be, of living out the time, which nature ordinarily alloweth men to live. And consequently it is a precept, or general rule of reason, *that every man, ought to endeavour peace, as far as he has hope of obtaining it; and when he cannot obtain it, that he may seek, and use, all helps, and advantages of war.* The first branch of which rule, containeth the first, and fundamental law of nature; which is, *to seek peace, and follow it*. The second, the sum of the right of nature; which is, *by all means we can, to defend ourselves*.

From this fundamental law of nature, by which men are commanded to endeavour peace, is derived this second law; that *a man be willing, when others are so too, as far-forth, as for peace, and defence of himself he shall think it necessary, to lay down this right to all things; and be contented with so much liberty against other men, as he would allow other men against himself*. For as long as every man holdeth this right, of doing any thing he liketh; so long are all men in the condition of war. But if other men will not lay down their right, as well as he; then there is no reason for any one, to divest himself of his: for that were to expose himself to prey, which no man is bound to, rather than to dispose himself to peace. . . .

From that law of nature, by which we are obliged to transfer to another, such rights, as being retained, hinder the peace of mankind, there followeth a third; which is this, *that men perform their covenants made:* without which, convenants are in vain, and but empty words; and the right of all men to all things remaining, we are still in the condition of war.

And in this law of nature, consisteth the fountain and original of JUSTICE. For where no covenant hath preceded, there hath no right been transferred, and every man has right to every thing; and consequently, no action can be unjust. But when a covenant is made, then to break it is *unjust;* and the definition of INJUSTICE, is no other than *the not performance of covenant*. And whatsoever is not unjust, is *just*.

But because covenants of mutual trust, where there is a fear of not performance on either part . . . are invalid; though the original of justice be the making of covenants; yet injustice actually there can be none, till the cause of such fear be taken away; which while men are in the natural condition of war, cannot be done. Therefore before the names of just, and unjust can have place, there must be some coercive power, to compel men equally to the performance of their covenants, by the terror of some punishment, greater than the benefit they expect by the breach of their convenant; and to make good that propriety, which by mutual contract men acquire, in recompense of the universal right they abandon: and such power there is none before the erection of a commonwealth. And this is also to be gathered out of the ordinary definition of justice in the Schools: for they say, that *justice is the constant will of giving to every man his own*. And therefore where there is no *own*, that is no propriety, there is no injustice; and where there is no coercive power erected, that is, where there is no commonwealth, there is no propriety; all men having right to all things: therefore where there is no commonwealth, there nothing is unjust. So that the nature of justice, consisteth in keeping of valid covenants: but the validity of convenants begins not but with the constitution of a civil power, sufficient to compel men to keep them: and then it is also that propriety begins. . . .

The only way to erect such a common power, as may be able to defend them from the invasion of foreigners, and the injuries of one another, and thereby to secure them in such sort, as that by their own industry, and by the fruits of the earth, they may nourish themselves and live contentedly; is, to confer all their power and strength upon one man, or upon one assembly of men, that may reduce all their wills, by plurality of voices, unto one will: which is as much as to say, to appoint one man, or assembly of men, to bear their person; and every one to own, and acknowledge himself to be author of whatsoever he that so beareth their person, shall act, or cause to be acted, in those things which concern the common peace and safety; and therein to submit their wills, every one to his will, and their judgments, to his judgment. This is more than consent, or concord; it is a real unity of them all, on one and the same person, made by covenant of every man with every man, in such manner, as if every man should say to every man, *I authorise and give up my right of governing myself, to this man, or to this assembly of men, on this condition, that thou give up thy right to him and authorise all his actions in like manner.* This done, the multitude so united in one person, is called a COMMONWEALTH, in Latin CIVITAS. This is the generation of that great LEVIA-THAN, or rather, to speak more reverently, of that MORTAL GOD, to which we owe under the *immortal God,* our peace and defence. For by this authority, given him by every particular man in the commonwealth, he hath the use of so much power and strength conferred on him, that by terror thereof, he is enabled to perform the wills of them all, to peace at home, and mutual aid against their enemies abroad. And in him consisteth the essence of the commonwealth; which, to de-fine it, is *one person, of whose acts a great multitude, by mutual covenants one with another, have made themselves every one the author, to the end he may use the strength and means of them all, as he shall think expedient, for their peace and common defence.*

And he that carrieth this person, is called SOVEREIGN, and said to have *sovereign power;* and every one besides, his SUBJECT.

. . . I observe the *diseases* of a commonwealth, that proceed from the poison of seditious doctrines, whereof one is, *That every private man is judge of good and evil actions.* This is true in the condition of mere nature, where there are no civil laws; and also under civil government, in such cases as are not determined by the law. But otherwise, it is manifest, that the measure of good and evil actions, is the civil law; and the judge the legislator, who is always representative of the com-monwealth. From this false doctrine, men are disposed to debate with them-selves, and dispute the commands of the commonwealth; and afterwards to obey, or disobey them, as in their private judgments they shall think fit; whereby the commonwealth is distracted and *weakened.*

Another doctrine repugnant to civil society, is, that *whatsoever a man does against his conscience, is sin;* and it dependeth on the presumption of making himself judge of good and evil. For a man's conscience, and his judgment is the same thing, and as the judgment, so also the conscience may be erroneous. Therefore, though he that is subject to no civil law, sinneth in all he does against his conscience, because he has no other rule to follow but his own reason; yet it is not so with him that lives in a commonwealth; because the law is the public conscience, by which he hath already undertaken to be guided. Otherwise in such diversity, as there is of private consciences, which are but private opinions, the commonwealth must needs be distracted, and no man dare to obey the sovereign power, further than it shall seem good in his own eyes. . . . There is [another] doctrine, plainly, and directly against the essence of a commonwealth; and it is this, *that the sovereign power may be divided.* For what is it to divide the power of a commonwealth, but to dissolve it; for powers divided mutually destroy each other. And for these doctrines, men are chiefly beholding to some of those, that making profession of the laws, endeavour to make them depend upon their own learning, and not upon the legislative power.

STUDY QUESTIONS

1   How does Hobbes define the word "good"? Could there be a common good for all persons?
2   Would Hobbes say that it is possible for someone to willingly give up his or her life? What would he say about martyrs and heroes?
3   "The trouble with Hobbes is that he bases his politics on man's worst impulses. Civil society should be organized so as to improve man's nature—to bring out and cultivate the emotion of love, the feeling of brotherhood, and acts of charity." How would Hobbes respond to this comment?
4   Hobbes argues that right and wrong, justice and injustice, would not exist prior to the founding of a commonwealth. Why is this? Do you agree?
5   Hobbes argues that the law takes precedence over conscience. Are there some cases where he cannot say this without inconsistency?
6   Evidently, Hobbes sees little danger of the sovereign using the position of power to attack his or her subjects. Assuming that Hobbes is essentially correct about human nature, could you convince a monarch to be strong but benevolent?

Why Choose Democracy?

Charles Frankel

Charles Frankel (1917–   ) Old Dominion Professor of Philosophy and Public Affairs at Columbia University, is one of America's outstanding political philosophers. He is active in governmental affairs, serving on several state and federal commissions, as well as international committees on education. From 1965 to 1967 he was Assistant Secretary of State for Education and Cultural Affairs. Among his many books are *The Case for Modern Man, The Faith of Reason, The Pleasures of Philosophy,* and a novel, *A Stubborn Case.*

Democratic institutions, Frankel claims, demand that we regard one another as probably rational, and that we accept our own fallibility. To live with the policies of those with whom we disagree, while we oppose them in socially acceptable ways, requires the citizen to adopt a scientific, hypothetical attitude. We are thus required to place our greatest allegiance in a *method,* rather than in a fixed doctrine. Above all we must value the search for truth, we must recognize that all the facts are not in, and we must allow our own values to stand the test of free and open criticism. These commitments allow for change within a system of civilized rules for competition—a competition of policies and ideas which allow mistakes to be corrected without social upheavals.

Above all, democratic policies demand that we treat others in ways which approximate the social dream of a free and equal society of people pursuing their own rational ideals. Democracy fosters democratic feelings toward others, Frankel says, and this is why it is the preferred system.

We have been overexposed to ideologies and political abstractions in this century, and have seen how much men are willing to sacrifice for the sake of ideological certainty. It is not surprising that sensitive men have developed something close to an ideology of uncertainty, and should look with a jaundiced eye on all questions about the justification of political systems. Why choose democracy? Trained in a hard school that has taught us the perils of belief, can we say anything more than that fanaticism is odious and that democracy should be chosen because it asks us to believe in very little?

On the contrary, it asks us to believe in a great deal. I do not believe we can show that the inside truth about the universe, human history, or the human psyche commands us to adopt democratic ideals. Choosing a political ideal is not like demonstrating the truth of a theorem in some geometry, and those who think that democracy needs that kind of justification are indirectly responsible for the uncertainty about it. Despite the semantic inflation from which the current discussion of political ideals suffers, the reasons for choosing democracy are neither mysterious nor difficult. But they are unsettling reasons, and they ask those who accept them to bet a great deal on their capacity to live with what they have chosen.

In an area so full of grandiose claims, it is safest to begin by using the word "democracy" in its narrowest sense. So conceived, democracy is the method of choosing a government through competitive elections in which people who are not members of the governing groups participate. Whatever may be said for or against democracy so conceived. it is surely not a supreme ideal of life. It is doubtful that anyone has ever treated the right to cast a ballot once every year or so as an end in itself. A society in which the democratic political method has been consolidated, to be sure, has a tremendous source of reassurance. It possesses a peaceful method for determining who shall hold power and for effecting changes in the structure of power. Yet even peace is only one value among others. It is worth something to have security and order, but how much it is worth depends on the kind of security and order it is. The importance of the democratic political method lies mainly in its nonpolitical by-products. It is important because a society in which it is well established will probably be different in at least four respects—in the conditions that protect its liberties, in the kind of consensus that prevails, in the character of the conflicts that go on within it, and in the manner in which it educates its rulers and citizens.

First, liberties. Construed strictly as a method for choosing governments, democracy does not guarantee the citizen's personal liberties. Democratic governments have attacked personal liberties, as in colonial New England, and undemocratic governments have often protected them, as in Vienna before World War I. Yet competitive elections have their points, and it is only one of their points that they allow a society to choose its government. For in order to main-

"Epilogue: Why Choose Democracy?" (pp. 166–179) from *The Democratic Prospect* by Charles Frankel. Copyright © 1962 by Charles Frankel. Reprinted by permission of Harper & Row, Publishers, Inc.

tain competitive elections, it is necessary to have an opposition, the opposition must have some independent rights and powers of its own, the good opinion of some people outside government must be sought, and at least some members of the society must have protections against the vengefulness of the powers that be. And this carries a whole train of institutions behind it—courts, a press not wholly devoted to promoting the interests of those in power, and independent agencies for social inquiry and criticism.

It is these necessitating conditions for elections that give elections their long-range significance. So far as political democracy is concerned, these conditions are only means to ends: they make competitive elections possible. But it is because a system of competitive elections requires and fosters such conditions that it justifies itself. The conditions required for maintaining an honest electoral system are the best reasons for wishing to maintain it. Indeed, a man might value such a system even though he thought all elections frivolous and foolish. He would have as good a reason to do so, and perhaps a better reason, than the man who always finds himself voting happily for the winning side. The outsider and the loser are the peculiar beneficiaries of a political system that creates institutions with a vested interest in liberty.

The democratic political method, furthermore, helps to foster a different kind of social consensus. There have been many kinds of political arrangement that have allowed men to feel that the government under which they live is *their* government. There is no clear evidence that democracy is necessarily superior to other systems in promoting a sense of oneness between rulers and ruled. But the special virtue of a democratic political system is that it permits men to feel at home within it who do not regard their political leaders as their own kind, and who would lose their self-respect, indeed, if they gave their unprovisional loyalty to any human institution. Despite all that is said about democratic pressures towards conformity—and a little of what is said is true—the democratic political system ceremonializes the fact of disagreement and the virtue of independent judgment. If it is to work, it requires an extraordinarily sophisticated human attitude—loyal opposition. The mark of a civilized man, in Justice Holmes' famous maxim, is that he can act with conviction while questioning his first principles. The ultimate claim of a democratic government to authority is that it permits dissent and survives it. In this respect, it dwells on the same moral landscape as the civilized man.

The democratic political method also changes the character of the conflicts that take place in a society. The perennial problem of politics is to manage conflict. And what happens in a conflict depends in part on who the onlookers are, how they react, and what powers they have. A significant fact about political democracy is that it immensely expands the audience that looks on and that feels itself affected and involved. This is why democratic citizens so often find democracy tiring and feel that their societies are peculiarly fragile. Hobbes, who said that he and fear were born as twins, recommended despotism in the interests of psychological security as well as physical safety.

But to say that democracy expands the scope of a conflict is also to say that democracy is a technique for the socialization of conflict. It brings a wider variety of pressures to bear on those who are quarreling and extends public control over private fights and private arrangements. And it does so whether these private fights are inside the government or outside. The association of democracy with the conception of private enerprise has something paradoxical about it. In one sense, there is more important enterprise that is private—free from outside discussion and surveillance—in totalitarian systems than in democratic systems. The persistent problem in a democratic system, indeed, is to know where to draw the line, where to say that outside surveillance is out of place. That line is drawn very firmly by those who make the important decisions in totalitarian societies.

But the final contribution that the democratic political method makes to the character of the society in which it is practiced is its contribution to education. Begin with the impact of political democracy on its leaders. The democratic method, like any other political method, is a system of rules for governing political competition. And such rules have both a selective and an educational force. They favor certain kinds of men, and make certain kinds of virtue more profitable and certain kinds of vice more possible. From this point of view, the significant characteristic of democratic rules of competition is that the loser is allowed to lose with honor, and permitted to live and try again if he wants. The stakes are heavy but limited. Such a system of competition gives men with sporting moral instincts a somewhat better chance to succeed. Even its typical kind of corruption has something to be said in its favor. The greased palm is bad but it is preferable to the mailed fist.

But enough of political systems. In any liberal view of men's business, politics is a subordinate enterprise. It has its soul-testing challenges and pleasures, and its great work to do. But like the work of commerce and industry, the work of politics is essentially servile labor. The State is not the place to turn if you want a free commentary on human experience, and governments do not produce science, philosophy, music, literature, or children—or at any rate they do not produce very convincing specimens of any of these things. Politics may achieve its own forms of excellence, but the more important human excellences are achieved elsewhere. And it is from this point of view, I think, that democracy should in the end be considered.

For the democratic idea is based on the assumption that the important ends of life are defined by private individuals in their own voluntary pursuits. Politics, for liberal democracy, is only one aspect of a civilization, a condition for civilization but not its total environment. That is probably why the air seems lighter as one travels from controlled societies to free ones. One receives an impression of vitality, the vitality of people who are going about their own business and generating their own momentum. They may be going off in more different directions than the members of a centrally organized society, but the directions are their own. The best reasons for choosing democracy lie in the qualities it is capable of bringing to our daily lives, in the ways in which it can furnish our minds, imaginations, and consciences. These qualities, I would say, are freedom, variety, self-consciousness, and the democratic attitude itself.

That democracy is hostile to distinction and prefers mediocrity is not a recent view. And there is an obvious sense in which it is true that democracy makes for homogeneity. Democracy erodes the clear distinctions between classes. It destroys ready-made status-symbols so rapidly that the manufacture of new ones becomes the occupation of a major industry. Most obvious of all, democracy increases the demand for a great many good things, from shoes to education. By increasing the demand, it also puts itself under pressure to cheapen the supply.

Yet certain pertinent facts must be set against these tendencies. First, more good things *are* more generally available in democracies. Second, egalitarianism's twin is the morality of achievement. There is a tension between the democratic suspicion of the man who sets himself apart and the democratic admiration for the man who stands out, but the egalitarian hostility towards ostentatious social distinctions is normally rooted in the belief that each man should be given a chance on his own to show what he can do. And finally, pressures towards uniformity are great in all societies. Is suspicion of the eccentric in egalitarian metropolitan America greater than in an eighteenth-century village? It is difficult to think so. "The fallacy of the aristocrat," Bertrand Russell has remarked, "consists in judging a society by the kind of life it affords a privileged few." Standing alone takes courage anywhere. Usually it also takes money; almost invariably it requires the guarantee that the individual will still retain his basic rights. In these respects modern liberal democracy, despite all the complaints about conformity, has made it easier for the ordinary unprivileged man to stand alone, if he has the will to do so, than any other kind of society known in history.

For however ambiguous some of the facts may be, the official commitment of liberal democracy is to the view that each man has his idiosyncrasies, that these idiosyncrasies deserve respect, and that if the individual does not know what is good for him, it is highly unlikely that a self-perpetuating elite will know better. And this is not just an official commitment. The institutions of liberal democracy go very far in giving it concrete embodiment. Assuming that the members of a democratic society have minimal economic securities, there is a flexibility in their situation which not many ordinary men have enjoyed in the past. If they fall out of favor with one set of authorities, they have a chance to turn around and look elsewhere.

It is unquestionable that there are great constellations of concentrated power in contemporary democratic societies; it is equally unquestionable that there is some freedom in any society. For in dealing with power, bright men learn how to work the angles. But in a democratic society there are more angles to work. Individual freedom of choice is not an absolute value. Any society must limit it; indeed, one man's freedom often rests on restricting the next man's. But while freedom of choice is not an absolute value, the democratic doctrine that each man has certain fundamental rights assigns an intrinsic value to his freedom of choice. If it has to be limited, it is recognized that something of value has been sacrificed. Social planning in a democracy is for this reason fundamentally different from social planning in undemocratic environments. The vague phrase "social utility," in a democratic setting, implicitly includes as one of its elements the value of freedom of choice.

What difference does this make? One difference is that variety is promoted;

a second is that individuals are educated in self-consciousness. Needless to say, variety, too, has its limits. We do not have to protect dope peddlers in its name. But the full import of variety, of the mere existence of differences and alternatives, is frequently overlooked. It does not merely give us more choices, or offer us a break in the routine. It affects the immediate quality of our experience; it changes our relation to whatever it is that we choose to have or do or be. This is what is forgotten when freedom is defined simply as the absence of felt frustrations, or when it is said that if a man has just what he wants, it makes little difference whether he has any choice or not. A good that is voluntarily chosen, a good which a man is always free to reconsider, belongs to him in a way that a passively accepted good does not. It is his responsibility.

And this means that democratic variety has another use as well. No one can say with assurance that democracy makes people wiser or more virtuous. But political democracy invites men to think that there may be alternatives to the way they are governed. And social democracy, in reducing the barriers of class, caste, and inherited privilege that stand between men, adds to the variety of people and occasions the individual meets and puts greater pressure on his capacity to adapt to the new and different. Political democracy and a socially mobile society thus invite the individual to a greater degree of consciousness about the relativity of his own ways and a greater degree of self-consciousness in the choice of the standards by which he lives. These are conditions for intensified personal experience. The role of democracy in the extension of these attitudes represents one of its principal contributions to the progress of liberal civilization.

The extension of such attitudes, to be sure, has its risks, which explains much of our uneasiness about what the democratic revolution means. Fads and fashions engage and distract larger groups in modern democratic societies. And social mobility, though it gives breadth and variety to men's experience, may well foreshorten their sense of time. Cut loose from fixed ranks and stations, each with its legends, rationale, and sense of historic vocation, the citizens of a modern democracy face a peculiar temptation to live experimentally, with the help of the latest book, as though no one had ever lived before. But these are the risks not simply of democracy but of modernity, and they can be controlled. The courts, the organized professions, the churches, and the universities are storehouses of funded experience. In a society in which they are given independence from the political urgencies of the moment, they can serve as protections against the dictatorship of the specious present. Modernity implies a revolution in human consciousness. Democratic social arrangements reflect that revolution and accept it; but they also provide instruments for guiding and controlling it. None of democracy's contemporary rivals possess these two qualities to the same extent.

In the end, indeed, the risks of democracy are simply the risks implicit in suggesting to men that the answers are not all in. Democracy gives political form to the principle that also regulates the scientific community—the principle that inquiry must be kept open, that there are no sacred books, that no conclusion that men have ever reached can be taken to be the necessary final world. Cant, obscurantism, and lies are of course a good part of the diet of most democracies. Man is a truth-fearing animal, and it would be a miracle if any social system could quickly change this fact. But the institutions of liberal democracy are unique in that they require men to hold no irreversible beliefs in anything except in the method of free criticism and peaceful change itself, and in the ethic on which this method rests. Such a social system permits men to give their highest loyalty, not to temporary human beliefs or institutions, but to the continuing pursuit after the truth, whatever it may be. The intellectual rationale of democracy is precisely that it does not need to make the foolish and arrogant claim that it rests on infallible truths. Men can believe in it and still believe that the truth is larger than anything they may think they know.

Yet the question that probably gnaws at us most deeply still remains. Freedom, variety, self-consciousness, a sane awareness of human fallibility, and loyalty to the principle that inquiry must be kept open—obviously, these have much in their favor. But they are refined values. Has liberal democracy priced itself out of the competition? Does it have anything to say, not to those who already know and enjoy it, but to the many more who must come to want it if human liberties are to be a little more secure in the world than they now are?

One of the debilitating illusions of many Western liberals is that the values of liberal culture are only our own values, that they have little point for those who look at the world differently, and no point at all for those whose lives are poor, mean, brutish, and short. Although colonialists used this view for different purposes, they shared it, and it betrays an inexact understanding of the nature of liberal values. Freedom, variety, self-consciousness, and the chance to seek the truth are all taxing experiences. Their virtues may be hard to conceive by those who have never enjoyed them. Yet in spite of the discomforts these values bring, the evidence indicates, I think, that most men would be happy to have them, and would think their lives enhanced. The difficulty with the most characteristic liberal values is not that they are parochial values. The difficulty is that men have other more imperious wants, like the need for medicines, schooling, bread, release from usurers, or a chance to get out from under corrupt and exploitative regimes. Illiberal programs promise these substantial material improvements and frequently deliver. And liberal programs, if they speak of freedom and leave out the usury and corruption, do not generally bring freedom either.

But let us assume, as there is every reason to assume, that liberal programs, if they are willing to recognize that they, too, must make a revolution, can also improve men's material condition. What can be said to the young man or the young—or old—nation in a hurry? What good reasons can we give, reasons that take account of their present condition and justified impatience, when we try to explain to them—and to ourselves—why the liberal path, despite its meanderings, is preferable to the authoritarian path?

One thing that can be said, quite simply, is that the authoritarian path closes up behind the traveler as he moves. The virtue of liberal democracy is that it permits second thoughts. To choose an authoritarian regime is to bet everything on a single throw of the dice; if the bet is bad, there is no way out save through violence, and not much hope in that direction. To choose a liberal approach, while it does not guarantee against errors, guarantees against the error so fatal that there is no peaceful way out or back. But there is another reason as well. The reason for choosing democracy is that it makes democrats.

The competition that takes place in a democracy is an instance of cooperative competition. It is a struggle in which both sides work to maintain the conditions necessary for a decent struggle. Accordingly, it rests on the assumption that there are no irreconcilable conflicts, that differences can be negotiated or compromised, if men have good will. Such a system requires men to deal with one another honestly, to make a serious effort to reach agreements, and to keep them after they have been made. It requires them to recognize, therefore, that the other side has its interests and to be prepared to make concessions to these interests when such concessions are not inconsistent with fundamental principles. A democratic ethic does not ask men to be fools. They do not have to assume that their opponents have put all their cards on the table. But democratic competition is impossible if the parties to the competition cannot assume that their opponents will recognize their victory if they win and will cooperate with them afterwards. The intention to annihilate the opposition or to win at all costs destroys the possibility of a regulated struggle. In this sense democracy is an exercise in the ethic of good faith. It is a system that makes it possible for men, not to love their enemies, but at least to live without fearing them. That kind of mutual trust between enemies is what authoritarianism destroys.

No doubt, such an argument may seem pathetically beside the point to men who live in societies that have been torn by distrust for centuries and that have known government only as a name for cruelty and dishonesty. If such men succeed in installing democratic regimes in their countries, they will do so by recognizing their enemies and distrusting them. But the harshness that goes with any deep social revolution is one thing if it is recognized as a bitter and dangerous necessity and is kept within limits. It is another if the violence is doctrinal, and the assumption is made that men can never cooperate unless they have the same interests and ideas. Such an assumption, as all the evidence suggests, encourages the adoption of terror as an official policy and condemns a society to an indefinite period in which power will be monopolistically controlled. In a diversified modern society, indeed in any society that has ever begun the movement towards modernity, the doctrine of governmental infallibility trains men in suspiciousness and conspiracy. Perhaps other objectives will be achieved, but under such circumstances their taste will be sour.

Nor does the doctrine of infallibility destroy only good faith. It is also incompatible with a belief in the probable rationality of others. To hold a democratic attitude is to proceed on the assumption that other men may have their own persuasive reasons for thinking as they do. If they disagree with you, this does not necessarily make them candidates for correction and cure. This is the homely meaning of the oft-repeated assertion that democracy has faith in the reasonableness and equality of human beings. The faith does not assert that all men are in fact reasonable, or that they are equal in the capacity to think well or live sensibly. The faith is pragmatic: it expresses a policy. And the policy is simply to credit others with minds of their own, and to hold them responsible for their actions, until there are strong and quite specific reasons for thinking otherwise. Such a policy allows room for the idiosyncrasies of men and permits the varieties of human intelligence to be recognized and used.

In the end, the man who asks himself why he should choose democracy is asking himself to decide with which of two policies he would rather live. One is the policy of normally thinking that his fellows are dangerous to him and to themselves. The other is the policy of thinking that they are reasonable until they show themselves dangerous. To act on either policy has its risks. Why should a man choose one rather than the other? One reason can be found if he asks himself about the consequences the policy he adopts will have for the elementary feelings he will entertain towards his fellows, not in some transfigured world to come, but here and now. The point of the democratic policy is that it makes for democratic feelings. Those who do not wish to see human society divided into exploiters and exploited, those who wish to see each man come into his own free estate, believe that in that ultimate condition men will treat each other with the respect and fellow-feeling that equals show to equals. It is in the name of such moral attitudes that they seek democracy. The final reason for choosing the democratic method is that it provides a training ground, here and now, in just these attitudes.

But arguments have their limits. It is not through disputation that men become convinced of the worth of a social system. It is through its capacity to exemplify a vision of human possibility and to move towards that vision. In the past the United States was a contagion. Its distinction, the quality that set it apart, was that it was a society moved by its prospect. The sense that American democracy has a prospect—that its future does not consist simply in rolling with the punches of its adversaries or in expanding its present sort of affluence still further—is most obviously absent from the present scene.

More than arguments about the advantages of democracy in comparison with other systems is required to restore that sense. At the end of his great book, Tocqueville wrote: "Let us, then, look forward to the future with that salutary fear which makes men keep watch and ward for freedom, not with that faint and idle terror which depresses and enervates the heart." The faint and idle terrors that depress and enervate us today are in part self-induced: they are not justified by a circumspect estimate of the resources of American democracy. But neither can such an estimate explain our spotty and undiscriminating affluence, or the bewilderment, scorn, and violence that lie a millimeter below the surface in the slums of our deteriorating cities, or the advancing bulldozed ugliness of our countryside, or the present condition of the public welfare, voluntary associations, the media of communication, and our work and play.

Like any social system, democracy must give men something in which to believe. They have to discern in what they are doing the intimation of a civic order that has beauty and design. That end cannot be accomplished by the currently fashionable technique of filling the air with words and filling words with air. Not even courage, good will, intelligence, and resolute action are enough. The action has to add up to a scheme of action; it has to be action lit by purposes that are visible, concrete, coherent, and deliberately chosen.

For in the modern world it is motion with a meaning, change in an identifiable and desired direction, which is the basic generator of belief in a social system. And the point about democracy, the point to it, is that it rests on the assumption that men have some choice about that direction, that it is not given to them or prearranged for them, but that, within limits, they can define it for themselves. When they do, when they use the chance for choice that makes democratic arrangements precious, the question "Why choose democracy?" becomes redundant.

STUDY QUESTIONS

1 According to Frankel, "the conditions for maintaining an honest electoral system are the best reasons for wishing to maintain it." What are some of these conditions and why are they valuable?

2 Frankel says that democracy promotes variety. Is this true, do you think?

3 Suppose Frankel were to confront a person from one of the developing nations where democratic institutions do not exist. How would he attempt to persuade this person that democracy was the best political system to solve the immediate economic and social problems which confront such nations?

4 "Nothing can do more harm to democracy than the thesis, so popular with many contemporary moral and religious leaders, that science is neutral, if not positively evil, with respect to human values. The truth of the matter is that the scientific attitude of mind is one of the highest values, and a primary value in democracy" (F. C. S. Northrop). Would Frankel agree with this? Why? What do you think is the "scientific attitude"? Do you agree that it is a value?

5 What do you think is the proper place of religion in a democracy? Do you think that religious beliefs are supportive of democratic ideals? Is the scientific attitude inconsistent with the "religious attitude"?

6 How would Hobbes respond to Frankel's argument? What are the crucial points of disagreement between them? Are there any shared values that you can detect?

Our Duty to the Law

Plato

In 404 B.C. the Peloponnesian War ended with the defeat of Athens. The victorious Spartans set up a puppet regime of thirty men who proceeded to terrorize the citizens with mass arrests and executions of dissenters. When the supporters of democracy came back into power and made peace with the Spartans, they, in turn, took reprisals against those who had sided with what became known as the *Tyranny of the Thirty*. Socrates, the friend and teacher of Plato (see biographies on pp. 136 and 189), was suspected of complicity in some of the brutalities of the Thirty. But this was untrue, and since nothing could be proved against him, he was accused of corrupting the youth and of being impious. Although he denied the charges, he was found guilty, and was executed in 399.

Plato knew that Socrates was innocent and that the legal process had been corrupted by prejudice. Nevertheless, in the following selection, Plato has Socrates defending the right of the state to take his life and arguing that he is obliged to allow it. Plato had seen what life was like when the rule of law disappeared—more Athenians were killed during the year-long reign of the Thirty than in the previous twenty-seven years of the war. The rule of law is our only protection against anarchy.

But the law can be unfair or the legal process can be perverted, and when this occurs, why should we surrender our own conscience and our own sense of justice—indeed our very lives—to some remote ideal of social order? Plato's answer to these questions may not satisfy you, but you can be sure that they were agonizingly reached by a man who saw his best friend unjustly executed by the Athenian court.

Crito: . . . But, oh! my beloved Socrates, let me entreat you once more to take my advice and escape. For if you die I shall not only lose a friend who can never be replaced, but there is another evil: people who do not know you and me will believe that I might have saved you if I had been willing to give money, but that I did not care. Now, can there be a worse disgrace than this—that I should be thought to value money more than the life of a friend? For the many will not be persuaded that I wanted you to escape, and that you refused.

Socrates: But why, my dear Crito, should we care about the opinion of the many? Good men, and they are the only persons who are worth considering, will think of these things truly as they occurred.

Crito: But you see, Socrates, that the opinion of the many must be regarded, for what is happening shows that they can do the greatest evil to any one who has lost their good opinion.

Socrates: I only wish it were so, Crito; and that the many could do the greatest evil; for then they would also be able to do the greatest good—and what a fine thing this would be! But in reality they can do neither; for they cannot make a man either wise or foolish; and whatever they do is the result of chance.

Crito: Well, I will not dispute with you; but please tell me, Socrates, whether you are not acting out of regard to me and your other friends: are you not afraid that if you escape from prison we may get into trouble with the informers for having stolen you away, and lose either the whole or a great part of our property; or that even a worse evil may happen to us? Now, if you fear on our account, be at ease; for in order to save you, we ought surely to run this, or even a greater risk; be persuaded, then, and do as I say.

Socrates: Yes, Crito, that is one fear which you mention, but by no means the only one.

Crito: Fear not—there are persons who are willing to get you out of prison at no great cost; and as for the informers, they are far from being exorbitant in their demands—a little money will satisfy them. My means, which are certainly ample, are at your service, and if you have a scruple about spending all mine, here are strangers who will give you the use of theirs; and one of them, Simias the Theban, has brought a large sum of money for this very purpose; and Cebes and many

From *The Crito,* in *The Dialogues of Plato,* Benjamin Jowett, trans. (The Macmillan Company, Ltd., 1892).

others are prepared to spend their money in helping you to escape. I say, therefore, do not hesitate on our account, and do not say, as you did in court, that you will have a difficulty in knowing what to do with yourself anywhere else. For men will love you in other places to which you may go, and not in Athens only; there are friends of mine in Thessaly, if you like to go to them, who will value and protect you, and no Thessalian will give you any trouble. Nor can I think that you are at all justified, Socrates, in betraying your own life when you might be saved; in acting thus you are playing into the hands of your enemies, who are hurrying on your destruction. And further I should say that you are deserting your own children; for you might bring them up and educate them; instead of which you go away and leave them, and they will have to take their chance; and if they do not meet with the usual fate of orphans, there will be small thanks to you. No man should bring children into the world who is unwilling to persevere to the end in their nurture and education. But you appear to be choosing the easier part, not the better and manlier, which would have been more becoming in one who professes to care for virtue in all his actions, like yourself. And indeed, I am ashamed not only of you, but of us who are your friends, when I reflect that the whole business will be attributed entirely to our want of courage. The trial need never have come on, or might have been managed differently; and this last act, or crowning folly, will seem to have occurred through our negligence and cowardice, who might have saved you, if you had been good for anything; and you might have saved yourself, for there was no difficulty at all. See now, Socrates, how sad and discreditable are the consequences, both to us and you. Make up your mind then, or rather have your mind already made up, for the time of deliberation is over, and there is only one thing to be done, which must be done this very night, and if we delay at all will be no longer practicable or possible; I beseech you therefore, Socrates, be persuaded by me, and do as I say.

Socrates: Dear Crito, your zeal is invaluable, if a right one; but if wrong, the greater the zeal the greater the danger; and therefore we ought to consider whether I shall or shall not do as you say. For I am and always have been one of those natures who must be guided by reason, whatever the reason may be which upon reflection appears to me to be the best; and now that this chance has befallen me, I cannot repudiate my own words: the principles which I have hitherto honoured and revered I still honour, and unless we can at once find other and better principles, I am certain not to agree with you; no, not even if the power of the multitude could inflict many more imprisonments, confiscations, deaths, frightening us like children with hobgoblin terrors. What will be the fairest way of considering the question? Shall I return to your old argument about the opinions of men?—we are saying that some of them are to be regarded, and others not. Now were we right in maintaining this before I was condemned? And has the argument which was once good now proved to be talk for the sake of talking— mere childish nonsense? That is what I want to consider with your help, Crito: whether, under my present circumstances, the argument appears to be in any way different or not; and is to be allowed by me or disallowed. That argument, which, as I believe, is maintained by many persons of authority, was to the effect, as I was saying, that the opinions of some men are to be regarded, and of other men not to be regarded. Now you, Crito, are not going to die tomorrow—at least, there is no human probability of this—and therefore you are disinterested and not liable to be deceived by the circumstances in which you are placed. Tell me then, whether I am right in saying that some opinions, and the opinions of some men only, are to be valued, and that other opinions, and the opinions of other men, are not to be valuable. I ask you whether I was right in maintaining this?

Crito: Certainly.

Socrates: The good are to be regarded, and not the bad?

Crito: Yes.

Socrates: And the opinions of the wise are good, and the opinions of the unwise are evil?

Crito: Certainly.

Socrates: And what was said about another matter? Is the pupil who devotes himself to the practice of gymnastics supposed to attend to the praise and blame and opinion of every man, or of one man only—his physician or trainer, whoever he may be?

Crito: Of one man only.

Socrates: And he ought to fear the censure and welcome the praise of that one only, and not of the many?

Crito: Clearly so.

Socrates: And he ought to act and train, and eat and drink in the way which seems good to his single master who has understanding, rather than according to the opinion of all other men put together?

Crito: True.

Socrates: And if he disobeys and disregards the opinion and approval of the one, and regards the opinion of the many who have no understanding, will he not suffer evil?

Crito: Certainly he will.

Socrates: And what will the evil be, whither tending and what affecting, in the disobedient person?

Crito: Clearly, affecting the body; that is what is destroyed by the evil.

Socrates: Very good; and is not this true, Crito, of other things which we need not separately enumerate? In questions of just and unjust, fair and foul, good and evil, which are the subjects of our present consultation, ought we to follow the opinion of the many and to fear them; or the opinion of the one man who has understanding? ought we not to fear and reverence him more than all the rest of the world: and if we desert him shall we not destroy and injure that principle in us which may be assumed to be improved by justice and deteriorated by injustice;—there is such a principle?

Crito: Certainly there is, Socrates.

Socrates: Take a parallel instance:—if, acting under the advice of those who have no understanding, we destroy that which is improved by health and is deteriorated by disease, would life be worth having? And that which has been destroyed is—the body?

Crito: Yes.

Socrates: Could we live, having an evil and corrupted body?

Crito: Certainly not.

Socrates: And will life be worth having, if that higher part of man be destroyed, which is improved by justice and depraved by injustice? Do we suppose that principle, whatever it may be in man, which has to do with justice and injustice, to be inferior to the body?

Crito: Certainly not.

Socrates: More honourable than the body?

Crito: Far more.

Socrates: Then, my friend, we must not regard what the many say of us: but what he, the one man who has understanding of just and unjust, will say, and what the truth will say. And therefore you begin in error when you advise that we should regard the opinion of the many about just and unjust, good and evil, honourable and dishonourable,—"Well," some one will say, "but the many can kill us."

Crito: Yes, Socrates; that will clearly be the answer.

Socrates: And it is true: but still I find with surprise that the old argument is unshaken as ever. And I should like to know whether I may say the same of another proposition—that not life, but a good life, is to be chiefly valued?

Crito: Yes, that also remains unshaken.

Socrates: And a good life is equivalent to a just and honourable one—that holds also?

Crito: Yes, it does.

Socrates: From these premises I proceed to argue the question whether I ought or ought not to try and escape without the consent of the Athenians: and if I am clearly right in escaping, then I will make the attempt; but if not, I will abstain. The other considerations which you mention, of money and loss of character and the duty of educating one's children are, I fear, only the doctrines of the multitude, who would be as ready to restore people to life, if they were able, as they are to put them to death—and with as little reason. But now, since the argument has thus far prevailed, the only question which remains to be considered is, whether we shall do rightly either in escaping or in suffering others to aid in our escape and paying them in money and thanks, or whether in reality we shall not do rightly; and if the latter, then death or any other calamity which may ensue on my remaining here must not be allowed to enter into the calculation.

Crito: I think that you are right, Socrates; how then shall we proceed?

Socrates: Let us consider the matter together, and do you either refute me if you can, and I will be convinced; or else cease, my dear friend, from repeating to me that I ought to escape against the wishes of the Athenians: for I highly value your attempts to persuade me to do so, but I may not be persuaded against my own better judgment. And now please to consider my first position, and try how you can best answer me.

Crito: I will.

Socrates: Are we to say that we are never intentionally to do wrong, or that in one way we ought and in another we ought not to do wrong, or is doing wrong always evil and dishonourable, as I was just now saying, and as has been already acknowledged by us? Are all our former admissions which were made within a few days to be thrown away? And have we, at our age, been earnestly discoursing with one another all our life long only to discover that we are no better than children? Or, in spite of the opinion of the many, and in spite of consequences whether better or worse, shall we insist on the truth of what was then said, that injustice is always an evil and dishonour to him who acts unjustly? Shall we say so or not?

Crito: Yes.

Socrates: Then we must do no wrong?

Crito: Certainly not.

Socrates: Nor when injured injure in return, as the many imagine; for we must injure no one at all?

Crito: Clearly not.

Socrates: Again, Crito, may we do evil?

Crito: Surely not, Socrates.

Socrates: And what of doing evil in return for evil, which is the morality of the many—is that just or not?

Crito: Not just.

Socrates: For doing evil to another is the same as injuring him?

Crito: Very true.

Socrates: Then we ought not to retaliate or render evil for evil to any one, whatever evil we may have suffered from him. But I would have you consider, Crito, whether you really mean what you are saying. For this opinion has never been held, and never will be held, by any considerable number of persons; and those who are agreed and those who are not agreed upon this point have no common ground, and can only despise one another when they see how widely they differ. Tell me, then, whether you agree with and assent to my first principle, that neither injury nor retaliation nor warding off evil by evil is ever right. And shall that be the premiss of our argument? Or do you decline and dissent from this? For so I have ever thought, and continue to think; but, if you are of another opinion, let me hear what you have to say. If, however, you remain of the same mind as formerly, I will proceed to the next step.

Crito: You may proceed, for I have not changed my mind.

Socrates: Then I will go on to the next point, which may be put in the form of a question:—Ought a man to do what he admits to be right, or ought he to betray the right?

Crito: He ought to do what he thinks right.

Socrates: But if this is true, what is the application? In leaving the prison against the will of the Athenians, do I wrong any? or rather do I not wrong those whom I ought least to wrong? Do I not desert the principles which were acknowledged by us to be just—what do you say?

Crito: I cannot tell, Socrates; for I do not know.

Socrates: Then consider the matter in this way: Imagine that I am about to play truant (you may call the proceeding by any name which you like), and the laws and the government come and interrogate me: "Tell us, Socrates," they say, "what are you about? are you not going by an act of yours to overturn us—the laws, and the whole state, as far as in you lies? Do you imagine that a state can subsist and not be overthrown, in which the decisions of law have no power, but are set aside and trampled upon by individuals?" What will be our answer, Crito, to these and the like words? Any one, and especially a rhetorician, will have a good deal to say on behalf of the law which requires a sentence to be carried out. He will argue that this law should not be set aside; and shall we reply, "Yes; but the state has injured us and given an unjust sentence." Suppose I say that?

Crito: Very good, Socrates.

Socrates: "And was that our agreement with you?" the law would answer, "or were you to abide by the sentence of the state?" And if I were to express my astonishment at their words, the law would probably add: "Answer, Socrates, instead of opening your eyes—you are in the habit of asking and answering questions. Tell us,—What complaint have you to make against us which justifies you in attempting to destroy us and the state? In the first place did we not bring you into existence? Your father married your mother by our aid and begat you. Say whether you have any objection to urge against those of us who regulate marriage?" None, I should reply. "Or against those of us who after birth regulate the nurture and education of children, in which you also were trained? Were not the laws, which have the charge of education, right in commanding your father to train you in music and gymnastic?" Right, I should reply. "Well then, since you were brought into the world and nurtured and educated by us, can you deny in the first place that you are our child and slave, as your fathers were before you? And if this is true you are not on equal terms with us; nor can you think that you have a right to do to us what we are doing to you. Would you have any right to strike or revile or do any other evil to your father or your master, if you had one, because you have been struck or reviled by him, or received some other evil at his hands?—you would not say this? And because we think right to destroy you, do you think that you have any right to destroy us in return, and your country as far as in you lies? Will you, O professor of true virtue, pretend that you are justified in this? Has a philosopher like you failed to discover that our country is more to be valued and higher and holier far than mother or father or any ancestor, and more to be regarded in the eyes of the gods and of men of understanding? Also to be soothed, and gently and reverently entreated when angry, even more than a father, and either to be persuaded, or if not persuaded, to be obeyed? And when we are punished by her, whether with imprisonment or stripes, the punishment is to be endured in silence; and if she leads us to wounds or death in battle, thither we follow as is right; neither may any one yield or retreat or leave his rank, but whether in battle or in a court of law, or in any other place, he must do what his city and his country order him; or he must change their view of what is just: and if he may do no violence to his father or mother, much less may he do violence to his country." What answer shall we make to this Crito? Do the laws speak truly, or do they not?

Crito: I think that they do.

Socrates: Then the laws will say, "Consider, Socrates, if we are speaking truly that in your present attempt you are going to do us an injury. For, having brought you into the world, and nurtured and educated you, and given you and every other citizen a share in every good which we had to give, we further proclaim to any Athenian by the liberty which we allow him, that if he does not like us when he has become of age and has seen the ways of the city, and made our acquaintance, he may go where he pleases and take his goods with him. None of us laws will forbid him or interfere with him. Any one who does not like us and the city, and who wants to emigrate to a colony or to any other city, may go where he likes, retaining his property. But he who has experience of the manner in which we order justice and administer the state, and still remains, has entered into an implied contract that he will do as we command him. And he who disobeys us is, as we maintain, thrice wrong; first, because in disobeying us he is disobeying his parents; secondly, because we are the authors of his education; thirdly, because he has made an agreement with us that he will duly obey our commands; and he neither obeys them nor convinces us that our commands are unjust; and we do not rudely impose them, but give him the alternative of obeying or convincing us;—that is what we offer, and he does neither.

"These are the sort of accusations to which, as we were saying, you, Socrates, will be exposed if you accomplish your intentions; you, above all other Athenians." Suppose now I ask, why I rather than anybody else? they will justly retort upon me that I above all other men have acknowledged the agreement. "There is clear proof," they will say, "Socrates, that we and the city were not displeasing to you. Of all Athenians you have been the most constant resident in the city, which, as you never leave, you may be supposed to love. For you never went out of the city either to see the games, except once when you went to the Isthmus, or to any other place unless when you were on military service; nor did you travel as other men do. Nor had you any curiosity to know other states or their laws; your affections did not go beyond us and our state; we were your special favourites, and you acquiesced in our govenment of you; and here in this city you begat your children, which is a proof of your satisfaction. Moreover, you might in the course of the trial, if you had liked, have fixed the penalty at banishment; the state which refuses to let you go now would have let you go then. But you pretended that you preferred death to exile, and that you were not unwilling to die. And now you have forgotten these fine sentiments, and pay no respect to us the laws, of whom you are the destroyer; and are doing what only a miserable slave would do, running away and turning your back upon the compacts and agreements which you made as a citizen. And first of all answer this very question: Are we right in saying that you agreed to be governed according to us in deed, and not in word only? Is that true or not?" How shall we answer, Crito? Must we not assent?

Crito: We cannot help it, Socrates.

Socrates: Then will they not say: "You, Socrates, are breaking the covenants and agreements which you made with us at your leisure, not in any haste or under any compulsion or deception, but after you have had seventy years to think of them, during which time you were at liberty to leave the city, if we were not to your mind, or if our covenants appeared to you to be unfair. You had your choice, and might have gone either to Lacedaemon or Crete, both which states are often praised by you for their good government, or to some other Hellenic or foreign state. Whereas you, above all other Athenians, seemed to be so fond of the state, or, in other words, of us her laws (and who would care about a state which has no laws?), that you never stirred out of her; the halt, the blind, the maimed were not more stationary in her than you were. And now you run away and forsake your agreements. Not so, Socrates, if you will take our advice; do not make yourself ridiculous by escaping out of the city.

"For just consider, if you transgress and err in this sort of way, what good will you do either to yourself or to your friends? That your friends will be driven into exile and deprived of citizenship, or will lose their property, is tolerably certain; and you yourself, if you fly to one of the neighboring cities, as, for example, Thebes or Megara, both of which are well governed, will come to them as an enemy, Socrates, and their government will be against you, and all patriotic citizens will cast an evil eye upon you as a subverter of the laws, and you will confirm in the minds of the judges the justice of their own condemnation of you. For he who is a corrupter of the laws is more than likely to be a corrupter of the young and foolish portion of mankind. Will you then flee from well-ordered cities and virtuous men? and is existence worth having on these terms? Or will you go to them without shame, and talk to them, Socrates? And what will you say to them? What you say here about virtue and justice and institutions and laws being the best things among well-governed states to Crito's friends in Thessaly, where there is great disorder and licence, they will be charmed to hear the tale of your escape from prison, set off with ludicrous particulars of the manner in which you were wrapped in a goatskin or some other disguise, and metamorphosed as the manner is of runaways; but will there be no one to remind you that in your old age you were not ashamed to violate the most sacred laws from a miserable desire of a little more life? Perhaps not, if you keep them in a good temper; but if they are out of temper you will hear many degrading things; you will live, but how?—as the flatterer of all men, and the servant of all men; and doing what?— eating and drinking in Thessaly, having gone abroad in order that you may get a dinner. And where will be your fine sentiments about justice and virtue? Say that you wish to live for the sake of your children—you want to bring them up and educate them—will you take them into Thessaly and deprive them of Athenian citizenship? Is this the benefit which you will confer upon them? Or are you under the impression that whey will be better cared for and educated here if you are still alive, although absent from them; for your friends will take care of them? Do you fancy that if you are an inhabitant of Thessaly they will take care of them, and if you are an inhabitant of the other world that they will not take care of them? Nay; but if they who call themselves friends are good for anything, they will—to be sure they will.

"Listen, then, Socrates, to us who have brought you up. Think not of life and children first, and of justice afterwards, but of justice first, that you may be justified before the princes of the world below. For neither will you nor any that belong to you be happier or holier or juster in this life, or happier in another, if you do as Crito bids. Now you depart in innocence, a sufferer and not a doer of evil; a victim, not of the laws but of men. But if you go forth, returning evil for evil, and injury for injury, breaking the covenants and agreements which you have made with us, and wronging those whom you ought least of all to wrong, that is to say, yourself, your friends, your country, and us, we shall be angry with you while you live, and our brethren, the laws of the world below, will receive you as an enemy; for they will know that you have done your best to destroy us. Listen, then, to us and not to Crito."

This, dear Crito, is the voice which I seem to hear murmuring in my ears, like the sound of the flute in the ears of the mystic; that voice, I say, is humming in my ears and prevents me from hearing any other. And I know that anything more which you may say will be in vain. Yet speak, if you have anything to say.

Crito: I have nothing to say, Socrates.

Socrates: Leave me then, Crito, to fulfil the will of God, and to follow whither he leads.

STUDY QUESTIONS

1   Socrates characterizes his relationship to the state as that of a child to its parent. What facts support this analogy? Do you agree with the comparison?

2   What are the limits of authority of parents over their children? When may a child rightfully reject the demands of parents? Do these considerations apply in Socrates's case?

3   Socrates argues that he is obliged to obey the law because he has contractually promised to do so. What facts are adduced to support the claim that he is under an implied contract to obey the law? Do you think the evidence is sufficient to demonstrate that a contract exists?

4   Surely contracts are not binding under any and all circumstances. What sorts of considerations would justify the breaking of a contract? Do you think that any of them obtain in this case?

5   Would Socrates grant amnesty to Vietnam draft resisters? Would you?

6   "An ordered society cannot exist if every man may determine which laws he will obey . . . that only 'just' laws need be obeyed and that every man is free to determine for himself the question of 'justness' " (Lewis F. Powell, Jr.). To what extent would Socrates agree with this? Would he accept it unqualifiedly?

In Defense of Anarchism

Robert Paul Wolff

Robert Paul Wolff (1933–   ) is a professor of philosophy at the University of Massachusetts. During his first year as a university professor, Wolff announced to his students that he would solve the fundamental problem of political philosophy. He writes: "I had no trouble formulating the problem—roughly speaking, how the moral autonomy of the individual can be made compatible with the legitimate authority of the state. . . . But mid-way through the semester, I was forced to go before my class, crestfallen and very embarrassed, to announce that I had failed to discover the grand solution." Eventually Wolff was led into the position of *political anarchism*—the view that no state has legitimate authority over its citizens.

Throughout history governments have ordered citizens into battle, and most of the time the wars people have fought have been unnecessary and immoral. Yet people usually submit to the demands of the state. Indeed, most often, this submission is based on the simple admission that the state *has the right to command.* This admission presents a dilemma: if the state has the *right* to command, then I am obliged to obey, even if I disagree with its orders. It makes no sense to say that someone has a *right* to do something, unless there is a corresponding obligation to allow that activity. To say that I have the right to free speech, for example, means that others have the obligation to allow me to speak freely, even if they disagree with what I say. Therefore, if I admit that the state has the right to command, that the state is a legitimate authority, then I give up moral independence and allow myself to be guided by the will of another. Wolff maintains that this forfeit of moral autonomy is never legitimate, and this means that no state has legitimate authority over its citizens. We, not the state, are the rightful arbiters of what we ought to do.

1. THE CONCEPT OF AUTHORITY

Politics is the exercise of the power of the state, or the attempt to influence that exercise. Political philosophy is therefore, strictly speaking, the philosophy of the state. If we are to determine the content of political philosophy, and whether indeed it exists, we must begin with the concept of the state.

The state is a group of persons who have and exercise supreme authority within a given territory. Strictly, we should say that a state is a group of persons who have supreme authority within a given territory or *over a certain population.* A nomadic tribe may exhibit the authority structure of a sate, so long as its subjects do not fall under the superior authority of a territorial state.[1] The state may include all the persons who fall under its authority, as does the democratic state according to its theorists; it may also consist of a single individual to whom all the rest are subject. We may doubt whether the one-person state has ever actually existed, although Louis XIV evidently thought so when he announced, *"L'état, c'est moi."* The distinctive characteristic of the state is supreme authority, or what political philosophers used to call "sovereignty." Thus one speaks of "popular sovereignty," which is the doctrine that the people are the state, and of course, the use of "sovereign" to mean "king" reflects the supposed concentration of supreme authority in a monarchy.

Authority is the right to command, and correlatively, the right to be obeyed. It must be distinguished from power, which is the ability to compel compliance, either through the use or the threat of force. When I turn over my wallet to a thief who is holding me at gunpoint, I do so because the fate with which he threatens me is worse than the loss of money which I am made to suffer. I grant that he has power over me, but I would hardly suppose that he has *authority,* that is, that he has a right to demand my money and that I have an obligation to give it to him. When the government presents me with a bill for taxes, on the other hand, I pay

[1] For a similar definition of "state," see Max Weber, *Politics as a Vocation.* Weber emphasizes the means—force—by which the will of the state is imposed, but a careful analysis of his definition shows that it also bases itself on the notion of authority ("imperative coordination").

it (normally) even though I do not wish to, and even if I think I can get away with not paying. It is, after all, the duly constituted government, and hence it has a *right* to tax me. It has *authority* over me. Sometimes, of course, I cheat the government, but even so, I acknowledge its authority, for who would speak of "cheating" a thief?

To *claim* authority is to claim the right to be obeyed. To *have* authority is then—what? It may mean to have that right, or it may mean to have one's claim acknowledged and accepted by those at whom it is directed. The term "authority" is ambiguous, having both a descriptive and a normative sense. Even the descriptive sense refers to norms or obligations, of course, but it does so by *describing* what men believe they ought to do rather than by *asserting* that they ought to do it.

Corresponding to the two senses of authority, there are two concepts of the state. Descriptively, the state may be defined as a group of persons who are *acknowledged* to have supreme authority within a territory—acknowledged, that is, by those over whom the authority is asserted. The study of the forms, characteristics, institutions, and functioning of *de facto* states, as we may call them, is the province of political science. If we take the term in its prescriptive signification, the state is a group of persons who have the *right* to exercise supreme authority within a territory. The discovery, analysis, and demonstration of the forms and principles of legitimate authority—of the right to rule—is called political philosophy.

What is meant by *supreme* authority? Some political philosophers, speaking of authority in the normative sense, have held that the true state has ultimate authority over all matters whatsoever that occur within its venue. Jean-Jacques Rousseau, for example, asserted that the social contract by which a just political community is formed "gives to the body politic absolute command over the members of which it is formed; and it is this power, when directed by the general will, that bears . . . the name of 'sovereignty.' " John Locke, on the other hand, held that the supreme authority of the just state extends only to those matters which it is proper for a state to control. The state is, to be sure, the highest authority, but its right to command is less than absolute. One of the questions which political philosophy must answer is whether there is any limit to the range of affairs over which a just state has authority. . . .

There are, of course, many reasons why men actually acknowledge claims of authority. The most common, taking the whole of human history, is simply the prescriptive force of tradition. The fact that something has always been done in a certain way strikes most men as a perfectly adequate reason for doing it that way again. Why should we submit to a king? Because we have always submitted to kings. But why should the oldest son of the king become king in turn? Because oldest sons have always been heirs to the throne. The force of the traditional is engraved so deeply on men's minds that even a study of the violent and haphazard origins of a ruling family will not weaken its authority in the eyes of its subjects.

Some men acquire the aura of authority by virtue of their own extraordinary characteristics, either as great military leaders, as men of saintly character, or as forceful personalities. Such men gather followers and disciples around them who willingly obey without consideration of personal interest or even against its dictates. The followers believe that the leader has the *right to command,* which is to say, *authority.*

Most commonly today, in a world of bureaucratic armies and institutionalized religions, when kings are few in number and the line of prophets has run out, authority is granted to those who occupy official positions. As Weber has pointed out, these positions appear authoritative in the minds of most men because they are defined by certain sorts of bureaucratic regulations having the virtues of publicity, generality, predictability, and so forth. We become conditioned to respond to the visible signs of officiality, such as printed forms and badges. Sometimes we may have clearly in mind the justification for a legalistic claim to authority, as when we comply with a command because its author is an *elected* official. More often the mere sight of a uniform is enough to make us feel that the man inside it has a right to be obeyed.

That men accede to claims of supreme authority is plain. That men *ought* to accede to claims of supreme authority is not so obvious. Our first question must therefore be, Under what conditions and for what reasons does one man have supreme authority over another? The same question can be restated, Under what conditions can a state (understood normatively) exist?

Kant has given us a convenient title for this sort of investigation. He called it a "deduction," meaning by the term not a proof of one proposition from another, but a demonstration of the legitimacy of a concept. When a concept is empirical, its deduction is accomplished merely by pointing to instances of its objects. For example, the deduction of the concept of a horse consists in exhibiting a horse. Since there are horses, it must be legitimate to employ the concept. Similarly, a deduction of the descriptive concept of a state consists simply in pointing to the innumerable examples of human communities in which some men claim supreme authority over the rest and are obeyed. But when the concept in question is nonempirical, its deduction must proceed in a different manner. All normative concepts are nonempirical, for they refer to what ought to be rather than to what is. Hence, we cannot justify the use of the concept of (normative) supreme authority by presenting instances.[2] We must demonstrate by an *a priori* argument that there can be forms of human community in which some men have a moral right to rule. In short, the fundamental task of political philosophy is to provide a *deduction of the concept of the state.*

To complete this deduction, it is not enough to show that there are circumstances in which men have an obligation to do what the *de facto* authorities command. Even under the most unjust of governments there are frequently good reasons for obedience rather than defiance. It may be that the government has commanded its subjects to do what in fact they already have an independent obligation to do; or it may be that the evil consequences of defiance far outweigh the indignity of submission. A government's commands may promise

---

[2] For each time we offered an example of legitimate authority, we would have to attach to it a nonempirical argument proving the legitimacy.

beneficent effects, either intentionally or not. For these reasons, and for reasons of prudence as well, a man may be right to comply with the commands of the government under whose *de facto* authority he finds himself. But none of this settles the question of legitimate authority. That is a matter of the *right* to command, and of the correlative obligations *to obey the person who issues the command.*

The point of the last paragraph cannot be too strongly stressed. Obedience is not a matter of doing what someone tells you to do. It is a matter of doing what he tells you to do *because he tells you to do it.* Legitimate, or *de jure,* authority thus concerns the grounds and sources of moral obligation.

Since it is indisputable that there are men who believe that others have authority over them, it might be thought that we could use that fact to prove that somewhere, at some time or other, there must have been men who really did possess legitimate authority. We might think, that is to say, that although some claims to authority might be wrong, it could not be that *all* such claims were wrong, since then we never would have had the concept of legitimate authority at all. By a similar argument, some philosophers have tried to show that not all our experiences are dreams, or more generally that in experience not everything is mere appearance rather than reality. The point is that terms like "dream" and "appearance" are defined by contrast with "waking experience" or "reality." Hence we could only have developed a use for them by being presented with situations in which some experiences were dreams and others not, or some things mere appearance and others reality.

Whatever the force of that argument in general, it cannot be applied to the case of *de facto* versus *de jure* authority, for the key component of both concepts, namely "right," is imported into the discussion from the realm of moral philosophy generally. Insofar as we concern ourselves with the possibility of a just state, we *assume* that moral discourse is meaningful and that adequate deductions have been given of concepts like "right," "duty," and "obligation."[3]

What can be inferred from the existence of *de facto* states is that men *believe* in the existence of legitimate authority, for of course a *de facto* state is simply a state whose subjects believe it to be legitimate (i.e., really to have the authority which it claims for itself). They may be wrong. Indeed, *all* beliefs in authority may be wrong—there may be not a single state in the history of mankind which has now or ever has had a right to be obeyed. It might even be impossible for such a state to exist; that is the question we must try to settle. But so long as men believe in the authority of states, we can conclude that they possess the concept of *de jure* authority. . . .[4]

[3] Thus, political philosophy is a dependent or derivative discipline, just as the philosophy of science is dependent upon the general theory of knowledge and on the branches of metaphysics which concern themselves with the reality and nature of the physical world.

[4] This point is so simple that it may seem unworthy of such emphasis. Nevertheless, a number of political philosophers, including Hobbes and John Austin, have supposed that *the concept* as well as the principles of authority could be derived from the concepts of power or utility. For example, Austin defines a command as a signification of desire, uttered by someone who will visit evil on those who do not comply with it *(The Providence of Jurisprudence Determined,* Lecture I).

2. THE CONCEPT OF AUTONOMY

The fundamental assumption of moral philosophy is that men are responsible for their actions. From this assumption it follows necessarily, as Kant pointed out, that men are metaphysically free, which is to say that in some sense they are capable of choosing how they shall act. Being able to choose how he acts makes a man responsible, but merely choosing is not in itself enough to constitute *taking* responsibility for one's actions. Taking responsibility involves attempting to determine what one ought to do, and that, as philosophers since Aristotle have recognized, lays upon one the additional burdens of gaining knowledge, reflecting on motives, predicting outcomes, criticizing principles, and so forth.

The obligation to take responsibility for one's actions does not derive from man's freedom of will alone, for more is required in taking responsibility than freedom of choice. Only because man has the capacity to reason about his choices can he be said to stand under a continuing obligation to take responsibility for them. It is quite appropriate that moral philosophers should group together children and madmen as beings not fully responsible for their actions, for as madmen are thought to lack freedom of choice, so children do not yet possess the power of reason in a developed form. It is even just that we should assign a greater degree of responsibility to children, for madmen, by virtue of their lack of free will, are completely without responsibility, while children, insofar as they possess reason in a partially developed form, can be held responsible (i.e., can be required to take responsibility) to a corresponding degree.

Every man who possesses both free will and reason has an obligation to take responsibility for his actions, even though he may not be actively engaged in a continuing process of reflection, investigation, and deliberation about how he ought to act. A man will sometimes announce his willingness to take responsibility for the consequences of his actions, even though he has not deliberated about them, or does not intend to do so in the future. Such a declaration is, of course, an advance over the refusal to take responsibility; it at least acknowledges the existence of the obligation. But it does not relieve the man of the duty to engage in the reflective process which he has thus far shunned. It goes without saying that a man may take responsibility for his actions and yet act wrongly. When we describe someone as a responsible individual, we do not imply that he always does what is right, but only that he does not neglect the duty of attempting to ascertain what is right.

The responsible man is not capricious or anarchic, for he does acknowledge himself bound by moral constraints. But he insists that he alone is the judge of those constraints. He may listen to the advice of others, but he makes it his own by determining for himself whether it is good advice. He may learn from others about his moral obligations, but only in the sense that a mathematician learns from other mathematicians—namely by hearing from them arguments whose validity he recognizes even though he did not think of them himself. He does not learn in the sense that one learns from an explorer, by accepting as true his accounts of things one cannot see for oneself.

Since the responsible man arrives at moral decisions which he expresses to himself in the form of imperatives, we may say that he gives laws to himself or is self-legislating. In short, he is *autonomous*. As Kant argued, moral autonomy is a combination of freedom and responsibility; it is a submission to laws which one has made for oneself. The autonomous man, insofar as he is autonomous, is not subject to the will of another. He may do what another tells him, but not *because* he has been told to do it. He is therefore, in the political sense of the word, *free*.

Since man's responsibility for his actions is a consequence of his capacity for choice, he cannot give it up or put it aside. He can refuse to acknowledge it, however, either deliberately or by simply failing to recognize his moral condition. All men refuse to take responsibility for their actions at some time or other during their lives, and some men so consistently shirk their duty that they present more the appearance of overgrown children than of adults. Inasmuch as moral autonomy is simply the condition of taking full responsibility for one's actions, it follows that men can forfeit their autonomy at will. That is to say, a man can decide to obey the commands of another without making any attempt to determine for himself whether what is commanded is good or wise.

This is an important point, and it should not be confused with the false assertion that a man can give up responsibility for his actions. Even after he has subjected himself to the will of another, an individual remains responsible for what he does. But by refusing to engage in moral deliberation, by accepting as final the commands of the others, he forfeits his autonomy. Rousseau is therefore right when he says that a man cannot become a slave even through his own choice, if he means that even slaves are morally responsible for their acts. But he is wrong if he means that men cannot place themselves voluntarily in a position of servitude and mindless obedience.

There are many forms and degrees of forfeiture of autonomy. A man can give up his independence of judgment with regard to a single question, or in respect of a single type of question. For example, when I place myself in the hands of my doctor, I commit myself to whatever course of treatment he prescribes, but only in regard to my health. I do not make him my legal counselor as well. A man may forfeit autonomy on some or all questions for a specific period of time, or during his entire life. He may submit himself to all commands, whatever they may be, save for some specified acts (such as killing) which he refuses to perform. From the example of the doctor, it is obvious that there are at least some situations in which it is reasonable to give up one's autonomy. Indeed, we may wonder whether, in a complex world of technical expertise, it is ever reasonable *not* to do so!

Since the concept of taking and forfeiting responsibility is central to the discussion which follows, it is worth devoting a bit more space to clarifying it. Taking responsibility for one's actions means making the final decisions about what one should do. For the autonomous man, there is no such thing, strictly speaking, as a *command*. If someone in my environment is issuing what are intended as commands, and if he or others expect those commands to be obeyed, that fact will be taken account of in my deliberations. I may decide that I ought to do what that person is commanding me to do, and it may even be that his issuing the command is the factor in the situation which makes it desirable for me to do so. For example, if I am on a sinking ship and the captain is giving orders for manning the lifeboats, and if everyone else is obeying the captain *because he is the captain,* I may decide that under the circumstances I had better do what he says, since the confusion caused by disobeying him would be generally harmful. But insofar as I make such a decision, I am not *obeying his command;* that is, I am not acknowledging him as having authority over me. I would make the same decision, for exactly the same reasons, if one of the passengers had started to issue "orders" and had, in the confusion, come to be obeyed.

In politics, as in life generally, men frequently forfeit their autonomy. There are a number of causes for this fact, and also a number of arguments which have been offered to justify it. Most men, as we have already noted, feel so strongly the force of tradition or bureaucracy that they accept unthinkingly the claims to authority which are made by their nominal rulers. It is the rare individual in the history of the race who rises even to the level of questioning the right of his masters to command and the duty of himself and his fellows to obey. Once the dangerous question has been started, however, a variety of arguments can be brought forward to demonstrate the authority of the rulers. Among the most ancient is Plato's assertion that men should submit to the authority of those with superior knowledge, wisdom, or insight. A sophisticated modern version has it that the educated portion of a democratic population is more likely to be politically active, and that it is just as well for the ill-informed segment of the electorate to remain passive, since its entrance into the political arena only supports the efforts of demagogues and extremists. A number of American political scientists have gone so far as to claim that the apathy of the American masses is a cause of stability and hence a good thing.

The moral condition demands that we acknowledge responsibility and achieve autonomy wherever and whenever possible. Sometimes this involves moral deliberation and reflection; at other times, the gathering of special, even technical, information. The contemporary American citizen, for example, has an obligation to master enough modern science to enable him to follow debates about nuclear policy and come to an independent conclusion.[5] There are great, perhaps insurmountable, obstacles to the achievement of a complete and rational autonomy in the modern world. Nevertheless, so long as we recognize our responsibility for our actions, and acknowledge the power of reason within us, we must acknowledge as well the continuing obligation to make ourselves the authors of such commands as we may obey. The paradox of man's condition in the modern world is that the more fully he recognizes his right and duty to be his own master, the more completely he becomes the passive object of a technology and bureaucracy whose complexities he cannot hope to understand. It is only several hundred years since a reasonably well-educated man could claim to un-

---

[5] This is not quite so difficult as it sounds, since policy very rarely turns on disputes over technical or theoretical details. Still, the citizen who, for example, does not understand the nature of atomic radiation cannot even pretend to have an opinion on the feasibility of bomb shelters; and since the momentous choice between first-strike and second-strike nuclear strategies depends on the possibility of a successful shelter system, the uninformed citizen will be as completely at the mercy of his "representatives" as the lowliest slave.

derstand the major issues of government as well as his king or parliament. Ironically, the high school graduate of today, who cannot master the issues of foreign and domestic policy on which he is asked to vote, could quite easily have grasped the problems of eighteenth-century statecraft.

3. THE CONFLICT BETWEEN AUTHORITY AND AUTONOMY

The defining mark of the state is authority, the right to rule. The primary obligation of man is autonomy, the refusal to be ruled. It would seem, then, that there can be no resolution of the conflict between the autonomy of the individual and the putative authority of the state. Insofar as a man fulfills his obligation to make himself the author of his decisions, he will resist the state's claim to have authority over him. That is to say, he will deny that he has a duty to obey the laws of the state *simply because they are the laws.* In that sense, it would seem that anarchism is the only political doctrine consistent with the virtue of autonomy.

Now, of course, an anarchist may grant the necessity of *complying* with the law under certain circumstances or for the time being. He may even doubt that there is any real prospect of eliminating the state as a human institution. But he will never view the commands of the state as *legitimate,* as having a binding moral force. In a sense, we might characterize the anarchist as a man without a country, for despite the ties which bind him to the land of his childhood, he stands in precisely the same moral relationship to "his" government as he does to the government of any other country in which he might happen to be staying for a time. When I take a vacation in Great Britain, I obey its laws, both because of prudential self-interest and because of the obvious moral considerations concerning the value of order, the general good consequences of preserving a system of property, and so forth. On my return to the United States, I have a sense of reentering *my* country, and if I think about the matter at all, I imagine myself to stand in a different and more intimate relation to American laws. They have been promulgated by *my* government, and I therefore have a special obligation to obey them. But the anarchist tells me that my feeling is purely sentimental and has no objective moral basis. All authority is equally illegitimate, although of course not therefore equally worthy or unworthy of support, and my obedience to American laws, if I am to be morally autonomous, must proceed from the same considerations which determine me abroad.

The dilemma which we have posed can be succinctly expressed in terms of the concept of a *de jure* state. If all men have a continuing obligation to achieve the highest degree of autonomy possible, then there would appear to be no state whose subjects have a moral obligation to obey its commands. Hence, the concept of a *de jure* legitimate state would appear to be vacuous, and philosophical anarchism would seem to be the only reasonable political belief for an enlightened man.

STUDY QUESTIONS

1   Wolff says that there are two concepts of the state. What are these two concepts? How are they related to the concept of "authority"?

2   How does Wolff characterize "obedience"? Why does the fact that I willingly obey the law because I believe that it is reasonable not solve the problem of political authority?

3   What is moral autonomy? Why must it be distinguished from moral responsibility? Why can autonomy be given up, but not responsibility?

4   Would it be possible, according to Wolff, to obey the commands of someone because you recognize the superior wisdom of that person and still remain autonomous? What would Wolff say about the claim that God is the foundation of all morality, and hence the supreme moral authority?

5   Would Jean-Paul Sartre agree with Wolff's anarchism? Would Hobbes? Do you think that Plato's reasons for submitting to the law are those of an autonomous agent?

6   "If autonomy is a virtue, then it is wrong to prevent it. But Adolph Hitler sincerely believed that Jews were corrupting Germany and that they had to be exterminated. Therefore he was acting autonomously and any state which tried to prevent him from murdering innocents would be acting illegitimately. This is where Wolff's theory leads: 'do your own thing, no matter what the consequences.' " Do you think this criticism of Wolff is correct?

7   "That which is anarchic within me (which is very strong) tunes in strongly on the idea of a society in which people decide for themselves what taxes to pay, what rules to obey, when to cooperate and when not to with the civil authorities. But that which is reasonable within me, which I am glad to say most often prevails, recognizes that societies so structured do not exist and cannot exist" (William Buckley). How would Wolff respond to Buckley? Do you think Buckley is right?

Liberty: The Search
for a Definition

PROBLEM INTRODUCTION

"No man is an island, entire of itself" are the often-quoted words from a poem by John Donne. In less poetic language—human beings are born, live out their lives, and die within structured groups called *societies*. The unwritten rules and customs of these societies are absorbed by us into our innermost being. As a result, it is no easy task to discover where the influence of social control ends and individual freedom actually begins. The problem is further complicated by the fact that no one has yet adequately determined what the word "freedom" really means. We, in the United States, tend to think of freedom as the ability to fix our personal ends according to our own lights. To be free is to be able to decide for ourselves what life-style, what values, what life's work we shall pursue. Probably most people, if asked, would value freedom from control more highly than security, public order, or even social justice. Why should this be so? After all, no one disputes the claim that some personal ends must be limited by social constraints: people must pay taxes, children are forced to go to school. A wide range of action—from murder to nudity to making a nuisance of oneself—is regulated by law. We justify these interferences with personal freedom by the supposition that

Editor's note: The introduction and editorial material of this section were written by Sarah Keating, professor of philosophy at California State University, Long Beach.

the value of certain social ends outweighs the evil of coercion, that some pursuits and sentiments are corrupting, and that intellectual and moral discipline must be achieved in order to lead a responsible and worthwhile life. The extent and form of social coercion which we tolerate is a reflection of our vision of humanity. To value personal freedom is to see it as a necessary condition for the development of something fundamentally good within human nature.

Personal freedom is a rare commodity in the world today chiefly because most of the dominant political philosophies do not share the assumption that freedom from control is necessary for the fullest expression of human potential. Plato, for example, placed no value on individual liberty. A society where people are allowed the broadest range of personal choices, he thought, soon becomes a collection of egoists, seeking personal fulfillment in the satisfaction of hollow impulses. New fads, cults, and "movements" spring up, as people try now this, now that style of life. As each desire is temporarily sated, and the old thrills grow stale, they are led into more intense and adventuresome pursuits. At last society collapses into anarchy as individuals who have been drained of all social and moral discipline become unrestrained libertines. Like Hobbes, Plato believed that people must be shaped by strong social institutions, for there is a dark side to human nature which, if not bridled, will devour self-control and rationality. To value personal liberty is therefore absurd: it is to give allegiance to self-destruction. True freedom, on the other hand, requires the development of the highest part of human nature. To be free is to be capable of arranging one's life so as to promote those desires and habits which create virtue. This freedom—freedom from irrationality, whimsy, and destructive drives—is achieved when the individual is shaped and disciplined by a social system which promotes definite ends and excludes others.

Now we seem to be confronted with two conceptions of freedom. The concept of *negative* freedom is basically that of being left alone. To be free is to have no external constraints upon one's desires. On the other hand, Plato's conception, called *positive* freedom, places the emphasis on the development of certain positive traits. What good is negative freedom to someone who lacks the psychological resources to benefit from it? A barbarian unleashed is still a barbarian. Plato insists that it is impossible to be free when corrupting desires and unedifying beliefs prevent us from seeing the world as it really is. But we cannot, by a sheer act of will, purge ourselves of corrupting influences, since our very consciousness is stained with them. Positive freedom, then, demands a great deal of social control over the factors which mold consciousness and self.

John Stuart Mill is perhaps the strongest voice for negative freedom. Writing in the middle of the last century, Mill was appalled at the uniformity of taste and opinion which seemed to characterize society. Although there was an increase in political democracies, he saw that the majority can be just as repressive as the most accomplished dictator. The world, he believed, was at a great turning point in history. With the emergence of modern capitalism and the industrial state, the old aristocratic tradition would soon be overthrown. The future direction of society, however, would depend upon the vision of a generation of men and women capable of grasping new ideas and new forms of life. Mill's fundamental faith was that a society which protects the eccentric, the bizarre, and the unpopular will produce creative people capable of exploring the breadth and depth of human potential. Consequently, he maintained that society must not seek to control the private affairs of the individual. Only when the actions of the individual harm others may society restrict freedom of action.

Mill's form of social experimentalism presupposes that the individual, when left alone, will develop internal resources which will lead to objective self-assessment and social appraisal. But this assumption was vigorously denied by Karl Marx and Friedrich Engels. Unlike Mill, Marx and Engels saw the increasing regimentation of society as the necessary result of powerful and subtle historical forces which shaped and controlled consciousness itself. Society organizes itself in a certain way so as to provide for the material needs of its members. A ruling class arises which determines the ways the productive forces will be used, initiates and promotes certain ruling ideas, and erects a political state to secure its power. Modern capitalism, for example, is a system of production which requires great freedom for producers to actively compete in a free market. The cry for freedom which characterized the rise of modern democracies was, in fact, Marx and Engels believed, a reflection of the demands of the capitalistic system of production. Owners demand freedom to hire cheap labor, freedom to fire whomever they wish, freedom to regulate prices and wages. The only freedom enjoyed by the working class is the freedom to be exploited.

Freedom in a capitalistic society, as depicted by Marx and Engels, is illusory. The consciousness of each individual becomes corrupted by false ideals. Aggression and selfishness are elevated to positive values, while community and sympathy are scorned. As long as society is economically organized into two classes—owners and workers—such traits will be valued above all others. In contrast, the community of revolutionary proletarians is a genuine community because all members of society participate in it as individuals, not as members of a class. Only in such a community will the consciousness of the individual reflect values indicative of the true nature of the human person. Only in such a community, therefore, is personal freedom for the individual truly possible.

In our own century, the conflict between the image of a human being as an autonomous individual and the recognition that certain social relations are necessary for meaningful self-exploration has become more acute. As the science of psychology advances, we become increasingly aware of the power and extent of the social forces that mold our conscious and unconscious lives. B. F. Skinner, one of the most noted psychologists of this century, believes that the demand for personal freedom reflects a tradition that is based on a false theory of human nature. Democratic ideals, he argues, must be reassessed in light of the discovery that human beings are not autonomous agents capable of resisting the controlling forces of the environment. Free will is a myth, and once we recognize this fact we can proceed to reorganize society to achieve human happiness. Using the techniques of behavior control, we shall be able to "engineer" any type of person we desire. While Skinner admits that in a totally engineered society, certain forms of behavior will no longer be possible, he does not regard this as a source of concern. Why should we mourn the passing of the accidental and the self-destructive?

The essay by Herbert Marcuse demonstrates how a Marxist sees contemporary American society. Marcuse thinks we already have a situation where the worst kind of social control is closing in on us. Without realizing what is happening, we are being programmed to fit into a one-dimensional world which is a grotesque caricature of Marx's classless society as well as a monstrous example of Skinner's human engineering gone awry. Constantly distracted by the ever-changing superficial differences in our society, we fail to see that beneath the variety of tastes and pursuits there exists a terrifying sameness. Through advertising and technology, modern society has created a plethora of artificial needs which are manipulated, catered to, and used against us. Marcuse believes that we are fast becoming the sort of democracy depicted by Plato: a collection of unhappy egoists, so dazzled by the immediate gratification of desires that lie at the surface of human nature that we cannot identify the deeper wants which are essential to being fully human.

On Liberty

John Stuart Mill

To all outward appearances, John Stuart Mill (1806–1873) was a paradigm of conventionality. He dressed somberly, had no outstanding vices, traveled in the best social circles, and held a responsible position in the East India Company. But as the general public discovered in 1859 with the publication of *On Liberty,* Mill was the most articulate champion of freedom and individualism of his age. The central claim of this book was that society had no right to interfere in the private affairs of the individual beyond what was required for self-protection. Mill stood firmly on the side of freedom of the press, freedom of association, and the freedom to hold and practice all sorts of bizarre and unconventional beliefs. The book was widely read and widely opposed. Carlyle, for example, was enraged. "As if," he cried, "it were a sin to control, or coerce into better methods, human swine in any way; . . . Ach Gott im Himmel!"

But if *On Liberty* made him many enemies, Mill's defense of women's rights in *The Subjection of Women* lost him many friends. Public reaction to his claim that women should enjoy all the rights and responsibilities of men ranged from shock to humor. What particularly exasperated Mill was the fact that so many women would not speak out for themselves or were actively hostile to the suffrage movement. Here was ample proof that the greatest enemy of freedom is the coercive force of custom. In a way which no dictator can imitate, custom creates sentiments which stand in the way of the full development of the faculties of observation and reason. Only by tolerating the widest possible range of character and life-style can society hope to discover the forms of human potential which will bring about the greatest happiness for all.

The subject of this essay is not the so-called liberty of the will, so unfortunately opposed to the misnamed doctrine of philosophical necessity; but civil, or social liberty: the nature and limits of the power which can be legitimately exercised by society over the individual. A question seldom stated and hardly ever discussed in general terms, but which profoundly influences the practical controversies of the age by its latent presence, and is likely soon to make itself recognized as the vital question of the future. It is so far from being new, that, in a certain sense, it has divided mankind almost from the remotest ages; but in the stage of progress into which the more civilized portions of the species have now entered, it presents itself under new conditions, and requires a different and more fundamental treatment.

The struggle between liberty and authority is the most conspicuous feature in the portions of history with which we are earliest familiar, particularly in that of Greece, Rome, and England. But in old times this contest was between subjects, or some classes of subjects, and the government. By liberty, was meant protection against the tyranny of the political rulers. The rulers were conceived

From *On Liberty* by John Stuart Mill, first published in 1859. Many editions.

(except in some of the popular governments of Greece) as in a necessarily antagonistic position to the people whom they ruled. They consisted of a governing
One, or a governing tribe or caste, who derived their authority from inheritance
or conquest, who, at all events, did not hold it at the pleasure of the governed,
and whose supremacy men did not venture, perhaps did not desire, to contest,
whatever precautions might be taken against its oppressive exercise. Their power
was regarded as necessary, but also as highly dangerous; as a weapon which they
would attempt to use against their subjects, no less than against external enemies.
To prevent the weaker members of the community from being preyed upon by
innumerable vultures, it was needful that there should be an animal of prey
stronger than the rest, commissioned to keep them down. But as the king of the
vultures would be no less bent upon preying on the flock than any of the minor
harpies, it was indispensable to be in a perpetual attitude of defense against his
beak and claws. The aim, therefore, of patriots was to set limits to the power
which the ruler should be suffered to exercise over the community; and this
limitation was what they meant by liberty. It was attempted in two ways. First,
by obtaining a recognition of certain immunities, called political liberties or
rights, which it was to be regarded as a breach of duty in the ruler to infringe, and
which if he did infringe, specific resistance, or general rebellion, was held to be
justifiable. A second, and generally a later expedient, was the establishment of
constitutional checks, by which the consent of the community, or of a body of
some sort, supposed to represent its interests, was made a necessary condition to
some of the more important acts of the governing power. To the first of these
modes of limitation, the ruling power, in most European countries, was compelled, more or less, to submit. It was not so with the second; and, to attain this,
or when already in some degree possessed, to attain it more completely, became
everywhere the principal object of the lovers of liberty. And so long as mankind
were content to combat one enemy by another, and to be ruled by a master, on
condition of being guaranteed more or less efficaciously against his tyranny, they
did not carry their aspirations beyond this point.

A time, however, came, in the progress of human affairs, when men ceased
to think it a necessity of nature that their governors should be an independent
power, opposed in interest to themselves. It appeared to them much better that
the various magistrates of the State should be their tenants or delegates, revoca-
ble at their pleasure. In that way alone, it seemed, could they have complete
security that the powers of government would never be abused to their disadvantage. By degrees this new demand for elective and temporary rulers became the
prominent object of the exertions of the popular party, wherever any such party
existed; and superseded, to a considerable extent, the previous efforts to limit the
power of rulers. As the struggle proceeded for making the ruling power emanate
from the periodical choice of the ruled, some persons began to think that too
much importance had been attached to the limitation of the power itself. *That* (it
might seem) was a resource against rulers whose interests were habitually opposed to those of the people. What was now wanted was, that the rulers should be
identified with the people; that their interest and will should be the interest and
will of the nation. The nation did not need to be protected against its own will.

There was no fear of its tyrannizing over itself. Let the rulers be effectually responsible to it, promptly removable by it, and it could afford to trust them with power of which it could itself dictate the use to be made. Their power was but the nation's own power, concentrated, and in a form convenient for exercise. This mode of thought, or rather perhaps of feeling, was common among the last generation of European liberalism, in the Continental section of which it still apparently predominates. Those who admit any limit to what a government may do, except in the case of such governments as they think ought not to exist, stand out as brilliant exceptions among the political thinkers of the Continent. A similar tone of sentiment might by this time have been prevalent in our own country, if the circumstances which for a time encouraged it had continued unaltered.

But in political and philosophical theories, as well as in persons, success discloses faults and infirmities which failure might have concealed from observation. The notion that the people have no need to limit their power over themselves, might seem axiomatic when popular government was a thing only dreamed about, or read of as having existed at some distant period of the past. Neither was that notion necessarily disturbed by such temporary aberrations as those of the French Revolution, the worst of which were the work of a usurping few, and which, in any case, belonged not to the permanent working of popular institutions, but to a sudden and convulsive outbreak against monarchical and aristocractic despotism. In time, however, a democratic republic came to occupy a large portion of the earth's surface, and made itself felt as one of the most powerful members of the community of nations; and elective and responsible government became subject to the observations and criticism which wait upon a great existing fact. It was now perceived that such phrases as "self-government," and the "power of the people over themselves," do not express the true state of the case. The "people" who exercise the power are not always the same people with those over whom it is exercised; and the "self-government" spoken of is not the government of each by himself, but of each by all the rest. The will of the people, moreover, practically means the will of the most numerous or the most active *part* of the people; the majority, or those who succeed in making themselves accepted as the majority: the people, consequently *may* desire to oppress a part of their number, and precautions are as much needed against this as against any other abuse of power. The limitation, therefore, of the power of government over individuals loses none of its importance when the holders of power are regularly accountable to the community, that is, to the strongest party therein. This view of things, recommending itself equally to the intelligence of thinkers and to the inclination of those important classes in European society to whose real or supposed interests democracy is adverse, has had no difficulty in establishing itself; and in political speculations "the tyranny of the majority" is now generally included among the evils against which society requires to be on its guard.

Like other tyrannies, the tyranny of the majority was at first, and is still vulgarly, held in dread chiefly as operating through the acts of the public authorities. But reflecting persons perceived that when society is itself the tyrant—society collectively over the separate individuals who compose it—its means of tyrannizing are not restricted to the acts which it may do by the hands of its political functionaries. Society can and does execute its own mandates; and if it issues wrong mandates instead of right, or any mandates at all in things with which it ought not to meddle, it practices a social tyranny more formidable than many kinds of political oppression, since, though not usually upheld by such extreme penalties, it leaves fewer means of escape, penetrating much more deeply into the details of life, and enslaving the soul itself. Protection, therefore, against the tyranny of the magistrate is not enough: there needs protection also against the tyranny of the prevailing opinion and feeling; against the tendency of society to impose, by other means than civil penalties, its own ideas and practices as rules of conduct on those who dissent from them; to fetter the development, and if possible, prevent the formation, of any individuality not in harmony with its ways, and compels all characters to fashion themselves upon the model of its own. There is a limit to the legitimate interference of collective opinion with individual independence; and to find that limit, and maintain it against encroachment, is as indispensable to a good condition of human affairs, as protection against political despotism.

But though this proposition is not likely to be contested in general terms, the practical question, where to place the limit—how to make the fitting adjustment between individual independence and social control—is a subject on which nearly everything remains to be done. All that makes existence valuable to anyone, depends on the enforcement of restraints upon the actions of other people. Some rules of conduct, therefore, must be imposed, by law in the first place, and by opinion on many things which are not fit subjects for the operation of law. What these rules should be is the principal question in human affairs; but if we except a few of the most obvious cases, it is one of those which least progress has been made in resolving. No two ages, and scarcely any two countries, have decided it alike; and the decision of one age or country is a wonder to another. Yet the people of any given age and country no more suspect any difficulty in it, than if it were a subject on which mankind had always been agreed. The rules which obtain among themselves appear to them self-evident and self-justifying. This all but universal illusion is one of the examples of the magical influence of custom, which is not only, as the proverb says, a second nature, but is continually mistaken for the first. The effect of custom, in preventing any misgiving respecting the rules of conduct which mankind impose on one another, is all the more complete because the subject is one on which it is not generally considered necessary that reasons should be given, either by one person to others or by each to himself. People are accustomed to believe, and have been encouraged in the belief by some who aspire to the character of philosophers, that their feelings, on subjects of this nature, are better than reasons, and render reasons unnecessary. The practical principle which guides them to their opinions on the regulation of human conduct, is the feeling in each person's mind that everybody should be required to act as he, and those with whom he sympathizes, would like them to act. No one, indeed, acknowledges to himself that his standard of judgment is his own liking; but an opinion on a point of conduct, not supported by reasons, can only count as one person's preference; and if the reasons, when given, are a mere appeal to a similar preference felt by other people, it is still only many people's liking instead of one. To an ordinary man, however, his own preference, thus supported, is not only a perfectly satisfactory reason, but the only one he generally has for any of his notions of morality, taste, or propriety, which are not expressly written in his religious creed; and his chief guide in the interpretation even of that. Men's opinions, accordingly, on what is laudable or blamable, are affected by all the multifarious causes which influence their wishes in regard to the conduct of others, and which are as numerous as those which determine their wishes on any other subject. Sometimes their reason, at other times their prejudices or superstitions; often their social affections, not seldom their antisocial ones, their envy of jealousy, their arrogance or contemptuousness: but most commonly their desires or fears for themselves—their legitimate or illegitimate self-interest. Wherever there is an ascendant class, a large portion of the morality of the country emanates from its class interests, and its feelings of class superiority. The morality between Spartans and Helots, between planters and Negroes, between princes and subjects, between nobles and roturiers, between men and women, has been for the most part of the creation of these class interests and feelings; and the sentiments thus generated react in turn upon the moral feelings of the members of the ascendant class, in their relations among themselves. Where, on the other hand, a class, formerly ascendant, has lost its ascendancy, or where its ascendancy is unpopular, the prevailing moral sentiments frequently bear the impress of an impatient dislike of superiority. Another grand determining principle of the rules of conduct, both in act and forbearance, which have been enforced by law or opinion, has been the servility of mankind towards the supposed preferences or aversions of their temporal masters or of their gods. This servility, though essentially selfish, is not hypocrisy; it gives rise to perfectly genuine sentiments of abhorrence; it made men burn magicians and heretics. Among so many baser influences, the general and obvious interests of society have of course had a share, and a large one, in the direction of the moral sentiments; less, however, as a matter of reason, and on their own account, than as a consequence of the sympathies and antipathies which grew out of them; and sympathies and antipathies which had little or nothing to do with the interests of society, have made themselves felt in the establishment of moralities with quite as great force.

The likings and dislikings of society, or of some powerful portion of it, are thus the main thing which has practically determined the rules laid down for general observance, under the penalties of law or opinion. And in general, those who have been in advance of society in thought and feeling, have left this condition of things unassailed in principle, however they may have come into conflict with it in some of its details. They have occupied themselves rather in inquiring what things society ought to like or dislike, than in questioning whether its likings or dislikings should be a law to individuals. They preferred endeavoring to alter the feelings of mankind on the particular points on which they were themselves heretical, rather than make common cause in defense of freedom, with heretics generally. . . . The great writers to whom the world owes what religious liberty it possesses, have mostly asserted freedom of conscience as an indefeasible right, and denied absolutely that a human being is accountable to others for his religious belief. Yet so natural to mankind is intolerance in whatever they really care about, that religious freedom has hardly anywhere been practically realized, except where religious indifference, which dislikes to have its peace disturbed by theological quarrels, has added its weight to the scale. In the minds of almost all religious persons, even in the most tolerant countries, the duty of toleration is admitted with tacit reserves. One person will bear with dissent in matters of church government, but not of dogma; another can tolerate everybody, short of a Papist or a Unitarian; another everyone who believes in revealed religion; a few extend their charity a little further, but stop at the belief in a God and in a future state. Wherever the sentiment of the majority is still genuine and intense, it is found to have abated little of its claim to be obeyed. . . .

The object of this essay is to assert one very simple principle, as entitled to govern absolutely the dealings of society with the individual in the way of compulsion and control, whether the means used by physical force in the form of legal penalties, or the moral coercion of public opinion. That principle is, that the sole end for which mankind are warranted, individually or collectively, in interfering with the liberty of action of any of their number, is self-protection. That the only purpose for which power can be rightfully exercised over any member of a civilized community, against his will, is to prevent harm to others. His own good, either physical or moral, is not a sufficient warrant. He cannot rightfully be compelled to do or forbear because it will be better for him to do so, because it will make him happier, because, in the opinions of others, to do so would be wise, or even right. These are good reasons for remonstrating with him, or reasoning with him, or persuading him, or entreating him, but not for compelling him, or visiting him with any evil in case he do otherwise. To justify that, the conduct from which it is desired to deter him must be calculated to produce evil to someone else. The only part of the conduct of anyone, for which he is amenable to society, is that which concerns others. In the part which merely concerns himself, his independence is, of right, absolute. Over himself, over his own body and mind, the individual is sovereign.

It is perhaps hardly necessary to say that this doctrine is meant to apply only to human beings in the maturity of their faculties. . . . Those who are still in a state to require being taken care of by others, must be protected against their own actions as well as against external injury. . . . Liberty, as a principle, has no application to any state of things anterior to the time when mankind have become capable of being improved by free and equal discussion. Until then, there is nothing for them but implicit obedience to an Akbar or a Charlemagne, if they are so fortunate as to find one. But as soon as mankind have attained the capacity of being guided to their own improvement by conviction or persuasion . . . , compulsion, either in the direct form or in that of pains and penalties for noncompliance, is no longer admissible as a means to their own good, and justifiable only for the security of others.

It is proper to state that I forego any advantage which could be derived to my argument from the idea of abstract right, as a thing independent of utility. I regard utility as the ultimate appeal on all ethical questions; but it must be utility in the largest sense, grounded on the permanent interests of a man as a progressive being. Those interests, I contend, authorized the subjection of individual spontaneity to external control, only in respect to those actions of each which concern the interest of other people. If anyone does an act hurtful to others, there is a *prima facie* case for punishing him, by law, or, where legal penalties are not safely applicable, by general disapprobation. There are also many positive acts for the benefit of others, which he may rightfully be compelled to perform: such as to give evidence in a court of justice; to bear his fair share in the common defense, or in any other joint work necessary to the interest of the society of which he enjoys the protection; and to perform certain acts of individual beneficence, such as saving a fellow-creature's life, or interposing to protect the defenseless against ill-usage, things which whenever it is obviously a man's duty to do, he may rightfully be made responsible to society for not doing. A person may cause evil to others not only by his actions but by his inaction, and in either case he is justly accountable to them for the injury. The latter case, it is true, requires a much more cautious exercise of compulsion than the former. To make anyone answerable for doing evil to others is the rule; to make him answerable for not preventing evil is, comparatively speaking, the exception. Yet there are many cases clear enough and grave enough to justify that exception. In all things which regard the external relations of the individual, he is *de jure* amenable to those whose interests are concerned, and, if need be, to society as their protector. There are often good reasons for not holding him to the responsibility; but these reasons must arise from the special expediencies of the case; either because it is a kind of case in which he is on the whole likely to act better, when left to his own discretion, than when controlled in any way in which society have it in their power to control him; or because the attempt to exercise control would produce other evils, greater than those which it would prevent. When such reasons as these preclude the enforcement of responsibility, the conscience of the agent himself should step into the vacant judgment seat, and protect those interests of others which have no external protection; judging himself all the more rigidly, because the case does not admit of his being made accountable to the judgment of his fellow-creatures.

But there is a sphere of action in which society, as distinguished from the individual, has, if any, only an indirect interest; comprehending all that portion of a person's life and conduct which affects only himself, or if it also affects others, only with their free, voluntary, and undeceived consent and participation. When I say only himself, I mean directly, and in the first instance; for whatever affects himself, may affect others through himself; and the objection which may be grounded on this contingency, will receive consideration in the sequel. This, then, is the appropriate region of human liberty. It comprises, *first,* the inward domain of consciousness; demanding liberty of conscience in the most comprehensive sense; liberty of thought and feeling; absolute freedom of opinion and sentiment on all subjects, practical or speculative, scientific, moral, or theological. The liberty of expressing and publishing opinions may seem to fall under a different principle, since it belongs to that part of the conduct of an individual which concerns other people; but, being almost of as much importance as the liberty of thought itself, and resting in great part on the same reasons, is practically inseparable from it. *Secondly,* the principle requires liberty of tastes and pursuits; of framing the plan of our life to suit our own character; of doing as we like, subject to such consequences as may follow: without impediment from our fellow-creatures, so long as what we do does not harm them, even though they should think our conduct foolish, perverse, or wrong. *Thirdly,* from this liberty of each individual, follows the liberty, within the same limits, of combination among individuals; freedom to unite for any purpose not involving harm to others: the persons combining being supposed to be of full age, and not forced or deceived.

No society in which these liberties are not, on the whole, respected, is free, whatever may be its form of government; and none is completely free in which they do not exist absolute and unqualified. The only freedom which deserves the name, is that of pursuing our own good in our own way, so long as we do not attempt to deprive others of theirs, or impede their effots to obtain it. Each is the proper guardian of his own health, whether bodily, or mental and spiritual. Mankind are greater gainers by suffering each other to live as seems good to themselves, than by compelling each to live as seems good to the rest. . . .

The time, it is to be hoped, is gone by, when any defence would be necessary of the "liberty of the press" as one of the securities against corrupt or tyrannical government. No argument, we may suppose, can now be needed, against permitting a legislature or an executive, not identified in interest with the people, to prescribe opinions to them, and determine what doctrines or what arguments they shall be allowed to hear. This aspect of the question, besides, has been so often and so triumphantly enforced by preceding writers, that it need not be specially insisted on in this place. Though the law of England, on the subject of the press, is as servile to this day as it was in the time of the Tudors, there is little danger of its being actually put in force against political discussion, except during some temporary panic, when fear of insurrection drives ministers and judges from their propriety; and, speaking generally, it is not, in constitutional countries, to be apprehended, that the government, whether completely responsible to the people or not, will often attempt to control the expression of opinion, except when in doing so it makes itself the organ of the general intolerance of the public. Let us suppose, therefore, that the government is entirely at one with the people, and never thinks of exerting any power of coercion unless in agreement with what it conceives to be their voice. But I deny the right of the people to exercise such coercion, either by themselves or by their government. The power itself is illegitimate. The best government has no more title to it than the worst. It is as noxious, or more noxious, when exerted in accordance with public opinion, than when in opposition to it. If all mankind minus one, were of one opinion, and only one person were of the contrary opinion, mankind would be no more justified in silencing that one person, than he, if he had the power, would be justified in silencing mankind. Were an opinion a personal possession of no value except to the owner; if to be obstructed in the enjoyment of it were simply a private injury, it would make some difference whether the injury was inflicted only on a few persons or on many. But the peculiar evil of silencing the expression of an opin-

ion is, that it is robbing the human race; posterity as well as the existing generation; those who dissent from the opinion, still more than those who hold it. If the
opinion is right, they are deprived of the opportunity of exchanging error for
truth: if wrong, they lose, what is almost as great a benefit, the clearer perception
and livelier impression of truth, produced by its collision with error. . . .

As it is useful that while mankind are imperfect there should be different
opinions, so is it that there should be different experiments of living; that free
scope should be given to varieties of character, short of injury to others; and that
the worth of different modes of life should be proved practically, when any one
thinks fit to try them. It is desirable, in short, that in things which do not primarily concern others, individuality should assert itself. Where, not the person's own
character, but the traditions or customs of other people are the rule of conduct,
there is wanting one of the principal ingredients of human happiness, and quite
the chief ingredient of individual and social progress.

In maintaining this principle, the greatest difficulty to be encountered does
not lie in the appreciation of means towards an acknowledged end, but in the
indifference of persons in general to the end itself. If it were felt that the free
development of individuality is one of the leading essentials of wellbeing; that it
is not only a co-ordinate element with all like that is designated by the terms
civilization, instruction, education, culture, but is itself a necessary part and condition of all those things; there would be no danger that liberty should be under-
valued, and the adjustment of the boundaries between it and social control would
present no extraordinary difficulty. But the evil is, that individual spontaneity is
hardly recognized by the common modes of thinking, as having any intrinsic
worth, or deserving any regard on its own account. . . .

He who lets the world, or his own portion of it, choose his plan of life for
him, has no need of any other faculty than the ape-like one of imitation. He who
chooses his plan for himself, employs all his faculties. He must use observation to
see, reasoning and judgment to foresee, activity to gather materials for decision,
discrimination to decide, and when he has decided, firmness and self-control to
hold to his deliberate decision. And these qualities he requires and exercises
exactly in proportion as the part of his conduct which he determines according to
his own judgment and feelings is a large one. It is possible that he might be
guided in some good path, and kept out of harm's way, without any of these
things. But what will be his comparative worth as a human being? It really is of
importance, not only what men do, but also what manner of men they are that do
it. Among the works of man, which human life is rightly employed in perfecting
and beautifying, the first in importance surely is man himself. Supposing it were
possible to get houses built, corn grown, battles fought, causes tried, and even
churches erected and prayers said, by machinery—by automatons in human
form—it would be a considerable loss to exchange for these automatons even the
men and women who at present inhabit the more civilized parts of the world, and
who assuredly are but starved specimens of what nature can and will produce.
Human nature is not a machine to be built after a model, and set to do exactly
the work prescribed for it, but a tree, which requires to grow and develop itself

on all sides, according to the tendency of the inward forces which make it a living thing. . . .

STUDY QUESTIONS

1 Why does Mill believe that the control of society over its members is more formidable than the political oppression of a dictatorship?

2 What is the sole justification for society interfering in the lives of its members? What are some illegitimate reasons?

3 Mill says that there are certain acts for the common good that society may demand of the individual. In effect he is saying that society may punish people for refusing to bring about some good, not only for doing harm. How does Mill justify this? Do you agree?

4 "It does me no injury for my neighbor to say there are twenty gods or no god. It neither picks my pocket nor breaks my leg" (Thomas Jefferson). But what if someone believed that atheism weakened the moral fiber of society? Couldn't they use Mill's criterion of self-protection to suppress this opinion? What do you think Mill would say?

5 Some people in the United States practice polygamy. Some members of religious cults believe that handling poisonous snakes is an exercise of faith. Naturally, some of the faithful have died in such displays of religious fervor. Both of these practices are unlawful. Using Mill's criterion, can you tell whether such practices should be permitted?

6 Mill believes that individuality is one of the chief ingredients of human happiness. Do you agree? Why do so many people seem not to value it?

7 Mill says that the men and women of today "are but starved specimens of what nature can and will produce." Obviously he thinks that the people of the future will be more individualistic and, hence, better. But surely eccentricity and difference are not intrinsically valuable, and inasmuch as they prevent the achievement of social unity and cooperation, they appear to be positively harmful. How would you define *individualism* so as to make its increase a positive good?

The Illusion of Capitalist Freedom

Karl Marx and Friedrich Engels

Having received his doctorate from the Univerity of Jena and after briefly serving as editor of a liberal newspaper in Cologne, Karl Marx (1818–1883) moved to Paris to begin his own political journal. In 1844 he began his lifelong collaboration and friendship with Friedrich Engels (1820–1895). In 1846, Marx and Engels produced *The German Ideology,* from which our reading is taken. In this work, the central ideas of dialectical materialism are set forth which culminated in the cry for revolution in *The Communist Manifesto* of 1848. But the world was not yet ready for revolution, and Marx moved to London with Engels where he lived out the rest of his life in dire poverty, supported largely by his generous friend.

In the following selection, Marx and Engels try to show that the most fundamental factor affecting all of human existence is the way in which the community is economically organized to provide for the material needs of its members. Ideologies—art, philosophy, religion, law—are forms of "consciousness" which evolve from the productive forces that exist in society. Democratic ideals—the ideals of personal freedom and social diversity—are in fact reflections of the capitalist system of free enterprise. This economic system leads to two classes, the capitalists and the proletariat, and the so-called freedom of the individual is simply the freedom of the capitalist to exploit the workers. Everyone in a capitalist system becomes increasingly enslaved to competition and money, until a genuine community is impossible. Since true freedom can be found only within the community, capitalist freedom is simply loneliness, hostility, and violence painted up to give the appearance of something valuable.

The premises from which we begin are not arbitrary ones, not dogmas, but real premises from which abstraction can only be made in the imagination. They are the real individuals, their activity and the material conditions under which they live, both those which they find already existing and those produced by their activity. These premises can thus be verified in a purely empirical way.

The first premise of all human history is, of course, the existence of living human individuals. Thus the first fact to be established is the physical organization of these individuals and their consequent relation to the rest of nature. Of course, we cannot here go either into the actual physical nature of man, or into the natural conditions in which man finds himself—geological, orohydorgraphical, climatic and so on. The writing of history must always set out from these natural bases and their modification in the course of history through the action of men.

Men can be distinguished from animals by consciousness, by religion or anything else you like. They themselves begin to distinguish themselves from animals as soon as they begin to *produce* their means of subsistence, a step which is conditioned by their physical organization. By producing their means of subsistence men are indirectly producing their actual material life.

The way in which men produce their means of subsistence depends first of all on the nature of the actual means of subsistence they find in existence and have to reproduce. This mode of production must not be considered simply as being the reproduction of the physical existence of the individuals. Rather it is a definite form of activity of these individuals, a definite form of expressing their life, a definite *mode of life* on their part. As individuals express their life, so they are. What they are, therefore, coincides with their production, both with *what* they produce and with *how* they produce. The nature of individuals thus depends on the material conditions determining their production. . . .

In direct contrast to German philosophy which descends from heaven to earth, here we ascend from earth to heaven. That is to say, we do not set out from what men say, imagine, conceive, nor from men as narrated, thought of, imagined, conceived, in order to arrive at men in the flesh. We set out from real, active

From Karl Marx and Friedrich Engels, *The German Ideology*, translated by W. Lough (Lawrence and Wishart, London, 1938).

men, and on the basis of their real life-process we demonstrate the development of the ideological reflexes and echoes of this life-process. The phantoms formed in the human brain are also, necessarily, sublimates of their material life-process, which is empirically verifiable and bound to material premises. Morality, religion, metaphysics, all the rest of ideology and their corresponding forms of consciousness, thus no longer retain the semblance of independence. They have no history, no development; but men, developing their material production and their material intercourse, alter, along with this their real existence, their thinking and the products of their thinking. Life is not determined by consciousness, but consciousness by life. In the first method of approach the starting-point is consciousness taken as the living individual; in the second method, which conforms to real life, it is the real living individuals themselves, and consciousness is considered solely as *their* consciousness. . . .

Since we are dealing with the Germans, who are devoid of premises, we must begin by stating the first premise of all human existence and, therefore, of all history, the premise, namely, that men must be in a position to live in order to be able to "make history." But life involves before everything else eating and drinking, a habitation, clothing and many other things. The first historical act is thus the production of the means to satisfy these needs, the production of material life itself. And indeed this is a historical act, a fundamental condition of all history, which today, as thousands of years ago, must daily and hourly be fulfilled merely in order to sustain human life. Even when the sensuous world is reduced to a minimum, to a stick as with . . . Bruno [Bauer], it presupposes the action of producing the stick. Therefore in any interpretation of history one has first of all to observe this fundamental fact in all its significance and all its implications and to accord it its due importance. . . .

The second point is that the satisfaction of the first need (the action of satisfying, and the instrument of satisfaction which has been acquired) leads to new needs; and this production of new needs is the first historical act. . . .

The third circumstance which, from the very outset, enters into historical development, is that men, who daily remake their own life, begin to make other men, to propagate their kind: the relation between man and woman, parents and children, the *family*. The family, which to begin with is the only social relationship, becomes later, when increased needs create new social relations and the increased population new needs, a subordinate one . . . and must then be treated and analyzed according to the existing empirical data, not according to "the concept of the family," as is the custom in Germany. These three aspects of social activity are not of course to be taken as three different stages, but just as three aspects . . . which have existed simultaneously since the dawn of history and the first men, and which still assert themselves in history today.

The production of life, both of one's own in labor and of fresh life in procreation, now appears as a double relationship: on the one hand as a natural, on the other as a social relationship. By social we understand the cooperation of several individuals, no matter under what conditions, in what manner and to what end. It follows from this that a certain mode of production, or industrial stage, is always combined with a certain mode of cooperation, or social stage, and this mode of cooperation is itself a "productive force." Further, that the multitude of productive forces accessible to men determines the nature of society, hence, that the "history of humanity" must always be studied and treated in relation to the history of industry and exchange. . . .

Only now, after having considered four moments, four aspects of the primary historical relationships, do we find that man also possesses "consciousness"; but, even so, not inherent, not "pure" consciousness. From the start the "spirit" is afflicted with the curse of being "burdened" with matter, which here makes its appearance in the form of agitated layers of air, sounds, in short, of language. Language is as old as consciousness, language *is* practical consciousness that exists also for other men, and for that reason alone it really exists for me personally as well; language, like consciousness, only arises from the need, the necessity, of intercourse with other men. Where there exists a relationship, it exists for me: the animal does not enter into *"relations"* with anything, it does not enter into any relation at all. For the animal, its relation to others does not exist as a relation. Consciousness is, therefore, from the very beginning a social product, and remains so as long as men exist at all. Consciousness is at first, of course, merely consciousness concerning the *immediate* sensuous environment and consciousness of the limited connection with other persons and things outside the individual who is growing self-conscious. At the same time it is consciousness of nature, which first appears to men as a completely alien, all-powerful and unassailable force, with which men's relations are purely animal and by which they are overawed like beasts; it is thus a purely animal consciousness of nature (natural religion).

We see here immediately: this natural religion or this particular relation of men to nature is determined by the form of society and vice versa. Here, as everywhere, the identity of nature and man appears in such a way that the restricted relation of men to nature determines their restricted relation to one another, and their restricted relation to one another determines men's restricted relation to nature, just because nature is as yet hardly modified historically; and, on the other hand, man's consciousness of the necessity of associating with the individuals around him is the beginning of the consciousness that he is living in society at all. This beginning is as animal as social life itself at this stage. It is mere herd-consciousness, and at this point man is only distinguished from sheep by the fact that with him consciousness takes the place of instinct or that his instinct is a conscious one. This sheep-like or tribal consciousness receives its further development and extension through increased productivity, the increase of needs, and, what is fundamental to both of these, the increase of population. With these there develops the division of labor, which was originally nothing but the division of labor in the sexual act, then that division of labor which develops spontaneously or "naturally" by virtue of natural predisposition (e.g., physical strength), needs, accidents, etc., etc. Division of labor only becomes truly such from the moment when a division of material and mental labor appears. From this moment onward consciousness *can* really flatter itself that it is something other than consciousness of existing practice, that it *really* represents something without representing something real; from now on consciousness is in a position to emancipate itself from the world and to proceed to the formation of "pure" theory, theology, philosophy, ethics, etc. But even if this theory, theology, philosophy, ethics, etc., comes into contradiction with the existing relations, this can only occur because existing social relations have come into contradiction with existing forces of production. . . .

Moreover, it is quite immaterial what consciousness starts to do on its own: out of all such muck we get only the one inference that these three moments, the forces of production, the state of society and consciousness, can and must come into contradiction with one another, because the *division of labor* implies the possibility, nay the fact that intellectual and material activity—enjoyment and labor, production and consumption—devolve on different individuals, and that the only possibility of their not coming into contradiction lies in the negation in its turn of the division of labor. . . .

The ideas of the ruling class are in every epoch the ruling ideas: i.e., the class which is the ruling *material* force of society, is at the same time its ruling *intellectual* force. The class which has the means of material production at its disposal, has control at the same time over the means of mental production, so that thereby, generally speaking, the ideas of those who lack the means of mental production are subject to it. The ruling ideas are nothing more than the ideal expression of the dominant material relationships, the dominant material relationships grasped as ideas; hence of the relationships which make the one class the ruling one, therefore, the ideas of its dominance. The individuals composing the ruling class possess among other things consciousness, and therefore think. Insofar, therefore, as they rule as a class and determine the extent and compass of an epoch, it is self-evident that they do this in its whole range, hence among other things rule also as thinkers, as producers of ideas, and regulate the production and distribution of the ideas of their age: thus their ideas are the ruling ideas of the epoch. For instance, in an age and in a country where royal power, aristocracy and bourgeoisie are contending for mastery and where, therefore, mastery is shared, the doctrine of the separation of powers proves to be the dominant idea and is expressed as an "external law."

The division of labor, which we already saw above as one of the chief forces of history up till now, manifests itself also in the ruling class as the division of mental and material labor, so that inside this class one part appears as the thinkers of the class (its active, conceptive ideologists, who make the perfecting of the illusion of the class about itself their chief source of livelihood), while the others' attitude to these ideas and illusions is more passive and receptive, because they are in reality the active members of this class and have less time to make up illusions and ideas about themselves. Within this class this cleavage can even develop into a certain opposition and hostility between the two parts, which, however, in the case of a practical collision, in which the class itself is endangered, automatically comes to nothing, in which case there also vanishes the semblance that the ruling ideas were not the ideas of the ruling class and had a power distinct from the power of this class. . . .

If now in considering the course of history we detach the ideas of the ruling class from the ruling class itself and attribute to them an independent existence, if we confine ourselves to saying that these or those ideas were dominant at a given time, without bothering ourselves about the conditions of production and the producers of these ideas, if we thus ignore the individuals and world conditions which are the source of the ideas, we can say, for instance, that during the time that the aristocracy was dominant, the concepts honor, loyalty, etc., were dominant, during the dominance of the bourgeoisie the concepts freedom, equality, etc. The ruling class itself on the whole imagines this to be so. This conception of history, which is common to all historians, particularly since the eighteenth century, will necessarily come up against the phenomenon that increasingly abstract ideas hold sway, i.e., ideas which increasingly take on the form of universality . For each new class which puts itself in the place of one ruling before it, is compelled, merely in order to carry through its aim, to represent its interest as the common interest of all the members of society, that is, expressed in ideal form: it has to give its ideas the form of universality, and represent them as the only rational, universally valid ones. The class making a revolution appears from the very start, if only because it is opposed to a *class,* not as a class but as the representative of the whole of society; it appears as the whole mass of society confronting the one ruling class. It can do this because, to start with, its interest really is more connected with the common interest of all other nonruling classes, because under the pressure of hitherto existing conditions its interest has not yet been able to develop as the particular interest of a particular class. Its victory, therefore, benefits also many individuals of the other classes which are not winning a dominant position, but only insofar as it now puts these individuals in a position to raise themselves into the ruling class. . . . Every new class, therefore, achieves its hegemony only on a broader basis than that of the class ruling previously, whereas the opposition of the nonruling class against the new ruling class later develops all the more sharply and profoundly. . . .

This whole semblance, that the rule of a certain class is only the rule of certain ideas, come to a natural end, of course, as soon as class rule in general ceases to be the form in which society is organized, that is to say, as soon as it is no longer necessary to represent a particular interest as general or the "general interest" as ruling. . . .

Finally, from the conception of history we have sketched we obtain these further conclusions: (1) In the development of productive forces there comes a stage when productive forces and means of intercourse are brought into being, which, under the existing relationships, only cause mischief, and are no longer productive but destructive forces (machinery and money); and connected with this a class is called forth, which has to bear all the burdens of society without enjoying its advantages, which, ousted from society, is forced into the most decided antagonism to all other classes; a class which forms the majority of all members of society, and from which emanates the consciousness of the necessity of a fundamental revolution, the communist consciousness, which may, of course, arise among the other classes too through the contemplation of the situation of this class. (2) The conditions under which definite productive forces can be applied are the conditions of the rule of a definite class of society, whose social power, deriving from its property, has its *practical*-idealistic expression in each case in the form of the State; and, therefore, every revolutionary struggle is directed against a class, which till then has been in power. (3) In all revolutions up till now the mode of activity always remained unscathed and it was only question of a different distribution of this activity, a new distribution of labor to other persons, while the communist revolution is directed against the preceding *mode* of activity, does away with *labor,* and abolishes the rule of all classes with the classes themselves, because it is carried through by the class which no longer counts as a class in society, is not recognized as a class, and is in itself the expression of the dissolution of all classes, nationalities, etc., within present society; and (4) both for the production on a mass scale of this communist consciousness, and for the success of the cause itself, the alteration of men on a mass scale is necessary, an alteration which can only take place in a practical movement, a *revolution;* this revolution is necessary, therefore, not only because the *ruling* class cannot be overthrown in any other way, but also because the class *overthrowing* it can only in a revolution succeed in ridding itself of all the muck of ages and become fitted to found society anew.

Communism differs from all previous movements in that it overturns the basis of all earlier relations of production and intercourse, and for the first time consciously treats all natural premises as the creatures of hitherto existing men, strips them of their natural character and subjugates them to the power of the united individuals. Its organization is, therefore, essentially economic, the material production of the conditions of this unity; it turns existing conditions into conditions of unity. The reality, which communism is creating, is precisely the true basis for rendering it impossible that anything should exist independently of individuals, insofar as reality is only a product of the preceding intercourse of individuals themselves. Thus the communists in practice treat the conditions created up to now by production and intercourse as inorganic conditions, without, however, imagining that it was the plan or the destiny of previous generations to give them material, and without believing that these conditions were inorganic for the individuals creating them. The difference between the individual as a person and what is accidental to him is not a conceptual difference but a historical fact. This distinction has a different significance at different times—e.g., the estate as something accidental to the individual in the eighteenth century, the family more or less too. It is not a distinction that we have to make for each age, but one which each age makes itself from among the different elements which it finds in existence, and indeed not according to any theory, but compelled by material collisions in life. What appears accidental to the later age as opposed to the earlier—and this applies also to the elements handed down by an earlier age—is a form of intercourse which corresponded to a definite stage of development of the productive forces. The relation of the productive forces to the form of intercourse is the relation of the form of intercourse to the occupation or activity of the individuals. (The fundamental form of this activity is, of course, material, on which depend all other forms—mental, political, religious, etc. The various shaping of material life is of course, in every case dependent on the needs which are already developed, and the production, as well as the satisfaction, of these needs is a historical process. . . .) The conditions under which individuals have intercourse with each other, so long as the above-mentioned contradiction is absent, are conditions appertaining to their individuality, in no way external to them; conditions under which these definite individuals, living under definite relationships, can alone produce their material life and what is connected with it, are thus the conditions of their self-activity and are produced by this self-activity. The definite condition under which they produce thus corresponds, as long as the contradiction has not yet appeared, to the reality of their conditioned nature, their one-sided existence, the one-sidedness of which only becomes evident when the contradiction enters on the scene and thus exists for the later individuals. Then this condition appears as an accidental fetter, and the consciousness that it is a fetter imputed to the earlier age as well. . . .

The transformation, through the division of labor, of personal powers (relationships) into material powers, cannot be dispelled by dismissing the general idea of it from one's mind, but can only be abolished by the individuals again subjecting these material powers to themselves and abolishing the division of labor. This is not possible without the community. Only in community [with others has each] individual the means of cultivating his gifts in all directions; only in the community, therefore, is personal freedom possible. In the previous substitutes for the community, in the State, etc., personal freedom has existed only for the individuals who developed within the relationships of the ruling class, and only insofar as they were individuals of this class. The illusory community, in which individuals have up till now combined, always took on an independent existence in relation to them, and was at the same time, since it was the combination of one class over against another, not only a completely illusory community, but a new fetter as well. In the real community the individuals obtain their freedom in and through their association.

It follows from all we have been saying up till now that the communal relationship into which the individuals of a class entered, and which was determined by their common interests over against a third party, was always a community to which these individuals belonged only as average individuals, only insofar as they lived within the conditions of existence of their class—a relationship in which they participated not as individuals but as members of a class. With the community of revolutionary proletarians, on the other hand, who take their conditions of existence and those of all members of society under their control, it is just the reverse; it is as individuals that the individuals participate in it. It is just this combination of individuals (assuming the advanced stage of modern productive forces, of course) which puts the conditions of the free development and movement of individuals under their control—conditions which were previously abandoned to chance and had won an independent existence over against the separate individuals just because of their separation as individuals, and because of the necessity of their combination which had been determined by the division of labor, and through their separation had become a bond alien to them. Combination up till now . . . was an agreement upon these conditions, within which the individuals were free to enjoy the freaks of fortune. . . . This right to the undisturbed enjoyment, within certain conditions of fortuity and chance has up till now been called personal freedom. . . .

This subsuming of individuals under definite classes cannot be abolished until a class has taken shape, which has no longer any particular class interest to assert against the ruling class.

Individuals have always built on themselves, but naturally on themselves within their given historical conditions and relationships, not on the "pure" individual in the sense of the ideologists. But in the course of historical evolution, and precisely through the inevitable fact that within the division of labor social relationships take on an independent existence, there appears a division within the life of each individual, insofar as it is personal and insofar as it is determined by some branch of labor and the conditions pertaining to it. (We do not mean it to be understood from this that, for example, the rentier, the capitalist, etc., cease to be persons; but their personality is conditioned and determined by quite definite class relationships, and the division appears only in their opposition to another class and, for themselves, only when they go bankrupt.) In the estate (and even more in the tribe) this is as yet concealed: for instance, a nobleman always remains a nobleman, a commoner always a commoner, apart from his other relationships, a quality inseparable from his individuality. The division between the personal and the class individual, the accidental nature of the conditions of life for the individual, appears only with the emergence of the class, which is itself a product of the bourgeoisie. This accidental character is only engendered and developed by competition and the struggle of individuals among themselves. Thus, in imagination, individuals seem freer under the dominance of the bourgeoisie than before, because their conditions of life seem accidental; in reality, of course, they are less free, because they are more subjected to the violence of things. . . .

STUDY QUESTIONS

1   How would you define Marx and Engels's concept of freedom for the individual? Why is it so closely tied up with the community? What kinds of social controls might exist in their genuine community?

2   Marx is well known for his view that we must abolish the division of labor. Exactly what is meant by this phrase? What kinds of divisions of labor are there and are all of them truly abolishable?

3   How would you evaluate Marx and Engels's notion of consciousness as being a social product? What do they mean when they say "Life is not determined by consciousness, but consciousness by life"?

4   In what ways might Marx and Engels agree with Mill? In what ways would they disagree?

5   "When Christian ideas succumbed in the eighteenth century to rationalist ideas, Feudal society fought its death battle with the then revolutionary bourgeoisie. The ideas of religious liberty and freedom of conscience merely gave expression to the sway of free competition within the domain of knowledge" (Marx and Engels). Interpret this passage from *The Communist Manifesto.*

6   "The Conservative has learned that the economic and spiritual aspects of man's nature are inextricably intertwined. He cannot be economically free, or even economically efficient, if he is enslaved politically; conversely, a man's political freedom is illusory if he is dependent for his economic needs on the state" (Barry Goldwater, *The Conscience of a Conservative*). How would Marx and Engels respond to this statement? What assumptions would they say Goldwater has made?

7   What would Marx and Engels think of Hobbes's account of human nature? What account of human nature do you think they would give?

Freedom and the Control of Men

B. F. Skinner

With the exception of Freud, B. F. Skinner (1904–   ) has aroused more interest in psychology than anyone in this century. Denounced as a charlatan, hailed as the new savior of humankind, Skinner has been in the center of controversy because of his commitment to behaviorism. Skinner believes that scientific psychology should not seek to explain behavior in terms of conscious or unconscious desires, wishes, or beliefs. Behavior is caused, he says, by the fact that it is reinforced by the environment. In other words, certain forms of behavior happen to be rewarded by the external environment, and become "conditioned responses." Some people, for example, when faced with a threatening situation, become "sick." If their "sick behavior" is rewarded by attention, love, and alleviation of responsibility, they will tend to become "sick" whenever they are faced with difficulties. They have been "conditioned" to become ill in this sort of situation, and they are "controlled" by the environment.

Skinner believes that everyone's behavior is controlled by a complex system of rewards and punishments which have accidentally come to bear upon us. Now that we are beginning to understand the forces that control us, he argues, we should use this knowledge to create a new society of people with "good" behavior patterns. In the following selection, he attempts to show that democratic political philosophy—the philosophy of personal freedom—is based on a false conception of humanity and must now be replaced by a philosophy which recognizes and uses the new technology of behavior control.

The second half of the twentieth century may be remembered for its solution of a curious problem. Although Western democracy created the conditions responsible for the rise of modern science, it is now evident that it may never fully profit from that achievement. The so-called "democratic philosophy" of human behavior to which it also gave rise is increasingly in conflict with the application of the methods of science to human affairs. Unless this conflict is somehow resolved, the ultimate goals of democracy may be long deferred.

From B. F. Skinner, "Freedom and the Control of Men," *The American Scholar*, Winter 1955–56, pp. 47–65. Reprinted by permission of the author.

I

Just as biographers and critics look for external influences to account for the traits and achievements of the men they study, so science ultimately explains behavior in terms of "causes" or conditions which lie beyond the individual himself. As more and more causal relations are demonstrated, a practical corollary becomes difficult to resist: it should be possible to *produce* behavior according to plan simply by arranging the proper conditions. Now, among the specifications which might reasonably be submitted to a behavioral technology are these: Let men be happy, informed, skillful, well behaved and productive.

This immediate practical implication of a science of behavior has a familiar ring, for it recalls the doctrine of human perfectibility of eighteenth- and nineteenth-century humanism. A science of man shares the optimism of that philosophy and supplies striking support for the working faith that men can build a better world and, through it, better men. The support comes just in time, for there has been little optimism of late among those who speak from the traditional point of view. Democracy has become "realistic," and it is only with some embarrassment that one admits today to perfectionistic or utopian thinking.

The earlier temper is worth considering, however. History records many foolish and unworkable schemes for human betterment, but almost all the great changes in our culture which we now regard as worthwhile can be traced to perfectionistic philosophies. Governmental, religious, educational, economic and social reforms follow a common pattern. Someone believes that a change in a cultural practice—for example, in the rules of evidence in a court of law, in the characterization of man's relation to God, in the way children are taught to read and write, in permitted rates of interest, or in minimal housing standards—will improve the condition of men: by promoting justice, permitting me to seek salvation more effectively, increasing the literacy of a people, checking an inflationary trend, or improving public health and family relations, respectively. The underlying hypothesis is always the same: that a different physical or cultural environment will make a different and better man.

The scientific study of behavior not only justifies the general pattern of such proposals; it promises new and better hypotheses. The earliest cultural practices must have originated in sheer accidents. Those which strengthened the group survived with the group in a sort of natural selection. As soon as men began to propose and carry out changes in practice for the sake of possible consequences, the evolutionary process must have accelerated. The simple practice of making changes must have had survival value. A further acceleration is now to be expected. As laws of behavior are more precisely stated, the changes in the environment required to bring about a given effect may be more clearly specified. Conditions which have been neglected because their effects were slight or unlooked for may be shown to be relevant. New conditions may actually be created, as in the discovery and synthesis of drugs which affect behavior.

This is no time, then to abandon notions of progress, improvement or, indeed, human perfectibility. The simple fact is that man is able, and now as never before, to lift himself by his own bootstraps. In achieving control of the world of which he is a part, he may learn at last to control himself.

II

Timeworn objections to the planned improvement of cultural practices are already losing much of their force. Marcus Aurelius was probably right in advising his readers to be content with a haphazard amelioration of mankind. "Never hope to realize Plato's republic," he sighed, ". . . for who can change the opinions of men? And without a change of sentiments what can you make but reluctant slaves and hypocrites?" He was thinking, no doubt, of contemporary patterns of control based upon punishment or the threat of punishment which, as he correctly observed, breed only reluctant slaves of those who submit and hypocrites of those who discover modes of evasion. But we need not share his pessimism, for the opinions of men can be changed. The techniques of indoctrination which were being devised by the early Christian Church at the very time Marcus Aurelius was writing are relevant, as are some of the techniques of psychotherapy and of advertising and public relations. Other methods suggested by recent scientific analyses leave little doubt of the matter.

The study of human behavior also answers the cynical complaint that there is a plain "cussedness" in man which will always thwart efforts to improve him. We are often told that men do not want to be changed, even for the better. Try to help them, and they will outwit you and remain happily wretched. Dostoevsky claimed to see some plan in it. "Out of sheer ingratitude," he complained, or possibly boasted, "man will play you a dirty trick, just to prove that men are still men and not the keys of a piano. . . . And even if you could prove that a man is only a piano key, he would still do something out of sheer perversity—he would create destruction and chaos—just to gain his point. . . . And if all this could in turn be analyzed and prevented by predicting that it would occur, then man would deliberately go mad to prove his point." This is a conceivable neurotic reaction to inept control. A few men may have shown it, and many have enjoyed Dostoevsky's statement because they tend to show it. But that such perversity is a fundamental reaction of the human organism to controlling conditions is sheer nonsense. . . .

Designing a new cultural pattern is in many ways like designing an experiment. In drawing up a new constitution, outlining a new educational program, modifying a religious doctrine, or setting up a new fiscal policy, many statements must be quite tentative. We cannot be sure that the practices we specify will have the consequences we predict, or that the consequences will reward our efforts. This is in the nature of such proposals. They are not value judgments—they are guesses. To confuse and delay the improvement of cultural practices by quibbling about the word *improve* is itself not a useful practice. Let us agree, to start with, that health is better than illness, wisdom better than ignorance, love better than hate, and productive energy better than neurotic sloth. . . .

III

But we are not yet in the clear, for a new and unexpected obstacle has arisen. With a world of their own making almost within reach, men of good will have been seized with distaste for their achievement. They have uneasily rejected opportunities to apply the techniques and findings of science in the service of men, and as the import of effective cultural design has come to be understood, many of them have voiced an outright refusal to have any part in it. Science has been challenged before when it has encroached upon institutions already engaged in the control of human behavior; but what are we to make of benevolent men, with no special interests of their own to defend, who nevertheless turn against the very means of reaching long-dreamed-of goals?

What is being rejected, of course, is the scientific conception of man and his place in nature. So long as the findings and methods of science are applied to human affairs only in a sort of remedial patchwork, we may continue to hold any view of human nature we like. But as the use of science increases, we are forced to accept the theoretical structure with which science represents its facts. The difficulty is that this structure is clearly at odds with the traditional democratic conception of man. Every discovery of an event which has a part in shaping a man's behavior seems to leave so much the less to be credited to the man himself; and as such explanations become more and more comprehensive, the contribution which may be claimed by the individual himself appears to approach zero. Man's vaunted creative powers, his original accomplishments in art, science and morals, his capacity to choose and our right to hold him responsible for the consequences of his choice—none of these is conspicuous in this new self-portrait. Man, we once believed, was free to express himself in art, music and literature, to inquire into nature, to seek salvation in his own way. He could initiate action and make spontaneous and capricious changes of course. Under the most extreme duress some sort of choice remained to him. He could resist any effort to control him though it might cost him his life. But science insists that action is initiated by forces impinging upon the individual, and that caprice is only another name for behavior for which we have not yet found a cause.

In attempting to reconcile these views it is important to note that the traditional democratic conception was not designed as a description in the scientific sense but as a philosophy to be used in setting up and maintaining a governmental process. It arose under historical circumstances and served political purposes apart from which it cannot be properly understood. In rallying men against tyranny it was necessary that the individual be strengthened, that he be taught that he had rights and could govern himself. To give the common man a new conception of his worth, his dignity, and his power to save himself, both here and hereafter, was often the only resource of the revolutionist. When democratic principles were put into practice, the same doctrines were used as a working formula. This is exemplified by the notion of personal responsibility in Anglo-American law. All governments make certain forms of punishment contingent upon certain kinds of acts. In democratic countries these contingencies are expressed by the notion of responsible choice. But the notion may have no meaning under governmental practices formulated in other ways and would certainly have no place in systems which did not use punishment.

The democratic philosophy of human nature is determined by certain political exigencies and techniques, not by the goals of democracy. But exigencies and techniques change; and a conception which is not supported for its accuracy as a likeness—is not, indeed, rooted in fact at all—may be expected to change too. No matter how effective we judge current democratic practices to be, how highly we value them or how long we expect them to survive, they are almost certainly not the *final* form of government. The philosophy of human nature which has been useful in implementing them is also almost certainly not the last word. The ultimate achievement of democracy may be long deferred unless we emphasize the real aims rather than the verbal devices of democratic thinking. A philosophy which has been appropriate to one set of political exigencies will defeat its purpose if, under other circumstances, it prevents us from applying to human affairs the science of man which probably nothing but democracy itself could have produced.

IV

Perhaps the most crucial part of our democratic philosophy to be reconsidered is our attitude toward freedom—or its reciprocal, the control of human behavior. We do not oppose all forms of control because it is "human nature" to do so. The reaction is not characteristic of all men under all conditions of life. It is an attitude which has been carefully engineered, in large part by what we call the "literature" of democracy. With respect to some methods of control (for example, the threat of force), very little engineering is needed, for the techniques of their immediate consequences are objectionable. Society has suppressed these methods by branding them "wrong," "illegal" or "sinful." But to encourage these attitudes toward objectionable forms of control, it has been necessary to disguise the real nature of certain indispensable techniques, the commonest examples of which are education, moral discourse, and persuasion. The actual procedures appear harmless enough. They consist of supplying information, presenting opportunities for action, pointing out logical relationships, appealing to reason or "enlightened understanding," and so on. Through a masterful piece of misrepresentation, the illusion is fostered that these procedures do not involve the control of behavior; at most, they are simply ways of "getting someone to change his mind." But analysis not only reveals the presence of well-defined behavioral processes, it demonstrates a kind of control no less inexorable, thought in some ways more acceptable, than the bully's threat of force.

Let us suppose that someone in whom we are interested is acting unwisely—he is careless in the way he deals with his friends, he drives too fast, or he holds his golf club the wrong way. We could probably help him by issuing a series of commands: don't nag, don't drive over sixty, don't hold your club that way. Much less objectionable would be "an appeal to reason." We could show him how people are affected by his treatment of them, how accident rates rise sharply at higher speeds, how a particular grip on the club alters the way the ball is struck and corrects a slice. In doing so we resort to verbal mediating devices which emphasize and support certain "contingencies of reinforcement"—that is, certain relations between behavior and its consequences—which strengthen the behavior we wish to set up. The same consequences would possibly set up the behavior without our help, and they eventually take control no matter which form of help we give. The appeal to reason has certain advantages over the authoritative command. A threat of punishment, no matter how subtle, generates emotional reactions and tendencies to escape or revolt. Perhaps the controllee merely "feels resentment" at being made to act in a given way, but even that is to be avoided. When we "appeal to reason," he "feels freer to do as he pleases." The fact is that we have exerted *less* control than in using a threat; since other conditions may contribute to the result, the effect may be delayed or, possibly in a given instance, lacking. But if we have worked a change in his behavior at all, it is because we have altered relevant environmental conditions, and the processes we have set in motion are just as real and just as inexorable, if not as comprehensive, as in the most authoritative coercion.

"Arranging an opportunity for action" is another example of disguised control. The power of the negative form has already been exposed in the analysis of censorship. Restriction of opportunity is recognized as far from harmless. As Ralph Barton Perry said in an article which appeared in the Spring, 1953, *Pacific Spectator,* "Whoever determines what alternatives shall be made known to man controls what that man shall choose *from.* He is deprived of freedom in proportion as he is denied access to *any* ideas, or is confined to any range of ideas short of the totality of relevant possibilities." But there is a positive side as well. When we present a relevant state of affairs, we increase the likelihood that a given form of behavior will be emitted. To the extent that the probability of action has changed, we have made a definite contribution. The teacher of history controls a student's behavior (or, if the reader prefers, "deprives him of freedom") just as much in *presenting* historical facts as in suppressing them. Other conditions will no doubt affect the student, but the contribution made to his behavior by the presentation of material is fixed and, within its range, irresistible.

The methods of education, moral discourse, and persuasion are acceptable not because they recognize the freedom of the individual or his right to dissent, but because they make only *partial* contributions to the control of his behavior. The freedom they recognize is freedom from a more coercive form of control. The dissent which they tolerate is the possible effect of other determiners of action. Since these sanctioned methods are frequently ineffective, we have been able to convince ourselves that they do not represent control at all. When they show too much strength to permit disguise, we give them other names and suppress them as energetically as we suppress the use of force. Education grown too powerful is rejected as propaganda or "brain-washing," while really effective persuasion is decried as "undue influence," "demagoguery," "seduction," and so on.

If we are not to rely solely upon accident for the innovations which give rise to cultural evolution, we must accept the fact that some kind of control of human behavior is inevitable. We cannot use good sense in human affairs unless someone engages in the design and construction of environmental conditions which affect the behavior of men. Environmental changes have always been the condition for the improvement of cultural patterns, and we can hardly use the more effective methods of science without making changes on a grander scale. We are all controlled by the world in which we live, and part of that world has been and will be constructed by men. The question is this: Are we to be controlled by accident, by tyrants, or by ourselves in effective cultural design? . . .

V

Those who reject the scientific conception of man must, to be logical, oppose the methods of science as well. The position is often supported by predicting a series of dire consequences which are to follow if science is not checked. A recent book by Joseph Wood Krutch, *The Measure of Man,* is in this vein. Mr. Krutch sees in the growing science of man the threat of an unexampled tyranny over men's minds. If science is permitted to have its way, he insists, "we may never be able really to think again." A controlled culture will, for example, lack some virtue inherent in disorder. We have emerged from chaos through a series of happy accidents, but in an engineered culture it will be "impossible for the unplanned to erupt again." But there is no virtue in the accidental character of an accident, and the diversity which arises from disorder can not only be duplicated by design but vastly extended. The experimental method is superior to simple observation just because it multiplies "accidents" in a systematic coverage of the possibilities. Technology offers many familiar examples. We no longer wait for immunity to disease to develop from a series of accidental exposures, nor do we wait for natural mutations in sheep and cotton to produce better fibers; but we continue to make use of such accidents when they occur, and we certainly do not prevent them. Many of the things we value have emerged from the clash of ignorant armies on darkling plains, but it is not therefore wise to encourage ignorance and darkness. . . .

Another predicted consequence of a science of man is an excessive uniformity. We are told that effective control—whether governmental, religious, educational, economic or social—will produce a race of men who differ from each other only through relatively refractory genetic differences. That would probably be bad design, but we must admit that we are not now pursuing another course from choice. In a modern school, for example, there is usually a syllabus which specifies what every student is to learn by the end of each year. This would be flagrant regimentation if anyone expected every student to comply. But some will be poor in particular subjects, others will not study, others will not remember what they have been taught, and diversity is assured. Suppose, however, that we someday possess such effective educational techniques that every student will in fact be put in possession of all the behavior specified in a syllabus. At the end of the year, all students will correctly answer all questions on the final examination and "must all have prizes." Should we reject such a system on the grounds that in making all students excellent it has made them all alike? Advocates of the theory of a special faculty might contend that an important advantage of the present system is that the good student learns *in spite of* a system which is so defective that it is currently producing bad students as well. But if really effective techniques are available, we cannot avoid the problem of design simply by preferring the status quo. At what point should education be deliberately inefficient? . . .

VI

Apart from their possibly objectionable consequences, scientific methods seem to make no provision for certain admirable qualities and faculties which seem to have flourished in less explicitly planned cultures; hence they are called "degrading" or "lacking in dignity." (Mr. Krutch has called the author's *Walden Two* an "ignoble Utopia.") The conditioned reflex is the current whipping boy. Because conditioned reflexes may be demonstrated in animals, they are spoken of as though they were exclusively subhuman. It is implied, as we have seen, that no behavioral processes are involved in education and moral discourse or, at least, that the processes are exclusively human. But men do show conditioned reflexes (for example, when they are frightened by all instances of the control of human behavior because some instances engender fear), and animals do show processes similar to the human behavior involved in instruction and moral discourse. When Mr. Krutch asserts that " 'Conditioning' is achieved by methods which by-pass or, as it were, short-circuit those very reasoning faculties which education proposes to cultivate and exercise," he is making a technical statement which needs a definition of terms and a great deal of supporting evidence.

If such methods are called "ignoble" simply because they leave no room for certain admirable attributes, then perhaps the practice of admiration needs to be examined. We might say that the child whose education has been skillfully planned has been deprived of the right to intellectual heroism. Nothing has been left to be admired in the way he acquires an education. Similarly, we can conceive of moral training which is so adequate to the demands of the culture that men will be good practically automatically, but to that extent they will be deprived of the right to moral heroism, since we seldom admire automatic goodness. Yet if we consider the end of morals rather than certain virtuous means, is not "automatic goodness" a desirable state of affairs? Is it not, for example, the avowed goal of religious education? T. H. Huxley answered the question unambiguously: "If some great power would agree to make me always think what is true and do what is right, on condition of being a sort of clock and wound up every morning before I got out of bed, I should close instantly with the offer." Yet Mr. Krutch quotes this as the scarcely credible point of view of a "protomodern" and seems himself to share T. S. Eliot's contempt for ". . . systems so perfect. / That no one will need to be good."

"Having to be good" is an excellent example of an expendable honorific. It is inseparable from a particular form of ethical and moral control. We distinguish between the things we *have* to do to avoid punishment and those we *want* to do for rewarding consequences. In a culture which did not resort to punishment we should never "have" to do anything except with respect to the punishing contingencies which arise directly in the physical environment. And we are moving toward such a culture, because the neurotic, not to say pyschotic, by-products of control through punishment have long since led compassionate men to seek alternative techniques. Recent research has explained some of the objectionable results of punishment and has revealed resources of at least equal power in "positive reinforcement." It is reasonable to look forward to a time when man will seldom "have" to do anything, although he may show interest, energy, imagination and productivity far beyond the level seen under the present system (except for rare eruptions of the unplanned).

What we have to do we do with *effort*. We call it "work." There is no other way to distinguish between exhausting labor and the possibly equally energetic but rewarding activity of play. It is presumably good cultural design to replace the former with the latter. But an adjustment in attitudes is needed. We are much more practiced in admiring the heroic labor of a Hercules than the activity of one who works without having to. In a truly effective educational system the student might not "have to work" at all, but that possibility is likely to be received by the contemporary teacher with an emotion little short of rage.

We cannot reconcile traditional and scientific views by agreeing upon *what* is to be admired or condemned. The question is whether anything is to be so treated. Praise and blame are cultural practices which have been adjuncts of the prevailing system of control in Western democracy. All peoples do not engage in them for the same purposes or to the same extent, nor, of course, are the same behaviors always classified in the same way as subject to praise or blame. In admiring intellectual and moral heroism and unrewarding labor, and in rejecting a world in which these would be uncommon, we are simply demonstrating our own cultural conditioning. By promoting certain tendencies to admire and censure, the group of which we are a part has arranged for the social reinforcement and punishment needed to assure a high level of intellectual and moral industry. Under other and possibly better controlling systems, the behavior which we now admire would occur, but not under those conditions which make it admirable, and we should have no reason to admire it because the culture would have arranged for its maintenance in other ways.

To those who are stimulated by the glamorous heroism of the battlefield, a peaceful world may not be a better world. Others may reject a world without sorrow, longing or a sense of guilt because the relevance of deeply moving works of art would be lost. To many who have devoted their lives to the struggle to be wise and good, a world without confusion and evil might be an empty thing. A nostalgic concern for the decline of moral heroism has been a dominating theme in the work of Aldous Huxley. In *Brave New World* he could see in the application of science to human affairs only a travesty on the notion of the Good (just as George Orwell, in *1984,* could foresee nothing but horror). In a recent issue of *Esquire,* Huxley has expressed the point this way: "We have had religious revolutions, we have had political, industrial, economic and nationalistic revolutions. All of them, as our descendants will discover, were but ripples in an ocean of conservatism—trivial by comparison with the psychological revolution toward which we are so rapidly moving. *That* will really be a revolution. When it is over, the human race will give no further trouble." (Footnote for the reader of the future: This was not meant as a happy ending. Up to 1956 men had been admired, if at all, either for causing trouble or alleviating it. Therefore—)

It will be a long time before the world can dispense with heroes and hence with the cultural practice of admiring heroism, but we move in that direction whenever we act to prevent war, famine, pestilence and disaster. It will be a long time before man will never need to submit to punishing environments or engage in exhausting labor, but we move in that direction whenever we make food, shelter, clothing and labor-saving devices more readily available. We may mourn the passing of heroes but not the conditions which make for heroism. We can spare the self-made saint or sage as we spare the laundress on the river's bank struggling against fearful odds to achieve cleanliness. . . .

STUDY QUESTIONS

1   What do you think of a world where human beings would be good almost automatically? What kinds of freedom might be increased in such a world? Would there be any increase in freedom?

2   Suppose we accept Skinner's thesis that since social conditioning exists, we might as well understand it and use it to our greatest advantage. Who, then, is going to be in charge of this social engineering? How could we prevent such techniques from being used to enslave us?

3   In your opinion, what is the depth of our present social conditioning? Would Skinner's type of control be any more encompassing? Would it need to be so?

4   In what ways could Mill's position on individual freedom conflict with Skinner's use of behavioral science?

5   If Marx could be consulted in regard to Skinner's method of achieving a better society, what do you think he would say?

6   "They say that habit is Second Nature; but perhaps Nature is only first Habit" (Pascal). To what extent do you agree with Pascal? Do you think that there is something called *human nature* which will resist all attempts to change it? Would Skinner agree?

7   Skinner says that education and persuasion are forms of control no less than force. Why does he say this? Why is this form of control less objectionable than force? Would Dewey agree with Skinner's notion of "control?"

The New Forms of Control

Herbert Marcuse

During the student demonstrations of the 1960s, one would frequently hear reference to the three M's: Marx, Mao, and Marcuse. Herbert Marcuse (1898–   ), born and educated in Germany, fled Nazi rule to become an American citizen in 1940. He is one of the outstanding contemporary Marxist critics of modern industrial society. Presently he is professor emeritus of political philosophy at the University of California, San Diego.

Marcuse reacts against the productive forces in our present-day technological society. He believes that instead of freeing individuals, the productive apparatus of advanced industrialized society is enslaving them. The individual is indoctrinated with false needs and life begins to have only one dimension. Worst of all, the inner freedom of the individual's mind is being gradually whittled down so that there is no place for resistance to take hold or for the individual to "become and remain 'himself.' " This entire trend is related, Marcuse says, to the development of operationalism in physical science and to behaviorism in social science. Marcuse also believes, like Skinner, that we have reached a stage where our traditional concepts of freedom are out of date and need to be replaced by newer modes of thought which more closely reflect the modern capabilities of our society. He defines some of the kinds of freedom individuals should have, but his main interest is in arousing us to the fact that there are "new forms of control" (technological ones) abroad in the world and that the result could be a totalitarian universe.

A comfortable, smooth, reasonable, democratic unfreedom prevails in advanced industrial civilization, a token of technical progress. Indeed, what could be more rational than the suppression of individuality in the mechanization of socially necessary but painful performances; the concentration of individual enterprises in more effective, more productive corporations; the regulation of free competition among unequally equipped economic subjects; the curtailment of prerogatives and national sovereignties which impede the international organization of resources. That this technological order also involves a political and intellectual coordination may be a regrettable and yet promising development.

The rights and liberties which were such vital factors in the origins and earlier stages of industrial society yield to a higher stage of this society: they are losing their traditional rationale and content. Freedom of thought, speech, and conscience were—just as free enterprise, which they served to promote and protect—essentially *critical* ideas, designed to replace an obsolescent material and intellectual culture by a more productive and rational one. Once institutionalized, these rights and liberties shared the fate of the society of which they had become an integral part. The achievement cancels the premises.

To the degree to which freedom from want, the concrete substance of all freedom, is becoming a real possibility, the liberties which pertain to a state of lower productivity are losing their former content. Independence of thought, autonomy, and the right to political opposition are being deprived of their basic critical function in a society which seems increasingly capable of satisfying the needs of the individuals through the way in which it is organized. Such a society may justly demand acceptance of its principles and institutions, and reduce the opposition to the discussion and promotion of alternative policies *within* the status quo. In this respect, it seems to make little difference whether the increasing satisfaction of needs is accomplished by an authoritarian or a non-authoritarian system. Under the conditions of a rising standard of living, non-conformity with the system itself appears to be socially useless, and the more so when it entails tangible economic and political disadvantages and threatens the smooth operation of the whole. Indeed, at least in so far as the necessities of life are involved, there seems to be no reason why the production and distribution of goods and services should proceed through the competitive concurrence of individual liberties.

Freedom of enterprise was from the beginning not altogether a blessing. As the liberty to work or to starve, it spelled toil, insecurity, and fear for the vast majority of the population. If the individual were no longer compelled to prove himself on the market, as a free economic subject, the disappearance of this kind of freedom would be one of the greatest achievements of civilization. The technological processes of mechanization and standardization might release individual energy into a yet uncharted realm of freedom beyond necessity. The very structure of human existence would be altered; the individual would be liberated from the work world's imposing upon him alien needs and alien possibilities. The individual would be free to exert autonomy over a life that would be his own. If the productive apparatus could be organized and directed toward the satisfaction of the vital needs, its control might well be centralized; such control would not prevent individual autonomy, but render it possible.

This is a goal within the capabilities of advanced industrial civilization, the "end" of technological rationality. In actual fact, however, the contrary trend operates: the apparatus imposes its economic and political requirements for defense and expansion on labor time and free time, on the material and intellectual culture. By virtue of the way it has organized its technological base, contemporary industrial society tends to be totalitarian. For "totalitarian" is not only a terroristic political coordination of society, but also a nonterroristic economic-technical coordination which operates through the manipulation of needs by vested interests. It thus precludes the emergence of an effective opposition against the whole. Not only a specific form of government or party rule makers for totalitarianism, but also a specific system of production and distribution which may well be compatible with a "pluralism" of parties, newspapers, "countervailing powers," etc.

Today political power asserts itself through its power over the machine process and over the technical organization of the apparatus. The government of advanced and advancing industrial societies can maintain and secure itself only when it succeeds in mobilizing, organizing, and exploiting the technical, scientific, and mechanical productivity available to industrial civilization. And this productivity mobilizes society as a whole, above and beyond any particular individual or group interests. The brute fact that the machine's physical (only physical?) power surpasses that of the individual, and of any particular group of individuals, makes the machine the most effective political instrument in any society whose basic organization is that of the machine process. But the political trend may be reversed; essentially the power of the machine is only the stored-up and projected power of man. To the extent to which the work world is conceived of as a machine and mechanized accordingly, it becomes the *potential* basis of a new freedom for man.

Contemporary industrial civilization demonstrates that it has reached the stage at which "the free society" can no longer be adequately defined in the traditional terms of economic, political, and intellectual liberties, not because these liberties have become insignificant, but because they are too significant to be confined within the traditional forms. New modes of realization are needed, corresponding to the new capabilities of society.

Such new modes can be indicated only in negative terms because they would amount to the negation of the prevailing modes. Thus economic freedom would mean freedom *from* the economy—from being controlled by economic forces and relationships; freedom from the daily struggle for existence, from earning a living. Political freedom would mean liberation of the individuals *from* politics over which they have no effective control. Similarly, intellectual freedom would mean the restoration of individual thought now absorbed by mass communication and indoctrination, abolition of "public opinion" together with its makers. The unrealistic sound of these propositions is indicative, not of their utopian character, but of the strength of the forces which prevent their realization. The most effective and enduring form of warfare against liberation is the implanting of material and intellectual needs that perpetuate obsolete forms of the struggle for existence.

The intensity, the satisfaction and even the character of human needs, beyond the biological level, have always been preconditioned. Whether or not the possibility of doing or leaving, enjoying or destroying, possessing or rejecting something is seized as a *need* depends on whether or not it can be seen as desirable and necessary for the prevailing societal institutions and interests. In this sense, human needs are historical needs and, to the extent to which society demands the repressive development of the individual, his needs themselves and their claim for satisfaction are subject to overriding critical standards.

We may distinguish both true and false needs. "False" are those which are superimposed upon the individual by particular social interests in his repression: the needs which perpetuate toil, agressiveness, misery, and injustice. Their satisfaction might be most gratifying to the individual, but this happiness is not a condition which has to be maintained and protected if it serves to arrest the development of the ability (his own and others) to recognize the disease of the whole and grasp the chances of curing the disease. The result then is euphoria in unhappiness. Most of the prevailing needs to relax, to have fun, to behave and consume in accordance with the advertisements, to love and hate what others love and hate, belong to this category of false needs.

Such needs have a societal content and function which are determined by external powers over which the individual has no control; the development and satisfaction of these needs is heteronomous. No matter how much such needs may have become the individual's own, reproduced and fortified by the conditions of his existence; no matter how much he identifies himself with them and finds himself in their satisfaction, they continue to be what they were from the beginning—products of a society whose dominant interest demands repression.

The prevalence of repressive needs is an accomplished fact, accepted in ignorance and defeat, but a fact that must be undone in the interest of the happy individual as well as all those whose misery is the price of his satisfaction. The only needs that have an unqualified claim for satisfaction are the vital ones—nourishment, clothing, lodging at the attainable level of culture. The satisfaction of these needs is the prerequisite for the realization of *all* needs, of the unsublimated as well as the sublimated ones.

For any consciousness and conscience, for any experience which does not accept the prevailing societal interest as the supreme law of thought and behavior, the established universe of needs and satisfactions is a fact to be questioned—questioned in terms of truth and falsehood. These terms are historical throughout, and their objectivity is historical. The judgment of needs and their satisfaction, under the given conditions, involves standards of *priority*—standards which refer to the optimal development of the individual, of all individuals, under the optimal utilization of the material and intellectual resources available to man. The resources are calculable. "Truth" and "falsehood" of needs designate objective conditions to the extent to which the universal satisfaction of vital needs and, beyond it, the progressive alleviation of toil and poverty, are universally valid standards. But as historical standards, they do not only vary according to area and stage of development, they also can be defined only in (greater or lesser) *contradiction* to the prevailing ones. What tribunal can possibly claim the authority of decision?

In the last analysis, the question of what are true and false needs must be answered by the individuals themselves, but only in the last analysis; that is, if and when they are free to give their own answer. As long as they are kept incapable of being autonomous, as long as they are indoctrinated and manipulated (down to their very instincts), their answer to this question cannot be taken as their own. By the same token, however, no tribunal can justly arrogate to itself the right to decide which needs should be developed and satisfied. Any such tribunal is reprehensible, although our revulsion does not do away with the question: how can the people who have been the object of effective and productive domination by themselves create the conditions of freedom?

The more rational, productive, technical, and total the repressive adminstration of society becomes, the more unimaginable the means and ways by which the administered individuals might break their servitude and seize their own liberation. To be sure, to impose Reason upon an entire society is a paradoxical and scandalous idea—although one might dispute the righteousness of a society which ridicules this idea while making its own population into objects of total administration. All liberation depends on the consciousness of servitude, and the emergence of this consciousness is always hampered by the predominance of needs and satisfactions which, to a great extent, have become the individual's own. The process always replaces one system of preconditioning by another; the optimal goal is the replacement of false needs by true ones, the abandonment of repressive satisfaction.

The distinguishing feature of advanced industrial society is its effective suffocation of those needs which demand liberation—liberation also from that which is tolerable and rewarding and comfortable—while it sustains and absolves the destructive power and repressive function of the affluent society. Here, the social controls exact the overwhelming need for the production and consumption of waste; the need for stupefying work where it is no longer a real necessity; the need for modes of relaxation which soothe and prolong this stupefication; the need for maintaining such deceptive liberties as free competition at administered prices, a free press which censors itself, free choice between brands and gadgets.

Under the rule of a repressive whole, liberty can be made into a powerful instrument of domination. The range of choice open to the individual is not the decisive factor in determining the degree of human freedom, but *what* can be chosen and what *is* chosen by the individual. The criterion for free choice can never be an absolute one, but neither is it entirely relative. Free election of masters does not abolish the masters or the slaves. Free choice among a wide variety of goods and services does not signify freedom if these goods and services sustain social controls over a life of toil and fear—that is, if they sustain alienation. And the spontaneous reproduction of superimposed needs by the individual does not establish autonomy; it only testifies to the efficacy of the controls.

The prevailing forms of social control are technological in a new sense. To be sure, the technical structure and efficacy of the productive and destructive apparatus has been a major instrumentality for subjecting the population to the established social division of labor throughout the modern period. Moreover, such integration has always been accompanied by more obvious forms of compulsion: loss of livelihood, the administration of justice, the police, the armed forces. It still is. But in the contemporary period, the technological controls appear to be the very embodiment of Reason for the benefit of all social groups and interests—to such an extent that all contradiction seems irrational and all counteraction impossible.

No wonder then that, in the most advanced areas of this civilization, the social controls have been introjected to the point where even individual protest is affected at its roots. The intellectual and emotional refusal "to go along" appears neurotic and impotent. This is the socio-psychological aspect of the political event that marks the contemporary period: the passing of the historical forces which, at the preceding stage of industrial society, seemed to represent the possibility of new forms of existence.

But the term "introjection" perhaps no longer describes the way in which the individual by himself reproduces and perpetuates the external controls exercised by his society. Introjection suggests a variety of relatively spontaneous processes by which a Self (Ego) transposes the "outer" into the "inner." Thus introjection implies the existence of an inner dimension distinguished from and even antagonistic to the external exigencies—an individual consciousness and an individual unconscious *apart from* public opinion and behavior.[1] The idea of "inner freedom" here has its reality: it designates the private space in which man may become and remain "himself."

Today this private space has been invaded and whittled down by technological reality. Mass production and mass distribution claim the *entire* individual, and industrial psychology has long since ceased to be confined to the factory. The manifold processes of introjection seem to be ossified in almost mechanical reactions. The result is, not adjustment but *mimesis:* an immediate identification of the individual with *his* society and, through it, with the society as a whole.

This immediate, automatic identification (which may have been characteristic of primitive forms of association) reappears in high industrial civilization; its

---

[1] The change in the function of the family here plays a decisive role: its "socializing" functions are increasingly taken over by outside groups and media. See my *Eros and Civilization* (Boston: Beacon Press, 1955), p. 96 ff.

new "immediacy," however, is the product of a sophisticated, scientific management and organization. In this process, the "inner" dimension of the mind in which opposition to the status quo can take root is whittled down. The loss of this dimension, in which the power of negative thinking—the critical power of Reason—is at home, is the ideological counterpart to the very material process in which advanced industrial society silences and reconciles the opposition. The impact of progress turns Reason into submission to the facts of life, and to the dynamic capability of producing more and bigger facts of the same sort of life. The efficiency of the system blunts the individuals' recognition that it contains no facts which do not communicate the repressive power of the whole. If the individuals find themselves in the things which shape their life, they do so, not by giving, but by accepting the law of things—not the law of physics but the law of their society.

I have just suggested that the concept of alienation seems to become questionable when the individuals identify themselves with the existence which is imposed upon them and have in it their own development and satisfaction. This identification is not illusion but reality. However, the reality constitutes a more progressive stage of alienation. The latter has become entirely objective; the subject which is alienated is swallowed up by its alienated existence. There is only one dimension, and it is everywhere and in all forms. The achievements of progress defy ideological indictment as well as justification; before their tribunal, the "false consciousness" of their rationality becomes the true consciousness.

This absorption of ideology into reality does not, however, signify the "end of ideology." On the contrary, in a specific sense advanced industrial culture is *more* ideological than its predecessor, inasmuch as today the ideology is in the process of production itself.[2] In a provocative form, this proposition reveals the political aspects of the prevailing technological rationality. The productive apparatus and the goods and services which it produces "sell" or impose the social system as a whole. The means of mass transportation and communication, the commodities of lodging, food, and clothing, the irresistible output of the entertainment and information industry carry with them prescribed attitudes and habits, certain intellectual and emotional reactions which bind the consumers more or less pleasantly to the producers and, through the latter, to the whole. The products indoctrinate and manipulate; they promote a false consciousness which is immune against its falsehood. And as these beneficial products become available to more individuals in more social classes, the indoctrination they carry ceases to be publicity; it becomes a way of life. It is a good way of life—much better than before—and as a good way of life, it militates against qualitative change. Thus emerges a pattern of *one-dimensional thought and behavior* in which ideas, aspirations, and objectives that, by their content, transcend the established universe of discourse and action are either repelled or reduced to terms of this universe. They are redefined by the rationality of the given system and of its quantitative extension.

[2] Theodor W. Adorno, *Prismen. Kulturkritik und Gesellschaft.* (Frankfurt: Suhrkamp, 1955), p. 24 f.

The trend may be related to a development in scientific method: operationalism in the physical, behaviorism in the social sciences. The common feature is a total empiricism in the treatment of concepts; their meaning is restricted to the representation of particular operations and behavior. The operational point of view is well illustrated by P. W. Bridgman's analysis of the concept of length:[3]

> We evidently know what we mean by length if we can tell what the length of any and every object is, and for the physicist nothing more is required. To find the length of an object, we have to perform certain physical operations. The concept of length is therefore fixed when the operations by which length is measured are fixed: that is, the concept of length involves as much and nothing more than the set of operations by which length is determined. In general, we mean by any concept nothing more than a set of operations; *the concept is synonymous with the corresponding set of operations.*

Bridgman has seen the wide implications of this mode of thought for the society at large:[4]

> To adopt the operational point of view involves much more than a mere restriction of the sense in which we understand "concept," but means a far-reaching change in all our habits of thought, in that we shall no longer permit ourselves to use as tools in our thinking concepts of which we cannot give an adequate account in terms of operations.

Bridgman's prediction has come true. The new mode of thought is today the predominant tendency in philosophy, psychology, sociology, and other fields. Many of the most seriously troublesome concepts are being "eliminated" by showing that no adequate account of them in terms of operations or behavior can be given. The radical empiricist onslaught (I shall subsequently, in chapters VII and VIII, examine its claim to be empiricist) thus provides the methodological justification for the debunking of the mind by the intellectuals—a positivism which, in its denial of the transcending elements of Reason, forms the academic counterpart of the socially required behavior.

Outside the academic establishment, the "far-reaching change in all our habits of thought" is more serious. It serves to coordinate ideas and goals with those exacted by the prevailing system, to enclose them in the system, and to repel those which are irreconcilable with the system. The reign of such a one-dimensional reality does not mean that materialism rules, and that the spiritual, metaphysical, and bohemian occupations are petering out. On the contrary, there is a great deal of "Worship together this week," "Why not try God," Zen, existentialism, and beat ways of life, etc. But such modes of protest and transcendence are no longer contradictory to the status quo and no longer negative. They are rather

---

[3] P. W. Bridgman, *The Logic of Modern Physics* (New York: Macmillan, 1928), p. 5. The operational doctrine has since been refined and qualified. Bridgman himself has extended the concept of "operation" to include the "paper-and-pencil" operations of the theorist [in Philipp J. Frank, *The Validation of Scientific Theories* (Boston: Beacon Press, 1954), Chap. II]. The main impetus remains the same: it is "desirable" that the paper-and-pencil operations "be capable of eventual contact, although perhaps indirectly, with instrumental operations."

[4] P. W. Bridgman, *The Logic of Modern Physics,* loc. cit., p. 31.

the ceremonial part of practical behaviorism, its harmless negation, and are quickly digested by the status quo as part of its healthy diet.

One-dimensional thought is systematically promoted by the makers of politics and their purveyors of mass information. Their universe of discourse is populated by self-validating hypotheses which, incessantly and monopolistically repeated, become hypnotic definitions or dictations. For example, "free" are the institutions which operate (and are operated on) in the countries of the Free World; other transcending modes of freedom are by definition either anarchism, communism, or propaganda. "Socialistic" are all encroachments on private enterprises not undertaken by private enterprise itself (or by government contracts), such as universal and comprehensive health insurance, or the protection of nature from all too sweeping commercialization, or the establishment of public services which may hurt private profit. This totalitarian logic of accomplished facts has its Eastern counterpart. There, freedom is the way of life instituted by a communist regime, and all other transcending modes of freedom are either capitalistic, or revisionist, or leftist sectarianism. In both camps, non-operational ideas are non-behavioral and subversive. The movement of thought is stopped at barriers which appear as the limits of Reason itself.

Such limitation of thought is certainly not new. Ascending modern rationalism, in its speculative as well as empirical form, shows a striking contrast between extreme critical radicalism in scientific and philosophic method on the one hand, and an uncritical quietism in the attitude toward established and functioning social institutions. Thus Descartes' *ego cogitans* was to leave the "great public bodies" untouched, and Hobbes held that "the present ought always to be preferred, maintained, and accounted best." Kant agreed with Locke in justifying revolution *if and when* it has succeeded in organizing the whole and in preventing subversion.

However, these accommodating concepts of Reason were always contradicted by the evident misery and injustice of the "great public bodies" and the effective, more or less conscious rebellion against them. Societal conditions existed which provoked and permitted real dissociation from the established state of affairs; a private as well as political dimension was present in which dissociation could develop into effective opposition, testing its strength and the validity of its objectives.

With the gradual closing of this dimension by the society, the self-limitation of thought assumes a larger significance. The interrelation between scientific-philosophical and societal processes, between theoretical and practical Reason, asserts itself "behind the back" of the scientists and philosophers. The society bars a whole type of oppositional operations and behavior; consequently, the concepts pertaining to them are rendered illusory or meaningless. Historical transcendence appears as metaphysical transcendence, not acceptable to science and scientific thought. The operational and behavioral point of view, practiced as a "habit of thought" at large, becomes the view of the established universe of discourse and action, needs and aspirations. The "cunning of Reason" works, as it so often did, in the interest of the powers that be. The insistence on operational and behavioral concepts turns against the efforts to free thought and behavior *from* the given reality and *for* the suppressed alternatives. Theoretical and practical Reason, academic and social behaviorism meet on common ground: that of an advanced society which makes scientific and technical progress into an instrument of domination.

"Progress" is not a neutral term; it moves toward specific ends, and these ends are defined by the possibilities of ameliorating the human condition. Advanced industrial society is approaching the stage where continued progress would demand the radical subversion of the prevailing direction and organization of progress. This stage would be reached when material production (including the necessary services) becomes automated to the extent that all vital needs can be satisfied while necessary labor time is reduced to marginal time. From this point on, technical progress would transcend the realm of necessity, where it served as the instrument of domination and exploitation which thereby limited its rationality; technology would become subject to the free play of faculties in the struggle for the pacification of nature and of society.

Such a state is envisioned in Marx's notion of the "abolition of labor." The term "pacification of existence" seems better suited to designate the historical alternative of a world which—through an international conflict which transforms and suspends the contradictions within the established societies—advances on the brink of a global war. "Pacification of existence" means the development of man's struggle with man and with nature, under conditions where the competing needs, desires, and aspirations are no longer organized by vested interests in domination and scarcity—an organization which perpetuates the destructive forms of this struggle.

Today's fight against this historical alternative finds a firm mass basis in the underlying population, and finds its ideology in the rigid orientation of thought and behavior to the given universe of facts. Validated by the accomplishments of science and technology, justified by its growing productivity, the status quo defies all transcendence. Faced with the possibility of pacification on the grounds of its technical and intellectual achievements, the mature industrial society closes itself against this alternative. Operationalism, in theory and practice, becomes the theory and practice of *containment.* Underneath its obvious dynamics, this society is a thoroughly static system of life: self-propelling in its oppressive productivity and in its beneficial coordination. Containment of technical progress goes hand in hand with its growth in the established direction. In spite of the political fetters imposed by the status quo, the more technology appears capable of creating the conditions for pacification, the more are the minds and bodies of man organized against this alternative.

The most advanced areas of industrial society exhibit throughout these two features: a trend toward consummation of technological rationality, and intensive efforts to contain this trend within the established institutions. Here is the internal contradiction of this civilization: the irrational element in its rationality. It is the token of its achievements. The industrial society which makes technology and science its own is organized for the ever-more-effective domination of man and nature, for the ever-more-effective utilization of its resources. It becomes irrational when the success of these efforts opens new dimensions of human realization. Organization for peace is different from organization for war; the institutions which served the struggle for existence cannot serve the pacification of existence. Life as an end is qualitatively different from life as a means.

Such a qualitatively new mode of existence can never be envisaged as the mere by-product of economic and political changes, as the more or less spontaneous effect of the new institutions which constitute the necessary prerequisite. Qualitative change also involves a change in the *technical* basis on which this society rests—one which sustains the economic and political institutions through which the "second nature" of man as an aggressive object of administration is stablized. The techniques of industrialization are political techniques; as such, they prejudge the possibilities of Reason and Freedom.

To be sure, labor must precede the reduction of labor, and industrialization must precede the development of human needs and satisfactions. But as all freedom depends on the conquest of alien necessity, the realization of freedom depends on the *techniques* of this conquest. The highest productivity of labor can be used for the perpetuation of labor, and the most efficient industrialization can serve the restriction and manipulation of needs.

When this point is reached, domination—in the guise of affluence and liberty—extends to all spheres of private and public existence, integrates all authentic opposition, absorbs all alternatives. Technological rationality reveals its political character as it becomes the great vehicle of better domination, creating a truly totalitarian universe in which society and nature, mind and body are kept in a state of permanent mobilization for the defense of this universe.

STUDY QUESTIONS

1   To what extent do you think technology represents a new danger to the individual? To what degree might we promote new types of freedom?

2   What does the phrase "one-dimensional man" mean to you? What kinds of elements in our society, if any, support the use of this phrase?

3   Marcuse presents a caustic indictment of our present society. In what ways do you think he is right? In what ways is he wrong? Which elements in our society should be corrected?

4   What arguments could Skinner confront Marcuse with in order to show that the science of behaviorism would actually improve life for the individual?

5   Taking into consideration the articles presented in this section, what kinds of control do you think the society should have over the individual?

6   "Let the student believe that he is always in control, though it is always you—the teacher—who really controls. There is no subjugation so perfect as that which keeps the appearance of freedom, for in that way one captures volition itself . . ." (Rosseau). Do you think American education is like this? Does Marcuse? How could education foster "self-control?"

SELECTED READINGS

While there are many useful anthologies in political philosophy, Robert Paul Wolff (ed.), *Political Man and Social Man* (New York: Random House, 1966) is one of the best. The bibliographies are especially interesting for bringing together provocative and unusual materials. Carl Cohen (ed.), *Communism, Fascism, and Democracy* (New York: Random House, 1966) also provides good coverage on the major political movements of this century. Besides the *Crito,* you will want to read Plato's *Republic* and *Laws* for an overview of his theory. Karl Popper, *The Open Society and Its Enemies* (Princeton, N. J.: Princeton University Press, 1950) is an excellent critique of Plato's position. It is always worthwhile to read Bertrand Russell's views on something, and the best summary of his political outlook is *Political Ideals* (New York: Barnes & Noble, 1963). If anything must be read on civil disobedience, it must be Henry David Thoreau's *Civil Disobedience* (1849). Other works that deserve consideration are Carl Cohen, *Civil Disobedience* (New York: Columbia, 1971); Abe Fortas, *Concerning Dissent and Civil Disobedience* (Cleveland: World Publishing, 1968); and Martin Luther King, "Letter from Birmingham Jail" in *Why We Can't Wait* (New York: Harper & Row, 1963).

In addition to his own autobiography, the best account of Mill's life is Michael St. James Packe, *The Life of John Stuart Mill* (New York: Capricorn Books, 1970). One of Mill's chief antagonists was Sir James Fitzjames Stephen, whose *Liberty, Equality, Fraternity* (London, 1874) contains a typical attack on Mill's distinction between private and public interests. Isaiah Berlin's "Two Concepts of Liberty" in *Four Essays on Liberty* (New York: Oxford University Press, 1969) is a famous account of the distinction between "positive" and "negative" freedom. The final chapter, entitled "John Stuart Mill and the Ends of Life," is an excellent exposition of Mill's views on individualism. Two good books which outline the intellectual difficulties in liberalism are Robert Paul Wolff, *The Poverty of Liberalism* (Boston: Beacon Press, 1968), and, as a balancing view, Peter Manicas, *The Death of the State* (New York: Putnam, 1974).

Two very good collections of the writings of Marx are L. D. Easton and K. H. Guddat (eds.), *Writings of the Young Marx on Philosophy and Society* (Garden City, N. Y.: Doubleday, 1967), and Frederic Bender (ed.), *Karl Marx: The Essential Writings* (New York: Harper & Row, 1972). For a collection which covers the most important documents of Marxism, see Arthur Mendel (ed.), *The Essential Works of Marxism* (New York: Bantam, 1961). Further books by B. F. Skinner which bring out his political thought are his utopian novel, *Walden Two* (New York: Macmillan, 1948), and *Beyond Freedom and Dignity* (New York: Knopf, 1971). For a somewhat grotesque view of the possibilities of technology for enslaving mankind, see Aldous Huxley's *Brave New World and Brave New World Revisited* (New York: Harper & Row, 1965). A more complete picture of Marcuse's philosophy can be gotten from his *A Critique of Pure Tolerance,* with R. P. Wolff and Barrington Moore, Jr. (Boston: Beacon Press, 1967), and *An Essay on Liberation* (Boston: Beacon Press, 1969). A good critical account of Marcuse's doctrines is Alasdair MacIntyre, *Herbert Marcuse: An Exposition and a Polemic* (New York: Viking, 1970).